THE ANDAMAN
ISLANDERS

THE ANDAMAN
ISLANDERS

A. R. RADCLIFFE-BROWN, M.A.

THE FREE PRESS, *New York*

First published 1922
Reprinted by permission of the Cambridge University Press

Printed in the United States of America

All rights reserved. No part of this book may be reproduced or transmitted in any form or by any means, electronic or mechanical, including photocopying, recording, or by any information storage and retrieval system, without permission in writing from the Publisher.

FIRST FREE PRESS PAPERBACK EDITION 1964

Second printing August 1967

TO

Dr A. C. HADDON, F.R.S.

AND

Dr W. H. R. RIVERS, F.R.S.

TO WHOSE INSTRUCTION AND KIND ENCOURAGEMENT
IS DUE WHATEVER VALUE IT MAY POSSESS, THIS
WORK OF APPRENTICESHIP IS DEDICATED.

PREFACE

THIS book is based on research carried out in the Andaman Islands in the years 1906 to 1908 as Anthony Wilkin Student in Ethnology of the University of Cambridge. In its original form the monograph was presented as a fellowship thesis at Trinity College. The work of rewriting it was interrupted by a period of field research in Western Australia and was only completed in 1914. In recent years I have been hoping to find leisure to rewrite and condense the whole book, but this is not possible at the present time, so that it is here reprinted without change save for the addition of a few pages on the Andaman languages.

In 1908–9, when the writing of this book was undertaken, anthropologists and ethnologists were concerned either with formulating hypotheses as to the origins of institutions or with attempts to provide hypothetical reconstructions of the details of culture history. In both types of enquiry the historical point of view was dominant. It was largely from this point of view that I approached the study of the Andaman Islanders and attempted, by an investigation of physical characters, language and culture, to make a hypothetical reconstruction of the history of the Andamans and of the Negritos in general. The appendix on technology in this book is an example of what was intended. During the course of my work a systematic examination of the methods available for such reconstructions of the unknown past convinced me that it is only in extremely rare instances that we can ever approach demonstrable conclusions and that speculative history cannot give us results of any real importance for the understanding of human life and culture. The work of the historical ethnologists of the last twenty-two years has only served to confirm me in that opinion.

While ethnologists were mostly thinking in terms of origins and history, as indeed many still are, there was developing out of the work of the French sociologists a different conception of the utilization of ethnological data for the understanding of human life. Perhaps the best brief definition of that approach is contained in the following passage written by the late Henri Hubert in 1904. "Nous disons donc que toute explication des phénomènes religieux doit être cherchée dans la série même des phénomènes. Il faudra considérer, s'il s'agit d'un mythe, non pas l'idée problématique qui suggéra les images qui le composent à leur premier assembleur, mais, entre autres choses, les conditions de temps et de lieu, les circonstances qui le rappellent régulièrement, rituellement à la mémoire d'un groupe d'hommes associés et les gestes que leur commande cette pensée présente. S'il s'agit d'un rite, on considérera non pas l'intention de celui qui l'exécute, mais les effets, quels qu'ils soient, images suggérées, modifications de rapports et de qualités, qui le suivent nécessairement. Le premier résultat de pareilles observations sera de faire rattacher les faits particuliers à des faits plus généraux....Mécanisme d'une part, effets produits ou fonction de l'autre, telles seront les bases de l'explication des faits religieux....Il ne s'agit en somme que de retrouver dans les faits particuliers des formes très générales d'activité. On ne sort pas du connaissable[1]."

It was the method thus defined by Hubert that I attempted to apply to the beliefs and customs of the Andaman Islanders in the fifth and sixth chapters of this book. These chapters deal with what I have called the "meaning" and the "function" of rites and myths, but no definitions of those terms are given. It seems desirable to supply them.

Just in the sense that words have meanings, so do some other things in culture—customary gestures, ritual actions and abstentions, symbolic objects, myths—they are expressive signs. The meaning of a word, a gesture, a rite, lies in what it expresses, and this is determined by its associations within a system of ideas, sentiments and mental attitudes. Ethnological field-workers have often been content to record myths and describe ceremonies

[1] Chantepie de la Saussaye, *Manuel d'Histoire des Religions*, Paris, 1904, p. xxxviii.

without concerning themselves with the meanings, with what these things express. The excuse for this procedure is that meanings are difficult to discover and that there is no standardized technique for their discovery. There is a danger that the ethnologist may interpret the beliefs of a native people not by a reference to *their* mental life but by reference to his own. My investigations led me to the conclusion that this was what Mr Man had done in his interpretation of some of the Andamanese myths. I did not question his records of what the natives told him but only the meanings that he attached to their statements. It therefore seemed to me necessary for ethnology to provide itself with a method of determining meanings as effective and free from "personal equation" as the methods by which a linguist determines the meanings of words or morphemes in a newly studied language. Ethnology is faced with the dilemma that it must either give up for ever all hope of understanding such things as myth or ritual, or it must develop proper methods for determining as accurately as can be what meanings they have for the people to whose culture they belong.

The notion of function in ethnology rests on the conception of culture as an adaptive mechanism by which a certain number of human beings are enabled to live a social life as an ordered community in a given environment. Adaptation has two aspects, external and internal. The external aspect is seen in the relation of the society to its geographical environment. The internal aspect is seen in the controlled relations of individuals within the social unity. It is convenient to use the term "social integration" to cover all the phenomena of internal adaptation. One of the fundamental problems of a science of culture or of human society is therefore the problem of the nature of social integration. This problem can only be approached by the study of a number of different cultures from this specific point of view, by an intensive investigation of each culture as an adaptive and integrative mechanism and a comparison one with another of as many variant types as possible.

The discovery of the integrative function of an institution, usage, or belief is to be made through the observation of its effects, and these are obviously in the first place effects on individuals, or their life, their thoughts, their emotions. Not all such effects are significant, or at least equally so. Nor is it the immediate effects with which we are finally concerned, but the more remote effects upon the social cohesion and continuity.

Thus "meaning" and "function" are two different but related things. We cannot discuss the social function of mythology or ritual without an understanding of the meanings of particular myths and ritual actions. In the two theoretical chapters of this book the discussion of meanings and the discussion of function are carried on together. Perhaps it would have been an advantage to separate them.

Strictly speaking the solution of any important functional problem requires the use of a comparative method, not however the juxtaposition of superficially similar particular usages or beliefs from two or more different cultures which is often spoken of as the comparative method. We formulate a hypothesis as to the nature and function of ritual or of myth. This requires to be tested, and may ultimately be proved, by a sufficient series of studies of cultures of different type, in each of which the whole system of ritual or of myth has to be considered in its relation to the culture as a whole. In this work I sought to formulate some hypotheses and test them by the simple culture of the Andamans. Later work in other culture regions would lead me to restate in somewhat different terms what is here written, particularly in the sixth chapter on myth. But I have found sufficient verification for the main hypothesis to encourage me to continue with the work of testing and developing it.

A. R. RADCLIFFE-BROWN

UNIVERSITY OF CHICAGO
1932

CONTENTS

CHAP.		PAGE
	INTRODUCTION	1
I.	THE SOCIAL ORGANISATION	22
II.	CEREMONIAL CUSTOMS	88
III.	RELIGIOUS AND MAGICAL BELIEFS	136
IV.	MYTHS AND LEGENDS	186
V.	THE INTERPRETATION OF ANDAMANESE CUSTOMS AND BELIEFS: CEREMONIAL	229
VI.	THE INTERPRETATION OF ANDAMANESE CUSTOMS AND BELIEFS: MYTHS AND LEGENDS	330
	APPENDIX A. THE TECHNICAL CULTURE OF THE ANDAMAN ISLANDERS	407
	APPENDIX B. THE ANDAMAN LANGUAGES	495
	INDEX	505

LIST OF PLATES AND MAPS

THE LISTED PLATES FOLLOW PAGE 50 OF THE TEXT

PLATE I. An Andaman Islander shooting fish with bow and arrow on the reefs at Port Blair.

PLATE II *(left)* A young man of the North Andaman. *(Right)* A young man decorated with white clay in readiness for a dance.

PLATE III. A young married woman.

PLATE IV. A man of the North Andaman and his son. (The man's height is 1438 mm., 4 feet 8 inches.)

PLATE V. A married woman of the Great Andaman wearing belts of *Pandanus* leaf and ornaments of *Dentalium* shell.

PLATE VI. A man of the *Akar-Bale* tribe with South Andaman bow and arrows, wearing belt and necklace of netting and *Dentalium* shells. (Height 1494 mm., 4 feet 9 inches.)

PLATE VII *(above)* A village of the Middle Andaman. *(Below)* A hut in the village of Moi-lepto, showing the mode of construction.

PLATE VIII. Portion of the village of Moi-lepto, *Akar-Bale* tribe. On the right is an unfinished mat of palm leaves for the roof of a new hut.

PLATE IX. Three men and a young woman decorated with *odu* clay.

PLATE X. Women decorated with *odu* clay.

PLATE XI. A man with a pattern of white clay on his face.

PLATE XII. A woman with her child.

PLATE XIII (left) A woman wearing clay on her forehead as a sign of mourning. *(Right)* A young married woman, showing pattern scarified on body and arms.

PLATE XIV. A girl wearing her sister's skull.

PLATE XV. The peace-making dance of the North Andaman.

PLATE XVI. A girl during the ceremony at puberty, decorated with strips of *Pandanus* leaf.

THE LISTED MAPS FOLLOW PAGE 510 OF THE TEXT

MAP I. South-eastern Asia, showing the present distribution of the Negrito Race.

MAP II. The Andaman Island, showing the distribution of tribes.

LIST OF FIGURES IN THE TEXT

	PAGE
Plan of Andamanese Village	34

		PAGE
Fig.	1. Section of Little Andaman bow, in the middle and near the end	420
,,	2. Shoulder of Little Andaman bow	420
,,	3. Bow-string of twisted fibre, Little Andaman	421
,,	4. Diagram showing the method of making the loop in the end of the Little Andaman bow-string	421
,,	5. Section of bow from North Sentinel Island	422
,,	6. Section of Jarawa bow	422
,,	7. Upper end of South Andaman bow	423
,,	8. Section across the blade of a South Andaman bow	424
,,	9. Loop of bow-string, South Andaman	425
,,	10. Ornament on South Andaman bow	426
,,	11. Section across the blade of a North Andaman bow	427
,,	12. North Andaman bow seen from the front	429
,,	13. North Andaman bow; A, in the half-strung or reversed position; B, in the fully strung position	429
,,	14. Toy bow of the North Andaman	432
,,	15. Section across the middle of four Semang bows	434
,,	16. Fish-arrow of the Great Andaman	437
,,	17. Head of pig-arrow, Great Andaman	437
,,	18. Pig-arrow with detachable head, Great Andaman	437
,,	19. Method of making the cord of the Great Andaman pig-arrow	437
,,	20. Pig-arrow, Little Andaman	440
,,	21. Head of Jarawa pig-arrow	440
,,	22. Arrow with head of *Areca* wood, Great Andaman	440
,,	23. Harpoon, Great Andaman	440
,,	24. Turtle net, South Andaman	442
,,	25. Knot used in making the North Andaman turtle net	443
,,	26. North Andaman fish-gig	444
,,	27. Boar's tusk, used as a spokeshave	448
,,	28. Adze and knife	449
,,	29. Method of making bamboo mat, Little Andaman	456
,,	30. Diagram showing the technique used in making mats of thatch	457
,,	31. Diagram showing the technique used in Great Andaman mats	457
,,	32 *a*, 32 *b*. Pot, tied up for carrying, North Andaman	459, 460

LIST OF FIGURES IN THE TEXT

		PAGE
Fig. 33.	Basket for carrying pot, South Andaman	461
„ 34.	Portion of basket of Little Andaman	462
„ 35.	Portion of basket of South Andaman	464
„ 36.	Pig's skull with basket-work, Jarawa	466
„ 37.	Diagram showing netting needle, and method of netting	471
„ 38.	Shape of North Andaman pot	473
„ 39.	Shape of South Andaman pot	474
„ 40.	Necklaces of mangrove seed-tops, Great Andaman	480
„ 41.	Diagram showing method of making ornamental cord, Little Andaman	481
„ 42.	Designs incised or painted on belts of *Pandanus* leaf, Great Andaman	484
„ 43.	Designs on bamboo necklace from the North Andaman	485
„ 44.	Transverse section of canoe and outrigger	487
„ 45.	Showing manner in which the boom is connected with the float	488
„ 46.	Paddle	489

INTRODUCTION

THE Andaman Islands are part of a chain of islands stretching from Cape Negrais in Burma to Achin Head in Sumatra. This line of islands forms a single geographical system, as it were a submarine range of mountains, the highest points rising here and there above the surface of the ocean. Some 80 miles or so from Cape Negrais lies the first of the islands in the chain, Preparis Island, between which and the mainland the sea depth does not exceed 100 fathoms. Southwards of this the submarine ridge sinks to a depth of about 150 fathoms, rising again to form the small group of islands known as the Cocos, some 50 miles from Preparis. Geographically the Cocos may be regarded as part of the Andaman Group. Landfall Island, the most northerly point of the Andamans proper, is only distant from them some 30 miles, and the sea depth between does not exceed 45 fathoms. The Andaman Group itself consists of the Great and Little Andaman with their outlying islets, and occupies a distance approximately north and south of about 210 miles. Eighty miles to the south of the Andamans lie the Nicobar Islands, a scattered archipelago occupying a distance of about 160 miles from north to south. The sea between the Andamans and the Nicobars is over 700 fathoms deep. Deep sea also divides the Nicobars from Sumatra, which is about 110 miles distant from the most southerly point of Great Nicobar.

This line of islands is part of a long fold extending from the eastern end of the Himalayas, which includes the Arakan Yomah Range of Burma and the Andaman and Nicobar

Islands and finds its continuation in the islands off the west coast of Sumatra[1].

On the west the Andamans are separated from the coast of Madras, 700 miles distant, by the Sea of Bengal. On the east the Andaman Sea, a depression with a depth of over 1000 fathoms, separates the Andamans and Nicobars from the Malay Isthmus and Peninsula. Across the Andaman Sea, less than 100 miles distant from the Andamans, there runs a line of volcanic activity, marked by two small islands, Barren Island in Lat. $12°\ 15'$ N. and Long. $93°\ 50'$ E., and Narkondam in Lat. $13°\ 26'$ N. and Long. $95°\ 15'$ E.[2]

The Cocos, the Andamans and the Nicobars are now part of the Indian Empire. The Cocos Islands are occupied by a station for wireless telegraphy. In the Andaman Islands there is a penal settlement at Port Blair, to which are sent the criminals of India and Burma. The Nicobars are treated as one with the Andamans for administrative purposes.

Until the nineteenth century the Cocos Islands were uninhabited. The Andamans and the Nicobars have for many centuries been inhabited by two entirely different races. The Andamanese belong to that branch of the human species known to anthropologists as the Negrito race. They are short of stature with black skins and frizzy hair. The Nicobarese, on the other hand, resemble the races of Indo-China and Malaya, and have brown skins and lank hair, and are of medium stature.

The Andaman Islands consist of the Great Andaman and the Little Andaman, and a number of smaller islands. The Great Andaman may be regarded as one island, although it is divided by narrow sea water creeks into four areas, often spoken of as separate islands and called North Andaman,

[1] The formation of the Arakan Fold (including the Andaman and Nicobar Islands), dates from the middle of the Tertiary Period, and was apparently connected with the great movements that produced the Himalaya-Alpine mountain system and the Circum-Pacific Fold. The Andaman Sea, in the later Tertiary period, was prolonged much further to the north, over the region now occupied by the Pegu Yomah.

[2] This line of volcanic activity is a minor continuation of the Sunda Range of volcanoes of Java and Sumatra. It is continued northward, parallel to the Arakan Fold, as far as the extinct volcano of Puppadoung, east of Pagan, not far from Lat. $21°$.

Middle Andaman, Baratang and South Andaman. It is a long narrow stretch of land with a much indented coast, surrounded by many smaller islands, of which the most important are Interview Island off the west coast, Ritchie's Archipelago on the east, Rutland Island at the extreme south, and the outlying North Sentinel Island. The length of the Great Andaman with Rutland Island is nearly 160 miles, while the breadth from sea to sea is nowhere more than 20 miles. The Little Andaman lies to the south of the Great Andaman, about 30 miles distant from Rutland Island, from which it is separated by a shallow strait with a maximum depth of only 21 fathoms. The island is about 26 miles long from north to south and about 16 miles wide.

Viewed from the sea the islands appear as a series of hills, nowhere of any great height, covered from sky-line to high-water mark with dense and lofty forest. The hill-ranges run approximately north and south, in the same direction as the islands themselves, and attain a greater elevation on the east than on the west. The highest point of the North Andaman is Saddle Peak (2402 feet), that of Middle Andaman is Mt Diavolo (1678 feet), while the South Andaman has the Mt Harriett Range (1505 feet), and in Rutland Island there is Mt Foord (1422 feet). There are no streams of any size. The water drains from the hills into tidal creeks running through mangrove swamps, often many miles in length. The coast is broken by a number of magnificent harbours. The shores are fringed with extensive coral reefs, and on these and in the creeks there is abundance of fish and molluscs.

The islands, save for the clearings of the Penal Settlement, are covered with dense tropical forest. There are few mammals, the only two of any size being a species of pig (*Sus andamanensis*, Blyth) and a civet-cat (*Paradoxurus tytlerii*, Tytler). The other mammals are a few species of rats, a tree-shrew and some species of bats. Of birds there are many different species, some of them peculiar to the islands. The reptiles include a considerable number of species of snakes, and a few species of lizards, of which the most noteworthy is the large Monitor lizard (*Varanus salvator*).

The climate is warm and moist, and fairly uniform throughout the year. The mean temperature for the year at Port Blair is about 86° F. (80° F. on the wet bulb thermometer). The lowest temperatures are recorded in January and February, and the highest in March, April, or May. The average lowest temperature in the South Andaman over a period of seven years is 66·7° F., the minimum during that period being 63° F. The average highest temperature in the shade for the same period was 96° F., the maximum being 97°. The average diurnal variation is 10°.

The average rainfall of seven stations in the Penal Settlement of Port Blair, for a period of seven years, was 138 inches per annum, the averages of the different stations varying from 104 to 172 inches. For the same period the average number of rainy days in the year was 177, the minimum being 160 and the maximum 196.

The islands are sufficiently far from the Equator to have a single well-defined rainy season. The greater part of the rain falls during the south-west monsoon, which lasts from the middle of May to the middle of November. The north-east monsoon extends over the other six months of the year, which include the dry and hot seasons.

The average weather can be shown most conveniently by means of a calendar.

January. Cool; little or no rain; wind N.N.E.; nights sometimes foggy.

February. Cool; little or no rain; wind N.N.E.; very clear; light airs.

March. Hot by day, cool nights; little or no rain; wind N.N.E.; light airs, occasional haze; the weather gets hotter as the month passes.

April. Very hot; little or no rain; wind variable, off-shore at night and on-shore by day; calm and hazy.

May. The first half of the month like April; the south-west monsoon sets in about the 15th; the remainder of the month cooler and with wind W.S.W.

June. Fairly cool; heavy rains; wind W.S.W., squally.

July.
August. } Do.   do.   do.   do.
September.

October. Variable wind and weather; generally some calm weather; waterspouts may occur.

November. During the first half of the month the wind and weather are very uncertain; a cyclone may occur; after the middle of the month the north-east monsoon sets in.

December. Fairly cool; not much rain; wind N.N.E.

Many of the violent cyclonic storms that sweep across the Sea of Bengal seem to form themselves a little to the south of the Andamans. Cyclones of exceptional violence struck Port Cornwallis in 1844 and Port Blair in 1864 and 1891.

The aborigines of the Andaman Islands have been in their present home for a great many centuries. It is not possible to say with any degree of certainty how or when they first reached the islands. Geological and other evidence would seem to show that the Andamans were united to the mainland along the line of the Arakan Fold in later Tertiary times, but even this is perhaps not quite certain[1]. In any case the period of past land connection seems to be so remote that it had probably ceased to exist at the time when the islands were peopled by the ancestors of the present natives. If the ancestors of the Andamanese reached the islands at the time of a past land connection, they can only have done so from the Arakan region of Burma. On the other hand, if they travelled by sea they must almost certainly have started from the Burmese coast (Pegu or Arakan). The north-east monsoon would drift them thence on to the Andamans. It is conceivable that they might have travelled from Sumatra by way of the Nicobars, but the north-east monsoon would have opposed their progress in this direction, while the south-west monsoon would have driven them to the east of the Andamans[2]. It is hardly possible to imagine them coming from the Malay Peninsula across the wide

---

[1] The flora of the Andamans and Cocos contains a number of species, the presence of which can only be explained by the supposition of a past land connection with the Arakan region. (See Prain, "The Vegetation of the Coco Group," *Journ. Asiatic Soc. of Bengal*, Vol. LX, Part II, pp. 283—406.) On the other hand, the paucity of mammalian fauna is such as to lead to the conclusion that the islands were isolated at a period when the mammals now typical of the mainland did not exist there. (See Miller, "Mammals of the Andaman and Nicobar Islands," *Proc. National Museum, U.S.A.* Vol. XXIV.)

[2] There is no evidence of the former existence of Negritos in the Nicobars, but on the other hand, there is equally no direct evidence of their former presence in Lower Burma.

stretch of the Andaman Sea. The balance of probability is in favour of the view that the Andamans were peopled, either by sea or by land, from the region of Lower Burma.

Of the Negrito race, to which the Andamanese belong, there are two other branches still in existence. The first of these consists of the people who may be conveniently spoken of as the Semang, inhabiting the interior of the Malay Peninsula between 5° and 7° N. Latitude. The other branch of this primitive race is found in the interior of the Philippine Islands. From their present distribution it is clear that the Negritos must at some long past time have wandered over a wide area in south-eastern Asia. The connection between the Andamanese and the Semang can only have been either through Sumatra and the Nicobars, or, more probably, by way of Lower Burma. Communication between the Malay Peninsula and the Philippine Islands must have been either by way of Borneo or Celebes, or else by way of Annam and Cochin China. It is certainly many centuries, and probably many thousands of years, since the three surviving branches of the race were cut off from all communication with each other[1].

In the Malay Peninsula and in the Philippines the Negritos have for a long time been living in contact with other races. They have been driven back from the coasts and fertile valleys into the less accessible districts. There is ample evidence that they have adopted many of the customs of the races around them, and have even adopted to a great extent the language of their alien neighbours. The original Negrito culture and language and even perhaps the original physical type have been modified in these two branches of the race.

In the case of the Andaman Islanders it is possible that they have been entirely isolated in their island home, and have not been affected by contact with other races, but have been free to develop their own culture in adaptation to their own environment. If a hypothesis to this effect were accepted we should see in the Andamanese the direct descendants, in physical character, in language, and in culture, of the original Negrito

[1] On the accompanying map of south-eastern Asia the regions now occupied by the Negritos are shown by the shading.

race. In historical times it is known that the islands have been avoided by mariners navigating the adjacent seas, owing to the fact that the natives attacked all strangers who landed or were wrecked upon their shores. Moreover, the islands offered little inducement to visitors or settlers. The coconut, which is one of the mainstays of life in tropical islands, was not found in the Andamans prior to the first European settlement.

The earliest authentic reference to the Andaman Islands seems to be that of two Arab travellers dating from A.D. 871. In the eighteenth century the Abbé Renaudot translated the account of these travels. Of the Andamans we read, " Au dela de ces deux Isles on trouve la mer appellée d'Andeman. Les peuples qui habitent sur la coste, mangent de la chair humaine, toute cruë. Ils sont noirs, ils ont les cheveux crespus, le visage et les yeux affreux, les pieds fort grands et presque longs d'une coudée, et ils vont tout nuds. Ils n'ont point de barques, et s'ils en avoient ils ne mangeroient pas tous les passants qu'ils peuvent attraper. Les vaisseaux se trouvant retardez dans leur route par les vents contraires, sont souvent obligez dans ces mers de mouiller à la coste où sont ces Barbares pour y faire de l'eau, lors qu'ils ont consommé celle qu'ils avoient a bord. Ils en attrapent souvent quelques-uns, mais la pluspart se sauvent[1]."

It would seem that the Chinese and Japanese knew the islands in the first millenium A.D., and referred to them by the names Yeng-t'o-mang and Andaban respectively[2]. Marco Polo gives a brief notice of the islands. "Angaman is a very large island, not governed by a king. The inhabitants are idolaters, and are a most brutish and savage race, having heads, eyes, and teeth resembling those of the canine species. Their dispositions are cruel, and every person, not being of their own nation, whom they can lay their hands upon, they kill and eat[3]." Some of Marco Polo's statements about the Andamans, as that the natives

---

[1] *Anciennes Relations des Indes et de la Chine*; De Deux Voyageurs Mahometans, qui y allerent dans le neuvième siècle; Traduites d'Arabe (par M. l'Abbé Renaudot). Paris, MDCCXVIII, pp. 5 and 6.
[2] Takakasu's Edition of I-tsing, pp. xxviii seq.
[3] *The Travels of Marco Polo*, Edited by John Masefield, *Everyman's Library*, 1908, p. 347.

live on rice and milk, and that they have coconuts, and plantains, are incorrect. It is evident that all he knew of the islands was derived from hearsay. The passage quoted is only of importance as showing that the reputation of the Andamanese was such as to cause them to be feared and avoided.

A more trustworthy account is that of Master Caesar Frederike, who passed near the Nicobars in 1566. "From Nicubar to Pegu is, as it were, a row or chain of an infinite number of islands, of which many are inhabited with wild people; and they call those islands the Islands of Andemaon, and they call their people savage or wild, because they eat one another: also, these islands have war one with another, for they have small barques, and with them they take one another, and so eat one another: and if by evil chance any ship be lost on those islands, as many have been, there is not one man of those ships lost there that escapeth uneaten or unslain. These people have not any acquaintance with any other people, neither have they trade with any, but live only of such fruits as those islands yield[1]."

There are numerous references to the Andamans in the seventeenth and eighteenth century, and all of them show that the islands were feared and avoided. During these and the previous centuries wrecks must have occurred in considerable numbers, and it is probable, from what is now known of the natives, that the mariners would be immediately slain. Visits were also paid by ships whose water supply had run out, and by Malay pirates. There is evidence that boats, either Malay or Chinese, sometimes visited the islands in search of edible birds' nests and trepang. In some cases Andamanese were captured and carried off as slaves. It is extremely improbable

---

[1] Extracts of Master Caesar Frederike: his Eighteene Yeeres' Indian Observations, *Purchas: his Pilgrimes*, London, 1625; Vol. II, p. 1710. In spite of the repeated descriptions of the Andamanese by early writers as ferocious cannibals, there is good reason to think that they have not deserved quite so evil a reputation. If they had ever been cannibals they had certainly abandoned the custom by the time the islands were occupied in 1858. It is improbable that such inveterate man-eaters, as they are supposed to have been, would have entirely altered their ways in the course of a century or two. The legend probably had its origin in the fact that the Andamanese attacked all strangers who landed on their coasts, and (in the North Andaman, at any rate) often disposed of the bodies of slain enemies by cutting them in pieces and burning them on a fire.

that such visitors ever succeeded in establishing friendly relations with the islanders.

There is one way in which the life of the Andamanese was affected by the vessels that visited or were wrecked upon their shores, since it was by this means that they learnt the use of iron.

It is impossible now to determine the date at which they became acquainted with the metal. The earliest reference to the subject is in an account of a visit to the Andamans in 1771, where it is shown that the natives were at that time aware of the value of iron[1]. Until the middle of the nineteenth century the only supply of the metal was from wrecks, of which there have always been a fair number.

Until the end of the eighteenth century there was no attempt made to open up communication with the Andaman Islands, although the Nicobar Islands were the scene of several attempts to establish a colony. In 1788, owing to the menace to shipping constituted by the islands and their inhabitants, the East India Company, under Lord Cornwallis, commissioned Archibald Blair to start a settlement, convicts being sent as labourers. The settlement was founded in September, 1789, in the harbour now known as Port Blair, but then called Port Cornwallis. In spite of the hostility of the natives the colony seems to have been successful. In 1792 it was transferred from the first site to the harbour in the North Andaman now known as Port Cornwallis. The transfer was made with the idea of creating a naval base, for which the spot chosen was well adapted. Unfortunately the new site proved to be very unhealthy, and in 1796 the scheme was abandoned, the convicts were transferred to Penang, and the settlers returned to India.

[1] The account is that of a visit to the Andamans in 1771 by John Ritchie, published in the *Indian Antiquary*, Vol. XXX, 1901, pp. 232 seq. Two natives came off to the ship in a canoe, and Ritchie writes: "I gave them some nails and bits of old iron which pleased them much; and about three in the afternoon, they went into the canoe, and tried hard to pull the chain plates from the vessel's side. They went astern when this would not do, and dragged strongly and long at the rudder chains; but these were too well fixed; and at last, they went towards the shore at an easy rate, looking at their nails, and singing all the way."

During the next sixty years the islands remained unoccupied save by the aborigines. There were a number of wrecks in different parts of the islands, and in some cases the crews were slain. In 1839 a geologist, Dr Helfer, visited the islands in the hope of finding minerals, and was killed by the natives. In 1844 two transports, the *Briton* and the *Runnymede*, were wrecked in a cyclone on Ritchie's Archipelago, one of the ships being thrown high up over a reef into a mangrove swamp. The crew and soldiers were safely landed, and were eventually rescued with hardly any loss of life. As they were a large party they were safe from the possible attacks of the natives, and they lived on stores rescued from the wrecks.

In view of the number of wrecks that occurred on the islands and the desirability of establishing there some harbour where vessels might safely call for water or shelter from storms, the East India Company again considered the question of colonizing the Andamans. When the Company, at the end of the Indian Mutiny, found themselves with a large number of prisoners on their hands, it was decided to create a new Penal Settlement, and the site of the settlement of 1788 was chosen for this purpose, and renamed Port Blair.

The Penal Settlement was established in March 1858, and has been in existence ever since. The aborigines were hostile from the outset, and gave much trouble by their raids. They made a determined effort to oust the invaders from their country. To establish friendly relations with them an institution known as the Andamanese Homes was founded, to provide free rations and lodging, and medical attendance, to such of them as could be induced to visit the Settlement. Through the efforts of successive officers in charge of these Homes friendly relations were established, first of all with the *Aka-Bea* tribe in the neighbourhood of Port Blair, then with other tribes of the South Andaman, and at a later date with the inhabitants of the North Andaman and the Little Andaman. At the present day there is only one body of Andamanese still persistently hostile, and these are the so-called *Jarawa* of the interior of the South Andaman. These *Jarawa*, since about 1870, have made repeated attacks on isolated parties of convicts and forest workers and on the friendly Andamanese. Punitive expeditions have been sent against them on several occasions, and attempts to set up friendly relations with them have been made by leaving presents in their huts, and by capturing some of them and keeping them for a time at Port Blair. At the present time the *Jarawa* are as hostile as ever.

Although of one race throughout, the Andaman Islanders are divided into several groups, with differences of language and culture. There are two main divisions, which will be spoken of as the Great Andaman Group and the Little Andaman Group respectively. The Great Andaman Group includes all the natives of the Great Andaman with the exception of those of the interior of the South Andaman who are known as *Jarawa*. The Little Andaman Group includes all the inhabitants of the Little Andaman, those of the North Sentinel Island and the *Jarawa* of the South Andaman.

These two different divisions exhibit many differences of language and culture. All the languages of the Great Andaman Group are closely related to one another. They have the same grammatical structure, and a large number of roots are the same in all or in several of them. In the same way the language of the *Jarawa*, so far as it is known, is very similar to that of the natives of the Little Andaman. On the other hand when the language of the Little Andaman is compared with the Great Andaman languages there is a very striking difference. Of a vocabulary of several hundred words collected in the Little Andaman there were less than a dozen in which the root or stem was clearly the same as that of words in the Great Andaman. While the grammatical structure of the languages of the two groups is fundamentally the same, this can only be shown in a somewhat detailed analysis, and there are many important differences.

With regard to technical culture the same grouping appears. There is a general similarity between all the tribes of the Great Andaman Group, while the *Jarawa* and the inhabitants of the Little Andaman have a technical culture of their own that is markedly different from that of the other division.

The natives of the Great Andaman Group are divided into tribes, of which there are ten, each with its own distinctive language or dialect, and with a name. The following is a list of these tribes, passing from north to south:—*Aka-Čari*, *Aka-Kọra*, *Aka-Bo*, *Aka-Jẹru*, *Aka-Kede*, *Aka-Kọl*, *Ọkọ-Jụwọi*, *A-Pučikwar*, *Akar-Bale*, and *Aka-Bea*. In each case the name is given in the form in which it is used by the tribe itself. Thus the *Aka-Bea* speak of the *A-Pučikwar* as *Aka-Bojig-yab*, and refer to the *Akar-Bale* as *Aka-Bala-wa*, and there are similar variants of other tribal names.

The natives of the Little Andaman refer to themselves as *Önge* (men). It is probable that the so-called *Jạrawa* of the South Andaman have the same word. In a vocabulary obtained by Colebrooke in 1790 from a *Jạrawa* near Port Blair, the word *Mincopie* is given as meaning a native of the Andaman Islands. This would seem to be simply the same phrase as the Little Andaman *M'önge-bi* = I am *Önge*, or I am a "man." The word *Jạrawa* is apparently derived from the *Aka-Bea* language, but is now used by all the friendly natives (i.e. the natives of the Great Andaman Group) to denote those of the Little Andaman Group. In the official publications dealing with the Andamans, however, the term *Jạrawa* has come to be applied solely to the hostile natives of the Great Andaman. It is in this sense that the word is used in the present work, the name *Önge* being reserved for the natives of the Little Andaman. It must be remembered, however, that the so-called *Jạrawa* probably call themselves *Önge*, while the *Önge* of the Little Andaman are called *Jạrawa* by the natives of the friendly tribes of the Great Andaman. The name *Mincopie* was at one time common in ethnological literature as a term for the Andaman Islanders.

It is convenient to divide the tribes of the Great Andaman Group into two subdivisions, to be spoken of as the Northern Group (including the first four tribes mentioned above) and the Southern Group (including the other six tribes). Between these two divisions there are a number of differences of culture. They have, for example, different forms of bow, and different kinds of baskets. The differences between them are much slighter than those between the Great Andaman tribes and the natives of the Little Andaman, but they are of sufficient importance to make it necessary to distinguish them from one another.

The different divisions of the Andamanese may for convenience be set out in the form of a table.

I. GREAT ANDAMAN GROUP.

 A. Northern Group, including the tribes:—

  Aka-Čari,
  Aka-Kọra,
  Aka-Bo,
  Aka-Jĕru.

 B. Southern Group, including the tribes:—

  Aka-Kede,
  Aka-Kọl,
  Okọ-Juwọi
  A-Pučikwar,
  Akar-Bale,
  Aka-Bea.

II. LITTLE ANDAMAN GROUP.

 A. The inhabitants of the Little Andaman (*Önge*).
 B. The *Jạrawa* of the South Andaman.
 C. The inhabitants of the North Sentinel Island.

The distribution of these different groups as it was in 1858 is shown on the map.

There is one important feature of this distribution that requires a few words of explanation, and that is the presence in the South Andaman of the *Jạrawa* who are allied by language and technical culture to the natives of the Little Andaman. There can be no doubt that the *Jạrawa* are the descendants of emigrants who at some time in the past made their way across from the Little Andaman and thrust themselves in upon the inhabitants of Rutland Island and the South Andaman, maintaining their footing in the new country by force of arms.

The identity of the flora and fauna of the Little Andaman with those of the Great Andaman and the shallowness of the strait between the islands, suggests that at no very remote period they have been united by a continuous land connection. Whether or not this connection existed at the time when the islands were first peopled, it is at any rate reasonable to suppose that the original ancestors of the present Andamanese had one language and one culture. Once the Little Andaman was peopled, the strait between it and the Great Andaman seems to have acted as an effective barrier, to keep the two divisions of the race apart for many centuries. During the period of this separation each division followed its own line of development, with the result that there arose the considerable differences of language and culture that now exist.

At a much later date than this separation of the Andamanese into two isolated groups, and after the typical differences of language and culture had been developed, a party of natives must have made their way by canoe from the north of the Little Andaman to Rutland Island. They would have found that country occupied by natives of the Great Andaman Group. In spite of this they succeeded in establishing themselves in the South Andaman, and became the progenitors of the present *Jarawa*. Owing to the difference of language all communication between the Little Andaman invaders and those already occupying the invaded country would be impossible. (At the present day a native of the Little Andaman cannot make himself understood to a native of one of the Great Andaman tribes.) The result has been that the *Jarawa* have lived in a state of constant warfare with their neighbours, and this hostility has lasted down to the present day.

It is only on the above hypothesis that it is possible to explain how it comes about that we find in the South Andaman people with language and technical culture very similar to that of the Little Andaman, and differing from that of the remaining inhabitants of the Great Andaman. It is impossible to say how long it is since this invasion from the Little Andaman took place. At the end of the eighteenth century the *Jarawa* were to be found in the neighbourhood of Port Blair. Lieutenant

Colebrooke in 1790 came across an individual of this tribe and obtained from him a vocabulary. A comparison of this vocabulary with the language of the Little Andaman shows it to be essentially the same language[1].

A few words must be said on the position of the natives of the North Sentinel Island. Almost nothing is known of these people. What little information is available concerning their weapons and implements seems to point to their belonging to the Little Andaman Division. There is no communication between them and either the Great Andaman or the Little Andaman. It is possible that they have been separated from the other Andamanese as long as those of the Little Andaman have been separated from those of the Great Andaman, and would therefore constitute a third separate division. The South Sentinel Island is uninhabited.

The total area of the Andamans is estimated to be about 2500 square miles. This area is divided as follows:—

	Sq. miles.
North Andaman, being the territory of the four tribes Aka-Cari, Aka-Kora, Aka-Bo, and Aka-Jeru	540
Middle Andaman and Baratang, occupied by four tribes, Aka-Kede, Aka-Kol, Oko-Juwoi and A-Pucikwar . .	790
The Archipelago, occupied by the Akar-Bale tribe .	140
The South Andaman, occupied by the Aka-Bea and the Jarawa	630
North Sentinel Island	30
Little Andaman	370
	2500

It is not possible to give accurately the area occupied by each tribe, as the boundaries are difficult to discover. The *Aka-Bea* is in an exceptional position, as there was no definite boundary between them and the *Jarawa*. The two parties of natives lived in the same territory at enmity with each other. It would seem that the *Aka-Bea* kept on the whole more to the coast, while the *Jarawa* lived in the interior.

[1] In 1906 some Little Andaman visitors to Rutland Island captured a *Jarawa* of that part. They told me that though he spoke differently from them, they could understand him fairly well.

Leaving aside the *Aka-Bea*, the largest of the Great Andaman tribes, as regards area of territory, was the *Aka-Kede*, which possessed over 300 square miles. After this tribe in order of size come the *A-Pučikwar*, *Aka-Jeru* and *Aka-Kọra* tribes, while the smaller ones are the *Okọ-Juwọi*, *Aka-Kọl*, *Aka-Bo*, *Akar-Bale* and *Aka-Čari*, the last being perhaps the smallest of all.

In 1901 an enumeration of the natives of the Great Andaman was attempted in connection with the census of India. Such an enumeration was of course very difficult, and liable to considerable error. The results are given in the following table:—

Name of Tribe	Adults		Children		Total
	Males	Females	Males	Females	
Aka-Cari	16	15	6	2	39
Aka-Kora	31	32	14	19	96
Aka-Bo	15	16	7	10	48
Aka-Jeru	98	80	26	14	218
Aka-Kede	24	30	3	2	59
Aka-Kol	6	2	3		11
Oko-Juwoi	21	19	7	1	48
A-Pucikwar	31	14	2	3	50
Akar-Bale	5	10	3	1	19
Aka-Bea	14	16	3	4	37
Total	261	234	74	56	625

These figures are likely to be more accurate for the southern tribes (the last five on the list) than for the northern tribes. It is probable that, in the North Andaman, some of the persons enumerated were entered under the wrong tribe. For many years the officers of the Andamans did not know of the existence of the *Aka-Kọra* and *Aka-Bo* tribes, and members of these tribes have fallen into the habit of describing themselves to Europeans as either *Aka-Jeru* or *Aka-Čari*. My own opinion is that the numbers given for the *Aka-Jeru* tribe are too large, while those of the *Aka-Kọra* and *Aka-Bo*, and perhaps also the *Aka-Kede*, are too small.

For the census of 1901 an attempt was made to estimate the numbers of the *Jarawa* and the natives of the Little Andaman, any attempt at enumeration being impossible. The estimate given was as follows:—

Little Andaman	.	.	.	.	672
South Andaman Jarawa		.	.	117
Rutland Island Jarawa		.	.	351
North Sentinel Island	.		.	.	117
Total			.	.	1257

This estimate is not of any great value. As regards the Little Andaman, my own information would lead me to estimate their numbers at between 600 and 700, thus agreeing with the estimate above. Concerning the North Sentinel Island nothing is known on which a satisfactory estimate could be based. The figures for the Rutland Island *Jarawa* are certainly very much too high. In 1907 I spent some weeks on Rutland Island trying to get into touch with the *Jarawa* there. At that time there were certainly not more than 50 all told on the island. I was only able to discover one camp, and that had been deserted just before it was discovered, but had not contained a dozen persons. The Rutland Island *Jarawa* have been cut off from the other *Jarawa* by the spread of the convict Settlement since about 1885. The majority of the *Jarawa* now inhabit the interior and western coast of the South Andaman north of Port Blair.

During the last fifty years the numbers of the Andamanese have been greatly diminished. This has been the result of the European occupation of the islands, and is chiefly due to new diseases that have been introduced amongst them. Syphilis was introduced among the tribes of the South Andaman about 1870, and this has now spread among all the Great Andaman tribes (that is, excluding the hostile *Jarawa*). A large number of natives are infected, and the disease is responsible directly and indirectly for a considerable increase in the death-rate. In March, 1877, an epidemic of measles broke out among the Andamanese, introduced with a batch of convicts from Madras, and spread rapidly from one end of the Great Andaman to the other. In six weeks 51 out of 184 cases treated in hospital proved fatal. It is almost certain that the proportion of deaths was much greater in the case of those, the vast majority, to whom no medical aid could be given. A writer on the Andamans[1] has

[1] Portman, M. V., *A History of Our Relations with the Andamanese*, Calcutta, 1899.

estimated that the mortality from measles and its sequelae was one-half if not two-thirds of the whole population of the Great Andaman. Other diseases which were formerly unknown to the islands seem also to have been introduced, including influenza.

While the death-rate amongst the friendly Andamanese has been enormously increased, the birth-rate has at the same time fallen to almost nothing. This is evident from the proportion of adults to children in the population table given above. In 1907, out of a total of about 500 natives whom I saw at different times, there were not more than a dozen children of less than five years old. A birth is a rare occurrence, and of the children born very few survive infancy.

This decrease of population has not as yet affected the Little Andaman. The natives of this island have had very little contact with the Penal Settlement or with the tribes of the Great Andaman, and have thus escaped the diseases which are mainly responsible for the depopulation of the larger island.

Several attempts have been made to estimate the former population of the Andamans. In the "Census Report" for 1901 the estimate given is 4800 for the whole group. Mr M. V. Portman has given an estimate of 8000. It seemed to me that one of these is too small and the other too large. Judging from what it is possible to learn about the habits of the natives, and the food supply available, I should estimate that the former population of the islands (in 1858) was about 5500[1]. An estimate for the proportion of the different groups is as follows:—

	Estimated former population.	Density per square mile.
North Andaman (four tribes)	1500	2·75
Middle Andaman with Baratang and Ritchie's Archipelago	2250	2·5
South Andaman (Aka-Bea and Jarawa)	1200	2·0
Little Andaman and North Sentinel	700	1·75
Total	5650	2·25

[1] This estimate is based on what the Andamanese were able to tell me of the conditions under which they formerly lived. Of course such an estimate can only be of small value. I think it is more probable that I have underestimated the former population than that I have overestimated it.

With regard to the comparative density per square mile of the different groups it may be pointed out that the reason for the smaller density of the South Andaman is the fact that the *Aka-Bea* and *Jarawa* were living there at war with one another, and the territory was therefore probably not so fully occupied as in other parts of the islands where boundaries between neighbouring tribes were well defined. The food supply of the Little Andaman does not seem to be so abundant as that of the Great Andaman in proportion to its area. It must be remembered that length of coast-line is of more importance to the Andamanese than the actual area of their country. The natives of the Little Andaman are not able to harpoon turtle and large fish, which constitute an important element of the food supply of the tribes of the Great Andaman.

If the figures of the above estimate be correct, it will be seen that the population of the North Andaman has been reduced in less than fifty years (1858–1901) to about 27 per cent. of its former volume, while in the same period the population of the Middle Andaman and South Andaman has been reduced to about 18 per cent. As the tribes in the south were the first to come into contact with the Settlement, their numbers have diminished more rapidly than those of the northern tribes. It is probable that in another fifty years the natives of the Great Andaman tribes will be extinct.

The diminution of population has combined with other causes to alter considerably the mode of life of the islanders. What were formerly distinct and often hostile communities are now merged together. The different languages have become corrupt, and some tribes have adopted customs of other tribes and have abandoned their own. Most of the younger men and women of the friendly tribes of the Great Andaman now speak a little Hindustani (Urdu) in a somewhat corrupt form. The friendly natives are under the charge of an officer of the Settlement, known as the Officer in Charge of the Andamanese. A Home and Hospital are provided for them in Port Blair, and natives from all parts, even from the extreme north, go there either to be treated in the Hospital or to stay at the Home. During certain parts of the year some of the natives are employed in collecting trepang (bêche de mer) under the direction of petty officers, who are natives of India or Burma. The trepang, together with wild honey and shells collected by the Andamanese, is sold, and the money is devoted to the service of the Andamanese Department. There is also a grant of money from the Government of India, in return for which the Officer in Charge must, when necessary, provide Andamanese to track and capture any convicts who may run away from the Penal Settlement. The funds thus made available serve to provide the natives with blankets, cloth, iron tools and scrap iron, rice, sugar, tea and tobacco. The result of this system is that there is a free circulation of natives in all parts of the Great Andaman. Whereas, formerly, the natives kept carefully to their own part of the country, they now make long journeys, either in their own canoes, or in Government launches, and members of the northern tribes are to be found at Port Blair and elsewhere in the south, while men and women of the southern tribes are to be found engaged in collecting trepang in the north.

The natives of the Little Andaman have as yet scarcely been affected by these changes. Within recent years, however, some of the natives of the northern part of the Little Andaman have been in the habit of making periodical visits to Rutland Island in their canoes, and occasionally come as far as Port Blair. Their chief reason for visiting the Settlement is to obtain iron for their arrows and adzes, but they have also begun to appreciate sugar and tobacco.

The manners and customs of the Andaman Islanders have formed the subject of a number of writings. By far the most important of these is a work by Mr E. H. Man, who was for some years an officer of the Penal Settlement of Port Blair, and for four years of that time was in charge of the Andamanese Home. Mr Man made a special study of the language of the *Aka-Bea* tribe and compiled an extensive vocabulary, which, however, has never been published. His observations on the manners and customs of this tribe and others of the South Andaman were published in the *Journal of the Anthropological Institute* of the year 1882 (Volume XII), and were reprinted in the form of a book *On the Aboriginal Inhabitants of the*

Andaman Islands. As the reprint is difficult to obtain, the references to Mr Man's work in the chapters that follow are all to the pages of the *Journal of the Anthropological Institute,* Volume XII.

Another writer on the Andamanese is Mr M. V. Portman, who was for some years an officer of the Andaman Commission, and was for a long time in charge of the Andamanese. His *Manual of the Andamanese Languages,* London, 1887, is full of errors and entirely unreliable. A later work, entitled *Notes on the Languages of the South Andaman Group of Tribes,* Calcutta, 1898, is of much greater value, and though not entirely free from errors, is on the whole useful and accurate. Mr Portman has also compiled *A History of Our Relations with the Andamanese* (2 volumes, Calcutta, 1899), which contains a mass of information on the subject with which it deals, but does not add very much to our knowledge of the Andamanese themselves. The British Museum possesses an excellent collection of photographs of the Andamanese taken by Mr Portman.

A good general description of the islands and of their inhabitants by Colonel Sir Richard Temple, who was for many years Chief Commissioner of the Andaman and Nicobar Islands, is contained in Volume III of the *Census of India,* 1901, here referred to as "Census Report" 1901.

CHAPTER I

THE SOCIAL ORGANISATION

IN the present chapter we are to deal with the customs and institutions by which the natives of the Great Andaman regulate the conduct of persons one to another. At the outset it is necessary to get as clear an idea as possible of the structure of the Andamanese society. That structure, as will be shown, is extremely simple.

What is really of interest to the ethnologist is the social organisation of these tribes as it existed before the European occupation of the islands. The changes that have taken place in recent years have been extensive, the most important being the great diminution in numbers and the merging together of what were formerly distinct and often hostile communities. It is fairly easy, however, to discover from the natives themselves what was the constitution of the society in former times, though there remain a few points about which no satisfactory information can be obtained.

When the islands were first occupied by the British, before depopulation had affected their institutions, the natives of the Great Andaman were to be found living in small communities scattered over the islands, mostly on the coast, but some of them in the forest of the interior of the island. Each such community, which will be spoken of as a "local group," was independent and autonomous, leading its own life and regulating its own affairs. Each group had occasional relations with other neighbouring groups; visitors might pass from one to another; or the two groups might meet together for a few days and join in feasting and dancing. On the other hand there were often quarrels between neighbouring groups, which might result in a state of feud between them for many months. Between communities separated from one another by a distance of only 50 miles or even less there were no direct relations whatever. The members of one community kept to their own part of the country, only leaving it to visit their friends within a narrow radius.

These local groups were united into what are here called tribes. A tribe consisted of a number of local groups all speaking what the natives themselves regard as one language, each tribe having its own language and its name. The tribe was of very little importance in regulating the social life, and was merely a loose aggregate of independent local groups.

The local groups are further distinguished by the natives themselves as being of two kinds according as they lived on the coast or inland. This division was independent of that into tribes. Some tribes consisted of coast-dwellers only, while others included both coast-dwellers and forest-dwellers.

Within the local group the only division was that into families. A family consists of a man and his wife and their unmarried children own or adopted.

These were the only social divisions existing among the Andamanese, who were without any of those divisions known as "clans" which are characteristic of many primitive societies.

The natives of the Great Andaman (leaving aside the *Jarawa*, who by language and culture belong to the Little Andaman division of the race) are divided into ten tribes, each occupying a certain area of country. Each tribe consists of a number of persons who speak what is regarded by the natives themselves as one language. That the tribe is fundamentally a linguistic group is shown by the tribal names. These are all formed from a stem with the prefix *aka-*, which prefix is used in the languages of the Great Andaman to convey a reference to the mouth and thereby to the function of speech. Thus in the *Aka-Jeru* language the stem *poy* means "a hole of any kind," and *aka-poy* means "the mouth," there being no other word for that part of the body. In the same language the stem *-ar-* meaning "to talk" can only be used with the prefix *aka-*, as *ak'-ar-ka*, "he says." The prefix which is characteristic of the tribal names, indicates, therefore, that these are really the names of languages.

The meanings or derivations of some of the tribal names have not been ascertained with certainty. The name *Aka-Čari* is derived from the word *čari* meaning "salt water," and therefore means "the salt-water language." Similarly the name *Aka-Jeru* is derived from *jeru*, a species of Sterculia from which canoes are made. In the Northern languages the word *ot-bo* means "the back" of anything, and *oy-kora* means "the hand." It is possible that the names *Aka-Bo* and *Aka-Kora* are derived from these stems (the *ot-* and the *oy-* being prefixes), but there is no evidence that they are associated with them in the minds of the natives of the present day. Among the Southern tribes the name *Akar-Bale* is derived from a word meaning "the other side" of a creek or strait, thus referring to their position in the Archipelago. The name *A-Pučik-war* (of which the *Aka-Bea* equivalent is *Aka-Bojig-yab*) means "those who speak our own language," from a stem *pučik* (*Aka-Bea, bojig*) which means "belonging to ourselves" as opposed to strangers of the same race. Mr Portman[1] gives the following meanings of the other tribal names of the South and Middle Andaman, but the derivations are somewhat doubtful.

Aka-Bea   Fresh water.
Oko-Juwoi   They cut patterns on their bows.
Aka-Kol   Bitter or salt taste.

I may take this opportunity of pointing out two errors in the names of the tribes given in the "Census Report" of 1901. The name *Aka-Čari* is given as *Aka-Chariar*; the stem *-ar-* means "to talk" and is not an essential part of the tribal name; *Aka-Čari-ar-bom* means "he talks the *Čari* language." The name *Aka-Bo* is given as *Aka-Tabo*; *t'a-Bo* means "I (am) *Aka-Bo*," just as *t'a-Jeru* means "I (am) *Aka-Jeru*," the prefix *aka-* being contracted to *a-* after the personal pronoun *t'* = I or my.

Although the natives themselves thus recognize and give names to ten distinct languages, all of them are closely related. There is, on the whole, not a great deal of difference between

---

[1] *Notes on the Languages of the South Andaman Group of Tribes*, p. 27.

two neighbouring languages. A man of the *Aka-Jeru* tribe could understand without any great difficulty a man speaking *Aka-Bo*. On the other hand many of the languages included two or even more distinct dialects. In the *Akar-Bale* tribe there were two dialects, one in the southern half of the Archipelago, which was allied to *Aka-Bea*, and the other in the northern half, showing affinities with *A-Pučikwar*. Even in such a small tribe as the *Aka-Čari* it would seem that there were differences of dialect. Thus, even from the point of view of language, the tribe was not entirely homogeneous.

Leaving aside the *Aka-Bea*, the average extent of territory occupied by a tribe was about 165 square miles. Of the nine tribes the largest, as regards area, was the *Aka-Kede*, with over 300 square miles, while the smallest was probably the *Aka-Čari*, with less than 100 square miles. Save in the case of the *Akar-Bale* tribe, which occupied the islands of Ritchie's Archipelago, it is difficult to find any marked geographical features that might be supposed to have determined the extent and the boundaries of the different tribes.

The *Aka-Bea* tribe was in an abnormal position as there was no recognized boundary between them and the *Jarawa*. Together, these two divisions of the Andamanese occupied an area of about 600 square miles. The *Aka-Bea* seem to have kept more to the coast while the *Jarawa* occupied the interior of the South Andaman and Rutland Island.

If the estimate previously given[1] of the former population of the islands be correct, the nine tribes (leaving aside the *Aka-Bea*) would have formerly contained about 3750 persons of all ages. At the present time the four tribes of the North Andaman number altogether about 400, of whom about 100 or less are children. The other six tribes taken together (including the almost extinct *Aka-Bea*) number about 200, of whom not more than 30 are children. Mr Man estimated the numbers of the *Aka-Bea* tribe (called by him *Bojig-ŋiji-da*) in 1882 at about 400, and supposes them to have numbered about 1000 in 1858. In 1901 that tribe consisted of only 37 persons.

[1] Page 18 above.

Besides the division into tribes, and independent of it, the Andamanese recognize another division into coast-dwellers and forest-dwellers. In the *Aka-Bea* language the coast-dwellers are called *Ar-yoto*, while the forest-dwellers are called *Erem-taga*. The difference between them is due solely to the difference of their food supply. The *Ar-yoto* obtain much of their food from the sea. They are expert in fishing and turtle hunting. They make canoes and use them not only for hunting but also for travelling from one camp to another. Some portion of their food they also obtain from the forest, edible roots and fruits and the flesh of the wild pig being the chief. On the other hand the *Erem-taga* rely solely on the forest and the inland creeks for their food supply. Their only use for canoes is in the creeks. They are entirely ignorant of such matters as turtle or dugong hunting, but they are more at home than the coast-dwellers in the forest, and are generally more skilful at pig-hunting. The advantage certainly rests with the coast-dwellers, for they have both the sea and the forest to draw upon for their sustenance.

Some tribes consist only of coast-dwellers, such as the *Aka-Čari*, the *Akar-Bale* and perhaps the *Aka-Kọl*. On the other hand the *Aka-Bo*, although their territory includes a part of the west coast, are, by their occupations and mode of life, forest-dwellers, and the same seems to have been the case of the *Okọ-Juwọi*. The *A-Pučikwar*, the *Aka-Kede*, the *Aka-Jeru* and perhaps also the *Aka-Kọra* tribes contained both coast-dwellers and forest-dwellers.

Each tribe formerly consisted of a number of independent local groups. The local group, and not the tribe, was the land-owning group, each one owning or exercising hunting rights over a certain recognized area. At the present time, owing to the breakdown of the local organisation, through the settlement of the islands and the resulting decrease of population, it is difficult to ascertain what area of country was occupied by each of these local groups. In many cases it would seem that the boundaries between two neighbouring groups are not very clearly defined, there being portions of forest over which the members of both hunted when the groups were at peace¹. There is no doubt that in the more favourable localities, particularly on the coast, the country occupied by a single group was smaller than in places of less abundant food supply. It is probable that the forest-dwelling local groups occupied considerably larger areas in each case than the coast groups. Some of the coast-dwelling groups seem to have occupied areas of less than ten square miles.

It is not easy to discover at this time exactly what number of persons would have been included in one local group. Mouat, who visited the islands in 1857–8, says of the natives, "They are rarely or never seen living alone, several of their little huts being raised in the same locality, where they dwell together in numbers varying between thirty and three hundred²." In another passage he states, "They are generally divided into small groups, the numbers of which vary considerably, some not containing more than ten individuals, while in others as many as two or three hundred may be found. The great majority of these groups of the natives consist on an average of from thirty to fifty men, women, and children, although sometimes as many as three hundred are found together³." It is probable that, if so small a party as ten were seen, they were a hunting party spending a day or a few days away from the main camp. On the other hand so large a number as three hundred could only be found together on the occasion of one of the periodical meetings of several local groups for purposes of festivity. Mouat's statement that the groups consisted on the average of from thirty to fifty persons, agrees very well with the statements of the natives themselves, and may be taken as being fairly accurate. Mr Man, writing in 1882, speaks of the Andamanese as divided into communities "each consisting of from twenty to fifty individuals," and elsewhere says that "permanent encampments vary in size and

---

[1] A few small areas were not occupied at all, for example the greater part of Saddle Peak in the North Andaman, which is covered with dense jungle and is supposed by the natives to be the haunt of large and deadly snakes and of evil spirits.
[2] Mouat, F. J., *Adventures and Researches among the Andaman Islanders*, London, 1863, p. 313.
[3] *Loc. cit.* p. 300.

consist of several huts, which in all are rarely inhabited by more than from fifty to eighty persons[1]."

From the information that I was able to obtain from the natives themselves I came to the conclusion that an average local group consisted of from 40 to 50 persons of all ages, the average number of local groups to a tribe being about 10. This would give the average extent of country occupied by each local group as about 16 square miles, but some groups certainly had a larger territory than this and some had smaller.

Mr M. V. Portman speaks of the tribes of the southern part of the Great Andaman as being divided into what he calls "septs," but he does not explain what he means by that term. He states that the *Aka-Bea* were divided into seven septs, the *A-Pučikwar* into four, the *Akar-Bale* into two, while the *Aka-Kol* and *Oko-Juwoi* had no real subdivisions[2]. Whatever Mr Portman may have meant by the term sept, it is clear that he did not use it to denote what is here called a local group, but some larger subdivision of the tribe. What these septs seem to have been are groups consisting each of four or five local groups having friendly relations with one another and meeting together occasionally at the festival gatherings to be described later in the present chapter.

There were, strictly speaking, no distinctive names for the local groups. A local group might be denoted by a reference to the district that it occupied or to one of its chief camping places. Thus, in the *Akar-Bale* tribe, those occupying the island of *Teb-juru* were spoken of as *Teb-juru-wa*, the word *wa* meaning "people," and the inhabitants of the east coast of Havelock Island were similarly denoted as *Puluga-l'ar-mugu-wa* from the name of the district that they occupied. In the tribes of the North Andaman the word equivalent to *wa* of the South is *koloko*. Some of the local groups of the *Aka-Bo* tribe were distinguished as *Teraut buliu koloko*, *Kelera buliu koloko*, *Teradikili buliu koloko* etc., from the names of the creeks (*buliu*) that they occupied. In the *Aka-Čari* tribe the local group occupying the island of *Tonmuket* and the

---

[1] *Journ. Anthrop. Inst.* Vol. XII, pp. 107 and 108.
[2] Portman, *Notes on the Languages of the South Andaman Group of Tribes*, p. 23.

adjoining mainland were called *Tarotọlo koloko*. When a man was asked to what part of the country he belonged he would generally answer by mentioning one of the chief camping places of his local group. Thus a man of the *Tarotọlo koloko* might say that he belonged to *Laropuli*, this being one of the chief camps of that country. A man of the *Teraut buliu koloko* might similarly say that he belonged to the village of Čaičue.

A man or woman is generally regarded as belonging to the local group in the country of which he or she was born. There is nothing, however, to prevent a person from taking up his residence with any other local group if he so wishes, and if the members of that group are willing to welcome him. It would seem that there were a fair number of such cases in which a man or a woman left his or her own local group to join another. In particular, when two young people belonging to different groups got married they might fix their residence either with his or with her parents.

The local group, as stated above, was characterised as the land-owning group. A man might hunt over the country of his own group at all times, but he might not hunt over the country of another group without the permission of the members of that group. Even at the present day, when the local organisation has largely broken down, some of these hunting rights are still observed. I noticed a case in which some of the men asked and obtained permission to hunt pig in a certain part from a man who was explained to be the owner of that part of the country, being one of the few survivors of the local group to which it belonged. It would, in former times, have been an offence that might easily have led to a serious quarrel for the men of one group to hunt or fish in the country or the waters of another group without having been granted permission to do so.

Within the territory of each local group there are a number of recognized camping places. During the greater part of every year the members of the local group would be found living together at one or other of these. Some of these camping-grounds have been in use for many centuries, as is shown by the heaps of refuse many feet deep, chiefly consisting of the shells of molluscs and the bones of animals. Such kitchen-middens, as they have been called, are to be found in numbers all around the coasts of the islands.

In the case of the coast-dwelling communities the camping sites are always close to the sea-shore or to a creek, so that they can be reached by canoe. In the case of those dwelling inland this is of course not so. In any case one of the chief factors determining the choice of the site is the existence of a supply of fresh water. This is of extreme importance in the case of a site to be occupied during the dry season when fresh water becomes scarce.

Within their own territory the local group is what we may speak of as semi-nomadic. The coast-dwellers rarely reside continuously at the same spot for more than a few months, but shift from one camp to another, moved by different causes. If a death occurs the camp is deserted for several months and a new one is occupied. A change of camp often takes place at a change of season, some spots presenting particular advantages, such as shelter from the prevailing wind, or better hunting or fishing, at certain times of the year. Another cause of the abandonment of a camp by the coast-dwellers is that all refuse is thrown away close to the camp, and after a few months the decaying animal matter thus accumulated renders the spot uninhabitable. The natives seem to find it easier to move their camp than to clear away their refuse. The truth is, perhaps, that they are so accustomed to change their camp from one spot to another, in order to make the best use of the natural resources available, that there is no necessity for them to take those sanitary measures that would be essential if they wished to remain for many months continuously at the same place.

The forest-dwellers are less nomadic in their habits than the coast-dwellers. One of the reasons for this is that as they cannot convey their belongings from one place to another by canoe, but must carry them overland, the moving of a camp is a more tiresome business with them than it is with the coast-dwellers. During a great part of the year the forest-dwellers were accustomed to remain at one camp, which was thus the chief camp of the group. In particular they would spend there the whole of the rainy season. During the cool and hot seasons they would leave the chief camp for a few months, leading during that time a more nomadic life, living in temporary hunting camps and paying visits to their friends in other groups. At the opening of the rainy season they would return once more to the main camp.

The camps of the natives of the Great Andaman may be distinguished as being of three kinds. Of the first kind are what may be spoken of as permanent encampments. Certainly every group of the forest-dwellers, and probably every group of the coast-dwellers had its permanent encampment, which was, so to speak, the headquarters of the group. At this spot there would be erected either a communal hut, or a carefully built village. Communal huts have in recent times fallen into disuse, as the natives now wander about the islands much more freely than was their wont. I did not see a single one in the Great Andaman during my visit, though I was told of one that was falling to ruins in the interior of the Middle Andaman. One such communal hut was photographed in 1895 by M. L. Lapicque, at a spot called *Lekera-l'un-ta*[1]. It was perhaps the last that the natives of the Great Andaman erected. What the communal hut was like it is possible to discover both from the statements of the natives and also from the fact that they are still to the present day used by the natives of the Little Andaman and by the *Jarawa*. The hut was roughly circular in form and might be as big as 60 feet in diameter and 20 or 30 feet high at the centre. The shape was somewhat that of a beehive. Two concentric circles, one of tall posts near the centre and the other of shorter posts near the circumference, were connected by horizontal and sloping roof-timbers, and on these were laid and fastened a number of mats of palm-leaves. These mats reached, as a rule, as far as the ground, a small doorway being left on one side.

Such communal huts, while still used in the Little Andaman

[1] The photograph is reproduced in *Le Tour du Monde*, 1895, p. 447.

and by the *Jarawa*, and formerly used by the forest-dwellers of the Great Andaman, were apparently not often erected by the coast-dwellers of the larger island at the time the islands were occupied in 1858. Mr Man seems to have regarded them as being peculiarly characteristic of the *Jarawa* and the natives of the Little Andaman[1]. There is evidence, however, that even the coast-dwellers formerly erected such huts, for in the *Akar-Bale* tribe there are several places with names such as *Paruŋ Bud* and *Golugma Bud*, which show that communal huts existed there at some time. The word *bud* is used to denote a communal hut, as compared with a village, which is called *baraij̆*.

A large communal hut took some little time to erect. The posts had to be cut and erected, this being the work of the men, and the palm-leaves had to be collected and then made into mats by the women. Once the hut was built it would last for several years, and if it were in fairly constant use, particularly if it were not abandoned in the rains, it might be used, with a little occasional patching, for ten years or even more.

Among the coast-dwellers it was more usual to erect at the headquarters a semi-permanent village. A portion of such a village is shown in the photographs reproduced in Plates VI and VII.

The village occupied a small clearing in the forest close to the sea-shore at a place called *Mọi-lepto* in the country of the *Akar-Bale* tribe. A spring or soak close to the village provided the fresh water. The site is a favourite one as it is well sheltered, and is within convenient distance of good fishing and turtle hunting grounds. It was formerly one of the chief camping places of the local group known as the *Boroin wa* (Hill people).

The village was composed of eight huts, ranged round a central open space, and all of them facing inwards towards the centre. This open space is kept clear and clean for dancing, and is simply the village dancing ground. Each of the single huts was occupied by a family group, consisting of

---

[1] See *Journ. Anthrop. Inst.* Vol. XII, p. 71.

a man and his wife with their children and dependants. One hut was occupied by an old widower and a bachelor.

The way the huts are built can be seen in the photographs. In the simplest form the hut consists of a sloping roof made of palm-leaves, erected on four posts, two taller ones at the front and two short ones at the back. A hut of this kind is shown in Plate VII. If more shelter is required a second roof is added in such a way that the top of one overhangs the top of the other. In some cases a third roof may be added on one side. In Plates VI and VII two mats of palm-leaf are shown in the course of construction, lying on the ground.

Huts such as these, in which the leaves are first made into a mat which is then attached to the rafters, will last for some time. Even if the village be deserted for several weeks, at any rate in the dry weather, very little work will be needed to make it habitable again when the occupants return to it.

A second kind of camp was made when the natives did not intend to stay more than two to three months. Such camps were erected by the forest folk during the dry season, or at any time when they were compelled to leave their chief camp through the death there of one of their number. Such a temporary camp is always put up in the form of a village, and never as a communal hut. The huts are similar to those already described, but are made more carelessly. The thatching leaves, instead of being made into mats, are simply tied in bundles on to the rafters. A hut of this kind will last quite well for three months or so and it can be built very rapidly at any place where there is a sufficient supply of thatching leaves. At the present day the natives rarely build a permanent camp for themselves, but are contented with temporary camps of the kind here described.

A third kind of camp remains to be briefly mentioned, which we may call the hunting camp. A hunting party (which may include women as well as men) spending a few days away from one of the main camps will erect for themselves a few huts or shelters consisting of nothing more than a simple lean-to of leaves.

Caves or rock shelters suitable for human occupation are

almost unknown in the Andamans. In the Archipelago there are one or two small rock shelters that are occasionally used by a hunting party away from home for a night. I was told by the natives that on one of the islands off the west coast of the North Andaman there is a rock shelter of a fair size that was formerly used as one of their chief camps.

The following figure will give an idea of the Andamanese village and its arrangement. In hunting camps which are intended only to be occupied for a few days or a few weeks, this arrangement is not observed, but the huts or shelters are placed

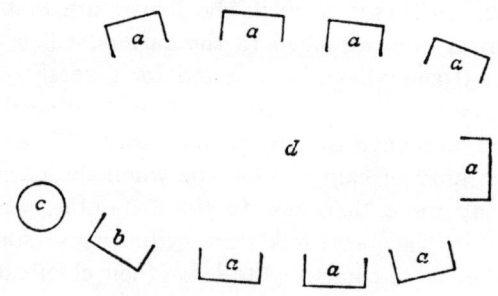

Plan of Andamanese Village

    a.   Huts of married people.
    b.   Bachelors' hut.
    c.   Public cooking place.
    d.   Dancing ground.

so as to give shelter from the prevailing wind with no particular regard to the respective position of the different units.

The constitution of the local group is illustrated by the arrangement of the village. The whole village consists of a number of separate huts, each hut occupied by a family. A family consists of a man and his wife and such of their children own or adopted as are not of an age to be independent. Besides the families each group necessarily contains a small number of unmarried men and widowers and some unmarried girls and widows. The unmarried men and widowers without children occupy a separate hut (or huts) which we may speak of as the bachelors' hut. Mr Man states that the spinsters (i.e., the unmarried women who are of marriageable age) and widows occupy a hut of their own similarly to the bachelors[1]. In the camps that I visited I did not find any such spinsters' hut. What unmarried females there were, I found attached to one or other of the families of the village, each one living in the hut of some married relative, generally the parent or foster-parent.

All the huts face inwards towards an open space which is the dancing ground of the village, and, except in exposed situations, are generally entirely open in front. At some convenient spot on one side of the dancing ground is to be found the communal cooking place of the village. This is generally close to the bachelors' hut, as it is the bachelors who attend to such cooking as is carried on there. Besides the public cooking place each family has its own fireplace in its own hut, on which a fire is kept continually alight. In the village two or more families may build their huts adjoining one another in such a way that they become for all practical purposes one hut, of which each family retains its own special portion. Two brothers will thus often make a sort of common household.

The communal hut, in the way in which it is arranged, and even in the way in which it is built, is really a village with all the huts drawn together so that each one is joined to the one next to it and the roofs meet in the middle. In the centre of the hut there is an open space corresponding to the dancing ground of the village. It is even used as a dancing ground, though for this purpose it is somewhat small. It is the public part of the hut. Around this are arranged the different families, each occupying its own special portion of the hut, which is marked off by means of short lengths of wood laid on the floor. The public cooking place is sometimes inside the hut, and there is the space marked off for the unmarried men. The advantage of the communal hut is that it affords a better protection from the weather; its disadvantage is that it leaves almost no room for dancing.

Thus it may be seen that the arrangement of the camp shows

[1] Man, *op. cit.* p. 108.

very plainly the constitution of a local group, consisting as it does of a few families. Each group seems to have contained, on an average, about ten families, with a few unmarried males and females.

The Andaman Islanders depend for their subsistence entirely on the natural products of the sea and the forest. From the sea they obtain dugong, turtle (both green and hawksbill), an enormous variety of different sorts of fish, crustaceans (crabs, crayfish and prawns) and molluscs. Fish and crabs are also to be found in the salt-water creeks which in many places penetrate inland for some miles. From the forest they obtain the flesh of the wild pig, wild honey, and a large number of vegetable foods—roots, fruits, and seeds.

The life of the forest folk is more simple and uniform than that of the coast people and we may therefore consider it first. During the rainy season, which lasts from the middle of May to the end of September, the local group lives at its headquarters camp, which, as we have seen, formerly often took the form of a communal hut. During this season animal food is plentiful, as the jungle animals are in good condition; on the other hand there is not much vegetable food to be obtained. The following brief account will give an idea of how the day is spent in such a camp at that time of year. Some time after sunrise the camp begins to be astir. The various members of the community make a meal of any food that may have been saved from the day before. The men start off for the day's hunting. At the present time dogs are used for pig-hunting. These dogs were obtained in the first instance from the Settlement of Port Blair, and their use in pig-hunting was learnt from the Burmese convicts. Nowadays every married man has at least one dog[1]. Before the dogs were obtained, hunting was a pursuit requiring a great deal more skill than it does at present. A hunting party consists of from two to five men. Each man carries his bow and two or three pig arrows, and one of the party carries a smouldering fire-brand. They make their way through the jungle until they find the fresh tracks of a pig, or follow up some of the usual pig runs

[1] In the North Andaman the times before the Settlement are spoken of as the time when there were no dogs, *Bibi poiye* = "Dog not."

until they come upon the animal feeding. In former days much skill was required to creep noiselessly through the jungle until they were sufficiently near either to discharge an arrow, or, if the jungle were more open, to rush in upon the animal shouting and shoot it before it could escape. At the present day it is the dogs that scent out the pig and bring it to bay, when the natives shoot it with their arrows.

When a pig has been killed it may be tied up and carried to the camp on the shoulders of one of the hunters, or a fire may be lighted then and there and the pig eviscerated and roasted. A cut is made in the abdomen and the viscera removed. The cavity is filled with leaves, the joints of the legs are half severed and the carcase is placed on the fire and turned over and shifted until every part is evenly roasted. It is then removed from the fire, the burnt skin is scraped clean and the meat is cut up. Meanwhile the intestines or some of the internal organs are cooked and eaten by the hunters. The meat is tied up in leaves and is carried to the camp. If the pig be carried home whole the process of roasting it and cutting it up is performed in exactly the same way at the public cooking place of the camp, the meat being distributed only after it has been thus partially cooked.

If the hunting party should come across a civet cat (*Paradoxurus*) or a monitor lizard they would endeavour to kill it[1], but the main object of every hunting party is to obtain pork. Snakes and even rats are killed and eaten. Birds, though plentiful in the islands, are not often obtained, for the density of the jungle and the height of the trees in which the birds conceal themselves, make it very difficult for the natives to shoot them with their bows and arrows. A man does not care to risk the loss of his arrow in a chance shot at a bird. The Andamanese do not trap either birds or animals, though some of the birds, particularly the rail, might be very easily caught in traps.

As the hunting party traverses the forest they may come across roots or fruits or seeds, or wild honey, and these are collected and carried home. In the rainy season only small

---

[1] They are only eaten in the rainy season.

combs of black honey are to be found[1], and these are generally consumed by the hunters on the spot.

The provision of the vegetable food of the community is the work of the women, who must also supply the camp with firewood and water. While the men are away hunting the women, attended by the children, cut and carry the firewood, and either remain in the camp making baskets or nets or other objects, or else go into the forest to look for fruits and seeds. Thus by midday the camp may be quite deserted, save perhaps for one or two old men and women, and a few of the children.

In the afternoon the women return with what food they have obtained and then the men come in with their provision. The camp, unless the hunters have been unsuccessful, is then busy with the preparation of the evening meal, which is the chief meal of the day. If a pig has been brought home whole it is cooked at the public cooking place and is then cut up. The meat is distributed amongst the members of the community and the woman of each family then proceeds to cook the family meal. The pork, after it has been roasted and cut up, is further cooked by being boiled. The family meal is prepared at the fire that each family has in its hut. The meal is a family one, partaken by a man and his wife and children. The bachelors cook and eat their own meal, and the unmarried women also eat by themselves.

After the meal is over, darkness having by this time fallen, the men may spend an hour or two in dancing to the accompaniment of a song sung by one of them with the help of a chorus of women. In that case they would probably eat another meal after the dance was over. Another favourite amusement for the evening is what may be called "yarning." A man sits down with a few listeners and tells them, with few words, and with many dramatic gestures, how he killed a pig. The same man may go on with tale after tale, till, by the time he finishes he has killed twenty or thirty pigs. Finally the whole camp retires to rest and nothing

[1] There are two kinds of wild bee in the Andamans. A small species makes black honeycombs in hollow trees, and these may be found at any time of the year. A larger species of bee builds white combs suspended from the underside of branches in tall trees. Such combs are found in abundance only in the hot season, and not at all in the middle of the rainy season.

is to be seen but the dim light of the little fires burning in each hut or in each of the family quarters.

On a day when there is plenty of food left from the day before, or on a day of stormy weather even when food is not too plentiful, the men may remain in camp instead of going hunting. They busy themselves with making weapons and implements, such as bows, arrows, adzes, etc.

On occasions when game is not very plentiful a party of hunters may stay away from the camp for a few days, not returning till they have been successful in obtaining a fair supply of food. The women and children and old men, with perhaps a few of the able bodied men also, remain at home and provide for themselves as well as they can, the women devoting their time to collecting what vegetable foods are in season.

At the end of the rainy season there comes a brief period of unsettled weather, called by the natives of the North Andaman *Kimil*, and by those of the South, *Gumul*. During this season some of the vegetable foods begin to be available, though not in any quantities. At this time of the year the natives are able to obtain and feast upon what they regard as great delicacies, the larvae of the cicada and of the great capricornis beetle. The cool season, when fruits and roots are plentiful, begins at the end of November. The forest dwellers leave their main encampment during this season. Some of them go off to pay visits to their friends of other local groups. Such visits may last two or three months. Those who remain occupy temporary camps in convenient places. The men join the women in looking for roots and fruits, and do not spend so much of their time in hunting. Some of the men visit the main camp at intervals of a few days to see that it is all right. As the cool season gives way to the hot season (March to May) honey begins to be plentiful. At that time hunting for pig is almost abandoned. The pigs are in poor condition, and even when one is killed it is often left in the jungle by the natives as not being good enough to eat. On the other hand everyone is busy collecting honey. This is work in which both men and women join, though it is the men who climb up the trees and cut down the honeycomb. The natives have no means of keeping the honey for more than a very short time, as it rapidly ferments. While it is plentiful they almost live on it, supplementing it with roots and fruits and with fish, if they are near a creek. Towards the end of the hot season the fruit of the *Artocarpus chaplasha*, which is a favourite food of the natives, becomes ripe. The men and women, at this time, spend much of their time collecting the fruit. When it is collected the fruit is broken open and each of the seeds is sucked to obtain the juicy pulp or aril with which it is surrounded, and which has a very pleasant taste. The seeds are then partly boiled and are buried in the ground to remain there for a few weeks, when they will be dug up again and cooked and eaten. Any natives who may have been away from home on a visit, return before the *Artocarpus* comes into fruit in order to take their share in collecting it and providing a supply of the seeds for consumption in the rainy season. The natives then return to the headquarters camp and make any necessary repairs to the hut in preparation for the rainy season, which begins about the middle of May.

The coast-dwellers are not quite so much influenced by the seasons as the forest-dwellers. They can fish and collect molluscs all the year round. In the rainy season they divide their time between hunting pig in the forest and fishing or turtle hunting. They do not need, however, to remain at the same camp during the whole of the rainy season, but after a month or two at one place can move to what they hope to find better hunting grounds. During the cool and hot seasons they pay visits to one another. In the fine weather the men often go off on turtle-hunting expeditions for several days, leaving the women and children and older men in the village, where they provide for themselves with vegetable food and with fish and molluscs from the reefs.

It is during the fine weather that there take place the meetings of two or more local groups that are an important feature of the social life of the Andaman Islanders. These meetings will be described later in the present chapter.

Besides their food, which they must find from day to day, the natives have need of nothing save their weapons and implements. Of these each person makes his own, each man making his own bow, arrows, adze, etc., while the wife makes her baskets, nets and so on.

The economic life of the local group, though in effect it approaches to a sort of communism, is yet based on the notion of private property. Land is the only thing that is owned in common. The hunting grounds of a local group belong to the whole group, and all the members have an equal right to hunt over any part of it. There exists, however, a certain private ownership of trees. A man of one of the local groups of the coast may notice in the jungle a tree suitable for a canoe. He will tell the others that he has noticed such a tree, describing it and its whereabouts. Thenceforward that tree is regarded as his property, and even if some years should elapse, and he has made no use of it, yet another man would not cut it down without first asking the owner to give him the tree. In a similar way certain men claim to possess certain *Artocarpus* trees, though how the ownership in these cases had arisen I was unable to determine. No one would pick the fruit off such a tree without the permission of the owner, and having received permission and gathered the fruit he would give some part of it to the owner of the tree.

A pig belongs to the man whose arrow first strikes it, though if the arrow merely glanced off and did not remain in the wound it would not give any claim to ownership. A turtle or a dugong or big fish belongs to the man who throws the harpoon with which it is taken. A honeycomb belongs to the man who climbs the tree and cuts it down. The fish that a man shoots belong to him, and to a woman belong the roots she digs up, the seeds that she collects, the fish or prawns that she takes in her net or the molluscs that she brings from the reefs. Any weapon that a man makes belongs to him alone to do what he pleases with, and anything that a woman makes is her own property. A man is not free to dispose of the personal property of his wife without her permission.

In the village each family erects and keeps in repair its own hut, and the wife provides the hut with the firewood and water needed. In the case of a communal hut it would seem that this is really an example of a possession common to the whole group.

This is so, however, only in appearance. The hut is built by all the different families, but each family is regarded as owning a certain portion of the hut when it is finished, and it is the family that keeps this part of the hut in repair.

A canoe is cut by a number of men together. From the outset, however, it is the property of one man, who selects the tree and superintends the operation of cutting it into shape. He is always one of the older men, and he enlists the services of the younger men to help him. When finished the canoe is his property, and he can do with it what he pleases, giving it away, if he wishes, and no one has any share of ownership in a canoe on the ground that he helped to make it.

While all portable property is thus owned by individuals, the Andamanese have customs which result in an approach to communism. One of these is the custom of constantly exchanging presents with one another. When two friends meet who have not seen each other for some time, one of the first things they do is to exchange presents with one another. Even in the ordinary everyday life of the village there is a constant giving and receiving of presents. A younger man or woman may give some article to an older one without expecting or receiving any return, but between equals a person who gives a present always expects that he will receive something of equal value in exchange. At the meetings that take place between neighbouring local groups the exchange of presents is of great importance. Each of the visitors brings with him a number of articles that he distributes amongst the members of the group that he visits. When the visitors depart they are loaded with presents received from their hosts. It requires a good deal of tact on the part of everyone concerned to avoid the unpleasantness that may arise if a man thinks that he has not received things as valuable as he has given, or if he fancies that he has not received quite the same amount of attention as has been accorded to others.

It is considered a breach of good manners ever to refuse the request of another. Thus if a man be asked by another to give him anything that he may possess, he will immediately do so. If the two men are equals a return of about the same value will have to be made. As between an older married man and a bachelor or a young married man, however, the younger would not make any request of such a nature, and if the older man asked the younger for anything the latter would give it without always expecting a return.

Almost every object that the Andamanese possess is thus constantly changing hands. Even canoes may be given away, but it is more usual for these to be lent by the owner to his friends.

It has been stated above that all food is private property and belongs to the man or woman who has obtained it. Every one who has food is expected, however, to give to those who have none. An older married man will reserve for himself sufficient for his family, and will then give the rest to his friends. A younger man is expected to give away the best of what he gets to the older men. This is particularly the case with the bachelors. Should a young unmarried man kill a pig he must be content to see it distributed by one of the older men, all the best parts going to the seniors, while he and his companions must be satisfied with the inferior parts. The result of these customs is that practically all the food obtained is evenly distributed through the whole camp, the only inequality being that the younger men do not fare so well as their elders. Generosity is esteemed by the Andaman Islanders one of the highest of virtues and is unremittingly practised by the majority of them.

Within the local group there is no such thing as a division of labour save as between the two sexes. In the coastal groups every man is expected to be able to hunt pig, to harpoon turtle and to catch fish, and also to cut a canoe, to make bows and arrows and all the other objects that are made by men. It happens that some men are more skilful in certain pursuits than in others. A skilful turtle-hunter, for example, may be an indifferent pig-hunter, and such a man will naturally prefer to devote himself to the pursuit in which he appears to most advantage.

The division of labour between the sexes is fairly clearly marked. A man hunts and fishes, using the bow and arrow and the harpoon; he makes his own bows and arrows, his adze and knife, cuts canoes and makes rope for harpoon lines. A woman collects fruits and digs up roots with her digging stick; she catches prawns and crabs and small fish with her small fishing net; she provides the firewood and the water of the family and does the cooking (i.e. the family cooking, but not the common cooking, which is entirely done by men); she makes all such objects as baskets, nets of thread, and personal ornaments either for herself or her husband.

There is no organised government in an Andamanese village. The affairs of the community are regulated entirely by the older men and women. The younger members of the community are brought up to pay respect to their elders and to submit to them in many ways. It has already been shown how, in the distribution of food, the elders get the best share. When it is a question of shifting camp to some better hunting ground the opinion of the older men would weigh against that of the younger if they disagreed. It must not be thought, however, that the older men are tyrannical or selfish. I only once heard a young man complain of the older men getting so much the best of everything. The respect for seniority is kept alive partly by tradition and partly by the fact that the older men have had a greater experience than the younger. It could probably not be maintained if it regularly gave rise to any tyrannical treatment of the younger by the elder.

The respect for seniors is shown in the existence of special terms of address which men and women use when speaking to their elders. In the languages of the North Andaman there are two such terms, *Mai* or *Maia*, applied to men, with a meaning equivalent to "Sir," and *Mimi*, applied to women. These words may be used either alone or prefixed to the personal name of the person addressed. A younger man speaking to an older one whose name was *Bora* would address him either as *Mai* (Sir), or as *Maia Bora* (Sir Bora).

In the tribes of the South Andaman there are exactly similar terms. In the *Aka-Bea* tribe *Maia* or *Maiola* is used in addressing men and *Čana* or *Čanola* in speaking to women. In *Akar-Bale* the equivalent terms are *Da* and *In*. Besides these terms there is in these tribes another, *Mam, Mama* or *Mamola*, which may be used in speaking to either men or women, and which implies a higher degree of respect than *Maia* or *Čana*. In these tribes also there is a special way of showing respect by adding the suffix *-la* to the name of the person addressed, as *Bia*, *Biala*, *Woičo*, *Woičo-la*, etc.

In the legends of the Andamanese these titles are nearly always prefixed to the names of the legendary ancestors, as *Maia Jutpu* and *Mimi Biliku* in *Aka-Jeru*, or *Da Duku* and *In Bain* in *Akar-Bale*. The moon is similarly spoken of as Sir Moon (*Maia Ogar* in *Aka-Bea*) and the sun as Lady Sun (*Čana Bodo*).

Besides the respect for seniority there is another important factor in the regulation of the social life, namely the respect for certain personal qualities. These qualities are skill in hunting and in warfare, generosity and kindness, and freedom from bad temper. A man possessing them inevitably acquires a position of influence in the community. His opinion on any subject carries more weight than that of another even older man. The younger men attach themselves to him, are anxious to please him by giving him any presents that they can, or by helping him in such work as cutting a canoe, and to join him in hunting parties or turtle expeditions. In each local group there was usually to be found one man who thus by his influence could control and direct others. Amongst the chief men of several friendly local groups it would generally happen that one of them, by reason of his personal qualities, would attain to a position of higher rank than the others. Younger men would be desirous of joining the local group to which he belonged. He would find himself popular and respected at the annual meetings of the different groups, and his influence would thus spread beyond the narrow limits of his own small community.

There was no special word to denote such men and distinguish them from others. In the languages of the North Andaman they were spoken of as *er-kuro* = "big."

Such men might perhaps be spoken of as "chiefs," but the term is somewhat misleading, as it makes us think of the organised chieftainship of other savage races.

The above statement is not quite in agreement with what has been written by Mr Man on the same subject, and what he says is therefore reproduced here. "Their domestic policy may be described as a communism modified by the authority, more or less nominal, of the chief. The head chief of a tribe is called *maia igla*, and the elders, or sub-chiefs, i.e. those in authority over each community, consisting of from 20 to 50 individuals, *maiola*. The head chief, who usually resides at a permanent encampment, has authority over all the sub-chiefs, but his power, like theirs, is very limited. It is exercised mainly in organising meetings between the various communities belonging to his tribe, and in exerting influence in all questions affecting the welfare of his followers. It is the chief alone, as may be supposed, who directs the movements of a party while on hunting and fishing expeditions, or when migrating. It is usually through his intervention that disputes are settled, but he possesses no power to punish or enforce obedience to his wishes, it being left to all alike to take the law into their own hands when aggrieved. The *aryoto* and *eremtaga* in each tribe have their own head chief, who are independent the one of the other. As might be assumed from the results of observations made of other savage races, whose sole or chief occupation consists in hunting or fishing, the power of the chiefs is very limited, and not necessarily hereditary, though, in the event of a grown-up son being left who was qualified for the post, he would, in most instances, be selected to succeed his father in preference to any other individual of equal efficiency. At the death of a chief there is no difficulty in appointing a successor, there being always at least one who is considered his deputy or right-hand man. As they are usually, on these occasions, unanimous in their choice, no formal election takes place; however, should any be found to dissent, the question is decided by the wishes of the majority, it being always open to malcontents to transfer their allegiance to another chief, since there is no such thing as forced submission to the authority of one who is not a general favourite. Social status being dependent not merely on the accident of relationship, but on skill in hunting, fishing, etc., and on a reputation for generosity and hospitality, the chiefs and elders are almost invariably superior in every respect to the rest. They and their wives are at liberty to enjoy immunity from the drudgery incidental to their mode of life, all such acts being voluntarily performed for them by the young unmarried persons living under their headship[1]."

Where Mr Man speaks of the "authority" of the chiefs it would be better to speak of "influence." Of authority the leading men have little or none, but of influence they have a good deal. Should any one venture to oppose a popular chief he would find the majority of the natives, including many of his friends, siding against him. The words "chief" and "authority" seem to imply some sort of organised rule and procedure, and of this there is nothing in the Andamans. Mr Man also implies that in each tribe there is always one recognized headman, but in reality each tribe may possess two or three leading men in different parts of the country, each with his own following. In any case a man's influence is largely confined to his own local group, for it is only at the annual meetings that the men of other groups come in contact with him.

The early officers of the Andamanese Homes (before the time of Mr Man) established a system of chieftainship in the islands by selecting a few of the more trustworthy and intelligent men, whom they dignified with the title of *raja*, and who acted as the intermediaries between the Officer in Charge of the Andamanese and the natives. This system has been continued to the present day, and the natives have adopted the title *raja* for these men, having themselves no word for a chief. Where a man is selected who is already respected and esteemed by the natives his influence is considerably increased through the position thus assigned to him. The natives themselves do not recognize that he has any authority over them, but if he be a man of generosity and tact, the majority will always support him, and his advice in any matters of moment will be readily followed.

Women may occupy a position of influence similar to that of the men. The wife of a leading man generally exercises the same sort of influence over the women as her husband does over the men. A woman, however, would not exercise any influence over the men in matters connected with hunting. They do have

---

[1] Man, in *Journ. Anthrop. Inst.* Vol. XII, p. 108.

a good deal of influence in connection with quarrels either of individuals or of local groups.

There are certain men, and possibly sometimes women, who have an influence over their fellows owing to their being credited with the possession of supernatural powers. These men, called in *Aka-Jeru oko-jumu* (literally "one who speaks from dreams"), will be described in a later chapter. As they are believed to have command over the powers that produce and cure sickness everyone tries to be on good terms with them, avoiding giving them offence in any way, and seeking their favour by presents of food or other things. It sometimes happens that a chief (the leading man of a local group) is at the same time a medicine-man or *oko-jumu*, but the two positions are entirely distinct and separate, and a man may be a medicine-man who possesses none of the qualities that are necessary for a head man.

There does not appear to have been in the Andamans any such thing as the punishment of crime. We may distinguish two kinds of anti-social actions which are regarded by the natives as being wrong. The first kind are those actions which injure in some way a private individual. The second are those, which, while they do not injure any particular person, are yet regarded with disapproval by the society in general.

Amongst the anti-social actions of the first kind are murder, or wounding, theft and adultery, and wilful damage of the property of another.

No case of one Andamanese killing another has occurred in recent years. Quarrels sometimes occur between two men of the same camp. A good deal of hard swearing goes on, and sometimes one of the men will work himself up to a high pitch of anger, in which he may seize his bow and discharge an arrow near to the one who has offended him, or may vent his ill-temper by destroying any property that he can lay his hands on, including not only that of his enemy but also that of other persons and even his own. At such a display of anger the women and children flee into the jungle in terror, and if the angry man be at all a formidable person the men occasionally do the same. It apparently requires more courage than the natives usually possess to endeavour to allay such a storm of anger. Yet I found that the slightest show of authority would immediately bring such a scene to an end. A man of influence in his village was probably generally equal to the task of keeping order and preventing any serious damage from taking place. It was probably rare for a man so far to give way to his anger as to kill his opponent.

Such murders did, however, occasionally take place[1]. The murderer would, as a rule, leave the camp and hide himself in the jungle, where he might be joined by such of his friends as were ready to take his part. It was left to the relatives and friends of the dead man to exact vengeance if they wished and if they could. If the murderer was a man who was much feared it is probable that he would escape. In any case the anger of the Andamanese is short-lived, and if for a few months he could keep out of the way of those who might seek revenge, it is probable that at the end of that time he would find their anger cooled.

A man who is liable to outbursts of violent anger is feared by his fellows, and unless he has other counterbalancing qualities, he is never likely to become popular. He is treated with outward respect, for every one is afraid of offending him, but he never acquires the esteem of others. There is a special nickname, *Tarenjek*, in the North Andaman, to denote such a man[2].

Quarrels were more likely to occur at the meetings of different local groups that took place in the fine weather, and such quarrels might occasionally end in the murder of some one. In such a case the quarrel would be taken up by the group

---

[1] The natives of the North Andaman were able to tell me of a few cases of murder which had occurred within the memory of those still living.

Mr Portman in his *History of Our Relations with the Andamanese* records a certain number of murders which occurred while he was in charge of the Andamanese. One man, who had been imprisoned at Port Blair for murder, committed another soon after his release and was hanged. Since that date there has been no case of murder among the Great Andaman tribes. This is perhaps in part due to the punishment with which they are now threatened by the Government, but another cause is probably the breakdown of the old social organisation which has in this respect rather improved their morals than the opposite.

[2] The nickname is applied, however, not only to those who deserve it by their character, but also to others; for instance, one man was called *Tarenjek* because his maternal uncle was a man of violent temper.

of the murdered man, and a feud would be set up between them and the local group to which the murderer belonged. Such was one of the common causes of origin of the petty warfare that formerly existed in the Andamans, which will be referred to later in the present chapter.

Cases of theft seem to have been rare. It was left to the aggrieved person to take vengeance upon the thief, but if he killed him or seriously wounded him he would have to expect the possible vengeance of the relatives and friends. Adultery was regarded as a form of theft. I gathered that a man had the right to punish his wife for unfaithfulness, but if the punishment were too severe it would be an occasion for a quarrel with her relatives. It was difficult for the aggrieved husband to punish the man who had offended against him. If he killed him he would lay himself open to the revenge of the relatives. The most he could do was to vent his anger in violent words.

Women also occasionally quarrel with one another and swear forcibly at one another, or even get so far as to destroy one another's belongings, or to fight with their fists or sticks. The men hesitate to interfere, and the quarrel can only be stopped by some woman of influence.

The frequent occurrence of serious quarrels is prevented both by the influence of the older men and by the fear that everyone has of the possible vengeance of others should he in any way offend them.

There are a number of actions which, while they do not offend any particular person, are regarded as being anti-social. One of these is laziness. Every man is expected to take his proper share in providing both himself and others with food. Should a man shirk this obligation, nothing would be said to him, unless he were a young unmarried man, and he would still be given food by others, but he would find himself occupying a position of inferiority in the camp, and would entirely lose the esteem of his fellows. Other qualities or actions that result in a similar loss of esteem are marital unfaithfulness, lack of respect to others and particularly to elders, meanness or niggardliness, and bad temper. One man was mentioned to me as being a bad man because he refused to take a wife after he had

PLATE I. An Andaman Islander shooting fish with bow and arrow on the reefs at Port Blair.

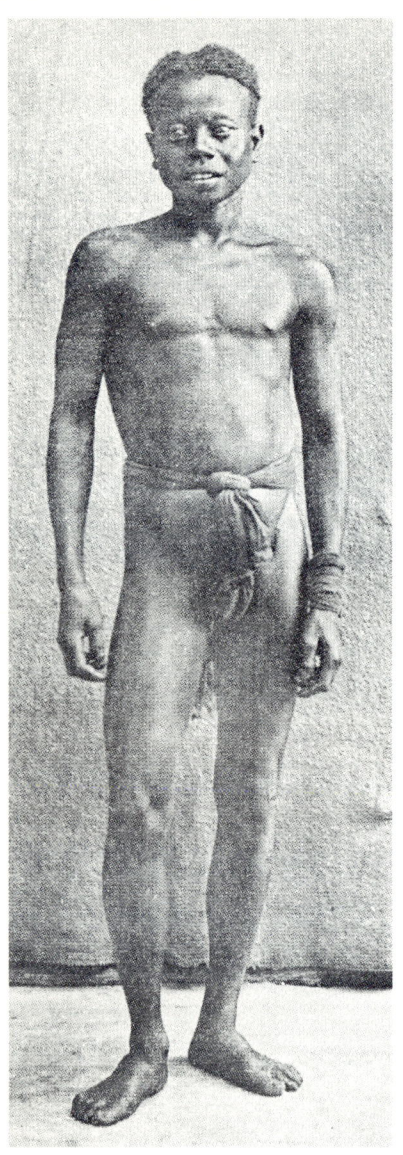

PLATE II *(left)*. A young man of the North Andaman. *(Right)* A young man decorated with white clay in readiness for a dance.

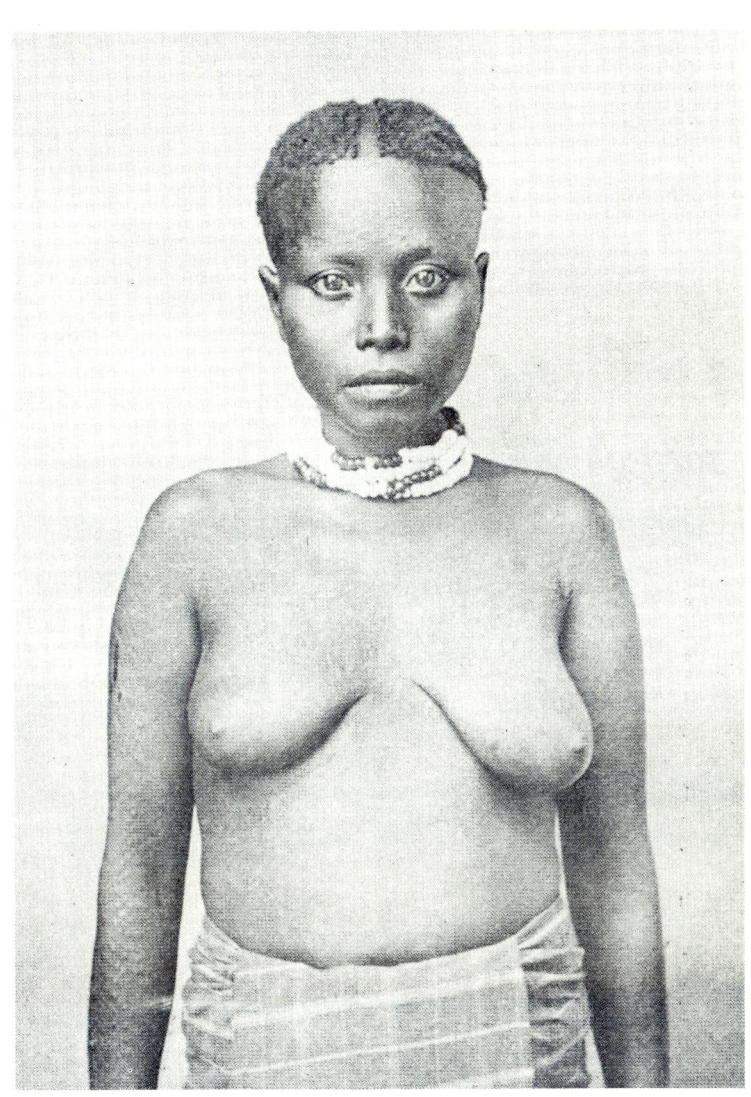

PLATE III. A young married woman.

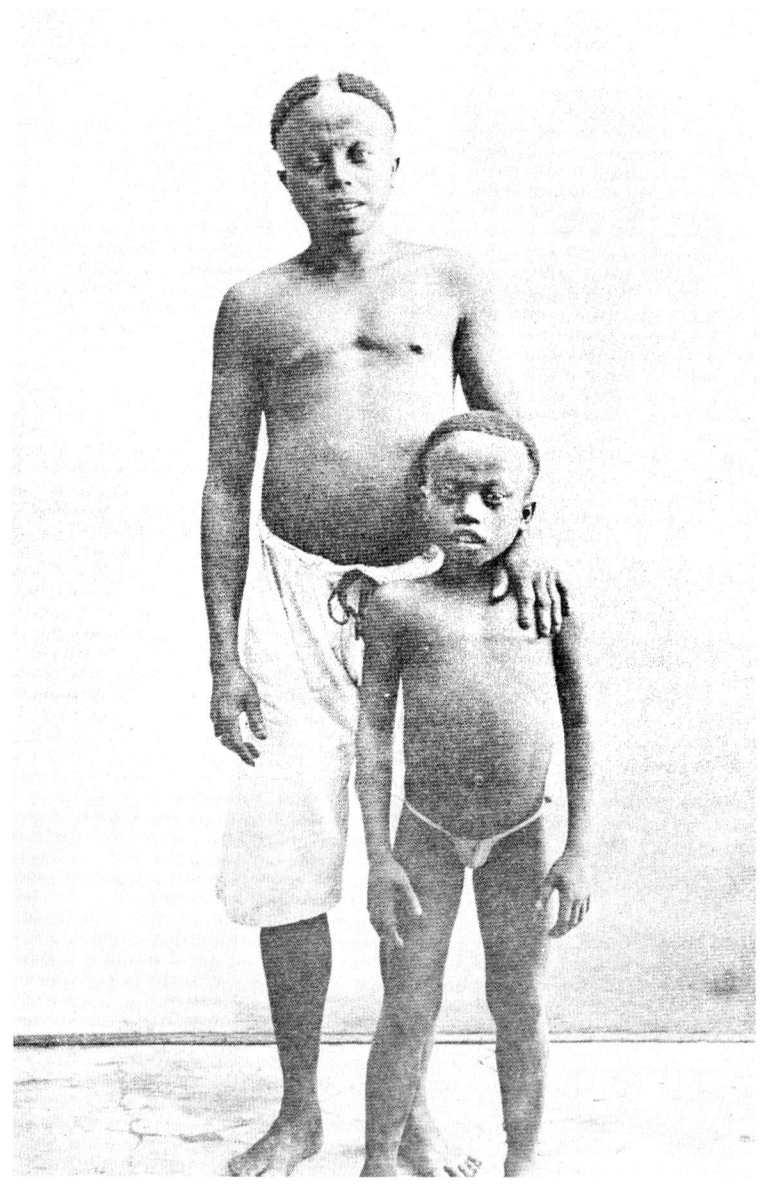

PLATE IV. A man of the North Andaman and his son. (The man's height is 1438 mm., 4 feet 8 inches.)

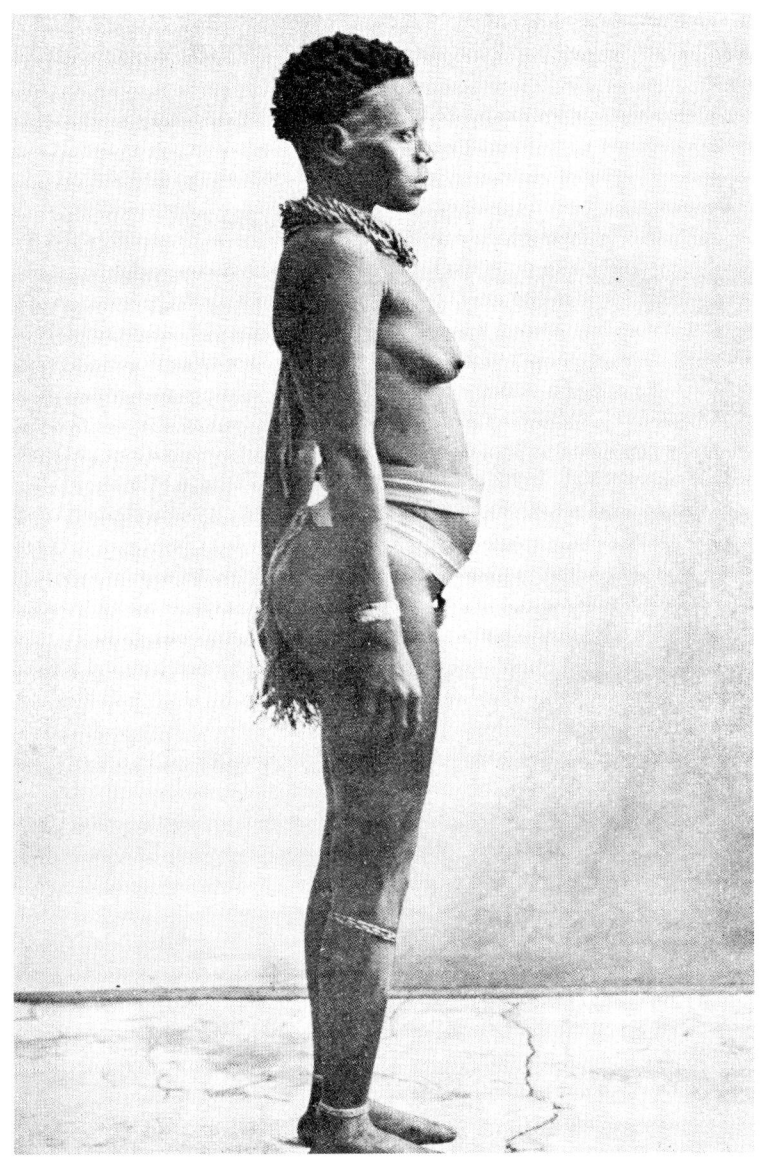

PLATE V. A married woman of the Great Andaman wearing belts of *Pandanus* leaf and ornaments of *Dentalium* shell.

PLATE VI. A man of the *Akar-Bale* tribe with South Andaman bow and arrows, wearing belt and necklace of netting and *Dentalium* shells. (Height 1494 mm., 4 feet 9 inches.)

PLATE VII *(above)*. A village of the Middle Andaman. *(Below)* A hut in the village of Moi-lepto, showing the mode of construction.

PLATE VIII. Portion of the village of Moi-lepto, *Akar-Bale* tribe. On the right is an unfinished mat of palm leaves for the roof of a new hut.

PLATE IX. Three men and a young woman decorated with *odu* clay.

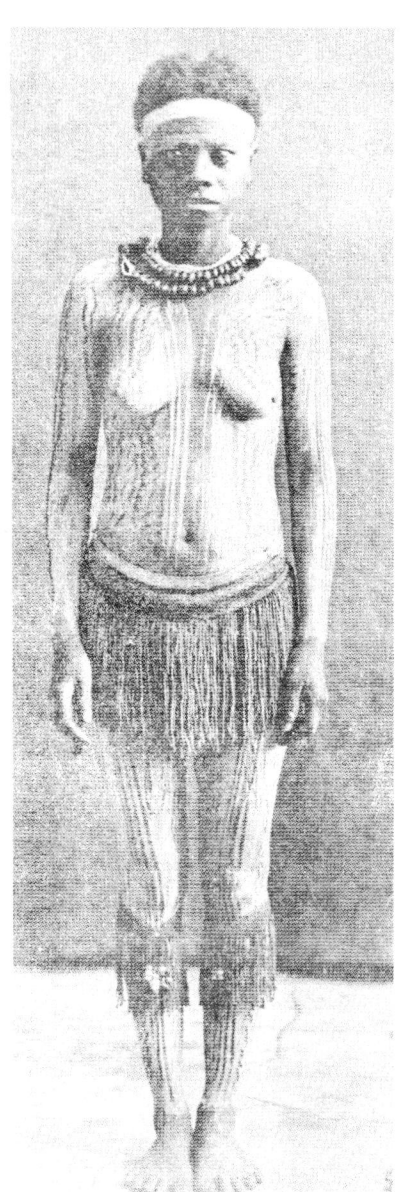

PLATE X. Women decorated with *odu* clay.

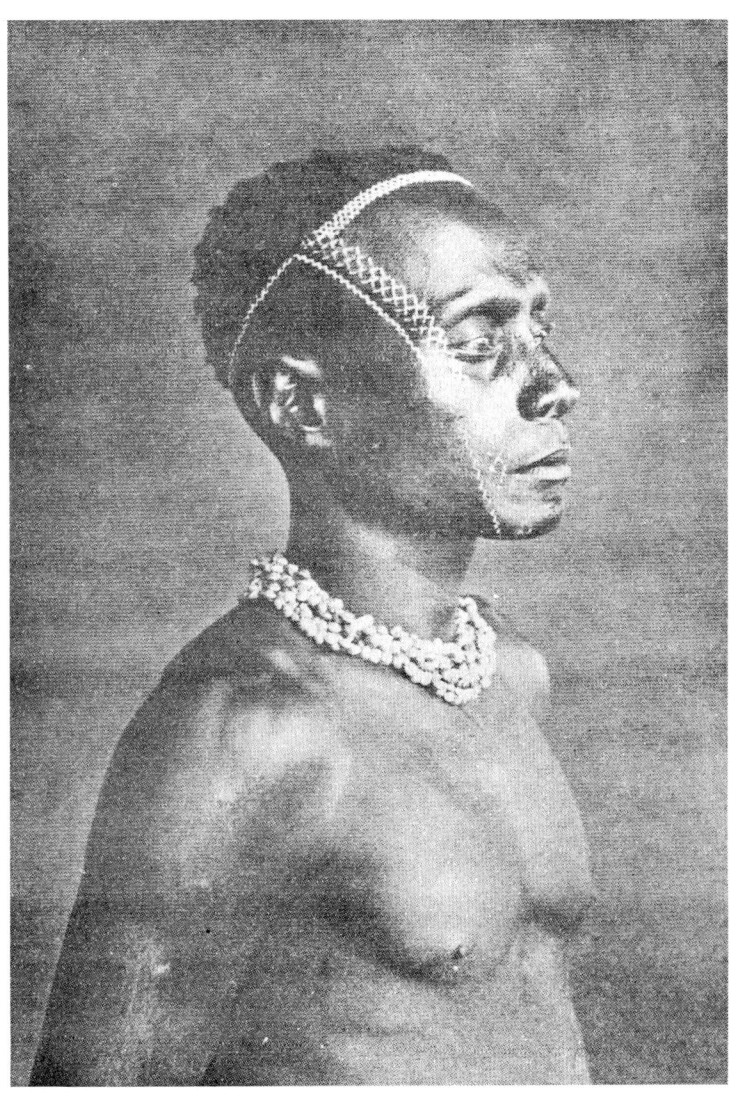

PLATE XI. A man with a pattern of white clay on his face.

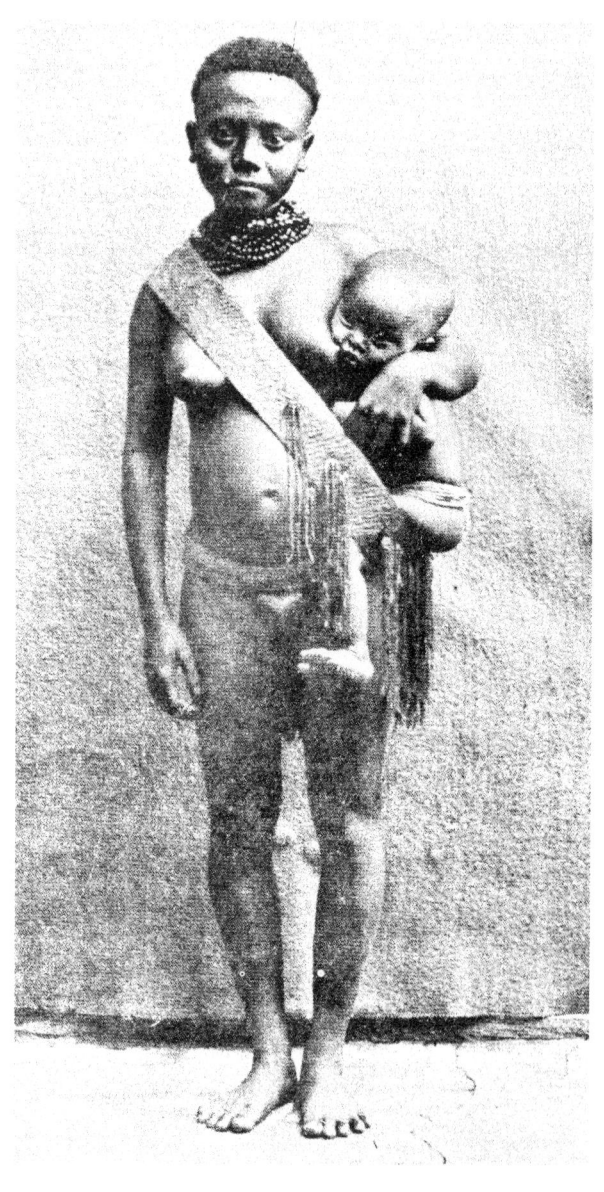

PLATE XII. A woman with her child.

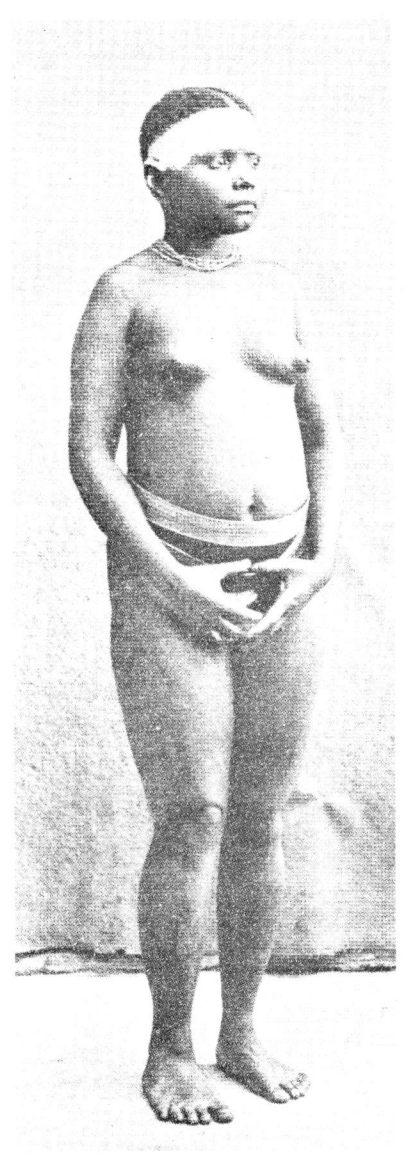 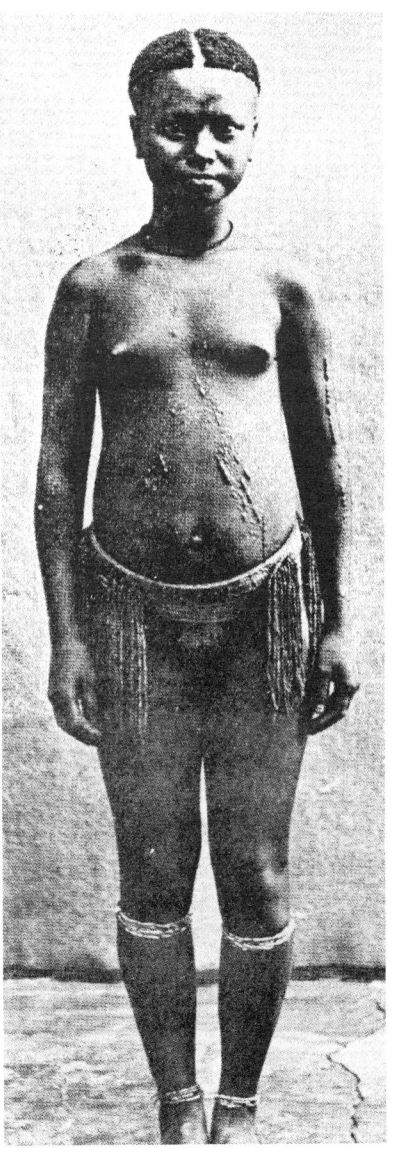

PLATE XIII (left). A woman wearing clay on her forehead as a sign of mourning. *(Right)* A young married woman, showing pattern scarified on body and arms.

PLATE XIV. A girl wearing her sister's skull.

PLATE XV. The peace-making dance of the North Andaman.

PLATE XVI. A girl during the ceremony at puberty, decorated with strips of *Pandanus* leaf.

reached the age when it is considered proper for a man to marry. In recent times at least one young man has refused to undergo the privations connected with the initiation ceremonies. This was of course a case of gross rebellion against the customs of the tribe, but there was no way of punishing him or of compelling him to conform, save by showing him that he was an object of contempt and ridicule to others. Probably such a refusal to conform to tribal customs could not have taken place before the British occupation of the islands.

Another class of wrong actions consists in the breaking of ritual prohibitions. There are, for example, as will be shown in a later chapter, a number of actions which it is believed may cause bad weather, such as burning bees'-wax or killing a cicada. There is, however, no punishment that can be meted out to any one who does any of these things. The punishment, if we may call it so, is a purely supernatural one, and it strikes not only the offender but every one else as well. In the legends of the Andamanese there are one or two stories related of how one of the ancestors, being angry, deliberately performed one of the forbidden actions and thus brought a storm that destroyed many human beings[1]. There are other ritual prohibitions the non-observance of which is supposed to bring its own punishment on the offender, who, it is believed, will be ill.

The medicine-men (*oko-jumu*) are credited with the power to work evil magic, and by its means to make other people ill, and even to kill them. A man suspected of evil magic might be liable to the vengeance of those who thought that they had been injured by him, but though the practice was regarded as reprehensible it does not seem that the society ever acted as a whole to punish a man suspected of it.

Children are reproved for improper behaviour, but they are never punished. During their years of infancy they are much spoilt, not only by their parents but by every one. During the period of adolescence every boy and girl has to undergo a somewhat severe discipline, to be described in a later chapter.

---

[1] See below, Chap. IV.

This probation, if it may be so called, is enforced by a unanimous public opinion. The discipline lasts until the man or woman is married and a parent, or if childless as so many now are, until he or she has settled down to a position of responsibility.

Thus, though the Andaman Islanders had a well developed social conscience, that is, a system of moral notions as to what is right and wrong, there was no such thing as the punishment of a crime by the society. If one person injured another it was left to the injured one to seek vengeance if he wished and if he dared. There were probably always some who would side with the criminal, their attachment to him overcoming their disapproval of his actions. The only painful result of anti-social actions was the loss of the esteem of others. This in itself was a punishment that the Andamanese, with their great personal vanity, would feel keenly, and it was in most instances sufficient to prevent such actions. For the rest, good order depended largely on the influence of the more prominent men and women.

We have so far considered only the general regulation of conduct in the local group, without giving any attention to the more special regulations dependent on relationships by blood and by marriage. In all human societies there is a system of rights and duties regulating the conduct towards one another of persons who are related either by consanguinity or through marriage. In primitive societies these particular rights and duties occupy a position of preponderating importance, owing, no doubt, to the small number of persons with whom any single person comes into effective social contact. When a large proportion of the men and women with whom any person comes in contact are related to him, it is clear that relationship must count for a good deal in regulating the everyday life of the people.

Different societies have different systems of relationship. This means, not only that they attach different duties to particular relations, but also that they have different ways of reckoning the relationships themselves. The vast majority of primitive peoples have some one or other form of what is known to ethnologists as the "classificatory system of relationship[1]." This system is intimately connected with the existence of the social divisions known as "clans." In the Andamans there are no clans, and the system of relationship is fundamentally different from all the classificatory systems.

To understand the Andamanese system it is necessary to examine the terms by which they denote the different kinds of relationship which are recognized[2]. In many societies having the classificatory system of relationship the terms which are used to denote relationship are also used as terms of address, just as we use the terms "Father" and "Mother." In the Andamans this is not so. There are special words that are used as terms of address, but these do not imply any relationship between the speaker and the person spoken to. In the North Andaman those terms are *Maia* (= Sir) and *Mimi* (= Lady). These are used by younger men and women in speaking to older persons. For the rest, persons are addressed freely by their personal names. There are no terms of address that imply any relationship of consanguinity between the person speaking and the person whom he addresses. This is an important feature of the Andamanese system, distinguishing it from the systems of many other primitive societies.

The following is a list of terms used to denote relationship in the North Andaman. There seems to be very little difference in this matter between the four tribes of the North (*Aka-Čari, Aka-Kǫra, Aka-Bo* and *Aka-Jeru*).

---

[1] The classificatory system of relationship was first studied and named by Lewis H. Morgan, in *Systems of Consanguinity and Affinity of the Human Family*, Washington, Smithsonian Institution, 1871. The subject is also discussed in the same author's *Ancient Society*. Although there has been a good deal of attention paid to the systems of relationship of savage tribes since the time of Morgan, there is no general work on the subject that supersedes these two books.

[2] The terms used in any society to denote relationships are of interest to the ethnologist as an important means to the discovery of the relationship system (i.e. the system of juridical and moral institutions) existing in the same society. Without a thorough knowledge of the terms in use and their exact meanings it is impossible to discover the rights and duties of relatives one to another. It is, however, sometimes forgotten that the study of terms of relationship is not an end in itself but a means to a more important study.

aka-mai	his father
aka-mimi	his mother
ot-tire	his child
ot-otoatue	his older brother
ot-otoatue-čip	his older sister
ot-arai-čulute	his younger brother
ot-arai-čulute-čip	his younger sister
ot-e-bui or *e-bui*	his wife (her husband)
e-pota-čiu	his father-in-law
e-pota-čip	his mother-in-law
ot-otone	his son-in-law.

Aka-mai and *aka-mimi*. The words for "father" and "mother" are derived from the terms of address *Maia* and *Mimi* by the addition in each case of the prefix *aka-*. By itself the term *Maia* is used by any man or woman in speaking to a man older than himself or herself without implying any relation between them beyond that of respective age. The addition of the prefix *aka-* changes the word, giving it the meaning "the father of somebody." Thus *Maia Bora* means "Mr Bora" or "Sir Bora," if we may so translate it, but *Bora aka-mai* means "Bora's father," and *aka-mai Bora* means "his or her father Bora." The *Aka-Jeru* equivalent for "my father" is *t'a-mai*, the *t'* being the personal pronoun "my," after which the prefix *aka-* is contracted to *a-*. Similarly "thy father" is *ŋ'a-mai* and "their father" or "their fathers" is *n'a-mai*. The word *aka-mimi* is in every respect exactly parallel to *aka-mai*. These two terms are only used when it is necessary to refer to the actual father or mother of anybody. For example, if a man be asked *Ačiu ŋ'a-mai bi?* (Who your father is?), he will reply by giving the name of his own father.

The stem *maia* clearly relates to the social position of the father of a family. A man who is a father, or while not having any children, is married and occupies an equivalent social position to a father, is addressed by the term which shows his social position, *Maia*. When I call a man *Maia*, I do not imply that he is *my* father nor that he is related to me at all, but only that he is *a* father. On the other hand, the prefix *aka-* added to the stem makes a possessive form, so that *aka-mai* means "his father" and *t'a-mai* means "my father." The word *mimi* is exactly parallel. By itself, the stem simply shows that the person addressed is *a* mother, while *aka-mimi* means "*his* mother."

Ot-tire. The word "child," when there is no reference to the child of some particular person, is translated *e-tire*, *-tire* being the stem and *e-* the prefix[1]. With a change of prefix from *-e* to *ot-*, a possessive form is made, so that *ot-tire* always means "his or her child," with reference to some particular person understood. Thus *Bora ot-tire* would mean "the child of Bora," while *Bora e-tire* or *e-tire Bora* would mean "the child Bora." The phrase *t'ot-tire* (my child) is used by either a man or a woman to denote his or her child.

Ot-otoatue and *ot-arai-čulute*. I was unable to find in the languages of the North Andaman any words which could properly be translated "brother" or "sister." The two words here given are used by the Andamanese to denote persons older or younger than the speaker, whether they be brothers and sisters or not. The derivation of *ot-otoatue* could not be ascertained, but the word means "he who was born before me," and it is used in this sense to denote any person of the speaker's generation who is older than himself. If it is necessary to emphasise the female sex of the person spoken of, the suffix *-čip* is added. An alternative word of exactly the same meaning is *ot-areupu* (fem. *ot-arep-čip*). The word *ot-arai-čulute* is formed from the stem *čulu* or *čulutu* meaning "following" or "after," which always takes the prefix *arai-*. (This prefix conveys a reference to position in time or space.) The stem is found in such phrases as *tio ŋ'arai-čulutu-bom*, "I will follow you" (literally *tio* = I, *ŋ'* = thou, *čulutu* = after, and *-bom*, verbal suffix), and *tarai-čulik* "afterwards" (*t-arai-čulu-ik*). The prefix *ot-*

---

[1] In the Andamanese languages a large number of words are formed from a stem and a prefix. *E-*, *ot-*, *aka-*, *ara-*, *ab-* etc. are prefixes of this kind. The function of the prefixes is (1) to show that the object denoted by the word is in a dependent relation to some other object understood, as for instance that it is part of that other object, and (2) to modify the reference of the stem, as for instance while *e-tire* means the offspring of an animal or an human being, *era-tire* means the offspring of a tree or plant (the young shoots). For a description of these prefixes the reader may be referred to the work of Mr Portman, *Notes on the Languages of the South Andaman Group of Tribes*.

added in front of the usual prefix *arai-* determines the particular use of the word as referring to human beings. Thus the word *ot-arai-čulute* means, literally, "he or she who was born after me." It is used in this sense by a man or woman to denote any person of the same generation who is younger than himself. The suffix *-čip* may be added to denote a female. Alternative words of the same meaning are *ot-ara-liču* and *ot-ara-bela*.

These words are not, properly speaking, terms of relationship, but serve only to denote the respective ages of two persons. I did not discover any terms whatever by which a man can distinguish his own brother or sister from any other man or woman of the same age.

Ot-e-bui. The stem *-bui* means "to marry," as in *n' e-bui-om* = they are married. "My husband" or "my wife" is simply *t'e-bui* or *t'ot-e-bui*.

E-pota-čiu and *e-pota-čip*. The derivation of these words was not discovered. They are the terms by which a man distinguishes his wife's father and mother, and a woman her husband's father and mother.

Ot-otone. The word and its meaning are somewhat doubtful. It was sometimes used by a man to denote his daughter's husband, and perhaps also his son's wife. I once heard it applied to a younger sister's husband. It may be compared with the same word as used in the South Andaman to be mentioned presently.

So far as could be discovered, there are no words in the languages of the North Andaman for grandfather, grandmother, uncle, aunt, cousin, etc. The terms given above can be combined to describe relatives of this kind, as

T'a-mimi aka-mai	my mother's father
Ot-e-bui ot-arai-čulute	his wife's younger brother
Ŋot-a-mai ot-arai-čulute	thy father's younger brother
T'ot-otoatue ot-tire	my older brother's child.

These compound terms are not often used, however.

The terms of relationship of the *Akar-Bale* tribe may be taken as representative of the tribes of the South Andaman. The following list contains all the more important of them.

da	father
ab-atr	father
in	mother
ar-bua	child
ar-kodire	child (father speaking)
ab-atet	child (mother speaking)
mama	grandparent
ǰat	grandchild
en-toaka-ŋa	older brother or sister
ar-dotot	younger brother or sister
otoni	son-in-law
oten	daughter-in-law
ab-i-ŋa	consort (husband or wife)
aka-yat	parent of child's consort
aka-bua	consort's younger brother or sister
ep-taruo-ŋa	step relative
ot-čat-ŋa	relative by adoption
aka-kuam	younger relative
ab-čuga	older relative (male)
ab-čupal	older relative (female).

Da and *in*. *Da* is the common term of address used when speaking to an older man to whom the speaker wishes to show respect. A man will speak of his own father as *dege da*, *dege* being the personal pronoun "my" as used before a word that has no prefix. The term *In* is the common term of address used in speaking to women. A man or woman will refer to his or her own mother as *deg' in*. The use of these two terms as applied to parents is very similar to the use of *aka-mai* and *aka-mimi* in the North Andaman, with the difference that in *Akar-Bale* the stem *da* or *in* does not take a prefix to modify its meaning. While the use of the terms *Da* and *In* as terms of address does not in the least imply that there is any relationship between the person speaking and the person addressed, yet the phrase *dege da* would in general be understood as referring to the speaker's own father.

Ab-atr. This is a word descriptive of the relationship of a father to his child. I never heard a man refer to his own father by this term, but it is heard in such phrases as *deg' in l'ab-atr* = my mother's father. It conveys a definite notion of the physiological relation between a father and his children, and might be translated "he who caused me to be conceived." There is probably a feminine equivalent meaning "mother," but it was not noted.

Ar-bua, ar-kodire and *ab-atet*. The *Akar-Bale* word for "infant" is *ab-liga* or *ab-dareka*. The latter word is the phonetic equivalent of the *e-tire* of the Northern languages. A parent often speaks of his or her infant son as *d'ab-bula*, and of his infant daughter as *d'ab-pal*, *ab-bula* and *ab-pal* being the terms for "male" and "female[1]." The exact use of the term *ar-bua* is difficult to determine. The stem *-bua* may be used by itself without a prefix. *Dege bua* (my child) would refer, I believe, only to the child of the speaker. On the other hand, a man would use the term *d'ar-bua* as referring not only to his own child but also to the child of a brother or a sister, or even to a person who was not related to him at all. So far as it could be determined, it seems that a man or woman might apply this term (*ar-bua*) to any person of the same generation as his or her children, whether a relative or not. It thus means "a person of the same generation as my own children," and describes, not relationship, but respective age. The word *ar-kodire* refers to the own child of a man, and *ab-atet* similarly refers to the own child of a woman. The two words together are thus equivalent to the *ot-tire* of the North Andaman, the *Akar-Bale* distinguishing between the offspring of a man (*ar-kodire*) and the offspring of a woman (*ab-atet*).

Mama. The word is translated above as meaning "grandparent," but it has a wider meaning than this. It is used as a term of address to convey more respect than is conveyed by the terms *Da* and *In*, and is thus used in addressing any man or woman who is considerably older than the speaker. With the personal pronoun, *dege mama*, it may be applied by a man or woman to any of his grandparents, and also to his father-in-law and mother-in-law, and to other senior relatives.

Jat. The word was explained to me by the natives as meaning "grandchild." It seems to be a sort of reciprocal of *mama*, and is apparently applicable by any old man or woman to any child of the same generation as his or her own grandchildren.

---

[1] *Dege bula* and *dege pal* mean "my husband" and "my wife" respectively.

En-toaka-ŋa and *ar-dotot*. These two words are used in exactly the same way as the words *ot-otoatue* and *ot-arai-čulute* of the North Andaman. They are not properly terms of relationship, but may be equally used in referring to non-relatives. *En-toaka-ŋa* means "he who was born before me," and *ar-dotot* means "he who was born after me." I was not able to discover any word by which a person could distinguish his own brother or sister from others of the same age. It is not certain, however, that such a word does not exist.

Otoni and *oten*. These are masculine and feminine forms of the same word, and are used to denote a daughter's husband and a son's wife. *Otoni* is also applied to a younger sister's husband, and *oten* to a younger brother's wife. The derivation of the words was not discovered.

Aka-yat. This is the native name for the relationship subsisting between a person's parents and his parents-in-law. My own mother or father is *aka-yat* to my wife's father or mother.

Aka-bua. The word is derived from the stem *bua*, meaning "child." It is applied by a man to the younger brothers and sisters of his wife, and by a woman to the younger brothers and sisters of her husband.

Ab-i-ŋa. The word is translated "consort," and means either husband or wife. It is derived from the verbal stem *-i-* meaning "to marry" (*on-i-re*), *ab-* being the prefix, and *-ŋa* the verbal suffix.

Ep-taruo-ŋa. The word is used to denote a step-child, or a younger step-brother or sister.

Ot-čat-ŋa. The word means "adopted." "My adopted child" is simply expressed as *d'ot-čat-ŋa*, while "my foster father" is *dege da ot-čat-ŋa*. The stem is *-čat-*, *-ŋa* being the verbal suffix and *ot-* the prefix.

Aka-kuam. In spite of several enquiries, I was unable to ascertain the significance of this word. I heard it applied on different occasions to a younger brother or sister, to a younger first cousin, and to the brothers and sisters of a wife. The only suitable translation would seem to be "my younger relative," but it is not certain that it even implies any relationship at all.

It is perhaps really a term denoting respective social status and is used by a married man to denote other married men who are somewhat younger than himself, and with whom he is on friendly terms.

Ab-čuga and *ab-čupal*. These are the masculine and feminine forms of one word. Mr Portman[1] gives them as meaning "married man" and "married woman." I heard them used, however, with the personal pronoun. Thus a man applied the term *ab-čuga* to his older brother, his older sister's husband, and to his father's brother. In this usage these two terms seem to be in a sense reciprocal to *aka-kuam*. A younger married man will refer to older married men and women as his *ab-čuga* and *ab-čupal*, while they will call him *aka-kuam*.

In his work on the Andamanese, Mr E. H. Man gives a long list of terms of relationship for the *Aka-Bea* tribe[2]. It will be of some interest to compare the terms there given with those of the *Akar-Bale* tribe described above.

D'ab-maiola (*D'ab-mai-ola*). This is translated by Mr Man as "father." In *Aka-Bea* the term *Maia* is the term of address corresponding to the *Da* of *Akar-Bale* and to the *Mai* of the North Andaman. The suffix *-ola*, added to this and other terms of address serves to convey additional respect, as *Maia*, *Mai-ola*, *Čana*, *Čan-ola*, *Mama*, *Mam-ola*. Thus *ab-mai-ola* corresponds to the *aka-mai* of the Northern languages.

Dia Maia. This is given by Mr Man as applicable to the following relatives:—my father's brother, my mother's brother, my father's sister's husband, my mother's sister's husband, my father's father's brother's (or sister's) son, my husband's grandfather, my wife's grandfather, my wife's sister's husband (if elder), my husband's sister's husband (if elder).

Dia maiola. My grandfather, my grandfather's brother, my grandmother's brother, my elder sister's husband.

It must be remembered that these terms are not properly terms of relationship at all. Any man who is older than the speaker is *Maia* or *Mai-ola* to him, the latter implying a slightly

---

[1] *Notes on the Languages of the South Andaman Group of Tribes.*

[2] Man, *op. cit.* p. 421. The *dia*, or the *d'* before a prefix, in the words of this list is the pronoun "my."

higher degree of respect than the former. It is probable that the three different terms given above are not used by the natives with the very precise distinctions that are drawn by Mr Man. It may be noted that Mr Portman writes in this connection:—
"*Maia* is an Honorific, equivalent to the English 'Sir,' and is used when addressing a male elder. A son calls his father 'Sir,' and uses no other word in speaking to, or of, him. A pronoun emphasises the relationship, as: $\dfrac{Dia\ maiola_1}{My\ Father}$."

D' ab-čanola. Given by Mr Man as meaning "my mother." It is the feminine equivalent of *d'ab-mai-ola*, *Čana* being the feminine of *Maia*, and corresponding to the *In* of *Akar-Bale* and the *Mimi* of *Aka-Jeru*.

Dia čanola. This is given as the *Aka-Bea* translation of the following:—my father's sister, my mother's sister, my father's brother's wife, my mother's brother's wife, my grandmother, my great aunt, my father's father's sister's daughter, my mother's mother's sister's daughter, my husband's grandmother, my wife's grandmother, my husband's sister (if senior and a mother), my elder brother's wife (if a mother). In its formation the term is the feminine equivalent of *dia mai-ola*, while in its use it is the equivalent both of this term and of *dia maia*. This serves to show that there is no real precise distinction between *dia maia* and *dia mai-ola*, such as Mr Man's list would seem to imply. *Dia čan-ola* is not, properly speaking, a term of relationship. Any married woman senior to the speaker is entitled to be addressed as *Čana* or *Čan-ola*.

D'ab-čabil. Mr Man gives this as translating "my father, my step-father." The feminine equivalent would seem to be *d'ab-čanola*, which is given for "my mother" and "my step-mother." Mr Portman gives *ab-čabil* and *ab-čana* as the *Aka-Bea* terms for "married man" and "married woman[2]." The two words are the equivalents of the *Akar-Bale ab-čuga* and *ab-čupal*.

D'ar-odi-ŋa. This word is given by Mr Man as one of the equivalents for "my father." It is parallel to the *Akar-Bale*

---

[1] Portman, *Notes on the Languages of the South Andaman Group of Tribes*, p. 255.
[2] *Op. cit.* p. 100.

term *ab-atr*, and is strictly a term of physiological relationship, meaning "he who caused me to be conceived."

D'ab-eti-ŋa. This is translated by Mr Man as "my mother." It is the corresponding term to *d'ar-odi-ŋa*, and refers to the physiological relationship.

D'ab-weji-ŋa or *d'ab-wejeri-ŋa*. This also means "my mother," and is only an alternative word for the above. The stems *eti* and *weji* or *wejeri* seem to be two stems meaning the same thing.

D'ar-odi-re or *d'ar-odi-yate*. Given by Mr Man as meaning "my son" (if over three years of age, father speaking). It is the equivalent of the *Akar-Bale ar-kodire*.

D'ab-eti-re, *d'ab-eti-yate*, *d'ab-weji-re*, *d'ab-weji-yate*, *d'ab-wejeri-re*, *d'ab-wejeri-yate*. These are all given by Mr Man as translating "my son" (if over three years of age, mother speaking). They are equivalent to the *Akar-Bale ab-atet*.

The above words seem to be derived from three stems, -*odi*-, -*eti*-, and -*weji*- (or -*wejeri*-), the stems -*eti*- and -*weji*- having exactly the same meaning, and belonging, perhaps, to different dialects. The words are formed by the addition of the prefixes *ar*- and *ab*-, and the verbal suffixes -*ŋa*, -*re*, -*yate*. Thus we have *ar-odi-ŋa*, "father," and *ar-odi-re* or *ar-odi-yate*, "son." Similarly we have *ab-eti-ŋa*, "mother," and *ab-eti-re* or *ab-eti-yate*, "son" (mother speaking), while similar equivalents are made from the stem -*weji*-. The words given as meaning "son" may also be used to mean "daughter," but when it is necessary to emphasise the female sex, the suffix -*pail* (meaning "female") is added, as *d'ar-odi-re-pail*, *d'ab-eti-re-pail*.

Dia ota and *dia kata*. These are given by Mr Man as meaning respectively "my son" and "my daughter" (if under three years of age, either parent speaking). *Ota* and *kata* are the terms for the male and female genitals.

Dia ba. This is given by Mr Man as meaning "my daughter" (if over three years of age, either parent speaking). It is the phonetic equivalent of *dege bua* in *Akar-Bale*.

Dia ba-lola. Given as the equivalent of:—my grandson (either grandparent speaking), my brother's grandson (male or female speaking), my sister's grandson (male or female speaking).

The same phrase with the addition of *-pail*, meaning "female," is given as equivalent to:—my granddaughter, my brother's granddaughter, and my sister's granddaughter (male or female speaking).

D'ar-ba. According to Mr Man this term is applicable by a male or female to the son of a brother, a sister, a half-brother, a half-sister, or of a male or female first cousin. With the addition of *-pail*, meaning "female," it is applicable to the daughter of any of the above.

Ad en-toba-re, ad en-toba-ŋa, ad en-toka-re, ad en-toka-ŋa. These terms are given by Mr Man as alternative equivalents for "my elder brother (male or female speaking)." The stem is *-toba-* or *-toka-*, with the prefix *en-* and the verbal suffix *-re* or *-ŋa*. The *ad* is a special form of the first personal pronoun, generally *d'*. With the addition of *-pail*, meaning "female," the term is applicable to an elder sister. The word corresponds, both phonetically and in meaning, to the *Akar-Bale en-toaka-ŋa*.

D'ar-doati-ŋa. Given as meaning "my younger brother (male or female speaking)." With the addition of *-pail*, it is applied to a younger sister. Mr Man gives the word as being also applicable to a first cousin, if younger than the speaker.

D'ar-weji-ŋa or *d'ar-wejeri-ŋa*. These are given by Mr Man as alternative terms for "younger brother," and, with the addition of *-pail*, for "younger sister." It is to be noted that the stem *-weji-* or *-wejeri-* is the same that occurs in one of the terms for "mother," but that the prefix is different, being in this case *ar-* instead of *ab-*.

Dia mama. This is given as meaning "my wife's brother, or my husband's brother (if of equal standing)."

Dia mam-ola. Given as the equivalent of the following:—my husband's father, my husband's mother, my wife's father, my wife's mother, my husband's elder brother, my wife's brother (if older), my husband's sister's husband (if older), my wife's sister (if older and a mother), my husband's brother's wife (if older), my wife's brother's wife (if older).

Mama and *Mam-ola* are terms of address in *Aka-Bea*. *Mam-ola* implies a somewhat greater degree of respect than

Mama, and this in its turn is more respectful than *Mai-ola* or *Maia*.

D'aka-kam. Mr Man gives this as a term applicable to the following relatives:—my younger brother, my younger half-brother. With the addition of *-pail*, it is applicable to a younger sister or half-sister.

Dia otoniya and *dia otin*. The first of these terms is given as meaning:—my son-in-law (male or female speaking), and my younger sister's husband (male or female speaking). The second term is feminine, and is given as applicable to the following:—daughter-in-law, husband's sister (if younger), husband's brother's wife (if younger). wife's brother's wife (if younger). The terms are thus equivalent, phonetically and in meaning, to the *Akar-Bale* terms *otoni* and *oten*.

Aka-yakat. This is given as the relationship subsisting between a married couple's fathers-in-law, and between their mothers-in-law. It is the equivalent of the *Akar-Bale* word *aka-yat*.

D'aka-ba-bula and *d'aka-ba-pail*. The meaning of the first of these is given as "my husband's brother (if younger)," and of the second as "my younger brother's wife." The suffixes *-bula* and *-pail* mean "male" and "female" respectively. The term *aka-ba* is the phonetic equivalent of the *Akar-Bale* word *aka-bua*. The latter seems to be applied to the younger brothers and sisters of a man's wife or of a woman's husband, and to these alone. The use of these terms and of the terms *otoni* and *oten*, as recorded from the *Akar-Bale* tribe, may be compared with the usage stated by Mr Man, as there is some disagreement. In the following table the *Aka-Bea* terms are given as they are found in Mr Man's list, while those of the *Akar-Bale* tribe are given from my own information.

	Aka-Bea	Akar-Bale
Husband's younger brother	*aka-ba-bula*	*aka-bua*
Husband's younger sister	*otin*	*aka-bua*
Wife's younger brother	....	*aka-bua*
Wife's younger sister	....	*aka-bua*
Younger brother's wife	*aka-ba-pail*	*oten*
Younger sister's husband	*otoniya*	*otoni*.

It will be observed that the *Akar-Bale* list is consistent and logical throughout. It seems probable that there is an error in Mr Man's list, and that "husband's younger sister" should be *aka-ba-pail* instead of *otin*, while "younger brother's wife" should be *otin* instead of *aka-ba-pail*. This would make the *Aka-Bea* list consistent with itself and with the *Akar-Bale* list.

Mr Man gives, in addition to the terms discussed above, a number of compound terms, which we may examine briefly.

D'ar-čabil-entoba-re. This is given as applicable to any first cousin or half-brother who is older than the speaker. The feminine form is given as *d'ar-čanol-a-entoba-yate*.

D'ar-čabil-entoba-re lai-ik-yate. This is applicable to the wife of any first cousin or half-brother, if older than the speaker. As *lai-ik-yate* means "his wife," this is a descriptive term. There is a similar term *dia čanol a-entoba-yate lai-ik-yate* for the husband of an older female cousin or half-sister.

D'ar-ba lai-ik-yate. This means "the wife of my *ar-ba*," and is therefore applicable to the wife of the son of a brother or sister or cousin, and to the husband of a daughter of a brother or sister or cousin.

There are a few other similar compounds that need not be given.

In Mr Man's list a step-son is given as *eb-aden-ire*. The word for adoption is *ot-čat-ya*, *d'ot-cat-ya* meaning "my adopted child" and *d'ab-mai-ot-čat-ya* "my adopted father."

The system of terms of relationship of the Andamanese is of great interest as being fundamentally different from the systems of other uncivilized peoples. It is by no means easy to discover the exact usage of the different terms that are mentioned above. It is, however, possible to gain a general idea, probably accurate in essentials, of the way in which the Andamanese languages express the notions of kinship.

We may consider first the terms of address and the terms of relationship formed from them. The terms of address are:—

Aka-Jeru	Aka-Bea	Akar-Bale	
Maia or *Mai*	Da	*Maia*	Sir
Mimi	In	*Cana*	Lady
......	Mama	*Mama* or *mamola*.	

The first of these is used in addressing males and the second in addressing females, while the third may be used either for males or for females and implies a higher degree of respect than the others.

In all the languages of the Great Andaman a man refers to his own father and mother by adding a personal pronoun to the words meaning "Sir" and "Lady." In *Aka-Jeru* a man speaks of his father as *t'a-mai*, and of his mother as *t'a-mimi*, the *a-* being a contracted form of the prefix *aka-*. This prefix is always used in this way in the Northern languages. It is not possible to say *tičo maia*, which would be the literal equivalent of *dege da* in *Akar-Bale*. In the *Akar-Bale* language the translation of "my father" and "my mother" is *dege da* and *deg' in*, the *dege* being the personal pronoun "my" as used before a word that has no prefix. The same formation is present also in the *A-Pučikwar* and *Aka-Kol* languages. For example in *Aka-Kol* "my father" is *tiye tao*, and "my mother" *tiye in*. In the *Aka-Bea* language, according to the information given by Mr Man, the word *maia* (or *maiola*) may be used combined with a prefix, as in *d'ab-maiola* = "my father," or it may be used simply with the personal pronoun as *dia maia* or *dia maiola*. According to Mr Man these last two terms are applied not to a man's own father, but to the other persons whom he addresses as *maia*. This is contradicted by Mr Portman who gives *dia maiola* as the *Aka-Bea* for "my father."

In the *Aka-Bea* and *Akar-Bale* languages (as also in *A-Pučikwar* and *Aka-Kol*) a man always addresses his grandparent or his father-in-law or mother-in-law by the term *Mama* or *Mamola*. He is therefore able to refer to these persons by adding the personal pronoun to the term of address, as *dege mama* in *Akar-Bale*. This cannot, however, be regarded as properly a term denoting relationship, for a man may apply the term *Mama* to a man or woman to whom he is not related at all[1].

The next kind of words that we may consider are those that describe the respective social position of two persons. Such are the words *ot-otoatue* and *ot-arai-čulute* in *Aka-Jeru*, meaning

---

[1] The natives commonly applied the term to me, in the form *Mam-jula*.

"he who was born before me" and "he who was born after me" respectively. These terms do not, strictly speaking, convey any idea of consanguinity, although they are commonly used to refer to a brother or a sister. Exactly equivalent terms are found in all the languages, for example the *en-toaka-ya* and *ar-dot-ot* of *Akar-Bale*. I was not able to discover in *Aka-Jeru* nor yet in *Akar-Bale* any term to denote a brother or a sister. In *Aka-Bea*, however, Mr Man records the term *ar-weji-ya* or *ar-wejeri-ya*. The stem *-weji-* or *-wejeri-*, as we shall shortly see, is a verbal stem referring to the act of birth, *-ya* is a verbal suffix, and the prefix *ar-* conveys a reference to position in space or time. The whole word seems to mean "he or she who was born in the same womb as myself," and is therefore strictly a word meaning "brother or sister." It is possible that similar words exist in *Akar-Jeru* and *Akar-Bale*, but I never came across them.

Other terms descriptive of social status are the *Akar-Bale* terms *ab-čuga* and *ab-čupal* which refer to married men and women particularly those older than the speaker. These also are not properly terms of relationship, though a man may refer to some of his relatives as *d'ab-čuga*, adding the personal pronoun to what is properly a word descriptive of the social position of the person in question. In *Aka-Bea* the equivalent terms are *ab-čabil* and *ab-čana*. It would seem that the term *aka-kuam* (*aka-kam* in *Aka-Bea*) is of the same kind, being applicable by an older married man to a younger. At any rate I was unable to discover that it conveyed to the natives any notion of relationship.

There are a certain number of terms that are descriptive of definite relationships. In the North *ot-e-bui*, and in *Akar-Bale* *ab-i-ya* are both of them derived from verbal stems meaning "to marry" and are used to denote a husband or a wife. In the North I did not discover any term descriptive of a father or a mother save those derived from the terms of address. In *Akar-Bale* and *Aka-Bea* there are such terms; *ab-atr* in *Akar-Bale* means "father" while the word for "mother" was not noted; in *Aka-Bea* a father is *ar-odi-ya*, and a mother is *ab-eti-ya*. These words are descriptive of the physiological relation between a parent and a child. A man's adopted mother could not be his *ab-eti-ŋa*, for this term applies only to the woman from whose womb he issued. Similarly an adopted father or a step-father could not be *ab-atr* or *ar-odi-ŋa*. There are similar words for child, which also refer to the physiological relation of a child to its parent. In the North the stem *-tire* means "offspring." The offspring of a plant, that is the young shoots, are denoted by the term *era-tire*, the prefix *era-* serving to convey a reference to trees and plants. The offspring of an animal or of a human being is *e-tire*. The word *e-tire* means "the child of somebody" without reference to any particular person as the parent. In the form *ot-tire* the word means "his or her child" with reference to some person understood. A man or woman cannot in strict accuracy apply the term *ot-tire* to his adopted child, though I believe that it might be used in this loose sense at times. An adopted child is "he whom I have adopted" *t'oi-čolo-kom*. In *Akar-Bale* and *Aka-Bea* there are different terms for "child" according as the reference is to the child of a man or to that of a woman. Thus in *Akar-Bale* the child (in the physiological sense) of a father is *ar-kodire*, and the child of a mother is *ab-atet*. In *Aka-Bea* the physiological relation of a father and child is denoted by the verbal stem *-odi-*. This stem takes the prefix *ar-*. The word for father is formed by adding the verbal suffix *-ŋa* (*ar-odi-ŋa*). The word for child (father speaking) is formed by means of the verbal suffix *-re* or *-yate* (*ar-odi-re* or *ar-odi-yate*). We may translate *d'ar-odi-ŋa* as meaning "he who caused me to be conceived" while *d'ar-odi-re* or *d'ar-odi-yate* means "him whom I caused to be conceived." In the same language the physiological relation of a mother and a child is denoted by the stem *-eti-*. This stem takes the prefix *ab-*. A mother is *ab-eti-ŋa*, and the child of a mother is *ab-eti-re* or *ab-eti-yate*, the verbal suffixes being used in a way similar to that in the case of the terms for father and child. In *Aka-Bea* there is also a stem *-weji-* or *-wejeri-* which has exactly the same meaning as *-eti-* and can be substituted for it in the terms meaning mother and child, as *ab-weji-ŋa* = mother, *ab-weji-re* = child.

Other descriptive words used to denote specific relationships are *e-pota-čiu* and *e-pota-čip* and *ot-otone* in the Northern languages. The derivations of these words has not been ascertained. Similar terms in *Akar-Bale* are *otoni* and *oten* and *aka-yat*. In this language I did not discover any word descriptive of the relationship of father-in-law or mother-in-law. Finally there are such terms as *ot-čat-ya* (adopted) and *ep-taruo-ya* (step-relative).

The most noteworthy feature of these terms is that it is impossible by means of them to deal with relationships that are at all distant. Thus there is no term by which a man can describe his grandfather. In *Akar-Bale* the phrase *dege mama* might mean a grandfather, but it might equally refer to a father-in-law. It is true that the simple terms may be combined as *Aka-Jeru* "*aka-mimi aka-mai*" = "his mother's father," or *Akar-Bale* "*deg' in l'ab-atr*" = "my mother's father," but these compounded terms are apparently not often used by the natives. A second noteworthy feature is the existence of terms to denote physiological relationships (as opposed to merely juridical relationships) such as the *Aka-Bea ar-odi-ya*, etc. Finally there is the apparent entire absence, so far as could be determined, of any classification of relatives such as is characteristic of the classificatory systems of relationship. Where there does seem to be some sort of approach to such classification, as in the use of the *Akar-Bale* term *dege mama*, we find that it is really based not on relationships of consanguinity and marriage, but on respective social status[1].

As, in the languages of the Andamans, there are few words serving to denote relationship, and on the contrary a

---

[1] The systems of relationship of savage peoples are often very difficult to study, even with a thorough mastery of the native language. My account of the Andamanese system is not perhaps complete and is therefore open to error. Since the above account was written I have had the opportunity of studying in Australia several examples of "classificatory" systems of relationship, and can now say very definitely that such a system presents an extreme contrast to the system of the Andamans. My failure fully to comprehend the Andamanese system was partly due to the difficulties of the language, in which I did not have time to become expert, and partly to the nature of the Andamanese terms, of which it is by no means easy to discover the meaning, even with careful observation.

developed system of terms denoting social status, so in the social organisation of the Andamans there are very few special duties between relatives, and the conduct of persons to one another is chiefly determined by their respective social positions. This will become evident as we proceed, and it will thus be shown that there is a close connection between the way the natives denote relationships and the way in which their social life is affected by questions of relationship.

We have already seen that in the Andamanese social organisation the family is of great importance. A family is constituted by a permanent union between one man and one woman. In one of its aspects this union is a sexual one. By marriage a man acquires the sole right to sexual congress with the woman who becomes his wife. At the same time it is the duty of a married man to avoid sexual relations with other women whether married or unmarried. Promiscuous intercourse between the sexes is the rule before marriage, and no harm is thought of it. The love affairs of the boys and girls are carried on in secret, but the older members of the camp are generally fully aware of all that goes on. What generally happens is that after a time a youth forms an attachment with some girl and a marriage between them results from their love affair.

It is impossible, at the present time, to discover exactly how the Andamanese formerly regarded infidelity on the part of a wife or husband. In the Great Andaman there is great laxity in this matter at the present day. Quarrels sometimes arise when a husband discovers an intrigue between his wife and another man, but very often the husband seems to condone the adultery of his wife. Mr E. H. Man, writing on this subject, says that "conjugal fidelity till death is not the exception, but the rule," and adds, "It is undoubtedly true that breaches of morality have occasionally taken place among a few of the married persons who have resided for any length of time at Port Blair, but this is only what might be expected from constant association with the Indian convict attendants at the various homes; justice, however, demands that in judging of their moral characteristics we should consider only those who have been uninfluenced by the vices or virtues of alien races[1]." At the present time conjugal infidelity is very common and is lightly regarded. It is almost certain that the establishment of the Penal Settlement amongst them has affected their morals in this particular, but there does not seem to be any very satisfactory evidence that their former morality was quite so strict as Mr Man would have us believe. One piece of evidence in this matter is that the spread of syphilis, when it was first introduced amongst them seems to have been very rapid, and yet this was before many of the tribes had been very seriously affected by the Settlement.

Besides the special sexual relation between a husband and wife there is a special economic relation, if we may speak of it as such. The two share one hut between them, or one portion of a communal hut. It is the duty of the wife to provide the fire-wood and the water for cooking and drinking, and to cook the meals at the family fire. It is the duty of the husband to provide flesh food for himself and for his wife, while it is her duty to provide and prepare vegetable food.

A marriage is not regarded as fully consummated until the birth of a child. Mr Man states that the survivor of a childless couple is not looked upon as the chief mourner. A father who has been away from home greets his wife first on his return and then greets his other relatives; but if no child has been born to him a husband first greets his blood-relatives (father, mother, brothers, etc.) and only after that does he visit his wife.

The only regulation of marriage is on the basis of relationship. Marriage is forbidden between near *consanguinei*. The exact rules, in this matter, if indeed there be any exact rules, are difficult to discover. It is quite clear that a man would not be permitted to marry his sister or half-sister, nor his father's or mother's sister, nor his brother's or sister's daughter. The question is more difficult when it comes to the matter of cousins. In 1908 I only found one pair of first cousins who were married to one another, this being in the *Aka-Bo* tribe. The husband

---

[1] Man, *op. cit.* p. 135. He speaks of the wives as "models of constancy."

and wife were the son and daughter of two brothers. Mr E. H. Man writes that "marriage is only permissible between those who are known to be not even distantly connected, except by wedlock, with each other; so inexorable, indeed is this rule, that it extends and applies equally to such as are related merely by the custom of adoption." He adds that marriage between first cousins is forbidden. I was not able to satisfy myself on this point, but it seemed to me that while such a marriage as that of first cousins was not actually regarded as wrong, and therefore forbidden, it was regarded as preferable that a man should marry a woman not so nearly related to him. No distinction is made between different kinds of cousin[1].

My observations did not confirm Mr Man's statement that persons related by adoption are forbidden to marry. It is necessary, however, to distinguish two different kinds of adoption. When the parents of a child of less than six or seven years of age die, the child is adopted into some other family. We may call this "orphan adoption." As will be explained later, there is another custom by which children of over seven or eight are adopted by a married couple belonging to a local group other than that of the parents, and live with them till they come of age. The parents of the child are still alive and they visit him or her at frequent intervals. No bar to marriage is set up by this kind of adoption. An adopted son may marry the daughter of his foster-parents. Indeed when children are betrothed it is the rule for the girl to be adopted by the boy's parents, at any rate for a time. On the other hand it is quite possible that a child adopted when of tender years (as an orphan) would not be permitted to marry a child of his or her foster-parents. I was unable to satisfy myself on this point.

There seems to be a prejudice against a woman marrying a man younger than herself. Some of the women with whom I talked expressed strong contempt at the idea of marrying a man younger than themselves. Unfortunately, I neglected

---

[1] I collected a number of genealogies from the natives, but unfortunately my own inexperience in the use of the genealogical method, and my consequent inability to surmount the difficulties with which I met, made this branch of my investigations a failure.

to obtain statistics as to the frequency with which such marriages occur, if they occur at all.

Beyond the prohibition of the marriage of near kin, I could not find any restriction on marriage. A man may marry a woman from his own local group or from another, from his own or from another tribe. That marriages between persons belonging to the same local group did occur in former times I was able to ascertain with certainty but I was not able to determine the proportion of such marriages to the whole number. It is probable that the majority of marriages, or at any rate a large proportion, were between persons belonging to different local groups.

Marriages are arranged by the older men and women. Children are sometimes betrothed by their parents while they are still infants. I found one such case in the North Andaman, and the betrothed couple, though they were yet small children, were spoken of as being "married." Such betrothals are not very common at the present time.

When the parents of a youth who is of suitable age to be married perceive that he has formed an attachment with a girl, they take it upon them to arrange a marriage. The matter is first of all talked over between the young man and his parents. The man's parents do not themselves speak to the girl's parents of the matter, but request some one or more of their friends to do so. From the moment that the possibility of a marriage exists the man's parents avoid speaking to the girl's parents. Any communication between them is carried on through a third person. They send presents to each other, of food and other objects. The recipient of such a present hastens to make a return of equal value. If the marriage is arranged the parents on each side become related to one another by the relationship denoted in *Akar-Bale* by the word *aka-yat*. The duties implied by this relationship will be described later.

When a marriage has finally been arranged an evening is appointed for the ceremony. In the North Andaman this is as follows. The bride is seated on a mat at one end of the dancing ground, her relatives and friends sitting near her. Torches or heaps of resin are lighted near by, so that the ceremony may be seen by the on-lookers. The bridegroom is seated with his friends at the other end of the dancing ground. One of the older and more respected men addresses the bride, telling her that she must make a good wife, must provide for her husband such things as it is the duty of a wife to obtain or make, must see that he does not run after other women, and must herself remain faithful to him. He then addresses the bridegroom to the same effect, and taking him by the hand or arm, leads him to where the bride is seated and makes him sit down beside her. The relatives and friends weep loudly, and the young couple look very self-conscious and uncomfortable. The shyness of the young man is such that he often attempts to run away, but he is caught by his friends, who are prepared for such an attempt. After some minutes the officiating elder takes the arms of the bride and bridegroom and places them around each other's necks. After a further interval he again approaches and makes the bridegroom sit on the bride's lap[1]. They sit so for some minutes and the ceremony is over. The other members of the community generally have a dance on such an occasion, but in this the newly wedded pair do not join. A hut has already been prepared for them, and all their friends make them presents of useful objects with which to start house-keeping. They retire shyly to their new hut, while their friends continue dancing. The day after the ceremony the bride and bridegroom are decorated by their friends with white clay. For a few days the newly married couple are very shy of each other, hardly venturing to speak to or look at one another: but they soon settle down to their new position in the life of the community. During the early days of their marriage they are abundantly supplied with food by their friends. They are not addressed or spoken of by name, but if their names be A and B, the husband is called " the husband of B " while the wife is called " the wife of A."

In the South Andaman the ceremony is much the same as in the North, the only difference being that the bridegroom is led to where the bride is sitting and is made to sit on her lap straightway, remaining there for a few minutes.

[1] When a husband and wife greet one another the man sits on the lap of the wife.

When a husband dies his widow may marry again if she wishes. As a rule I believe that it is not considered fitting that she should take another husband before the end of her mourning for her former one. Mr Man says "it is not considered decorous that any fresh alliance should be contracted until about a year had elapsed from the date of bereavement[1]." I knew of one case, however, of a woman with a young child who married again only a fortnight or so after her husband's death.

Mr Man speaks of a custom " which all but compels a bachelor or widower to propose to the childless widow of his elder brother or cousin (if she be not past her prime), while she has no choice beyond remaining single or accepting him ; should she have no younger brother-in-law (or cousin by marriage), however, she is free to wed whom she will. It should be added that marriage with a deceased wife's younger sister is equally a matter of necessity on the part of a *childless* widower[2]."

I was not able to come across a case in which a man had actually married his elder brother's widow in recent years. The natives whom I questioned confirmed Mr Man's statement, which, moreover, was based on at least one instance known to him as having occurred. It may be noted that in his description of this instance Mr Man says that the woman married her husband's " brother or cousin," leaving us in doubt as to which of these two relatives it really was. There is an ambiguity in the use of the term "younger brother," for the Andamanese have no word meaning simply " younger brother," but only such terms as *ot-arai-čulute* and the equivalents in other languages, which apply to any younger person, whether actually a brother or cousin or not.

The recent changes in the social life of the Andamanese render it difficult to determine what was the former practice in matters of this sort, but I believe that the custom was this, that when a man of a local group died the older men selected one of the unmarried men and required him to marry the widow. They selected a man who was younger than the deceased, that is who was his *ot-arai-čulute*, and gave the preference to an unmarried younger brother if there were one, or to a relative of the deceased, such as a father's brother's son.

[1] Man, *op. cit.* p. 139.   [2] *Ibid.*

It may be noted that this custom may conflict with the other custom, previously mentioned, that a woman objects to marrying a man younger than herself. In the case mentioned by Mr Man a young man was compelled to marry a woman who was considerably his senior[1].

I believe that, in connection with, or underlying this custom there was an objection against a widow marrying a man who was older than her former husband (and who would therefore be his *ot-otoatue*). I regret that I cannot speak with certainty on these matters.

We may turn now to the duties to one another of parents and children. During their infancy the children are in the care of the mother. Children are, however, such favourites with the Andamanese that a child is played with and petted and nursed not only by his own father and mother but by everyone in the village. A woman with an unweaned child will often give suck to the children of other women. Babies are not weaned till they are three or four years old.

Before the children can walk, they are carried about by the mother, and sometimes by the father or other persons, in a bark sling (called *čiba* in *Aka-Jeru*), which is shown in Plate XIV. After they can walk the children generally accompany their mothers in their expeditions near the camp for firewood or vegetables. When they are not with their mothers they amuse themselves with games in the village or on the beach. All the children of the coast villages learn to swim when they are very young, in fact almost as soon as they learn to walk, and many of their games are conducted in the water.

When a boy reaches the age of five or six his father makes him a toy bow and arrows, and sometimes a toy canoe. From this time the boy begins to learn the occupations of men and begins to pick up knowledge about the animals and trees and fishes of his country. The girl, accompanying her mother on her expeditions to gather roots and seeds, or to catch fish or pick up molluscs on the reefs, learns what it is necessary for women to know.

Until the age of about eight to ten a child lives with his

[1] Man, *op. cit.* p. 139.

parents, having a place in the family hut, and a share of the family meal. The children are treated with extreme kindness, and are never punished, and hardly ever scolded. Should the parents die the children are adopted by friends or relatives, and such adopted children are treated by the foster-parents in exactly the same way as their own children.

At the age of ten, or a little before, a change is often brought about in the life of a child, owing to the custom of adoption. Mr Man writes of this custom as follows:

"It is said to be of rare occurrence to find any child above six or seven years of age residing with its parents, and this because it is considered a compliment and also a mark of friendship for a married man, after paying a visit, to ask his hosts to allow him to adopt one of their children. The request is usually complied with, and thenceforth the child's home is with his (or her) foster-father: though the parents in their turn adopt the children of other friends, they nevertheless pay continual visits to their own child, and occasionally ask permission (!) to take him (or her) away with them for a few days. A man is entirely at liberty to please himself in the number of children he adopts, but he must treat them with kindness and consideration, and in every respect as his own sons and daughters, and they, on their part, render him filial affection and obedience. It not unfrequently happens that in course of time permission to adopt a foster-child is sought by a friend of the *soi-disant* father, and is at once granted (unless any exceptional circumstance should render it personally inconvenient), without even the formality of a reference to the actual parents, who are merely informed of the change, in order that they may be enabled to pay their periodical visits[1]."

The above passage is quoted because Mr Man had better opportunities of observation in this matter than myself. At the present day there are not many children in the Andamans, and this is an obstacle in the way of this custom of adoption. From my own observation, however, I should put the age at which it is customary for children to be adopted at higher than six or seven. I found children of about seven or eight still

[1] Man, *op. cit.* p. 125.

living with their own parents. The usual age of adoption seemed to me to be from nine or ten years upwards.

A man and his wife adopt in this way children belonging to a local group other than their own. The adopted child lives with his or her foster-parents, having a place in their hut and a share of their meals. From about the age of ten children of both sexes begin to be of service to their parents or foster-parents in many ways. The foster-parents treat their adopted children in exactly the same way that they would treat their own children, and the children on the other hand show the same regard and affection to their foster-parents that they do to their own parents, and assist them in every way that they can. Their own parents come to visit them at regular intervals.

The period of childhood is brought to an end at about the age of puberty by certain ceremonies to be described in the next chapter. After the beginning of these ceremonies a boy ceases to live in the hut of his parents or his foster-parents, and must live with the young unmarried men and widowers in what has been called the bachelors' hut. From this time until he marries, his services are constantly required by his parents or by his foster-parents, and he is expected to obey them and help them in any way he can, It is only after his marriage that he becomes relatively independent and free to please himself in his own actions, and even then he is required to provide his parents or his foster-parents with food, and to serve them in any way they may need.

A girl, during the period between the beginning of the initiation ceremonies and her marriage, continues, at any rate, in some cases, and in these days, to live with her parents or with foster-parents. Mr Man states that the unmarried women and girls occupy a spinsters' hut similar to the bachelors' hut. It is possible that this was the former custom. I found instances of an unmarried girl occupying a place in the hut of a married couple who made use of her services and controlled her conduct, regarding her in the light of a foster-daughter. On one occasion I found two unmarried girls occupying a separate hut adjoining that of a married couple, who looked after the girls who occupied it.

The position of an unmarried girl is very similar to that of an unmarried youth. She is required to help her elders, in particular either her parents or her foster-parents, i.e. the married couple under whose care she is for the time being.

After marriage a son continues to help his parents, providing them with food and seeing that they are comfortable. If either a man or a woman lives in a local group other than that of his or her parents, he or she pays frequent visits to them.

From the time that a youth or girl ceases to belong to the family household, his or her duties to the parents are really only the same in kind as the duties that every young man and woman owes to all the older men and women. Though there is no difference in kind, yet a man or woman is expected to show more affection and respect for his or her own parents than to other persons of the same social standing.

The only other relationship, besides that of husband and wife and that of parents and children, which exists inside the family, is that between children of the same parents. The conduct of brothers to one another depends on their respective ages. The younger is expected to give way to the elder, while the latter protects and looks after the former. The relation of sisters to one another is similar.

The duties of a man and woman to his or her relatives, other than those to parents, brothers and sisters, and even to some extent the duties to these near relatives, are not distinguishable in kind from the duties he or she owes to other persons who are not relatives. Thus a young married man owes certain duties to all the older married men of about the age of his father. These duties are the same in kind as those towards his own father and his foster-father, the only difference being that he must defer more to his own father than to other men, and must be more constant in his attentions to him. I could not discover any way in which a man distinguished, in his dealings with them, his father's brother from his mother's brother. They are both of them older men whom he must respect and to whom he must make presents of food. Similarly a father's sister is not distinguished, so far as I could discover, from a mother's sister. A man treats both of them in much the same way that he treats his own mother, or any other woman of the same age. There is only a slight difference in connection with parents-in-law. A man would not be so familiar with his parents-in-law as he would with his parents or their brothers or sisters, and treats them with more deference and respect. This is borne out by the *Akar-Bale* custom of applying to a father-in-law or mother-in-law the same term of address (*Mama*) that is used in speaking to grandparents and others to whom it is required to show particular deference.

In the same way there is very little difference between the way a man conducts himself towards his elder brother and his conduct towards any other man of the same age. Brothers are often close comrades, putting their huts next to one another in the same village, joining together whenever possible in hunting or fishing expeditions, and so on; but a man may have a comrade who is not his brother, whom he will treat in exactly the same way.

The general attitude of a married man to other married men somewhat younger than himself is very much that towards a younger brother. As between men and women one special duty appears in this connection. A married man may not and will not have any close dealings with the wife of a man younger than himself. It is not considered fitting that he should speak to her. If he wished to have any communication with her, he would do so through some third person. It would be regarded as a wrong thing to do if he were ever to touch her. The only explanation that the natives give of this custom is by saying that a man feels "shy" or "ashamed" towards his younger brother's or friend's wife. The custom is exactly the same with respect to the wife of any younger man, whether a brother, a cousin, or a stranger.

This custom depends on the distinction between older and younger. A man may be on terms of familiarity with the wife of a man older than himself, whom he would treat much as he would an elder sister.

There is one special relationship which has peculiar duties attaching to it, and this is the relationship between the father and mother of a man on the one hand and the father and mother of the man's wife on the other. In the *Akar-Bale* language such persons are said to be *aka-yat* to one another. A man or a woman will not have any immediate dealings with a person who is his *aka-yat*. He will not speak to him, and if they should meet or be sitting near to one another they would avoid looking at each other. On the other hand a man is constantly sending presents to his *aka-yat*. The natives say that two persons in this relation feel "shy" or "ashamed." (There is only one word in Andamanese for these two English words, *ot-jete* in *Aka-Jeru*.) The shyness begins at the moment when a marriage between their respective children is first discussed as a possibility, and lasts apparently till death.

As throwing a little light on this peculiar relation it may be mentioned that a similar relation exists between two men who have been through either the turtle-eating ceremony or the pig-eating ceremony (to be described in the next chapter) on the same occasion. Two such men will avoid any contact with one another, not speaking to nor looking at each other when they chance to meet, but on the other hand they will be constantly giving each other presents of all kinds, sending them through some third person.

The main features of the relationship system of the Andaman Islanders may be briefly summed up. The duties that one person owes to another are determined much less by their relation to one another by consanguinity and marriage, than by their respective ages and social status. Even within the family, which nevertheless is of importance, the duty of a child to a parent is very little different from his duty to any other person of the same age. There is very little of any special customs relating to conduct towards different kinds of relatives. Corresponding to this we find very few terms to denote relationships and a considerable development of the terms which denote age and social status. Thus a man's duties to his elder brother are much the same as those towards the other men of the same age, and we find that there is no word for "elder brother" but only a term by which a man distinguishes all the men of his own generation older than himself from those who are younger. Similarly there are no duties that a man owes to his father's brother or to his mother's brother which he does not also owe, in perhaps a less degree, to other men of the same age, and there is no term by which he can distinguish his father's brother from those others.

If this account of the system of relationship be accurate it will be seen that the Andamanese society contrasts very strongly, in this matter, with other primitive societies[1].

It remains for us only to examine the social relations between the different local groups. Two neighbouring groups, whether of the same tribe or of different tribes, might be either friendly towards one another or unfriendly. Friendly relations were kept alive by several of the customs of the Andamanese, by the intermarriage of members of different groups, by the adoption of children from one group to another, and by the fact that a man of one group might take up his residence more or less permanently with another (particularly when he married a woman of that group, or was adopted when a boy by one of the men belonging to it). All these customs served to bind some persons in the one group to persons in the other, and thus prevent the two groups from becoming entirely unfriendly to one another.

When two neighbouring local groups were friendly to one another communication between them was kept up by visitors from one group to another, and by occasional meetings of the whole of the two groups.

Either a single person or a family might at any time pay a visit to another camp, staying a few days or weeks or even longer. A man would, however, only go visiting when he was sure of a welcome. Such visits were most frequent in the fine months of the year (December to May). As a husband and wife in many instances belonged to different local groups they

[1] It would not be safe, however, to base any arguments of importance to sociology on the above description of the Andamanese system of relationship alone. Although I tried to learn all that I could on the subject, it is quite certain that I did not learn all that was to be learnt, and it is possible that further enquiry might have shown that I was mistaken in some of my observations. The difficulty of being really sure on these matters is due (1) to the fact that the breaking-up of the old local organisation has produced many changes in their customs, and (2) to the difficulty of questioning the natives on matters connected with relationships when they have no words in their language to denote any but the simplest relationships.

would, if living with the man's parents, pay a visit every year to the parents or other relatives of the wife. The parents of a child that had been adopted by a member of another local group would make a point of visiting the child when they could. Visitors to a camp would always take with them presents to be given to their hosts. A visitor was hospitably entertained, being given the best of the food, and joined his hosts in their hunting and fishing expeditions. The duty of hospitality is one upon which the Andamanese lay stress.

The meetings of two or more local groups were organised from time to time by the more prominent men. The time and place of the meeting would be fixed and invitations sent out to the neighbours. The visitors, men, women and children, would arrive at the appointed time, and would be accommodated as well as possible by the hosts. During the first few hours, as the natives themselves told me, everyone would feel a little shy and perhaps frightened, and it would take some time for this feeling to wear off. The visitors would bring with them various objects, such as bows, arrows, adzes, baskets, nets, red paint, white clay, and so on. These were given by the visitors to their hosts, and other presents were received in return. Although the natives themselves regarded the objects thus given as being presents, yet when a man gave a present to another he expected that he would receive something of equal value in return, and would be very angry if the return present did not come up to his expectations. A man would sometimes mention, when giving his present, that he would like some particular object in exchange, but this was the exception and not the rule, and the process cannot be spoken of as barter. In certain cases it undoubtedly served a useful economic purpose. Thus if a local group had no red ochre or white clay in their own country they could obtain these commodities by exchange with others who had. In the case of a meeting between forest and coast dwellers, the former could obtain such things as shells, red paint made with turtle fat, and other objects with which they could not provide themselves in any other way. It was in this way also that the iron obtained from a wreck on one part of the coast would be spread over a large area. For the most part, however, as each local group, and indeed each family, was able to provide itself with everything that it needed in the way of weapons and utensils, the exchange of presents did not serve the same purpose as trade and barter in more developed communities.

The purpose that it did serve was a moral one. The object of the exchange was to produce a friendly feeling between the two persons concerned, and unless it did this it failed of its purpose. It gave great scope for the exercise of tact and courtesy. No one was free to refuse a present that was offered to him. Each man and woman tried to out-do the others in generosity. There was a sort of amiable rivalry as to who could give away the greatest number of valuable presents.

The visitors remained with their hosts for a few days. The time was spent in hunting, feasting and dancing, and in the exchange of presents above described. The hosts made every effort to provide the camp with plenty of good things. The guests took their share in the hunting and fishing expeditions. Every evening was spent in singing and dancing. Some of the men were sure to have composed new songs for such an occasion.

Such meetings as these were sometimes the means of bringing to an end past quarrels between the local groups, but occasionally they were the cause of new quarrels. The hosts, or some of them, might think that they had been shabbily treated in the matter of presents, or the guests might complain that they were not well enough entertained. It often needed a man of strong influence to maintain harmony in the camp. Angry words might lead to the rapid breaking up of a meeting, and even result in a feud between the two groups.

Quarrels between individuals, as we have seen, were often taken up by friends on each side. This was particularly the case when the two opponents belonged to different local groups. Before the days of the settlement of the islands there often arose in this way petty quarrels between neighbouring local groups. In some instances there appear to have been feuds of long standing; in others there was a quarrel, a fight or two, and the enemies made peace with one another, until a fresh cause of disagreement should arise.

It does not seem that there was ever such a thing as a stand-up fight between two parties. The whole art of fighting was to come upon your enemies by surprise, kill one or two of them and then retreat. A local group that had some grievance against another would decide to make an attack. They might seek and obtain the aid of friends from other local groups. The men who were to take part in the expedition would paint themselves and put on various ornaments and join in a dance[1]. They would then set out, either by land or by sea, in the direction of the encampment they meant to attack. Their weapons consisted of bows and arrows, and they carried no shields or other defensive weapons. They would not venture to attack the enemy's camp unless they were certain of taking it by surprise. For this reason such attacks were generally made either in the evening when the camp would be busy with the preparation of the evening meal, or at early dawn, when every one would be asleep. The attacking party would rush the camp and shoot as many men as they could. If they met with any serious resistance or lost one of their own number they would immediately retire. Those attacked, if they were really taken by surprise, were generally compelled to save themselves by flight. Though the aim of the attacking party was to kill the men, it often happened that women or children were killed. The whole fight would last only a few minutes, ending either with the retirement of the attackers before resistance, or the flight of those attacked into the jungle. A wounded enemy would be killed if found.

Such attacks and counter-attacks might be continued for some years, thus establishing a feud between two neighbouring local groups. More usually, however, after one or two such fights peace would be made. In the tribes of the North Andaman there was a special peace-making ceremony, that will be described in the next chapter. All peace negotiations were conducted through the women. One or two of the women of the one group would be sent to interview the women of the other group to see if they were willing to forget the past and make friends. It seems that it was largely the rancour of the

---

[1] The dance is described in the next chapter.

women over their slain relatives that kept the feud alive, the men of the two parties being willing to make friends much more readily than the women.

An example of a long-continued feud, which, to all appearance, has been in existence for several centuries, is that between the *Aka-Bea* and the *Jarawa* of the South Andaman. The *Jarawa* have the advantage over the *Aka-Bea* that their camps are situated in the dense forest and are difficult to find, while the camps of the *Aka-Bea* are mostly along the sea-coast. At the present day the *Jarawa* take some precautions against being surprised in their camp by a hostile party. The camp is often placed on the top of a hill and the trees in the neighbourhood are cut down so that they have a good view. The paths leading to the camp are also cleared and made wider than is usual in a native path. At times it would seem that they keep sentries on the look-out.

The *Aka-Bea* and the *Jarawa* were inveterate enemies. Whenever two parties of them met by any chance, or came in the neighbourhood of one another, the larger party would attack the other. When the Settlement of Port Blair was established, friendly relations were set up with the *Aka-Bea*, and since that time the hostility of the *Jarawa* has been directed not only against the friendly Andamanese (*Aka-Bea*, etc.) but also against the inhabitants of the Settlement[1].

Such a thing as fighting on a large scale seems to have been unknown amongst the Andamanese. In the early days of the Penal Settlement of Port Blair, the natives of the South Andaman

[1] In the years 1872 to 1902 inclusive the *Jarawa* made eight attacks on camps of the friendly Andamanese in different places, in which two of the friendly Andamanese men and one girl were killed and three men and one boy were wounded. There were also one or two casual meetings between *Jarawa* and friendly Andamanese. One of the friendlies was surprised and killed while turtle hunting in 1894. During the same years the *Jarawa* made on different occasions about twenty attacks on parties of convicts or on separate individuals, killing altogether 27 convicts and two police constables, and wounding six other convicts. In these skirmishes and in the expeditions to which they gave rise three *Jarawa* were killed and seven wounded on various occasions, and several times *Jarawa* men, women or children were captured and afterwards released. A number of convicts have at different times run away from the Settlement and as some of those were never after heard of they may be supposed to have been killed by the *Jarawa*. For an official record of dealings with the *Jarawa* see the "Census Report" 1901, pp. 68—90.

combined in large numbers to make an attack on the Settlement, but this seems to have been an unusual course of action in order to meet what was to them an altogether unusual contingency, their territory having been invaded by a large force of foreigners. Their only fights amongst themselves seem to have been the brief and far from bloody skirmishes described above, where only a handful of warriors were engaged on each side and rarely more than one or two were killed. Of such a thing as a war in which the whole of one tribe joined to fight with another tribe I could not find any evidence in what the natives were able to tell me of their former customs.

As showing within what narrow limits the different local groups held communication with one another, it may be mentioned that till the year 1875 the *Aka-Bea* natives of Port Blair did not know of the existence of the *Aka-Kọl* tribe, less than fifty miles distant, nor of any of the tribes further north. As a general rule it may be said that no man knew anything of any of the natives living more than twenty miles from his own part of the country.

CHAPTER II

CEREMONIAL CUSTOMS

IN such a society as that of the Andaman Islanders it is possible to distinguish three different ways in which the actions of individuals are regulated or determined by the society. There are, first of all, what we may distinguish as "moral customs," whereby the actions of individuals in relation to one another are regulated on principles of right and wrong conduct. It was with customs of this kind that we were concerned in the last chapter. Secondly, the activities by which the natives obtain their food and make the various objects of which they have need are determined by tradition. Such activities are purely utilitarian and they are regulated, not by commandments similar to those of the moral law, but by accumulated technical knowledge as to the means by which a particular object may be attained. These we may speak of as the "technical customs" of the society.

There are customs of a third kind which are distinguishable both from moral customs and from technical customs. For example, when a man dies, his near relatives observe certain mourning customs, such as covering their bodies with clay. Such customs are distinguished from technical customs by having no utilitarian purpose. They are distinguished from moral customs by this, that they are not immediately concerned with the effects of the action of one person upon another.

It is difficult to find a satisfactory name for all the customs of this kind. A large number of them may be spoken of as "ceremonial customs," and it is this that explains the title of the present chapter.

It is not pretended that this division of social customs into three different kinds is of any great or permanent value, and it is only introduced as an aid to the exposition of the customs of the Andamanese. It will be argued in a later chapter that many of the customs described in the present chapter have a common psychological basis.

Of any customs in connection with the birth of children I was able to learn very little, as no births at which I could be present occurred during my stay at the islands. Earlier writers have given very little information on this subject.

During the latter part of the period of pregnancy, and for about a month after the birth of the child, the mother and father must observe certain restrictions. In particular there are certain foods that they may not eat. The statements of different informants on this matter did not quite agree with each other, and it seems that there were slightly different rules in different tribes. According to an *Akar-Bale* informant the man and woman may not eat dugong, honey and yams; they may eat the flesh of small but not of full-grown pigs and turtle. An informant of one of the Northern tribes said that the woman may not eat full-grown pig, *Paradoxurus*, turtle, dugong, the fish *komar*, monitor lizard, honey and yams; her husband may eat these things but must carefully avoid eating certain fishes.

The natives give two different reasons for these rules. One is that if these foods be eaten by the parents the child will be ill. The other is that the parents themselves will be ill. The latter is the explanation most commonly offered.

The baby is named some time before it is born, and from that time the parents are not addressed or spoken of by name. For example, if the name chosen be *Rea*, the father will be spoken of as *Rea aka-mai* (Rea's father) instead of by his own name. The mother may be referred to as *Rea it-pet*, from the word *it-pet* meaning "belly." This practice is continued till some weeks after the birth, when the use of the names of the parents is once more resumed.

In child-birth the woman is assisted by the matrons of the camp. She is seated in her hut in the village on fresh leaves, and a piece of wood is placed at her back for her to lean against.

Her legs are flexed so that her knees may be clasped by her arms. The only manipulation is pressure exerted on the upper part of the abdomen by one of the attendant women. The umbilical cord is severed with a knife, formerly of cane or bamboo, but in these days of iron. The after-birth is buried in the jungle. The infant is washed and then scraped with a *Cyrena* shell. After a few days he (or she) is given a coating of clay (*odu*).

If a baby dies and within a year or two the mother again becomes pregnant, it is said that it is the same baby born again, and the name of the deceased child is given to it. Thus one woman had three children of the same name, the first two having died soon after birth. According to the native ideas this was really the same child born three times. It is only those who die in infancy that are thus reincarnated.

In the Northern tribes it is believed that a woman can tell the sex of her unborn child. If she feels it on the left side it is a male, because men hold the bow (the typical masculine implement) in the left hand. If she feels it on the right side it is a female, because it is in her right hand that a woman holds her fishing net.

A married man who is childless and desires a child will wear a *čiba* (sling of bark used for carrying children) round his shoulders when he is sitting in camp. The *čiba* and the way it is used for carrying children may be seen in the photograph in Plate XIV. If a childless woman wishes to have a child she may catch, cook and eat a certain species of small frog.

At a place called *Tonmuket* in the North Andaman there is a spot to which it is said that women may resort if they wish to become pregnant. On the reef at this spot there are a large number of stones which, according to the legend, were once little children. The woman who desires a child walks out on to the reef when the tide is low and stands upon these stones. It is believed that one of the baby souls will enter her body and become incarnate[1].

---

[1] I could not obtain any definite legend about these stones, but one informant said that when *Biliku* got angry and destroyed the world (see later, Chap. IV) the children all became stones at this place.

In the North Andaman there is some sort of association between the unborn souls of babies, the green pigeon and the *Ficus laccifera* tree. The same name, *Reŋko*, is used to denote both the green pigeon and also the *Ficus laccifera*, of the fruit of which the pigeon is very fond. The belief of the natives is sometimes stated by saying that the souls of unborn children live in the *Ficus* trees, and that if a baby dies before it has been weaned its soul goes back to the tree. Another statement of the natives is that it is when the green pigeon is calling that the soul of a baby goes into its mother. The *Ficus* is to a certain extent tabu. I was told that the tree must not be cut or damaged. Nevertheless the natives do cut the tree in order to obtain the bark of the aerial roots from which they prepare a fibre that they use for making personal ornaments. There is no tabu in connection with the green pigeon, which may be killed and eaten.

In most primitive societies, if not in all, there are ritual or ceremonial observances in connection with the change by which a boy or girl becomes a man or woman. The ceremonies that are performed to mark this change are commonly spoken of in ethnological literature as "initiation ceremonies." The term is not perhaps the best that could be chosen, but usage has rendered it familiar.

The life of an Andaman Islander is divided into three well-marked periods, corresponding roughly with the physiological periods of childhood, adolescence, and maturity. The first period lasts from birth till about the advent of puberty; the second lasts from puberty till after marriage; the third extends from marriage to death.

During the period of childhood the boy or girl lives with his or her parents, or, in the later years of the period, with adopted parents, having a place in the family hut and a share in the family meal. A girl continues to live with her parents or with her adopted parents until she marries. When boys have finished growing, and have reached the condition of young men, they cease to live with their parents or adopted parents and, until they are married, they occupy a bachelors' hut of their own, and have their own meal.

Every boy and girl has to undergo the operation of scarification. This is begun when the child is quite young, and a small portion of the body is operated on. The operation is repeated at intervals during childhood, until the whole body has been scarified. A small flake of quartz or glass is used, and a series of fine incisions are made in the skin. The usual method is to cover a small portion of the skin with a number of parallel rows of short cuts. The choice of the design (if it can be called such) rests entirely with the person who performs the operation, who is in all cases a woman. The incisions leave scars that can usually only be seen when close to the person. In the photograph of Plate XV a pattern of scars may be seen. In this case the incisions became infected and raised scars were produced, and it is for this reason that they are visible in the photograph. In ordinary cases raised scars are not produced and the scarification is hardly visible in a photograph.

The only reason that the natives give for this custom is either that it improves the personal appearance, or else that it helps to make the child grow strong.

In the case of a girl the period of childhood is brought to a close by a ceremony that takes place on the occasion of her first menstrual discharge. The ceremony I describe is that in use in the Northern tribes, but I believe that the ceremony of the Southern tribes is very similar. On the occurrence of the first menstrual discharge the girl tells her parents, who weep over her. She must then go and bathe in the sea for an hour or two by herself. After that she goes back to her parents' hut or to a special shelter that is put up for the occasion. She is not required to go away from the camp. All ornaments are removed from her, only a single belt of *Pandanus* leaf being left, with an apron of *čainyo* leaves. Strips of *Pandanus* leaf are attached round her arms near the shoulders and round her wrists, and others are placed as bands crossing her chest from the shoulder to the waist on the opposite side, and crossing her abdomen from the iliac crest on the one side to the trochanter on the other. These are so attached that the long loose ends hang down at the girl's side. Bunches of leaves, either *čelmo* (*Tetranthera lancæfolia*) or, if these be not obtainable, *poramo* (*Myristica longifolia*) are fastened beneath her belt before and behind. Other leaves of the same kind are placed for her to sit upon. The strips of *Pandanus* leaf and the bundle of leaves are visible in the photograph reproduced in Plate XVI.

Thus covered with leaves the girl must sit in the hut allotted to her, with her legs doubled up beneath her and her arms folded. A piece of wood or bamboo is placed at her back for her to lean against, as she may not lie down. If she is cramped she may stretch one of her legs or one of her arms, but not both arms or both legs at the same time. To feed herself she may release one of her hands, but she must not take up the food with her fingers; a skewer of *čainyo* wood[1] is given her with which to feed herself. She may not speak nor sleep for 24 hours. Her wants are attended to by her parents and their friends, who sit near her to keep her from falling asleep.

The girl sits thus for three days. Early every morning she leaves the hut to bathe for an hour in the sea. At the end of the three days she resumes her life in the village. For a month following she must bathe in the sea every morning at dawn.

During the ceremony and for a short time afterwards the girl is not addressed or spoken of by name, but is referred to as *Alebe* or *Toto*. The meaning of the first word is not known. *Toto* is the name of the species of *Pandanus* from which women's belts are made and the leaves of which are used in the ceremony. On the occasion of this ceremony the girl is given a new name, her "flower-name," and from this time till after the birth of her first child she is never addressed or spoken of by the name which she had as a child, but only by the name given to her at this ceremony. The name given is that of a plant or tree which is in flower at the time. If the ceremony takes place when the *Jili* is in flower she is called *Jili*; if when the *Jeru* is in flower she is named *Jeru*, and so on. These names will be mentioned again later in the present chapter.

---

[1] This is the plant (not identified) of which the leaves were, till recent times, worn by the women of the North Andaman to cover the pudenda. In the South Andaman the leaves of the *Mimusops littoralis* are in use for this purpose, and the Northern tribes have recently given up their own custom and adopted that of the South.

After this ceremony the girl is said to be *aka-nJu-kolọt*. For some time afterwards she must not have her head shaved, and she must not use red paint or white clay.

I was not able to learn much about the native ideas in connection with the menstrual function. According to the account given me by one informant I gathered that the girl's first menstrual discharge is supposed to be due to sexual intercourse. The man's breath goes into her nose and this produces the discharge. It is believed that if a man were to touch a girl during this period, either during the ceremony or for some time after it, his arm would swell up.

At every recurrence of the menstrual period a woman is required to abstain from eating certain foods. According to an *Akar-Bale* informant these are, in that tribe, pork, turtle, *Paradoxurus*, honey and yams. An *Aka-Čari* informant added to the above list dugong, monitor lizard, and the fish *komar*. If she ate any of these things at such a time she would be ill. This continues throughout her life till the climacteric. A menstruating woman is not required to leave the camp, as she is in many savage communities.

From the moment of the ceremony just described the girl enters a new condition which is denoted in the *Aka-Jeru* language by the word *aka-op* (*aka-yaba* in *Aka-Bea*). This word means that the person to whom it is applied is under certain ritual restrictions, chiefly concerned with foods that may not be eaten.

In the case of a boy there is no physiological event so clearly marked as there is in that of a girl. It rests with the relatives and friends to decide when the boy is to become *aka-op*. It would seem that in the Southern tribes there is no ceremony on this occasion. Among the Northern tribes the boy is made *aka-op* by means of a ceremony that consists of making the scars on his back that are customary in these tribes[1].

When the friends and relatives of a boy decide that he is old enough to have the incisions made in his back a dance is held in the evening, and the boy is required to dance through the

---

[1] Unfortunately I was not able to see this ceremony performed, and my information is therefore derived from the statements of the natives.

whole night till he is tired. As soon as morning breaks he is made to bathe in the sea for two hours or so. He is then seated in some convenient place, not in a hut. The boy kneels down and bends forward till his elbows rest on the ground in front. One of the older men takes a pig-arrow and with the sharpened blade makes a series of cuts on the boy's back. Each cut is horizontal, and they are arranged in three vertical rows, each row consisting of from 20 to 30 cuts. When the cutting is finished the boy sits up, with a fire at his back, until the bleeding stops. During the operation and for a few hours following it the boy must remain silent. There is no treatment of the wounds to produce raised scars. The scars are much more noticeable on some men than on others.

The boy does not receive a new name on this occasion, but for a few weeks his own name is dropped and he is addressed and spoken of as *Ejido*. From this time the boy is described as being *oko-taliŋ-kolot*, this being the masculine term corresponding to *aka-ndu-kolot* for girls. From the time the cuts are made on his back the boy becomes *aka-op* and is under certain restrictions as to what foods he may eat.

When the wounds on his back are thoroughly healed similar cuts are made on his chest. I found a certain number of men who had no visible scars on their chests, but in the North Andaman every man has the three rows of scars on his back. Some of the women of the North Andaman have similar scars on their chests and a very few have them also on the back. These scars on women are not regularly made as part of the initiation ceremonies, and may be made after the woman has been married for some years.

During the period that a boy or girl is *aka-op* he or she is required by the customs of the tribe to abstain from eating certain foods. The exact rules in this matter differ from tribe to tribe. More particularly there are important differences between the coast-dwellers on the one hand and the jungle-dwellers on the other. The general principle, however, is in all cases the same. The boy (or girl) must abstain from all the chief foods of the people, and since he could not abstain from them all at one time without starving, he takes them in turn. It is in the order in which the different foods are forbidden that the chief differences occur.

In the *Aka-Čari* tribe of the North Andaman, where all are coast-dwellers, the boy or girl, during the first part of the *aka-op* period must not eat turtle, dugong, porpoise, *komar* (a fish), hawksbill turtle, the two kinds of edible grubs (*pata* and *čokele*), the monitor lizard, the flying fox (*Pteropus*), certain birds (perhaps all birds), certain shell-fish, the four varieties of mangrove seed (*kao, čimi, kabal* and *kaplo*), three edible roots (*mino, labo* and *mikulu*), and a large number of other vegetable foods, including *loitok, poroto* (if cooked, but it may be eaten raw), *bijo, čoroyo, celet, buroy, bui, bakle, čo, čatali,* and *kata*. A certain number of fishes must be added to this list. This period is brought to a end by the turtle-eating ceremony which will be presently described. After this ceremony, turtle, which is one of the chief foods of the *Aka-Čari*, may be eaten, although certain parts of the turtle (such as the intestinal fat) are still forbidden, and the youth is also allowed to eat many of the other foods previously forbidden. On the other hand he is now required not to eat pork and a number of other foods both animal and vegetable. During this second period certain minor ceremonies take place, as for instance on the first occasion on which turtle's eggs are eaten. This period is brought to an end by the pig-eating ceremony. After that the youth is again free to eat pork. As turtle and pork are the two most important foods the ceremonies and observances in connection with these occupy a position of greater importance. After the pig-eating ceremony the youth is made free of one food after another, until some time after he is married he becomes free to partake of any of the foods available. In the case of some of the more important foods, such as honey, dugong, porpoise, the fish *komar*, etc., there is a sort of minor ceremony. The only ceremonies of any great importance in this tribe are the turtle-eating and the pig-eating ceremonies.

In the forest-dwelling communities of the North Andaman things are necessarily different. These people only eat such foods as turtle, dugong, etc. when they are visiting their friends on the coast. The three most important ceremonies amongst these people are the *ṅyuri*-eating, the pig-eating and the honey-eating ceremonies. (The *ṅyuri* is a fish that is found in the creeks.) According to my informants of the *Aka-Bo* tribe the foods that must be avoided during the first part of the abstention period are all species of fish found in inland creeks (*ṅyuri, burto, bari, bol, kuato*), the monitor lizard, sucking-pig, two species of snake (*or-čubi* and *uluku-čubi*), a number of vegetable foods and also honey. After the *ṅyuri*-eating ceremony the different kinds of fish mentioned may be eaten, but the youth or girl must then abstain from pork.

These examples, without entering into further details, will suffice to show what is the nature of the *aka-op* period. During that period the youth must abstain for a certain length of time from each one of the more important foods of his community. After a certain period of abstention he is permitted to eat the particular food. On each occasion of thus eating a food for the first time after the abstention, there are certain ritual customs that must be observed, and these customs are more important in some cases (such as pig, turtle and honey) than in others. In the case of some of the foods the only ritual observed is that the food must be given by an older man, who is himself free to eat it, that it must be eaten in silence, and that the man must be painted afterwards with clay (*odu*). In the case of pork and turtle, however, there are fairly elaborate ceremonies. The ceremonies are very similar in different parts of the islands. The description given below applies to the coast-dwellers of the North Andaman. In these communities the period of abstention from turtle and other foods begins in the case of a girl at the first menstruation, and in the case of a boy when his back is cut. It may last only one year or several years, according to circumstances, and is brought to a close by the turtle-eating ceremony. The details of this are exactly the same in the case of a girl and a boy.

When the older men decide that it is time for a boy who has been abstaining from turtle to be released from the restriction, a turtle-hunting expedition is arranged, and this is continued until a fair number of good turtle are captured. The best of these is selected, killed, and cooked. The youth is seated in a hut, either that of his parents, or one placed at his disposal by a friend or one specially built[1]. All his ornaments are removed. (In the case of a girl one belt of *Pandanus* leaf is retained.) He is seated on leaves of the *Hibiscus tiliaceus*, or if these be not obtainable, on those of the *Myristica longifolia*, and a bundle of the same leaves is placed under his folded arms so as to cover his belly, while another bundle is placed at his back where there is some sort of rest provided for him to lean against. He must sit still with folded arms and with legs stretched out in front, the two big toes clasping each other. He sits facing towards the open sea, and a fire is placed near him, generally just beyond his feet.

Some man is chosen to take charge of the ceremony. This may be one of the older men of the community to which the youth belongs or a distinguished visitor, if there be any such present in the camp at the time. This man selects some of the meat and fat of the cooked turtle, placing them in a wooden dish. He comes to where the youth is seated, while the friends and relatives gather round. Taking some of the fat he rubs it first over the lips and then over the whole body of the youth, while the female relatives of the latter sit near and weep loudly. When the youth's body is thoroughly covered with fat the man who is performing the ceremony takes some burnt oxide of iron, such as is used for making red paint, and rubs it over the youth's whole body, except the hair of his head. He then takes a piece of turtle fat and places it in the youth's mouth, feeding him thus with a few mouthfuls which the youth eats in silence. At this point the weeping of the relatives is taken up again with renewed vigour and then gradually comes to an end. Having fed the youth the man then proceeds to massage him. He first stands behind him and placing his hands on his shoulders presses down on them with all his weight. Then he seizes a roll of flesh on each side of the youth's belly and shakes it up and down as though to shake down what has been eaten. The arms are next massaged and the wrists and knuckles are forcibly flexed so as to make the joints "crack." The legs are similarly massaged, either with the hands or with the feet, the performer

---

[1] There is no secrecy about any of the proceedings; the whole ceremony is performed in the village and may be witnessed by anybody.

(in the latter case) standing on the outstretched legs of the youth and rolling the muscles beneath his feet[1]. The joints of the toes are forcibly bent with the hand to make them "crack" if possible. A mixture of clay (*odu*) and water has been prepared in a wooden dish. The performer dips his hands into this and spatters it over the youth's body from head to foot, either by holding his hands near the youth and clapping them together, or by jerking the clay off his fingers with a flicking motion. During the whole of these proceedings the youth sits passive and silent.

The first part of the ceremony is now over. The food tray containing turtle meat and fat, cut into small pieces, is placed beside the youth and he is provided with a skewer of the wood of the *Hibiscus tiliaceus*, as he may not touch the meat with his fingers. He must sit in the same position with legs outstretched and arms folded and surrounded with *Hibiscus* leaves. To feed himself he may unloose one arm, and when his legs are cramped he may double them up beneath him. He may not lie down nor speak nor sleep for 48 hours. During this period he may eat nothing but turtle and drink nothing but water[2]. The man in charge of the ceremony sits behind him and gives him instructions as to what foods he may and what he may not eat after the ceremony. Some of the men and women take it in turn to sit beside the youth, attending to his wants and talking or singing to keep him awake.

On the morning of the third day a belt and necklace are made of pieces of the creeper called *terkobito-balo*, i.e. "centipede creeper" (*Pothos scandens*), and these are placed round the youth's waist and neck. On this day he is permitted to sleep. Either on the same day, or early the next morning, he has a bath in the sea, to remove some of the red paint and clay, and he is then decorated with red paint made of red ochre and turtle fat, and with white clay (*tǫl-odu*). The red paint is put on in stripes over his body, and his ears are daubed with it. The white clay

---

[1] In the Southern tribes large stones are placed on the youth's thighs.

[2] In these days the natives are very fond of tea, which they obtain from the Andamanese Homes; during the ceremony described above the youth or girl is not permitted to drink tea.

is put on in a zig-zag pattern to be described later, the lines of white clay alternating with those of red paint. This decoration is done by female relatives.

Early on the morning of the fourth day, soon after daybreak, the whole village is astir. One of the older men takes his stand by the sounding-board used for marking time at dances, and the women sit down near him. The youth comes out from his hut and stands in the middle of the dancing ground, and five or six men stand round him in a circle, each of them facing towards the youth. Each of the men, including the youth, holds in each hand a bundle of twigs of the *Hibiscus tiliaceus* or, if such be not obtainable, of the *Myristica longifolia*. The man at the sounding-board sings a song, beating time with his foot, in the usual way, on the sounding-board, and at the chorus the women join in and mark the time by clapping their hands on their thighs. The song may be on any subject and is selected by the singer from his own repertory. A song referring to turtle-hunting is preferred. During the first song the dancers stand at their positions on the dancing ground, lifting up their leaf bundles at short intervals and bringing them down against their knees. The singer then commences a new song or repeats the former one, and when the song comes to an end the youth and those with him begin their dance. Each dancer flexes his hips so that his back is nearly horizontal. He raises his hands to the back of his neck so that the two bundles of leaves in his hands rest on his back. With knees flexed he leaps from the ground with both feet, keeping time to the beating of the sounding-board, which is about 144 beats to the minute. At the end of every eight jumps or so, the dancer brings his hands forwards, downwards and backwards, giving a vigorous sweep with the bundles of leaves, which scrape the ground at each side of his feet, and then brings back the bundles to their former position. They dance thus for 15 or 30 seconds and then pause to rest. The dance is repeated several times, until the youth is tired out. As the dance is extremely fatiguing this does not take long[1].

---

[1] I believe that the dance is intended to imitate the movement of a turtle as it swims through the water.

The youth then returns to his hut and resumes his former position. He may now, if he wishes, talk to his friends and he may sleep. He must retain the bundles of *Hibiscus* leaves and the necklace and belt of *Pothos* leaves. The dance is sometimes repeated in the afternoon. It is in any case repeated on each of the two days following, and after that the youth resumes his ordinary life. For a week or two he may not touch a bow and arrow. The *Pothos* leaves are worn till they are faded and are then discarded. The paint on the body wears off and is not renewed, but his ears are kept painted with red paint. For some weeks the youth is supposed to be in an abnormal condition and is carefully watched by his friends.

At the turtle-eating ceremony a new name is given to the youth. This name, however, never seems to be used afterwards either in speaking of or to the person to whom it belongs. A youth of the *Aka-Jeru* tribe whose birth name was *Čop* (from a species of tree) and whose nick-name or second name was *Komar* (from a species of fish) had two new names given to him on the occasion of the turtle-eating ceremony, *Čokbi-čiro* (meaning turtle-liver) and *Pilečar* (high-tide). Neither of these names was ever used in addressing him.

The turtle-eating ceremony is called in the Northern tribes either *Čokbi-jo*, *Čokbi-kimil*, or *Kimil-jo*. The word *čokbi* means "turtle," and *jo* means "eating." The word *kimil* is more difficult to translate. With the prefix *ot-* or *er-* it means "hot" as in *T'ot-kimil-bom*, "I am hot." From the time of the commencement of the ceremony the youth or girl is said to be in a condition denoted by the word *aka-kimil*. During this time, i.e. during the ceremony and for some months afterwards, he or she is not addressed or spoken of by name but is referred to as "*Kimil*," the word being thus used as a term of address or a substitute for the personal name. A person who is in this condition is described as *aka-kimil-kolot*. (Before the ceremony the youth is *oko-taliŋ-kolot* and the girl is *aka-ndu-kolot*.) In the *Aka-Bea* tribe the turtle-eating ceremony is called *Yadi-gumul* or *Gumul-leke*, *yadi* being the word for "turtle" in that language, and *leke* being the equivalent of the *jo* of *Aka-Jeru*, that is "eating." A youth or girl who is passing or has recently passed through the ceremony is said to be *aka-gumul*, and is addressed and spoken of, not by name, but by the term *Guma*[1].

In the coast-dwelling communities of the Northern tribes, the youth or girl who has passed through the turtle-eating ceremony is thereafter free to eat turtle flesh (though not the liver nor the intestinal fat of the turtle) and a certain number of the other foods that were previously forbidden. On the other hand, he or she is now forbidden to eat pork and a number of other foods which previously were permitted. The period during which these new prohibitions are in force may last for a few months or for a year or even longer. It is, however, generally shorter than the first period of abstention from turtle. It is brought to an end by a pig-eating ceremony which is similar in many ways to the turtle-eating ceremony already described. A boar must be killed if the initiate be a youth, or a sow if it be a girl who is to go through the ceremony. The youth is seated in a hut on leaves of the *čelmo* (*Tetranthera*) and the carcase of the boar is brought and pressed upon the youth's shoulders and back by one of the men. The girl is not treated in this way. The pork is then cooked and the youth is first anointed and then fed with some of the fat. He is then rubbed with red ochre, massaged and splashed with clay, just as in the turtle-eating ceremony. He must sit silent with arms crossed, and covered with *Tetranthera* leaves for a day and a night. During this time he may only eat pork, and must not touch his food with his hands but must use a skewer of *Tetranthera* wood. On the following day he is decorated with white clay (*tọl-odu*) and with red paint, and takes part in a dance. The dance is almost exactly the same as the dance on the occasion of the turtle-eating ceremony, the only differences being that instead of *Hibiscus* leaves those of the *Tetranthera* are used, and that the dancer does not leap with both feet from the ground, but raises one foot and stamps with it.

In the Northern tribes these are the two most important ceremonies. After the pig-eating ceremony the youth is free to eat pork and a certain number of previously forbidden foods.

---

[1] The meaning of the word *kimil* (or *gumul*) will be discussed in a later chapter.

There remain a considerable number of foods, however, which he is still forbidden. In connection with each of these there is some sort of minor ceremony. The older men, when occasion arises, offer the youth or girl some of the forbidden food, first rubbing it over his or her mouth. The food is then eaten in silence. I only saw one such ceremony, when a man ate for the first time after his abstention the intestinal fat of the turtle. The man was about 24 years of age and had long since been through the chief ceremonies, and was married. The ceremony is perhaps more elaborate in the case of the similar first eating of honey, dugong and a few other foods. One after another of the food prohibitions is removed until the man or woman is free to eat anything. There is no regular order in which this takes place, as in each case it is determined by chance circumstances. The only order that is rigorously observed is that of the two chief ceremonies connected with pork and turtle. These two are the principal meat foods of the coast-dwellers.

The above description applies strictly only to the coast-dwellers of the North Andaman (*Aka-Čari*, *Aka-Jeru* and *Aka-Kọra*). I was not able to see any ceremonies performed by the jungle-dwellers. The old men of the *Aka-Bo* tribe told me that the period of abstention begins when a boy or girl is forbidden to eat the fish *ṅyuri* (*Plotosus sp.* probably *P. arab*), and a certain number of other foods, not including pork. The first ceremony is the eating of the *ṅyuri*. The boy or girl is seated on leaves (*kibir* or *tare* or *ra-čiro*) and bundles of these are placed in his belt before and behind. A belt of *Pandanus* leaf is worn by the boys at this ceremony as well as by the girls. The initiate sits with his legs doubled up beneath him, and is fed with the fish. The ceremony lasts only one day. There is no special dance, but the initiate joins in an ordinary dance at the end of the ceremony, being decorated for this purpose with white clay. After this ceremony the youth must abstain from pork and other foods. The pig-eating ceremony, which closes this period of abstention, lasts altogether for three or four days, the initiate remaining awake for one night. The leaves used are the same as those of the first (fish-eating) ceremony. The third important ceremony of these communities is the honey-eating. The initiate sits cross-legged and honey is rubbed over his or her shoulders and chest, and he or she is fed with it.

I was told by one of my informants that in the *Aka-Kede* tribe the pig-eating ceremony precedes the turtle-eating, but I could not obtain reliable information about the ceremonies of this tribe.

My informants of the *Akar-Bale* tribe, which consists of coast-dwelling communities only, told me that the period of abstention begins with turtle, honey, turtle's eggs, yams, and a number of fruits and seeds. This period lasts for three or four years. Then comes the turtle-eating ceremony, which is said to be similar in its details to that already described from the North Andaman. After this ceremony the initiate may not eat dugong, porpoise and a considerable number of fishes (including *Tetrodon sp., Plotosus sp., Anguilla bengalensis, Trygon bleekari, T. siphen, Urogymnus asperrimus, Carcharias gangeticus,* etc.). He must also abstain from turtle's eggs, pig, yams, honey, and certain fruits (e.g. *Artocarpus chaplasha, Mimusops littoralis, Baccaurea sapida,* etc.). A few months after the turtle-eating ceremony there is a minor ceremony of eating turtle's eggs, the eggs being eaten in silence and the meal followed by a dance. After another period follows the ceremony of eating pig's kidney-fat. Then, as opportunity occurs, the initiate eats dugong, honey and the other forbidden foods, one after another. The ceremony in each case is not elaborate except in connection with such important foods as dugong and honey.

Mr E. H. Man has given a description of the ceremonies of the *Aka-Bea* tribe, which shows that they are essentially similar to those of the North. He does not distinguish between the ceremonies of the *aryoto* (coast-dwellers) and those of the *eremtaga* (jungle-dwellers). He states that the fasting period (*aka-yaba*) is divided into three parts, the first ending with the *yadi-* (turtle) *gumul*, the second with the *aja-* (honey) *gumul*, and the third with the *reg-jiri-* (kidney-fat of pig) *gumul*.

As I was not able to witness the honey-eating ceremony, I venture to reproduce below the description that Mr Man gives of this ceremony as it is conducted in the *Aka-Bea* tribe.

"When the honey fast is to be broken a quantity of honey-combs, according to the number assembled, are on the appointed day procured: the *aka-yab* being placed in the midst of the group, the chief or other elder goes to him with a large honeycomb wrapped in leaves; after helping the novice to a large mouthful, which he does by means of a bamboo or iron knife, he presents the remainder to him, and then leaves him to devour it in silence: this he does, not, however, by the ordinary method, for it is an essential part of the ceremony that he should not use his fingers to break off pieces, but eat it bear-fashion, by holding the comb up to his mouth and attacking it with his teeth and lips. After satisfying his present requirements, he wraps what is left of the comb in leaves for later consumption. The chief then takes another comb and anoints the youth by squeezing it over his head, rubbing the honey well into his body as it trickles down. The proceedings at this stage are interrupted by a bath, in order to remove all traces of the honey, which would otherwise be a source of considerable inconvenience by attracting ants. Beyond the observance of silence, and continued abstention from *reg-jiri* (pig's kidney-fat), the youth is under no special restrictions, being able to eat, drink and sleep as much as he pleases. Early the following morning the lad decorates himself with leaves of a species of *Alpinia*, called *jini*[1], and then, in the presence of his friends, goes into the sea (or, if he be an *eremtaga*, into a creek) up to his waist, where, locking his thumbs together, he splashes as much water as possible over himself and the bystanders, occasionally ducking his head under the surface as well. This is considered a safeguard or charm against *snakes*, and the onlookers cry "*ọto-pedike, kinig wara-jobo lọtike*" (Go and splash yourself, or *Wara-jobo*[2] will get inside you), for they imagine that unless they go through this splashing performance, this snake will by some means enter their stomachs and so cause death. The only difference between the sexes with respect to the *aja-gumul* is that with females it cannot take place until

---

[1] This plant is selected because it is associated with honey-gathering; its bitter sap, being extremely obnoxious to bees, is smeared over their persons when taking a comb, and enables them to escape scot free with their prize. (Note by Mr Man.)
[2] This is believed to be the *Ophiophagus elaps*. (Note by Mr Man.)

after the birth of the first child; they are also required to abstain from honey during each subsequent pregnancy; and in their case, too, a chief or elder (preferably a relative) officiates, and not a woman[1]."

We may now proceed to the ritual customs connected with death and burial. In all the Great Andaman tribes disease and death are supposed to be due to the spirits of the jungle and the sea. The subject will be dealt with in the next chapter.

On the occurrence of a death the news quickly spreads through the camp, and all the women collect round the body and, sitting down, weep loudly until they are exhausted. The women then retire and the men come and weep over the corpse. All the adult members of the community then proceed to cover themselves with a wash of common clay smeared evenly over their bodies and limbs. This clay is of the kind called *odu* in *Aka-Jeru* and *og* in *Aka-Bea*. The nearer relatives and more intimate friends of the deceased also plaster some of the same clay on their heads.

Some of the women, generally, but not necessarily, relatives, remove any ornaments the dead person may have been wearing, shave the head and decorate the body. This decoration consists of lines of fine pattern in white clay alternating with bands of red paint. A band of red paint is placed across the upper lip passing from ear to ear and the ears themselves are smeared with the pigment. The greater the estimation in which the deceased person is held the greater is the care lavished upon this the last decoration.

Thus decorated the body is prepared for burial. The legs and arms are flexed so that the knees come up under the chin and the fists rest against the cheeks. A *Cyrena* shell (or sometimes in these days a steel knife) is placed in the closed hand. A sleeping mat is wrapped round the body, and over this a number of the large palm leaves known as *kobo* (*Aka-Jeru*) are arranged and the whole is made into a bundle and tied up with rope. Before the ropes are all tied the relatives of the dead person take their last farewell by gently blowing on the face of the corpse.

---

[1] Man, *op. cit.* p. 133.

The male relatives and friends then proceed to the spot selected for the burial, one of them carrying the corpse slung on his back. If the burial place can be reached by canoe, no hesitation is shown in making use of a canoe for the purpose. There are not, so far as could be discovered, any rules as to which of the men shall undertake the burial. Such relatives as brother, father, son or husband generally take the leading part. The women take no part in the actual burial. There are two modes of disposing of the body, in a grave dug in the ground, or upon a platform placed in a tree. The latter is considered the more honourable form of burial, and is only adopted in the case of a man or woman dying in the prime of life. The same grave is not used twice, in the case of interment, though a new grave may be made close to an old one. The natives said that the same tree might be used several times for platform-burial, but there was no opportunity of proving this statement. There are not, generally speaking, any regular burying grounds. Any convenient spot may be chosen so long as it is at some little distance from the camp. It does happen, however, that certain spots are fairly regularly used. In the case of one burial that I witnessed the spot chosen was about a mile distant from the camp, the journey being made in a canoe, and there were already five or six graves at the same place.

In the case of interment a hole is dug three or four feet in depth, the digging being done with an adze and a digging stick, and sometimes a wooden dish is used to scoop out the soil. The body is placed in the hole and the ropes tied round it are severed. The body is placed slightly on its side facing the east. I asked some of the natives the reason for this orientation, and was told that if the custom were not observed the sun would not rise and the world would be left in darkness. A pillow of wood is placed under the head, and a log of wood at each side of the corpse. Sometimes some object that has been worn by the deceased, such as a belt or necklace, is placed in the grave. The soil is then replaced, all present helping. Beside the grave a fire is lighted and some water contained in a bamboo vessel or in a nautilus shell is left for the corpse. In some cases the bow belonging to the deceased, if it be a man, and a few arrows are placed on the grave. In the *Aka-Čari* tribe a harpoon and line are substituted for the bow and arrows, and a bamboo harpoon shaft is erected vertically in the grave near the right hand of the body. In the same tribe it is usual to suspend near the grave a bundle of the prepared fibre of *Anadendron paniculatum* such as is used for making thread. There are probably slight variations of custom in this respect in different tribes or even in different cases in the same tribe.

In the case of platform-burial a platform of sticks is erected in a tree, twelve feet or so above the ground, and the body is placed thereon, lying sideways facing the east. Water and fire are placed beneath the tree. Mr Man states that in cases of tree-burial they are careful not to select a fruit tree or one of a species used for the manufacture of their canoes, bows and other implements. Such natives as I questioned on this point said that this was not so and that they would use any suitable tree whether one that was useful or not. I was unable definitely to prove the point, as I did not see a single instance of tree-burial during my stay in the islands. A tree that is sometimes used for this purpose is the *Ficus laccifera*, which as we have seen has a special connection with the spirits of new-born children. On the coast, mangrove trees, such as the *Rhizophora* or *Bruguiera*, are said to be used.

When the burial is completed, whether in a grave or a tree, plumes made of shredded palm-leaf stem *koro* (*Aka-Jeru*) or *ara* (*Aka-Bea*) are attached near the graves to the branches of trees or shrubs or to sticks put up for the purpose. This is done, it is said, to show any native, who might inadvertently approach, that there has been a burial at the spot. The undergrowth is cleared for a short distance round the grave.

The men then return to the camp, where the women have been busy packing up all belongings. Plumes of shredded palm-leaf stem (*koro*) are put up at the entrance to the camp, to show chance visitors that there has been a death. The camp is then deserted, the natives moving to some other camping ground until the period of mourning is over, when they may, if they wish, return to the deserted village. No one goes near the grave again until the period of mourning is over.

In the case of very young children the burial ceremony is different. There is no general mourning of the whole camp. Only the father and mother and a few other relatives weep over the dead body. The head of the corpse is shaved and the body is decorated in the same way as that of an adult. The body is wrapped up in palm leaves (*Licuala*), the limbs being flexed. The fire is then removed from its customary place and a grave is dug there in the floor of the hut. In this the child's body is placed, the grave is filled in and the fire replaced above it. Not only is the camp not deserted, but there seems to be an obligation on the parents not to leave the place until the bones have been dug up, or at any rate for some weeks after the death. If the mother went away, the natives say, the baby would cry for its mother's milk. This is the custom of the Northern tribes. Referring to the Southern tribes, Mr Man says that the baby is buried beneath the fireplace and the camp is then deserted, the mother placing beside the grave a shell containing some milk squeezed from her breasts. Some of my informants of the Southern tribes (*Akar-Bale*, etc.) told me however that the camp would not be deserted in the case of the death of an infant, thus contradicting Mr Man's statement. As there was no opportunity of testing the point by reference to an actual case, it must be left as doubtful. In the Northern tribes when an older child dies the body is buried away from the camp, but the latter is not, at any rate in all instances, deserted, though the hut in which the death occurred may be destroyed and a new one built a short distance away. It is only in the case of the death of an adult that the camp is abandoned.

In connection with the burial of a baby beneath the hearth there is a belief that the soul of the dead baby may re-enter the mother and be born again. This would seem to be one of the reasons why the mother does not leave the camp when her baby dies.

Should a person die while on a visit, he or she is buried in the usual way and news of the death and place of burial is sent to the relatives. A stranger who dies or is killed is buried unceremoniously or is cast into the sea. Among the Northern tribes the body of such a one used in former days to be disposed of by cutting it into pieces and burning it on a fire. The natives say that if this be done the 'blood' and the 'fat' of the dead man go up to the sky and this removes all danger to the living from the dead man. The blood of persons so burnt is seen in the sky at sunset. If a man were killed in a fight between two communities and his body remained with the enemy, they would dispose of it in this way. If the friends secured the body they would bury it in the usual way. It may be worthy of remark that this custom of burning the bodies of slain enemies is perhaps the real origin of the belief that the Andamanese are or were cannibals. We can well imagine that when, as must have often happened, sailors venturing to land on the islands have been killed and the survivors have seen the bodies of their companions cut up and placed on fires, they would readily conclude that they were witnessing a cannibal feast. There can be no doubt whatever that since the islands were occupied in 1858 the inhabitants have not practised cannibalism, and there is no good reason to suppose that they once followed the custom and then abandoned it.

The burial is conducted, if possible, on the day of the death. If it has to be deferred till the morrow all the inhabitants of the camp keep awake. The relatives sit round the corpse weeping at intervals, while some of the men take it in turn to sing songs during the hours of darkness. This, so they say, is to keep away the spirits that have caused the death, and so prevent them from further mischief. When a man or woman dies in the prime of life after a short illness the friends and relatives often break out in anger which they express in different ways. A man will shout threats and curses at the spirits that he conceives to be responsible for the death of his friend. He may pick up his bow and discharge his arrows in all directions, or in some other way give expression to his angry feelings. On the occasion of a death in one of the *Akar-Bale* villages the relatives expressed their grief by cutting down a coconut tree that grew there.

The period of mourning for near relatives—parent, adult child, consort, brother or sister—lasts for several months. In the case of a young child only the parents mourn. The essentials of mourning are (1) the use of clay (*odu*), and (2) abstention from certain foods, from dancing, and from the use of white clay (*tǫl*) and red paint. As stated above, every adult in the camp covers himself or herself with clay on the death of an adult member of the community, but when this wears off, or is washed off in the course of two or three days, it is not renewed. The near relatives retain this covering of clay for many weeks, constantly renewing it. The clay is smeared evenly over the body, and is not put on in patterns, as on other occasions. The relatives, but not the others, plaster some of the same clay on their heads. A widow mourning for her husband covers her whole head with a thick layer of clay, renewing it from time to time. For a lesser degree of mourning, the custom is to plaster clay on the forehead only. After some weeks or months of mourning, the near relatives discontinue the use of clay on their bodies, but retain a band of clay over the forehead as shown in Plates IX, X, and XVII.

The name of the clay thus used is *odu* in the Northern languages, and a mourner is called *aka-odu*. In the *Aka-Bea* language the name of the clay is *og* and the term for a mourner is *aka-og*.

During the period of mourning the name of the dead person is carefully avoided and no one uses it. If it is necessary to refer to the dead this is done by using some such phrase as "he who is buried by the big rock" or "he who is laid in the fig tree" or by mentioning the name of the place of burial. There is no prohibition against mentioning the name itself in other connections. Thus if a man were called *Buio*, from the name of a species of *Mucuna*, it is not necessary to avoid the word *buio* when speaking of the plant. Further if there is another person alive of the same name as the dead man it is not necessary to avoid the name in referring to the living individual. The custom is that a dead person must not be spoken of unless it is absolutely necessary, and then must not be spoken of by name. After the period of mourning is over the dead person may again be spoken of by name.

During the period of mourning a near relative of the deceased is never addressed or spoken of by name. There are certain terms which are used for this purpose, being terms of address that can be substituted for the names that are avoided. Thus in the *Aka-Jeru* language one such term is *Bolok*, meaning "orphan," used in addressing or speaking of a person who has lately lost a parent. Another term of the same language is *Ropuč*, applicable to one who has lost a brother or sister. After the period of mourning is over the use of the personal name of the mourner is resumed.

During the period of mourning the near relatives of the deceased are required by custom to abstain from dancing and from using red paint or white clay. The white clay here referred to is that called *tǫl* or *tǫl-odu* in *Aka-Jeru* and *tala-og* in *Aka-Bea*, and is used for decorating the body on ceremonial occasions, such as that of a big dance. Further, the mourners must abstain from eating certain foods. The customs with regard to the foods to be avoided are different in different parts. There is however the universal rule that coast-dwellers must not eat turtle, and jungle-dwellers must avoid pork. Other foods that are included amongst those to be avoided are dugong, certain fishes such as that called *komar* in *Aka-Jeru*, and in some parts yams and honey.

The exact duration of the period of mourning is difficult to discover. It seems to vary considerably in different cases. In all cases it must last long enough for the flesh to decay from the bones. The proceedings at the end of mourning consist of (1) digging up the bones of the dead man or woman and (2) a dance in which all the mourners join. The bones are generally dug up by the men who performed the burial. They cover themselves with clay (*odu*) and proceed to the grave or tree and dig up or take down the bones and weep over them. These are then washed in the sea or a creek and are taken back to camp. Here they are received by the women who weep over them in their turn. The skull and jawbone are decorated with red paint and white clay, and each separately has a band of ornamental netting attached to it so that it may be worn around the neck. Additional ornament is frequently added in the form of strings of *Dentalium* or other shells. The skulls and jawbones of deceased relatives are preserved for a long time, and are worn round the neck either in front or behind. The photograph in Plate XVIII shows a woman wearing the skull of her deceased sister. Like all their other possessions these relics are lent or exchanged, passing from one person to another, until sometimes a skull may be found in the possession of a man who does not know to whom it belonged. The other bones are also preserved. The limb bones are generally painted with red paint and white clay and are kept in the roof of the hut. They are not treasured as much as the skull and jaw, and are often mislaid. Thus, while every camp is sure to contain a number of skulls and jaw-bones it is comparatively rarely that the limb bones are to be found. The other bones are made into strings, such bones as those of the hand and foot being used as they are, while ribs and vertebrae are broken up into pieces of convenient size. The bones or pieces of bone are attached to a length of rope by means of thread and the string thus produced is often ornamented with the dried yellow skin of the *Dendrobium* and with shells. The whole is covered with red paint. These strings of bone are worn as cures for and preventives of illness. If a man has a head-ache, for instance, he will attach one of the strings round his head. They are in almost constant use in every camp and every man and woman is sure to possess one or two. The bones are made into strings by the female relatives of the deceased and are then given away as presents.

In the North Andaman the skull of a baby is preserved by enclosing it in a small basket just big enough to contain it, the top of the basket, which is narrower than the lower part, being only finished after the skull is placed inside, so that it cannot fall out and can only be removed by unfastening the rim of the basket. Mr Man states that children's skulls are not carried in baskets, except temporarily as when travelling, fishing, etc., but are preserved from injury by being entirely covered with string[1]. This applies only to the tribes of the South and Middle Andaman.

At about the time that the bones are recovered there takes place a special ceremony referred to as "taking off the clay" or

---

[1] Man, *loc. cit.* p. 143.

"the shedding of tears." The object of this ceremony is to release the mourners from the restrictions that they have had to observe. The ceremony takes place in the evening, and an occasion is chosen when there are plenty of people in the camp. The mourners, male and female, remove the *odu* clay from their foreheads and decorate themselves with red paint and white clay in the way described in connection with dancing. They also put on what ornaments of *Pandanus* leaf or netting and *Dentalium* shell they may possess or be able to borrow. When all the members of the camp are assembled around the dancing ground one of the male mourners takes his stand at the sounding-board and sings a song. This song does not refer in any way to the dead man or woman; it is just an ordinary song of hunting or canoe-cutting or any other subject, though it may have been specially composed for the occasion. Those women who are not in mourning sit near the singer and take up the chorus. When the song is fairly started the mourners, male and female, begin to dance. There is nothing special about the dance, which is exactly like any other dance. After dancing for a short time the mourners seat themselves at one end of the dancing ground and their friends begin to weep and wail. Everybody present joins in the lamentation until they are tired. The mourners then rise and again dance. After a time the women retire and seat themselves with the chorus, but the men continue the dance (in which they are joined by the other men present), till they are tired, which often means till near dawn. After this ceremony the mourners are free to eat any of the foods up till then forbidden, and are free once more to use red paint and white clay and to take their part in all dances and other festivities.

It has been seen from the preceding descriptions that the Andamanese have a number of ritual customs relating to food. There are certain occasions in the life of every individual when he or she must abstain from eating certain foods. A person mourning for the death of a relative is subjected to restrictions of this kind, and so are the parents of a new-born child for a short period before and after the birth. A woman must not eat certain things when she is menstruating. Restrictions as to diet are imposed by custom on all persons who are ill. The most important restrictions, however, are those imposed on every boy and girl during the period of adolescence. During this period of life, as we have seen, the initiate is required to abstain for a longer or shorter period from all the most important foods of the Andamanese.

Mr Man states that "every Andamanese man or woman is prohibited all through life from eating some one (or more) fish or animal: in most cases the forbidden dainty is one which in childhood was observed (or imagined) by the mother to occasion some functional derangement; when of an age to understand it the circumstance is explained, and cause and effect being clearly demonstrated, the individual in question thenceforth considers that particular meat his *yat-tub*, and avoids it carefully. In cases where no evil consequences have resulted from partaking of any kind of food, the fortunate person is privileged to select his own *yat-tub*, and is of course shrewd enough to decide upon some fish, such as shark or skate, which is little relished, and to abstain from which consequently entails no exercise of self-denial[1]."

Although I made repeated enquiries amongst the natives of both the North and the South Andaman I was not able to confirm this observation of Mr Man. It is quite true that if a certain food is observed to disagree with a child he or she is taught to avoid that food for the rest of life, but it is not necessary for every person to have some forbidden food. Many men told me that they were under no such prohibition and might eat any food they liked, apart from the restrictions on special occasions. On a minor point it may be noted that skate and even shark are not by any means so little relished as the statement of Mr Man would imply. The liver of skates and rays, and even the liver of sharks is rather regarded as a delicacy.

I noticed on several occasions that men would not eat certain foods when they were away from their own part of the islands.

---

[1] Man, *op. cit.* p. 354. Mr Man adds in a note that "it is believed that *Puluga* would punish severely any person who might be guilty of eating his *yat-tub*, either by causing his skin to peel off (*wainyake*) or by turning his hair white and flaying him alive." On *Puluga* see later, Chaps. III and IV.

Thus one man of the North Andaman told me that he would not eat dugong when he was with me in the South Andaman. Another said that though he would eat the fish *komar* when he was at home, he would not eat it when he was in a strange place, as at the Settlement of Port Blair, for fear that it would make him ill.

In the North Andaman I was told that when a dugong is caught and the people feast on it they do not leave the camp till some hours after the meat is all finished, either to go fishing or hunting. The reason they give for this is that the spirits of the jungle and the sea may smell them, attracted by the odour of the food they have eaten and may cause them to be ill. They therefore remain in the camp and eat up all the dugong and do not venture out till they begin to feel hungry and must go in search of food. I believe that the same custom is observed in the South Andaman also.

A few other customs connected with food may be mentioned here. There is only one way in which a turtle may be killed[1]. It must be laid on its back with its head pointing towards the open sea, and a skewer of wood is then thrust through the eye-socket into the brain. The natives say that if a turtle were killed in any other way than this, the meat would be "bad," i.e., uneatable.

Turtle meat may only be cooked on a fire of the wood of the *Hibiscus tiliaceus*.

A pig is killed as it runs, without ceremony, but there is one special way in which it must be cut up. The pig is first disembowelled, and the joints of the legs are severed. The abdominal cavity is then filled with leaves, of which only certain special kinds are used. It is placed on a fire and roasted whole, and is then cut up. Should the carcase be cut up by any other than the traditional method, the natives believe that the meat would be "bad," and they would not eat it.

A number of beliefs relating to vegetable foods will be mentioned in the next chapter.

In several of the ceremonies described in this chapter it will be noticed that the weeping of relatives and friends occurs

[1] Turtle are captured alive by means of harpoons, and may be kept alive several days before they are killed and eaten.

as an essential part of the ceremony. The female relatives of a youth or girl who is being initiated come and weep over him or her at the turtle-eating ceremony. Their friends weep over, or with, the mourners at the dance at the end of mourning. The friends of a bride and bridegroom weep over them when they are married. The friends and relatives weep over a corpse before it is buried and over the bones when they are recovered. In all cases it is real weeping. The man or woman sits down and wails or howls, and the tears stream down his or her face. On one occasion I asked the natives to show how it was done and two or three of them sat down and were immediately weeping real tears at my request. The weeping in this way is really a ceremony or rite. When two friends or relatives meet who have been separated from one another for a few weeks or longer, they greet each other by sitting down, one on the lap of the other, with their arms around each other's necks, and weeping and wailing for two or three minutes till they are tired. Two brothers greet each other in this way, and so do father and son, mother and son, mother and daughter, and husband and wife. When husband and wife meet, it is the man who sits on the lap of the woman. When two friends part from one another, one of them lifts up the hand of the other towards his mouth and gently blows on it.

Reference has already been made in this chapter to a number of customs relating to personal names. It will be useful to bring together the scattered references, and give a general account of the whole matter.

Every Andaman Islander has a personal name that is given to him or her before birth, and which we may speak of as the birth-name. As soon as a woman realises that she is pregnant, she and her husband begin to think of a name for the child. The name is selected by the parents, but the suggestions of their friends and relatives are always considered. It is regarded as a compliment to name the child after some man or woman. Sometimes a man may request the parents that the child shall be named after him, and such a request is rarely, if ever, refused. The names given before birth are of course applicable to both sexes, there being no difference between the names of men and those of women. There are a considerable number of names in common use, but some of them are more popular at a given time and place than others. It therefore happens that there are several persons, both men and women, bearing the same name.

Each of the names in common use has a meaning, but it is not always easy to obtain an adequate and accurate explanation of the meaning from the natives themselves[1]. In a certain number the derivation is obvious. Many names are the names of objects such as trees, fish or other animals, or even such objects as rope or mats. A few examples from the North Andaman are:—

Buio	*Mucuna sp.*, a plant with edible beans.
Bol	*Hibiscus tiliaceus*.
Čop	a tree with edible nuts.
Konmo	*Dioscorea sp.*
Čokbi	turtle.
Maro	honey.
Meo	a stone.
Čeo	a knife.
Bani	the oriole.

In the case of a number of names it is not possible to discover with certainty the derivation, and the statements of the natives regarding them do not always agree. Such names in the North Andaman, with their meanings as stated by the natives, are:—

Kea	one who turns in his sleep.
Boičo	one who wrestles.
Elpe	one who comes and goes.
Kijeri	one who walks backwards and forwards.
Nimi	one who catches hold.

Some time after a child is born it is given a nick-name. Nick-names may be given at any time of life, and some persons may have several nick-names given to them at different times. New nick-names are from time to time invented, but there are

---

[1] Mr M. V. Portman gives a list of personal names in use in the South Andaman in his *Notes on the Languages of the South Andaman Group of Tribes*, p. 70. The derivations of many of the names as there given, are, however, of doubtful accuracy.

a certain number of recognized names from which a choice is usually made. A few examples from the North Andaman are:—

Ra-ťot-betč	pig's hair.
Renya-čope	much baggage, or many possessions.
Poičo-tomo	the wood (literally flesh) of the *Sterculia* (*poičo*) tree.
Lau-tei	spirit blood.
Luremo	rope.
Remu-toi	a piece of iron.
Čokbi-čiro	turtle liver.
Tarenjek	angry.

During childhood boys and girls are addressed by either the birth-name or the nick-name.

When a girl reaches the age of puberty she receives a new name. This is one of a limited number of names, each of which is the name of a tree or plant. The name given to the girl is that of the tree or plant that is in flower at the time of her first menstruation.

There is a succession of trees and plants flowering one after another throughout the year. The natives describe the different parts of the year by reference to the plants in flower at the time. The plants selected as typical of the different seasons all have flowers from which the native bees make honey. Each of them has a distinctive scent and gives to the honey made from it a distinctive flavour. The flower-names are given below in *Aka-Bea* and *Aka-Jeru*.

Aka-Bea	Aka-Jeru	
Čilipa	Čelibi	From the middle of November to the middle of February.
Moda	Mukui	
Ora	Okor	
Jidga		From the middle of February to the middle of
Yere	Jeru	May, in order.
Pataka	Botek	
Balya	Puliu	
Reće	Re	From the middle of May to the end of August.
Čagara	Čokoro	
Čarapa	Čarap	
Čenra	Torok?	September, October and the first half of November.
Yulu	Jili	

From the time that a girl receives her flower-name her birth-name and nick-name fall entirely out of use. No one would address an unmarried girl by any name except the flower-name. This continues until some time after the girl is married. Properly speaking a woman should be known by her flower-name from the advent of puberty until after the birth of her first child. In these days of childless women the flower-name drops out of use after a few years of married life. After the birth of her first child the woman is known by her birth-name or by a nick-name. Thus a woman who was named before her birth *Kaba* (from *kabal*, a species of mangrove) was called by that name until puberty; thereafter she was called *Jili* (her flower-name) until the birth of her first child; after this event she is again called *Kaba*, and no one would think of addressing her as *Jili*. A woman named *Ele* (lightning) at birth was known by this name until puberty, and thereafter was called *Boṭek*. When I knew her she had been married for three years or so, but had not had a child. A few of the younger men and women addressed her as *Ele*, but the older people still called her *Boṭek*. If she should bear a child, the name *Boṭek* would fall entirely out of use and she would be known as *Ele* by both her juniors and her seniors.

In the case of a boy there is nothing corresponding to the flower-names of girls. He continues to be known by his birth-name and his nick-name from the time he is born until he dies. During adolescence a youth has to pass through certain ceremonies of initiation as described in the present chapter. At the turtle-eating ceremony the youth is given a new name, of the nature of a nick-name. The name given in this way is never used either in addressing the youth or in speaking of him. It is possible that he also receives a new name on the occasion of the pig-eating ceremony, but of this I am not sure. Though girls pass through the same ceremonies as boys, I did not discover whether or not they also are given new names on these occasions.

Names are used freely in speaking of and to one another. An older person always speaks of or to the younger one by the name alone. When a younger person is speaking to an older one it is customary and polite to use one of the terms of address, either by itself, or prefixed to the name of the person spoken to, as *Maia Buio, Mimi Kaba*, etc. A native generally hesitates to tell his own name, and if asked the question "What is your name?" often asks a bystander to give the required information. There is, however, no hesitation about mentioning the name of any other person, except under certain special conditions.

There are certain occasions when the name of a man or woman is temporarily avoided. After the death of a relative and during the period of mourning, a mourner's name is not mentioned, either in speaking to him or of him. There are a few terms that may be used instead. One who has lost a parent is addressed as *Bolok*, one who has lost a brother or sister as *Ropuč*. For a short time before and after the birth of a child the names of the father and mother are not mentioned. A bride and bridegroom are not addressed or spoken of by name for a short period after their marriage, though if their names be A and B there seems to be no harm in referring to A as "the husband of B," or to B as "the wife of A." During the initiation ceremonies through which every boy and girl must pass, the name of the initiate is avoided. Thus on the occasion of the turtle-eating ceremony or the pig-eating ceremony, during the few days the ceremony lasts and for a few weeks afterwards, the youth or girl is never addressed or spoken of by name, but is referred to as *Kimil*. During the ceremony that takes place on the occasion of the advent of puberty, and for some weeks after, a girl is not spoken of or to either by her birth-name or her flower-name, but is called *Toto*. When a boy, in the Northern tribes, has the scars made on his back, which show him to be no longer a child, his name is avoided for a few weeks and he is called *Ejido*.

The name of a dead man or woman is not mentioned during the period of mourning, which lasts for some months after the death.

In the preceding portions of the chapter reference has been made several times to the ornamentation of the body with clay and pigment. In the Great Andaman three different substances are used for painting the body. These are (1) a common clay of which different specimens are gray, yellow or pink, called *odu* in *Aka-Jeru* and *og* in *Aka-Bea*; (2) a fine white pipe-clay which is rarer than the common clay and is more highly prized, called *tǫl* or *tǫl-odu* in *Aka-Jeru* and *tala-og* in *Aka-Bea*; (3) a red pigment made by mixing burnt oxide of iron with animal or vegetable fat or oil, called *keyip* in *Aka-Jeru* and *kǫiob* in *Aka-Bea*.

The common clay (*odu*) is used in three different ways. After the death of a relative a man or woman smears himself all over with this clay and plasters it on his head. From this custom a person who is mourning for a dead relative is called *aka-odu* in *Aka-Jeru* or *aka-og* in *Aka-Bea*. The same clay is used at a certain stage of the initiation ceremonies, as described above, being spattered over the initiate in the turtle-eating and pig-eating ceremonies. The third and most common use of this clay is to decorate the bodies of men and women with patterns called (in *Aka-Jeru*) *ęra-puli*. These patterns are always made by the women, who decorate each other and their male relatives. The clay is mixed with water in a wooden dish or a shell and the mixture is applied to the body with the fingers. There is an almost indefinite variety in the patterns employed, although there are a certain number of what may be called usual designs. Each woman vies with others in her endeavours to produce some novelty of detail in her designs, and a successful innovation is immediately copied by others. I was able to watch the rise and development and ultimate disappearance of "fashions" in this connection in one of the camps of the North Andaman.

The design is made in one of two ways. It may, in some cases, be formed by painting with the finger on the body, that is by tracing white (or gray) lines on a black surface. A design of this kind is shown on the back of the man on the right in the photograph of Plate XI. On the other hand, an equally common method is to cover a part of the body with an even smear of clay and then to scrape it away either with the fingers or with a small fish-bone or with a little instrument made of small strips of bamboo, so as to leave a design of black lines where the skin shows through the smeared clay. Two not very striking designs of this kind are shown in Plates IX and X. As a rule the designs are more or less symmetrical, the right and the left sides of the body being treated alike, but in a few cases different patterns are made on the two sides, and I have seen a man with one side of his body painted and the other not. The painting may cover the whole of the body and limbs with the exception of the hands and feet, or it may be confined to the front and back of the trunk, or it may be on the front only. The face is often painted, the designs being made with greater care than those on the body.

These patterns are made in the afternoon after the men return from their day's hunting, and always either just before or just after a meal.

If a man be asked what pattern he is painted with, he replies by mentioning the food that he has just eaten. A man who has been eating turtle will say that the painting on his body is *čokbi-t'era-puli*, turtle pattern, while if he has been eating pork he will call it *ra-t'era-puli*, pig pattern. There is not, however, a strict uniformity in the use of particular patterns in connection with special foods. When the whole camp has been feasting on turtle many different and (apparently) unrelated designs are to be seen on the bodies of the men and women. I did not find it possible, even after a study of the matter, to distinguish by means of the design a man who has been eating turtle from one who has been eating pork. There is one design, or group of closely related designs, that seemed to be based on the pattern of the plates on a turtle's carapace. A pattern of this distinctive kind was never, so far as my experience went, used except after eating turtle. Other patterns, however, which were used after eating turtle, did not seem to me to be related in any way to what I may call the specific turtle pattern. In some of the patterns used after eating pork I noticed a tendency to make use of vertical lines or bands on the back and chest. There may be a connection here with the longitudinal markings on the back of the wild pig.

Of special patterns I was only able to discover two. One of these is called *kimil-t'era-puli* and is only used to paint a person who is *aka-kimil*, i.e., who has just been through one of the initiation ceremonies. This pattern is shown on the back of a man in the photograph reproduced as Plate XI (the second figure from the left). Another special pattern is called *toto-t'era-puli* (*Pandanus* pattern), and is used, I believe, to decorate a girl after the ceremony at her first menstruation.

The fine white clay called *tol-odu* in *Aka-Jeru* is used in a different way and on different occasions. When it is used to ornament the body it is always applied in one customary pattern. The name of this pattern in *Aka-Jeru* is *or-čubi-t'era-bat*, from the name of a species of snake, *or-čubi*. Exactly the same name is used in *A-Pučikwar*, *wara-čupi-l'ar-par*. Mr Man gives the *Aka-Bea* name as *jobo-tartaŋa*, from *jobo* the name for snake in general. A man decorated with this "snake pattern," as it may be called, is shown in Plate XII, and a pattern of the same kind is shown on the head of the man in Plate XIII. The pattern is built up of zig-zag lines. They are made by taking a little of the clay mixed with water between the thumb and first finger; by a movement of the thumb the space between the nail and the skin of the finger is filled with the clay, and the end of the finger is then applied to the skin so that it leaves a short and fine line of clay. A zig-zag line is thus built up of short lines each a finger's breadth in length. A second line is then added, not parallel to the first, but opposed to it, so that the two lines together form a row of lozenges. A third and sometimes a fourth or fifth line are similarly added. As shown in Plate XII the lines of pattern are carried down the front of the body, down the sides of the arms, and down the front of the legs, and they are similarly worked on the back of the body, and the back of the legs. The face also is decorated. These patterns are made by the women. It is one of the duties of a wife to decorate her husband in this way when occasion requires.

The only reason that the natives give for ornamenting themselves in this way is that it makes them "look well." On the occasion of a big dance many of the performers are thus ornamented. This is always so at the dances held when two or more local groups meet together. There are certain special occasions, already mentioned in this chapter, when the use of the "snake pattern" is required by custom. One of these is the dance at the end of mourning. During the period of mourning the mourners are forbidden to make use of this form of decoration.

The same pattern is used to decorate a bride and bridegroom after their marriage. In the initiation ceremonies the youth or girl is decorated in this way before the dances at the turtle-eating and pig-eating ceremonies. The same pattern is also made on a corpse before burial.

In all these cases the whole body is decorated. On less ceremonial occasions, such as an ordinary dance when there are no visitors of importance in the camp, a man frequently has his face alone decorated with white clay, as in the photograph of Plate XIII.

The third kind of material used for painting the body is red paint. This is applied in two different ways. When a man or woman is ill he or she is generally to be seen with some part of his body smeared with red paint. For colds and coughs the chest and neck are painted. In fevers red paint is smeared on the upper lip. Besides the medical use of red paint, if we may call it so, there is a ceremonial use, the pigment being used in combination with white clay, lines of red paint being applied to the body between the lines of clay of the snake pattern. It is used in this way to decorate the body of a dead person for burial, and on ceremonial occasions such as the dance at the end of mourning and the dances in connection with the initiation ceremonies.

Most of the ornaments worn at various times by the Andaman Islanders have a ceremonial or a magical purpose. The only things worn by men that can be considered to have a utilitarian value are the belt of rope and the necklet of string. The belt may be a plain piece of rope, or it may be ornamented with the yellow skin of a species of *Dendrobium*. It serves as a receptacle in which the natives carry such things as adzes, fish, roots, or even arrows. It is the one object that is constantly worn by men. The string necklet is simply a length of thin string tied round the neck. It serves as a means of carrying a knife and skewer. The knife, in former days made of a slip of cane, but in these times from a piece of scrap iron, is attached to a skewer of *Areca* wood by a short length of rope or stout string. By sliding either the knife or the skewer under the necklet at the back of the neck the double implement hangs securely in a position where it is not likely to get lost when running through the jungle, and where it is immediately accessible when wanted. The necklet also serves as a means of carrying bees'-wax, which is in constant use amongst the natives, a small ball of the wax being attached to one of the ends of the string of which the necklet is made.

As a rule, in everyday life, the men wear only a belt, or a belt and necklace. Those natives who visit the Settlement of Port Blair have been required by the European officers to wear a strip of cloth over the genitals. It has now become the rule to wear such a loin cloth whenever they are in the neighbourhood of a European. This, however, is a modern custom, and in former times the men went freely with no covering whatever, as do the inhabitants of the Little Andaman at the present time. As showing the extent to which the natives have been influenced in this matter by outside opinion, it may be mentioned that at the present day many of the younger men, particularly those who have been brought up at Port Blair, regard it as very immodest to be seen without some covering over the genitals.

On ceremonial occasions, such as the dance at the end of mourning, or a big dance-meeting, the men put on a number of ornaments. A common costume on such occasions consists of a belt, necklace, bracelets, and garters of netting and *Dentalium* shell. A belt and necklace of this kind are to be seen in Plate V, and garters are worn by the woman in Plate IX. An alternative costume for men consists of a set of ornaments of *Pandanus* leaf (belt, chaplet, bracelets and garters), decorated with *Dentalium* and other shells. Garters of this kind are shown in Plate XII.

Other objects are worn by the natives for magical purposes. Chief amongst these are the strings made of human bones which are worn to prevent and cure sickness. The bones are attached to a length of rope, and this is generally decorated with shells or with *Dendrobium* skin. These strings of bones are worn most commonly as chaplets, necklaces or belts, but they may also be made into garters and bracelets. The bones of animals, such as pig, turtle, dugong, etc., are treated in exactly the same way as human bones, and ornaments made of them are commonly worn.

There are a number of other ornaments that are commonly worn, not only on ceremonial occasions, which, unlike the strings of human bones, do not obviously have a magical purpose. Such are necklaces made of various kinds of shells, and of mangrove seeds. At the present time the natives obtain beads from Port Blair and make ornaments of these.

The ordinary costume of the women is different from that of the men. Every woman and girl wears at least one belt of *Pandanus* leaf. There is one kind of belt that is always worn by married women and which may not be worn by unmarried girls. There is another kind of belt that may only be worn by unmarried girls. The women of the Southern tribes wear a bundle of leaves of the *Mimusops littoralis* laid one over another suspended from the front of the belt so as to cover the pudenda. In the Northern tribes it was formerly the custom for the women to wear a similar apron of the leaves of a plant called *čainyo*, and over this they also wore a tassel of shredded palm-leaf stem (*koro*). Within recent years the Northern tribes have given up their own custom in this matter and have adopted the custom of the Southern tribes.

Women often wear round the neck a piece of string similar to that worn by the men, but as they do not carry knives it does not serve the same purpose. It is more usual for a woman to wear a necklace of some sort. Nowadays they are rather fond of necklaces of beads which they obtain from the Settlement at Port Blair. In former times different kinds of shells were used, such as the *Dentalium octogonum*.

With the exception that men wear the belt of rope, and women wear the belt of *Pandanus* leaf and the apron of leaves, there is no difference between the ornaments worn by men and by women. On the occasion of a dance or other ceremony a woman may wear any of the objects described as being worn by men on such occasions. They also wear in the same way strings of human or animal bones.

One object which would seem to have a purely utilitarian purpose is the sling used for carrying children (called in *Aka-*

Jeru čiba). This object, however, seems to have its ceremonial uses also. In one of the initiation ceremonies that I saw, the man who was officiating wore such a sling round his shoulders during the ceremony.

In the earlier parts of this chapter reference has been made several times to the dance of the Andaman Islanders. For the natives the dance is both a means of enjoyment and also a ceremony. The period of mourning for the dead is brought to a close by a dance, in which all the mourners join. As will be shown later, a dance was generally held before a fight, in former times when fights occurred. The ceremony by which two hostile local groups made peace with one another was a dance.

In the initiation ceremonies there are special dances, which have already been described, in connection with the pig-eating and turtle-eating ceremonies. With the exception of these special dances, and the peace-making dance to be described later, there is only one kind of dance in any given tribe. Thus the dance at the end of mourning, or before setting out on an attack on enemies, is in all essentials exactly the same as the dance in which the natives indulge when the day's hunting has been successful and the evening is fine.

The time for dancing, except in connection with certain ceremonies, is at night, after the evening meal. The dance takes place on the open ground in the centre of the village. This is swept clean by the women and the younger men. One or two fires are lighted, and little heaps of resin are placed in convenient situations to provide lights. These have to be replenished from time to time as the dance proceeds. Near one end of the dancing ground is placed a sounding-board, upon which it is the duty of one man to beat time with his foot. A sounding-board is a piece of wood somewhat of the shape of a large shield, cut from the hard *Pterocarpus* tree. One is shown in Plate VI. Behind the sounding-board, or a little to one side of it, the women, who form the chorus, sit in a row, with their legs stretched out in front of them, facing the dancing-ground. The men who intend to dance sit or stand round the edge of the space reserved for the dance.

When all is ready a man who has volunteered to sing the first song takes his stand at the sounding-board, and sings his song through. When he reaches the chorus the women take it up and repeat it after him, and as they do so each woman marks time by clapping her hands on the hollow formed by her thighs, the legs being crossed one over the other at the ankle. The singer continues to sing, thus leading the chorus, and at the same time marks the time of the song by beating on the sounding-board with his foot. As soon as the chorus begins the dancers begin to dance. The step of each dancer is the same, but there is very little attempt to form a figure. When the singer and the chorus get tired, the singing ceases, but the man at the sounding-board continues to mark time for the dancers. The singer repeats his song several times, and he may sing several songs, each repeated several times. When he gets tired he is relieved by another man. In a dance that lasts for any time, one singer succeeds another, and the singing and dancing are kept up continuously, sometimes for five or six hours.

The above description applies to all the tribes of the Great Andaman, but there are some differences between the four tribes of the North Andaman, and the tribes of the Middle and South Andaman.

In the North Andaman the song is sung through once from beginning to end by the singer, and is then repeated three or four times by the chorus. In the South Andaman each song consists of one verse and a refrain, if we may speak of them thus. The singer sings the verse and the refrain, and then the refrain only is repeated an indefinite number of times by the chorus.

In the dance of the Southern tribes, each dancer dances alternately on the right foot or on the left. When dancing on the right foot the first movement is a slight hop with the right foot, then the left foot is raised and brought down with a backward scrape along the ground, then another hop on the right foot. These three movements, which occupy the time of two beats of the song, are repeated until the right leg is tired, and the dancer then changes the movement to a hop with the left foot, followed by a scrape with the right and another hop with the left. The time of the movement is as follows, the upper line being the rhythm of the dance, while the lower line shows the beats of the song, which is marked on the sounding-board and by the clapping of the women.

The body of the dancer is bent slightly forward from the hips, the legs being flexed at the knees and the back being curved well inwards. There are several ways of holding the hands and arms, one of the commonest being to hold the arms outstretched in front on a level with the shoulders, while the thumb and forefinger of one hand are interlocked with those of the other. When a man does not wish to cease altogether from dancing but desires to have a short rest, he marks the time by raising each heel alternately from the ground. As a man dances he remains in one spot for a short time, and then, still continuing the same step, moves for a yard or two around the circle of the dancing ground. Every now and then a dancer is to be seen trotting from one position to another across the dancing ground, abandoning the step of the dance, but still keeping time to the song.

The Northern tribes have now adopted the same kind of dance as the tribes of the South, but formerly their dance was slightly different. There was a little more attempt at forming a figure, the dancers moving for the most part in a circle, some in one direction and others in the other. The step was as follows : a step forward with the right foot, a hop on the right foot, a scrape with the left, then another hop with the right, a step forward with the left foot, a hop with the left, a scrape with the right and a hop with the left. The rhythm is as follows :—

The lower line shows the beats on the sounding-board.

Some of the dancers occasionally break into the regular Southern step. A dancer sometimes changes from the usual step to another called *koi*, in which each foot is alternately struck on the ground and scraped backwards. Other slight variations of the movement may be introduced.

In both the Southern and the Northern dance each dancer pleases himself as to the direction in which he moves, and the step that he adopts at any given moment. All the dancers, however independently of one another they dance, keep strict time to the music.

Women do not, as a rule, join in the ordinary dances held in the evening. Their share in the entertainment consists of forming the chorus. When they do dance, as they do on certain occasions, such as the dance at the end of mourning, their step is different from that of the men. In the Southern tribes the female dancer stands at one spot with knees flexed and lifts her heels alternately from the ground in time to the music, thus producing a slight swaying or swinging motion of the hips. After dancing thus at one spot for a few moments, she moves forward a few steps to a new position, keeping time to the music in all her movements, and then repeats the same performance. The arms are swung in time to the dance, or else are held before the breast with one wrist crossed over the other.

In the Northern tribes the common dance of the women is a sort of modification of that of the men. A woman advances across the ground in regular time, but at every third step she gives a peculiar little hop which has something of the effect of a bobbing curtsey. The time is as follows :—

l and r standing for left and right foot, and the accent indicating the hop or curtsey. Every now and then a dancer stops and remains at one spot, alternately scraping each foot backwards, holding her knees flexed, and swinging both arms together.

The ordinary dance of the Andamanese, as described above, must always be accompanied by a song, and the purpose of every song is to serve as the accompaniment to a dance. Every man composes his own songs. No one would ever sing (at a dance) a song composed by any other person. There are no traditional songs. Women occasionally compose songs, but I never heard a woman sing at a dance except in the chorus.

Every man composes songs, and the boys begin to practise themselves in the art of composition when they are still young. A man composes his song as he cuts a canoe or a bow or as he paddles a canoe, singing it over softly to himself, until he is satisfied with it. He then awaits an opportunity to sing it in public, and for this he has to wait for a dance. Before the dance he takes care to teach the chorus to one or two of his female relatives so that they can lead the chorus of women. He sings his song, and if it is successful he repeats it several times, and thereafter it becomes part of his repertory, for every man of any age has a repertory of songs that he is prepared to repeat at any time. If the song is not successful, if the chorus and dancers do not like it, the composer abandons it and does not repeat it. Some men are recognized as being more skilful song-makers than others.

The songs all deal with everyday subjects such as hunting or cutting a canoe. The important thing about a song is not its sense, but its sound, i.e., its rhythm and melody. A translation of an *Akar-Bale* song, which is quite typical, is "*Pọio*, the son of *Mam Golat*, wants to know when I am going to finish my canoe. He comes every day. That is why I make haste to get it launched as soon as possible." Another on the same subject runs: "Knots are very hard to cut with an adze. They blunt the edge of the adze. How hard I am working cutting these knots." The singer here refers to the cutting of a canoe. A number of songs in the native languages with translations, are given by Mr Portman[1]. To these the reader may refer for further information.

According to the statements of the natives it was formerly the custom to have a dance before setting out to a fight. There was no special war-dance, the warriors joining in an ordinary dance such as has just been described. Those who intended

---

[1] Portman, *Notes on the Languages of the South Andaman Group of Tribes*, pp. 166—188.

to take part in the attack on their enemies, i.e., all the able-bodied adult males, decorated themselves with red paint and white clay, and put on ornaments of *Pandanus* leaf or netting and shells. Each man held in his hands or placed in his belt or head-dress plumes of shredded *Tetranthera* wood called (čelmo in Aka-J̌eru, uǰ in Aka-Bea). These plumes of shredded wood are now often worn or carried in an ordinary dance, but I believe that in former times they were the distinctive sign of a war-dance. To make them, a short length of the wood is taken (generally a piece of an old broken pig-arrow) and the wood is carefully shredded with a *Cyrena* shell, care being taken not to break any of the longitudinal fibres. One end is then tied with a piece of string or fibre. Similar plumes are made from *Pandanus* wood, and are carried or worn in a similar manner.

When the attacking party set out from their village each man wears a plume of shredded *Tetranthera* wood thrust into the back of his belt. They rub their bows with the shredded wood, and say that this has the effect of making their own bows shoot well and those of their enemies shoot badly.

If a man kills another in a fight between two villages, or in a private quarrel, he leaves his village and goes to live by himself in the jungle, where he must stay for some weeks, or even months. His wife, and one or two of his friends may live with him or visit him and attend to his wants. For some weeks the homicide must observe a rigorous tabu. He must not handle a bow or arrow. He must not feed himself or touch any food with his hands, but must be fed by his wife or a friend. He must keep his neck and upper lip covered with red paint, and must wear plumes of shredded *Tetranthera* wood (čelmo) in his belt before and behind, and in his necklace at the back of his neck. If he breaks any of these rules it is supposed that the spirit of the man he has killed will cause him to be ill. At the end of a few weeks the homicide undergoes a sort of purification ceremony. His hands are first rubbed with white clay (tọl-odu) and then with red paint. After this he may wash his hands and may then feed himself with his hands and may handle bows and arrows. He retains the plumes of shredded wood for a year or so.

In the North Andaman, and possibly in the South also, there was a ceremony by which two hostile local groups made peace with one another. When the two groups have agreed to make friends and bring their quarrel to an end, arrangements are made for this ceremony. The arrangements are made through the women of the two parties. A day is fixed for the ceremony, which takes place in the country of the group that made the last attack. In the village of this group the dancing ground is prepared, and across it is erected what is called a *koro-čop*. Posts are put up in a line, to the tops of these is attached a length of strong cane, and from the cane are suspended bundles of shredded palm-leaf (*koro*). The appearance of this construction may be seen from the photograph reproduced in Plate XIX. The women of the camp keep a look-out for the approach of the visitors. When they are known to be near the camp, the women sit down on one side of the dancing ground, and the men take up positions in front of the decorated cane. Each man stands with his back against the *koro-čop*, with his arms stretched out sideways along the top of it. None of them has any weapons.

The visitors, who are, if we may so put it, the forgiving party, while the home party are those who have committed the last act of hostility, advance into the camp dancing, the step being that of the ordinary dance. The women of the home party mark the time of the dance by clapping their hands on their thighs. I was told that the visitors carry their weapons with them, but when the dance was performed at my request the dancers were without weapons. The visitors dance forward in front of the men standing at the *koro-čop*, and then, still dancing all the time, pass backwards and forwards between the standing men, bending their heads as they pass beneath the suspended cane. The dancers make threatening gestures at the men standing at the *koro-čop*, and every now and then break into a shrill shout. The men at the *koro* stand silent and motionless, and are expected to show no sign of fear.

After they have been dancing thus for a little time, the leader of the dancers approaches the man at one end of the *koro* and, taking him by the shoulders from the front, leaps vigorously up and down to the time of the dance, thus giving the man he holds a good shaking. The leader then passes on to the next man in the row while another of the dancers goes through the same performance with the first man. This is continued until each of the dancers has "shaken" each of the standing men. The dancers then pass under the *koro* and shake their enemies in the same manner from the back. After a little more dancing the dancers retire, and the women of the visiting group come forward and dance in much the same way that the men have done, each woman giving each of the men of the other group a good shaking.

When the women have been through their dance the two parties of men and women sit down and weep together.

The two groups remain camped together for a few days, spending the time in hunting and dancing together. Presents are exchanged, as at the ordinary meetings of different groups. The men of the two groups exchange bows with one another.

CHAPTER III

RELIGIOUS AND MAGICAL BELIEFS

The Andaman Islanders believe in the existence of a class of supernatural beings which I propose to denote by the term "spirits." The native name for these spirits is *lau, lao* or *yau* in the languages of the North and Middle Andaman, and *čauga* in the South Andaman. While all spirits are denoted together by the term *lau* or *čauga*, there are certain special classes of spirits. There are, for instance, spirits that haunt the jungles of the islands. These are called in the North Andaman *Ti-miku Lau*, from the word *ti-miku* meaning the forest, or more accurately "land." (The only land known to the Andamanese is covered with forest.) In *Aka-Bea* the name for these jungle spirits is *E̱rem Čauga*, the word *e̱rem* being the equivalent in that language of the Northern *ti-miku*. In the North Andaman the *Ti-miku Lau* are often called *Bido Teč Lau*, i.e., spirits of the *Calamus* leaf, *bido* being the name of the *Calamus tigrinus*. This cane is armed with strong thorns, and in some parts of the jungle forms absolutely impenetrable thickets. The natives say that the spirits haunt these thickets, and hence their name.

There are other spirits that live in the sea. Although these may be included under the term *Lau* or *Čauga*, when it is used in a general sense, yet there is a special name for the sea spirits, *J̌urua* in the North Andaman, and *J̌uruwin* in *Aka-Bea*. The *J̌urua* are beings of the same nature as the *Ti-miku Lau*, with the difference that they live in the sea, while the latter live in the forest.

In the South Andaman the natives also speak of another class of spirits who live in the sky and are called *Mo̱rua* or *Mo̱rowin*.

When an Andamanese man or woman dies he or she becomes a spirit, i.e., a *Lau* or *Čauga*. The bones of a dead person, which are dug up after the flesh has decayed, are called *Lau tọi* in the North Andaman, *tọi* being the word for "bone." The skull is *Lau t'ẹr-čo*, from the word *ẹr-čo* meaning "head." Exactly similar terms are in use in *Aka-Bea*, the bones of a dead man being called *Čauga ta* (spirit bones).

The Andamanese relate legends, to be described in the next chapter, which concern the doings of mythical ancestors. As all Andamanese, when they die, become *Lau*, these ancestors are of course included under that term. They are often distinguished from the spirits of persons recently dead by being denoted as *Lau t'ẹr-kuro*, from the word *ẹr-kuro* meaning "big," and applied to human beings to denote importance of social position. Just as a man who occupies a prominent position in his tribe is called a "big" man (*ẹr-kuro*), so the ancestors of the Andamanese legends are called "big" spirits. The *Aka-Bea* use a similar term, *Čauga tabaya*, to distinguish the ancestors from the spirits of ordinary persons.

The name *Lau* or *Čauga* is also applied by the Andamanese to the natives of India and Burma whom they see in the Penal Settlement of Port Blair. The *Aka-Jeru* name for the Penal Settlement is *Lau-t'ara-nyu*, literally "the village of the spirits." At the present time the term *Lau* or *Čauga* is not applied to Europeans, who are generally spoken of in the North Andaman by the Hindustani word "sahib." Natives of the North Andaman told me that in former times (before 1875) they applied the term *Lau* to Europeans also not distinguishing them from other light-skinned aliens. The necessity for distinguishing between Asiatics, such as natives of India, and Europeans, has only arisen since they have come to have dealings with the Penal Settlement.

The term *Lau* is not applied by the Andamanese to aliens of their own race. Nor would it be applied, I believe, to men of other black races such as the African negro. I showed the natives photographs of Semang from the Malay Peninsula and also of natives of Africa and New Guinea, and in all cases they called them *Jarawa*, that being the term applied by the Great

Andaman tribes to the natives of the Little Andaman. On the other hand they called Polynesians *Lau*.

For many centuries the Andaman Islanders have been accustomed to see light-skinned men visit their shores in ships, Europeans, natives from the coasts of India, Burma and Malaya, and occasionally perhaps Chinese. To these aliens they gave the name of *Lau*, apparently regarding them as visitors from the only other world they knew of, the world of spirits[1]. The clothes that these "spirits" wore they called *Lau ot-julu*, the word *ot-julu* meaning "cold."

The spirits of the forest and the sea are believed to be generally invisible, but there are tales of men and women who have seen them, and their personal appearance is sometimes described. The descriptions vary considerably from one informant to another. One of the commonest statements is that they are light or white skinned. (The Andamanese vocabulary does not allow of any distinction between white and a light gray or a light shade of colour.) One man, however, said that the forest spirits are black (or dark), while the sea spirits are white (or light). I was told several times that the spirits have long hair and beards (the Andamanese having, as a rule, no beard, and their hair, being frizzy, never growing to any length). Their arms and legs are said to be abnormally long, while they have only small bodies. Though there is no uniformity in the way in which the natives describe the spirits of the jungle and the sea, there is a notable tendency to associate them with the grotesque, the ugly, and the fearful. There is a common belief that the spirits, both of the jungle and of the sea, carry about with them lights, which several men and women claim to have seen.

In reply to the question as to how the spirits of the forest and the sea originated, the natives all agree in saying that they are the spirits of dead men and women.

The jungle spirits live in a village (or villages) in the forest. There is a belief that mortals wandering by themselves in the jungle have been captured by the spirits. Should the captive

---

[1] A similar custom is found in many savage tribes. Thus in many parts of Australia the aborigines call white men by the same name that they apply to the spirits of the dead.

show any fear, my informants said, the spirits would kill him, but if he were brave they would take him to their village, detaining him for a time, and then releasing him to return to his friends. A man to whom such an adventure has happened will be endowed for the rest of his life with power to perform magic. He will pay occasional visits to his friends the spirits. The natives told me of one such man who died not many years ago. At irregular intervals he used to wander off into the jungle by himself and remain absent for a few hours, sometimes for a day or two. He returned to the village after such an absence looking strange and wearing ornaments of shredded palm-leaf (*koro*) which he claimed had been placed upon him by the spirits.

Save for persons who have made friends with them, and have thereby become endowed with magical powers, all contact with the spirits of the jungle and the sea, or with the spirit of a dead man, is dangerous. The spirits are believed to be the cause of all sickness and of all deaths resulting from sickness. As a man wanders in the jungle or by the sea, the spirits come invisibly and strike him, whereupon he falls ill, and may die. A man or woman is more likely to be attacked by the spirits if he or she is alone, and it is therefore always better to be in company when away from the village. The spirits rarely venture into the village itself, though they may prowl round it, particularly at night. They are more dangerous at night than during the day.

There are many objects that are believed to have the power of keeping spirits at a distance, and thus of preserving human beings from the danger of sickness. Amongst the most important of these are fire, arrows, human bones, bees'-wax, and red paint. A man or a woman leaving a hut to go only a few yards at night will always carry a fire-brand as a protection against spirits that may be prowling in the neighbourhood. If the night be dark a torch is carried in addition to the fire-stick.

The Andamanese will never whistle at night, as they believe that the noise of whistling would attract spirits. On the other hand they believe that singing will keep the spirits away.

The spirits that haunt the woods and waters of a man's own home are regarded as being less dangerous to him than those of a country in which he is a stranger. A man of the *Aka-Čari* tribe who was with me in Rutland Island had a cold on his chest. He asked me for permission to return to his own country, explaining that the spirits of Rutland Island were, so to speak, at enmity with him, and that if he stayed longer he would be seriously ill, and perhaps die, while on the other hand, the spirits of his own country were friendly towards him, and once he was amongst them he would quickly recover.

There is a belief that the spirits feed on the flesh of dead men and women. The jungle spirits eat those who are buried on land, and the *Jurua* devour those who are drowned or otherwise lost in the sea.

Mr Man's account of the spirits of the jungle and sea contains an important error, which needs to be pointed out. He writes as though there were only one *Erem Čauga* (jungle spirit) and only one *Juruwin* (sea spirit), whereas each of these names is the name not of a single individual but of a class of supernatural beings of which there is an indefinite number. The following is Mr Man's account:—*Erem-čauga-la*, the "evil spirit of the woods, has a numerous progeny by his wife *Čana Badgi-lola*, who remains at home with her daughters and younger children, while her husband and grown up sons roam about the jungles with a lighted torch attached to their left legs, in order that the former may injure any unhappy wights who may meet them unprotected, and in the dark; he generally makes his victims ill, or kills them by wounding them internally with invisible arrows, and if he is successful in causing death, it is supposed that they feast upon the raw flesh." "As regards *Juruwin*, the evil spirit of the sea, they say that he too is invisible, and lives in the sea with his wife and children, who help him to devour the bodies of those who are drowned or buried at sea; fish constitute the staple of his food, but he also occasionally, by way of variety, attacks the aborigines he finds fishing on the shores or by the creeks. The weapon he uses is a spear, and persons who are seized with cramp or any sudden illness, on returning from, or while on the water are said to have been 'speared' by *Juruwin*. He has various submarine residences, and boats for travelling under the surface of the sea, while he carries with him a net, in which he places all the victims, human or piscine, he may succeed in capturing[1]."

Mr Portman correctly translates the word *Juruwin* as meaning "the spirits of the sea" using the plural and not the singular[2].

Further references to the Andamanese beliefs about the spirits will be found later in the chapter. It is necessary at this point to consider an entirely different class of beings.

The Andaman Islanders personify the phenomena of nature with which they are acquainted, such as the sun and the moon. Before relating in detail what could be learnt about their beliefs on these matters, it is necessary to call attention to one feature of these beliefs. Different statements, not only of different informants, but even of the same informant, are often quite contradictory. For example, it is sometimes said that lightning is a person, and at other times it is said that lightning is a firebrand thrown across the sky by a mythical being named *Biliku*. These two statements, which to all logical thinking are incompatible, are both given, and apparently both equally believed, by the same person. Many examples of such contradictions will be found in what follows, and it is important to point out their existence beforehand.

About the sun and moon, the most usual statement in all the tribes is that the sun is the wife of the moon and the stars are their children. In the North Andaman the moon is *Maia Dula* (*Aka-Čari*) or *Maia Čirikli* (*Aka-Jeru*), the sun is *Mimi Diu* and their children the stars are *Čatlo*, the larger ones, and *Katan* the smaller. *Čatlo* is the name of a species of finely marked beetle, and *katan* is the name of the common fire-fly. Individual stars or constellations are not recognized.

Another version from the same tribes is that the moon (*Dula*) is female, and has a husband named *Maia Tok*, while the sun (*Diu* or *Torodiu*) is male.

In the *Aka-Jeru* tribe there is a belief that the moon (*Maia Čirikli*) can, when he wishes, turn himself into a pig, and come down to earth and feed on the things that the pigs eat. There

---

[1] Man, *op. cit.* pp. 158, 159.
[2] Portman, *Notes on the Languages*, etc. p. 183.

is a legend that on one occasion the moon thus turned himself into a pig and came down to earth to eat the *čuei* fruit. A man named *Maia Čoinyop* met the moon (in the form of a pig) in the forest, and shot him with an arrow. *Čirikli* (the moon) took out his knife and killed the unfortunate *Čoinyop*, cutting off his head, which he left behind, and taking the body up to the sky where he ate it.

In the *A-Pučikwar* tribe the most common statement is that the moon (*Puki*) is male and that the sun (*Puto*) is his wife. A different statement from the same tribe is that the moon is female and is the wife of a being named *Tomo*. *Tomo* seems to be to some extent identified with the sun. Thus one informant said that it is *Tomo* who sends the fine weather, and that it is he who sends the daylight every day. Where *Tomo* lives, in the sky, it is always day and is always fine. When the natives die their spirits go up to the sky and live with *Tomo*. We shall see in the next chapter that, according to some of the legends, *Tomo* is the first ancestor of the Andamanese.

Yet another version is that the moon was made by *Tomo* out of opalescent stone, and it is *Tomo* who, in some way, regulates its passage across the sky.

A belief about the moon which is found in all the tribes, both of the North and the South, is that he will be very angry if there is any fire, or any bright light, visible when he rises in the evening shortly after sundown. At such times the natives are careful to cover up their fires so that they only smoulder without flame. Mr Man refers to this custom. "From fear of displeasing *Maia Ogar* (Mr Moon), during the first few evenings of the third quarter, when he rises after sundown, they preserve silence, cease from any work on which they may be engaged—even halting should they be travelling—and almost extinguishing any light or fire that may be burning. This is owing to the belief that he is jealous of attention being distracted to other objects than himself at such a time, or of any other light being employed than that which he had been graciously pleased to afford so abundantly. By the time the moon has ascended a few degrees, however, they restore their fires and resume their former occupations, as they consider that they have sufficiently complied with *Maia Ogar's* wishes and requirements. The glowing aspect of the full moon on its first appearance above the horizon is supposed to indicate that *Maia Ogar* is enraged at finding some persons neglecting to observe these conciliatory measures; there is also an idea that, if he be greatly annoyed, he will punish them by withdrawing or diminishing the light of his countenance[1]."

As regards the waxing and waning of the moon, Mr Man says that these are explained by the *Aka-Bea* "by saying that they are occasioned by 'his' applying a coating of cloud to his person by degrees, after the manner of their own use of *koiob* (red paint) and *tala-og* (white clay) and then gradually wiping it off[2]." In the *Aka-Kede* tribe the natives say that as *Maia Čirike* (Sir Moon) goes across the sky, his tongue hangs out of his mouth, sometimes more, sometimes less, and that it is the tongue that is visible, that gives the light. I did not hear any explanation of the waxing and waning of the moon in the tribes of the North Andaman. In these tribes the new moon is called *Dula e-tire*, i.e. the "baby moon," the word *e-tire* denoting the young offspring of an animal or a human being.

With regard to a lunar eclipse Mr Man writes that "in case *Maia Ogar* should be so ill-advised as permanently to withhold his light or render himself in other ways still more disagreeable, whenever the moon is eclipsed some persons at once seize their bows and twang them as rapidly as possible, thereby producing a rattling sound as if discharging a large number of arrows, while others commence at once sharpening their *rata* (arrows). Of course this hostile demonstration is never lost upon the moon, who does not venture to hurt those who show themselves ready to give him so uncomfortable a reception. Their immunity from harm on these occasions has given rise to some joking at the expense of the luminary in question, for, during the continuance of the eclipse, they shout in inviting tones to the hidden orb as follows:—*Ogar, laden balak ban lebe ŋ'idoati! doati! doati!* (O Moon, I will give you the seed of the *balak!* show yourself! appear! appear!) This is said derisively, for, although these

[1] Man, *op. cit.* p. 152.   [2] *Ibid.* p. 160.

seeds are largely consumed by the pigs, the aborigines do not consider them fit for food[1]."

It may be noted that the invitation to the moon to eat *balak* seeds is not perhaps derisive, but may be connected with the belief that the moon can turn himself into a pig in order to feed on the things that pigs eat.

There was no eclipse of the moon during my stay in the islands. The natives of the North Andaman told me that on such an occasion they frighten the moon into showing himself again by lighting the end of a bamboo arrow-shaft, and shooting it from a bow in the direction of the moon. Another custom of which they told me is to take plumes of shredded *Tetranthera* wood (*čelmo* or *uj*) and blow on them towards the moon.

Mr Man states that "a solar eclipse alarms them too much to allow of their indulging in jests or threats, &c.: during the time it lasts they all remain silent and motionless, as if in momentary expectation of some calamity[2]."

There are several different accounts in the North Andaman of the phenomena of day and night. The night is often personified and is called *Mimi Bat* (Lady Night). One version is that it is she who makes the night while *Maia Ţorodiu* makes the day. *Diu* is the name of the sun, and *ţoro-diu* really means "the full sun" and refers to the middle part of the day when the sun is well up in the sky.

Another Northern version is that the daylight is made by a being named *Tautǫbitatmo* who lives in the sky. He shuts up the day under a stone every evening and lets it out every morning. Of *Tautǫbitatmǫ* I was told that he is sometimes to be seen in the evening sky, but I was not able to discover to what natural phenomenon reference was made. I was also unable to discover the meaning of the name, which is a compound, *tau* being the sky.

Still another version from the same tribes is that it is a being named *Maia Čara* who makes the daylight. *Čara* seems to be the equivalent of the *Tomo* of the *A-Pučikwar* and other Southern tribes. He is sometimes said to have been the first ancestor, and sometimes the creator, of the Andamanese. He lives in the sky.

[1] Man, *op. cit.* p. 160.   [2] *Ibid.* p. 161.

Another belief about the night connects it with the spirits. The *Lau* (spirits) in the sky, wrap up the night in a cloth or mat. When they unroll the cloth it becomes dark. The natives of the North Andaman formerly called cloth *lau-ot-ju̇lu*, from a stem *-ju̇lu* meaning "cold." They were only acquainted with cloth through seeing it used by the aliens who visited their shores, and whom they called spirits (*Lau*).

In the North Andaman thunder and lightning are commonly personified. The lightning is *Ele* or *Ali*, and the thunder is *Korude* or *Korule*. Some of the natives spoke of *Mimi Ele* (female) and others of *Maia Ele* (male). He lives in the sky, which is regarded as being made of stone (or rock) and is called *tau-meo* (the sky-stone). The lightning is due to his shaking his foot. One rather obscure statement was to the effect that *Ele* spends most of his time asleep or lying down and doing nothing. When the weather gets bad *Lato* (a being that I could not identify), comes and worries *Ele* and wakes him up. Then *Ele* gets angry and shakes his leg. This is the lightning.

Thunder (*Korude*) also lives in the sky. It is said that he makes the thunder by means of a large round stone. One account is that he rolls the stone about over the sky. Another is that he makes the stone hot, and this produces the thunder.

An entirely different explanation of thunder and lightning, which is found in all the tribes, is that they are made by two beings named *Tarai* and *Biliku*, to be described later on in this chapter.

I never heard the rain (*jiċer*) spoken of as a person in the same way as thunder and lightning. One explanation of rain is that the sky-stone (*tau-meo*) gets cold, and this turns the mist (*milite*) into rain. Another is that in the sky there is a large hollow or pool, which gets filled with water and then overflows. Still another version is that the rain is made by a being (or beings) named *Čaitoŋ*, who seems to be female and lives in the sky. I could not obtain any satisfactory information about her.

In all parts of the islands the rainbow is believed to have some connection with the spirits of the jungle or of the sea. One very common statement is that it is a bridge of cane that stretches between this world and the world of departed spirits.

It is along the rainbow that the spirits travel when they visit the earth. It is necessary to correct a statement by Mr Portman on this matter. In connection with the *Aka-Bea* word for the rainbow, *pidga-l'ar-čauga*, he says "The root *pidga* (a rainbow) must not be confounded with the root *pidga* 'a cane' or 'rattan.' The Andamanese have certain legends regarding the uses of the rainbow, and these have been hitherto understood as referring to 'canes.' *Pidga-l'ar-čauga* means 'the rainbow (bridge) by which the spirits (cross)'[1]." Mr Portman is in error. The word *pidga* means "cane" and the whole word means "the cane of the spirits." It is the whole word that is the name of the rainbow, and not the word *pidga*. An exactly similar compound name for the rainbow exists in each of the languages of the Great Andaman. The name of the particular species of large cane varies, being *pidga* in *Aka-Bea*, *peta* in *A-Pučikwar*, *pir* in *Aka-Jeru*, and so on. Apart from the fact that the natives themselves say that the rainbow is a "cane," Mr Portman would have us believe that in each of the different languages there are two exactly similar words, different in the different languages, one of which means "cane" and the other "rainbow," while there is no connection between the words. Thus *Aka-Bea* would have *pidga* meaning "a kind of cane" and *pidga* meaning "a rainbow." *Aka-Jeru* would have *pir* meaning "cane" and *pir* meaning "rainbow."

The rainbow is generally regarded as an evil omen, being believed to be a precursor of sickness. One *Aka-Jeru* statement is that it is made by a being called *Toliton* and that when it appears somebody will be ill.

The only explanation of the tides that I heard was to the effect that they are caused by a fish, a species of *Tetrodon*, called *čolmo* in *Aka-Jeru* and *pit* in *Aka-Kede*, which drinks up the water and then lets it out again.

The Andaman Islands are occasionally visited by earthquakes. An *Aka-Kede* account of how earthquakes are caused is that when a man dies he goes to the spirit world which is beneath the earth. The spirits hold a ceremony. My informant spoke of the ceremony as *Kimil*, which is the name of the

---

[1] Portman, *Notes on the Languages of the South Andaman*, p. 328.

initiation ceremonies. At this ceremony they have a dance similar to the peace-making dance described in the last chapter, but instead of erecting a screen such as is used in that ceremony, they make use of the rainbow. As they shake the rainbow in dancing this causes earthquakes. The ceremony which newly-arrived spirits have to undergo in the world after death is a *poroto kimil*, i.e., the initiate eats *poroto* (*Caryota sobolifera*).

Among the most important of the Andamanese beliefs are those relating to the weather and the seasons. These are under the control of two beings named *Biliku, Bilik* or *Puluga*, and *Tarai, Teriya*, or *Daria*. There are a certain number of points in which the statements of one informant may differ from those of another in connection with these two mythical beings, but there are also a certain number of points on which there is absolute unanimity in all the tribes of the Great Andaman.

The first belief in which there is entire unanimity is that of the connection of *Biliku* and *Tarai* with the two chief winds that are known in the Andamans. *Biliku* lives in the north-east and is connected with the north-east monsoon. *Tarai* lives in the south-west and is connected with the south-west monsoon. The connection is shown in the names of these winds, which are as follows:—

Language	N. E. Wind	S. W. Wind
Aka-Cari, Aka-Bo, Aka-Kora, Aka-Jeru	Biliku boto	Tarai boto
Oko-Juwoi, Aka-Kol and A-Pucikwar	Bilik to	Teriya
Akar-Bale	Puluga toa	Daria
Aka-Bea	Puluga ta	Deria

In the Northern tribes the word *boto* means "wind." *Biliku boto* must be translated "the *Biliku* wind," and *Tarai boto* is similarly "the *Tarai* wind." It would be incorrect to translate the name *Biliku boto* as "the wind of *Biliku*," for this would be rendered in *Aka-Jeru* by *Biliku ičo boto*. In *A-Pučikwar* the south-west wind is called *Teriya* simply, the name of the mythical being connected with the wind being used as the name of the wind itself, just as is the case with the name *Ele* (lightning). On the other hand the north-east wind is called not *Bilik* but *Bilik to*. The same thing occurs also in the *Akar-Bale* and *Aka-Bea* languages.

Mr Portman translates the *Aka-Bea* term *Puluga ta* as "God's wind," and he adds, in explanation, "*Puluga ta* means 'God's wind,' and the reason for the name is not known. Some vague ideas regarding the direction of God's dwelling in the sky are the probable origin of the term[1]." As regards the translation of the Andamanese name *Puluga* by the English "God" more will be said later. Leaving that aside, it is important to note that *Puluga ta* does not mean "*Puluga's* wind." The word for wind in *Aka-Bea* is given by Mr Portman himself as *wul-ŋa*, and the *Akar-Bale* and *A-Pučikwar* equivalents are *poat-ŋa* and *pọte*, being forms of the same stem as the Northern *bọto*. The translation of "*Puluga's* wind" in *A-Pučikwar* would be *Bilik l'iye pọte*, but this is not a phrase that the natives ever use. It is not possible to translate "*Puluga's* wind" accurately in *Akar-Bale*. *Puluga poat-ŋa* would mean "*Puluga* blowing" the *-ŋa* being a verbal ending. In any case *Bilik tọ*, and *Puluga toa* are not to be translated as meaning "*Puluga's* wind."

It may be observed, in reference to Mr Portman's statement, that the notions of the Andamanese as to the direction of the dwelling of *Puluga* in the sky are very far from vague. The natives all agree that *Puluga* or *Biliku* lives in the direction from which the north-east wind blows, really N.N.E. This is shown in geographical names. For example the side of Havelock Island that faces north-east is called *Puluga-l'ar-mugu*, meaning "the side that faces *Puluga*," from *ar-mugu* meaning "front" or "face."

There are two matters, then, on which there is absolute unanimity in all the tribes of the Great Andaman, one being the connection of *Biliku* (or *Puluga*) with the north-east and of *Tarai* (or *Deria*) with the south-west, and the other being the connection of these two beings with the winds that blow from these two opposite points of the compass.

The connection of these two beings with winds is shown in another way in the *A-Pučikwar* tribe, where the winds are divided into two divisions. One division contains only the south-west wind, which is of extreme regularity, and blows steadily for about five months in every year. This wind is

---

[1] Portman, *Notes on the Languages of the South Andaman*, p. 314.

called *Teriya*. The other division contains all the other winds, and they are collectively denoted by the term *Bilik*. They are distinguished by names, as *Jila Bilik* (the east *Bilik*, from *jila*, east) *Koico Bilik* (the west *Bilik*), *Metepur Bilik*, *Coliatum Bilik*, *Rartear Bilik*, and *Koičor-toŋ Bilik*. Here we find the name *Bilik* used not as the name of a single person, but as a common name for a class of beings who are the winds personified. The same use of the term is found also in the *Aka-Kol* tribe.

Even in the *Akar-Bale* tribe something of the same kind is found. One *Akar-Bale* man said that *Puluga* has two brothers, *Jila Puluga* (East *Puluga*) and *Koaičo Puluga* (West *Puluga*); the one sends all the easterly winds and the other all the westerly ones.

In the Andamans the year is divided into two nearly equal portions. During the season of the south-west monsoon, which lasts from May to September, the wind blows steadily from the south-west. This is the rainy season. Violent storms never or only very rarely occur during the season of the south-west wind. From December to March the wind blows mostly from the N.N.E., occasionally changing to E.N.E. or N.E. In the periods at the change of the monsoon (from N.E. to S.W. in April and May, and from S.W. to N.E. in October and November) the wind is variable, and may blow at times from E.S.E. or W.N.W.

The south-west wind (properly speaking W.S.W.) is identified, as we have seen with *Tarai* (*Deria*). Although *Biliku* (*Puluga*) is specially connected with the north-east wind, yet all the winds other than the south-west are commonly supposed to be sent by *Biliku*. Thus we have seen that in the *A-Pučikwar* tribe the different winds are named, each of them (with the exception of the south-west) being a *Bilik*.

It comes about, in this way, that the year is divided into two portions, one of which is specially connected with *Biliku* (*Puluga*), while the other is specially connected with *Tarai* (*Deria*). These two seasons are not quite of equal length. The *Tarai* season lasts only while the south-west monsoon is blowing, which, in an average year, is between four and five months. The other seven months are connected with *Biliku* and are divided into three portions, (1) the stormy season of October and November, (2) the cold season of December to February, and (3) the hot season of March and April.

There are many points relating to *Biliku* and *Tarai* about which there is no general agreement amongst the tribes, or, in some cases, even within the same tribe. In the North Andaman *Biliku* is regarded as female, and is called *Mimi Biliku*, while *Tarai* is male and is called *Maia Tarai*. This is so in all the four tribes, *Aka-Čari*, *Aka-Bo*, *Aka-Kọra* and *Aka-Jeru*. A statement that is frequently made by the natives of these tribes is that *Tarai* and *Biliku* are husband and wife. While this is the most common statement, there are, however, other versions of the matter. In order to show the lack of uniformity in statements about *Biliku* and *Tarai* in the Northern tribes I reproduce a few extracts from my note-books written down exactly as they were given to me.

(1) *Biliku* is the wife of *Tarai* and they have a child named *Perjido*. (This statement was made to me a great many times in the North Andaman, and may be regarded as the most usual form of the belief.)

(2) *Biliku* is the wife of *Tarai*. Their children are the sun and moon. (Heard only once.)

(3) The husband of *Biliku* is *Perjido* and her children are *Totaimo*, *Mite* (cicada) and *Tarai*.

(4) *Biliku* is unmarried, but she has a son *Perjido*, and her other children are *Tọrọi*, *Čelene*, *Čotọt*, and *Čerei*. These four are the names of birds.

(5) *Biliku* is the wife of *Tarai*. Their children are *Tọrọi*, *Taka*, *Čotọt*, *Poruatọko*, *Kelil*, *Cọpcura*, *Benye*, *Biratkoro*, *Čereo*, *Milidu*, *Bobelo*, *Kọlo*. These are all names of birds.

(6) *Biliku* has a husband *Tọrọi* (a bird). *Tarai* has a wife *Kelil* (a bird).

In the *Aka-Kede* tribe the most common statement, at any rate in the northern part of the tribe, is that *Bilika* is female, and that *Tarai* is male. One *Aka-Kede* man, from the southern part of the tribe said that *Bilika* was male.

In the *Aka-Kọl* and *A-Pučikwar* tribes *Bilik* is generally spoken of as being male, and *Teriya* is also male. Other versions from these tribes are as follows:—

(1) *Bilik* is female and *Teriya* is her husband. Their children are the winds, *Čoliatum Bilik*, *Metepur Bilik*, and *Woičol'arpat Bilik*.

(2) There is a male *Bilik* and a female *Bilik*, who are husband and wife. Their children are *Koičor-toy Bilik*, *Koičo Bilik*, *Jila Bilik*, *Metepur Bilik*, *Rartear Bilik*, and *Teriya*. These are the winds.

(3) *Bilik* is male. His wife is *In Čaria*, and their children are *Kao* (prawn) and *Morua* (the sky).

In the *Akar-Bale* tribe the most usual statement is that both *Puluga* and *Daria* are male, and this was apparently also the common belief of the *Aka-Bea*.

In the North Andaman the name *Biliku* is also the word for "spider," but no meaning (save as the name of the mythical being) was discovered for the name *Tarai*. In the South and Middle Andaman no meaning was discovered, either for the name *Bilik* or *Puluga*, or for the name *Teriya* or *Deria*. Although this book does not deal with the Little Andaman, it is worth while to mention that there also the natives believe in a mythical person who lives in the north-east and sends the storms. This being is female and is named *Öluga*. The monitor lizard is also called *öluga* in the language of the Little Andaman. It is obvious, however, that the names *Biliku*, *Puluga*, *Öluga* are all of them different forms of the same word.

As we have already seen, it is *Biliku* and *Tarai* who send the winds. *Tarai* sends the south-west wind, which brings the rain. *Biliku* sends the other winds which bring either fine weather, or, at times, violent storms. One *Akar-Bale* account of the matter (literally translated as told to me) is as follows. "Once upon a time *Puluga* and *Daria* were great friends, but they quarrelled. *Puluga* said that he was the bigger (more important). *Daria* said that he was. So now they are always quarrelling. *Puluga* sends the wind for one period. Then *Daria* sends his wind."

According to the statement of an *Akar-Bale* man, *Puluga* makes the wind by fanning with a very large *kwar-toy* leaf.

Rain and thunder and lightning that come with the south-west wind are believed to be due to *Tarai*. Storms that come during the season connected with *Biliku* are made by *Biliku* and are due to her anger. When a big storm comes the natives say "*Biliku* is angry." Lightning is explained as being a fire-brand thrown by *Biliku* across the sky when she is angry, and thunder is said to be her voice growling. Another explanation of lightning is that it is a pearl-shell, called *be* in the North Andaman, thrown by *Biliku*, the bright flash of the mother-of-pearl being seen as it crosses the sky. Still another statement from the North Andaman is that *Biliku* makes the lightning by striking a pearl-shell (*be*) against a stone.

Although *Biliku* is generally mentioned when a native is asked about lightning, yet *Tarai* also wields the lightning and the thunder. On one occasion when I was talking to a native I referred to the thunder and lightning that were at the moment coming up from the south-west, making a remark to the effect that *Biliku* was getting angry about something, and was corrected by him with "No, that is *Tarai*."

There are a certain number of actions that are believed by the natives to arouse the anger of *Biliku* (*Puluga*), and thereby cause storms. There are three of these that are of importance.

(1) Burning or melting bees'-wax.

(2) Killing a cicada, or making a noise, particularly a noise of cutting or banging wood, during the time that the cicada is "singing" in the morning and evening.

(3) The use of certain articles of food, of which the chief are the seeds of the *Entada scandens*, the pith of the *Caryota sobolifera*, two species of *Dioscorea* (yam), and certain edible roots, of which may be mentioned those called in *Aka-Jeru labo*, *mikulu*, *ji* and *loito*.

In this matter there is an entire unanimity of belief in all the tribes of the Great Andaman. All the natives agree in saying that any of these three actions causes the anger of *Biliku* or *Puluga* and so brings bad weather.

The natives do, as a matter of fact, melt all the bees'-wax they obtain, in order to purify it, and render it suitable for use in the various ways in which they employ it. Also they do make use of all the plants mentioned under (3) whenever they are in season. They give various explanations of this variance between their precepts and their actions. Some of my informants said that though these actions may bring rain and storms, yet they would rather submit to the bad weather than go without some of their most prized vegetable foods. Others again say that there is always a chance that *Biliku* may not notice that the plants have been disturbed, particularly if no fragments are left lying about the camp, and if, when taking the roots, the creepers are not disturbed. Another statement is that it is really only during the season of storms, called the *Kimil* season in *Aka-Jeru*, that it is dangerous to eat these foods, that is, during the months of October and November. After this season has passed there is no longer any danger of violent storms and the foods in question may be freely eaten. Nevertheless the natives do eat these foods in the months of October and November.

Mr Man records the native beliefs about bees'-wax and the plants in question. "There is an idea current that if during the first half of the rainy season they eat the *Caryota sobolifera*, or pluck or eat the seeds of the *Entada pursætha*, or gather yams or other edible roots, another deluge would be the consequence, for *Puluga* is supposed to require these for his own consumption at that period of the year; the restriction, however does not extend to the fallen seeds of the *Entada pursætha*, which may be collected and eaten at any time with impunity. Another of the offences visited by *Puluga* with storms is the burning of bee's wax, the smell of which is said to be peculiarly obnoxious to him. Owing to this belief it is a common practice secretly to burn wax when a person against whom they bear ill-will is engaged in fishing, hunting, or the like, the object being to spoil his sport and cause him as much discomfort as possible; hence arises the saying amongst them, when suddenly overtaken by a storm, that some one must be burning wax[1]."

It must be noted that it is not only the "burning," but also the melting of bees'-wax that angers *Puluga*. As regards the plants mentioned by Mr Man none of these is available for food during the early part of the rainy season. At that time the yams are not formed, the pith of the *Caryota* palm is not ripe

---

[1] Man, *op. cit.* pp. 153, 154.

and is uneatable, and the only available seeds of the *Entada* would be those of the last season that had not fallen from the pods or that had lain on the ground without having germinated. Thus the prohibition as stated by Mr Man amounts to nothing. The subject will be discussed in a later chapter. It may be remarked, however, that it is a fact easily to be observed that the natives do regard the gathering of these vegetable foods during the later portion of the rainy season and during the first part of the cool season (i.e. from October to December), as being an action that may offend *Biliku*. I was myself able to observe this on several occasions, as when once, at the very end of the rainy season, I, not then knowing the belief, asked a native to cut for me one of the pods of the *Entada* as a botanical specimen, whereupon the native, after fulfilling my request, explained to me that there would probably be a storm next day as the result of our action.

In all the tribes of the Great Andaman I found a belief that *Biliku* or *Puluga* will be angry if anybody makes a noise, particularly a noise of chopping, breaking or banging wood, during the time the cicada is singing. The cicada "sings" as the natives call it, during the short interval between dawn and sunrise, and during that between sunset and darkness. It is at these times that no noise may be made. The Andamanese do observe this custom, and refrain from making any noise at such times. For instance, if a man were singing, he would cease until the cicada were silent again. In all the tribes I found that this prohibition was connected in the minds of the natives with *Puluga*, the reason of the custom being always explained to me by saying that any breach of it would infallibly bring bad weather. In the North Andaman the cicada (*mite*) is commonly spoken of as the "child" of *Biliku, Biliku ot-tire.*

Mr Man refers to this custom. In one place he says that the first parents of the Andamanese were told by *Puluga* "that, though they were to work in the wet months, they must not do so after sundown, because by doing so they would worry the *butu*, which are under *Puluga's* special protection. Any noise, such as working (*kopke*) with an adze, would cause the *butu's* head to ache, and that would be a serious matter. During the cold and dry seasons work may be carried on day and night, as the *butu* is then seldom seen, and cannot be disturbed [1]."

The *butu* here mentioned is the cicada. The prohibition is not, however, as Mr Man says, against working, but against making a noise. Nor does the prohibition against noise extend to the whole night, but only to the short interval between sunset and darkness, for it is during this interval that the cicada is singing. As soon as the cicada is silent you may make as much noise as you please.

Another reference by Mr Man to the same custom is as follows: " Between dawn and sunrise they will do no work, save what is noiseless, lest the sun should be offended and cause an eclipse, storm, or other misfortune to overtake them. If, therefore, they have occasion to start on a journey or hunting expedition at so early an hour, they proceed as quietly as possible, and refrain from the practice, observed at other times of the day, of testing the strength of their bow-strings, as the snapping noise caused thereby is one of those to which the sun objects [2]."

This is really the same prohibition as that already mentioned, against making a noise when the cicada is singing. The interesting point, which will be discussed in a later chapter, is that Mr Man's informant associated the prohibition not with *Puluga*, but with the sun. All the natives with whom I talked on the matter said that they would make no noise at such a time for fear of offending the cicada, and therefore *Puluga* or *Biliku*, and so bringing a storm.

As regards the prohibition against killing the cicada, this seems to refer only to the imago. So far as I was able to observe, the natives do carefully avoid killing the cicada in its full-grown form. On the other hand the grub of the cicada is regularly killed and eaten, being regarded as a delicacy. It is only eaten during the months of October and November.

In connection with the cicada, and with the weather, there is a rite which was described to me, but which I did not see performed. According to the account given of this rite, which is called "killing the cicada," its purpose is to produce fine weather. It takes place in December, at the end of the season

[1] Man, *op. cit.* p. 165. [2] *Ibid.* p. 153.

during which they eat the grub. When the time agreed upon for the performance of the ceremony arrives, all the members of the community are careful to be in the camp before sunset. As soon as the sun sets and the cicadæ begin their shrill cry, all the men, women and children present begin to make as much noise as they possibly can, by banging on the sounding-board, striking the ground with bamboos, beating pieces of wood together, or hammering on the sides of canoes, while at the same time shouting. They continue the noise, which entirely drowns that of the cicada, until after darkness has fallen. The rite may be performed, I believe, two or more times, on successive evenings. My informant explained the rite by saying that the natives have been eating the cicada, and the rite is intended to "kill" those that are left. After the rite the cicada disappears and is not seen or heard for some weeks, and there follow four months of fine weather with little rain.

The beliefs relating to bees'-wax, to the various edible roots, and to the cicada, are the same in all the Great Andaman tribes, and are by far the most important of those connected with *Biliku*. In the North Andaman *Biliku* is supposed to be angry if any one kills a *biliku* (spider) a *reo* (a species of insect making a noise like a cicada, during the daytime, which I often heard, but never saw), or a *čatlo* (a species of beetle). There is also a bird, which I was not able to identify, called *tǫrǫi*, which belongs to *Biliku* and may not be killed.

In the *A-Pučikwar* tribe it is said that two species of fish, called *unakoro* and *liwat* belong to *Bilik* and may not be killed. A mollusc, called *towa*, also belongs to *Bilik*, and is for that reason never eaten. A bird called *Bilik-l'ar-dala* (probably the same bird that is called *tǫrǫi* in the North Andaman) may not be killed.

In the *Akar-Bale* tribe I was told that two kinds of wood, *bukura* and *worago*, must not be used for firewood, for fear of offending *Puluga*, to whom they belong. *Bukura* is a species of *Diospyros* (ebony).

The only punishment that *Biliku* ever inflicts on human beings when she is angry with them for any reason, is to send violent storms. The way to stop a storm seems to be to frighten

Biliku. One means of doing this is to throw the leaves of the *Mimusops littoralis* in the fire. These leaves explode with the heating of the juices and make a crackling or popping noise, which it is said that *Biliku* dislikes. I believe, however, that if any one were thus to burn *Mimusops* leaves during fine weather, it would be regarded as likely to cause a storm. The most efficacious means of stopping a storm is to do some of the things that *Biliku* most dislikes. To burn bees'-wax, or to go into the jungle and damage or destroy the creepers that belong to her, these are the heroic remedies against *Biliku's* anger.

The question of the Andamanese beliefs about storms is complicated by the fact that although all storms are said to be made by *Puluga* or *Biliku*, yet there is an alternative and contradictory belief that storms are made by the spirits of the sea (*Jurua*). It is said that if a piece of the *Anadendron paniculatum* creeper were to be burnt there would be a great cyclone, but this appears to be associated, not with *Biliku*, but with the spirits of the sea. It will be shown later that there is a special connection between the *Jurua* and this plant. The belief that a storm will arise if turtle fat be allowed to burn in the fire seems also to be connected with the *Jurua* and not with *Biliku*. The same is probably the case with a belief that rain will come if a *Ficus laccifera* tree be damaged.

Some of the methods used to stop storms are also probably connected with the spirits and not with *Biliku*. One such method is to go into the sea and swish arrows about in the water. One *oko-jumu* (medicine-man) of the North Andaman is reputed to have stopped a big cyclone by taking a few pieces of *Anadendron paniculatum* and crushing them, and then diving into the sea and placing the crushed creeper under a stone. An *oko-jumu* who died while I was in the islands is supposed to have been able to stop a storm by similarly placing leaves and twigs of the *Ficus laccifera* (*reŋko*) under a rock in the sea.

To complete the account of this part of the Andamanese beliefs it is necessary to quote what Mr Man writes about the tribes of the South Andaman. Mr Man describes *Puluga* as a "Supreme Being" and says that some of the beliefs of the Andamanese relating to him "approximate closely to the true faith concerning the Deity." Mr Portman, following Mr Man, in this as in many other matters, translates the name *Puluga* by the English word " God." Mr Man's statements are as follows :—

" Of *Puluga* they say that—

" I. Though His appearance is like fire, yet He is (nowadays) invisible.

" II. He was never born and is immortal.

" III. By him the world and all objects, animate and inanimate were created, excepting only the powers of evil.

" IV. He is regarded as omniscient while it is day, knowing even the thoughts of their hearts.

" V. He is angered by the commission of certain sins, while to those in pain or distress he is pitiful, and sometimes deigns to afford relief.

" VI. He is the Judge from whom each soul receives its sentence after death, and to some extent, the hope of escape from the torments of *Jereg-l'ar-mugu* is said to affect their course of action in the present life.

" *Puluga* is believed to live in a large stone house in the sky, with a wife whom he created for himself: she is green in appearance and has two names, *Čana Aulola* (Mother Fresh-water Shrimp), and *Čana Palak* (Mother Eel); by her he has a large family, all, except the eldest, being girls ; these last, known as *morowin* (sky spirits or angels), are said to be black in appearance, and, with their mother, amuse themselves from time to time by throwing fish and prawns into the streams and sea for the use of the inhabitants of the world. *Puluga*'s son is called *Pijčor* : he is regarded as a sort of archangel, and is alone permitted to live with his father, whose orders it is his duty to make known to the *morowin*.

"*Puluga* is said to eat and drink, and, during the dry months of the year, to pass much of his time in sleep, as is proved by his voice (thunder) being rarely heard at that season ; he is the source whence they receive all their supplies of animals, birds, and turtles ; when they anger him he comes out of his house and blows, and growls, and hurls burning faggots at them—in other words, visits their offences with violent thunderstorms and heavy squalls; except for this purpose he seldom leaves home, unless it be during the rains, when he descends to earth to provide himself with certain kinds of food; how often this happens they do not know since, nowadays, he is invisible[1]."

Mr Man's comparison between the Andamanese belief in *Puluga* and the Christian belief in a God, will be discussed in a later chapter when we come to deal with the interpretation of the Andamanese beliefs. It is to be noted that Mr Man does not make any reference to *Deria* (*Tarai*), nor does he mention the association of *Puluga* with the north-east.

As regards the personal appearance of *Puluga*, the statements of different informants are not in agreement. One *A-Pučikwar* man described *Bilik* as being very big, about the height of one of the posts of my hut (which was eighteen feet), white-skinned like a European, having a long beard, and carrying a bow of the *Jarawa* type.

The legends connecting *Puluga* with the creation of the world will be given in the next chapter.

I am not able to confirm Mr Man's statement that *Puluga* is omniscient, and in fact there are some customs of the natives that are in contradiction with any such belief. When they dig up yams (which belong to *Puluga*) they take the tuber and replace the "crown" with the attached stem in the ground, and explain this by saying that if they do so *Puluga* will not notice that the yam has been taken. Whenever they do any of the things that displease *Puluga*, they seem to believe that there is a possibility that *Puluga* may not discover what has been done. It may be noted that there is no means of distinguishing in Andamanese between "all" and "a great deal." Thus a statement the *Puluga* knows "everything" may be equally well translated "*Puluga* knows a great deal." Between these two statements there is no difference for the Andamanese, but there is a great difference for us, and for this reason the use of the word "omniscient" is misleading.

Mr Man says that *Puluga* "is angered by the commission of certain sins." In this connection it is necessary to refer to another passage in Mr Man's work. "That they are not entirely devoid of moral consciousness may, I think, in some

[1] Man, *op. cit.* p. 157.

measure, be demonstrated by the fact of their possessing a word, *yub-da*, signifying sin or wrong-doing, which is used in connection with falsehood, theft, grave assault, murder, adultery, and—burning wax (!), which deeds are believed to anger *Puluga-la*, the Creator[1]." Although I made very careful and repeated enquiries, I was unable to meet with a single native who believed that such actions as the murder of one man by another, or adultery, aroused the anger of *Puluga*. The only actions at which *Puluga* is angry are those purely ritual offences, such as burning or melting wax, killing a cicada, digging up yams, etc., which have already been mentioned.

The Andamanese beliefs connected with the life after death will be described later in the present chapter.

As regards the "stone house" in which *Puluga* is said to live, this really means, I believe, a cave. In the North Andaman *Biliku* is frequently spoken of as living in a cave (*era-poŋ*). Also, it may be recalled, the sky is generally regarded as consisting of stone or rock, and it is in the sky the *Puluga* lives.

The son of *Puluga*, mentioned by Mr Man, *Pijčor*, is a being about whom I was able to learn very little. In the North Andaman the same being is named *Perjido*, and is said to be the son of *Biliku*. The *Morowin*, whom Mr Man describes as the daughters of *Puluga*, are sky spirits. The most usual belief in the South Andaman is that there are both male and female *Morowin*. They are beings of somewhat the same nature as the jungle spirits and the sea spirits. An *Akar-Bale* informant told me, "The *Morua* are sky spirits. They eat only pork and nothing else. They are angry if pork is roasted, and make the people ill. They used to live in the big *baja* (*Sterculia*) trees, but now they live in the sky."

In this connection it may be mentioned that there is a belief throughout the Andamans that it is dangerous to roast pork. In the North Andaman the natives commonly say that the spirits of the jungle are angry if pork be roasted, and may be attracted to the spot and cause the natives to be ill. An *Akar-Bale* belief, connecting the danger with the spirits of the sky has just been mentioned. Mr Man's version of the matter is as follows :—

[1] Man, *op. cit.* p. 112.

"...there is a company of evil spirits who are called *čol*, and who are much dreaded. They are believed to be descendants of *Maia Čol* who lived in antediluvian times. They generally punish those who offend them by baking or roasting pig's flesh, the smell of which is particularly obnoxious to them, as it is also to *Puluga*, who therefore, often assists them in discovering the delinquent; the same risk does not attend *boiling* pork, which the olfactory nerves of the fastidious *čol* are not keen enough to detect. While the Andamanese say that they are liable to be struck by *Erem-čauga-la* or *Juruwin* at any time or in any place, the *čol* strike those only who offend them, and that during the day while they are stationary, this being necessitated by the distance from the earth of their abode, whence they hurl their darts; an invisible spear is the weapon they always use, and this is thrown with unerring aim at the head of their victims, and is invariably fatal. As these demons are considered especially dangerous on the hottest days, they are apparently held accountable for the deaths from sunstroke which happen from time to time [1]."

It may be remarked that *Čol* is the name of a species of bird (probably the racket-tailed drongo), which is named from its call—*čol, čol, čol*. I did not hear the name used to denote what Mr Man calls demons, except in so far as the birds themselves are supposed to have supernatural powers. There is, perhaps, some sort of connection between the *čol* (the birds, that is) and the sky-spirits, *Morowin* or *Morua*, but I was not able to satisfy myself on the point. The connection of them both with *Puluga* is still more obscure.

Another belief in connection with pigs is that any person who cuts up a pig badly is liable to be punished. Mr Man states, on this subject, "*Puluga* never himself puts any one to death, but he objects so strongly to seeing a pig badly quartered and carved that he invariably points out those who offend him in this respect to a class of malevolent spirits called *Čol*, one of whom forthwith despatches the unfortunate individual [2]."

I was not able to find any evidence that *Puluga* is believed to be angry if a pig is badly quartered. From the natives with

[1] Man, *op. cit.* p. 159. [2] *Ibid.* p. 158.

whom I talked on the subject I received two different statements. One was to the effect that if a pig is badly cut up the meat will be bad and anyone who eats it will be ill. The other was that if a pig is badly cut up the spirits of the jungle will be angry and will punish the offender. In neither case was there any reference to *Puluga* or *Biliku*.

In general it may be said that the natives believe that the only punishment that *Puluga* or *Biliku* ever sends against those who offend him or her in any way is bad weather, and I did not myself meet with any exception to this rule.

One other observation by Mr Man may be mentioned. He says, "When they see a dark cloud approaching at a time when rain would prove very inconvenient, as when hunting, travelling, etc., they advise *Puluga* to divert its course by shouting '*Wara-Jobo kopke, kopke, kopke*' (*Wara-Jobo* will bite, bite, bite (you)). If in spite of this a shower falls they imagine that *Puluga* is undeterred by their warning [1]."

It is clear from the above discussion of the matter that there is not any complete agreement in the beliefs concerning *Puluga* (*Biliku*) even in any one tribe of the Andamans. There are many different statements about this being which cannot be made consistent with one another without doing violence to the evidence. At the same time, amid all the differences and inconsistencies there are a certain number of points about which there is a general agreement throughout the whole of the tribes of the Great Andaman. One of these is the connection of *Puluga* and *Daria* with the weather, with the two chief winds, and with the points of the compass from which these winds blow. The other is the belief that certain actions, such as melting bees'-wax, digging up yams, etc., are disliked by *Puluga*, and are punished by him (or her) with stormy weather. On these matters there is entire agreement amongst the natives of all the tribes, and they are to the natives themselves by far the most important part of the beliefs concerning *Puluga*.

We have seen that the Andamanese believe in two different kinds of what may be called, for want of a better term, super-

[1] Man, *op. cit.* p. 153.

natural beings. In the first place there are the spirits, the *Lau* or *Čauga*, and the *Jurua*, inhabiting the forest and the sea respectively. These are all associated by the natives with ghosts, i.e. with the spirits of dead men and women. In the second place there are other beings connected with the sun and moon, lightning and thunder and the monsoons (*Biliku* and *Tarai*). These are all associated with the phenomena of nature. There are many points of contact between these two classes of beings. Thus there are two alternative explanations of bad weather, one that it is due to the spirits (particularly the spirits of the sea), the other that it is due to the anger of *Biliku*. This is a point that will be referred to again in a later chapter.

It is possible that there are beliefs in other supernatural beings who are neither spirits of the dead nor connected with natural phenomena. The only being of such a nature that I was able to discover anything about is one called *Nila* or *Ńila*. This is the name of an evil being who is supposed to live in hollow *Pterocarpus* trees. When he smells human beings near his tree he comes out and kills them with his knife. I found this belief in the *A-Pučikwar* tribe, but was not able to find any trace of a similar belief in the North Andaman, though of course I cannot say that it does not exist there. Mr Man mentions this same being. "This spirit *Nila* is supposed to live in ant-hills, and to have neither wife nor child; he is not regarded as such a malevolent personage as *Erem-čauga-la*, and, though he is always armed with a knife, he rarely injures human beings with it, or when he does so, it is not in order to feed upon their bodies, for he is said to eat earth only [1]." Mr Man adds, in a footnote that "cases have been cited of persons who have been found stabbed, whose deaths have been attributed to *Nila*: the possibility of the individuals in question having been murdered is scouted."

The version given by Mr Man is not quite in agreement with the information given to me, but I was unfortunately not able to learn anything more about the nature of *Nila*.

As throwing some additional light on the way in which the Andamanese think of the supernatural beings that have been

[1] Man, *op. cit.* p. 159.

mentioned above, I add here a brief description of a sort of dramatic or pantomimic dance that I witnessed in the North Andaman. Many savage tribes in different parts of the world are in the habit of performing dances or pantomimes in which the performer represents a supernatural being. In the Andamans there are no regular performances of this kind. The solitary one that I witnessed was entirely exceptional.

The performer was a man named *Kobo*. This man, according to the statements of the natives, had, at one time of his life, died and come back to life again. Owing to this fact he was endowed with special magical powers, and had some reputation as a magician or medicine-man (*oko-jumu*). During the time that he was dead (probably a few hours of unconsciousness), he is supposed to have visited the world of spirits, and while there he saw many things and learnt much about the spirits. Among other things he witnessed a dance in which the spirits and other supernatural beings took part. All these things he was able to remember when he returned to life.

The performance was given one afternoon on the ordinary dancing ground of the village. The performer sat on his haunches in a hut at one end of the dancing ground. Thrust into the back of his belt he wore a bunch of leaves sticking out somewhat after the manner of a cock's tail, but he had no other ornament. The spectators, consisting of men, women and children, were seated round the edge of the dancing ground, which had been swept clean. On one side sat a few women who acted as chorus. There was no sounding-board.

The performer began to sing a song, composed on the model of the songs of the South Andaman (with a short refrain) which has now for some years been adopted by the Northern tribes in preference to their own. As he finished the song the women of the chorus took up the refrain, repeating it over and over again, and marking time by clapping their hands on their thighs. The performer came out of his hut and performed a dance. At a signal from him the chorus ceased and he returned to his hut. In this way he sang several songs, repeating each one several times, and performed a number of short dances. In nearly every case the step of the dance was some simple modification of the step in common use at an ordinary dance. Thus in one dance he danced very violently and pretended to hurt his leg through the violence of his dancing, making angry signs to the chorus to stop their clapping, of which, of course, they took no notice. In another dance he stopped at short intervals and violently scratched his sides and then doubled himself up with laughter. In yet another, he danced with the step of the women's dance, covering his face with his hands and pretending to be very bashful. In still another he stood on tiptoe on the right foot and stamped with his left foot in time to the chorus of women. In some of the dances he walked round the open space within the circle of spectators, sometimes in a crouching attitude, and at other times in other attitudes. All these dances aroused great amusement amongst the spectators. It was unfortunately impossible for me to understand them all or to obtain an adequate explanation of them either at the time or later.

Of the songs that were sung one was "The tide has gone down over the reef. I walk round the world. There is great wind and rain."

Some of these dances I was able to understand even without explanation. One of them represented *Biliku*. The performer held in his right hand a shell, and as he danced grotesquely round the open space he looked fiercely at the spectators and threatened to throw the shell at them. Many of the women and children could not prevent themselves from starting backwards when he thus threatened them, but their fears were immediately dispelled in laughter. The shell was not a pearl-shell (*be*) but a *Cyrena* shell (*bun*), but I believe that this was because there was no pearl-shell available. The representation of *Biliku* was thus reduced to a single gesture, that of threatening the natives with her pearl-shell (lightning).

Another dance represented the jungle spirits (*Bido-teč Lau*). In this he first hid himself behind a screen of *bido* leaves (*Calamus tigrinus*) that had been prepared, singing a song. The leaves represented a clump of the *Calamus* palm such as is supposed to be the favourite haunt of the jungle spirits. After having sung for some time behind his screen of leaves, he came out with a bow and arrow in his hand, and as he danced in front of the spectators he pretended to shoot at them.

In another dance he represented *Ele*, the lightning. He sat on a stone that had been placed in the middle of the open space, swinging his arms to the time of the chorus, and every now and then shaking his leg.

This observation is an important one in several ways. Although I asked the man to repeat it, in order that I might make fuller notes and obtain explanations of many obscure points, and although he grudgingly said that he would, yet he did not do so. He was, moreover, very reserved over the matter, and not very willing to talk about his own performance.

I believe that the performance was an entirely exceptional affair. I never at any other time either saw or heard of one man or even several men, giving a dance for the amusement of others. I think that the whole thing was entirely the invention of the performer. He had given the same performance, or one very similar, at least once before the occasion on which I saw it.

We may now turn to the Andamanese beliefs relating to the soul and the life after death.

The vital principle is at different times identified by the Andamanese with the pulse, the breath, with the blood and with the fat, particularly the kidney-fat. Thus the body of a slain enemy is burnt so that the blood and fat may be consumed in smoke and ascend to the sky where they will no longer be a danger to those who have slain him.

The nearest approach to our notion of a soul that the natives possess is their belief concerning the double or reflection seen in a mirror. In the Northern tribes the word *ot-jumulo* means "reflection," and also "shadow," and is also nowadays applied to a photograph. The word *ot-jumu*, in the same languages, means "a dream" or "to dream." We may perhaps translate the word *ot-jumulo* as meaning "soul." In the *Aka-Bea* language *ot-yolo* is "reflection," while there is a different word, *ot-diya* or *ot-lere*, for "shadow," and neither of the words has any connection with the word "dream" which is *taraba*. Mr Man translates the word *ot-yolo* as "soul."

The fact that the words for dream and reflection, double or shadow are from the same root in the Northern languages is of interest. Dreams are sometimes explained by saying that the sleeper's double (*ot-jumulo*) has left his body and is wandering elsewhere. Dreams are regarded as being veridical, or at any rate, as having importance. One man told me how, in a dream the night before, his *ot-jumulo* had travelled from where we were to his own country and had there seen the death of the baby of a woman of his own tribe. He was fully convinced that the baby must really have died.

An Andamanese will never, or only with the very greatest reluctance, awaken another from sleep. One explanation of this that was given to me was that the *ot-jumulo* or double of the sleeper may be wandering far from his body, and to waken him suddenly might cause him to be ill.

The principle on which dreams are interpreted is a very simple one. All unpleasant dreams are bad, all pleasant ones are good. The natives believe that sickness is often caused by dreams. A man in the early stages of an attack of fever, for instance, may have a bad dream. When the fever develops he explains it as due to the dream. If a man has a painful dream he will often not venture out of the camp the following day, but will stay at home until the effect has worn off. The natives believe that they can communicate in dreams with the spirits, but the power to do this regularly is the privilege of certain special individuals, known as *oko-jumu* (dreamers). However, an ordinary individual may occasionally have dreams of this kind.

I found that any attempt to study the dreams of such a people as the Andamanese is made very difficult by the fact that it is never possible to tell how far the original dream has been arranged and altered by the waking imagination. So far as my observations went the majority of dreams are either visual or motor, or both. Further reference to dreams will be made later in connection with magic.

When a man or woman dies the double (or as some of the natives explain it, the breath) leaves the body and becomes a spirit (*lau* or *čauga*). By death a man ceases to exist as a man, and begins a new existence as a spirit.

Whenever I asked the natives whence came the spirits of the jungle and the sea I received the answer that they are the spirits of dead men and women. On the other hand, when I put in another form what might seem to be the same question, and asked what became of a man's spirit after his death, I received many different and inconsistent answers. As it would take too much space to transcribe every answer that I received to this question, a number of typical ones are selected. Any attempt to reconcile the statements of different men or of the same men on different occasions can only produce a false impression of the real condition of the native beliefs, and therefore the statements are kept separate, and each one is given as it was taken down.

The first is from the Northern tribes. Exactly similar statements were made to me by men of several tribes. "When a man dies he becomes a *Lau* and wanders about the jungle. At first he keeps near the grave or the place where he died, but after a while he finds that is no good, and so he goes to live with the other spirits. If he is drowned he becomes a *Jurua*." A second account, varying from the above in only one particular, is also from one of the Northern tribes (*Aka-Čari*). "When a man dies he becomes a *Lau* or a *Jurua* and lives with the other spirits. If he be a jungle-dweller he becomes a *Lau* and lives in the jungle. If he be a coast-dweller he becomes a *Jurua* and lives in the sea. All the *Aka-Čari* become *Jurua* when they die. The spirit stays in his own country. The spirits of a man's own country (whether *Lau* or *Jurua*) are friendly to him, but those of another country are dangerous and will make him ill."

An entirely different statement frequently made to me by men of the Northern tribes is that when a man dies the spirit (*Lau*) either immediately, or after the lapse of some time, goes to another world that lies under this one and is called *Maramiku*. This world of spirits is said to be just like the actual world, with forest and sea, and all the familiar animal and vegetable species. The inhabitants spend their time just as the Andamanese do on earth, hunting, fishing and dancing.

Still another statement that is commonly made in the North is that the spirits of the dead go to live in the sky. Two such statements are as follows: "When a man dies his *ot-ǰumulo* (double) goes up to the sky and becomes a *Lau* (spirit)." "A man's spirit wanders in the jungle till the flesh has rotted from the bones, and then goes away to the sky." Other statements were very similar to these two.

Turning now to the Southern tribes, one informant of the *A-Pučikwar* tribe gave me the following account: "When a man or woman dies the spirit goes away to the east or north-east and goes over the edge of the world, remaining in a place called *Lau-l'uŋ-ciŋ* (Spirit's House) where there is a large hut in a jungle similar to that on earth. There they live just as men do on earth, hunting and fishing, and so on. Beyond the home of the spirits is *Puta-ko̧iča*, the home of the sun and moon. The rainbow is the path by which the spirits come to visit their friends on earth, which they do in dreams. The rainbow is made of canes (? a cane)."

Another version from the same tribe was to the effect that after death the spirits of the dead go to live in the sky with a mythical being named *Tomo*. This *Tomo*, according to some of the legends, was the first ancestor of the Andamanese. By one of my best informants he was identified to some extent with the sun, and consequently with light and with fine weather. This man stated that in the world of the spirits it is never night as *Tomo* is always there. The spirits always have plenty of pork and turtle, and spend their time dancing and enjoying themselves.

One old man of the *A-Pučikwar* tribe, who had some reputation as a medicine-man, said that the spirits of medicine-men lived apart from the spirits of ordinary men and women, and are called not *Lau* but *Bilik*. He told me how he had been visited in a dream by *Bo̧ičo Bilik*, that is by the spirit of one *Bo̧ičo* who had, when he lived, been a great medicine-man, and who, now that he was dead, had become a *Bilik*, as distinguished from an ordinary *Lau*. It is the *Bilik* who control the weather. They can also cause or cure sickness in living men. The *Bo̧ičo* mentioned above was alive when my informant was a young man.

In the *Akar-Bale* tribe one man told me that the breath (*ig-peti*) of a dying person goes up to the sky and becomes a spirit. Another belief of the same tribe is that the spirits of the dead go to *Jereg-l'ar-mugu*, which is under the earth. From the same tribe comes the following account: "When a man or woman dies, the spirit first of all goes southward to the country of the *Aka-Bea*, and then returns to *Gudna-l'ar-boŋ* in *Kuaičo-bur* (in the *Akar-Bale* country). It then goes to *Jila-buaro* in *Jila* (East Island) and from there to *Kere-tuaur*. The inhabitants of the last-named place are warned of the approach of the spirit by the cries of the birds *tao* (*Eudynamis honorata*, Indian koel or brain-fever bird) and *bil* (Australian goggle-eyed plover). At one time the people of *Luŋ-tauar* used to catch the spirits in big nets made for the purpose. They were taught to do this by a wise woman named *In Golat*. The spirits try to run away, but they get caught at the place called *Guamo-leber*. The people then throw them into the sea, and they (the spirits) then go to *Čauga-l'uŋ-jiŋa* (Spirit's Home) and remain there." The above is given exactly as it was translated to me by an *Akar-Bale* man who knew English and who acted as my interpreter on the occasion. There is much in it that I do not understand and that my questions failed to elucidate. It is given as an example of the nature of some of the more obscure of the Andamanese beliefs. To understand fully many of their statements on this and other matters would need a more complete knowledge of the language than I possessed, and a longer time than I was able to give.

The various examples given above are sufficient to show the general nature of the Andamanese beliefs. In every tribe there are alternative and inconsistent beliefs as to the place where spirits go, which by different accounts is in the sky, beneath the earth, out to the east where the sun and moon take their rise, or in the jungle and sea of their own country. One thing is clear, that the Andamanese ideas on the subject are floating and lacking in precision. There is no fixity or unanimity of belief amongst them.

To these various accounts from the natives themselves, must be added the description of the beliefs of the *Aka-Bea* tribe as recorded by Mr Man. This may best be given in the writer's own words. "The world, exclusive of the sea, is declared to be flat and to rest on an immense palm-tree (*Caryota sobolifera*) called *barata*, which stands in the midst of a jungle comprising the whole area under the earth. This jungle, *čaitan* (Hades) is a gloomy place, for, though visited in turn by the sun and moon, it can, in consequence of its situation, be only partially lighted: it is hither the spirits (*čauga*) of the departed are sent by *Puluga* to await the Resurrection.

"No change takes place in *čaitan* in respect to growth or age; all remain as they were at the time of their departure from the earth, and the adults are represented as engaged in hunting, after a manner peculiar to disembodied spirits. In order to furnish them with sport the spirits of animals and birds are also sent to *čaitan*, but as there is no sea there, the *čauga* of fish and turtle remain in their native element and are preyed upon by *juruwin*. The spirits (*čauga*) and souls (*ot-yolo*) of all children who die before they cease to be entirely dependent on their parents (i.e. under six years of age) go to *čaitan*, and are placed under a *rau* tree (*Ficus laccifera*) on the fruit of which they subsist. As none can quit *čaitan* who have once entered, they support their stories regarding it by a tradition that in ages long past an *oko-paiad* was favoured in a dream with a vision of the regions and of the pursuits of the disembodied spirits.

"Between the earth and the eastern sky there stretches an invisible cane bridge (*pidga-l'ar-čauga*) which steadies the former and connects it with *jereg* (paradise); over this bridge the souls (*ot-yolo*) of the departed pass into paradise, or to *jereg-l'ar-mugu*, which is situated below it: this latter place might be described as purgatory, for it is a place of punishment for those who have been guilty of heinous sins, such as murder. Like Dante, they depict it as very cold, and therefore a most undesirable region for mortals to inhabit. From all this it will be gathered that these despised savages believe in a future state, in the resurrection, and in the threefold constitution of man.

"In serious illness the sufferer's spirit (*čauga*) is said to be hovering between this world and Hades, but does not remain permanently in the latter place until some time after death, during which interval it haunts the abode of the deceased and the spot where the remains have been deposited. In dreams it is the soul which, having taken its departure through the nostrils, sees or is engaged in the manner represented to the sleeper.

"The Andamanese do not regard their shadows but their reflections (in any mirror) as their souls. The colour of the soul is said to be red, and that of the spirit black, and, though invisible to human eyes, they partake of the form of the person to whom they belong. Evil emanates from the soul, and all good from the spirit; at the resurrection they will be re-united and live permanently on the new earth, for the souls of the wicked will then have been reformed by the punishments inflicted on them during their residence in *jereg-l'ar-mugu*.

"The future life will be but a repetition of the present, but all will then remain in the prime of life, sickness and death will be unknown, and there will be no more marrying or giving in marriage. The animals, birds, and fish will also re-appear in the new world in their present form.

"This blissful state will be inaugurated by a great earthquake, which, occurring by *Puluga's* command, will break the *pidga-l'ar-čauga* and cause the earth to turn over: all alive at the time will perish, exchanging places with their deceased ancestors[1]."

This account given by Mr Man, must, I think, be received with great caution. To one who has talked to the Andamanese on these subjects it seems probable that Mr Man has here combined into a single consistent version, a number of independent statements, which, as the natives believe them, are not parts of an organised doctrine, but are separate from and often inconsistent with each other. Added to this there is the fact that Mr Man has so written down the native beliefs as to bring out the greatest possible degree of resemblance to the Christian mythology. This is clear from his use of the words Hades, paradise, etc. Allowance must therefore be made for the fact that Mr Man evidently found some pleasure in tracing analogies between the mythology of the Andamanese and the Christian doctrines.

Owing to the importance attaching to all Mr Man's statements it is necessary to examine critically the account tran-

[1] Man, *op. cit.* p. 161.

scribed above. We may begin with what is said of the doctrine of the threefold nature of man. By this it would seem to be meant that man is regarded as composed of body, soul and spirit. It is quite certain that the Andamanese mean different things by the words *ot-yolo* (reflection) here translated "soul," and *čauga* translated "spirit." The difference is this, that a man, while he is still alive, *has* a "double" or "soul" if the latter word be preferred, while when he is dead he *becomes* a spirit. Thus the spirit is not a part of a man while he is alive. The word *čauga* (or *lau*) is simply the name of a particular class of beings which includes all dead men and women. The bones of a man become "spirit-bones" (*čauga-ta*) when he dies, just as he becomes a spirit. To compare the Andamanese belief with the Christian doctrine that each man possesses, while he is alive, both a soul and a spirit, these being different things, is therefore misleading. For this reason it is perhaps unfortunate to translate the Andamanese *čauga* as meaning spirit, but there does not seem to be any other convenient English word.

Mr Man's account would seem to imply that the native belief is that at death the soul (reflection) of a man goes to one place (*Jereg* or *Jereg-l'ar-mugu*) while his spirit goes elsewhere (to *Čaitan*). In the case of children however, Mr Man makes a difference, for both the souls and spirits of children go to *Čaitan*. Mr Man compares *Čaitan* to Hades, *Jereg* to paradise and *Jereg-l'ar-mugu* to purgatory.

I do not think that the Andamanese have any such complicated doctrine as this. It seems to me almost certain that Mr Man has received from the natives several different statements, similar to some of those given earlier, and that he has combined and reconciled them as well as he could. Some of his informants, apparently, described the world after death as being beneath the earth, and gave the name of it as *Čaitan*[1]. Other informants seem to have spoken of *Jereg* or *Jereg-l'ar-mugu*. I think it improbable that any one native should have stated, as Mr Man's account would seem to imply, that the *soul* of a dead

---

[1] I could not obtain any information about the word that Mr Man gives as *chaitan*. Some men of the South Andaman whom I questioned did not seem to recognize the word, except as their way of pronouncing the Urdu word *shaitan* = devil.

man goes to one place, while the man himself (now a *spirit*) goes somewhere else. Mr Man's description of *Čaitan* corresponds almost exactly to the descriptions given to me by the *Akar-Bale* and *A-Pučikwar* of *Jereg-l'ar-mugu*, and to the descriptions of *Maramiku* given by the Northern tribes. If *Čaitan* be really an *Aka-Bea* word, it would seem to be only another name for *Jereg-l'ar-mugu*.

One of the most important points in Mr Man's statement is that while the souls of good men go to paradise as he puts it, the souls of bad men are condemned to torture in purgatory[1]. In my own enquiries I did not come across any definite belief of this nature, but I am not prepared to deny its existence. All that I can say is that I did not find any evidence whatever that good men and bad men (in any meanings in which those words could be used by the natives) receive different treatment after death. In talking to men of the *Akar-Bale* and *A-Pučikwar* tribes I did not hear of *Jereg* as a distinct place from *Jereg-l'ar-mugu*. The latter name is of course a compound, from *ar-mugu* = front, and might mean either "the place fronting or facing *Jereg*" or "the place *Jereg*, fronting us."

Mr Man states that the souls and spirits of young children go to *Čaitan* where they subsist on the fruit of a *rau* tree (*Ficus laccifera*). In the North Andaman I found a belief that the souls of children, before they are born, live in the *Ficus* trees, but these are the real trees on earth that are in question, and not a mythical tree in the next world. It is commonly believed that if a baby dies the soul enters the mother again and is born a second time. It is possible that what Mr Man relates as to the souls of children after death living in a *Ficus* tree in *Čaitan* may really refer to real fig trees on earth.

As regards the resurrection spoken of by Mr Man, I was also so unfortunate as to obtain no information. As will be shown in a later chapter, there are several myths of the world coming to an end and starting afresh, and these myths are generally

---

[1] In the "Census Report" 1901, p. 62, Sir Richard Temple writes, "The Andamanese have an idea that the 'soul' will go under the earth by an aerial bridge after death, but there is no heaven nor hell nor any idea of a corporeal resurrection in a religious sense."

associated with *Puluga* or *Biliku*. All the versions that I heard, however, referred to the past and not to the future[1].

The Andamanese speak of unconsciousness as "death," and regard a person who has been unconscious for some time as having been dead and returned to life again. I was once told that an old man in the village was "dead" and found him in a state of coma from which he recovered and lived for several days. There are stories of persons having returned to life even after they have been buried. One such tale was told me in the North Andaman. A man died and was buried. As his friends and relatives, after packing up their belongings, were leaving the camp in their canoes, the man's voice was heard calling. His wife and mother turned back and met him and took him in their canoe. He lived for some time after this and then he died and was buried again. Again the same thing happened, the dead man re-appearing just as they were setting off in their canoes from the camp that they were deserting on account of his death. Finally the man died a third time. When he was buried this time the men dug a very deep hole some distance from the camp, and then hurried back to the camp and hastily gathered up their belongings and left it. Nothing more was seen of the dead man, but when, after the lapse of some months, they went to dig up the bones, they found the mat and leaves and rope in which the corpse had been bound, but there were no bones.

Amongst the coast-dwellers of the North Andaman I found a belief that the soul of a dying man goes out with the ebbing tide.

There are, amongst the Andamanese, certain individuals who are distinguished from their fellows by the supposed possession of supernatural powers. These specially favoured persons

[1] It may be noted that in the Andamanese languages there is no future tense of the verb, and it is often very difficult to know whether a speaker is referring to the present or to the future. Further, although there is a past tense, a native often uses the present tense in a narrative relating to the past, so that a statement relating to the past and one relating to the future may have exactly the same grammatical form. Mr Ellis, writing in the *Journal of the Philological Society* (1882) from information supplied by Mr Man, gives a verbal suffix -*ngabo* denoting the future in the *Aka-Bea* language. Mr Portman points out that this is an error. (*Notes on the Languages of the South Andaman*, p. 88.)

correspond, to some degree, with the medicine-men, magicians or shamans of other primitive societies. The name for these medicine-men in the North Andaman is *oko-jumu*, meaning literally "dreamer" or "one who speaks from dreams" from a stem *-jumu* the primary meaning of which refers to the phenomena of dreams. In *Aka-Bea* the corresponding term is *oko-paiad*, and according to Mr Man, this term also means "dreamer." Mr Portman, however, gives *taraba* as the *Aka-Bea* word for "dream" or "to dream."

According to a statement by Mr Man, only men can possess the powers that entitle them to be regarded as *oko-paiad*[1]. The natives whom I questioned told me that a woman may possess the same powers, though it is more usual for men to become famous in this way than women. There is no very clear dividing line between those who are *oko-jumu* or *oko-paiad* and those who are not; one person may possess the powers in only a slight degree, so as scarcely to differentiate him from others, while another may be much more highly gifted.

At the present time it is no longer possible to obtain full and satisfactory information on this subject. Most of the old *oko-jumu* and *oko-paiad* are now dead. Amongst the younger men there are a few who pretend to the position, but the recent intercourse with foreigners has produced a degree of scepticism in such matters that makes it difficult or nearly impossible to obtain any reliable information as to the former beliefs from any but the very old men. To this difficulty must be added that in talking to some of the very few old men who could have given more valuable information I had to make use of an interpreter, and though they might have been willing to confide to me some of the secrets of their profession they would not do so before a younger man of their own race.

The powers of a dreamer, supernatural as they are, can only be acquired by supernatural means, through contact in one way or another with the spirits (i.e. the *Lau* or *Čauga*). One way of coming into contact with the spirits is by death. If a man should, as the natives put it, die and then come back to life again,

---

[1] Man, *op. cit.* p. 96.

he is, by that adventure, endowed with the power that makes a medicine-man. One man of the *Aka-Kǫra* tribe was pointed out to me as having obtained his powers in this way. It would seem that during a serious illness he was unconscious for some twelve hours or so, and his friends thought that he was dead. A medicine-man whom I met with in the *A-Pučikwar* tribe was said to have died and come to life again three times. Another man, whom I did not meet, was described to me as a great *oko-jumu*, and from the description given it seemed to me that he was subject to epileptic fits. As against this, however, Mr Man states that "epilepsy is a recognised form of malady, but the fits are not regarded in a superstitious light[1]."

Another way in which a man can acquire magical powers is by direct communication with the spirits. A man who died a few years ago was believed by the natives to have once met with some spirits in the jungle, and to have acquired in this way the powers of an *oko-jumu*. He used to go off into the jungle by himself at intervals and hold communication with the spirits with whom he had made friends. From such a visit he had returned with his head decorated with shredded palm-leaf fibre (*kǫro*) which had, so he said, been placed on him by the spirits. This man had a reputation as a powerful *oko-jumu*.

In a less degree the powers of an *oko-jumu* may be obtained through dreams. It is believed that certain men have the power of communicating with the spirits in dreams, and such men are *oko-jumu*. If a man or boy experiences dreams that are in any way extraordinary, particularly if, in his dreams he sees spirits, either the spirits of dead persons known to him when alive, or spirits of the forest or the sea, he may acquire in time the reputation of a medicine-man.

A man may claim some degree of magical power, and yet his claims may not be recognized by others. Each *oko-jumu* has to make his own reputation, and to sustain it when made. This he can only do by demonstrating his power to others. Once this reputation is his, he not only receives the respect of others but also makes a considerable personal profit. Every one is anxious to be on good terms with one who is believed to

[1] Man, *op. cit.* p. 83.

have extraordinary powers. Hence a man who is an acknowledged *oko-jumu* is sure to receive a good share of the game caught by others, and presents of all kinds from those who seek his goodwill.

As the name implies, and in whatever way his power may have been obtained, an *oko-jumu* is privileged to dream in a way that less favoured persons do not. In his dreams he can communicate with the spirits of the dead. In dreams, also, so the natives say, he is able to cause the illness of an enemy or to cure that of a friend.

By his communication with the spirits, in dreams, or in waking life, the *oko-jumu* acquires magical knowledge that he is able to turn to account in curing illness and in preventing bad weather. When a person is ill the *oko-jumu* is often consulted as to the best means of treating the patient. His treatment is often limited to the recommendation, or the application, of some one or other of the recognized remedies. He may undertake to dispel the spirits that are supposed to be the cause of the disease, which he does by addressing them and conjuring them to go away, or by the use of one or other of the substances and objects that are believed to have the power of keeping spirits at a distance. Sometimes the *oko-jumu* will promise to cure the patient by means of dreams. It is believed that in his dreams he can communicate with the spirits and can persuade them to help him to cure the sick person.

Besides their power of causing or curing sickness, the *oko-jumu* are credited with being able to control the weather. As has been shown, the Andamanese believe that the weather is under the control of two beings named *Biliku* and *Tarai*. There is, however, an alternative and contradictory belief, which is also held, that the weather is controlled by the spirits, and particularly by those of the sea. The means taken by magicians or others to prevent bad weather can be divided into two kinds according as they are directed against *Biliku* or *Tarai*, or against the spirits of the sea. As an example of the very simple rites which are performed for this purpose, two cases may be quoted. One of the *oko-jumu* of the Northern tribes, now dead, once stopped a very violent storm by crushing between two stones a piece of the *Anadendron paniculatum* and diving with it into the sea where he placed it under a rock on the reef. A more recent example is very similar. A man still living, named *Jire Pilečar*, who was, in a way, the successor of the man formerly mentioned, is said to have stopped a violent storm by using the leaves and bark of the *Ficus laccifera* in the same way, that is by crushing them and placing them under a rock in the sea. In both these cases it would seem that the rite was directed not against *Biliku* and *Tarai*, but against the *Jurua*.

Apart from his power to communicate directly with the spirits, the *oko-jumu* owes his position to a superior knowledge of the magical properties of common substances and objects. This knowledge he is supposed to obtain from the spirits. However, a lesser degree of knowledge on such matters is possessed by everybody. Thus in the treatment of sickness there are a number of magical remedies of which anyone can make use without consulting an *oko-jumu*.

A complete enumeration of all the things that are believed to possess magical properties is, of course, not possible, but the following notes refer to all the most important.

We may consider first of all the magical properties of mineral substances. One of the most important of these is red ochre. Yellow ochre, which is found in pockets in many parts of the islands, is collected and burnt, when it turns red, and the powder so obtained is either used by itself or is made into a paint with pig or turtle fat. The powder is mixed with water and taken internally. Red paint is applied to the throat and chest for coughs and colds and sore throats, and round the ear for ear-ache. When a man feels unwell he often smears red paint on his upper lip just below his nostrils. In this way, the natives say, the "smell" of the paint cures his sickness. The paint is sometimes used as a dressing for wounds or centipede bites. Its use for ornamenting the body on ceremonial occasions has already been noted in the last chapter.

In the North Andaman a soft red stone is found, called *talar*. This is used as a substitute for red paint. It is rubbed on the body, or it is powdered and the powder is mixed with water and taken internally.

White clay (*tọl-odu* in *Aka-Jeru*) is sometimes used medicinally, both externally and internally. The commoner clay (*odu* in *Aka-Jeru*) is plastered on sores, and has the effect of keeping off flies, if it does nothing else.

An olive-coloured earth (called *čulya* in *Aka-Bea*), found in certain springs, is prized as a remedy. It is mixed with water and taken internally as a general remedy for all sorts of complaints.

Turning now to the magical properties of vegetable substances, there are a large number of these, and some of them have not been botanically identified.

The *Anadendron paniculatum* is a plant from which the Andamanese obtain a valuable fibre, which they use for their bow-strings, and for thread with which to make their arrows and harpoons. A number of magical properties are attributed to this plant. Rheumatism is supposed to be due to the "smell" of the plant getting into the system when the fibre is being prepared[1]. The "smell" of the green plant, or of the fibre until it has been thoroughly dried for some days, is believed to frighten away turtle. A man who has been preparing the fibre would not dream of joining a turtle-hunting expedition, for his presence in the canoe would be sufficient to drive away all the turtle. A turtle-hunting expedition would be a failure if a piece of the green creeper were in the canoe. A man who has been handling the plant may not cook turtle, for the meat would be "bad," i.e., uneatable. The same thing would happen if turtle meat accidentally came in contact with a piece of the plant. All this applies only to the green creeper, and not to the fibre after it has been properly prepared and dried. The fibre itself is used for binding the heads of turtle-harpoons, so it is evidently regarded as harmless.

If a piece of the *Anadendron* creeper were burnt in the fire the natives believe that it would drive all the turtle away from the neighbourhood, or, according to another statement, that there would be a great storm.

So far we have considered the properties of the plant only in

---

[1] In preparing the fibre, the skin or bark of the young shoots of the plant is torn off in strips and these are placed on the thigh and scraped with a *Cyrena* shell.

so far as they make it dangerous to handle. It has other and beneficial properties. It is said that a man swimming in waters infested with sharks would be safe from them if he had a piece of the *Anadendron* creeper with him, in his belt or necklace. The creeper is also supposed to preserve anyone who carries it from the attacks of the sea spirits (*Jurua*).

The *Hibiscus tiliaceus* is a small tree from which the natives obtain the fibre which they make into rope, used now for harpoon lines and in former times for turtle-nets. The leaves of this tree are believed to have the power of keeping away the spirits of the sea. They have no efficacy, however, against the spirits of the forest. Leaves of the *Hibiscus tiliaceus* are used in the turtle-eating ceremony described in the last chapter. For cooking turtle the only wood that may be used is the *Hibiscus*. If any other wood were used the meat would not be good. In this connection it is necessary to point out an error in the statements of Mr Man. He says that the wood of the *alaba* must never be used for cooking turtle, though it may be used for cooking pig, and that *Puluga* is angry if this commandment is not observed and sends either the sun or moon to punish the offender[1]. There is evidently an error here. The *alaba* is the *Hibiscus tiliaceus*. Mr Man identifies it with the *Melochia velutina*, but this is an error. Now the custom in connection with the *Hibiscus* (*alaba*) is not that it may not be used for cooking turtle, but that no other kind of wood must be used. It is difficult to see how Mr Man fell into the error, unless he mistook a statement regarding the *yolba* (*Anadendron paniculatum*) for a statement relating to *alaba* (*Hibiscus tiliaceus*). We have just seen that if the *Anadendron* comes in contact with turtle meat the meat will be bad, and that if it is burnt there will be a storm.

Another plant that provides fibre for thread is the *Gnetum edule*. There is a belief that the green creeper of this plant will drive away turtle, if a piece of it be taken in a canoe.

Magical properties are attributed to the *Ficus laccifera* tree. These trees are believed to be the home of the yet unborn souls of children. I was told in the North Andaman that if a tree of

[1] Man, *op. cit.* pp. 153 and 172.

the species were cut there would be a storm. The bark of the aerial roots of the tree affords a fibre used in the Little Andaman for bow-strings, but only used in the Great Andaman for making personal ornaments. It is possible that some magical properties are attributed to the ornaments made from this fibre.

The *Pterocarpus dalbergioides* is one of the most striking trees of the Andamans. It has a very hard red wood, from which the natives make their sounding-boards. There is an obscure belief in the *A-Pučikwar* tribe (and possibly also in other tribes) that it is dangerous to look at the tree when it is in flower. I was twice told a story of how some people were affected by looking at the flowers, and either went mad or died. On one occasion my interpreter translated the words of my informant by saying "They saw the flowers, and went giddy, and they all went to hell (*Jereg-l'ar-mugu*)." Men must be careful when the tree is in flower, not to look at it too long. In the North Andaman I was told that string games (*jipre*) must not be played when the *Pterocarpus* tree is in flower. They may be indulged in with safety at any other time of the year. (String games, according to one statement, were invented by the *Lau*, while another account attributes the invention to the crab.)

The *Tetranthera lancæfolia* is a small tree from which the natives obtain the wood for the shafts of their pig arrows. The leaves of this tree are believed to have the power to keep away the spirits of the forest. They are used in the pig-eating ceremony described in the last chapter. The wood is shredded and made into plumes, and these plumes are believed to have magical properties. They are worn by a man who has killed another, and are believed to protect him from the vengeance of the spirit of the dead man.

A common remedy for sickness of different kinds is a small tree called *gugma* in *Aka-Bea*, which Mr Man identifies as being *Trigonostemon longifolius*. The leaves of this tree are made into a bed for the patient to lie upon. They are also crushed and rubbed over the patient's body, or he is made to inhale the odour of the crushed leaves. The natives say that it is the "smell" of the plant that possesses medical properties. The "smell" will drive away turtle, and leaves should therefore not be taken in a canoe. A man who has been handling the leaves would not go turtle-hunting.

Another remedy is a species of *Alpinia*. The leaves and stems of this plant are chewed and the juice swallowed for certain ailments. The plant is also used when taking honey. A man takes some of the leaves in his mouth and chews them well. Before taking the honeycomb he sprays the saliva from his mouth over and around it. He may also rub the chewed leaves over his body. The natives say that in this way they are able to prevent the bees from stinging them.

Magical properties are attributed to a number of plants that have not been botanically identified. Thus the leaves of a small tree called *tare* in *Aka-Jeru* are crushed and moistened with water and rubbed over the body as a remedy for illness. A strip of bark from the same tree is tied round the chest of a man with a pain in his chest. The bark of two trees called (in *Aka-Jeru*) *tip* and *laro* is crushed and moistened and rubbed over a sick man's body. The leaves of a plant called *pare* are crushed with water and the infusion is drunk by persons suffering from diarrhœa and abdominal pains. A creeper called *korotli* is crushed and tied round a limb in cases of snake-bite. The seeds of the *Entada scandens* are heated in the fire and applied (while hot) to such wounds as that from the tusk of a boar.

There are a certain number of trees and plants about which the natives say that any person cutting them will become blind. The names of four of these in *Aka-Jeru* are *jin, burut, dey*, and *mit*.

We may turn now to animals and animal substances. Magical properties are attributed to bees'-wax, particularly to black bees'-wax. In a case of pleurisy black bees'-wax was heated until it was soft, and then smeared over the man's chest. Bees'-wax is believed to keep away the spirits of the forest.

If a man be bitten by a snake and the snake be killed it is skinned and the inner surface of the skin is applied to the wound.

A hiccough is supposed to be the result of inadvertently swallowing a tree lizard, whose call rather resembles the sound of a person hiccoughing.

The condition popularly called "pins and needles" or described as an arm or leg "going to sleep" is believed by the Andamanese to be due to the bite of a rat. If a man wakes up in the night with one of his limbs benumbed in this way, he believes that a rat has bitten him while he slept.

The Andamanese say that the bite of a civet-cat (*Paradoxurus*) will produce cramp. I was once told that if a man eats the flesh of the civet-cat and then goes into the water he will become "lame." This means, I think, that he will have cramp, and so will be unable to swim.

The flesh and particularly the fat of the flying fox (*Pteropus*) is believed to be a remedy for rheumatism. An old man who was suffering from this ailment once asked me to shoot for him some of these bats, which he cooked and ate.

If turtle-fat be permitted to burn in the fire there will be a storm.

Mention has already been made of the magical value attributed to human bones. They are esteemed as a means of driving away spirits, and therefore of curing or preventing sickness. A human jaw-bone was hanging in my hut in such a position that it could swing in the wind. The natives attributed to this the illness from which I and several of them were suffering at the time, and asked me to put the bone away in a basket, where it could not move.

Bones of animals are made into ornaments in the same way as human bones, and magical properties of a similar kind seem to be attributed to them.

Of other objects possessing magical properties the most important is fire. Fire is believed to have the power of keeping away spirits of the sea and of the forest. A fire is always kept alight beside a sick man or woman. For dysentery stones are heated in a fire and the patient is required to defecate on to these.

In conclusion, mention must be made of one favourite remedy

of the Andamanese, namely scarification. The part of the body that is the seat of pain is scarified, as the forehead for headaches, the cheek for toothache. A number of very small incisions are made in the skin close together, with a sharp flake of quartz or glass. The incisions are just deep enough to cut through the skin and cause a little blood to ooze out, but not so deep as to produce a flow of blood. The operation is the work of women. It is probably more frequently used than any other remedy except red paint and human bones.

CHAPTER IV

MYTHS AND LEGENDS

THE Andamanese have a number of stories which are told to the younger people by their elders and relate to the doings of their ancestors in a time long ago. Some of these stories are recorded in the present chapter. A difficulty in the way of giving any clear and readable account of them is the fact that there are many slightly different versions of one and the same legend. To some extent the variations are local, each tribe, and even each portion of a tribe having its own set of legendary stories. Besides these local variations there are also individual variations. Two men of the same tribe may relate what is substantially the same story, yet each chooses his own words and gestures, and to some extent they may even arrange the incidents differently.

In the last chapter it was mentioned that there are certain individuals, known as *oko-jumu* in the North Andaman and *oko-paiad* in the South, who are believed to have special knowledge as to the spirits and as to the magical efficacy of remedies for sickness. It is these *oko-jumu* also who are the authorities on the legendary lore of the Andamanese. In the case of magical remedies there is a certain common stock of beliefs as to the efficacy to be attributed to different substances, such as leaves of different plants, and on the basis of these beliefs the *oko-jumu* elaborates the remedies that he uses in particular cases. Each *oko-jumu*, however, prides himself on being, to some extent, original. An example of this has been already mentioned. When a great storm arose an *oko-jumu* of one of the Northern tribes succeeded in stopping it (in the belief of the natives) by placing a piece of the crushed stem of the *Anadendron* creeper under a particular stone in the sea. On a later occasion another storm arose, and the successor of the first-mentioned *oko-jumu* was appealed to that he might exert his powers. He did not simply imitate his predecessor, but he placed a piece of crushed bark and twigs of the *Ficus laccifera* in the sea under a different stone. In very much the same way there is a common stock of beliefs as to the events that took place in the time of the ancestors, but each *oko-jumu* builds up on this basis his own particular set of legends, so that it is rarely that two of them tell the same story in the same way. An *oko-jumu* may obtain for himself a reputation by relating legends of the ancestors in a vivid and amusing way. Such a man would be able to invent new stories by combining together in his own way some of the traditional incidents. The desire on the part of each *oko-jumu* to be original and so to enhance his own reputation is a fertile source of variation in the legends.

This lack of traditional form, which is a very important characteristic of the Andamanese mythology, may be compared with their lack of traditional songs. Just as every man composes his own songs, so, within certain limits, every *oko-jumu* relates in his own way the legends of his tribe. But whereas every man is a composer of songs, only a certain number are regarded as having authority to speak on the legends.

Underlying the legends of any tribe there are a certain number of beliefs or representations with which every native is familiar. It is on the basis of these that the *oko-jumu* elaborates his own doctrine, if we may call it so, which he hands on to his followers, who in turn may become *oko-jumu* and produce further slight modifications of their own. Thus the legends are continually being changed, though in any one generation the changes introduced are slight, and it would take a long time for important changes in belief to be brought about. There is evidence, however, that a succession of leading men in the *A-Pučikwar* tribe have succeeded in introducing a new doctrine as to the weather, making *Bilik* the name of a class of beings instead of the name of a single being, and that this doctrine, while it has not entirely ousted the former beliefs, has yet succeeded in gaining currency not only in the *A-Pučikwar* tribe, but also in the *Aka-Kọl* and *Ọkọ-J̌uwọi* tribes.

At the present time it is only possible to recover a small part of the many different legends with their variants. The introduction of many new interests into the lives of the natives, through the European settlement and the many changes it has produced, has caused the ancient legends to be neglected. Most of the old *oko-jumu* have died without leaving any followers to take their place. Many of the legends recorded here are merely what some of the men not specially skilled in legendary lore can remember of the stories told them in former days by *oko-jumu* who are now dead.

One feature of the legends that must be pointed out is their unsystematic nature. The same informant may give, on different occasions, two entirely different versions of such a thing as the origin of fire, or the beginning of the human race. The Andamanese, to all appearance, regard each little story as independent, and do not consciously compare one with another. They thus seem to be entirely unconscious of what are obvious contradictions to the student of the legends. It is necessary to emphasise the fragmentary and unsystematic nature of the Andaman mythology because Mr Man, in his work on the Andamanese, has brought together a number of legends from the tribes of the South Andaman and has combined them into a continuous and fairly consistent narrative, and has thus, undoubtedly not intentionally, given a wrong impression to the reader of what the nature of the disconnected stories really is. While each of the stories included in Mr Man's account is derived directly from the natives, it would seem certain that the arrangement of them into a more or less consistent narrative is due to Mr Man.

In recording the legends in this chapter, only the English translation is given. In some cases the legends were translated on the spot and written down in English. In other cases they were written down in the native language and then translated. When I was recording the legends I very frequently had to ask what was meant by a particular statement, the meaning of which might be quite clear to a native, but which was obscure to one not accustomed to thinking in the same way as the natives. In some cases I could obtain no satisfactory explanation, and such legends are given in this chapter in as nearly as possible an exact literal translation of the original. In other cases the explanations given by the natives have been incorporated in the translation itself.

In order to give the reader a fair idea of the nature of the legends as they are told, one is here given in the native language (*Aka-Čari*) with a word-for-word translation.

A Maia Dik ijokoduko;	*o kǫnmo teč injuktertǫia;*	
Sir Prawn makes fire;	yam leaf catches fire;	
kǫnmo teč bi ikterbie;	*kete uijoko;*	*uijokobiko;*
yam leaf is dry;	that one it burns;	he makes a fire;
Maia Dik ubenoba;	*Maia Totemo emato;*	*ujokil uektebalo;*
Sir Prawn slept;	Sir Kingfisher takes;	he fire with he runs away
Maia Totemo jokobiko;	*Maia Totemo tajeo ubiko;*	
Sir Kingfisher makes a fire;	Sir Kingfisher fish (food) cooks;	
upetil ubeno;	*Maia Mite juktebalo uemato.*	
his belly in he sleeps;	Sir Dove runs away taking.	

The above translation is hardly comprehensible without a little explanation. The word *ijoko* means "something burns," the word *ubiko* means "he cooks (by roasting)." The compound *ijokobiko* may mean either "he makes a fire and cooks something at it" or it may simply mean "he makes up a fire (by adding firewood)." The word *ijokoduko* has a quite different meaning, "to produce fire." The derivation of *injuktertǫia* is uncertain, as I am not sure of the proper use of *er-tǫia*; it is translated on the basis of the explanation given me by the man who told the story. The word *ikterbie* is descriptive of the dryness of dead leaves.

A free translation would be as follows: "It was Sir Prawn who first produced or obtained fire. Some yam leaves, being shrivelled and dry by reason of the hot weather, caught fire and burnt. The prawn made a fire with some firewood and went to sleep. The kingfisher stole fire and ran away with it. He made a fire and cooked some fish. When he had filled his belly he went to sleep. The dove stole fire from the kingfisher and ran away." It is implied that it was the dove who gave the fire to the ancestors of the Andamanese.

Versions of legends of the origin of fire are given by Mr Portman, in each of the languages of the Southern group of tribes[1].

All the legends relate to events that are supposed to have happened in the past, and deal with the doings of the ancestors of the Andamanese. In the North Andaman the ancestors are sometimes called *Lau t'er-kuro*, i.e. the big spirits, "big" being used in the sense of our word "chief." Another term for them is *N'a-mai-koloko*, from *n'* or *nio* = they, *aka-mai* = father, and *koloko* = people, so that the phrase literally means "the father people," or the ancestors. In the South Andaman the ancestors are sometimes called *Čauga tabaŋa*, which is the equivalent of *Lau t'er-kuro*. Mr Man seems to have misunderstood the exact meaning of this term. He writes: "*Lači Lora-lola*, the chief of the survivors from the Deluge[2], gave, at his death, the name of *Čauga tabaŋa* to their descendants.......The *Čauga tabaŋa* are described as fine tall men with large beards, and they are said to have been long lived, but, in other respects and in their mode of living they did not differ from the present inhabitants. The name seems to have been borne till comparatively recent times, as a few still living are said to remember having seen the last of the so-called *Čauga tabaŋa*[3]."

Mr Man has evidently not realised that the term *čauga* cannot be applied to any living Andamanese, but may be applied to every dead one. The *Čauga* are the spirits of dead natives, and new *Čauga* are continually coming into existence by death. Any person who is of such importance when alive as to form the subject of legends or stories after his death may be distinguished (after his death only) as a *Čauga tabaŋa*. The name may thus be applied to the purely mythical ancestors of the legends, and also to the spirits of men recently dead

---

[1] Portman, *Notes on the Languages*, etc. p. 97.
[2] The legend will be given later.
[3] Man, *op. cit.* p. 169.

whose memory is preserved owing to fame acquired in some way when they were alive. It is thus possible that some of the natives with whom Mr Man formerly conversed are now *Čauga tabaya*, i.e. big spirits, having been "big men" when they were alive.

Another name sometimes used in the South Andaman to denote the ancestors is *Tomo-la*[1]. This word, however, is sometimes used in the singular to denote the mythical first man. Its use is thus similar to that of the name *Bilik* in the *A-Pučikwar* tribe, which is used both as the name of a single mythical being and also as the name of a class of beings. Only the early ancestors of the Andamanese, i.e. those about whom the legends are related, can be called *Tomo-la*.

Among the ancestors who appear in the legends there are a few who bear names that are used as personal names of men and women at the present time, and who appear in the legends simply as men and women. The larger number of the ancestors, however, bear names that are those of species of animals. In each case the ancestor is identified with the species which bears the same name. Yet others of the mythical ancestors have names that are neither personal names at the present day, nor names of animals. It may perhaps be supposed that in all such cases the name has some sort of meaning, but in many instances it was not found possible to discover the meaning with certainty.

When speaking of the ancestors, the natives generally add to the name the appropriate title. These titles are, in the North Andaman *Maia* (Sir) and *Mimi* (Lady), in Akar-Bale *Da* (Sir) and *In* (Lady), and in Aka-Bea *Maia* and *Čana*.

There are legends as to the origin of mankind, i.e., of their own race, for they did not recognize, until recently, the existence of any men of other races than their own, calling aliens *Lau* (spirits). There is, however, no unanimity in their beliefs as to how mankind originated, even in any one tribe. An *Aka-Bo* legend is as follows:

[1] The suffix *-la* is added to personal names and to terms of address in order to express respect.

"The first man was *Ĵutpu*¹. He was born inside the joint of a big bamboo, just like a bird in an egg². The bamboo split and he came out. He was a little child. When it rained he made a small hut for himself and lived in it. He made little bows and arrows. As he grew bigger he made bigger huts, and bigger bows and arrows. One day he found a lump of quartz and with it he scarified himself. *Ĵutpu* was lonely, living all by himself. He took some clay (*kọt*) from a nest of the white ants and moulded it into the shape of a woman. She became alive and became his wife. She was called *Kọt*. They lived together at *Teraut-buliu*. Afterwards *Ĵutpu* made other people out of clay. These were the ancestors. *Ĵutpu* taught them how to make canoes and bows and arrows, and how to hunt and fish. His wife taught the women how to make baskets and nets and mats and belts, and how to use clay for making patterns on the body."

The same story was told me by *Aka-Ĵeru* men, the only difference being that they gave the name of the place where *Ĵutpu* lived differently, mentioning a spot in the *Aka-Ĵeru* country.

From the *Aka-Ĵeru* I also obtained what is really another version of the same legend, though the name of the first ancestor is given differently. "The first man came out of the buttress of a *pọičo* (*Sterculia*) tree, and was called *Pọičotobut* (*Sterculia* buttress). He had no wife, so he cohabited with an ant's nest (*kọt*) and thus obtained a large number of children. These were the first Andamanese, and *Pọičotobut* taught them all their arts and customs. *Pọičotobut* lived at *Bọroŋ Buliu* (in *Aka-Ĵeru* country)."

The association between the origin of the Andamanese and an ant's nest (*kọt*) is retained in another legend, told by an *Aka-Ĵeru* man. "*Tarai* (the south-west monsoon) was the first man. His wife was *Kọt*. They lived at *Tarai-era-*

---

[1] The name seems to mean "alone."

[2] The giant bamboo does not grow in the Andamans, but pieces of it are often drifted ashore, having come from the coast of Burma. The natives pick up these drift-wood bamboos and make buckets of them. It is possible that the bamboo from which the first man was born was just such a piece drifted up from the sea. Unfortunately I neglected to enquire on this point when taking down the legend.

poŋ[1]. Their children were *Tau* (the sky), *Bǫto* (wind), *Piribi* (storm), and *Air* (the foam on a rough sea)."

An entirely different legend, of which, however, I could not obtain a detailed version, is also found in the *Aka-Jẽru* tribe. This is to the effect that the first living being was *Maia Čara*[2]. He made the earth, and caused it to be peopled with inhabitants. He also made the sun and moon. In the last chapter *Čara* was mentioned as a mythical being associated with the sun, with daylight and with fine weather. One of my informants of the *Aka-Jẽru* tribe said that *Čara* had a wife named *Nimi* (a common personal name), and that his children were *Čeo* (knife), *Ino* (water), *Loto*, and *Luk*. It is *Maia Čara*, according to one commonly received account, who makes the daylight every day.

I could not obtain any *Aka-Kede* legend as to the origin of mankind. One informant of that tribe said that it was *Bilika* (the north-east monsoon) who made the world and the first men and women, but he could give me no detailed legend.

In the *Aka-Kǫl* and *A-Pučikwar* tribes there are several versions of a legend that makes the monitor lizard (*Varanus salvator*) the progenitor of the Andaman race. In all the versions there is no mention of how the lizard himself originated. The following was told me by an *Aka-Kǫl* man. "When *Ta Pẹti* (Sir Monitor Lizard) was *aka-gǫi* (i.e. unmarried, but having completed the initiation ceremonies), he went into the jungle to hunt pig. He climbed up a *Dipterocarpus* tree, and got stuck there[3]. *Beyan* (civet-cat, *Paradoxurus*) found him there, stuck in the tree. She released him and helped him to get down. The two got married. Their children were the *Tomo-la* (i.e. the ancestors)."

Another legend telling how the monitor lizard obtained a wife was related to me on more than one occasion by *A-Pučikwar* men. "The first of the ancestors (*Tomo-la*) was *Ta Pẹtie* (Sir Monitor Lizard). He lived at *Tomo-la-tog*. At first he had

[1] The meaning of the name is "the cave of *Tarai*"; I believe that this is the name of a spot in the *Aka-Jẽru* country.

[2] The meaning of the name was not discovered.

[3] The lizard was caught in some way by his genital organs, but I was unable to understand the story completely.

no wife. One day, when he was out fishing, he found a piece of black wood of the kind called *kolotat* (*Diospyros* sp.). He found it in the creek, and brought it to his hut, where he put it on the little platform over the fire[1]. He sat down by the fire and set to work over an arrow that he was making. As he bent over his work he did not see what was happening. By and by he heard some one laugh, and looked up. Then he saw that the piece of wood had turned into a woman. He got up and took her down from the platform. She sat down with him and became his wife. They had a son named *Poi* (a species of small bird, possibly a woodpecker), and afterwards many other children. They lived together for a long time at *Tomo-la-tog*. One day *Ta Petie* went fishing and was drowned in the creek. He turned into a *kara-duku*."

There is some doubt about the translation of the word *kara-duku*. It is an *Aka-Bea* word, although it was used as given above, by an *A-Pučikwar* man. Mr Man translates it "cachalot." Mr Portman says that *kara-duku* is "crocodile," but that the cachalot, the proper name of which is *biriga-ta*, is also sometimes called *kara-duku*[2]. The only authority for the existence of crocodiles in the Andamans is the statement of Mr Portman, who says that the natives killed one in the Middle Andaman and brought the bones to him. Although I was in many of the creeks of the Andamans at different times I never saw a crocodile, and none of the other officers of the Settlement, who have repeatedly explored a large part of the islands, ever seems to have seen one, so that the one recorded by Mr Portman may possibly have been a single one that had come oversea from the mainland of Asia.

Another *A-Pučikwar* account of the origin of the first woman *Kolotat*, is as follows: "At first there were no women, only men. A man called *Kolotat* came to live in the *A-Pučikwar* country. *Ta Petie* (Sir Monitor Lizard) caught him and cut off his genitals and made him into a woman. She became his wife. Their children were the first of the ancestors (*Tomo-la*)."

---

[1] This is the small platform of sticks placed near or above the fire, on which the natives keep their food, and on which they often place objects that they desire to dry.

[2] *Notes on the Languages*, etc. p. 227.

Another account given by members of the *A-Pučikwar* tribe is that the first man was *Tomo*, or *Tomo-la*. One version that I heard is that *Tomo* made the world and peopled it with the ancestors. He made the moon (*Puki*) who is his wife. *Tomo* and his wife invented all the arts of the Andamanese and taught them to the ancestors. After his death *Tomo* went to live in the sky, where he now is. It is *Tomo* who sends the fine weather, while *Bilik* sends the bad weather. In the world where *Tomo* now lives it is always daylight and is always fine. When men die their spirits go up to the sky and live with *Tomo*. The man who gave me this version said that he did not know how *Tomo* originated, but was quite sure that he was not made by *Bilik*. *Tomo* came first and *Bilik* came afterwards. The Andamanese are all the children of *Tomo*[1].

In disagreement with this story, another man of the same tribe said that *Tomo* was made by *Bilik*. He (i.e., *Tomo*) had a wife *Mita* (Dove), and they were the ancestors of the Andamanese. Yet another informant said: "*Ta Tomo* was the first man. He made bows and arrows and canoes. His canoes were made of the wood of the Pandanus tree. *Mita* (Dove) was his wife. It was she who first made nets and baskets and discovered the uses of red paint and white clay." When I asked how *Tomo* and his wife originated my informant replied that he did not know.

A species of bird (perhaps a woodpecker), called *Poi* in *A-Pučikwar* and *Koio* in *Aka-Kol*, is often said to have been the son of *Tomo*. I was once told that *Koio* was the first of the Andamanese, from whom they are all descended, and that his wife was *Mita*. Another informant said that *Petie* (Monitor Lizard) was the first man and *Mita* was his wife, while still another stated that *Ta Mita* (Sir Dove) was the progenitor of the race, making the dove male instead of female. These different versions will give some idea of the

---

[1] When an old man of the *A-Pucikwar* tribe was giving me the information repeated above, an Andamanese man was with us who had been brought up as a Christian and had some knowledge of the doctrines of that faith. He explained to me that *Tomo* is the equivalent of the Christian God. This man belonged to the *Akar-Bale* tribe.

contradictory nature of the statements of the Andamanese. All of them come from only two tribes, the *A-Pučikwar* and the *Aka-Kọl*.

From the *Akar-Bale* tribe I obtained the following legend. "*Puluga* made the first of the ancestors. He made one man and one woman called *Nyali* and *Irap*[1]. He gave them fire, and taught them how to hunt and fish, and how to make bows and arrows and baskets and nets. The place where they lived is called *Irap* because they lived there[2]."

Another *Akar-Bale* version is that the first man was *Da Duku* (Sir Monitor Lizard), and that his wife was *In Bain* (Lady Civet-cat).

Mr E. H. Man, in his account of the South Andaman, says that there are a few discrepancies in their accounts of the creation and origin of the human species, but in the main features all the natives with whom he spoke are agreed. The world was created by *Puluga*, who then made a man named *Tomo*, the first of the human race. *Tomo* was black, like the present Andamanese, but was much taller and bearded. *Puluga* showed him the various fruit-trees in the jungle, which then existed only at *Wota-emi*, a spot in the country of the *A-Pučikwar* tribe. The wife of *Tomo* was *Čana Elewadi* (Lady Crab), and as to her origin there are different legends. According to some, *Puluga* created her after he had taught *Tomo* how to sustain life; others say that *Tomo* saw her swimming near his home and called to her, whereupon she landed and lived with him; while a third story represents her as coming pregnant to Kyd Island, where she gave birth to several male and female children, who subsequently became the progenitors of the present race. *Tomo* had two sons and two daughters by *Čana Elewadi*; the names of the former were *Biro-la* and *Bọro-la*, and of the latter *Rie-la* and *Čọrmi-la*.

A story that tells how *Tomo* came to his end states that

---

[1] These names are common personal names among the aborigines of the present day. Mr Portman derives *Nyali* from *nam-da*, the name of a tree, and *Irap* from *pira-da* meaning "scattered," but these derivations are far from being authenticated. (Portman, *Notes on the Languages of the South Andaman Group of Tribes*, p. 70.)

[2] The place called *Irap* is at the north end of Havelock Island.

one day, while hunting, he fell into the creek called *Yara-tig-jig* and was drowned. He was at once transformed into a *kara-duku* (which Mr Man translates as "cachalot"). *Čana Elewadi*, ignorant of the accident that had befallen her husband, went in a canoe with some of her grandchildren to ascertain the cause of his continued absence; on seeing them, *Kara-duku* upset their skiff and drowned his wife and most of her companions. She became a small crab, of a description still named after her, *elewadi*, and the others were transformed into lizards (*duku*). Another version of this story is that, wearied with an unsuccessful day's hunting, *Tomo* went to the shore, where he found a *čidi* (Pinna) shell-fish; while playing with it, it fastened on him, and he was unable to free himself until a *baian* (Paradoxurus) seized the *čidi* and liberated him at the expense of one of his members. Shortly after this he saw his wife and some of their children coming after him in a canoe; unwilling that they should become aware of the misfortune that had befallen him he upset the canoe, drowning its occupants and himself. He then became *kara-duku*, and the others *duku*, which are now plentiful in the jungles[1].

In some of the preceding legends reference is made to *Biliku* or *Puluga*. There is a very general belief, in all parts of the islands, that in the time of the ancestors, *Biliku* or *Puluga* lived on earth. Each tribe has at least one spot in its territory that is pointed out as the place where *Biliku* (or *Puluga*) lived. In some tribes there are three or four such places, each of which is claimed as the original home of *Biliku* by the people living in the neighbourhood. In many cases the name of the spot contains a reference to the legend, as *Puluga l'od-baraij* (the village of *Puluga*) in *Akar-Bale* or *Biliku era-poŋ* (the cave of *Biliku*) in the North Andaman.

I was able to obtain a few legends relating to the time when *Biliku* lived on earth, though there were probably many more that I was not fortunate enough to hear.

The following is an *Aka-Jeru* legend:

"In the time of the ancestors *Biliku* lived at *Ar-kọl*. One day the people caught a turtle and brought it to the camp.

[1] Man, *op. cit.* p. 164.

Biliku was sitting there. They asked her if she would eat some of it. She said 'No.' They put the meat in the roof of the hut and went away. When they had gone *Biliku* ate the whole turtle. Then she went to sleep. The people came back and found the turtle gone. They said '*Biliku* has eaten it.' They left the camp and all went to *Tebi-ċiro*. They left *Biliku* asleep. Some of the people went to hunt for turtle. Their canoe passed near *Ar-kọl*. *Biliku* saw the people in the canoe. She called to them and asked to be taken with them. The people refused saying 'You ate up all the turtle.' *Biliku* had a round stọne and several *be* shells (pearl shells). She threw the shells at the people in the canoe. The first shell did not hit them but came back and fell at her feet; and so also with the second. Then *Biliku* got very angry and threw a third time. The shell struck the canoe and killed all the people in it. The canoe and its occupants became a reef of rocks that is still there. The other people at *Tebi-ċiro* called across to *Biliku* saying 'Come over here.' She answered 'Very well! I am coming.' She took the stone that she had and put it in the sea, and it floated. She got on to it to cross over. When she had got half way across *Biliku* and her stone sank in the sea. They became two big rocks that are there still." This legend refers to the west coast of the North Andaman. The pearl shells that *Biliku* throws seem to be lightning, and the round stone the one that she rolls about to make thunder.

A few other statements about *Biliku* and *Tarai* from the four tribes of the North Andaman are given below just as they were taken down in my note-books.

(1) "*Biliku* lived at *Pura-'ra-poŋ* in the time of the ancestors. Her husband was *Pẹrjido* and her children *Totaimo*, *Mite* (cicada) and *Tarai*. She made the sun and the moon. It was she who first invented all the things that are now made and used by women, such as baskets, nets, etc., and it was she who discovered fire, and who first discovered the use of edible roots such as *kọnmo* and *mino* (two species of *Dioscorea*)."

(2) "*Biliku* used to live at *Ċaura*. She had a husband

Tarai and a son *Perjido*, and a daughter *Mite*. She used to live only on certain vegetable foods, *loito, pata, bui, čo, konmo* and *mino* and others. It was *Biliku* who made the earth (the forest, *ti-miku*). She began at *Čaura*."

(3) "*Biliku* lived at *Ar-Kol* in the time of the ancestors. Her husband was *Tarai* and their children were the birds, *Toroi, Taka, Čotot, Poruatoko, Kelil, Mite, Čopčura, Benye, Biratkoro, Čereo, Milidu, Bobelo, Kolo,* and *Teo*." (*Aka-Jeru.*)

(4) "*Biliku* lived at *Poroket*. She was unmarried. She had a son *Perjido*, and her other children were *Toroi, Čelene, Čotot* and *Čerei*. (These four are the names of birds.) It was *Perjido* who invented all the arts of the Andamanese such as their bows and arrows, etc." (*Aka-Bo*?.)

(5) "*Biliku* used to live at *Peč-meo* with her husband *Toroi* (a bird). She used to eat *loito*, and when anyone else ate that root she was angry. *Tarai* lived at *Čaroya* with his wife *Kelil* (a bird). He ate only *mikulu*." (*Aka-Kora.*)

(6) "*Tarai* has very long legs and a short body. He used to live on a small island beyond Interview Island, which is now submerged. When *Tarai* goes to sleep he breathes very heavily and this makes the wind."

The next is an *Aka-Kede* legend. "In the days of the ancestors *Bilika* lived at *Purum-at-čape* in the *Aka-Kede* country, with her husband *Porokul*. One day *Porokul* was out hunting. He returned with a pig that he had killed and came to the creek on the other side of which was his home (*Coti-ter-buli Buliu*). Laden as he was with the pig he could not swim across the creek. *Bilika* was sleeping, but her children were playing near and saw their father on the other side of the creek. They ran and told their mother that their father was coming but could not cross the creek. *Bilika* went and lay down on one bank of the creek and stretched out her leg so that it reached the other bank. *Porokul* walked across her leg and so reached home."

While it is clear from this legend that *Bilika* was of superhuman size, the same was also true of her husband, if we may judge from another legend. "*Porokul* made for himself a bow (of the large southern pattern), with which to shoot pig. At this time the sky was low down near the earth, only just above the tops of the trees. When *Porokul* had finished his bow he lifted it upright. The top of it struck the sky and lifted it up to its present position where it has remained ever since."

In another legend from another part of the *Aka-Kede* tribe *Bilika* is spoken of as being male. "*Bilika* lived at *Poroy-et-čo* with his wife *Mite*. They had a child. The ancestors ate *Bilika's* food, *loito* and *kata* and other plants. *Bilika* was very angry. He used to smell their mouths to see if they had eaten his food. When he found a man or woman who had done so he would cut his throat. The ancestors were very angry with *Bilika*, because he killed the men and women when they ate his foods. They all came together and killed *Bilika* and his wife *Mite*. *Maia Burto* (a species of fish) took the child (of *Bilika*) away to the north-east."

Owing to my lack of knowledge of the *Aka-Kede* language there are some points of the above legend that remain obscure. I think that the child of *Bilika* is also named *Bilika*, and that it is he (or she) who now lives in the north-east and sends the storms. The plants (*loito, kata,* etc.), called here the "food" of *Bilika*, are those mentioned in the last chapter as specially belonging to *Bilika*, who is angry when the natives eat them. As regards the name, *Mite*, of *Bilika's* wife, I do not know whether this is the name of the bronze-winged dove, or of the cicada. In some of the Andamanese languages the names of these two are very similar, the only difference being a very slight one in the way of pronouncing the two vowels.

The *A-Pučikwar* people who live on the east coast of Baratang Island say that in the beginning the ancestors lived at a place called *Wota-emi*, and *Bilik* lived opposite to them across the strait at a place called *Tol-l'oko-tima*. In a rock at *Wota-emi* there is a large peculiarly shaped hollow. This is said to be where *Bilik* used to sit when he was on earth.

An *Akar-Bale* legend is as follows. "In the days of the ancestors *Puluga* lived at *Jila* off the east coast of Henry Lawrence Island and the ancestors lived at *Puluga l'od-baraij* (the village of *Puluga*) on the main island just opposite to *Jila*. *Puluga* was always getting angry with the ancestors, because they dug up yams and ate *čakan* (*Entada scandens*) and *barata* (*Caryota sobolifera*). When he was angry he used to destroy their huts and property. So the people sent him out of the world, saying 'We do not want you here. You are always angry with us.' *Puluga* went away to the north-east."

It is worth while to note that *Jila* is north-east from *Puluga l'od-baraij*, just as *Tọl-l'oko-tima* is north-east from *Wota-emi*. In both cases there is a narrow strait between the place where the ancestors lived and the home of *Puluga* or *Bilik*.

There are a number of different legends that relate how the ancestors first obtained fire[1]. In many of these legends there is a reference to *Biliku* or *Puluga*. A common statement in the North Andaman is that "Fire was stolen from *Biliku* by *Maia Tiritmo* (Sir Kingfisher)." Some of the legends give further details. An *Aka-Čari* legend is as follows:

"*Biliku* had a red stone and a pearl shell (*be*). She struck them together and obtained fire. She collected firewood and made a fire. She went to sleep. *Mite* (the bronze-winged dove) came and stole fire. He made a fire for himself. He gave fire to all the people in the village. Afterwards fire was given to all the places. Each village had its own."

The next is an *Aka-Jeru* version.

"In the days of the ancestors they had no fire. *Biliku* had fire. While *Biliku* slept *Maia Lirčitmo* (Sir Kingfisher) came and stole fire. As he was taking the fire *Biliku* awoke and saw him. *Lirčitmo* swallowed the fire. *Biliku* took a pearl shell (*be*) and threw it at *Lirčitmo* and cut off his head. The fire came out (of his neck). The ancestors got the fire. *Lirčitmo* became a bird."

The next is also, I believe, an *Aka-Jeru* story. "*Maia Tiritmo* (Sir Kingfisher) lived at *Tolepar Buruin*. He had no fire. When he caught fish he had no fire with which to cook it. He went to the place where *Čokčura* (heron) lived. There was no fire there. *Tiritmo* took some rotten wood of the *piṅ*

---

[1] Until the settlement of Europeans on the islands the Andamanese had no knowledge of any means of producing fire. It is necessary to remember this to understand some of their legends which relate how in the time of the ancestors the fire was very nearly lost in a heavy storm.

tree and hit it on a rock, and thus made fire. He gave fire to *Čokčura*. *Čokčura* gave fire to *Totemo* (a species of kingfisher). *Totemo* gave it to all the others.

A slightly different and less detailed version of the same story is as follows:

"*Tiritmo* made fire. *Totemo* stole fire (from *Tiritmo*) and gave it to *Moičo* (Rail). *Moičo* gave fire to all the people."

The next version, which was taken down in *Aka-Jeru*, I did not fully understand.

"Some one shot an arrow. The arrow hit the hill of fire. *Tirin* (a species of kingfisher) found the arrow. It was on fire. He took the fire to his camp. He would not give fire to any one. The others asked him. They went to their homes. At night they came to *Tirin's* hut and stole fire. They went away, each to his own place."

There is a certain amount of obscurity about two other versions, which are given in a translation as nearly literal as possible. "*Maia Dik* (Sir Prawn) made fire. Some *konmo* (yam) leaves caught fire, being dry. *Maia Dik* made a fire. *Maia Dik* slept. *Maia Totemo* (Sir Kingfisher) stole fire and ran away. *Maia Totemo* made a fire. He cooked fish. When he had eaten, he slept. *Maia Mite* (Sir Dove) stole fire (from *Totemo*) and ran away.

The other is as follows. "*Piribi* got fire from a stone. He threw fire at *Bilika*. It set some *konmo* (yam) leaves on fire. *Corolo* (Parrot) got fire (from the burning leaves). He gave it to the ancestors."

These two legends were taken down in *Aka-Čari*, but they are perhaps really *Aka-Kora* or *Aka-Jeru* stories. I have the word *piribi* in my notes as meaning a storm, but the translation is doubtful.

The next is an *Aka-Kede* version of what is the most widespread of the legends.

"The ancestors had no fire. *Bilika* had fire. The ancestors tried to steal fire from *Bilika*. *Lirtit* (Kingfisher) went one night while *Bilika* was sleeping and stole fire. *Bilika* awoke and saw him going away with the fire. She threw a pearl shell (*ba*) at him, which cut off his wings and his tail. *Lirtit* dived into the water and swam with the fire to *Bet-'ra-kudu* and gave it to *Tepe*. *Tepe* gave fire to *Mite* (the bronze-winged dove). *Mite* gave it to the others[1]."

An *Aka-Kede* legend of the origin of the sun may conveniently be given in this place, as it is connected with the possession of fire by *Bilika*. "*Bilika* made fire of *purum* wood. One day, when she was very angry, she started throwing fire about. One large fire-brand she threw into the sky, and there it became the sun." This legend explains the name of the place *Purum-at-čape*, at which *Bilika* is said to have lived when on earth. *Purum* is the name of a tree, not identified; *at* means either "fire" or "fire-wood," and *čape* means a village or a hut. The whole word therefore means "*Purum* fire village."

I did not obtain any legend of the origin of fire from the *Oko-Juwoi* and *Aka-Kol* tribes, but a version from each of these tribes has been given by Mr Portman. A translation of Mr Portman's *Oko-Juwoi* story is as follows[2]. "*Mom Mirit*[3] stole a fire-brand from *Kuro-t'on-mika* while *Bilik* was sleeping. He gave the brand to the late *Leč*, who then made fire at *Karat-tatak-emi*."

Mr Portman's *Aka-Kol* story is somewhat obscure. "*Bilik* was sleeping at *Tol-l'oko-tima*. *Luratut* (Kingfisher) took away fire to *Oko-emi*. *Kolotat* went to *Min-toŋ-ta* (taking with him fire from *Oko-emi*). At *Min-toŋ-ta* the fire went out. *Kolotat* broke up the charred firewood and made fire again (by blowing up the embers). They (the people there) became alive. Owing to the fire they became alive. The ancestors (*Jaŋil*) thus got fire at *Min-toŋ-ta* village."

From the *A-Pučikwar* tribe I only obtained one version of the fire legend. "When the ancestors lived at *Wota-emi*, *Bilik* lived at *Tol-l'oko-tima* across the strait. In those days the ancestors had no fire. *Bilik* took some wood of the tree called *perat* and broke it and made fire for himself. *Luratut* (Kingfisher) came to *Tol-l'oko-tima* while *Bilik* was sleeping and stole some fire. *Bilik* awoke and saw *Luratut*. He (*Bilik*) took

---

[1] I understood that *Lirtit*, by the loss of his wings and tail, became a man.
[2] Portman, *loc. cit.*
[3] *Mom* is a title indicating respect, aud *Mirit* is the imperial pigeon.

up a lighted brand and threw it at *Luratut*. It hit him in the back of the neck and burnt him. *Luratut* gave the fire to the people at *Wota-emi*. *Bilik* was very angry about this and went away to live in the sky."

The kingfisher of the story (*Alcedo beavani*?) has a patch of bright red feathers on its neck. This is where it was burnt by the brand thrown by *Bilik*.

Mr Portman gives a slightly different version from the same tribe[1]. "*Bilik* was sleeping at *Tọl-l'oko-tima*. *Luratut* went to bring fire. He caught hold of the fire, and in doing so burnt *Bilik*. *Bilik* awoke and seized some fire. He hit *Luratut* with the fire. Then he hit *Tarčal* (a fish) with the fire. *Čalter* (another species of kingfisher) caught hold of the fire. He gave it to the ancestors at *Wota-emi*. The ancestors made fires."

From the *Akar-Bale* tribe I obtained the following legend: "The people had no fire. *Dim-dọri* (a fish) went and fetched fire from *Jereg-l'ar-mugu* (the place of departed spirits). He came back and threw the fire at the people and burnt them, and marked them all. The people ran into the sea and became fishes. *Dim-dọri* went to shoot them with his bow and arrows, and he also became a fish." This story is supposed to account for the bright colouring of certain species of fish.

Mr Portman gives a somewhat similar version from the same tribe[2]. *Dim-dọra* (a fish), a very long time ago, at *Keri-l'oŋ-tower*, was bringing fire from *Puluga's* platform (fireplace). He, taking the fire, burnt everybody with it. *Bolub* and *Tarkọr* and *Biličau* fell into the sea and became fishes. They took the fire to *Rokwa-l'ar-toŋa* village and made fires there."

Another *Akar-Bale* legend is that fire was given to the first ancestors (*Da Duku* and *In Bain*) by *Puluga*. Still another is that fire was obtained by the ancestors from *Aga*, the skink (*Mabuia tytleri*). The mist that is often seen hanging over the jungle in small patches, after rain or at dawn, is said to be the smoke of *Aga's* fire. An island in the Archipelago is called *Aga l'od-baraij*, *Aga's* village.

---

[1] Portman, *loc. cit.*   [2] *Ibid.*

Mr Portman gives an *Aka-Bea* legend, which, however, relates that the events took place at *Wota-emi* in the *A-Pučikwar* country[1].

"*Puluga* was asleep at *Tọl-l'oko-tima*. *Luratut* came, stealing fire. The fire burnt *Puluga*. *Puluga* awoke. *Puluga* seized some fire. Taking the fire he burnt *Luratut* with it. *Luratut* took the fire. He burnt *Tar-čeker* (another kind of kingfisher) with it in *Wota-emi* village. The ancestors lit fires. They (the ancestors) were the *Tomo-la.*"

Mr Man gives three different versions of legends as to the origin of fire. According to the first of these, *Puluga*, after he had made the first man, *Tomo*, gave him fire and taught him its use. *Puluga* obtained fire by stacking in alternate layers two kinds of wood known as *cọr* and *ber*, and then bidding the sun to come and sit on or near the pile until she ignited it, after which she returned to her place in the sky[2]. The second version is that *Puluga* came to *Tomo* with a spirit named *Lači Puŋa Ablola* to instruct *Tomo*, who at his direction, prepared a pyre and then struck it, on which the fire was kindled and *Puŋa Ablola* proceeded to teach him how to cook food[3]. This legend contains an obvious contradiction. *Lači Puŋa Ablola*, as is shown by the name itself (*Lači* = the late), is the name of some one who is supposed to have lived and died and so become a spirit. Yet at the same time *Tomo* is supposed to have been the first of the Andamanese. There is the possibility, however, that this inconsistency is due not to the natives themselves, but to Mr Man's transcription. It is possible that the legend is that fire was discovered and was given to the ancestors (the *Tomo*) by a person who, being dead, is now *Lači Puŋa Ablola*, but who was then alive and one of the ancestors (*Tomo*) themselves.

A third legend about fire given by Mr Man is associated by him with another legend about a flood that once overwhelmed the ancestors. According to Mr Man's version the fires were all extinguished by the flood, so that the few survivors were left without fire. "At this juncture one of their recently deceased

---

[1] Portman, *loc. cit.*   [2] Man, *op. cit.* p. 164.   [3] *Ibid.*

friends appeared in their midst in the form of a bird named *Luratut*. Seeing their distress he flew up to *Moro*, the sky, where he discovered *Puluga* seated beside his fire; he thereupon seized and attempted to carry away in his beak a burning log, but the heat, or weight, or both, rendered the task impossible, and the blazing brand fell on *Puluga*, who, incensed with pain, hurled it at the intruder; happily for those concerned, the missile missed its mark and fell near the very spot where the survivors were deploring their condition. As *Luratut* alighted in their midst at the same moment, he gained the full credit for having removed the chief cause of their distress[1]."

We may now consider a group of legends that relate how a great catastrophe overwhelmed the ancestors. In many of the versions the legend relates how the ancestors were transformed into animals. Some of the legends are connected with *Biliku* or *Puluga* and others are connected with the first discovery of fire. Beginning with the North Andaman, the following is, I believe, an *Aka-Jeru* version. "*Mimi Cara* once broke some firewood in the evening (while the cicada was singing). A great storm came and killed many people, who were turned into fishes and birds. The water rose up till it covered the trees. *Mimi Čara* and *Mimi Kota* took the fire and went up the hill to the cave at *Ŋaram*. They carried the fire under a cooking-pot. They kept the fire alight in the cave, until the storm was over."

Another *Aka-Jeru* legend was taken down hurriedly and the full details were not obtained. "The people made a noise in the evening when *Mite* (the cicada) was singing. *Mite* went to see her mother *Biliku*. Her mother saw her eyes and face. She looked bad. Her eyes were red (with weeping). *Biliku* was very angry. There was a big storm and heavy rain. *Biliku* threw her pearl shells (lightning). She went mad. She destroyed the whole world. *Biliku* went up to live in the sky. The earth was bare (literally, empty). One day *Biliku* dropped a *Dipterocarpus* seed from the sky. Out of this all the different kinds of tree grew, and the earth was again covered with

[1] Man, *op. cit.* p. 167.

forest." There was more of the legend, which I was unable at the time to understand, and which I did not hear again. My informant added "It was on this occasion that *Maia Taolu* saved the fire."

An *Aka-Cari* legend relates how the birds and beasts and fishes arose. "*Maia Dik* (Sir Prawn) once got angry and threw fire at the people (the ancestors). They all turned into birds and fishes. The birds flew into the jungle. The fishes jumped into the sea. *Maia Dik*[1] himself became a large prawn which is still called by the same name." In connection with this legend it must be remembered that it was *Maia Dik*, according to one legend, who first discovered the use of fire. One version of the story said that he made fire by striking a piece of *parayo* wood. Then he threw the burning wood about amongst the ancestors and they turned into birds and fishes.

An *Aka-Jeru* version is very similar. "The people were all asleep. *Maia Kǫlo* (Sir Sea-eagle) came and threw fire amongst them. They awoke in a fright and all ran in different directions. Some ran into the sea and became fishes and turtle; others ran into the jungle and became birds."

The *Aka-Kede* version of the catastrophe that overtook the ancestors is as follows. "It was at the place called *Čilpet*. The people collected a lot of honey. They refused to give any to *Kǫpo-tera-wat* (a bird, not identified). The latter got very angry, and in the evening, when the cicadæ were singing he made a great noise and disturbed their song. Then there arose a great storm, and it rained very heavily, and the sea rose over the land. It rose very rapidly till only the top of a big *Dipterocarpus* tree showed above the water. The people took refuge in the branches of this tree. *Mima Mite* (Lady Dove) managed to rescue some fire and keep it alight under a cooking pot. The waters at length subsided. Then the people did not know how to get down from the tree. *Mima Čarami-lebek* made a long piece of string and with this she lowered the people

---

[1] *Dik* was one of the ancestors. He was a giant and was so big that he could go into the deepest water and never needed a canoe. He used to shoot dugong and porpoise with his bow and arrow. (The natives shoot small fish with a bow and arrows, but large fish and dugong and porpoise they take with harpoons.)

safely to the ground." The *čarami-lebek*, which was not identified, is a species of bird that lives, so the natives say, only at the top of the very tallest trees of the forest.

An *Aka-Kọl* version of the same legend is as follows: "At first there were no birds in the jungle and no fish in the sea. The ancestors were playing one evening and making a noise while the *peti* (cicada) was singing. Then *Bilik* got angry and sent a great cyclone. All the people were turned into birds and fishes and turtles and jungle beasts."

There is an *A-Pučikwar* legend that, in the days of the ancestors, there was a big cyclone. There was a flood at *Wota-emi* and the water rose up over the trees. Some of the ancestors climbed up into a big *Dipterocarpus* tree and remained there till the waters had subsided. I was not able to hear any more detailed version of the legend.

The following legend explaining how the ancestors were turned into animals was told me by an *A-Pučikwar* man, but it is probably really of *Akar-Bale* origin.

"It was in the days of the ancestors. *Ta Kọlwọt* (Sir Tree-lizard) went over to a big meeting at *Teb-juru* (in the Archipelago). There was a lot of dancing. *Kọlwọt* decided to give a big dancing party of his own. He invited everybody and they all came to his place. *Kọlwọt* danced a great deal. He began to get wild. All the people were afraid, because he was very strong. They caught hold of him by the arms. *Kọlwọt* got very angry. He threw the people from him. He threw them so violently that some fell in the sea and became fishes and turtle. Others fell on different islands and became birds and animals. No one could hold *Kọlwọt*. At last *Berep* (a species of crab) caught hold of his arm and would not let go. And thus *Berep* stopped him. Before this there had been no birds in the jungles nor any fish in the sea."

A more complete version of this story was obtained from the *Akar-Bale* tribe. "*Da Tigbul* (Sir Dugong) took all the people to dance at *Kwaičo*. *In Bain* (Lady Civet-cat) told *Da Kwọkọl* (Sir Tree-lizard) that people were coming from *Tar-mugu* to dance and that *Da Karami*[1] would quarrel with

---

[1] *Karami* is the name of a bird that was not identified.

him. *Da Kwǫkǫl* replied 'Oh! I don't care. I can fight all those people easily enough.' All the people came together for the dance and *Karami* quarrelled with *Kwǫkǫl*. The latter got very angry. The people were afraid. *Tigbul* (Dugong) caught hold of *Kwǫkǫl* by the arm. *Kwǫkǫl* threw him from him with such force that *Tigbul* fell into the sea and became a dugong. Then *Kočurag-boa* caught hold of *Kwǫkǫl* and *Kwǫkǫl* threw him into the jungle¹. *Kwǫkǫl* threw all the people into the sea or into the jungle and they became birds and beasts and fishes. No one could hold him. *Da Kwǫkǫl* went away to *Teb-juru*. The people told *Da Berag* (Sir Crab) what had happened at *Kwaičo* and how no one could hold *Da Kwǫkǫl*. *Da Berag* went after him to *Teb-juru*. *Da Kwǫkǫl* had covered himself with *kǫiob* (red paint)². *Da Berag* pretended that he wanted some paint to put on his upper lip, saying that he was sick. There was no more red paint in the place, so *Da Kwǫkǫl* said 'You had better come and take some off me.' *Da Berag* put his nose to *Kwǫkǫl's* arm as though to get some paint, and bit deeply into *Kwǫkǫl's* shoulder. *Kwǫkǫl* could not get loose, and so he died. The people at *Teb-juru* attacked *Da Berag* and beat him. They could not kill him, because his skin was too hard, so they threw him into the sea. When *Kwǫkǫl's* mother, *Kegya*, came and found her son dead she was very angry. She wept for a long time. Then she went into the jungle and cut the plant *tǫkul* which belongs to *Puluga*. *Puluga* was angry because the *tǫkul* was cut and sent a big storm which killed *Kegya* and all the other people in that place."

Mr Man records another version of this legend.

"To explain the origin of certain fish, they say that one day before the Deluge, *Maia Kǫlwǫt* went to visit an encampment of the *Tomola* situated in the Archipelago. While engaged in his song the women, through inattention to his instructions, marred the effect of the chorus, so, to punish them, he seized

---

[1] *Kočurag-boa* is the *Akar-Bale* name for a huge legendary animal.

[2] When a man has killed another, either in a personal or a tribal quarrel, he has to observe several customs of which one is to keep himself painted with red paint for several weeks.

his bow, whereupon the whole party in terror fled in all directions; some escaping into the sea were changed into dugongs, porpoises, sharks, and various other fish which till then had not been seen[1]."

Mr Man gives still another version of the same story. "One day, at the commencement of the rainy season, a *tomola* named *Berebi* came to visit *Kǫlwǫt's* mother, *Čana Erep*, with the express intention of seeing her son, of whom he was extremely jealous. When he appeared *Berebi* treacherously bit him in the arm, but his teeth became fixed in the flesh and he was therefore unable to detach himself from his victim, whose friends promptly avenged his murder, and disposed of the corpses by throwing them into the sea. (*Kǫlwǫt*, after death, was transformed into a species of tree-lizard, which is still named after him, and *Berebi* became a fish called *Koyo*, which is armed with a row of poisonous barbs in its back.) The bereaved mother, in her rage, grief and despair, committed various acts, against which *Tomo* had been warned by *Puluga*, and while so doing incited others to follow her example by the following words:—

> *e, e, e, dia ra-gumul l'ab-dala,*
> *e, e, e, ŋul kaja pij pugatken,*
> *e, e, e, ŋul čoaken toaiken,*
> *e, e, e, ŋul boarato aga-kolaken,*
> *e, e, e, ŋul gono boaŋken,*
> *e, e, e, ŋul toŋ čoara boaŋken,*
> *e, e, e, ŋig arlot pulaijoken.*

The translation of which is:—

> e, e, e (sobbing)—My grown-up handsome son,
> ,,   ,,   Burn the wax,
> ,,   ,,   Grind the seed of the *čakan* (*Entada*),
> ,,   ,,   Destroy the *barata* (*Caryota*),
> ,,   ,,   Dig up the *gono* (yam),
> ,,   ,,   Dig up the *čati* (yam),
> ,,   ,,   Destroy everything."

Thereupon *Puluga* was exceeding wroth, and sent the flood, that which destroyed all living things with the exception of two men and two women.

---

[1] Man, *op. cit.* p. 171.

"This tradition is preserved in the following lines:—

> *Keledoat ibaji lar čora,*
> *Ra-gumul ab-gorga en ig-boadi*
> *Ra-gumul le liga koarna*
> *Ra-gumul ab-gorka*
> *Toala arbo eb dagan čoarpo.*

The meaning of which is:—

> Bring the boat to the beach
> I will see your fine grown-up son,
> The grown-up son who threw the youths (into the sea)
> The fine grown-up son,
> My adze is rusty, I will stain my lips with his blood.

In this, as in all their songs and chants, a good deal is left to the imagination, but from their explanations which have been given by the aborigines, the following appear to afford some light on the subject:—*Berebi*, being jealous of the renown *Kǫlwǫt* had won for himself by his numerous accomplishments and great strength, took advantage of meeting him and his mother one day on the water to ask them to let him enter their boat. On their complying with his request, he provided himself with a rusty adze and hone, remarking on the rusty condition of the former; then taking *Kǫlwǫt* by the arm he sniffed it from the wrist to the shoulder as if admiring the development of the muscles; while doing so he muttered the threat of staining his lips with blood, which he shortly after fulfilled in the manner already described[1]."

As the songs given in this legend are in the *Akar-Bale* language (Southern dialect), it is probable that the legend is an *Akar-Bale* one. It is really another version of the legend already given.

Another *Akar-Bale* story tells how the first ancestors *Duku*, the monitor lizard, and *Bain* the civet-cat, managed to keep the fire alight when a flood overwhelmed them. "One day in the time of the ancestors there came a great storm, and the water rose over the land. The rain put out the fires. *Da Duku* (Sir Monitor Lizard) took a smouldering log and tried to climb up a tree with it. He could not climb with the fire in his hand. His wife *In Bain* (Lady Civet-cat) took the fire from him and took it

[1] Man, *op. cit.* pp. 167—169.

up to the top of a hill and there kept it alight till the rain stopped and the water went away. The hill is called *Bain l'it-čapa* (Bain's fire) to the present day." The hill is a rather steep-sided hill of no great height in Havelock Island.

Mr Portman[1] connects the story of the flood with the story of the dispersion of the ancestors over the islands. Referring to the names of the tribes he says, "The Andamanese state that these names were given to the different tribes by *Maia Tomo-la* when they were dispersed after a cataclysm. They have a tradition that this group of tribes was once all one tribe, and that the Andaman Islands were much larger than at present. Some great cataclysm occurred during which part of the islands subsided and many aborigines were drowned, the remainder being separated into different territories as at present by the orders of *Maia Tomo-la*, apparently the chief at that time of the collected tribe. (The above is of course a matter-of-fact version of the fanciful and impossible legends of the Andamanese.)"

The dispersion legend in the South Andaman is connected with the name of the *A-Pučikwar* tribe. The name (of which the *Aka-Bea* equivalent is *Aka-Bojig-yab*) means "those who talk the original language," it being believed that the *A-Pučikwar* language was the one originally spoken by the ancestors.

The only version of the dispersion legend that I heard was from the *Aka-Kede* tribe. It was to the effect that *Bilika* once seized all the ancestors and put them in a netted bag (such as the natives use for carrying small objects of various kinds). She (or he) took them out a few at a time and put them in different parts of the country, where their descendants have been ever since.

Mr Man speaks of a legend of how the tribes came to be dispersed over the islands. From his account it would seem that there were two different dispersions, one before the Deluge, and a second after it. Mr Man's account is as follows. "*Tomo* lived to a great age, but even before his death his offspring became so numerous that their home could no longer accommodate them. At *Puluga's* bidding they were furnished with all necessary weapons, implements, and fire, and then scattered in

[1] *Notes on the Languages*, etc. p. 27.

pairs all over the country. When this exodus occurred *Puluga* provided each party with a distinct dialect. It would almost seem that, without straining the legend to suit facts, we might discern in this a faint echo of the Biblical account of the confusion of tongues and dispersion at Babel[1]."

"Consequent on the disappearance of *Tomo* and his wife, the duties of headship over the community at *Wota-emi* devolved on one of their grandchildren, named *Kolwot*, who was distinguished by being the first to spear and catch turtles. The *tomola* remained on the islands long after *Tomo's* transformation, but after *Kolwot's* death, according to one legend, they grew disobedient, and as *Puluga* ceased to visit them, became more and more remiss in their observance of the commands given at the creation. At last *Puluga's* anger burst forth, and, without any warning, he sent a great flood that covered the whole land, and destroyed all living. Four persons (two men, *Lora-lola* and *Poi-lola*, and two women, *Ka-lola* and *Rima-lola*), who happened to be in a canoe when the catastrophe occurred, were able to effect an escape. When the waters subsided, they found themselves near *Wota-emi*, where they landed and discovered that every living thing on earth had perished; but *Puluga* re-created the animals, birds, etc.[2]"

"When, for the second time in their history, their numbers had increased to so great an extent that it became impossible for them to remain together in one spot, an exodus, similar to the first, took place; each party being furnished with fire and every other essential, started in a different direction, and on settling down adopted a new and distinct dialect. They each received a tribal name, and from them have sprung the various tribes still existing on the islands[3]."

In the Southern tribes there is a legend to account for the origin of night. The following version was obtained from the *A-Pučikwar* tribe. "In the early days of the world, in the time of the ancestors, there was no night; it was always day. *Ta Petie* (Sir Monitor Lizard) went into the jungle to dig up yams. He found some yams. He also found some resin (*teki*), and a cicada (*roto*). He brought them to the camp of the ancestors at

---

[1] Man, *op. cit.* p. 166.   [2] *Ibid.*
[3] Man, *op. cit.* p. 169.

Wota-emi. He sat down and the people came round him. *Ta Petie* took the cicada and rubbed it between his hands and crushed it. As he did this the cicada uttered its cry. Then the day went away and it was dark. It remained dark for several days. The ancestors came together and tried to get back the day. They made torches of resin, and danced and sang songs. First *Kotare* (a bird) sang a song, but he could not get back the daylight. Then *Bumu* (a beetle?) sang, but the day would not come. Then *Pecerol* (the bulbul, *Otocompsia emeria*) sang, and after him *Koio* (a bird), but both in vain. Then *Koŋoro* (a species of ant) sang a song and morning came. After that, day and night followed one another alternately."

A similar legend was obtained from the *Akar-Bale* tribe. "*Da Teŋat*[1] lived at *Golugma Bud.* He went fishing one day and got only one small fish of the kind called *čelau* (*Glyphidodon sordidus?*): He turned to go home, and as he went he shot his arrows before him into the jungle[2]. Then he went after his arrows to find them again. As he went he spoke to the fruits of the jungle, asking them their names. In those days the ancestors did not know the names of the fruits and trees. First he asked the *puiam*, and then the *guluba*, and then the *čakli*, but none of them replied to him. Then he found his first arrow. It was stuck fast in a big yam (*gono*). He took the arrow and said to the yam 'What is your name?' At first the yam did not answer. *Teŋat* turned to go away. He had gone a few steps when the yam called him back, saying 'My name is *gono.*' *Teŋat* replied 'Oh! I did not know. Why did not you say so before?' He dug up the yam, which was a very big one. He went off to look for his second arrow. As he went he spoke to the stones of the jungle, asking their names, but none of them replied. Then he found his second arrow fixed in a large lump of resin (*tug*)[3]. He took the arrow, and as he was going away

---

[1] This is the name of some creature that I did not identify, perhaps a kind of spider.

[2] An Andaman Islander will often, when walking along the shore, shoot his arrows before him, either aiming at some object, or trying to send each one as far as possible. I have never seen them do this in the jungle, for they might easily lose the arrows.

[3] The Andamanese classify resin as a "stone" although they know its vegetable origin.

the resin called him back, saying 'Here! my name is *tug*; you can take me along with you.' So *Teŋat* took the resin. Then *Teŋat* found a cicada (*rita*), and he took that also. When *Teŋat* got to the hut (*bud*), everyone came to look at the things he had brought. He showed them the yam. He told them its name and showed them how to cook it. This was the first time that the ancestors ate *gono*. Then *Teŋat* took in his hand the cicada and squashed it between his palms. As he killed it the cicada uttered its cry and the whole world became dark. When the people saw that it was dark they tried to bring back the daylight. *Teŋat* took some of the resin and made torches. He taught the people how to dance and sing. When *Da Koŋoro* (Sir Ant) sang a song the day came back. After that the day and night came alternately."

Mr Man records a different version of this story.

"The manner in which the world was illuminated at the beginning is not clearly to be ascertained from their legends, for one story states that the sun and moon were subsequently created at *Tomo's* request, as he found that, under the then existing circumstances, it was impossible to catch fish by night or to hunt by day; while, in direct disagreement with this, another story tells us that night was a punishment brought upon mankind by certain individuals who angered *Puluga* by killing a caterpillar. The tale informs us that the sun, one day, burned so fiercely as to cause great distress. Two women named *Čana Limi* and *Čana Jaraŋud*, became exceedingly irritable, and while in this unhappy frame of mind they discovered a caterpillar (*gurug*) and a certain plant called *utura*. By way of venting their spleen, one crushed the helpless grub, and the other destroyed the plant. These wanton acts so displeased *Puluga* that he determined to punish them, and to teach them to appreciate the privilege of daylight, which they had hitherto uninterruptedly enjoyed. He accordingly visited the earth with a long-continued darkness, which caused every one much inconvenience and distress. At last their chief, *Maia Kọlwọt*, to whom reference has already been made, hit upon a happy expedient of inducing *Puluga* to restore the former state of things by trying to assure him that they were quite unconcerned, and could enjoy themselves in spite of light being withheld from them. To accomplish this, he invented the custom of dancing and singing, the result of which was that *Puluga*, finding that they had frustrated his intention, granted, as a first concession alternate periods of day and night, and subsequently, moved by the difficulties often occasioned by the latter, created the moon to mitigate their troubles. It is in this way that they account for the same word being used to denote a caterpillar and night¹."

From the *Akar-Bale* tribe I obtained a legend about the origin of death. No other version of the same legend was obtained.

"At *Jǫyo-l'ar-bǫy* lived *In Kalwadi* with her sons *Yaramurud* and *Toau*². *Yaramurud* went to hunt pig for his mother, but was unsuccessful. When he came home his mother brought him some pork that was in the hut. As he took his knife from the back of his neck to cut the meat with it, he cut himself³. Then his mother knew that he was dead. She said to him 'You are dead now. You had better go away. We do not want you here any more.' She took him up and carried him into the jungle and buried him, returning home. Very soon *Yaramurud* returned. His mother exclaimed 'Oh! I thought you had gone.' He replied 'Mother, I did not die. Why did you bury me?' But she knew he was dead, so she took him and buried him again. He came back again. This happened three times. Then *Kalwadi* took him into the jungle to a big *dumla* tree (*Pisonia excelsa*), in which there was a big hole. She kicked the tree with her foot and said 'You go in there.' *Yaramurud* went inside. 'Well! Have you gone?' his mother asked. He answered 'Yes!' 'Tell me how the spirits (*čauga*) talk' she asked him, and he replied '*Tǫ kit*⁴.' Then his mother knew that he was with the spirits, and said 'Oh! my child, you are

---

¹ Man, *op. cit.* p. 172.

² *Kalwadi* is a small crab, *yaramurud* is the crow pheasant (*Centropus andamanensis*), and *toau* is the hawksbill turtle.

³ Knives are generally carried slipped into a string that is tied round the neck, the knife, with a skewer of sharpened wood that is attached to it, hanging at the back of the neck, where it is easily accessible and not likely to get lost.

⁴ I could obtain no explanation of the phrase, or word, *tǫ kit*. My informant only said "That is the way the spirits talk."

finished now. You will never come back again.' After a few days *Yaramurud* came back (as a spirit) to see his brother *Toau*. *Toau* was busy building a hut. When *Yaramurud* saw him he killed him. Before this there had been no death. But *In Kalwadi* told the people, saying 'You see what has happened; well, we shall all of us die like this, like these two have done'."

There is a widespread legend to account for the origin of creeks and islands. The following is an *A-Pučikwar* version.

"At first there was only one big island with the sea all round it. There were no small islands and no creeks. *Koyoro* (a species of ant) made a turtle net and went fishing. He caught a very big fish of the kind called *koro-yiti-čau* in his net, and dived down and attached a rope to its tail. The fish got very angry and made furious plunges to get away, striking the land in its struggles, and each time knocking off a bit of the land or making a long split. This is the origin of the smaller islands and the creeks."

Mr Man records the same legend, but says it was *Tomo* who caught the fish[1]. In an *Akar-Bale* version it was *Da Pečerol* who caught the fish (*koroyadi*). *Pečerol* is the bulbul (*Otocompsia emeria*). I have the name *koroyadi* in my notes as being *Sphyraena acutipinnis*, but the identification is a doubtful one. In the *Aka-Kede* tribe there is a version in which it is stated that one of the ancestors captured a fish called *talepo*. This does not seem to be the same species of fish as that called *koro-yiti-čau* or *koroyadi* in the South. In the North Andaman the legend is that *Perjido*, the son of *Biliku*, shot a large eel (*bol*) with an arrow, and in its endeavours to get free from the arrow the eel wriggled about till it made all the creeks.

In the Southern tribes there is a legend that relates how the pig first got its senses. A version from the *A-Pučikwar* tribe is as follows.

"*Ta Mita* (Sir Dove) went into the jungle and found a lot of pigs. They did not run away when he came because they had no eyes to see him, no ears to hear, and no nostrils with which to smell. They had no mouths. *Mita* made mouths for them and gave them tusks which he made of *tobur* wood. He made

[1] Man, *op. cit.* p. 165.

eyes and ears and nostrils in their heads and taught them how to grunt and how to sneeze[1]."

Another version from the same tribe is as follows.

"At first the pigs had neither nose nor ears nor eyes. They used to stand about at *Wota-emi* when the ancestors lived there. The people ate a great many of them. They were such a nuisance that *Mita* (Dove), the wife of *Tomo*, thought of a plan to get them out of the way. She bored holes in their heads, two for eyes, two for ears, and two for nostrils. The pigs ran off into the forest where they have been ever since."

I did not obtain any version of this legend from the Northern tribes. The *Aka-Kede* have a different legend about the pigs.

"At first there were no pigs. One of the ancestors, *Mimi Čau* (Lady Civet-cat), invented a new game, and made the ancestors run on all fours and grunt. Those playing were turned into pigs, and went to live in the jungle. *Mimi Čau* became a civet-cat (*čau*)."

In the North Andaman there is a legend connected with the pig which explains the origin of the dugong.

"*Perjido* was the first man to catch a pig. He went into the forest and found a pig. *Perjido* was hungry. He caught the pig and took it home. The pig had no eyes nor ears nor mouth. *Perjido* did not disembowel the pig, nor did he sever the joints of its legs[2]. He made a fire and put the pig on it. The pig swelled up in the heat of the fire and burst. This made holes in the pig's head, two for ears, two for eyes, two for nostrils. The pig perceived that it was being burnt. It jumped up from the fire and ran away. *Perjido* threw a *kobo* (*Licuala*) leaf at it. The pig ran into the sea and became a dugong. The leaf became its flipper."

In the *Aka-Čari* tribe there is a legend describing the origin of turtles.

"At first there was only one big turtle. He came to the camp of the *Aka-Čari* people and called them, saying 'Bring your canoes and catch me.' They got into their canoes and

---

[1] The sneezing (the word is translated literally) is a sort of whistling noise that the wild pigs make when they suspect danger.

[2] The Andamanese always disembowel a pig and sever the joints of its legs before they place it on a fire.

followed the turtle. They could not catch him. The turtle swam away and the canoes followed. When the canoes were far from land the big turtle came and upset the canoes. The men were all turned into turtles of the same kind and size as those that are seen now. The canoes (and the big turtle?) were turned into a reef."

In the South Andaman it is supposed that the custom of scarifying the skin was invented by the first ancestor of the Andamanese, the monitor lizard. An *Akar-Bale* version of the story is as follows.

"*Duku* (Monitor Lizard) lived with his wife *Bain* (Civet-cat). *Duku* said 'I am going to scarify myself.' His wife tried to dissuade him. He would not listen to her. He went into the jungle and found a piece of *tolma* (quartz) and scarified himself all over. His wife was very angry and asked him why he had done it. *Duku* replied 'I look very well like this, and you will see, all the other people will do the same'."

Mr Man gives a version of the same legend.

"*Maia Duku*, who appears to be identical with *Tomo*, is said to have been the first to tattoo himself. One day, while out on a fishing expedition, he shot an arrow; missing its object it struck a hard substance which proved to be a piece of iron, the first ever found. With it *Duku* made an arrow-head and tattooed himself, after which he sang the ditty:—

> *Toŋ ma lir pireŋa? toŋ yitiken! toŋ yitiken!*
> *toŋ ma lir pireŋa? toŋ yitiken!*

the interpretation of which is

> 'What can now strike me?
> I am tattooed, I am tattooed!' etc. (Da capo)[1]."

It would seem that Mr Man, or else his informant, was not very clear about the details of the legend. In the South Andaman scarification is never performed with an arrow-head, nor with any instrument of iron, but with a flake of quartz or glass. It is only in the North and Middle Andaman that an arrow-head is used for such a purpose, and even then it is only so used to make the big scars on the back and chest, the ordinary scarifica-

---

[1] Man, *op. cit.* p. 170.

tion being performed with a flake of stone or glass. The legend is certainly a Southern one, and the song given is in the *Aka-Bea* language. The accuracy of the transcription of the legend therefore seems very doubtful.

Yams and honey, being two of the most important foods of the Andaman Islanders, are the subject of several legends. A common belief about yams is that they were made, or their qualities were first discovered, by *Biliku* or *Puluga*. We have already seen that there is a special connection between *Biliku* (or *Puluga*) and the yams and other edible roots. There are also other legends, however, on the same subject. An account of the first discovery of the yam called *gono* is contained in the *Akar-Bale* legend of the origin of night, already given[1].

In the North Andaman the following tale is told about the discovery of one kind of yam.

"*Maia Dik* (Sir Prawn) discovered *kǫnmo* (*Dioscorea* sp.). He was very hungry and went to look for something to eat. He found a very large *kǫnmo*. There was only one *kǫnmo*. He cooked it in the fire and ate as much as he could. He dashed the remainder on a rock, and the fragments scattered everywhere and grew into fresh plants. After this there were plenty of *kǫnmo* everywhere."

A legend is also told in the North Andaman about the first discovery of another kind of yam.

"*Maia Pulimu* (Sir Fly) and *Maia Mǫičo* (Sir Rail) went to hunt pig. They killed one pig. There was nothing to tie up the pig (to carry it home). *Maia Pulimu* went to look for a creeper (with which to tie up the pig). He caught hold of a creeper and pulled it and found it was a *mino* (*Dioscorea* sp.). *Maia Pulimu* was a long time away. *Maia Mǫičo* went and found some creeper for himself and tied up the pig and carried it home. When *Maia Pulimu* came back he found that *Maia Mǫičo* had gone and taken the pig. He followed him and went home. He showed the ancestors how to cook and eat *mino*."

I believe that there is a fuller version of this legend, which I was unable, however, to obtain. Another of my informants told me the story as follows.

[1] Page 214.

"*Mimi Moičo* (Lady Rail) had a son *Pulimu* (Fly). *Pulimu* found a *mino* in the forest and brought it to his mother. They roasted it in the fire."

Mr Man gives a story from the South Andaman.

"Another of their antediluvian ancestors was famous for propagating yams. This was *Maia Bumroag*, who in shooting an arrow, struck the creeper belonging to the favourite variety called *gono*; his curiosity being excited he dug up the root, and tasted it: the result being satisfactory, he informed his friends of his discovery, and they all feasted upon it; when they had had sufficient, he scattered the remains in different directions; this apparent waste so angered his mother that, on pretence of shaving him, she split his head open with a flint. After his death it was found that the act for which he had suffered had tended to the spread of the plant which is now plentiful[1]."

In the North Andaman it is supposed that honey was discovered by *Perjido* the son of *Biliku*.

"*Perjido* was the first to eat honey. One day he went to shoot fish. He saw a *nyuri* (*Plotosus* sp.). The *nyuri* disappeared amongst the roots of the mangrove trees. *Perjido* was looking for the fish. There was a honeycomb in a mangrove tree. *Perjido* saw its reflection in the water. He took some fire and tried to get the honey out of the water[2]. The water put out the fire. He could not get the honey. He went home and told his mother what he had been doing. She went with him and saw the honey. 'What a fool you are' she said, 'don't you see that it is in the trees.' *Perjido* took some fire and smoked out the bees and took the honey. After that *Perjido* used to go and collect honey. He ate it all himself. He did not tell the others (the ancestors) about it. *Maia Porubi* (Sir Frog) found out that *Perjido* was getting honey and eating it. He went in to the forest to look for some. He found five or six combs. He ate them all and brought none home to his children. *Beret* (a smaller species of frog) was the child of *Porubi*. One day *Beret* said to his father 'Bring us some honey.' The children went with their father and showed him the combs in the trees.

[1] Man, *op. cit.* p. 170.
[2] In taking a honeycomb the natives often drive away the bees with fire or smoke.

Pǫrubi went up the tree, and each time he ate the honey in the tree and did not bring any of it down for his children. Then *Bęręt* saw another honeycomb in a very tall tree. He pointed it out to his father. *Pǫrubi* went up to get it. *Bęręt* cut the creeper up which his father had climbed[1]. *Pǫrubi* wrapped up the honeycomb to bring it down. *Bęręt* said 'Father, this creeper is bad. How will you come down?' *Pǫrubi* replied 'How can it be bad, when I have just climbed up it?' *Bęręt* made some sharp stakes of *čǫm* (*Areca*) wood, and put them round the tree. *Pǫrubi* jumped (or fell) from the tree on to the stakes and was killed. *Bęręt* took the honey and ran away home."

In the *Aka-Čari* tribe there is another legend connected with the frog (*pǫrubi*) which may conveniently be given here.

"The ancestors were at enmity with *Maia Pǫrubi*. They went to kill him. They shot him with their arrows, but they could not kill him. *Maia Pǫrubi* caught hold of them all in his arms, and jumped into the sea. He jumped from the hill called *Čauanara*. He found a big round stone (boulder) and put the people under it and left them there. All the people turned into stone, and may be seen there now. The next night some more of the people went to hunt turtle near *Maia Pǫrubi's* place. They caught a turtle and shouted[2]. *Maia Pǫrubi* heard them shouting. 'They are coming again to kill me,' he said. While they were catching turtle he threw a round stone at them. The stone sank the canoe. The canoe and the people in it were turned to stone."

A story in which there is a connection between honey and a toad is given by Mr Man.

"Another curious fable is told to account for a drought from which their early ancestors suffered: it relates that once upon a time, in the dry season, a woodpecker discovered a black honeycomb in the hollow of a tree; while regaling himself on this dainty he observed a toad eyeing him wistfully from below, so he invited him to join in the feast; the toad gladly accepted, whereupon the woodpecker lowered a creeper, giving instructions to

---

[1] In climbing a tall tree the Andamanese choose a stout cane or other creeper depending from one of the branches of the tree, and climb up it.

[2] The natives express their joy at a success in hunting by shouting.

his guest to fasten his bucket (*dakar*) thereto, and then to seat himself in it, so that he might be drawn up. The toad complied with the directions and the woodpecker proceeded to haul him up; but just when he had brought him near the comb he mischievously let go the creeper, and his confiding and expectant guest experienced an unpleasant fall. The trick so exasperated him that he at once repaired to the streams far and near in the island and drained them, the result of which was that great distress was occasioned to all the birds, as well as to the rest of the animate creation. The success of his revenge so delighted the toad that, to show his satisfaction, and to add to the annoyance of his enemies, he thoughtlessly began to dance, whereupon all the water flowed from him, and the drought soon terminated[1]."

One of the incidents of the North Andaman story of the frog (*Pọrubi*) and his son (*Beret*) appears in a different story from the South and Middle Andaman. The following is an *Aka-Kọl* version of this legend.

"*Ta Mita* (Sir Dove) and *Ta Kọio* (a species of small bird) went hunting together and got a great number of pigs. *Ta Kọio* told *Ta Mita* to get some canes to tie up all the pigs. As soon as *Ta Mita* had gone to look for the cane, *Ta Kọio* went up a big *Dipterocarpus* tree, taking half the pigs with him. He came down and took the rest of the pigs. He stayed up in the tree with the pigs. When *Ta Mita* came back he found that the pigs had disappeared. He was very angry and went home. As there was nothing to eat, *Mita* and his two children, *Čada* and *Čoda* (two species of fish) went fishing. *Kọio* was still up the tree. He was cooking the pigs up there. *Mita* and his children passed under the tree and some burning resin[2] fell on them. In this way they discovered that *Kọio* was in the tree. *Mita* planned to punish *Kọio*. He cut a great number of sharp stakes of *Areca* wood and fixed them all round the tree, pointing upwards. *Kọio* was asleep. *Mita* made the tree sink into the ground. As soon as it was low enough he took some water and threw it into the

[1] Man, *op. cit.* p. 173.
[2] The narrator said "resin." The *Dipterocarpus* tree does not produce resin, but a sort of oil. The marks on the two fishes owe their origin to this incident.

ear of the sleeping *Koio*, who awoke in a fright and jumped from the tree. He was impaled on the stakes of wood and so died."

Another version of the same tale was obtained from the *Akar-Bale* tribe.

"*Da Bumu* (a species of bird) went hunting pig with *Da Berakwe* (another species of bird), and they got a large number of pigs. Then *Berakwe* said to *Bumu* 'We want some cane to tie up all these pigs. You go and get it.' When *Bumu* had gone *Berakwe* climbed up into a big *Dipterocarpus* tree, taking all the pigs with him, except one very small one which he left behind. When *Bumu* came back with the cane he found only one small pig, and he was very angry. He went home with the pig. *Bumu's* wife *Yakoy* (a species of fish) said 'I am very hungry. We will go and get some fish by night.' At night *Yakoy* went out to get some fish and she passed under the tree where *Berakwe* was cooking his pigs. Some burning resin fell on her and burnt her. She looked up and saw *Berakwe* and said 'Oh! there you are; you stole all my husband's pigs.' She went home and told *Bumu*. In the morning *Bumu* got up very early and cut a number of pointed stakes of *Areca* (*čam*) wood, and fixed them all round the tree where *Berakwe* was, with the sharp points upwards. Then *Bumu* made the tree sink gradually into the ground. *Berakwe* fell from the tree on to the stakes and so was killed. *Bumu* and his wife got the pigs."

Mr Man records a version of the same story.

"The legend regarding the origin of the evil spirits known as *Čol* is as follows :—Their ancestor, *Maia Čol*, one day stole a pig which had been captured by *Maia Kolwot*, and climbed up into a gurjon-tree with his prize. Now *Maia Kolwot* was remarkable for his great strength, and being enraged, determined to revenge himself; he thereupon planted a number of spikes all round the tree in which the thief had taken refuge, and then proceeded to force it into the ground. On finding that if he remained where he was, he must inevitably be buried alive, *Maia Čol* sprang off the tree, and thereby met a more terrible fate, for he was impaled on the spikes, and perished miserably. His disembodied spirit did not pass to *Čaitan* (Hades), but took up its abode on the invisible bridge, where, by *Puluga's* orders, numbers of his descendants were sent to join him, in the form of black birds with long tails[1]."

In reference to this version it may be noted that the *Čǫl* are not "spirits" if that word is used to translate the native term *čauga* or *lau*. *Čǫl* is the name of a species of bird, which I believe is the racket-tailed drongo. These birds, though according to Mr Man they live on the rainbow, are to be seen every day in the jungle, and may be heard calling *čǫl! čǫl! čǫl!*

Throughout the Great Andaman there is a belief in a huge animal that haunts the jungles, or that haunted them in the days of the ancestors. In the North Andaman this beast is called *Jĭrmu*. In the days of the ancestors it is supposed to have lived at *Ulibi-taŋ*, where it attacked and killed any men and women who came in its way. No detailed legend about the *Jĭrmu* was obtained.

In the *Akar-Bale* language *Kočurag-boa* is the name of the same or a similar monster. In the *A-Pučikwar* language it is called *Uču*. This is the name applied to two rocks of limestone which are situated about two or three miles south of *Wota-emi*, one being in a mangrove swamp, and the other some little way out in the sea. The following legend is told about these rocks.

"In the early days of the Andamanese, *Ta Pętie* (Sir Monitor Lizard), the first ancestor, went into the jungle and found a *čoti* tree, up which he climbed to eat the fruit. The other people (who lived with him at *Wota-emi*) came and found him, and *Ta Pętie* threw down some of the fruit to them, which they ate. The people began to bully *Pętie* to make him throw down more of the fruit. *Pętie* got angry and said 'If you bully me like that I will call the *Uču*, and they will kill you all.' The people only laughed at him. *Pętie* called the *Uču*, calling '*Dire! dire!*' The *Uču* came, one male and one female. They caught all the people and ate them. Only *Pętie* they did not eat because he was up in the high tree. The *Uču* went off to cross the strait to *Tǫl-l'oko-tima*. They had eaten so much that they were very heavy and stuck in the sand and mud at the edge of the mangrove swamp. When *Pętie* came down from the tree he found all the people gone. He said 'Hallo! the *Uču* must have eaten

---

[1] Man, *op. cit.* p. 173.

them all.' He went to look. He found the *Uču* stuck fast at the edge of the mangrove swamp, so that they could not move. He cut open their bellies and all the people came out, for the *Uču* had swallowed them whole. The *Uču* are there to this day."

When elephants were first introduced into the Andamans for the use of the Forest Department, they were named *Uču* by the natives, and have ever since retained that name. Similarly the natives of the Northern tribes call them *Jirmu*.

In the *Akar-Bale* tribe there is a legend to account for the origin of a rock standing in the sea at a place called *Kwaičo-bur*.

"*Ra-gumul Kwokol* went fishing with his bow and arrows in the sea. His bow and arrows and he himself were turned into stone, and may be seen there to the present day."

Kwokol is the common tree-lizard. *Ra-gumul* is the term applied to a youth or girl who has just passed through the pig-eating ceremony described in Chap. II. A youth is not permitted to handle a bow for some days after the ceremony in question. A version of the same legend is recorded by Mr Man.

"The story regarding certain *Tomola* who failed to observe the rules for neophytes, states that, on the day after they broke their fast of *reg-jiri* (kidney-fat of pig), they left the encampment without giving notice of their intention to their friends, and the result was that, when they were missed and searched for, it was found that they had gone to the shore to fish, and had there met a sad fate; the body of one was discovered adhering to a large boulder, and turned into stone, while the other, likewise in a state of petrifaction, was standing erect beside it[1]."

A reef on the east side of Ritchie's Archipelago is said to have originated as follows.

"The people of *Kwaičo* went to *Jila* to hunt turtle, taking two canoes. While they were away their wives made up a big fire in the evening at *Kwaičo*. The hunters and their canoes were turned to stone, and formed the reefs that are now there."

I believe that the explanation of this story is the belief that the moon is angry when a bright fire is visible at the time when he rises in the evening shortly after sunset[2].

[1] Man, *op. cit.* p. 169. [2] *Vide supra*, p. 142.

There seems to be a legend relating to a large snake called *ǫr-čubi* in the North Andaman, but I was not able to obtain a detailed version. The following was told me in *Aka-Jeru*.

"At *Dalamio*, in the time of the ancestors, there used to be a big snake of the kind called *ǫr-čubi*. He used to catch men and women when they were gathering honey, and kill them and eat them."

An *Akar-Bale* version is a little fuller.

"There was a man named *Biča* who went to look for honey in the jungle. He saw a big snake (*wara-jobo*) and from its neck was hanging a honeycomb. The snake was as big as a tree. 'Why don't you make your honey in the trees?' *Biča* said to the bees. He went home and called several of the men. They took their bows and arrows. They found the snake, and shot it with a great many arrows. They could not kill the snake, which ran away and was never seen again."

An *Akar-Bale* story relates how the first murder came to pass.

"*Da Ko* (Sir Crow) was the first of the Andamanese. He lived at *Kared-čar-buaro* with his wife *In Mud* (Lady Dove). He had a friend, *Badgi-beria* (Hawk). *Badgi-beria* had no wife and was jealous of *Da Ko* and wanted to get his wife. When *Da Ko* knew this he was very angry. He went into the jungle and hid himself. By and by he saw *Badgi-beria* and *Mud* coming along the path together. He took his bow and arrows and killed them."

Another *Akar-Bale* story about the dove is as follows.

"*Mud* and *Kulal* were cooking pig and got very hot. They went to bathe and were turned into birds."

Mud is the bronze-winged dove, *Chalcophaps indica*, and *kulal* is the teal, *Nettium albigulare*.

In the North Andaman there are tales about the sea-eagle (*kǫlo*). One is to the effect that at first he used *kǫbo* (*Licuala*) leaves to fly with. This was before he had wings of his own. Another story is as follows.

"*Maia Kǫlo* (Sir Sea-eagle) lived at *Čona* in *Tau-'ra-miku*. He had a hut in the top of a *tǫrǫktato* tree. He was unmarried.

When the men went fishing he used to steal their wives. He would only take good-looking girls. He would call out to a girl to come and catch hold of his foot, saying 'I have a fish for you.' If an old or ugly woman came, he would say 'No! not you; go away.' When a young woman came and caught hold of his foot he flew away with her to his hut in the tree."

CHAPTER V

THE INTERPRETATION OF ANDAMANESE CUSTOMS AND BELIEFS: CEREMONIAL

THE present chapter is devoted to an attempt to interpret some of the beliefs and customs of the Andaman Islanders, as they have been described in the earlier part of this work. By the interpretation of a custom is meant the discovery, not of its origin, but of its meaning. The system of beliefs and customs that exists to-day in the Andamans is the result of a long process of evolution. To seek the origin of these customs, as the word origin is here used, is to seek to know the details of the historical process by which they have come into existence. In the absence of all historical records, the most that we could do would be to attempt to make a hypothetical reconstruction of the past, which, in the present state of ethnological science, would be of very doubtful utility[1].

It is otherwise with the meaning of these customs. Every custom and belief of a primitive society plays some determinate part in the social life of the community, just as every organ of a living body plays some part in the general life of the organism. The mass of institutions, customs and beliefs forms a single whole or system that determines the life of the society, and the life of a society is not less real, or less subject to natural laws, than the

---

[1] The making of such hypothetical reconstructions of the past has been regarded by a number of writers as the principal if not the sole task of ethnology. My own view is that such studies can never be of any great *scientific* value. Although, within narrow limits, particularly when the method is applied to the facts of language and material culture, it is possible to reach conclusions of some degree of probability, yet by their very nature all such hypotheses are incapable of verification. Moreover, the purpose of scientific studies is to discover general laws, and hypotheses as to events in the past of which we have and can have no certain knowledge will not provide suitable material from which to draw generalisations.

life of an organism. To continue the analogy, the study of the meaning of savage customs is a sort of social physiology, and is to be distinguished from the study of origins, or changes of custom in just the same way that animal physiology is distinguished from the biology that deals with the origin of species, the causes of variation, and the general laws of evolution.

The problems that this chapter presents are therefore not historical but psychological or sociological. We have to explain why it is that the Andamanese think and act in certain ways. The explanation of each single custom is provided by showing what is its relation to the other customs of the Andamanese and to their general system of ideas and sentiments.

Thus the subject of the present chapter is not in any way affected by questions of the historical origin of the customs with which it deals, but is concerned only with those customs as they exist at the present day. Nor are we concerned with the comparison of the customs of the Andamanese with those of other savage races. Such comparisons are not only valueless for our purpose, but might be misleading. To draw any valid conclusion from the comparison of two apparently similar customs in two different societies, we must be sure that they are really similar, and to do this we need to know the true meaning of each of them considered by itself. The true comparative method consists of the comparison, not of one isolated custom of one society with a similar custom of another, but of the whole system of institutions, customs and beliefs of one society with that of another. In a word, what we need to compare is not institutions but social systems or types.

It is often urged that in ethnology description and interpretation should be most carefully separated. So far as this means that the facts observed by the ethnologist should be recorded free from all bias of interpretation, the necessity cannot be too often or too strongly urged. If, however, it is meant to imply that efforts at interpretation are to be excluded from works of descriptive ethnology, there is much to be said against such an opinion. In trying to interpret the institutions of a primitive society the field ethnologist has a great advantage over those who know the facts only at second hand. However exact and detailed the description of a primitive people may be, there remains much that cannot be put into such a description. Living, as he must, in daily contact with the people he is studying, the field ethnologist comes gradually to "understand" them, if we may use the term. He acquires a series of multitudinous impressions, each slight and often vague, that guide him in his dealings with them. The better the observer the more accurate will be his general impression of the mental peculiarities of the race. This general impression it is impossible to analyse, and so to record and convey to others. Yet it may be of the greatest service when it comes to interpreting the beliefs and practices of a primitive society. If it does not give any positive aid towards a correct interpretation, it at least prevents errors into which it is only too easy for those to fall who have not the same immediate knowledge of the people and their ways. Indeed it may be urged, with some reason, that attempts to interpret the beliefs of savages without any first-hand knowledge of the people whose beliefs are in question, are at the best unsatisfactory and open to many possibilities of error.

The present position of ethnological studies may well be regarded as anomalous. Many of the observers engaged in recording the customs of primitive people are very imperfectly acquainted with modern theories of sociology. One result of this is that they often neglect to record anything concerning matters that are of fundamental importance for the theorist[1]. On the other hand those engaged in elaborating hypotheses do not, as a rule, observe for themselves the facts to be explained, but have to rely on what are in many cases imperfect documents, being thus unwittingly led into errors that might have been avoided. In this science, as in others, if progress is to be made, the elaboration of hypotheses and the observation and classification of facts must be carried on as interdependent parts of one process, and no advantage, but rather great disadvantage, results from the false division of labour whereby theorists and observers

---

[1] It may be worth while to mention that the interpretation of Andamanese customs given in this chapter was not worked out until after I had left the islands. Had it been otherwise I should have made careful enquiries into subjects which, as it was, escaped my notice.

work independently and without systematic cooperation. The most urgent need of ethnology at the present time is a series of investigations of the kind here attempted, in which the observation and the analysis and interpretation of the institutions of some one primitive people are carried on together by the ethnologist working in the field.

It is clear that such studies need to be based on a scientific and carefully elaborated method. Unfortunately ethnologists are not yet agreed as to the methods of their science. The question of method is therefore, at the present time, of the greatest importance, and for this reason I have tried, in the present chapter, to present the argument in such a way that the various steps of the analysis shall be immediately apparent, so that the reader may be able not only to judge the value of the conclusions, but also to form a clear idea of the psychological methods by which they are reached.

Any attempt to explain or interpret the particular beliefs and customs of a savage people is necessarily based on some general psychological hypothesis as to the real nature of the phenomena to be explained. The sound rule of method is therefore to formulate clearly and explicitly the working hypothesis on which the interpretation is based. It is only in this way that its value can be properly tested.

The hypothesis that seems to be most usually adopted by English writers on anthropology is that the beliefs of savage peoples are due to attempts on the part of primitive man to explain to himself the phenomena of life and nature. The student of human customs, examining his own mind, finds that one of the motives most constantly present in his consciousness is the desire to understand, to explain—in other words what we call scientific curiosity. He concludes that this motive is equally insistent in the mind of primitive man. Thus he supposes that primitive man, wishing to explain the phenomena of death and of sleep and dreams, framed a hypothesis that every man possesses a soul or spiritual double[1]. The hypothesis, once formulated, is supposed to have been accepted and believed

---

[1] Tylor, *Primitive Culture*, I, 387.

because it satisfied this need of comprehension. On this view the belief in a soul (animism) is exactly similar in character to the scientific belief in atoms, let us say. The same general hypothesis appears in the explanation of totemism as having arisen as a theory invented by primitive man in order to explain the phenomena of pregnancy and childbirth[1].

On this hypothesis the beliefs are primary, arising first merely as beliefs and then acquiring the power to influence action and so giving rise to all sorts of ceremonies and customs. Thus these customs are only to be explained by showing that they depend on particular beliefs. This hypothesis, which we may call the intellectualist hypothesis, has never, so far as I am aware, been very clearly formulated or defended, but it does seem to underlie many of the explanations of the customs of primitive man to be found in works on ethnology.

A second hypothesis explains the beliefs of primitive man as being due to emotions of surprise and terror[2], or of awe and wonder[3] aroused by the contemplation of the phenomena of nature.

Both these hypotheses may be held together, one being used to explain some primitive beliefs and the other to explain others[4].

Doubtless there are other psychological hypotheses underlying the many attempts that have been made to explain the customs of primitive peoples, but these two seem to be the most important and the most widespread. They are mentioned here, not in order to criticise them, but in order to contrast them with the hypothesis to be formulated in the present chapter[5].

Stated as briefly as possible the working hypothesis here adopted is as follows. (1) A society depends for its existence on the presence in the minds of its members of a certain system of

[1] Frazer, *Totemism and Exogamy*, IV.
[2] Max Müller, *Physical Religion*, p. 119.
[3] Marett, *Threshold of Religion*.
[4] McDougall, *Introduction to Social Psychology*, Chap. XIII, seems to combine the two hypotheses.
[5] For a criticism of the hypotheses of animism and naturism as explanations of primitive religion see Durkheim, *Les Formes Élémentaires de la Vie Religieuse*, Book I, chapters 2 and 3.

sentiments[1] by which the conduct of the individual is regulated in conformity with the needs of the society. (2) Every feature of the social system itself and every event or object that in any way affects the well-being or the cohesion of the society becomes an object of this system of sentiments. (3) In human society the sentiments in question are not innate but are developed in the individual by the action of the society upon him. (4) The ceremonial customs of a society are a means by which the sentiments in question are given collective expression on appropriate occasions. (5) The ceremonial (i.e. collective) expression of any sentiment serves both to maintain it at the requisite degree of intensity in the mind of the individual and to transmit it from one generation to another. Without such expression the sentiments involved could not exist.

Using the term "social function" to denote the effects of an institution (custom or belief) in so far as they concern the society and its solidarity or cohesion, the hypothesis of this chapter may be more briefly resumed in the statement that the social function of the ceremonial customs of the Andaman Islanders is to maintain and to transmit from one generation to another the emotional dispositions on which the society (as it is constituted) depends for its existence.

The present chapter contains an attempt to apply this hypothesis to the ceremonial customs of the Andaman Islanders. An attempt will be made to show that there is a correspondence between the customs and beliefs of the Andamanese and a certain system of social sentiments, and that there is also a correspondence between these sentiments and the manner in which the society is constituted. It is an attempt to discover necessary connections between the different characters of a society as they exist in the present. No attempt will be made to discover or imagine the historical process by which these customs have come into existence.

For the clearer understanding of the argument it is necessary to draw attention to a few rules of method that will be observed. (1) In explaining any given custom it is necessary to take

---

[1] Sentiment,—an organised system of emotional tendencies centred about some object.

into account the explanation given by the natives themselves. Although these explanations are not of the same kind as the scientific explanations that are the objects of our search yet they are of great importance as data. Like the civilised man of Western Europe the savage of the Andamans seeks to rationalise his behaviour; being impelled to certain actions by mental dispositions of whose origin and real nature he is unaware, he seeks to formulate reasons for his conduct, or even if he does not so when left to himself he is compelled to when the enquiring ethnologist attacks him with questions. Such a reason as is produced by this process of rationalisation is rarely if ever identical with the psychological cause of the action that it justifies, yet it will nearly always help us in our search for the cause. At any rate the reason given as explaining an action is so intimately connected with the action itself that we cannot regard any hypothesis as to the meaning of a custom as being satisfactory unless it explains not only the custom but also the reasons that the natives give for following it. (2) The assumption is made that when the same or a similar custom is practised on different occasions it has the same or a similar meaning in all of them. For example, there are different occasions on which a personal name is avoided; it is assumed that there is something in common to all these occasions and that the meaning of the custom is to be discovered by ascertaining what that common element is. (3) It is assumed that when different customs are practised together on one and the same occasion there is a common element in the customs. This rule is the inverse of the last. As an example may be mentioned the different customs observed by mourners, which may be assumed to be all related to one another. The discovery of what is common to them all will explain the meaning of each. (4) I have avoided, as being misleading as well as unnecessary, any comparison of Andamanese customs with similar customs of other races. Only in one or two instances have I broken this rule, and in those I believe I am justified by special considerations.

We can conveniently begin by considering the Andamanese marriage ceremony, which is one of the simplest and most easily understood. The main feature of it is that the bride and bridegroom are required publicly to embrace each other. In the North Andaman the embrace is made gradually, by stages as it were, each stage being more intimate than the preceding. At first the two sit side by side, then their arms are placed around each other, and finally the bridegroom is made to sit on the bride's lap[1].

Everywhere in human life the embrace is employed as an expression of such feelings as love, affection, friendship, i.e. of feelings of attachment between persons. There is no need to enquire into the psycho-physical basis of this expression. It is probably intimately related to the nursing of the infant by the mother, and is certainly very closely connected with the development of the sex instinct. It is sufficient for our purpose to satisfy ourselves that the embrace in all its forms does always express feelings of one generic kind. Nor is it necessary for us to consider the peculiar form of the Andamanese embrace, in which one person sits down and extends his or her legs, while the other person sits on the lap so formed and the two wrap their arms round one another's necks and shoulders.

The meaning of the marriage ceremony is readily seen. By marriage the man and woman are brought into a special and intimate relation to one another; they are, as we say, united. The social union is symbolised or expressed by the physical union of the embrace. The ceremony brings vividly to the minds of the young couple and also to those of the spectators the consciousness that the two are entering upon a new social relation of which the essential feature is the affection in which they must hold one another.

The rite has two aspects according as we regard it from the standpoint of the witnesses or from that of the couple themselves. The witnesses, by their presence, give their sanction to the union that is thus enacted before them. The man who conducts the ceremony is merely the active representative of the community; in what he does and says he acts as a deputy and not as a private individual. Thus the ceremony serves to make it clear that the marriage is a matter which concerns not only those who are entering into it, but the whole community,

[1] See p. 73 above.

and its occasional performance serves to keep alive this sentiment with regard to marriage in general. The existence of the sentiment is shown in the reprobation felt and often expressed at an irregular marriage, in which the couple unite without a ceremony; such a union showing a contemptuous or careless thrusting aside of an important social principle.

For the witnesses, then, the ceremony serves to awaken to activity and to express this sentiment; but it also serves as a recognition on their part of the change of status of the marrying pair. It makes them realise that henceforward the young couple must be treated no longer as children but as responsible adults, and it is thus the occasion of a change of sentiment towards those whose social position is being changed. For in the society of the Andamans there is a very marked division between married and unmarried persons in the way in which they are regarded by others, and in respect of their place in the community.

The married couple are made to realise, in a different way and with a much greater intensity of feeling, these same two things; first, that their union in marriage is a matter that concerns the whole community, and second, that they are entering a new condition, with new privileges but also with new duties and obligations. For them, indeed, the ceremony is a sort of ordeal from which they would only too gladly escape, and which, by the powerful emotions it evokes in them very vividly impresses upon them what their marriage means.

The wedding gifts that are bestowed upon the young couple are an expression of the general good-will towards them. The giving of presents is a common method of expressing friendship in the Andamans. Thus when two friends meet after separation, the first thing they do after having embraced and wept together, is to give one another presents. In most instances the giving is reciprocal, and is therefore really an exchange. If a present be given as a sign of good-will the giver expects to receive a present of about equal value in return. The reason for this is obvious; the one has expressed his good-will towards the other, and if the feeling is reciprocated a return present must be given in order to express it. So also it would be an insult to refuse a present offered, for to do so would be equivalent to rejecting the good-will it represents. At marriage the giving is one-sided, no return being expected, for it is an expression not of personal friendship on the part of the givers, but of the general social good-will and approval. It is for this reason that it is the duty of everybody who is present to make some gift to the newly-married pair.

In another simple ceremony, the peace-making ceremony of the North Andaman[1], the meaning is again easily discovered; the symbolism of the dance being indeed at once obvious to a witness, though perhaps not quite so obvious from the description given. The dancers are divided into two parties. The actions of the one party throughout are expressions of their aggressive feelings towards the other. This is clear enough in the shouting, the threatening gestures, and the way in which each member of the "attacking" party gives a good shaking to each member of the other party. On the other side what is expressed may be described as complete passivity; the performers stand quite still throughout the whole dance, taking care to show neither fear nor resentment at the treatment to which they have to submit. Thus those of the one side give collective expression to their collective anger, which is thereby appeased. The others, by passively submitting to this, humbling themselves before the just wrath of their enemies, expiate their wrongs. Anger appeased dies down; wrongs expiated are forgiven and forgotten; the enmity is at an end.

The screen of fibre against which the passive participants in the ceremony stand has a peculiar symbolic meaning that will be explained later in the chapter. The only other elements of the ceremony are the weeping together, which will be dealt with very soon, and the exchange of weapons, which is simply a special form of the rite of exchanging presents as an expression of good-will. The special form is particularly appropriate as it would seem to ensure at least some months of friendship, for you cannot go out to fight a man with his weapons while he has yours.

The purpose of the ceremony is clearly to produce a change

[1] Page 134.

in the feelings of the two parties towards one another, feelings of enmity being replaced through it by feelings of friendship and solidarity. It depends for its effect on the fact that anger and similar aggressive feelings may be appeased by being freely expressed. Its social function is to restore the condition of solidarity between two local groups that has been destroyed by some act of offence.

The marriage ceremony and the peace-making dance both afford examples of the custom which the Andamanese have of weeping together under certain circumstances. The principal occasions of this ceremonial weeping are as follows: (1) when two friends or relatives meet after having been for some time parted, they embrace each other and weep together; (2) at the peace-making ceremony the two parties of former enemies weep together, embracing each other; (3) at the end of the period of mourning the friends of the mourners (who have not themselves been mourning) weep with the latter; (4) after a death the relatives and friends embrace the corpse and weep over it; (5) when the bones of a dead man or woman are recovered from the grave they are wept over; (6) on the occasion of a marriage the relatives of each weep over the bride and bridegroom; (7) at various stages of the initiation ceremonies the female relatives of a youth or girl weep over him or her.

First of all it is necessary to note that not in any of the above-mentioned instances is the weeping simply a spontaneous expression of feeling. It is always a rite the proper performance of which is demanded by custom. (As mentioned in an earlier chapter, the Andamanese are able to sit down and shed tears at will.) Nor can we explain the weeping as being an expression of sorrow. It is true that some of the occasions are such as to produce sorrowful feelings (4 and 5, for example), but there are others on which there would seem to be no reason for sorrow but rather for joy. The Andamanese do weep from sorrow and spontaneously. A child cries when he is scolded or hurt; a widow weeps thinking of her recently dead husband. Men rarely weep spontaneously for any reason, though they shed tears abundantly when taking part in the rite. The weeping on the occasions enumerated is therefore not a spontaneous expression of individual emotion but is an example of what I have called ceremonial customs. In certain circumstances men and women are required by custom to embrace one another and weep, and if they neglected to do so it would be an offence condemned by all right-thinking persons.

According to the postulate of method laid down at the beginning of the chapter we have to seek such an explanation of this custom as will account for all the different occasions on which the rite is performed, since we must assume that one and the same rite has the same meaning in whatever circumstances it may take place. It must be noted, however, that there are two varieties of the rite. In the first three instances enumerated above the rite is reciprocal, i.e. two persons or two distinct groups of persons weep together and embrace each other, both parties to the rite being active. In the other four instances it is one-sided; a person or group of persons weeps over another person (or the relics of a person) who has only a passive part in the ceremony. Any explanation, to be satisfactory, must take account of the difference between these two varieties.

I would explain the rite as being an expression of that feeling of attachment between persons which is of such importance in the almost domestic life of the Andaman society. In other words the purpose of the rite is to affirm the existence of a social bond between two or more persons.

There are two elements in the ceremony, the embrace and the weeping. We have already seen that the embrace is an expression, in the Andamans as elsewhere, of the feeling of attachment, i.e. the feeling of which love, friendship, affection are varieties. Turning to the second element of the ceremony, we are accustomed to think of weeping as more particularly an expression of sorrow. We are familiar, however, with tears of joy, and I have myself observed tears that were the result neither of joy nor of sorrow but of a sudden overwhelming feeling of affection. I believe that we may describe weeping as being a means by which the mind obtains relief from a condition of emotional tension, and that it is because such conditions of tension are most common in feelings of grief and pain that weeping comes to be associated with painful feelings. It is impossible here to discuss this subject, and I am therefore compelled to assume without proof this proposition on which my explanation of the rite is based[1]. My own conclusion, based on careful observation, is that in this rite the weeping is an expression of what has been called the tender emotion[2]. Without doubt, on some of the occasions of the rite, as when weeping over a dead friend, the participants are suffering a painful emotion, but this is evidently not so on all occasions. It is true, however, as I shall show, that on every occasion of the rite there is a condition of emotional tension due to the sudden calling into activity of the sentiment of personal attachment.

When two friends or relatives meet after having been separated, the social relation between them that has been interrupted is about to be renewed. This social relation implies or depends upon the existence of a specific bond of solidarity between them. The weeping rite (together with the subsequent exchange of presents) is the affirmation of this bond. The rite, which, it must be remembered, is obligatory, compels the two participants to act as though they felt certain emotions, and thereby does, to some extent, produce those emotions in them. When the two friends meet their first feeling seems to be one of shyness mingled with pleasure at seeing each other again. This is according to the statements of the natives as well as my own observation. Now this shyness (the Andamanese use the same word as they do for "shame") is itself a condition of emotional tension, which has to be relieved in some way. The embrace awakens to full activity that feeling of affection or friendship that has been dormant and which it is the business of the rite to renew. The weeping gives relief to the emotional tension just noted, and also reinforces the effect of the embrace. This it does owing to the fact that a strong feeling of personal attachment is always produced when two persons join together in sharing and simul-

[1] In a few words the psycho-physical theory here assumed is that weeping is a substitute for motor activity when the kinetic system of the body (motor centres, thyroid, suprarenals, etc.) is stimulated but no effective action in direct response to the stimulus is possible at the moment. When a sentiment is stimulated and action to which it might lead is frustrated, the resultant emotional state is usually painful, and hence weeping is commonly associated with painful states.

[2] McDougall, *Social Psychology*.

taneously expressing one and the same emotion[1]. The little ceremony thus serves to dispel the initial feeling of shyness and to reinstate the condition of intimacy and affection that existed before the separation.

In the peace-making ceremony the purpose of the whole rite is to abolish a condition of enmity and replace it by one of friendship. The once friendly relations between the two groups have been interrupted by a longer or shorter period of antagonism. We have seen that the effect of the dance is to dispel the wrath of the one group by giving it free expression. The weeping that follows is the renewal of the friendship. The rite is here exactly parallel to that on the meeting of two friends, except that not two individuals but two groups are concerned, and that owing to the number of persons involved the emotional condition is one of much greater intensity[2]. Here therefore also we see that the rite is an affirmation of solidarity or social union, in this instance between the groups, and that the rule is in its nature such as to make the participants feel that they are bound to each other by ties of friendship.

We now come to a more difficult example of the rite, that at the end of mourning. It will be shown later in the chapter that during the period of mourning the mourners are cut off from the ordinary life of the community. By reason of the ties that still bind them to the dead person they are placed, as it were, outside the society and the bonds that unite them to their group are temporarily loosened. At the end of the mourning period they re-enter the society and take up once more their place in the social life. Their return to the community is the occasion on which they and their friends weep together. In this instance also, therefore, the rite may be explained as having for its purpose the renewal of the social relations that have been interrupted. This explanation will seem more convincing when we have considered in detail the customs of mourning. If it be accepted, then it

---

[1] Active sympathy, the habitual sharing of joyful and painful emotions, is of the utmost importance in the formation of sentiments of personal attachment.

[2] It is a commonplace of psychology that a collective emotion, i.e. one felt and expressed at the same moment by a number of persons, is felt much more intensely than an unshared emotion of the same kind.

may be seen that in the first three instances of the rite of weeping (those in which the action is reciprocal) we have conditions in which social relations that have been interrupted are about to be renewed, and the rite serves as a ceremony of aggregation.

Let us now consider the second variety of the rite, and first of all its meaning as part of the ceremony of marriage. By marriage the social bonds that have to that time united the bride and bridegroom to their respective relatives, particularly their female relatives such as mother, mother's sister, father's sister and adopted mother, are modified. The unmarried youth or girl is in a position of dependence upon his or her older relatives, and by the marriage this dependence is partly abolished. Whereas the principal duties of the bride were formerly those towards her mother and older female relatives, henceforth her chief duties in life will be towards her husband. The position of the bridegroom is similar, and it must be noted that his social relations with his male relatives are less affected by his marriage than those with his female relatives. Yet, though the ties that have bound the bride and bridegroom to their relatives are about to be modified or partially destroyed by the new ties of marriage with its new duties and rights they will still continue to exist in a weakened and changed condition. The rite of weeping is the expression of this. It serves to make real (by feeling), in those taking part in it, the presence of the social ties that are being modified.

When the mother of the bride or bridegroom weeps at a marriage she feels that her son or daughter is being taken from her care. She has the sorrow of a partial separation and she consoles herself by expressing in the rite her continued feeling of tenderness and affection towards him in the new condition that he is entering upon. For her the chief result of the rite is to make her feel that her child is still an object of her affection, still bound to her by close ties, in spite of the fact that he or she is being taken from her care.

Exactly the same explanation holds with regard to the weeping at the initiation ceremonies. By these ceremonies the youth (or girl) is gradually withdrawn from a condition of dependence on his mother and older female relatives and is made an independent

16—2

member of the community. The initiation is a long process that is only completed by marriage. At every stage of the lengthy ceremonies therefore, the social ties that unite the initiate to these relatives are modified or weakened, and the rite of weeping is the means by which the significance of the change is impressed upon those taking part in it. For the mother the weeping expresses her resignation at her necessary loss, and acts as a consolation by making her feel that her son is still hers, though now being withdrawn from her care. For the boy the rite has a different meaning. He realises that he is no longer merely a child, dependent upon his mother, but is now entering upon manhood. His former feelings towards his mother must be modified. That he is being separated from her is, for him, the most important aspect of the matter, and therefore while she weeps he must give no sign of tenderness in return but must sit passive and silent. So also in the marriage ceremony, the rite serves to impress upon the young man and woman that they are, by reason of the new ties that they are forming with one another, severing their ties with their families.

When a person dies the social bonds that unite him to the survivors are profoundly modified. They are not in an instant utterly destroyed, as we shall see better when we deal with the funeral and mourning customs, for the friends and relatives still feel towards the dead person that affection in which they held him when alive, and this has now become a source of deep grief. It is this affection still binding them to him that they express in the rite of weeping over the corpse. Here rite and natural expression of emotion coincide, but it must be noted that the weeping is obligatory, a matter of duty. In this instance, then, the rite is similar to that at marriage and initiation. The man is by death cut off from the society to which he belonged, and from association with his friends, but the latter still feel towards him that attachment that bound them together while he lived, and it is this attachment that they express when they embrace the lifeless corpse and weep over it.

There remains only one more instance of the rite to be considered. When the period of mourning for a dead person is over and the bones are recovered the modification in the relations between the dead and the living, which begins at death, and is, as we shall see, carried out by the mourning customs and ceremonies, is finally accomplished. The dead person is now entirely cut off from the world of the living, save that his bones are to be treasured as relics and amulets. The weeping over the bones must be taken, I think, as a rite of aggregation whereby the bones as representative of the dead person (all that is left of him) are received back into the society henceforth to fill a special place in the social life. It really constitutes a renewal of social relations with the dead person, after a period during which all active social relations have been interrupted owing to the danger in all contact between the living and the dead. By the rite the affection that was once felt towards the dead person is revived and is now directed to the skeletal relics of the man or woman that once was their object. If this explanation seem unsatisfactory, I would ask the reader to suspend his judgment until the funeral customs of the Andamans have been discussed, and then to return to this point.

The proffered explanation of the rite of weeping should now be plain. I regard it as being the affirmation of a bond of social solidarity between those taking part in it, and as producing in them a realisation of that bond by arousing the sentiment of attachment. In some instances the rite therefore serves to renew social relations when they have been interrupted, and in such instances the rite is reciprocal. In others it serves to show the continued existence of the social bond when it is being weakened or modified, as by marriage, initiation or death. In all instances we may say that the purpose of the rite is to bring about a new state of the affective dispositions that regulate the conduct of persons to one another, either by reviving sentiments that have lain dormant, or producing a recognition of a change in the condition of personal relations.

The study of these simple ceremonies has shown us several things of importance. (1) In every instance the ceremony is the expression of an affective state of mind shared by two or more persons. Thus the weeping rite expresses feelings of solidarity, the exchange of presents expresses good-will. (2) But the ceremonies are not spontaneous expressions of feeling; they are all customary actions to which the sentiment of obligation attaches, which it is the duty of persons to perform on certain definite occasions. It is the duty of everyone in a community to give presents at a wedding; it is the duty of relatives to weep together when they meet. (3) In every instance the ceremony is to be explained by reference to fundamental laws regulating the affective life of human beings. It is not our business here to analyse these phenomena but only to satisfy ourselves that they are real. That weeping is an outlet for emotional excitement, that the free expression of aggressive feelings causes them to die out instead of smouldering on, that an embrace is an expression of feelings of attachment between persons: these are the psychological generalisations upon which are based the explanations given above of various ceremonies of the Andamanese. (4) Finally, we have seen that each of the ceremonies serves to renew or to modify in the minds of those taking part in it some one or more of the social sentiments. The peace-making ceremony is a method by which feelings of enmity are exchanged for feelings of friendship. The marriage rite serves to arouse in the minds of the marrying pair a sense of their obligations as married folk, and to bring about in the minds of the witnesses a change of feeling towards the young people such as should properly accompany their change of social status. The weeping and exchange of presents when friends come together is a means of renewing their feelings of attachment to one another. The weeping at marriage, at initiation, and on the occasion of a death is a reaction of defence or compensation when feelings of solidarity are attacked by a partial breaking of the social ties that bind persons to one another.

In the ceremonial life of the Andamans some part is played by dancing, and it will be convenient to consider next the meaning and function of the dance. It is necessary, however, to deal very briefly with this subject and omit much that would have to be included in an exhaustive study. Thus the ordinary Andaman dance may be looked upon as a form of play; it also shows us the beginnings of the arts of dancing, music and poetry; and therefore in any study pretending to completeness it would be necessary to discuss the difficult problem of the relation between art, play and ceremonial in social life, a subject of too wide a scope to be handled in such an essay as this. For our present purpose we are concerned with the dance only as a form of social ceremonial.

If an Andaman Islander is asked why he dances he gives an answer that amounts to saying that he does so because he enjoys it. Dancing is therefore in general a means of enjoyment. It is frequently a rejoicing. The Andaman Islanders dance after a successful day of hunting; they do not dance if their day has been one of disappointment.

Pleasurable mental excitement finds its natural expression in bodily activity, as we see most plainly in young children and in some animals. And in its turn mere muscular activity is itself a source of pleasure. The individual shouts and jumps for joy; the society turns the jump into a dance, the shout into a song.

The essential character of all dancing is that it is rhythmical, and it is fairly evident that the primary function of this rhythmical nature of the dance is to enable a number of persons to join in the same actions and perform them as one body. In the Andamans at any rate it is clear that the spectacular dance (such as the performance described on page 164) is a late development out of the common dance. And it is probable that the history of the dance is everywhere the same, that it began as a common dance in which all present take some active part, and from this first form (still surviving in our ball-room dances) arose the spectacular dance in which one or more dancers perform before spectators who take no part themselves.

In the Andamans the song is an accompaniment of the dance. The dancing and singing and the marking of the rhythm by clapping and by stamping on the sounding-board are all parts of the one common action in which all join and which for convenience is here spoken of as the dance. It is probable that here again the Andamanese practice shows us the earliest stage in the development of the song, that song and music at first had no independent existence but together with dancing formed one activity. It is reasonable to suppose that the song first came into general use in human society because it provides a means by which a number of persons can utter the same series of sounds together and as with one voice, this being made possible by the fixed rhythm and the fixed pitch of the whole song and of each part of it (i.e. by melody). Once the art of song was in existence its further development was doubtless largely dependent upon the esthetic pleasure that it is able to give. But in the Andamans the esthetic pleasure that the natives get from their simple and monotonous songs seems to me of quite secondary importance as compared with the value of the song as a joint social activity.

The movements of the ordinary Great Andaman dance do not seem to me to be in themselves expressive, or at any rate they are not obviously mimetic like the movements of the dances of many primitive folk. Their function seems to be to bring into activity as many of the muscles of the body as possible. The bending of the body at the hips and of the legs at the knees, with the slightly backward poise of the head and the common position of the arms held in line with the shoulders with the elbows crooked and the thumb and first finger of each hand clasping those of the other, produce a condition of tension of a great number of the muscles of the trunk and limbs. The attitude is one in which all the main joints of the body are between complete flexion and complete extension so that there is approximately an equal tension in the opposing groups of flexor and extensor muscles. Thus the whole body of the dancer is full of active forces balanced one against another, resulting in a condition of flexibility and alertness without strain.

While the dance thus brings into play the whole muscular system of the dancer it also requires the activity of the two chief senses, that of sight to guide the dancer in his movements amongst the others and that of hearing to enable him to keep time with the music. Thus the dancer is in a condition in which all the bodily and mental activities are harmoniously directed to one end.

Finally, in order to understand the function of the Andamanese dance it must be noted that every adult member of the community takes some part in it. All the able-bodied men join in the dance itself; all the women join in the chorus. If anyone through ill-health or old age is unable to take any active part, he or she is at least necessarily a spectator, for the dance takes place in the centre of the village in the open space towards which the huts usually face[1].

The Andamanese dance (with its accompanying song) may therefore be described as an activity in which, by virtue of the effects of rhythm and melody, all the members of a community are able harmoniously to cooperate and act in unity; which requires on the part of the dancer a continual condition of tension free from strain; and which produces in those taking part in it a high degree of pleasure. We must now proceed to examine very briefly the chief effects on the mental condition of those taking part[2].

First let us consider some of the effects of rhythm. Any marked rhythm exercises over those submitted to its influence a constraint, impelling them to yield to it and to permit it to direct and regulate the movements of the body and even those of the mind. If one does not yield to this constraining influence it produces a state of restlessness that may become markedly unpleasant. One who yields himself utterly to it, as does the dancer when he joins in the dance, still continues to feel the constraint, but so far from being unpleasant it now produces a pleasure of a quite distinct quality. The first point for us to note therefore is that through the effect of rhythm the dance affords an experience of a constraint or force of a peculiar kind acting upon the individual and inducing in him when he yields himself to it a pleasure of self-surrender. The peculiarity of the force in question is that it seems to act upon the individual both from without (since it is the sight of his friends dancing and the sound of the singing and marking time that occasions it), and also from within (since the impulse to yield himself to the constraining rhythm comes from his own organism).

A second effect of the rhythm of the dance is due to the well-known fact that a series of actions performed rhythmically

---

[1] It will be shown later in the chapter that when individuals are excluded from participation in the dance it is because they are in a condition of partial exclusion from the common life.

[2] The psychology of dancing offers a wide field for study that has as yet, so far as I know, been barely touched. The following brief notes are therefore necessarily incomplete and somewhat unsatisfactory.

produces very much less fatigue than actions not rhythmical requiring the same expenditure of muscular energy. So the dancer feels that in and through the dance he obtains such an increase of his personal energy that he is able to accomplish strenuous exertions with a minimum of fatigue. This effect of rhythm is reinforced by the excitement produced by the rapid movements of the dancers, the loud sounds of the song and clapping and sounding-board, and intensified, as all collective states of emotion are intensified, by reason of being collective; with the result that the Andaman Islanders are able to continue their strenuous dancing through many hours of the night[1].

There is yet a third most important effect of rhythm. Recent psychology shows that what are called the esthetic emotions are largely dependent upon motor images. We call a form beautiful when, through the movements of the eye in following it, we feel it as movement, and as movement of a particular kind which we can only describe at present by using such a word as 'harmonious.' Similarly our esthetic appreciation of music seems to be largely dependent on our feeling the music as movement, the sounds appealing not to the ear only but to stored-up unconscious motor memories. With regard to dancing, our pleasure in watching the graceful, rhythmical and harmonious movements of the dancer is an esthetic pleasure of similar nature to that obtained from the contemplation of beautiful shapes or listening to music. But when the individual is himself dancing it does not seem quite fitting to call his pleasure esthetic. Yet the dance, even the simple dance of the Andamans, does make, in the dancer himself, partly by the effect of rhythm, partly by the effect of the harmonious and balanced tension of the muscles, a direct appeal to that motor sense to which the contemplation of beautiful forms and movements makes only an indirect appeal. In other words the dancer actually feels within himself that harmonious action of balanced and directed forces which, in the contemplation of a beautiful form we feel as though it were in the object at which we look. Hence such dancing as that of the Andaman

---

[1] I have known a dance to be continued for seven or eight hours, each dancer taking only short periods of rest; and it must be remembered that the Andamanese dance is more strenuous than our ball-room dances.

Islanders may be looked upon as an early step in the training of the esthetic sense, and to recognize all that the dance means we must make allowance for this fact that the mental state of the dancer is closely related to the mental state that we call esthetic enjoyment.

Let us now consider the effects of the dance as a social or collective activity. First, the dance affords an opportunity for the individual to exhibit before others his skill and agility and so to gratify his personal vanity. It is very easy to observe the action of this harmless vanity in the dancers, and particularly in the man who takes the place at the sounding-board and acts as soloist or leader of the chorus. The dancer seeks to feel, and does feel, that he is the object of the approbation and admiration of his friends. His self-regarding sentiments are pleasantly stimulated, so that he becomes conscious, in a state of self-satisfaction and elation, of his own personal value. This stimulation of the self-regarding sentiment is an important factor in the total effect produced by the dance.

Secondly, the dance, at the same time that it stimulates pleasantly the self-regarding sentiment, also affects the sentiments of the dancer towards his fellows. The pleasure that the dancer feels irradiates itself over everything around him and he is filled with geniality and good-will towards his companions. The sharing with others of an intense pleasure, or rather the sharing in a collective expression of pleasure, must ever incline us to such expansive feelings. It is certainly a readily observable fact that in the Andamans the dance does produce a condition of warm good-fellowship in those taking part in it. There is no need to enquire more closely into the mental mechanisms by which this is brought about.

The Andaman dance, then, is a complete activity of the whole community, in which every able-bodied adult takes some part, and is also an activity in which, so far as the dancer himself is concerned, the whole personality is involved, by the innervation of all the muscles of the body, by the concentration of attention required, and by its action on the personal sentiments. In the dance the individual submits to the action upon him of the community; he is constrained, by the immediate effect of rhythm as well as by custom, to join in, and he is required to conform in his own actions and movements to the needs of the common activity. The surrender of the individual to this constraint or obligation is not felt as painful, but on the contrary as highly pleasurable. As the dancer loses himself in the dance, as he becomes absorbed in the unified community, he reaches a state of elation in which he feels himself filled with energy or force immensely beyond his ordinary state, and so finds himself able to perform prodigies of exertion. This state of intoxication, as it might almost be called, is accompanied by a pleasant stimulation of the self-regarding sentiment, so that the dancer comes to feel a great increase in his personal force and value. And at the same time, finding himself in complete and ecstatic harmony with all the fellow-members of his community, experiences a great increase in his feelings of amity and attachment towards them.

In this way the dance produces a condition in which the unity, harmony and concord of the community are at a maximum, and in which they are intensely felt by every member. It is to produce this condition, I would maintain, that is the primary social function of the dance. The well-being, or indeed the existence, of the society depends on the unity and harmony that obtain in it, and the dance, by making that unity intensely felt, is a means of maintaining it. For the dance affords an opportunity for the direct action of the community upon the individual, and we have seen that it exercises in the individual those sentiments by which the social harmony is maintained.

It was formerly the custom, I was told, always to have a dance before setting out to a fight. The reason for this should now be clear. When a group engages in a fight with another it is to revenge some injury that has been done to the whole group. The group is to act as a group and not merely as a collection of individuals, and it is therefore necessary that the group should be conscious of its unity and solidarity. Now we have seen that the chief function of the dance is to arouse in the mind of every individual a sense of the unity of the social group of which he is a member, and its function before setting out to a fight is therefore apparent. A secondary effect of the dance before a fight is to intensify the collective anger against the hostile group, and thereby and in other ways to produce a state of excitement and elation which has an important influence on the fighting quality of the Andaman warrior.

An important feature of the social life of the Andamans in former times was the dance-meetings that were regularly held and at which two or more local groups met together for a few days. Each local group lived for the greater part of the year comparatively isolated from others. What little solidarity there was between neighbouring groups therefore tended to become weakened. Social relations between two groups were for the most part only kept up by visits of individuals from one group to another, but such visits did not constitute a relation between group and group. The function of the dance-meetings was therefore to bring the two groups into contact and renew the social relations between them and in that way to maintain the solidarity between them. Those meetings, apart from the provision of the necessary food, were entirely devoted to the exchange of presents and to dancing, the two or more parties of men and women joining together every night in a dance. We have already seen that the exchange of presents is a means of expressing solidarity or mutual good-will. It is now clear that the dance serves to unite the two or more groups into one body, and to make that unity felt by every individual, so creating for a few days a condition of close solidarity. The effects of the meeting would gradually wear out as months went by, and therefore it was necessary to repeat the meeting at suitable intervals.

Thus it appears that not only the ordinary dance, but also the war-dance, and the dance-meetings owe their place in the life of the Andaman Islanders to the fact that dancing is a means of uniting individuals into a harmonious whole and at the same time making them actually and intensely experience their relation to that unity of which they are the members. The special dances at initiation ceremonies and on other occasions will be dealt with later in the chapter, on the basis of the general explanation given above.

On the occasion of a dance, particularly if it be a dance of some importance, such as a war-dance, or a dance of two groups together, the dancers decorate themselves by putting on various ornaments and by painting their bodies with red paint and white clay. The explanation of the dance cannot therefore be regarded as complete till we have considered the meaning of this personal adornment connected with it.

If the Andaman Islander be asked why he adorns himself for the dance, his reply is invariably that he wishes to look well, to improve his personal appearance. In other words his conscious motive is personal vanity.

One of the features of the dance, and a not unimportant one, is that it offers an opportunity for the gratification of personal vanity. The dancer, painted, and hung over with ornaments, becomes pleasantly conscious of himself, of his own skill and agility, and of his striking or at least satisfactory appearance, and so he becomes also conscious of his relation to others, of their admiration, actual or possible, and of the approval and good-will that go with admiration. In brief, the ornamented dancer is pleasantly conscious of his own personal value. We may therefore say that the most important function of any such adorning of the body is to express or mark the personal value of the decorated individual.

This explanation only applies to certain bodily ornaments and to certain ways of painting the body. It applies to the painting of white clay, with or without red paint, that is adopted at dances and on other ceremonial occasions. It applies to such personal ornaments as those made of netting and *Dentalium* shell which constitute what may be called the ceremonial costume of the Andamanese. It is of these that the natives say that they use them in order to look well.

The occasions on which such personal decoration is used are strictly defined by custom. In other words the society dictates to the individual when and how he shall be permitted to express his own personal value. It is obvious that personal vanity is of great importance in directing the conduct of the individual in his dealings with his fellows, and much more amongst a primitive people such as the Andamanese than amongst ourselves, and it is therefore necessary that the society should have some means of controlling the sentiment and directing it towards social ends. We have seen that the dance is the expression of the unity and harmony of the society, and by permitting at the dance the free expression of personal vanity the society ensures that the individual shall learn to feel, even if only subconsciously, that his personal value depends upon the harmony between himself and his fellows.

The bride and bridegroom are painted with white clay, and wear ornaments of *Dentalium* shell on the day following their marriage. We have seen that marriage involves a change of social status, and we may say that it gives an increased social value to the married pair, the social position of a married man or woman being of greater importance and dignity than that of a bachelor or spinster. They are, after marriage, the objects of higher regard on the part of their fellows than they were before. It is therefore appropriate that the personal value of the bride and bridegroom should be expressed so that both they themselves and their fellows should have their attention drawn to it, and this is clearly the function of the painting and ornaments.

After the completion of any of the more important of the initiation ceremonies, such as the eating of turtle, the initiate is painted with white clay and red paint and wears ornaments of *Dentalium* shell. This is exactly parallel to the painting of the bride and bridegroom. The initiate, by reason of the ceremony he has been through, has acquired new dignity and importance, and by having fulfilled the requirements of custom has deserved the approval of his fellows. The decoration of his body after the ceremony is thus the expression of his increased social value.

A corpse, before burial, is decorated in the same manner as the body of a dancer. This, we may take it, is the means by which the surviving relatives and friends express their regard for the dead, i.e. their sense of his value. We need not suppose that they believe the dead man to be conscious of what they are doing. It is to satisfy themselves that they decorate the corpse, not to satisfy the spirit. When a man is painted he feels that he has the regard and good-will of his fellows, and those who see him, at any rate in the instance of a bridegroom or initiate, realise that he has deserved their regard. So, to express their regard for the dead man they paint the inanimate body. Hence it is that the greater the esteem in which the dead man or woman is held, the greater is the care bestowed on the last painting.

We may conclude therefore that the painting of the body with white clay and the wearing of ornaments of *Dentalium* shell is a rite or ceremony by which the value of the individual to the society is expressed on appropriate occasions. We shall find confirmation of this later in the chapter.

Before passing on to consider the meaning of other methods of decorating the body there is one matter that is worthy of mention. It is often assumed or stated that both personal ornament and dancing, amongst uncivilised peoples, are connected with sexual emotion. It is, of course, extremely difficult to disprove a statement of this sort. So far as the Andamanese are concerned I was unable to find any trace whatever of a definitely sexual element in either their dances or their personal adornment. It may be recalled that both men and women wear exactly the same ornaments on ceremonial occasions, and this is to some extent evidence that such have no sexual value. It is possible that some observers might see in the dance of the women (which is only performed on rare occasions) a suggestion of something of a sexual nature. I was unable to find that the natives themselves consider that there is anything suggestive of sex in either the dance of the men or that of the women. If it were true that the most important feature of the dance was that it appealed in some way to sexual feelings it is difficult to see how we are to explain the different occasions on which dancing takes place, as before a fight, at the end of mourning, etc., whereas these are adequately accounted for by the hypothesis that the dance is a method of expressing the unity and harmony of the society. Similarly the explanation of personal ornament as being connected with sexual feeling would fail to account for the occasions on which it is regarded as obligatory. There is therefore, I believe, no special connection between the dancing and personal ornament of the Andamanese and sexual feeling. It would still be possible to hold that there is a general connection of great importance between the affective dispositions underlying these and other customs and the complex affective disposition that we call the sex instinct. The nature of that connection, important as it is, lies outside the scope of this work.

I remarked above that the explanation which I have given of the meaning of personal ornament does not apply to all the objects that the Andaman Islanders wear on their body, but only to certain of them. If an Andaman Islander be asked why he paints himself with white clay, or why he wears a belt or necklace of *Dentalium* shell he replies that he does so in order to look well; but if he be asked why he wears a string of human bones round his head or neck or waist, he gives quite a different answer, to the effect that he does so in order to protect himself from dangers of a special kind. According to circumstances he will say either that he is wearing the bones to cure himself of illness, or else that he wears them as a protection against spirits. Thus while some things are worn on the body in order to improve the personal appearance, and consequently, as explained above, to give the individual a sense of his own value, others are worn because they are believed to have a protective power, and thereby arouse in the person a sense of security. Exactly the some sort of protective power is attributed to things that cannot be worn on the body, such as fire, and it will therefore be convenient to consider together all the things that afford this kind of protection, whether they can be worn on the body or not.

The interpretation here offered is that the customs connected with this belief in the protective power of objects of various kinds are means by which is expressed and thereby maintained at the necessary degree of energy a very important social sentiment, which, for lack of a better term, I shall call the sentiment of dependence. In such a primitive society as that of the Andamans one of the most powerful means of maintaining the cohesion of the society and of enforcing that conformity to custom and tradition without which social life is impossible, is the recognition by the individual that for his security and well-being he depends entirely upon the society. Now for the Andaman Islander the society is not sufficiently concrete and particular to act as the object of such a sentiment, and he therefore feels his dependence upon the society not directly but in a number of indirect ways. The particular way with which we are now concerned is that the individual experiences this feeling of dependence towards every important possession of the society, towards every object which for the society has constant and important uses.

The most prominent example of such an object is fire. It may be said to be the one object on which the society most of all depends for its well-being. It provides warmth on cold nights; it is the means whereby they prepare their food, for they eat nothing raw save a few fruits; it is a possession that has to be constantly guarded, for they have no means of producing it, and must therefore take care to keep it always alight; it is the first thing they think of carrying with them when they go on a journey by land or sea; it is the centre around which the social life moves, the family hearth being the centre of the family life, while the communal cooking place is the centre round which the men often gather after the day's hunting is over. To the mind of the Andaman Islander, therefore, the social life of which his own life is a fragment, the social well-being which is the source of his own happiness, depend upon the possession of fire, without which the society could not exist. In this way it comes about that his dependence on the society appears in his consciousness as a sense of dependence upon fire and a belief that it possesses power to protect him from dangers of all kinds.

The belief in the protective power of fire is very strong. A man would never move even a few yards out of camp at night without a fire-stick. More than any other object fire is believed to keep away the spirits that cause disease and death. This belief, it is here maintained, is one of the ways in which the individual is made to feel his dependence upon the society.

Now this hypothesis is capable of being very strictly tested by the facts, for if it is true we must expect to find that the same protective power is attributed to every object on which the social life depends. An examination of the Andamanese beliefs shows that this is so, and thereby confirms the hypothesis.

In their daily life the Andamanese depend on the instrinsic qualities of the materials they use for their bows and arrows and harpoons and other hunting implements, and it can be shown that they do attribute to these implements and to the materials from which they are made powers of protection against evil. Moreover it is even possible to apply a quantitative test and show that the more important the place a thing occupies in the social life the greater is the degree of protective power attributed to it. Finally I shall be able to show that as different materials are used for special purposes so they are supposed to have certain special powers of protection against certain sorts of danger. Thus the hypothesis I have stated is capable of being as nearly demonstrated as is possible in such psychological enquiries as the one we are engaged in.

A man carrying his bow and arrows is supposed to be less likely to fall a victim to the spirits than one who has no weapons with him. One way of stopping a violent storm is to go into the sea (storms being supposed to be due to the spirits of the sea) and swish the water about with arrows. The natives sometimes wear a necklace formed of short lengths of the bamboo shaft of a fish-arrow. All the examples of such necklaces that I met with had been made from an old arrow. I asked a native to make one for me, and although he could readily have made one from bamboo that had never served as an arrow he did not do so, but used the shaft of one of his arrows. Such a necklace may therefore be described as an arrow in such a form that it can be worn round the neck and thus carried continually without trouble. The protective power of the bow is at first sight not quite so evident, but the material used for the string is regarded as possessing protective power, and to this I shall return shortly.

The best demonstration of the truth of the explanation offered is to be found by considering the different vegetable fibres of which use is made. The most important of these are the *Anadendron paniculatum* (used for bow-strings and for fine string), the *Hibiscus tiliaceus* (used for rope) and the *Gnetum edule* (used for string, and inferior to the *Anadendron*). All these fibres are believed to possess power to keep away dangers, but there is a sort of specialisation in their use.

The fibre of the *Hibiscus* is used mainly in the hunting of turtle and big fish. Consequently the tree itself from which the fibre is obtained is believed to possess the power of warding off all dangers connected with turtle and the sea. There is a custom that turtle flesh may only be cooked with wood of the *Hibiscus*, otherwise it will be uneatable. In the turtle-eating ceremony the initiate who, as we shall see later, is in a condition of danger by reason of having eaten turtle for the first time after a period of abstention, is seated on *Hibiscus* leaves and holds a bundle of the same leaves before him. At the same ceremony the leaves of this tree are used in the dance, and the initiate is given a skewer made from its wood with which to feed himself. If for any reason the leaves of the *Hibiscus* are not obtainable when the ceremony is performed those of the *Myristica longifolia* are used instead. Now this is the tree from which the natives always make their canoe paddles, which, like ropes of *Hibiscus* fibre, are used in hunting turtle. This specialisation is therefore easy to understand; the natives habitually make use of the *Hibiscus* and the *Myristica* in turtle-hunting; they use the intrinsic qualities of these trees in their actual struggles with turtle and large fish, and by means of these qualities they are able to succeed in overcoming their prey; they therefore come to believe that these trees possess special powers which not only enable them to conquer the turtle itself but also are able to protect them from the evil influences that they believe (for reasons to be explained later) result from the eating of its flesh.

This explanation is readily verified by considering an exactly parallel instance. In the pig-eating ceremony at initiation the leaves of the *Hibiscus* or the *Myristica* are not used, and are regarded as valueless. Paddles and ropes are of no use in hunting pigs. The leaves that are used in this ceremony are those of the *Tetranthera lancæfolia*. It is from this tree that are obtained the shafts of pig-arrows. Hence the relation of the tree to the pig is exactly parallel to that of the *Hibiscus* to turtle. It is by making use of the qualities of the wood that they are able to destroy the pig and so they believe that its leaves will enable them to destroy the dangers that result from the eating of the animal.

The leaves of the *Tetranthera* are also used, however, in the ceremony at a girl's first menstruation, and I cannot pass over this without an explanation. It is to be found in the fact that pig-arrows are used in fighting, so that the tree comes to have a special relation to the shedding of blood. Plumes of shredded *Tetranthera* wood (made from an old arrow-shaft) must be worn by a homicide during the period of "purification" as a protection against the dangers that are believed to threaten him because he has shed blood. The same plumes were formerly always carried in a dance preceding a fight, and at such times the natives used to rub their bows with the shredded wood in order to ensure success in battle. Thus it is clear that there is a special connection between this tree and the shedding of blood, due to the fact that pig-arrows, of which the shafts are made from it, are used in fighting as well as for killing pigs and other animals. It is probable that this is the explanation of the use of the leaves during the ceremony at a girl's first menstruation.

These examples afford a crucial test of the hypothesis here maintained. Not only is the protective power of these substances explicable by the fact that they are things on which the society depends in its daily life, but the special uses of each of them as amulets are only explicable when we consider the different uses to which they are put as materials.

The fibre of the *Anadendron paniculatum* is used for making thread, bow-strings, the cords of pig-arrows, and for binding the heads and barbs of harpoons and arrows. It has therefore no special relation to either pig or turtle. There is a belief, however, that the plant does possess special protective powers that make it efficacious against certain dangers coming from the sea. A piece of the plant tied round the neck or worn in the belt of a swimmer is believed to protect him from sharks and other dangerous fish. A piece of it crushed and placed in the sea is said to have stopped a violent storm on one occasion. Thus the *Anadendron* seems to possess a special power which makes it a source of protection against dangers from the sea. The same is true of the *Gnetum edule*, though, as this fibre is less valued than that of the *Anadendron*, it is not supposed to be so powerful in its effects. In regard to the specialisation in the use of these two plants as amulets it seems likely that it is due to a notion of opposition between the things of the forest and the things of the sea. The Andamanese live in a double environment; the jungle-dwellers live entirely in the forest and have dealings with forest things; they develop knowledge and powers that make them better woodsmen than the coast-dwellers. The latter live by the sea and are chiefly occupied with things of the sea, being skilled in the occupations of fishing and canoeing. There is thus a contrast or opposition between the life of the forest and the life of the shore that runs through all the social life, and I believe that it is this opposition which explains the belief that the *Anadendron* and the *Gnetum*, which are essentially forest things, are possessed of a quality that makes them contrary or opposed to all things of the sea.

Personal ornaments are made from the fibres that have been mentioned (*Hibiscus, Anadendron, Gnetum*), and we are justified, I think, in regarding such ornaments as being to some extent amulets. I purchased from a man in the Little Andaman a charm that was hanging round his neck, which he seemed to value highly. I imagined that it might contain a human bone, but when I had unwound the ornamental thread with which it was bound and opened out the covering of bark I found inside the parcel only a carefully folded length of rope made from *Hibiscus* fibre.

There is one fibre from which the natives of the Great Andaman make themselves ornaments, which they do not regularly use in any other way, namely that of the *Ficus laccifera*. We may perhaps regard this as a genuine and demonstrable example of a survival in custom. The natives of the Little Andaman, who, until their recent contact with those of the Great Andaman, did not know the use of the *Anadendron*, use the fibre of the *Ficus* for their bow-strings. We are justified in assuming, I believe, that the natives of the Great Andaman made a similar use of the same fibre before they had learnt to use the *Anadendron*. In those days much of the power that is now attributed to the *Anadendron*, because of its service as the material for bow-strings, must then have been attributed to the *Ficus*. When the substitution of the superior *Anadendron* fibre came about, the belief in the efficacy of the *Ficus* did not disappear, although the ground of the belief (if we may call it so) had ceased to exist. If this be so, then the present use of the *Ficus* fibre as an amulet is an example of survival. It may be noted that the qualities of the *Ficus* are supposed to be similar to those of the *Anadendron*. Thus while one medicine-man stopped a storm with *Anadendron*, another did the same thing on another occasion with *Ficus*.

The above examples are sufficient to justify the generalisation that the Andamanese attribute protective power to all those substances on the strength and other qualities of which they rely in order to obtain their food or overcome their enemies. There are one or two other positive instances that have not been mentioned. Bees'-wax, which is used for waxing thread and bow-strings, is believed to have power to keep spirits away and to cure sickness. Cane, which is used by the natives for many different purposes, seems also to have its use as an amulet, for belts and other personal ornaments are made of pieces of cane attached to a length of rope.

Negative instances are more difficult to discover. When I was in the Andamans I had not formulated the explanation that is offered here, and I therefore did not make any search for negative instances that might have afforded a means of testing the value of the hypothesis. I have no satisfactory evidence that protective power is attributed to iron, or to the shells that were formerly used, as iron now is, for the heads and barbs of arrows, but it is quite possible that I may have overlooked evidence that was really there. I do not think that any particular protective properties are attributed to such things as the materials from which baskets are made and the clay that is used for pottery. These things, however, may be regarded as luxuries rather than necessities; they are not of the same immediate service to the society in its fundamental activity (that of providing food) as are weapons and the materials used in them.

There are still two important kinds of amulets that remain to be considered. First, protective power is attributed to the bones of animals, which are made into personal ornaments; these cannot be dealt with until we have considered some of the beliefs relating to food. Secondly, a very high degree of protective power is attributed to human bones, but the discussion of this belief must wait till we have discovered the meaning of the funeral customs of the Andamanese.

To conclude the present argument, it would seem that the function of the belief in the protective power of such things as fire and the materials from which weapons are made is to maintain in the mind of the individual the feeling of his dependence upon the society; but viewed from another aspect the beliefs in question may be regarded as expressing the social value of the things to which they relate. This term—social value—will be used repeatedly in the later part of this chapter, and it is therefore necessary to give an exact definition. By the social value of anything I mean the way in which that thing affects or is capable of affecting the social life. Value may be either positive or negative, positive value being possessed by any thing that contributes to the well-being of the society, negative value by anything that can adversely affect that well-being.

The social value of a thing (such as fire) is a matter of immediate experience to every member of the society, but the individual does not of necessity consciously and directly realise that value. He is made to realise it indirectly through the belief, impressed upon him by tradition, that the thing in question affords protection against danger. A belief or sentiment which finds regular outlet in action is a very different thing from a belief which rarely or never influences conduct. Thus, though the Andaman Islander might have a vague realisation of the value of *Hibiscus*, for example, that would be something very different from the result on the mind of the individual of the regular use of the leaves of that tree in initiation ceremonies as a protection against unseen dangers. So that the protective uses of such things are really rites or ceremonies by means of which the individual is made to realise (1) his own dependence on the society and its possessions, and (2) the social value of the things in question.

I have had to postpone to the later parts of the chapter the consideration of some of the objects possessing protective power, but I venture to state here three propositions some part of the evidence for which has already been examined, and which will be sufficiently demonstrated, I hope, before the end of the chapter. They are as follows : (1) any object that contributes to the well-being of the society is believed to afford protection against evil; (2) the degree of protective power it is believed to possess depends on the importance of the services it actually renders to the society; (3) the kind of special protection it is supposed to afford is often related to the kind of special service that it does actually render.

We were led to the consideration of the protective power of objects through an attempt to understand the meaning of the methods of ornamenting the body in the Andamans. We have seen that some ornaments are worn in order to express the personal value of the individual, while others are worn for the sake of the protection they are believed to afford. We have also seen that one method of painting the body (with white clay) is a means of expressing the personal value of the painted individual. We will next consider the use of the clay called *odu*. This clay is painted on the body of a mourner and is the outward sign of mourning; it is used at certain stages of the initiation ceremonies; it is also regularly used for painting the body with the designs known as *era-puli*. According to the rule of method laid down at the beginning of the chapter we must seek some common explanation of these different uses of the same substance.

We may consider, first of all, the patterns (*era-puli*) that are made with this clay on the body and face after eating certain foods such as pork and turtle.

Mr Man gives two explanations of the use of these paintings of clay. During the hot season, he says, the natives "endeavour to lessen the discomfort caused by the heat by smearing their bodies with a white-wash of common white clay and water." He adds: "it has long been erroneously believed that they have recourse to this expedient in order to allay the inconvenience which they would otherwise suffer from the bites of mosquitoes and other jungle pests; but the true reason for the practice is, I am well assured, that which I have given above[1]." In another place he says: "After eating pork or turtle they are in the habit of smearing *og* over their bodies with their fingers, in the belief that it affects their breath, and that evil spirits will be unable to detect, and therefore will not be attracted to, them by the

[1] Man, *op. cit.* p. 76.

savoury smell of the food of which they have partaken. Again, when heated by travelling or by hunting or dancing, they have recourse to the same wash, but in these cases it is applied thinly[1]."

There are here two explanations of fundamentally different character. First the Andamanese practice of painting their bodies with clay is explained as having a purely utilitarian purpose, being intended to cool them when they are heated. In the second statement the explanation given is that the custom is intended to protect them from danger.

My own observations do not altogether agree with the statements of Mr Man. I found that the natives painted themselves just as much in the cold season as in the hot season. The principal, if not the sole, occasion on which the clay is used is after or immediately before a meal, and therefore generally in the late afternoon or evening when the heat of the day is past. I do not feel so satisfied as Mr Man appears to be, that the clay really has the effect of keeping a person cool, particularly when it is remembered that the painting may consist of a few lines each as broad as a finger. Moreover, Mr Man's explanation does not afford any reason for the fact that the clay is always applied in some sort of pattern. If it were merely to keep himself cool, we should expect to see a man cover himself all over with a plain coating evenly spread over the body. Such an even coating is never used, in the Great Andaman tribes, except by persons mourning for the dead, and is the essential mark of a mourner.

It is easy to explain how Mr Man has fallen into an error in this matter. On many occasions, when I questioned the natives as to their reason for painting themselves with clay I received the answer, "When we have eaten pork or turtle or dugong, we become *ot-kimil* and so we take clay and paint ourselves." Now the word *ot-kimil* in the *Aka-Jeru* language is the word that the natives use to express what we mean by the word "hot." But while "hot" may always be translated by *ot-kimil* or *er-kimil*, the latter word cannot always be adequately rendered in English by the word "hot." Mr Man seems to have supposed that when an Andaman Islander says "hot" he means by the word only what we mean, whereas he really means a great deal more.

[1] Man, *op. cit.* p. 333.

Let us examine briefly the word in question. In the languages of the North Andaman the stem is -*kimil*. With the prefix *ot*- or *er*- it is used to mean "hot" as in *T'ot-kimil-bom*, "I am hot," or *Ino ot-kimil bi* or *Ino er-kimil bi*, "The water is hot." Used by itself the stem *kimil* is the name of the latter part of the rainy season, when the weather is not hot but cool. A youth or girl who is passing through the initiation ceremonies is said to be *aka-kimil*, and is addressed or spoken of as *Kimil*, instead of by his or her proper name. The turtle-eating ceremony is called *čokbi-kımil*, or *čokbi-jo* or *kimil-jo*, *čokbi* meaning "turtle" and *jo* meaning "eating." The word "hot" is used by the natives in several unusual ways when they are talking their own language or Hindustani. Thus a stormy or rough sea is said to be "hot," and one native in describing to me (in Hindustani) the cessation of a cyclone said "the sea became cold." A person who is ill is said to be hot, and getting well is expressed by the phrase "getting cool."

In the *Aka-Bea* language the word "hot" is translated by Mr Portman by the stem *uya*. The stem *kimil* appears in the form *gumul* in only some of the uses it has in the Northern languages. *Gumul* is the name of the latter part of the rainy season. A youth passing through the initiation ceremonies is said to be *aka-gumul* and is addressed or spoken of as *Guma*. The turtle-eating ceremony is called *gumul-le-ke*, *le-ke* meaning "eating." The word thus means "the *gumul* eating" and is the literal equivalent of the *kimil-jo* of the North.

The uses of the word *kimil* may be summarised as follows:

(1) to mean "hot" in the sense of the English word;

(2) in connection with illness;

(3) in speaking of stormy weather;

(4) as the name of the latter part of the rainy season;

(5) to denote the condition of a youth or girl who is passing through or has recently passed through the initiation ceremonies, and to denote the ceremonies themselves;

(6) to denote a condition in a person consequent on eating certain foods, and perhaps sometimes due to other causes, to remedy or obviate which the natives make use of clay painted in patterns on their bodies.

It is probable, then, that when a native says that after eating food he is *ot-kimil* and therefore paints himself with clay he does not mean simply that he is hot. This will be still more evident when we consider the second explanation of the custom that is given by the natives. Many of those whom I questioned stated that after eating dugong, pork, turtle, etc., the body emits an odour, that this odour may attract the spirits of the jungle or the sea, and that to obviate this they paint themselves with clay. This agrees exactly with what Mr Man says in the second passage quoted above. It is confirmed by other customs. I was told that a man who has eaten dugong will not leave the camp until some time after the dugong meat is all finished, for fear that the spirits may smell him and do him harm. It is to be noted in passing that painting the body with clay does not by any means remove the odour that does actually characterise a native after he has been eating fat meat of any kind. We must be careful, in this instance also, not to assume that an Andaman Islander means by "smell" exactly what we mean by it and nothing more. It will be shown later in the chapter that the Andamanese identify the smell of an object with its active magical principle. One example may be given here to show this. The origin of rheumatism in the legs is explained by the natives as being the result of the common practice of preparing the fibre of the *Anadendron paniculatum* by scraping it on the thigh. During this process, they say, the "smell" of the plant enters the thigh and is the cause of rheumatic or sciatic pains.

The natives give yet a third statement of their reasons for using clay. On many occasions I asked them what would happen if they ate pork or turtle and did not paint themselves. In every case I received the reply that any man who did such a thing would almost certainly be ill.

When a number of persons give three different reasons for one and the same action, and are equally sincere throughout, it is to be presumed that the three different statements are so many different ways of saying one and the same thing. We may therefore conclude that the Andaman Islanders believe that there is a peculiar power in foods (or in some foods) which makes it dangerous to eat them. This danger may be expressed by saying that the person who has eaten food will, unless he takes certain precautions, be liable to be ill. Now sickness is believed to be caused by the spirits of the jungle and the sea, and therefore an alternative or equivalent statement of the same belief is that after a person has eaten food he is in danger from the spirits. We may therefore conclude that the word *ot-kimil*, when it is used to describe the condition of a person who has eaten food, denotes simply this condition of danger, and nothing more. For this we shall find ample confirmation later on. Subject to such later confirmation I will here state what has been maintained, which is (1) that the *era-puli* patterns are to be explained as being protective, (2) that the eating of food is regarded as dangerous, and (3) that this danger is associated in the minds of the natives with sickness and with the spirits. It will be convenient to leave the first of these three propositions for later discussion and take up the second, seeking to find the meaning of this belief in the dangerous properties of food.

Not all foods are equally dangerous. I was able to establish roughly a sort of scale. The most dangerous foods are dugong; the fish called *komar*; some of the snakes; the internal fat such as the kidney-fat or the intestinal fat of pig, turtle, monitor lizard and *Paradoxurus*; the liver of sharks, sting-rays and *Plotosus*; and honey. Next in order come the flesh of pigs, turtle, monitor lizard and *Paradoxurus* and of the fishes mentioned above; also the eggs of turtle. To these should perhaps be added the edible grubs and some vegetable foods such as the yams and the *Artocarpus* fruit and seed. Lowest in the scale, that is, least dangerous, are molluscs and the commoner sorts of fish and vegetable foods.

The principles underlying this grading of foods are two. Those foods that are difficult or dangerous to procure are considered more dangerous than others. Thus all the fishes that are thought most dangerous to eat are actually dangerous, such as the sharks, the sting-rays, the armed *Plotosus*, and the fish *komar* that has a powerful spike on its head with which it can inflict a dangerous wound. Secondly the foods that are most prized are regarded as being more dangerous than those that are less prized. The internal fat of animals is regarded as a great delicacy and therefore occupies a high place in the scale. It is this also that explains the position of honey and of the edible grubs. The dugong, which is of all foods the most difficult and dangerous to procure, and is at the same time more highly prized than any other, is regarded as more dangerous to eat than any other.

It is this difference in the danger attributed to different foods that gives the clue to the explanation of the beliefs relating to them. The hypothesis I wish to put forward is that the custom of painting the body after eating food is an expression of the social value of food.

In a simple community such as that of the Andaman Islands, in which the necessary food has to be provided from day to day, food occupies a predominant position, and is the chief source of those variations or oscillations between conditions of euphoria and dysphoria that constitute the emotional life of the society. Food is obtainable only by the expenditure of effort, and the effort is a communal one. The obtaining of food is the principal social activity and it is an activity in which every able-bodied member of the community is required by custom to join. A man's first duty to the society may be defined as the duty of providing food for himself and others, and no one is looked on with more contempt than one who is lazy or careless in this respect. On the contrary the man who stands highest in the esteem of others is the skilful hunter who is generous in distributing to others the food he obtains. The food provides the community with its chief joys and sorrows. When food is scarce the whole community suffers. The men spend all their time in hunting but are disappointed. They have to fall back upon foods that are little relished, such as the commoner kinds of molluscs. On the contrary when there is plenty of food the whole society rejoices together. Every one has as much as he or she can eat. Hunting and fishing become pleasant sports instead of arduous labour.

Viewing the matter from its relation to the feelings of the individual we may say that it is particularly in connection with food that he is made to feel that he is a member of the community, sharing with others their joys and sorrows, taking part in a common activity, often dependent upon others for the satisfaction of his hunger, and obliged by custom to share with those others what he himself obtains. Thus food is, for the Andaman Islander, the one object above all others that serves to awaken in him day after day the feeling of his relation to his fellows. It is also the source of a very large proportion of his joys and sorrows, his excitements and disappointments. Thus it is that when the natives wish to amuse each other it is by tales of hunting that they do so, and a large proportion of their songs relate to the getting of food.

It is thus clear that food becomes an important secondary object of the fundamental affective dispositions that regulate the emotional attitude of the individual to the society to which he belongs. It is connected very closely with the feeling of moral obligation; the most valued moral qualities in the Andaman Islands are energy in providing food and generosity in distributing it; among the worst faults are laziness in hunting and meanness in giving to others. Similarly food is closely associated with the feeling of dependence. During childhood, particularly, the individual has to depend on others for his food; even later in life the food that a man eats is more often provided by others than by himself; he depends on the community even for his daily nourishment.

Different foods have different social values. Thus a dugong provides a large supply of a highly-prized delicacy, but on the other hand can only be obtained by strenuous and dangerous efforts of skilful hunters. At the other end of the scale the social value of shell-fish is very little. They are not relished and are only eaten when there is nothing better, while the labour of obtaining them is simply one of drudgery requiring little skill.

Finally it must be pointed out that the value of food is both positive and negative. It is the source of conditions of social euphoria when it is plentiful; while it is equally the source of social dysphoria when it is lacking. In other words, on different occasions it is the source of both pleasurable and painful states of the fundamental social sentiments.

All these experiences connected with food organise themselves around the notion that foods, or the animals that are used for food, are things to be treated carefully, with respect, or, in other words, with ritual precautions. The sense of the social value of food reveals itself as a belief that food may be a source of danger unless it is approached with circumspection, and this belief, translated into action, gives rise to the rite of painting the body after eating. This does not mean that when the Andaman Islander eats turtle he is actually in a state of fear; he feels that he would have reason to be afraid if it were not that the society has provided him with a means of avoiding the dangers of turtle eating. What he does feel, then, as I have tried to show, is not a fear of food but a sense of the value of food.

This interpretation will, I hope, be amply justified later, and the psychological processes assumed by it will be further illustrated. One point needs to be emphasised here, namely that the suggested interpretation affords, as no other would seem to do, an explanation of the fact that some foods are believed to be more dangerous than others, and that while it is obligatory to paint the body after eating the more dangerous foods, it is not necessary to do so after eating those that are less dangerous. If the rite is simply the expression of the social value of foods, it will follow that different food substances, having different social values, must be subject to differences in ritual treatment.

There are a few other customs connected with food, recorded in an earlier chapter, which show that in general food is regarded as something that may only be approached with ritual precautions. A turtle must be killed with its head towards the open sea, and must be cut up in one particular way, otherwise the meat would be "bad." A pig must also be cut up in a particular way, and must be stuffed with certain leaves before it is roasted. A man will not eat certain foods when he is away from his own country, as he is afraid that to do so might make him ill. (This corresponds to the belief that there is less chance of illness in one's own country than away from it, and that the spirits of a strange place are more dangerous than those that haunt the jungles and the waters of a man's own home.) All these customs, I believe, are so many different expressions of the social value of food.

I have maintained earlier in the chapter that the sense of the social value of such things as fire and the materials used for weapons translates itself into the belief that these things afford protection against danger. This would seem, at first sight, to be contradicted by the explanation that I have just given of the belief in the danger of food. The apparent contradiction must be faced and resolved before we can proceed further.

First, it can be shown that the various things that are regarded as affording protection when used according to custom, are also believed to be dangerous, just in the same way that food is dangerous. One example of this will suffice. The fibre of the *Anadendron paniculatum*, which is used for bow-strings and other purposes, has been shown to possess a power which gives it efficacy against dangers of the sea such as sharks. This same power, however, may have injurious effects if the plant is handled without proper precautions. Thus, if a piece of the green creeper, or a person who has recently been handling it, should be in a canoe, it would be impossible to capture turtle from that canoe, as they would be driven away by the "smell" of the plant. If a piece of the creeper were burnt in the fire there would be a great storm, according to one statement, or all the turtle would be driven away from the vicinity, according to another. The handling of the plant in the preparation of the fibre, by scraping it on the thigh, is believed to be the cause of rheumatism. Turtle meat that might by accident come in contact with the plant would be dangerous and would therefore not be eaten. These different beliefs show us that while this plant possesses powers that make it of service to the society, both directly as a material for weapons, and indirectly as a magical protection against evil, it is also dangerous, i.e. it will produce undesirable effects unless treated with the proper ritual precautions.

Now just as materials such as the *Anadendron* are dangerous but may yet be used protectively, so it can be shown that the things used for food are also capable of affording protection against evil. It may be recalled that an important element of the treatment of sickness is by the use of special foods. Yams, honey, the fat of turtle and dugong and other foods are believed to possess curative properties. The flesh of the flying-fox is used as a remedy for rheumatism. But the clearest evidence is provided by the custom of wearing ornaments made of the bones of animals that have been eaten. These ornaments are believed to possess protective powers of the same kind as those attributed to human bones, but they are considered to be more particularly of value to the hunter when he is in the forest or on the sea. They are made chiefly from the bones of those animals that are believed to be most dangerous to eat. These animals are difficult and often dangerous to capture or kill. When obtained they become very important sources of well-being to the society. The Andamanese express their sense of the social value of these animals in the belief that it is necessary to adopt certain measures of ritual precaution in dealing with them. When these due precautions are taken, however, then the society is able to make use of the flesh to serve its own ends. So, when an animal has been eaten, and has thus been made to serve as a source of advantage, of strength, the bones, which are the permanent remains of the feast, acquire a symbolic value as evidence of past social well-being, and omens of future security. They are a visible proof of the ability of the society to protect itself and its members from the dangers that are believed to threaten the human being in the most important activity of his life, the obtaining and eating of food.

Formerly the Andamanese preserved the skulls of all large animals such as pigs, turtle and dugong. At the present day they no longer preserve the skulls of pigs, giving as their reason that owing to the dogs obtained from Europeans they now have little difficulty in killing pigs; but they still preserve the skulls of dugongs, and a fair proportion of the skulls of turtle. The *Jarawa* still seem to preserve with great care the skulls of all the pigs they kill, going to the pains of enclosing each one in a case of basket-work. These skulls, we must conclude, are more than mere trophies of the chase. As visible proofs of the ability of the society in the past to overcome the hostile powers of nature, they form, as it were, the guarantee of a similar ability in the future, and I believe that their preservation is regarded as a means of ensuring success in hunting as well as protection for the hunters. The turtle skulls that are often suspended under the forward platform of a canoe, are, I believe, intended both to protect the occupants of the canoe from the dangers of the sea and to help them to obtain a good catch.

The Andamanese belief in the power of the bones of animals

to protect them from danger and to bring them luck, is therefore very similar to their belief in the protective power of the materials used for weapons and implements. The consideration of the apparent contradiction mentioned above has led us to a more exact statement of the real beliefs in these matters. They believe, we may say, that all the things from the jungle and the sea of which they make use as food or as materials, are dangerous unless approached with proper ritual precautions, but when so approached they become sources of strength and well-being and also of protection from unseen dangers.

To return to the main argument, which was concerned with the meaning of the patterns of clay painted on the body after eating the more dangerous foods, it would seem that this action is really a rite or ceremony, of the same general character as other ceremonial customs of the Andamans. It is an action required by custom, the performance of which on appropriate occasions serves to keep alive in the mind of the individual a certain system of sentiments necessary for the regulation of conduct in conformity to the needs of the society. By it the individual is made to feel (or to act as though he felt) that his life is one of continually repeated dangers from which he can only be preserved by conforming to the customs of the society as they have been handed down by tradition. He is made to feel that the eating of food is not merely the satisfaction of an animal appetite, but an act of communion, that the food itself is something "sacred" (if we may use that word in the sense of the original Latin "sacer"). It serves also, like any other rite in which all join, to make the individual feel the solidarity and unity of the community; all share in the common repast and the common danger, and each man sees on his neighbour the clay with which he himself is daubed.

Of course it is probable that the Andamanese custom of painting the body after eating, like our own grace before and after meat, with which it is parallel, tends to become a formality accompanied by little real feeling, but it can be shown, I believe, that such customs do possess a real value—a real psychological function—in keeping alive ideas and sentiments that will on occasion play an important part in influencing conduct.

We have not yet completed the study of the Andamanese beliefs about food. To do so we must examine the initiation ceremonies. I hope to show that these ceremonies are the means by which the society powerfully impresses upon the initiate the sense of the social value of food, and keeps the same sense alive in the minds of the spectators of the ceremony.

The position in the social life occupied by a child is different from that of an adult; the child is dependent upon and closely united to his parents, and is not an independent member of the community. To this difference in social position there corresponds a difference in the attitude of a person towards a child and towards an adult, and also a difference in the attitude of a child and that of an adult towards the society. As the child grows up a change takes place in his position in the social life, and this must be accompanied by a change in the emotional dispositions of the child himself in so far as these regulate his attitude towards the society, and by a change in the attitude towards the child of the other members of the group. The initiation ceremonies are the means by which these changes are brought about, and by which, therefore, the child is made an independent member of the society.

The ceremonies have two aspects according as we regard them from the point of view of the society or from that of the initiate. For the society they are to be described as the recognition of the change of status of the initiate, just as the marriage ceremony is the social recognition of the change of status by marriage. For the initiate they constitute a sort of moral or social education.

To fit a child for his proper place in the community he needs to be educated. Part of the process consists of learning how to hunt, how to make bows and arrows, and so on. This necessary knowledge he acquires gradually by imitation of his elders, in which he is guided and encouraged by them. But in addition to this he has to acquire those sentiments or emotional dispositions which regulate the conduct of members of the society and constitute morality. Part of this education in morality, this education of the sentiments, takes place gradually as the child grows up, less by any actual instruction than by processes of imitation and suggestion; but in this connection an extremely important part is played by the initiation ceremonies. That the long series of abstentions and ceremonies does have a very powerful emotional effect on the youth or girl may be readily observed by an eye-witness; that their permanent effect is to create in his or her mind a number of sentiments that previously existed not at all or only in an undeveloped condition will be shown in the course of the present argument.

Since in the life of the Andamans by far the most important social activity is the getting of food, and it is in connection with food that the social sentiments are most frequently called into action, it is therefore appropriate that it should be through his relation to food that the child should be taught his relation to the society, and thus have those sentiments implanted in him or brought to the necessary degree of strength. During his infancy the child is almost entirely unrestrained and acts with great comparative freedom. He does not realise, in any adequate manner, that the food with which he is freely provided (for children are the last to suffer hunger) is only obtained by skill and effort, nor does he realise that he will one day be required to labour to supply food for others. There follows a period of restraint, during which the growing boy or girl has to give up eating certain relished foods, and has to pass through a number of ceremonies, some of them painful, and all solemn and awe-inspiring. These restraints on the action of the individual are not imposed by one person, but by the whole society backed by the whole force of tradition. Through a series of years, just at what is, for physiological reasons, the most impressionable age, the individual learns to subordinate his own desires to the requirements of the society or of custom, as explained to him by his elders. He is thus impressed, in a forcible manner, with the importance of the moral law, and at the same time he is impressed with a sense of the social value of food. The ceremonies thus afford a moral education adapted to the requirements of life as it is lived in the Andamans. It would need a very lengthy analysis to show all the effects of the ceremonies on the emotional life of those who undergo them, and for the purpose of this chapter such an analysis is unnecessary. It will suffice merely to mention a few of the more important. As stated above, the ceremonies teach the boy or girl self-control or self-restraint, and they do so in relation to one of the two fundamental human instincts,—hunger. The cutting of the boy's back in the North Andaman gives a still sharper lesson in self-control in the endurance of pain. Secondly the ceremonies teach the initiate, for the first time in life, to view life and its duties and obligations seriously. The various ceremonies are all very solemn affairs for the initiate. Again, the growing boy or girl is made to feel very strongly the importance of conforming to the customs of the community to which he belongs, thus having implanted in his mind what is certainly one of the most powerful of the sentiments that regulate conduct in the Andamans. In this connection there may also be mentioned the respect for elders which is a most important element in the regulation of social life in all savage communities, and which is strongly impressed on the initiate throughout the ceremonies. And yet again, the ceremonies awaken and develop in the adolescent that fear of unseen danger which, as we shall see later, has a very important place in the mental life of the Andamanese and an important function in their moral life. Finally, the whole series of abstentions and ceremonies serves to develop in the mind of every new member of the society that sense of the social value of foods with which our argument has been concerned, which may be briefly described as being a realisation that food is a possession of the society, that not only the power to obtain food, but also the power to use it without danger is something that the individual owes to the society, and that the bestowal upon him of this power involves the acceptance on his part of corresponding obligations.

We may say, to look at the matter under another aspect, that the initiation ceremonies teach the youth or girl to realise what is implied in being a member of the society by putting him or her during the period of adolescence in an exceptional position, and, as it were, outside the society. The youth is no longer a child and may not act as a child; but he is not yet an adult and may not act as adults do. He feels himself cut off, as it were, from the ordinary life of the group, having as yet no share in it. As a child he was not yet aware of what it means to be a member of a society, but now, by means of the ceremonies, his attention is directed to the society and its life, by his being placed in a position of isolation outside it. He begins to look forward to the time when he will take his proper place as an adult, and his share in the common life of the camp. At each step of the ceremonies he feels that he is brought a little closer, until at last he can feel himself a man amongst men. Thus he is brought to a consciousness of all that it must mean to him to be a member of the community; he is taught the significance and value of social communion.

Since the greater part of social life is the getting and eating of food, to place a person outside the social life would be to forbid him from partaking of the food that is obtained by the society and consumed by it. This, however, would result in his starvation. The same object is attained, however, by making the initiate abstain for a period from a number of the most important and relished foods, and then making him abstain for a second period from the others. This is not the only way however in which the initiate is cut off from social communion. A youth or girl who is *aka-op* is not permitted to dance, nor to be decorated with red paint and white clay. It is in the dance that the community expresses most completely its own unity. Being forbidden to join in the dance is therefore to be excluded from the common life. Painting the body with red paint and white clay is, as we have seen, a way of expressing that the individual is aware of his own position as a member of the group having the approval and good-will of his fellows. Thus these other prohibitions reinforce and supplement the prohibition against eating certain foods during the period of adolescence, and the consideration of them serves to confirm the interpretation just given. I believe that the *aka-op* is also forbidden to use *odu* clay as a sign of mourning, and if this be so it is of considerable significance, as will be evident after we have considered the meaning of this use of clay. Unfortunately I am not quite sure of the facts, and so the point must be left.

To discuss in detail all the features of these ceremonies would take much space. I propose therefore to take as typical of the others the ceremony of turtle-eating and to explain its various features. When this ceremony is performed the youth has been compelled for many months to abstain from eating turtle, and has thus learnt to realise the social value of food in general and of turtle in particular. He is now to have the same lesson impressed upon him in a different way. The previous part of his education has been the continuous action over a long period of a not very powerful emotion. He has had to sit quietly while others regaled themselves with turtle meat and to be satisfied with less tasty food. At times he has probably gone hungry because the only food in camp was of kinds that were forbidden to him. The ceremony he is now to go through acts by producing in the space of a few days a very intense emotional experience. We have seen that the sense of the social value of food takes the form of a belief that food is dangerous to eat, and that its dangers may only be avoided by ritual precautions. At the turtle-eating ceremony the initiate is eating turtle for the first time as an adult, and is therefore exposed to great danger which makes it necessary to guard him with every possible ritual precaution. This, at any rate, is what the initiate himself is made to feel, and it is through this that the ceremony has its emotional effects. The initiate is not, of course, himself possessed by a simple feeling of fear, though the emotional state of his mind is built up on the basis of the fear instinct. What he is about to do is a matter of great danger to himself, but at the same time the precautions that are to be taken are such as entirely to remedy that danger if they are properly observed. Thus what he experiences is an intense feeling of the importance and solemnity of the ritual in which he is to take part.

All the details of the ceremony are readily to be explained as so many different ways of warding off the danger that threatens the initiate. He is seated on leaves of the *Hibiscus tiliaceus*, which, as we have seen, possess special efficacy against dangers connected with turtle. Leaves of the same kind are placed under his arms so as to cover his belly, where, we may suppose, the danger is most intense. A fire is placed near him, between him and the open sea. It has already been shown that fire is believed to afford protection against dangers of this sort, and the appropriateness of the position is due to the fact that in this instance it is from the sea and the things of the sea that danger is to be feared. He may not feed himself with his fingers, but must use a skewer of *Hibiscus* wood. This is clearly only one more precaution against danger, though the ideas connected with it are somewhat obscure. At the beginning of the ceremony the initiate is fed with turtle by a man who conducts the ceremony and who represents the society, that latter fact being sometimes symbolised by his wearing round his shoulders a bark sling such as is used for carrying children. This means, I think, that it is the society that "gives" the food to the initiate, giving him at the same time the power to use it with safety. The older man hands on to the younger the right and the power to eat which he himself possesses. He makes himself responsible, as it were, for the action of the initiate. At one stage of the performance the initiate is rubbed over with red ochre. This is to be understood by recalling that red ochre and red paint are regarded by the natives as valuable remedies against sickness and against the spirits that cause sickness. Immediately afterwards the body of the initiate is spattered with *odu* clay. The use of this clay after eating food was explained as a method of avoiding the dangers supposed to result from eating such foods as turtle. It is clear that exactly the same explanation will apply to its use in the initiation ceremonies. I have not found a satisfactory explanation of the peculiar manner in which it is applied. That the youth is not allowed to sleep for the first two days of the ceremony will be explained later in the chapter, when it will be shown that sleep itself is regarded as a condition of danger.

A notable incident is that at the beginning of the ceremony the female relatives of the initiate are required by custom to come and weep over him. An explanation of this has already been given, but may well be repeated. At each stage of the initiation ceremonies the initiate is withdrawn from the position of dependence that the child necessarily occupies, and as children are, for the most part, under the care of their elder female relatives, the ceremonies result in a partial destruction of those bonds that unite the initiate to his mother or his foster-mother and her sisters or to his own elder sisters. The weeping of the female relatives is as it were a reaction against this lessening of solidarity. It is evident why the rite is necessarily one-sided. The female relatives need to feel that they are not being entirely cut off from the initiate, and so they affirm their attachment to him by weeping over him. On the other hand the important thing for the initiate himself is to feel that the bonds that united him as a child to the women who cared for him are now severed or modified ; he must no longer depend on them but must learn to depend on himself; hence it is necessary that he should not weep but should remain passive and as it were indifferent under the tears that are shed over him.

The last part of the ceremony consists of a dance, in which the youth dances in the middle surrounded by a ring of men. As we have seen that dancing is in general an affirmation of solidarity between those taking part, and an expression of the unity of the society, we may well regard this dance as an affirmation of the solidarity that now exists between the youth and the other dancers, who are representatives of the society of adults. There is something more in the dance than this however. I pointed out that one of the results of taking part in a dance is to produce in the individual an experience of increased personal force, and it is obvious that this is a very appropriate feeling for the initiate who, by his long abstention from turtle, and by the ceremony he has just been through, has acquired an increase of personal force, an addition to his social personality. Before the dance the initiate is decorated with white clay (the snake pattern) and red paint. I have explained this particular method of painting the body as being a means of expressing and so producing or reinforcing the feeling of elation accompanying the recognition by an individual of his own social value, of the fact that he has deserved and obtained the good-will and regard of his fellows. The youth who has been through the period of restraint and the ordeal of the ceremony has done his duty and has earned the approbation of his friends. It is for this reason that he alone of the dancers is decorated with the painting that serves to express or arouse the elation or self-satisfaction that it is right for him to feel. The painting is the mark of the increase in social value of the initiate brought about by the turtle-eating ceremony.

There is one aspect of the dance that may be mentioned as being of importance, and which will be referred to again later, namely that the movements seem to be in a way imitative of the movements of turtle in the water. The leaves used in the dance are those that possess magical efficacy against dangers from turtle.

I have not been able to satisfy myself as to the meaning of the belt and necklace of *Pothos scandens* worn by the initiate in the dance and for some days afterwards. It is probable that the clue to this lies in the resemblance of the leaves to the shape of a phallus, but I have no clear evidence that this is the real explanation, and therefore offer it as merely a surmise.

If the natives be asked the reason for these ceremonies they often reply that their purpose is to make the youth or girl grow up strong. By this word "strong" they seem to mean in the first instance able-bodied, skilful (in hunting, etc.) and above all able to avoid or resist disease. They believe that anyone who did not pass through the ceremonies would be certain to die at an early age, and they recall the instance of one young man who refused to submit to the ceremonies who died before reaching maturity. Now, since the danger that they fear in eating food is said to be sickness, we may translate their statement into other terms by saying that the purpose of the initiation ceremonies is to endow the initiate with the power to eat the dangerous foods with comparative safety.

It would seem that an infant, being completely dependent upon his parents, is protected by that dependence from the danger of foods, but the adult is only able to make use of food with safety by reason of the possession within himself of a special power with which it is the purpose of the initiation ceremonies to endow him. Each kind of food has its own kind of dangerous power, and therefore every individual needs to be endowed with the special power to avoid each kind of danger. For this reason there is a separate ceremony for each of the important kinds of food. Thus we see very clearly that, for the Andamanese, food, or the power to make use of food without danger, is essentially a possession of the society, and one function of the initiation ceremonies is to keep alive this sentiment.

But there is a further meaning, I think, lying behind the statement that the initiation ceremonies endow the youth or girl with strength. I have already argued that all the most important social sentiments are closely associated with the sense of the social value of food, and although the initiation ceremonies are chiefly concerned with food, that is only because that is the easiest way by which to get at the main system of social sentiments. So that behind the special meaning of the ceremonies with relation to food we must look for a more general meaning in relation to the social life in general. This may be conveniently stated by saying that the purpose of the ceremonies is to endow the individual with a social personality. By the social personality of a person I mean the sum of those qualities by which he is able to affect the society. It is, in other words, what gives him his social value. The social personality depends in the first place on the social status of the individual. A young child seems to be regarded as having no social personality. He is not an independent member of the society, and therefore has no immediate social value, no direct effect on the general social life. At any rate the social personality of a child is something very different from that of an adult. So, since the initiation ceremonies provide the passage from childhood to manhood or womanhood we may describe them as the means by which the society endows the child with an adult social personality.

But the social personality of an individual also depends on his personal qualities, his strength and intelligence, his skill as a hunter, and on his moral qualities, whether he is mean or generous, quarrelsome or good-tempered, and so on, for all these things help to determine the place he occupies in the social life and the effects he has upon it. Above all, the social personality depends upon the development in the individual of those sentiments by which the social life is regulated and by which the social cohesion is preserved. Now we have seen that the initiation ceremonies do serve to develop these sentiments in the mind of the initiate, and we may therefore say that in this respect also it is true that the initiation ceremonies serve to develop in the child the social personality of an adult.

The consideration of the initiation ceremonies has served to confirm the hypothesis that the Andamanese customs relating to food are all of them different modes of expressing the social value of foods. We have now to consider the nature of the dangers that are supposed to accrue from the eating of food if due precautions be not taken. One statement of the natives is that the danger they fear is sickness. Now sickness of all kinds is believed by the Andamanese to be caused by certain supernatural beings called *Lau* or *Čauga*,—the spirits of the dead; and further, we have seen that the danger connected with food is sometimes said to be the danger of an attack by the spirits. So that it is evident that to understand the meaning of the fear of foods it is first of all necessary to understand the notions they have about the spirits, and to do this we shall have to consider the various customs relating to death and burial.

For the society a death is the loss of one of its members, one of its constituent parts. A person occupies a definite position in society, has a certain share in the social life, is one of the supports of the network of social relations. His death constitutes a partial destruction of the social cohesion, the normal social life is disorganised, the social equilibrium is disturbed. After the death the society has to organise itself anew and reach a new condition of equilibrium. In reference to the small community of the Andamans we may translate the above statement into terms of personal feeling by saying that the death removes a person who was the object of feelings of affection and attachment on the part of others and is thus a direct offence against those sentiments in the survivors.

Though the dead man has ceased to exist as a member of the society, it is clear that he has by no means ceased to influence the society. On the contrary he has become the source of intense painful emotions. Where the affection that was felt towards him was previously a source of pleasure it now becomes a source of pain. Defining the "social personality" of an individual as being the sum of characteristics by which he has an effect upon the social life and therefore on the social sentiments of others, we may say that by death the social personality is not annihilated but undergoes a profound change, so that from being an object of pleasurable states of the social sentiments it becomes an object of painful states. This is expressed by the Andamanese by saying that by death a man or woman becomes a *Lau*.

The burial customs of the Andaman Islanders, however, are

not to be regarded as simply the expression of natural personal feeling. They are a collective and ritual expression of a collective feeling. This is evident from the fact that they are regulated in every detail by custom. It is the duty of the relatives and friends to mourn, whether they feel sorrow or not, and it is equally their duty to mourn only for a certain period.

The cohesion of a social group, by which is maintained its existence as a group, depends directly on the existence of a collective system of sentiments or affective dispositions that bind every member to every other. The death, or removal by any other means, of a member of the group is a direct attack against these sentiments. Now whenever a sentiment of any kind is subjected to an attack of such a kind as this there are only two possible alternatives; either the sentiment must suffer a diminution of its intrinsic energy, and thus be less capable of controlling behaviour in the future; or it must find an outlet in an expressive action of some sort which serves as a reaction of defence or compensation and restores the sentiment to its former condition of strength. The typical example of such an emotional reaction is anger; anything that wounds our self-regarding feelings arouses our anger; if it did not do so those feelings would gradually weaken. This law holds true of collective sentiments as well as of individual sentiments. If the society permitted its solidarity to be attacked, whether by death or by any other means, without reacting in such a way as to give relief to wounded social feelings and so to reinstate them in their former condition, these sentiments would lose their strength and the society its cohesion. The burial customs of the Andamanese are to be explained, I believe, as a collective reaction against the attack on the collective feeling of solidarity constituted by the death of a member of the social group.

The man being dead, the first thing that the society does is to sever its connection with him, and the first step in this process is to get rid of the body by burying it or placing it in a tree, to abandon the camp at which he died, and temporarily to drop the use of his name. It is often supposed that customs such as these, which are found in many primitive societies, are due to the fear of the dead man's spirit. That there is an element of fear present is undoubtedly true, but this fear does not seem to be by any means instinctive, and therefore comparable to the fear that some animals exhibit towards the dead body of one of their species. On the contrary the fear itself needs to be explained, and this will have to be attempted later.

There is one group of facts which show very clearly that the burial customs are not solely due to an instinctive fear of dead bodies, namely that the customs vary according to the social position of the deceased. A child plays very little part in the general life of the community; hence on the death of a child the camp is not deserted and only the parents are subjected to the mourning ritual. Similarly the death of a person who has for long been so ill as not to be able to take any important part in social life has very little effect on the community as a whole; the body of such a one is disposed of with scant ceremony and mourning is perfunctory. On the other hand the death of a noted hunter in the prime of life, of a man who is esteemed as a leader, is a much greater loss; the whole community mourns for him; his body is placed on a tree instead of in the ground, showing that his death is regarded as something different from the death of a person who is interred. The body of a stranger who dies or is killed is not buried, but is thrown into the sea or cut up and burnt. The explanation that the natives give of this custom of burning the body is that it serves to dispel danger that might accrue from the presence of the dead body of a stranger. The blood and the fat of the dead man, from which they appear to fear evil influences, are, they say, driven up to the sky in the smoke of the fire and are thus rendered harmless.

There is, then, a close correspondence between the manner of burial and the social value of the person buried, and it is evident that the differences in the mode of disposing of the body are quite inexplicable on the assumption that the funeral customs are solely due to the fear of the dead.

Before burial the corpse is decorated with white clay and red paint. We have already seen that this is an expression on the part of the survivors of their regard for the deceased. A living man or woman is decorated in this way when, for some special reason, it is desired to express the fact that he or she has the good-will and regard of others, and it is applied to the dead body with exactly the same meaning. Fire and water are placed beside the grave. It is not necessary to suppose that the Andamanese believe that the spirit of the dead man makes any use of these, any more than it is necessary for us to believe that the spirit enjoys the flowers that it is our custom to place upon the grave. The action in each case is symbolical.

The dead man was bound by ties of solidarity to those still living. Now that he is dead those ties have not ceased to exist, but continue until the society has recovered from the effects of the death, for they are based on deep-seated and elaborately organised sentiments. I believe that the mourning customs of the Andamanese are to be explained on this basis, as being the means by which the social sentiments of the survivors are slowly reorganised and adapted to the new condition produced by the death. The severance of the dead man from the society is not a sudden but a gradual process, during which his relatives and friends, being still attached to him by social ties, are in an abnormal condition which may be defined as a partial separation from the world of living men and women and a partial aggregation to the world of the dead (i.e. the spirit world). This abnormal condition of the mourner is shown chiefly in his or her withdrawal from participation in the ordinary life of the society. We have seen that the eating of food is, for the Andamanese, one of the most important of social actions, a kind of communion of the society, and that during the period of adolescence a youth is separated or withdrawn from the common life of the group by being forbidden to eat certain foods. So, in strict conformity with the same set of notions, the mourner is separated from the normal life of the society by being forbidden to eat pork or turtle, these being the most important foods that the Andamanese have[1]. Like the *aka-op*, also, the mourner is

---

[1] In a number of tribes of Western Australia I found an exactly similar custom. It was formerly the rule that after the death of a near relative the mourner must abstain from eating kangaroo, that being the largest game animal. Since the establishment of sheep stations in their country, with the consequent great decrease in numbers of the kangaroo, it has come about that the animal which now provides their most important supply of meat is the sheep, and the modern rule is that a mourner must not eat mutton.

forbidden to take part in a dance, or to decorate himself with red paint and white clay, for by these actions the Andaman Islander becomes conscious of his position as a member of a closely unified group, and it is necessary for the mourner, as for the *aka-op*, to feel that for the time being he is cut off from the ordinary life of the group. The disuse, during the period of mourning, of the name of a mourner is to be explained, as we shall see more plainly later, on the same principle, the personal name being what marks the person's position in the social life, so that the temporary dropping of the name shows that for the time being the person is not occupying his normal social position.

The distinctive sign of a mourner is the use of clay, which is smeared over the body and head, and from the name of this clay is derived the term that denotes a mourner (*aka-odu*). It is possible to explain this also as a symbolic expression of the separation of the mourner from the world of living men and his aggregation to the world of the dead. In his everyday life the Andaman Islander is black from head to foot. During mourning he turns himself as nearly as possible white from head to foot, by covering his body all over with clay. It must be remembered that the spirits of the dead are said to be white or light in colour. This is undoubtedly one of the reasons why the (light-coloured) natives of India are called spirits (*Lau*), while men of such a dark-coloured race as the African negroes are not referred to by this term. The use of clay would therefore seem to serve not only to make the mourner unlike his ordinary self, but to make him like the spirits of the dead.

Of course, the natives explain all these customs of mourning as being expressions of sorrow for their loss, and this is, from the simple standpoint of everyday life, an adequate and true explanation. From the standpoint of psychology, however, what we need to know is why the sorrow is expressed in just these ways and no others. Moreover, the natives give as a further reason for the mourning customs that if they did not observe them they would be liable to sickness or even death.

I have said that the Andamanese believe that by death a man or woman becomes a *Lau*, but there is a little uncertainty in the statements of the natives as to whether he becomes a spirit at once, immediately after the death, or whether he does so only after the flesh of the body has decayed. Both statements are sometimes made, but it seems common to think of the dead person during the period of mourning not as a spirit (*Lau*) but as a dead man (*empilo*). We may best express the ideas of the natives by saying that the process by which a man becomes a spirit is one that takes some months to complete, and is only ended when the bones are dug up. An interesting insight into their notions in this matter is afforded by a belief, about which unfortunately I have very scanty information, to the effect that when a man dies he is initiated into the world of the dead by a ceremony resembling the ceremonies by which a youth is initiated into manhood. In the statement of an *Aka-Kede* informant the ceremony was spoken of by the term *kimil*, which is generally used for the initiation ceremonies, and was described as a *poroto-kimil*, i.e., a ceremony in which the dead man ate *poroto* (*Caryota sobolifera*) in just the same way that a youth eats turtle (*čokbi*) at the *čokbi-kimil*. There is independent evidence that there is a special connection between the spirits of the dead and the *Caryota* palm[1].

The description of this ceremony (of initiation into the world of the dead) that was given to me stated that in it the shredded fibre named *koro* was used in just the same way as the leaves of the *Hibiscus* are used in the turtle-eating ceremony. Further, as in the peace-making ceremony men stand against a suspended cane from which depend bunches of this same *koro*, so in the initiation into the spirit world the initiate has to stand against the rainbow while the dancing spirits shake it and him. It is this shaking of the rainbow (according to my informant) that causes earthquakes. It may be recalled that the rainbow is regarded as a sort of bridge between this world and the spirit world, and that its name is "the spirit's cane," so that it would seem that it is regarded as like a cane with *koro* fibre suspended from it, such as is used in the peace-making ceremony.

The explanation of the use of this *koro* fibre was postponed earlier in the chapter, and may well be undertaken here. It serves

[1] Page 171.

as a sign that the spot where it is placed is tabu, or, in more precise terms, that the spot must be avoided because of the presence there of a force or power that makes things dangerous. This force is present at the grave of a dead man, and therefore the fibre is placed at the grave to mark the fact, while a bunch is similarly suspended at the entrance to a village that is deserted after a death. In the peace-making ceremony the members of the one party stand against a suspended cane to which are attached strips of the fibre. The meaning of this, I think, is that it thus forbids the members of the other party from attacking them. If a man were to leave the screen of *koro*, he would, I believe, be liable to be killed by the enemy party; it is only as long as he stands against it with his arms outstretched that he is safe, because while there he is tabu.

How then does this belief in the fibre as a mark of tabu come about? The fibre is worn by the women of the Little Andaman to cover their pudenda, and it was formerly worn in this way by the women of the North Andaman. We may conclude that this was an old element in the Andaman culture dating back to the remote period when the inhabitants of the Little Andaman became separated from those of the Great Andaman. Now in a very special sense the sexual organs of women are tabu, and, without discussing the matter in detail, we may suppose that the Andaman Islander regards the genitals of women as a spot in which resides the same sort of force or power that makes the spirits, or the body of a dead man, dangerous. One point may be mentioned as throwing light on this subject, and helping forward the argument, namely that the natives of the North Andaman often use the expression *Lau-buku* (meaning literally "spirit-women" or "female spirits") to denote women collectively instead of the phrase that might be expected—*n'e-buku*. It would seem that by reason of their sex and the special ideas that are associated with it, women are regarded as having a very special relation with the world of spirits. We may conclude that the *koro* fibre, being a convenient material for the purpose, was first used as a covering for the women, and in this way came to be used as a sign of tabu in general, or else that for some unknown reason the fibre was selected as a suitable material to mark any kind of tabu, and so came to be used both as a covering for women and also as a sign of warning at the grave and the village that has been visited by death[1].

To return from this digression to the question of the initiation of the dead man into the world of spirits, it is clear that since such ceremonies take time to accomplish there is a period during which the dead man is in an indeterminate position; he is no longer a member of the society of the living, and has not yet become a member of the society of the dead. As long as he is thus situated his relatives and friends are still attached to him, so that he still remains as it were in partial contact with the living. During this time the society is still suffering the ill effects of the death, and the process of readjustment by means of the customs of mourning is still taking place. At the end of it the dead man becomes completely absorbed in the spirit world, and as a spirit he has no more part in or influence over the social life than any other spirit, and the mourning is brought to a close by means of a ceremony.

This ceremony has two parts. One is the recovery of the bones and their reaggregation to the society, a rite which we may regard as the final settling of the dead man in his proper place. All that is left of him, who was once a source of strength to the community, who had once—as it is here expressed—a social value, are the bones, his name, and the memory of him that his friends retain. We may suppose that the bones still have something of the value that originally attached to their owner, and indeed it is evident that they have, for after they are recovered they are affectionately treasured as relics by the relatives. By the end of the period of mourning the painful feelings aroused by the death have died down, so that the dead man is now the object only of memories that are pleasant, or, at the worst, bittersweet. The bones, then, are visible evidences of the fact that the society has recovered from the disruptive shock of the death, and this is why they are dug up as soon as the recovery is complete, or rather in order to complete it, and are thereafter treasured.

[1] The brakes formed by the cane (*bido*) from the leaves of which the *koro* fibre is obtained seem to be regarded as lurking places of the spirits. The natives often speak of the *Bido-teč-lau* (*Calamus* leaf spirits).

It should now be clear why the Andamanese attribute to the bones of dead persons the power to protect them from unseen dangers. Like the bones of animals that have been eaten they are visible and wearable signs of past dangers overcome through the protective action of the society itself, and are therefore a guarantee of similar protection in the future. And as the death of a member is an enormously more important event for the community than the mere killing and eating of a dugong, so an enormously greater protective power is attributed to the human bones than to those of any animal.

The bones, then, are dug up, and brought into camp, where they are wept over just as a friend who has been absent is wept over. All that is left of the former person returns to the social life, henceforward to occupy a definite place in it, and the weeping is the rite of aggregation, the expression of the attachment of those who weep to the bones that now return to them from the grave. The skull and jawbone and the long bones are then decorated with red paint and white clay, this being the way in which the relatives express their sense of the value of them. The other bones are made up into strings and distributed to be used on occasion as amulets.

Soon after the digging up of the bones the other part of the ceremony of the end of mourning takes place. We have seen that while the dead man was in an indeterminate position his relatives were still attached to him by social bonds, but now that he has finally become a spirit, and is for ever definitely cut off from the human society, these bonds cease to exist. The mourners, therefore, who have been cut off from the normal social life are free to return to it and even if they should not so desire, yet it is their duty to do so. The return of the mourners to the society is marked by a dance. The clay that has marked their condition is taken off, and they are decorated with white clay and red paint and all the ornaments usual on ceremonial occasions. Thus decorated they dance, the women on this occasion being required to dance as well as the men. The dance is interrupted shortly after it is begun in order that those who have not been mourning may weep with the mourners. The weeping, according to the explanation at the beginning of the chapter is a rite of aggregation by which the mourners are welcomed back to the society, just as returning friends are welcomed after an absence. It has nothing whatever to do, I believe, with the dead person for whom they have been mourning, but is merely an expression of solidarity between those still alive. Dancing and the decorations used in the dance, I have argued, are means by which the society expresses its own unity, and makes the individual realise what it means to be one of a group, so that in this dance we see the society once more coming together to continue its common life, and compelling those who have been cut off from it to feel, even against their inclinations, that they have become once more units of the social body. After this ceremony the mourners are relieved from the restrictions to which they were subjected.

In order to complete this discussion of the burial customs it is necessary to explain why a person's name should be dropped from use after his death, and although this will require a digression of some length, this seems the most convenient point at which to deal with it. There is a very special relation between the name of anything and its fundamental characteristics, which in logic we describe by saying that the latter are included in the connotation of the name. The way in which the Andamanese represent this relation to themselves is shown in one of the legends. At a time when the ancestors did not know either the names or the uses of the different objects to be found in their country, one of them, *Da Teyat* by name, walked through the forest enquiring of the objects he met what were their names. From most of them he received no reply, but the yam and the resin replied to him and gave him their names. The legend shows that as soon as the hero of the tale knew the name of the yam he immediately knew that it was of use as a food and that it required to be cooked in a particular way, although he was till then ignorant of those important properties. Similarly, having discovered the name of the resin he knew that it could be made into a torch and so used to give light.

There is, to the mind of the Andaman Islander, a somewhat similar and very important connection between a person's name and what is here called his social personality, and this is exhibited in the customs whereby the name is avoided on certain occasions. A consideration of the different instances will show, I think, that the name is always avoided whenever the owner is for any reason prevented from taking his or her usual place in the life of the society. At such times the social personality is as it were suppressed, and the name which represents it is therefore also suppressed.

From the moment of her first menstruation to the date of her marriage, or more strictly to the date of her first parturition, the birth-name of a woman is dropped from use and she is called by her flower-name. A woman only attains her complete social personality as a mother. As a child she has not the power to become a mother. She acquires that power at her first menstruation and therefore from that time until this new virtue is actively exercised she is in a position in which one of her virtues, one of the qualities making up her social personality, is in abeyance. Therefore her name (her birth-name) is not used and she is given a temporary name in its place, a flower-name. She is, as it were, in blossom, and only when her body ripens to its fruit is she a complete woman.

At certain stages of the initiation ceremonies the name of a youth or of a girl (the flower-name in this instance) is avoided for a certain period. Such occasions are during, and for some time after, any of the more important ceremonies, such as the cutting of the boy's back, the puberty ceremony of the girl, the turtle-eating and pig-eating ceremonies. After a boy's back is cut he is addressed and spoken of for some time as *Ejido*, his own name not being spoken. Similarly during and after the turtle-eating or the pig-eating ceremony he is addressed and spoken of by the name *Kimil*. The explanation of these customs is that at these times the initiate is in an abnormal position by reason of the ceremony that has taken place, and is not permitted to take an ordinary part in social life. After the initiation ceremony, for example, the youth is not permitted to handle a bow for some weeks (the bow being the typical masculine implement).

The names of a newly-married couple are avoided for a few days after their marriage. Marriage produces an important change in the social personality, and this change is expressed in the marriage ceremony, but all such changes take time, and it is some days at least before the married couple can be expected to have settled down in their new positions. For these days, therefore, their names are not used. The same sort of explanation will hold for the custom of dropping the names of a father and mother before and after the birth of a child, particularly the first born.

At the turtle-eating ceremony of the North Andaman coast-dwellers the youth is given a new name. It is possible that a girl is also given a new name at this time, and that another name is also given to the youth at the pig-eating ceremony, but on these points I neglected to make sufficient enquiry. The name given at the turtle-eating ceremony is never used and is not likely to be known except to those who were present at the ceremony, and therefore serves no such purpose as the flower-name of the girl. The giving of the name is simply the mark of the change of social personality brought about by the ceremony. The youth receives an addition to his personality and therefore receives an additional name. It is significant that all the names given at this ceremony have reference to the sea and to things of the sea, particularly to turtle, such as *Čokbi-čiro*, turtle-liver, *Čokbi-tei*, turtle-blood, etc.

During the period of mourning, when, as we have seen, the mourner is withdrawn from the ordinary life of the society, his name is not used, showing that during this period his social personality is in a state of partial suppression. After the mourning period is over the mourner, when he resumes his social personality, resumes at the same time his name.

Now death is the most fundamental modification of the social personality that is possible and therefore the name of a person recently dead is strictly avoided. Death, however, does not destroy the social personality utterly and for ever, but produces in it a profound change, which begins at the death itself and is only completed at the end of and by means of the customs of mourning. After the mourning is over the virtues of the dead man affect the survivors through memory, and his bones form a precious possession of the community, thus constituting for him a new social value, a new personality. During the period of change, while the personality does not exist in the same form as before the death, but does not yet exist in the form in which it will when he lives only in the memory of his friends, the name is not used. After the mourning period is over the name may again be used.

In general then, it may be said that at any period in which a person is undergoing a critical change in his condition in so far as it affects the society his name falls out of use, to be resumed when the period of change is over. The reason for this is that during such periods of change the social personality is suppressed or latent and therefore the name which is closely associated with the social personality must be suppressed also.

The customs of burial and mourning are therefore seen to be not simply the result of natural feelings of fear and sorrow but ritual actions performed under a sense of obligation and strictly regulated by tradition. They are means by which the society acts upon its members, compelling them to feel emotions appropriate to the occasion. Since the dead person has, by his death, become a cause of social disruption, all contact with him must be avoided. But the dead man had a certain value to the society, and as a thing of any kind cannot be valued unless its loss is felt as a source of pain, so if the community did not mourn when it lost one of its members that feeling of the social value of individuals on which the existence of the society depends would soon diminish in strength, thereby weakening the social cohesion.

It is now possible for us to understand the Andamanese beliefs about the spirits. The basis of these beliefs, I wish to maintain, is the fact that at the death of an individual his social personality (as defined above) is not annihilated, but is suddenly changed. This continuance after death is a fact of immediate experience to the Andaman Islanders and not in any way a deduction. The person has not ceased to exist. For one thing his body is still there. But above all he is still the object of the social sentiments of the survivors, and thereby he continues to act upon the society. The removal of a member of the group is felt not as something negative but as the positive cause of great social disturbance.

The spirits are feared or regarded as dangerous. The basis of this fear is the fact that the spirit (i.e. the social personality of a person recently dead) is obviously a source of weakness and disruption to the community, affecting the survivors through their attachment to him, and producing a condition of dysphoria, of diminished social activity. The natural impulse of the Andaman Islander or of any other human being, would be, I believe, not to shun the dead body of a loved one, but to remain near it as long as possible. It is the society, acting under a quite different set of impulses, that compels the relatives to separate themselves from the remains of the one they loved. The death of a small child has very little influence on the general activity of the community, and the motive for severing connection with the dead that is present in the case of an adult, either does not exist or is so weak as to be overruled by the private feelings of affection, and so the child is buried in the hut of the parents, that they may continue to keep it near them. This affords a good test of the hypothesis, and gives strong support to the view that the fear of the dead man (his body and his spirit) is a collective feeling induced in the society by the fact that by death he has become the object of a dysphoric condition of the collective consciousness.

If the Andamanese are asked what they fear from the spirit of a dead man they reply that they fear sickness or death, and that if the burial and mourning customs are not properly observed the relatives of the dead person will fall sick and perhaps die.

The basis of this notion of the spirits is that the near relatives of the deceased, being bound to him by close social ties, are influenced by everything that happens to him, and share in his good or evil fortune. So that when by sickness and resulting death he is removed from the community, they are as it were drawn after him. For this reason they are, during the period of mourning, between life and death, being still attached to the dead man. Contact with the world of the dead is therefore regarded as dangerous for the living because it is believed that they may be drawn completely into that world. Death is a process by which a person leaves the living world and enters the world of the spirits, and since no one dies willingly he is conceived as being under a compulsive force acting from the world of spirits. Now sickness is a condition that often ends in death, a first stage of the way leading to the world of spirits. Hence sickness is conceived by the Andamanese as a condition of partial contact with that world. This is what is meant by the statement that sickness and death come from the spirits.

The way the Andamanese think about the spirits is shown in the *Akar-Bale* legend of the origin of death[1]. *Yaramurud*, having died through an accident, self-caused, becomes a spirit, but he does so only under the compulsion exercised upon him by his mother, who, now that he is dead, insists that he must go away from the world of the living and become a spirit. The spirit then comes back to see his brother and by this contact causes the brother's death. The story implies that it was not because *Yaramurud* was evilly disposed towards his brother that he killed him, but on the contrary it was his attachment to his relative that caused him to return to visit him, and death followed as a result of this contact of the living man with the spirit. Since that time deaths have continued to occur in the same way. Thus it appears that the Andamanese conceive that the spirits do not cause death and sickness through evil intention, but through their mere proximity, and, as the legend very clearly shows, the burial customs are intended to cut off the unwilling spirit from contact with the living. This explains also why during the period of mourning the relatives of a dead person are thought to be in danger of sickness, and have more to fear from the spirit than others, for since it is they who were most attached to him during life it is they who are most likely to suffer from contact with him after he is dead. It was *Yaramurud's* brother who was the first to die through the influence of the spirits.

The feelings of the living towards the spirits of the dead are therefore ambivalent, compounded of affection and fear, and this must be clearly recognized if we are to understand all the Andamanese beliefs and customs. We may compare the relation between the society of the living and the society of the dead to that between two hostile communities having occasional friendly relations. That the Andamanese themselves look upon it in some such way is shown by the belief that the ceremony by which a dead man is initiated into the world of spirits resembles the peace-making ceremony. The dead man, up to the time of his death, has been living in a state of enmity with the spirits, and before he can enter their community and share their life he

[1] Page 216.

has to make peace with them in the same way that men make peace with one another after they have been at war.

This notion of hostility between the society and the world of spirits is found in other primitive societies, and seems everywhere to have a definite social function. The removal of a member of the community either by death or otherwise is a direct attack on the social solidarity and produces in primitive societies an emotional reaction of the same general character as anger. This collective anger, if freely expressed, serves as a compensating mechanism, satisfying and restoring the damaged sentiment[1]. But this can only happen if there is some object against which the anger can be directed. In the instance of homicide the social anger is directed against the person responsible for the death and against the social group to which he belongs. In the instance of death from sickness some other object has to be found, and amongst primitive peoples there are two chief ways in which this is done. An example of one method is afforded by the tribes of Australia, amongst whom there is a strong and constant hostility between neighbouring local groups, with a result that the anger at a death from sickness directs itself against some community with which the group of the dead man is at enmity and it is believed that some member of that community has caused the death by magic. The Andamans afford an example of the second method. Amongst them it would seem that the enmity between different local groups (except as concerns the *Jarawa* in the South Andaman) was never very strong and the belief in evil magic was not highly developed, so that the anger at a death is directed against the spirits, and sometimes find expression in violent railings against them, accompanied by all the bodily manifestations of extreme rage and hatred.

Now though the Andamanese regard the spirits with fear and hatred, and believe that all contact with them is dangerous for living men, yet they do not look on them as essentially evil, for that would conflict with their own feelings of attachment to their dead friends.

---

[1] The psychological function of individual anger is to restore to their normal condition the wounded self-regarding sentiments. The function of collective anger is similarly to restore the collective sentiments on which the solidarity of the society depends.

I gathered a few hints that they even believe that at times the spirits can and will help them. Thus a man will call on the sea-spirits of his own country to send plenty of turtle (over which the spirits seem to be assumed to have power) when he is going hunting. A very important fact in this connection is the different way in which a native regards the spirits of his own country and of other parts, the latter being thought to be much more dangerous than the former because presumably they are the spirits not of relatives and friends but of strangers at the best or enemies at the worst.

There is other evidence that the Andamanese do not regard the power that is possessed by the spirits as being essentially evil. This power, whereby the spirits are able to cause sickness, seems to be shared by the bones of dead men. Indeed the Andamanese call such bones "spirit-bones" (*lau-toi, čauga-ta*). Now this power in the bones (though it may at times be supposed to cause sickness) is more commonly made use of in order to prevent or cure it.

The most conclusive evidence that the power of the spirits is not intrinsically evil, but may be used to produce both good and evil is afforded by the beliefs about medicine-men or dreamers (*oko-jumu*). There are three ways in which a man can become a medicine-man. The first is (as the natives put it) by dying and coming back to life. Now when a man dies he becomes a spirit and therefore acquires the peculiar powers and qualities of a spirit, which he retains if he returns to life. Secondly, if a man straying in the jungle by himself be affronted by the spirits, and if he show no fear (for if he is afraid they will kill him) they may keep him with them for a time and then let him go. Such a man, on his return, is regarded as being a medicine-man, and possessing all the powers of medicine-men. I was told of one man who became a medicine-man in this way within living memory, and it was stated that when he returned from the forest where he had been kept by the spirits for two or three days he was decorated with *koro* fibre. We have seen that this fibre is used by the spirits in the ceremony by which they initiate dead men, and its presence on the returned warrior was perhaps accepted by his friends as evidence that he had been initiated by the spirits. The third and last way in which a man may become a medicine-man is by having intercourse with the spirits in his dreams. This is a point to which it will be necessary to return later. For the present it is sufficient to note that in every instance the power of the medicine-man is believed to be derived from his contact with the spirits in one of the three possible ways.

We are justified in concluding that the special power of the medicine-man, by which he is distinguished from his fellows, is simply the same power that is possessed by the spirits, from contact with whom he has obtained it. The medicine-man is believed to be able both to cause and to cure sickness, to arouse and to dispel storms. In other words he has power for both good and evil, and we must conclude that the spirits have the same. Moreover, it is commonly said that the medicine-man is able to produce the effects he does, whether they be harmful or beneficial to his fellows, by communicating with the spirits in dreams and enlisting their aid. This would seem to prove the point that I am here concerned with, that the power possessed by the spirits, though contact with it is always dangerous, may yet in certain circumstances be of benefit to the society, and is therefore not essentially evil in nature.

The Andamanese believe that a medicine-man communicates with the spirits in sleep, and this is not the only evidence that they believe sleep to be a condition in which contact with the world of spirits is easier than in waking life. It is believed that sickness is more likely to begin during sleep than when awake. During the initiation ceremonies the initiate is required to abstain from sleep after eating pork or turtle, and this would seem to be because sleep is regarded as generally dangerous and therefore to be avoided on such occasions as this when every precaution needs to be taken.

The explanation of this belief seems to lie in the fact that sleep is a condition of diminished social activity, in which the individual is withdrawn from active social life, and is therefore also withdrawn from the protection of the society. After eating turtle the initiate is in urgent need of the protection of the society, which would be lost to him if he were permitted to sleep. After a death, when the corpse remains in the camp all night the people remain awake, and since there is no other common activity in which they can join, they sing, and thus protect themselves from the spirits that are present as the cause of the death.

This explanation implies that all conditions of diminished social activity on the part of an individual are dangerous. One example of such a condition is sickness, in which the sick person is unable to pursue his ordinary occupations. Other examples are afforded by a mother, and to a certain extent a father during the period preceding and following the birth of a child, and by a woman during the menstrual period. All these, as various customs show, are believed by the Andamanese to be conditions of danger in which it is necessary to take ritual or magical precautions. A better example for our purpose is that of an adolescent during the period covered by the initiation ceremonies, when, as we have seen, he is as it were cut off from the society, and there is abundant evidence that the Andamanese believe this to be a state of danger. Another example is the condition of a homicide during the period of his isolation. Lastly, we have seen that a mourner is cut off from the ordinary social life, and it may now be noted that the native explanation of the restrictions observed in that state is that if things were not done thus the mourner would be ill; in other words the condition of mourning is one of danger, and the ritual referring to it is the means by which the danger (from the spirit world) is avoided. This explanation does not conflict with the one previously given but on the contrary we can now see that the notion that the mourner is in a position partly withdrawn from active participation in social life necessarily involves the belief that he is in a condition of danger.

We may conclude that every condition in which the individual is withdrawn from full participation in active social life is regarded as dangerous for him, and that this is at least one of the reasons why sleep is so regarded. We have already noted that all conditions of danger tend to be thought of as due to contact with the spirits, and sleep is therefore supposed to be a state in which such contact is easier than in waking life. Now sleep is visited by dreams and it comes about that the dream-life, by reason of its contrast with waking-life, is seized upon by the Andamanese as a means by which the nature of the spirit world may be represented to the imagination.

The Andaman Islander seems to regard the dream-world as a world of shadows or reflections, for he uses the same word to denote a shadow, a reflection in a mirror, and a dream (the stem *-jumu* in *Aka-Jeru*). Now when a man enters this shadow-world in sleep he is, as we have seen, conceived as coming into partial contact with the world of spirits. Hence the Andaman Islander believes that in dreams he may communicate with the spirits, that dreams may be a cause of sickness, and that in dreams a medicine-man can cause or cure sickness in his fellows. In this shadow-world the man himself becomes as it were a shadow, a mere reflection of himself; it is not he that lives and acts in his dreams but his *ot-jumulo*, his double, his shadow-self, or, as we might say, his soul. It is but a step from this to the representation of the spirit-world as a similar world of shadows and dream-shapes, and to the conclusion that when a man dies it is his *ot-jumulo* that becomes the spirit.

To summarise the argument, the belief in the world of spirits rests on the actual fact that a dead person continues to affect the society. As the effect is one of disorganisation, whereby the social sentiments are wounded, the dead are avoided and the spirits are regarded with fear. But as a recently dead person is still regarded with feelings of attachment by his friends, the resulting final attitude towards the spirits is ambivalent. By a simple step the spirits come to be regarded as the cause of sickness and death, and therefore as hostile to living men. Yet, as the beliefs about medicine-men show, it is possible for exceptional individuals to be on terms of friendship with the spirits. Finally, the dream-life affords a means by which the spirit-world may be represented in a simple and concrete manner. This last feature (the association of the spirits with dreams) I believe to be a secondary elaboration of the primary or fundamental belief which shows itself in the ritual of death and mourning, serving only to rationalise it and make it more concrete. This need of concrete representation of the spirit-world shows itself in other beliefs, in which may be seen the tendency to become self-contradictory that is often the mark of ideas that arise as the result of attempts to rationalise conative and affective impulses. The spirits are, on the one hand, as it were shadows or images of living men, and yet, since they are feared and disliked, they are often represented as being repulsive and inhuman, with long legs and short bodies, with long beards and ugly faces[1]. The spirits must be thought of as somewhere, but there is no consistency in the statements as to where that somewhere is; one man will say that they live in the sky, another that they are under the earth, a third will point to a particular island as their home; at the same time it is evident from other statements that they vaguely conceive them as being everywhere, in the forest and the sea.

We are now in a position to understand what the Andaman Islander means when he says that the danger he fears from food is from the spirits. The greatest evil that can happen to the community is the sickness or death of its members, and these are believed to be the work of the spirits. The sense of the social value of food takes the form of a belief that food is dangerous, and inevitably the danger comes to be conceived as that of sickness or death, and is therefore associated in their minds with the spirits.

But there is a more fundamental reason than this. I have tried to show that it is because food has such important effects for good and evil on the social life that it is believed to be endued with a peculiar power which makes it necessary to approach it with ritual precautions. If this thesis be valid it should be capable of generalisation, and we should find the same power attributed to every object or being that is capable of affecting in important ways the well-being of the society. We should expect that the Andamanese would attribute this power not only to the more important things used for food but also to such things as the weather and dead men (i.e., the spirits). Now this, if the argument has been correct, is exactly what we do find, and we have here the reason why the Andaman Islander, when asked what he fears from eating dangerous foods, replies that he fears sickness or the spirits of the dead.

We may formulate in precise language the beliefs that underlie the ceremonial, remembering always that the Andaman Islanders

---

[1] I once drew a few grotesque figures for the amusement of some Andamanese children, and they at once pronounced them to be "spirits."

themselves are quite incapable of expressing these beliefs in words and are probably only vaguely conscious of them. (1) There is a power or force in all objects or beings that in any way affect the social life. (2) It is by virtue of this power that such things are able to aid or harm the society. (3) The power, no matter what may be the object or being in which it is present, is never either essentially good or essentially evil, but is able to produce both good and evil results. (4) Any contact with the power is dangerous, but the danger is avoided by ritual precautions. (5) The degree of power possessed by anything is directly proportioned to the importance of the effects that it has on the social life. (6) The power in one thing may be used to counteract the danger due to contact with the power in some other thing.

We have studied this power in the animals and plants used for food and the things used as materials. It is this that makes turtle dangerous to eat and *Anadendron* fibre dangerous to prepare, and it is this also that makes animal bones or the leaves of *Hibiscus* available for protection. We have now seen that the same power is present in dead men, in their bodies, their bones, and in the spirit-world to which dead men go. All contact with the world of the dead is highly dangerous, and yet we have seen that human bones may be used for protection and that even the spirits may be induced to heal sickness or allay storms. We have also seen that the same power is present in the *oko-jumu*, and we have made the important discovery that it is through contact with the spirits that he acquires the power. This reveals another important principle. (7) If an individual comes into contact with the power in any thing and successfully avoids the danger of such contact, he becomes himself endowed with power of the same kind as that with which he is in contact. Now although the *oko-jumu* possesses a very special social value, yet every man and woman has some social value, some of that power which makes any being capable of affecting the society for good or ill, and we can now see that the initiation ceremonies are the means by which the individual is endowed with power (or, as the natives say, made strong) by being brought into contact with the special power present in each of the important kinds of food. The initiation of the ordinary man or woman is parallel to the initiation of the *oko-jumu* save that in one instance it is the power in foods and in the other that in the spirits with which the initiation is concerned.

It has been held in this chapter that the society or the social life itself is the chief source of protection against danger for the individual. If this be so then the society itself possesses this same power with which we are dealing, and we must expect to find that contact with this power is also dangerous for the individual. Now the occasion on which the individual comes into contact with the power in the society is in the dance, and I found evidence that the natives believe that dancing is dangerous in exactly the same way as eating food. Confirmation of this will appear later.

It would seem that for the Andaman Islander the social life is a process of complex interaction of powers or forces present in the society itself, in each individual, in animals and plants and the phenomena of nature, and in the world of spirits, and on these powers the well-being of the society and its members depends. By the action of the principle of opposition the society —the world of the living—comes to be opposed to the spirits— the world of the dead. The society itself is the chief source of protection to the individual; the spirits are the chief source of danger. Hence all protection tends to be referred to the society and all danger to the spirits. In the initiation ceremonies it is the society that protects the initiate against the dangers of food, and those dangers are referred, generally if not quite consistently, to the spirits, with which at first sight they would seem to have nothing to do.

It is now at last possible to understand the uses of the word *ot-kimil* which were first discussed on page 267 above. When the word is used in reference to a person who has just partaken of food it denotes a condition of danger produced by contact with the power in foods. This condition results at any time from the eating of any of the more important foods, but is clearly produced in an extreme form when a food such as turtle or pork is being eaten for the first time at a ceremony of initiation. Hence the initiate is most intensely *kimil* and is therefore addressed and spoken of by that term, or as we might say " the *kimil* person."

Used in reference to sickness the word denotes a condition of danger due to contact with that power (in the spirits or in food) which is the cause of sickness. Used in reference to storms it again denotes a condition of danger for the society. Storms are sometimes said to be caused by the spirits[1]. This is also the explanation of the use of the word to denote a particular season of the year. The *Kimil* season is by no means hot, but cool; it is, however, the season at which violent cyclones are most likely to occur, being the period of the change from the south-west to the north-east monsoon. It is therefore a season of danger to the society from that power which produces storms.

Finally, a man who has joined in a dance is said to be *ot-kimil* and seems to be regarded as being in a condition of danger similar to that produced by food. It might be thought that in this instance the word is only used in its literal meaning of "hot," but I believe that this is not so. The dance is the occasion on which the individual comes most closely into contact with the power in the society itself, and I believe that this contact is regarded as dangerous and therefore as making the individual *ot-kimil*.

Thus we see that in its various uses the word *ot-kimil* denotes a condition of danger due to contact with that power on the interaction of the different manifestations of which the well-being of the society depends.

How is it then that to denote this condition the Andamanese use a word which, primarily, seems to mean "heat"? The answer is that they conceive the qualities that give to objects their social values as being the manifestations of a kind of energy, and as being similar to the kind of energy which they know best, that of heat. The psychological basis of this is not difficult to discover. The eating of food is productive of bodily heat (the Andamanese live in a hot climate and eat much fat, it must be remembered), so that the power present in foods is inevitably thought of as a sort of heat or heat-producing energy. In the dance the Andaman Islander experiences, as we have seen, an increase in his own personal force or energy, and this also is associated with

[1] The Andamanese beliefs about storms and the weather generally will be dealt with in the next chapter.

the sensation of bodily heat produced by dancing. All other bodily activities result in the sensation of heat (in hunting and work of all kinds) and as it is in his activities that the social value of the individual is manifested this value is itself conceived as a sort of heat-producing energy. Further the Andamanese seem to associate with the idea of heat all conditions of mental activity and excitement. We ourselves do the same, as shown by such words as " ardour," " zeal," etc. and such phrases as "the heat of anger, or enthusiasm," and there is good ground for thinking that all such associations or symbolisms (sensory metaphors) have a physiological basis. Finally, fire which (as we shall see better in the next chapter) is regarded by the Andamanese as the most important possession of the society, and which (as we have already seen) has in a very high degree the power that makes objects capable of affecting the society, is for this reason in a suitable position to become the archetype of all forms of energy, activity or force. This system of notions of the Andamanese that the world is the arena of a continual struggle of forces present in the society itself, in each individual, in the substances that are used for foods and materials, in fire, in storms and sunshine, and in the spirits and bones of the dead, is, as I have tried to show, the result not of any process of reasoning but of the immediate social experience, and as it is in the heat of his own body, and in states of excitement of his own mind, that the individual does actually experience the effects of these forces upon himself he uses the same word to denote all conditions of heat and all conditions of the manifestation of this energy, organising around that word as well as he can his somewhat vague conceptions.

In case this symbolism should still seem strange, and the explanation of it unsatisfactory, it is as well to show by means of a couple of quotations that in other primitive societies differing widely from the Andamanese similar uses of the words hot and heat are to be found. In his work on the Achehnese (Vol. I, p. 305) C. Snouck Hurgronje writes thus of the natives of the Malay Archipelago: "In the native language of the E. Archipelago all happiness, rest and well-being are united under the concept of 'coolness,' while the words 'hot' and 'heat' typify all the powers of evil. Thus when a person has either just endured the attack of a 'hot' influence or has luckily contrived to escape it, the adat prescribes methods of 'cooling' in order to confirm him in the well-being which he has recovered or escaped losing. The same methods are also adopted for charming away evil things and baneful influences, the removal of which is regarded as an imperative necessity. For instance, the completion of a house, and various domestic festivities, are made the occasion for a process of 'cooling'; so also with a ship when newly built or after holding of a kanduri on board; and before the padi is planted out the ground must be purified from 'hot' or dangerous influences." In this instance we find the word "hot" used only in reference to evil forces. In the Andamans there is no line drawn between good and evil forces. In spite of the differences between them it is clear that the same mental process is responsible for the symbolic use of the word "hot" in the Andamans and in the Malay Archipelago.

In Codrington's *The Melanesians*, p. 191, we find an example of the same mode of thought. "That invisible power which is believed by the natives to cause all such effects as transcend their conception of the regular course of nature and to reside in spiritual beings, whether in the spiritual part of living men or in the ghosts of the dead, being imparted by them to their names and to various things that belong to them, such as stones, snakes, and indeed objects of all sorts, is that generally known as mana. By means of this men are able to control or direct the forces of nature, to make rain or sunshine, wind or calm, to cause sickness or remove it, to know what is far off in time and space, to bring good luck or prosperity or to blast and curse. In the New Hebrides, the Banks' Islands, the Solomon Islands about Florida as in New Zealand and many of the Pacific Islands the word in use is mana. In Santa Cruz a different word malete is used, which bears however the same meaning. At Saa in Malanta all persons and things in which this supernatural power resides are said to be saka, that is, hot. Ghosts that are powerful are saka; a man who has knowledge of the things which have spiritual power is himself saka; one who knows a charm which is saka mutters it over water, saru'e and makes the water 'hot, ha'asaka.

The people of Mala Masiki, the lesser part of the island, which is cut in two not far from its south-eastern end by a narrow channel, think that the men of the larger part, Mala Paina, are very saka. If one of these visiting the Saa people points with his finger, suisui, there is danger of death or calamity; if one of them spits on a man he dies at once." Here again there are important differences, as might be expected in such different cultures as those of Melanesia and the Andamans, and yet it is clear that there is a fundamental similarity of mental process.

The nature of this symbolic representation of the forces that affect the social life may be made clear by considering another example. The natives say that they use *odu* clay after eating because their bodies give off an odour which would attract the spirits if they did not paint themselves. The power of an object, by virtue of which it has what may be called magical efficacy, is sometimes identified with its odour. A number of the plants that are used as remedies for sickness, such as the *Trigonostemon*, are possessed of strong and characteristic odours, and the natives think that it is through the odour that they effect a cure. Similarly the powerful properties attributed to the *Anadendron*, whereby it will cause rheumatism, keep away sharks and spirits, and turn turtle-meat bad, or stop a storm, are all said to be the results of its "smell." The stimulating power of olfactory sensations probably has much to do with the development of these beliefs, but the discussion of their psycho-physiological basis would lead us too far away from the main subject, interesting as it would be.

In the jungles of the Andamans it is possible to recognize a distinct succession of odours during a considerable part of the year as one after another the commoner trees and lianas come into flower. When, for example, the species of *Sterculia* called in the North Andaman *jeru* comes into blossom, it is almost impossible to get away from the smell of it except on the seashore when the wind is from the sea. Moreover these various flowers give their scent to the honey that is made from them, so that there is also a succession of differently flavoured kinds of honey. The Andamanese have therefore adopted an original method of marking the different periods of the year by means of the different odoriferous flowers that are in bloom at different times. Their calendar is a calendar of scents[1].

Now they seem to regard each flower-period as possessing its own particular kind of force, of which the scent is the manifest sign, and to think that the succession of these different forces produces the succession of different fruits, the whole generative energy of nature being conceived as the result not of one force but of many, following one another in regular rotation. When a girl reaches puberty the natives think of her as having blossomed as it were, the later ripening being the birth of her children, and so she, like the plants of the jungle, is under the influence of the same natural forces that produce the successive blossoming and fruiting of the different species. Therefore, when a girl reaches her blossoming time she is given, for a name, to be used until she bears her fruit, the name of that particular odoriferous plant that is in flower at the time, it being this particular one of the successive forces of the forest life that has brought her childhood to an end.

Under the influence of muscular exertion the human body gives off a characteristic odour, of one generic kind, but differing somewhat in every individual. The odour of the body, being the immediate result of activity, may therefore well be regarded by the Andamanese as being closely connected with the virtue or energy of the person. Further, the eating of certain foods, such as dugong, turtle and pork, causes the body of the Andaman Islander to give out a noticeable and recognizable odour, different from that of mere perspiration. The natives themselves seem to distinguish different odours for these different foods, but I was not myself able to appreciate such differences. The Andamanese see in this odour given off after eating a manifestation of the energy that has been absorbed with the food, which energy it is that makes the food both necessary for life and also a source of danger. This seems to be the meaning of the belief that the spirits are attracted to a man by the odour of the food he has eaten unless he paint himself with clay.

We can now at last return to the rite of painting the body with *odu* clay after eating. I have suggested that the use of this

[1] See above, p. 119.

clay in mourning is a means by which the mourner marks the fact that he is in a peculiar relation to the spirit-world, spirits being believed to be light in colour. The mourner is in contact with the spirit-world through his connection with the dead person, and to mark his condition he paints himself to resemble the spirits, thereby affirming his solidarity with them. The clay protects him from the danger that results from any contact with the spirit-world. According to the rule of method laid down at the beginning of the chapter we must find a similar explanation of the use of *odu* after eating.

We have seen that it is the same kind of force in the spirits and in the animals used for food that makes them both dangerous. Yet at the same time there is a sense in which it is true that each kind of thing has its own peculiar kind of force. The ceremony of turtle-eating endows a youth with power to avoid the dangers of turtle but it does not give him the power to avoid the dangers of pork. *Hibiscus* leaves are efficacious against turtle, but against the pig *Tetranthera* leaves must be used. In describing the patterns painted on the body after eating it was stated that there is a tendency to connect particular types of pattern with particular kinds of food. Thus a design commonly used after eating turtle suggests the plates of the turtle's carapace, and a pattern used after eating pork similarly suggests the longitudinal markings on the pig's back. This would seem to indicate that when a man has eaten turtle he paints himself so as to identify himself with the animal he has eaten, and similarly with other foods, just as in mourning he paints himself so as to identify himself with the spirit-world. In other words, the painting of the body with *odu* serves to show that there is a relation between the individual and some source of power, which relation can best be described as one of solidarity with the species, whether of animals or supernatural beings, in which the power resides. The mourner is in contact with the dangerous powers of the world of death, and by expressing his solidarity with that world he avoids the dangers that might result from his condition. For the fear of any being and a feeling of solidarity towards that being are incompatible with one another. Similarly a man who has eaten turtle is in contact with the power that resides in the turtle species, a power that may be dangerous, but which when mastered and made use of by proper precautions is a source of well-being, of strength. By painting himself with a pattern that reminds him in some way of the turtle he expresses his solidarity with the turtle species and so obviates the dangers of his condition.

This interpretation is made more probable by the consideration of the dances of the initiation ceremonies. In the dance at the turtle-eating ceremony the movements of the dancers suggest the movements of a turtle swimming. If the resemblance be not imaginary we may regard this as another method of affirming the solidarity of the dancers with the turtle species. We should then have to conclude that the dance at the pig-eating ceremony is similarly imitative of the movements of a pig, and though this is quite possible it is not so obvious.

This same kind of clay is used in the initiation ceremonies. At the turtle-eating and pig-eating ceremonies it is spattered over the body of the initiate from head to foot. I have no explanation to offer for this peculiar method of application. After the ceremony is over the initiate is painted with clay in a pattern called *kimil-t'era-puli* which consists of a background of the clay on which a pattern of separate spirals is made with the finger. The pattern is to be seen in Plate XI. I cannot put forward with any confidence the explanation I have to offer of this pattern, for I have no means of confirming it, and it is therefore little more than a guess. It is that the spiral or circle is a symbol of the camp and therefore of the society and the social life in general, the basis of the symbolism being the roughly circular or elliptical form of the village or communal hut, and the circular form of the dance (more noticeable in the Little Andaman than in the Great Andaman). If this be really the meaning of the symbol then the explanation of its use in the initiation ceremonies would be that in these ceremonies the youth is preserved from danger by the force inherent in the society, which affords protection to all its members, and the use of the symbol of the society would therefore be most appropriate.

The act of painting the body with *odu* clay is therefore a rite which advertises the fact that an individual is in intimate contact with some source of that power which belongs to the things that affect the social life, and it thereby serves to keep alive the sentiments associated with that notion of power. The painting after eating reminds the individual of his dependence upon and obligation towards the society, and, since all join in the rite, it serves also to maintain the unity of the community.

We may now return to the question of the meaning of personal ornament in general. It is a commonplace of psychology that the development of the sense of self is closely connected with the perception of one's own body. It is also generally recognized that the development of the moral and social sentiments in man is dependent upon the development of self-consciousness, of the sense of self. These two important principles will help us to appreciate the hypothesis to which the discussion has now led, that in the Andamans the customary regulation of personal ornament is a means by which the society acts upon, modifies, and regulates the sense of self in the individual.

There are three methods of ornamenting the body in the Andamans, (1) by scarification, (2) by painting, and (3) by the putting on of ornaments.

The natives give two reasons for the custom of scarification, that it improves the personal appearance and that it makes the boy or girl grow up strong. Both these mean that scarification gives or marks an added value. The explanation of the rite would therefore seem to be that it marks the passage from childhood to manhood and is a means by which the society bestows upon the individual that power, or social value, which is possessed by the adult but not by the child. The individual is made to feel that his value—his strength and the qualities of which he may be proud—is not his by nature but is received by him from the society to which he is admitted. The scars on his body are the visible marks of his admission. The individual is proud or vain of the scars which are the mark of his manhood, and thus the society makes use of the very powerful sentiment of personal vanity to strengthen the social sentiments.

Turning now to the painting of the body, we have seen that the pattern of white clay serves to make both the painted individual and those who see him feel his social value, and we have seen that this interpretation explains the occasions on which such painting is used. To complete the argument it is necessary to consider the occasions on which the use of white clay is forbidden.

Those to whom this prohibition applies are (1) a youth or girl who is *aka-op*, i.e., who is abstaining from certain foods during the initiation period, (2) a mourner, (3) a homicide during the period of isolation, and (4) a person who is ill. All these persons are excluded from full participation in the active social life, and therefore the social value of each of them is diminished. It would obviously be wrong for a person in such a condition to express by decorating himself a social value that he did not at the time possess.

The occasions on which this style of painting is used or forbidden are thus all satisfactorily explained by our hypothesis. It remains to consider the nature of the painting itself, and how far it is an appropriate means of expression. To do this we must discuss very briefly some of the processes of symbolic thought of the Andamanese. Conditions of well-being (both individual and social) are associated in the minds of the Andamanese with fine weather, both directly (through physiological action) and indirectly (through the effect of fine weather on the social life). Hence *Tomo*, who, as we shall see in the next chapter, is a personification of fine weather, is a being who is connected with goodness and happiness. With fine weather, and therefore with individual and social well-being, the Andamanese associate brightness and whiteness (for which they have only one word) and any bright or light colour. The association of light and dark with euphoric and dysphoric conditions respectively has a psycho-physical basis, for it seems to be universal in human nature. Now the clay that the Andamanese call *tol-odu* is the whitest substance they know, and is for this reason fitted to be symbolical of conditions of well-being. Fine weather is associated, in the minds of the Andamanese with honey, because in the season of fine weather honey is plentiful, and is also associated for a similar reason with snakes. Sweetness itself is universally associated with pleasant things, again through a psycho-physical link. The Andamanese believe in a special connection between honey and a species of large snake called *wara-jobo* or *or-čubi*[1], so that this snake comes to be representative of fine weather and sweetness and therefore generally of states of well-being. Now, throughout the Great Andaman the pattern in which white clay is painted on the body is called after this snake, and the zig-zags of which the pattern is composed may be supposed to be representative of the snake itself. When, therefore, a man paints himself with white clay in a pattern which he regards as representing the snake *wara-jobo*, it is evident that the painting is meant to express a condition of well-being, with which the snake itself, and whiteness, are, by a number of links, closely associated. This is not all, however. The Andamanese, we may not doubt, derive from the painted pattern an esthetic pleasure due to its rhythmical character, its shape as an arrangement of lines and spaces. Further it provides the pleasure that we obtain from a thing elegantly and skilfully made, and this explains why so much care is taken in the making of the pattern. This pleasure at what we may call the beauty of the pattern heightens the effect produced by its symbolic references. The real value of the pattern, its pleasure-giving quality, is transferred to the man on whose body it is executed. He himself is pleased with it, proud of it, and so becomes pleased with and proud of himself, for the pattern by being imprinted on his body becomes part of him. The sense of self attaches to it, as with us the sense of self attaches to our clothes.

It would be interesting to carry the analysis of the mental processes involved in all this a stage or two further, but enough has been said, I hope, to show that the nature of the painting with clay is appropriate to its use as marking or expressing value.

Patterns are sometimes painted with this same white clay on the face alone, such patterns being built up either of the zig-zags of the snake pattern, or of rhythmically arranged series of short lines. The use of such paintings is regulated by a sort of etiquette. By so having his face decorated a man expresses that he is pleased with himself, and obviously there are occasions on which it is appropriate and others on which it is inappropriate

[1] See p. 227.

that he should feel thus. A man who has been successful in the day's hunting, for example, is quite justified in having his face ornamented in this way, and it is on such occasions as this that the custom is observed.

When a man is painted for a dance, or on any other ceremonial occasion, with white clay, he is also painted at the same time with red paint. In these instances we must suppose that the red paint serves the same purpose as the pattern of white clay with which it is combined, namely to make the decorated person pleasantly aware of his or her social value. Red paint is also used, however, in sickness, and on other occasions, as affording protection against evil, particularly evil from the spirit-world.

This double use of red paint is to be explained by reference to the colour symbolism of the Andaman Islanders. For them the colour red is pre-eminently the colour of blood and of fire. There is ample evidence of this which it is perhaps not necessary to state. Now blood is identified with the warmth of the body and with life; the blood and the fat are sometimes spoken of as the two vital principles. Fire, as I have already shown, is taken as a symbol of activity and of mental excitement. Thus the colour comes to be associated in the minds of the Andamanese with all euphoric conditions, with excitement, vitality, mental and bodily activity, and with energy or force in general. It is possible that this symbolism, which seems to be much the same in all divisions of mankind, has a psycho-physical basis in the stimulating dynamogenic power of sensations of redness.

When a person is sick he is in need of vitality, of energy, and so his body is daubed with the red paint that is a symbol of the things that he needs, and by a simple mental process he comes to believe that by applying the paint to his body he increases his energy and vitality, and so helps himself to get rid of the sickness. At a dance, or on other ceremonial occasions, it is required that the individual shall have a sense of his own value, and for this he must experience that sense of personal force and vitality that is produced, as we have seen, by the action of the dance. This effect is reinforced by the use of the red paint which is the symbol of that condition of energy and vitality that it is (for some special reason) necessary for him to feel. As the value of the individual depends upon his strength or force, the red paint is thus a suitable means of expressing the value of him on whose body it is painted, and really expresses, though by different means, exactly the same thing as the pattern of white clay with which it is combined.

We are now in a position to understand the use of white clay and red paint in the purification of a homicide. This takes place at the end of a period of isolation, during which the man is entirely cut off from the social life, and lives in a condition of supposed extreme danger on account of the blood that he has shed. During this time he may not use his hands to touch food, and at the end his hands are purified by the application to them of red paint and white clay. It is clearly because these two substances are both of them in different ways symbols of conditions of well-being that magical virtue is ascribed to their use in this instance. It is perhaps worth while to recall that both red ochre and white clay are sometimes given internally as remedies against sickness.

For the sake of the argument it has been necessary to separate the two motives underlying the use of personal ornament, the desire for protection and the desire for display. But we now see that these two motives are very intimately related and are really both involved in every kind of ornament. All ornament in some way marks the relation of the individual to the society and to that force or power in the society to which he owes his well-being and happiness. When painting or ornament is used to give protection, it is, as we have seen, the protective power of the society itself that is appealed to, and what is expressed is the dependence of the individual on the society. When ornament or paint is used for display it is again the dependence on the society that is expressed, though in a different way and on occasions of a different kind. We have seen that scarification is also a means of marking the dependence of the individual on the society, and it is very important to note that the Andamanese sometimes explain it as due to the desire for display and sometimes to the need of protection (enabling the child to grow strong and so avoid the dangers of sickness), showing very clearly that there is some intimate connection between these two motives, or at any rate that one and the same method of ornamentation can satisfy both. There is the further example of red paint, which is combined with the pattern of white clay for purposes of display, and is also constantly used in many ways as affording protection.

We are thus brought to the final conclusion that the scarification and painting of the body and the wearing of most if not all of the customary ornaments are rites which have the function of marking the fact that the individual is in a particular permanent or temporary relation to that power in the society and in all things that affect the social life, the notion of which we have seen to underlie so much of the Andaman ceremonial.

The scarification of a boy or girl leaves permanent marks of the permanent relation between the adult and the society. By means of it and the initiation ceremonies that follow or accompany it, and of which it may really be considered to be a part, the society gives the individual his social value, of which the scars remain as a visible sign for him to be proud of, and at the same time endows him with the power to avoid the dangers with which his life is beset.

The paintings of clay after food mark the temporary relation between the individual and the power present in the food he has eaten. It is chiefly thought of by the natives themselves as protective, as we have seen, but it also gives an opportunity for the exercise of personal vanity, for much care is taken in the designing and execution of the pattern, which therefore affords the painted individual much the same sort of satisfaction as the snake pattern of white clay. It calls his attention to his own appearance, and makes him feel pleased or satisfied with himself, conscious of his own personal value. A condition of unity and harmony is produced in the community by a feast as well as by a dance, and in each instance that harmony is expressed by the painting of every member with the same material in a similar design. The relation of the individual to the society is made visible on his body. By means of the paintings after food the society not only protects itself from danger but also rejoices in the well-being that is produced by a supply of relished food.

Inversely it can now also be shown that the painting of white clay and red paint worn at a dance and after marriage and initiation is not only a means of display but is also protective. Both red paint and white clay are used to give protection in sickness, and they are similarly used in the purification of the hands of a homicide. Moreover we have seen, in reference to the word *ot-kimil*, that the dance is a condition of danger by reason of the contact it involves between the individual and the power of the society. The few days following an initiation ceremony are definitely believed to be a period of danger for the initiate, and during this time the pattern of white clay and red paint must not be washed off but must be allowed to wear off. By the time the last traces of the pattern have disappeared the danger is considered to be over. There is evidence that the first few days of marriage are regarded as a period of danger. It would seem that the natives do attribute to the painting with white clay and red paint some power of protection, but this is hidden under the importance of such painting as a means of display.

Of the various ornaments that are worn on the body some would seem to be worn almost solely for purposes of display, because they are pleasing to the eye. Such are the necklaces and other ornaments of small shells. It would seem that the same motive is also responsible for the use of the yellow skin of the *Dendrobium* of which the Andamanese are so fond. The ornaments of netting and shell seem to be worn primarily for display, but it is quite possible that some protective power is attributed to them, as to the paintings of white clay with which they are regularly worn. The belts of *Pandanus* leaf that are worn by women are a mark of the sex, and the style of belt worn differs with the social status of the woman. They thus serve to exhibit the special social value of the woman in so far as it depends upon her sex and her social status, but I believe that the Andamanese attribute to the belt and to the apron of leaves worn with it a power of protection against the special dangers to which women are believed to be subject. Ths is suggested by the use of the *Pandanus* leaf in the ceremony at a girl's first menstruation[1]. I failed to discover any special ideas connected

[1] I am unfortunately obliged to leave a big gap in this chapter and in the book, owing to my inability to discuss the Andamanese notions about sex. The natives of

with the ornaments of *Pandanus* leaf that are sometimes worn by both men and women at dances. The ornaments that are worn primarily for their protective power are those made of human and animal bones and those of pieces of canes or of fibres of *Hibiscus* or *Ficus*. These are always made decorative by the addition of shells and yellow *Dendrobium* skin, and therefore besides their primary function also serve as means of display.

It is clear then that in the various methods of ornamenting the body the two chief motives that we have considered are so combined that they can hardly be estimated separately, and it is this mingling of motives that has led us to the final understanding of the meaning and social function of bodily ornament. Each of the different kinds of ornament serves to make manifest the existence of some special relation between the individual and the society, and therefore of some special relation between him and that system of powers on which the welfare of the society and of the individual depends. One of the most important aspects of the relation of the individual to the society is his dependence upon it for his safety and well-being and this is revealed in all painting and ornament worn for protection. But the society not only protects the individual from danger; it is the direct source of his well-being; and this makes itself felt in the customary regulation by which the use of the more important ornaments used for display is confined to occasions on which it is quite clear that his happiness is directly due to the society, such as a dance or feast. Thus the customs relating to the ornamentation of the body are of the kind that I have here called ceremonial. They are means by which the society exercises on

the Great Andaman at the present time show an unusual prudery in their conversation and dealings with white men, but there is good reason to suspect that this is due to the influence of officers who have been in charge of the Andaman Home in former years. At the present time all the men except a few of the oldest in remote parts are very careful never to appear before a white man without some covering although formerly they wore nothing. In their conversation in the presence of a white man they are careful to avoid reference to sexual matters. The men of the Little Andaman who have not come under the influence of the Andamanese Homes, still go naked and unashamed, and indulge in obscene gestures and jokes. At the time I was in the Andamans I failed to realise the very great importance of a thorough knowledge of the notions of a primitive people on matters of sex in any attempt to understand their customs, and therefore failed to make the necessary enquiries.

appropriate occasions some of the important social sentiments, thereby maintaining them at the necessary degree of energy required to maintain the social cohesion.

To complete the discussion of ornament in general it is necessary to refer very briefly to the ornamentation of objects such as bows, canoes and baskets. Such ornamentation consists of (1) incised patterns (on bows, etc.), which may be compared with the scarification of the body, (2) painting with red paint and white clay (bows, canoes, skulls, etc.), or with prepared wax (Nautilus shell cups, etc.), (3) patterns made with the yellow skin of the *Dendrobium* (baskets, etc.), and (4) shells attached by thread (baskets, baby-sling, etc.). The important point to note is that the decoration applied to utensils is of the same character throughout as that which, when applied to the body, has been shown to be an expression of the social value of the person. Thus the pattern painted on a canoe with white clay and red paint is the same as that on the body of a dancer. It would seem, therefore, that the ornamentation of utensils is a means of expressing or marking the social value of the decorated object, and it might even be held that the application of ornament to utensils is really a matter of ceremonial. Just as a newly married man is painted with the snake pattern which wears off and is not renewed, so a new canoe or a new South Andaman bow is painted with the same pattern as soon as it is finished, and after this pattern wears off it is not renewed. It is the act of bringing a new canoe or bow into use that is the occasion of the ceremonial expression of its value, if we may so regard the painting. A new relation is established between the society and an object, which thereby acquires a special social value, just as a youth acquires a special new social value at the conclusion of one of the initiation ceremonies. This example is sufficient to show that at least there is nothing in the ornamentation of utensils that conflicts with the explanation of bodily ornament given in this chapter[1].

[1] In order to carry the analysis further it would be necessary to consider in detail the whole question of the relation of art and ceremonial, and that of the social function of art which is involved in it, and also to deal with the notion of "value" as it appears in primitive societies. The material from the Andaman Islands is not suitable for the discussion of these problems.

It is time to bring the argument to a conclusion. It should now, I hope, be evident that the ceremonial customs of the Andaman Islands form a closely connected system, and that we cannot understand their meaning if we only consider each one by itself, but must study the whole system to arrive at an interpretation. This in itself I regard as a most important conclusion, for it justifies the contention that we must substitute for the old method of dealing with the customs of primitive people,—the comparative method by which isolated customs from different social types were brought together and conclusions drawn from their similarity,—a new method by which all the institutions of one society or social type are studied together so as to exhibit their intimate relations as parts of an organic system.

I have tried to show that the ceremonial customs are the means by which the society acts upon its individual members and keeps alive in their minds a certain system of sentiments. Without the ceremonial those sentiments would not exist, and without them the social organisation in its actual form could not exist. There is great difficulty, however, in finding a suitable method of describing these sentiments. In attempting to put into precise words the vague *feelings* of the Andaman Islander there is always the danger that we may attribute to him *conceptions* that he does not possess. For he is not himself capable of thinking about his own sentiments.

In the attempt to exhibit the meaning of the ceremonial I have shown that it implies a complex system of beliefs about what I have called power, and have stated those beliefs in more or less precise terms. But the Andaman Islander is of course quite incapable of making similar statements or even of understanding them. In his consciousness appear only the very vaguest conceptions, such as those associated with the word *kimil* or with odours. We, in order to understand his customs must substitute for such vague notions others capable of precise statement, must formulate in words the beliefs that are revealed in his actions, but we must be careful not to fall into the error of attributing to him the conceptions by which we make clear to ourselves his indefinite sentiments and notions and the ceremonies in which they are expressed.

With this qualification, then, the ceremonial of the Andaman Islands may be said to involve the assumption of a power of a peculiar kind, and we have been able to formulate certain principles which, although the native is quite incapable of stating them as principles, are revealed in the ceremonial. This power, though in itself neither good nor evil, is the source of all good and all evil in human life. It is present in the society itself and in everything that can affect in important ways the social life. All occasions of special contact with it are dangerous, i.e., are subject to ritual precautions.

It should already, from the course of the argument, be plain that this power or force, the interaction of whose different manifestations constitutes the process of social life, is not imaginary, is not even something the existence of which is surmised as the result of intellectual processes, but is real, an object of actual experience. It is, in a few words, the moral power of the society acting upon the individual directly or indirectly and felt by him in innumerable ways throughout the whole course of his life[1].

One of the most important ways in which the individual experiences the moral force of the society of which he is a member is through the feeling of moral obligation, which gives him the experience of a power compelling him to subordinate his egoistic desires to the demands of social custom. The individual feels this force acting upon him both from outside and from inside himself. For he recognizes that it is the society with its traditions and customs that constrains him through the force of public opinion, and yet the conflict between customary duty and selfish inclination takes place in his own mind and is experienced as the clash of antagonistic mental forces. The moral sense within impels towards the same end as the social opinion without.

This force of moral obligation is felt not only in relation to right and wrong conduct towards other persons, but is also felt in all ritual, whether negative or positive.

[1] The exposition of this important thesis can only be given here in the most abbreviated form. The thesis itself, as applied to primitive ritual in general, owes its origin to Professor Émile Durkheim, and has been expounded by him (more particularly in his work *Les Formes élémentaires de la Vie religieuse*) and by Messieurs H. Hubert and M. Mauss.

The moral force of the society is also felt, in a quite different way, in all states of intense collective emotion, of which the dance affords a good example. I have shown how in the dance the individual feels the society acting upon him, constraining him to join in the common activity and regulate his actions to conform with those of others, and, when he so acts in harmony with them, giving him the experience of a great increase of his own personal force or energy. All ceremonies in which the whole community takes part give the individual the experience of the moral force of the society acting upon him in somewhat the same way as the dance.

Thus in these and other ways the individual does experience the action of the society upon himself as a sort of force, not however as a physical force, but as a moral force, acting directly in his own mind and yet clearly felt as something outside his own self, and with which that self may be in conflict.

How is it, then; that this force comes to be projected into the world of nature? The answer to that question, which can only be very briefly indicated here, is to be found in the conclusions at which we have arrived with regard to social values. The moral force of the society is experienced by the individual not only directly but also as acting upon him indirectly through every object that has social value. The best example of this process is found in the things used for food. Thus, in the Andamans, food is very closely connected with the feeling of moral obligation, as we have seen. Further, food is one of the principal sources of those alternations of social euphoria and dysphoria in which, through the action of the collective emotion, the individual experiences the action of the society upon his own well-being. When food is plentiful happiness spreads through the community and the time is spent in dancing and feasting so that the individual feels a great increase in his own personal force coming to him from the society or from the food. On the other hand, when food is scarce and hunting unsuccessful the community feels itself thwarted and restrained and experiences a sense of weakness, which collective feeling has for its immediate object the food the lack of which is its origin.

Similarly with the phenomena of the weather and all other

objects that have social value, they are all associated in the mind of the individual with his experience of the action of the society upon himself, so that the moral force of the society is actually felt as acting through them.

But it is really through the ceremonial that this is mainly brought about. It is in the initiation ceremonies that the moral force of the society acting through foods is chiefly felt, and the same experience is repeated in a less intense form in the rite of painting the body after food. It is similarly through the protective use of the materials used for weapons and through the various ritual prohibitions connected with them that the moral force of the society acting through them is chiefly felt. The argument has been that it is by means of the ceremonial that the individual is made to feel the social value of the various things with which the ceremonial is concerned. Putting this in other words we can now define the ceremonial as the means by which the individual is made to feel the moral force of the society acting upon him either directly, or in some instances indirectly through those things that have important effects on the social life. By its action upon the individual the ceremonial develops and maintains in existence in his mind an organised system of dispositions by which the social life, in the particular form it takes in the Andamans, is made possible, using for the purpose of maintaining the social cohesion all the instinctive tendencies of human nature, modifying and combining them according to its needs.

As an example of such modification of primary instincts let us briefly consider that of fear, to which, from the time of Petronius[1] to the present day, so much importance has been attributed in relation to the origin of religion. In childhood any fear of danger makes the child run to its mother or father for protection, and thus the instinct of fear becomes an important component of that feeling of dependence that the child has towards its parents. The primitive society uses the fear instinct in much the same way. The Andaman Islander, through the ceremonies and customs of his people, is made to feel that he is in a world full of unseen dangers,—dangers from the foods he

[1] Primus in orbe deos fecit timor.

eats, from the sea, the weather, the forest and its animals, but above all from the spirits of the dead,—which can only be avoided by the help of the society and by conformity with social custom. As men press close to one another in danger, the belief in and fear of the spirit-world make the Andaman Islander cling more firmly to his fellows, and make him feel more intensely his own dependence on the society to which he belongs, just as the fear of danger makes the child feel its dependence upon its parents. So the belief in the spirit-world serves directly to increase the cohesion of the society through its action on the mind of the individual. An important law of sociology is that the solidarity of a group is increased when the group as a whole finds itself opposed to some other group; so, enmity between two tribes or nations increases the solidarity of each; and so also, the antagonism between the society of the living and the world of the dead increases the solidarity of the former.

The argument is now concluded. I have examined, as fully as space would permit, all the more important features of the Andaman ceremonial, and have tried to show what part they play in the social life of the Andamans. At the end of our enquiry it is well to ask if any definition of ceremonial can be given more exact than the vague one with which we started. The chapter has shown that what I have denoted as ceremonial consists of (1) collective actions, (2) required by custom, (3) performed on occasions of changes in the course of social life, and (4) expressing the collective sentiments relating to such social change. By the first part of the definition we exclude the magical practices of the medicine-men, which however it has been convenient to consider in connection with the ceremonial, as it has helped us to understand some of the ideas underlying both magic and ceremonial. If we are not to exclude the rite of painting after eating food we must regard the obtaining of a good supply of food as being a change in the course of social life even though it occurs very frequently, and even every day for weeks together. It must be admitted, however, that the definition does not give us any very clear dividing line between ceremonial and art, play, or morals. The painting of the body with white clay after marriage or initiation must, I think, be regarded as ceremonial, while the painting of a new bow or canoe with the same clay in the same pattern should perhaps more conveniently be called art. But what are we to say of the painting worn at a dance or the face-painting that a man occasionally wears when there is no special reason? The dance at the end of mourning is clearly a ceremony, but can we say the same of the ordinary dance after a successful hunt? And if it be not ceremonial, shall we call it art or play? When friends are required to give presents to a newly-married couple are we to call this obligation one of ceremonial, of etiquette or of morals? These and similar questions are perhaps incapable of a satisfactory answer, nor does it seem necessary to attempt to find one. Those elements of culture that we now differentiate and call by different names were, in primitive societies, undifferentiated and not clearly to be distinguished from one another, and a striving after too great a precision of definition in dealing with such a culture as that of the Andamans leads, I think, not to a clearer understanding, but to the opposite. The main thing is to keep close to the facts. In this chapter I have examined a number of facts which are plainly related and the question of how we are to label them is one that may well be left till such time as we shall have acquired a more profound insight into the nature of culture in general and the complex forces involved in its existence and growth. For the present, some vagueness in our provisional classifications need not greatly perturb us.

CHAPTER VI

THE INTERPRETATION OF ANDAMANESE CUSTOMS AND BELIEFS: MYTHS AND LEGENDS

IN the last chapter I tried to explain, by reference to psychological principles, the more important ritual and ceremonial observances of the Andamanese; in the present chapter I shall deal in a similar manner with the legends recorded in Chapter IV. That is to say, I propose to explain, not how the legends arose, but what they mean, what part they play at the present time in the mental life of the Andaman Islander. Customs that seem at first sight meaningless or ridiculous have been shown to fulfil most important functions in the social economy, and similarly I hope to prove that the tales that might seem merely the products of a somewhat childish fancy are very far indeed from being merely fanciful and are the means by which the Andamanese express and systematise their fundamental notions of life and nature and the sentiments attaching to those notions.

I propose to analyse a few of the more important legends, and will begin with the *Akar-Bale* story of the origin of night and day[1]. The explanation of this story depends on the connection of day and night with the cicada. This species of cicada, of which I do not know the scientific name, always makes a noise ("sings" as the natives say) during the short interval of twilight between sunset and darkness and between dawn and sunrise. It is possible that individual insects of the species make a noise at other times of the day and night, but I do not remember to have heard them, and it is only at the beginning and end of the day that they are all to be heard singing together.

[1] Page 214.

CH. VI] CUSTOMS AND BELIEFS: MYTHS AND LEGENDS 331

The song of the cicada, as day gives place to night and as night changes to day is one of the most familiar of all natural phenomena to the Andamanese. Another fact that is made use of in the legend is that if one of these insects be crushed as was the cicada of the story, or even if it be taken up in the hand, it will utter its shrill and plaintive note, not unlike the cry of a human being in pain. Finally, fully to understand the tale, it is necessary to remember that in all the tribes of the Great Andaman Division there is a prohibition against killing the cicada. The meaning of this prohibition will have to be discussed in connection with the legend.

The facts stated above enable us to understand what may be called the skeleton of the legend. One of the ancestors killed a cicada (a forbidden act), the cicada uttered its cry (as it does when hurt), and as a result, darkness covered the world (as it always does when the cicada sings in the evening). Leaving aside, for the present, the rest of the story, we may try to make clear to ourselves just what this part of it expresses. The explanation that I propose is to the effect that the legend is simply an expression or a statement of the "social value" of the phenomenon of the alternation of day and night. By the social value of anything I mean, as explained in the last chapter, the way in which that thing affects the life of the society (either beneficially or adversely) and therefore the way in which it affects the social sentiments of the individuals who compose the society. There is no need to discuss at length and in all its bearings, the way in which the alternation of day and night affects the social life of the Andamanese. The one outstanding feature of first importance is that the day is the time of social activity whereas the night is a period when the society is, as a rule, not active. It was shown in the last chapter that one of the most important elements in the mental complex revealed by a study of the ceremonial is the recognition of the fact that it is on the activity of the society that the individual depends for his security and well-being. So long as he can feel that he is an active member of an active community the individual feels that he has for his support (morally and physically) a great force on which he can rely. If, for any reason, he is temporarily cut off from the society and from participation in its life, he is in a position of insecurity, and believes himself to be in danger from the powers of the world of spirits. It is an inevitable result of this that the daytime, when the society is active, should be felt to be a period of comparative security, while the night, when all social activity ceases, should be felt to be a period of comparative insecurity. That the day and night are so regarded is shown in the belief of the natives that the spirits are more to be dreaded during the night than during the day.

The Andaman Islander, like many other savages, is afraid of the dark. It might perhaps be thought that this fear is immediate and instinctive, a result of the physiology of the human nervous system, but that, I think, would be a false assumption. Many infants would seem not to be at first afraid of darkness, but to learn to fear it, as they learn to fear many other things. It is not possible here to enter into a discussion of the matter, but I would hold that in the Andaman Islanders and probably in other savages, the fear of darkness, of night, is a secondary or induced feeling, not by any means instinctive, and is in large part due to the social sentiments, to the fact that at night the social life ceases. The savage feels, and rightly so, that for everything he has and is, for the safety and well-being of his body and the comfort of his soul, he depends on the communal life in which his own life is merged. When, at the close of day, the social life ceases, he feels, should anything occur to direct his attention to his own condition, less secure than when the social life is proceeding actively around him[1].

The interpretation that I would offer of the *Akar-Bale* legend is that it is an expression of these sentiments relating to the night, an expression that takes advantage of the connection between the song of the cicada and the alternation of night and day. One feature of the manner of expression will be explained later in the chapter, namely that it takes the form of a story relating to a mythical period of the past. For the present the necessity of this particular form must be accepted

---

[1] We have seen, in the last chapter, that any condition of the individual in which he is withdrawn from active participation in the common life is regarded as one of danger from magico-religious forces antagonistic to the society.

as a postulate. Granting this it remains only to show that the legend does express the social value of night as defined above.

The fear of night, or rather, since that fear is rarely more than potential, the feeling that night is a time of insecurity, is part of the general attitude of fear or respect towards the forces of nature that are believed to be possible sources of danger to the society. Now it has been shown that this particular attitude to nature finds expression in ritual prohibitions of various kinds. For instance, the Andaman Islander translates his feeling of the social value of food substances into the belief that such things must be treated with ritual precautions. Applying this to the case before us, we must first recognize that to the Andaman Islander the alternation of day and night and the singing of the cicada are not separate phenomena but are two parts or aspects of one and the same recurring event. Now, the night and the day are things that cannot be handled, i.e., cannot be immediately subject to the actions of human beings, while the cicada can be handled. Hence it is to the cicada that the need of precaution is referred. Any interference with the cicada is forbidden, and this prohibition serves as a mark or expression of the social value of that alternation of night and day with which the cicada is so intimately associated[1].

The legend of the *Akar-Bale* tribe is simply an elaboration of this theme. In the beginning there was no night, no darkness. Social life was continuous and was not subject to periods of diminished intensity. Then one of the ancestors (apparently in a fit of temper owing to his lack of success in fishing) crushed a cicada, and the cry of the insect brought darkness upon the world. The darkness, with its inhibition of activity, is clearly regarded as an evil, i.e., as a manifestation of force hostile to the society, and this accords with the definition of the social value of night given above, where it was shown that this value is negative, that night is a source of social dysphoria.

[1] It will be shown later in the chapter that some part of the respect paid to the cicada is due to its connection not with the day and night but with the seasons of the year.

This interpretation is confirmed by the statements about the night made in the North Andaman (where this legend does not seem to exist), such as that the night is made by the spirits (*Lau*) who draw a mat or cloth across the sky. When we remember that the spirits are the embodiment of the forces hostile to the society we see how this statement expresses the feeling that night is the time when such hostile forces are in the ascendant.

The *Akar-Bale* story, besides giving an account of the origin of night, relates the invention of singing and dancing. There is no specific reference to dancing in the story as recorded from my *Akar-Bale* informant. The reference is found, however, in the version recorded by Mr Man[1] and it is implicit even in the *Akar-Bale* version. Dancing is always accompanied by a song, and every song is composed with the express intention of being sung at a dance. Thus, for the Andamanese, singing and dancing are merely two aspects of one and the same activity.

Dancing, except on a few special ceremonial occasions, always takes place at night. Night, as we have seen, is a source of social dysphoria. It prevents the pursuit of the common social activities, such as hunting or making canoes or weapons. The condition produced by darkness can be neutralised by means of singing and dancing, the dance being a condition of intense social euphoria, in which social activity is at its maximum, and all the social sentiments are pleasurably and intensely excited.

This belief that dancing and singing are means by which the evil influence of darkness can be overcome is shown in the custom observed when a corpse remains in a camp all night, of sitting round it and singing, in order (so the natives say) to keep away the spirits that have caused the death. They do not dance, because the pleasurable excitement of the more intense activity would be incompatible with the condition naturally resulting from a death. This custom affords clear evidence that singing, and in a yet higher degree the combined activity of singing and dancing, possess magical efficacy against the dangers prevalent at night.

[1] Page 215.

This relation between the (negative) social value of night and the (positive) social value of dancing and singing is simply and clearly expressed in the legend. It was the "singing" of the cicada that produced the darkness. The ancestors, finding themselves overwhelmed with darkness, set to work to remedy this evil by singing (and, it is to be presumed, by dancing to the song). One after another they sang a song, just as at a dance one man after another sings until he is tired. Finally, after the dance had gone on for a number of hours, *Koyoro* took his turn at singing and the night came to an end and day appeared. So effectual was the means adopted of neutralising the evils of darkness that it finally resulted in the return of the daylight in which ordinary social life is possible.

The reference to resin in the legend can be easily understood. The Andamanese use resin to provide the light by which they dance, as well as for torches for fishing on dark nights. It is their only artificial light, and without resin a dance would be a very poor affair. Thus the social value of resin is that it affords a means of neutralising to a certain extent the effects of darkness.

These are, I think, all the essential elements of the story. One of the ancestors, under the influence of an anti-social passion, killed a cicada, which uttered its cry, and thereupon the world was covered with darkness. The ancestors then made torches of resin which enabled them to neutralise the darkness to some extent. They then invented dancing and singing and after they had continued for a number of hours the light came back. Since that time day and night regularly alternate with one another, and the cicada sings at each period of change. Men have learnt how to use resin for artificial light, and how to remedy the effects of darkness by dancing and singing.

The legend is thus simply the expression in a particular form of the relation between the society and a certain natural phenomenon in terms of what have been called social values. We find expressed the social values of night and of resin and dancing. It may be noted that the legend also gives a special social value to the ancestors, different from and greater than that of men or women at the present day. The ancestors of the Andamanese were able to do many things that men cannot do now; they were able to affect the processes of nature in a way that is no longer possible. This notion of the social value of the ancestors, of the past, will be shown to be one of the most important elements in the legends, it being this that is responsible for the general form of the stories. The consideration of this subject, however, must be postponed.

There are still a number of points of the legend that have not been considered. It is not easy to account for the inclusion in this story of the discovery of the yam. It is possible that there is some ground of association between the yam and the cicada, but I do not certainly know of any such. There is a legend recorded by Mr Man from the *Aka-Bea* tribe, and given above[1], in which an account is given of the lucky discovery of the first yam by the chance shooting of an arrow. It is therefore quite likely that the yam story first existed quite independently, and that it has become incorporated in the legend of the origin of night on account of the fact that the incident of the shooting of an arrow was found in both of them.

There is one reason for the inclusion of the yam incident that it is worth while to note. By its means it is told how *Da Teŋat* discovered a new object of each of the three kinds—animal, vegetable, and mineral. The new animal was the cicada, the new vegetable was the yam, and the new mineral was the resin, which, as the story shows, the natives classify as a "stone," although they know its vegetable origin. The story is thus rounded off and given an air of completeness and symmetry.

The incident of the shooting of the three arrows is of some interest as giving us an idea of how the Andamanese think of chance or luck. Arrows, it must be remembered, are regarded as being possessed of magical power. Further, the ancestors themselves possessed powers that do not belong to living men, as is shown repeatedly in the legends. The ancestor shoots an arrow, and, by reason of his power and that of the arrow, it strikes an important object and leads him to a discovery. The mere striking of the object by the arrow seems to give him a certain degree of power over the object, whereby he forces it to reveal its name. (We have already seen, by a reference to this very

[1] Page 221.

story, that there is an important connection between the name of an object and its social value¹.) Thus, in common with other primitive peoples, the Andaman Islanders regard what we call luck or chance as due to the action of the magical powers possessed by objects and by human beings.

There is one point that is not very plain in the *Akar-Bale* version, but I think we must take it that *Da Teŋat* was disgusted at his lack of success in fishing. His irritation was not diminished but rather increased by the fact that he did succeed in procuring one small and worthless fish. His shooting of the arrows must be regarded, I think, as the result of his anger. He might be supposed to address his arrows as follows : "You have not succeeded in hitting any fish at which I aimed you ; let me see if you can hit anything on your own account, when I take no aim." In this way he was led to the discovery of the yam, the resin and the cicada, for though it is not explicit, it is evident that it was the third arrow that led him to the cicada. His irritation was not yet appeased however, and he crushed the cicada, thus bringing darkness over the world. We must infer that he was aware of what he was doing, for as soon as he had discovered the yam and the resin he learnt their names and thereby learnt all there was to know about them and their properties, and we must suppose that he similarly learnt the name of the cicada, and that to injure it would cause darkness. In the *Aka-Bea* legend recorded by Mr Man it is expressly stated that the ancestors who performed the actions that led to the first darkness did so because they were annoyed by the continuous heat of the sun².

Now we have here a very important feature of the legend which it will not do to overlook. We shall find that it is a principle of the Andaman legends that evil results follow from evil actions. Night, which, by reason of its negative social value, is regarded as an evil, is shown to be the result of the misbehaviour of one of the ancestors in giving way to anti-social feelings of anger or annoyance. It is a case of like producing like. When an individual gives way to such feelings as anger he becomes a source of danger to the society, or at any rate a

---

¹ Page 294. ² Page 215.

source of social dysphoria by disturbing the harmony of the community. Thus, in the legend, it was the wickedness of the ancestor in giving way to his feeling of irritation that led to the social disaster. Inversely, it was through the combined effort of the ancestors joining in a harmonious action (singing and dancing) that the day was brought back.

The events of the legend are supposed to have taken place at a spot named *Golugma*. I only visited this spot once and did not take particular note of it, nor have I information about the position it occupied in the social life of that part of the island in former times. We do know, however, from the name *Golugma Bud*, that at one time it was the site of a communal hut and was therefore an important camping place. It may have been a place at which dance-meetings were frequently held, and this would be a sufficient reason for its selection as the legendary site of the first dance.

One of the minor motives of the *Akar-Bale* version of this story is the identity of the ancestor who appears as the chief actor. I regret to say that I have never found the exact meaning of the word *teɲat*. Though I asked the natives to bring me a specimen they did not do so. It is probably either a species of spider or of ant. However, even if I had succeeded in identifying the *teɲat*, it is possible that I should not have discovered the reason why this particular creature was selected as the hero of the story. This can be shown by considering another of the incidents of the story. All the ancestors who sang and tried to bring back the day failed except the *koɲoro*. This is a species of small red ant. Whenever I heard this story told or referred to, this particular incident (the successful singing of *koɲoro*) caused great amusement amongst the listeners. It was obvious that it was a good joke. Yet in spite of my endeavours on more than one occasion I was unable to see what the joke was.

In the *A-Pučikwar* version of the same legend[1] it was *Peṭie*, the monitor lizard, who crushed the cicada and brought darkness. This is to be explained not on the basis of any particular characteristic of the lizard, but as being due to the position that

[1] Page 213.

this animal occupies in the *A-Pučikwar* mythology in general as the first ancestor of the Andamanese. As the first progenitor he is made responsible for the origin of all sorts of things. The story of the origin of night must have a chief actor, and in the absence of any important ground for selecting any other of the ancestors the *A-Pučikwar* story-teller falls back on the monitor lizard.

In the above analysis I have drawn a distinction between what may be called major and minor motives of the story. The validity of the interpretation of the legends offered in this chapter depends on the validity of this distinction, and it is therefore important to provide a method by which we can separate major from minor motives. This can only be done when there are several versions of the same legend. Major motives may be defined as those which appear in all the versions of one legend, while minor motives are those which may vary from one version to another without producing any fundamental change in the legend itself. Thus, by a comparison of the *Akar-Bale* and the *A-Pučikwar* versions it can be shown that the identity of the chief actor is a minor and not a major motive.

If we compare the *Akar-Bale* legend with the *Aka-Bea* version recorded by Mr Man we see that they have in common (1) the explanation of the origin of night as due to the breaking of a rule, (2) the tracing back of the trouble to the anti-social passion of anger on the part of the actor or actors, (3) the account of the origin of dancing and singing as a means of neutralising the effects of darkness. All the other elements of the story are different in the two versions. In the *Aka-Bea* story it is the killing of a grub (*gurug*) that brings on the night, which is itself called *gurug*. What the meaning of this may be I cannot say. I did not hear this version of the story, and was not able to make any enquiries concerning it. All that it is necessary to note is that both the legends express the social value of night, and they both express it in very much the same way, the difference being that the *Akar-Bale* version makes use of the connection between night and day and the cicada, while the *Aka-Bea* story makes a similar use of some connection (not yet explained) between the night and a grub.

Thus the comparison of different versions confirms the interpretation here given. The legend expresses the negative social value of night as a period when social activity is diminished and the power of protection of the society therefore lessened. It does so by telling how the night first arose as the result of disobedience to a ritual prohibition, i.e., of meddling with the forces of nature. It traces the original cause yet further back to the anger of one of the ancestors, anger being itself a source of social disturbance. It passes on to express the social value of the dance, with its accompanying song, and exhibits the relation, within the system of social values, of dancing and darkness. Thus, although the manner of expression may differ, yet what is expressed is the same in both versions, and we are therefore justified in regarding this as the essential content of them.

An exactly parallel explanation can be given of the Andaman notions relating to the moon. The social value of moonlight is due to the fact that it enables the natives to fish and catch turtle and dugong by night. A clear moonlight night affords the best opportunity for harpooning dugong. During the second quarter the light of the moon steadily increases, and the period of moonlight falls in the first part of the night. After the change to the third quarter the light steadily diminishes, and moreover there is a gradually increasing period of complete darkness at the beginning of the night. The natives do not care to get up in the middle of the night to go fishing or hunting turtle. Therefore the second quarter is the time when they undertake such expeditions, and after the change to the third quarter they abandon them largely or entirely, and if they do go out they have to depend on torches. Therefore we may say that during the second quarter the moon gives valuable help to the natives, but during the third quarter withdraws that help.

At the beginning of the third quarter the moon rises in the evening with a ruddy hue. The natives explain this red and swollen appearance by saying that the moon is angry. When a man does something that hurts or damages another it is generally (in Andamanese life) because he is angry. So to say that the moon is angry is equivalent to saying that he is damaging or hurting someone, as he is indeed damaging the society by withdrawing the light by which for the past week or so they have been able to capture fish and turtle. The phenomena of the change of the moon in so far as they affect the social life are represented as if they were the actions of a human being. We may describe this briefly by saying that the moon is personified, using that term in a special sense to be defined more exactly later. Amongst the Andamanese, as amongst ourselves, anger is associated with heat, and this explains why the red glow of the moon when he rises during the first few nights of the third quarter is regarded as the visible sign of his anger.

Even the moon, however, is not to be expected to be angry without a cause. The natives say that the anger is due to some bright light having been visible at the time the moon rises. The personification is thus further elaborated. The moon gives the light by which fishing and turtle hunting at night are possible. This light has a positive social value, and its withdrawal is an evil. They therefore regard the moon as jealous, so jealous that if anyone makes use of an artificial light, as of a fire or torch or burning resin, the moon immediately is consumed with anger and withdraws the light that has been of so much use and has not been sufficiently appreciated. This belief is a means by which the value of the moonlight is recognized. Thus the beliefs about the moon can be interpreted in exactly the same way as the legend about night; both express, in accordance with the same psychological laws, the social values of natural phenomena.

I will next consider not a single legend but a number of different stories, running through all of which we can find a single major motive. I have recorded[1] three legends which relate, with some differences of detail, how in the beginning the ancestors had no fire, how fire was introduced by one of them, and how many of them, being burnt or frightened, were turned into animals of different kinds. In one version[2] the sea-eagle came into the camp of the ancestors and threw fire amongst them; whereby many of them being frightened were turned into animals. Another version is very similar, the chief actor, however, being the prawn[3]. In an *Akar-Bale* version *Dim-dǫri*, now

[1] Pages 207 and 204.   [2] Page 207.   [3] *Ibid.*

a fish, obtained the fire and burnt some of the ancestors with it so that they became fishes[1].

This legend is a widespread one, being found both in the north and in the south of the islands. The fact that the actor is different in the three recorded versions proves that the identity of the hero of the tale is a minor motive, i.e., one that may be varied without affecting the essential meaning of the myth.

The story serves as an explanation of the markings on birds and fishes, these being where the ancestor who became the species was burnt by the fire. Thus the legend is of the kind that is often called etiological. The common method of explaining such legends is to say that they are crude attempts on the part of primitive man to explain the natural phenomena with which they deal, in this case the bright colours of birds and fishes. Such an interpretation cannot be regarded as adequate. Why should the Andaman Islanders want to explain the markings of animals? Why should they explain them in the form of a legend, and why should the legend take this peculiar form?

The clue to the true interpretation of the three stories mentioned must be sought in the social value of fire. It was shown in the last chapter that fire is regarded as the symbol of social life and social activity, the centre around which the social life revolves, the source from which it draws its force. We may say, in a word, that it is the possession of fire that makes social life (as the Andamanese know it) possible. It was shown that it is on account of this relation of the society to fire that the latter is believed to be a source of security, of protection against the spirits. Now amongst all the creatures that inhabit the world, man is the only one that possesses and makes use of fire. Here, then, is the fundamental notion that is expressed in these legends. At first, so the story runs, animals and human beings were one, were not distinguished. Then came the discovery of fire. Some of the (undifferentiated) ancestors fled from the fire, because they were afraid of it, or because it burnt them. They became birds and beasts and fishes, retaining their fear of the fire, and being cut off for ever from the human society which, from that moment, constitutes itself around the fire. It is the

[1] Page 204.

possession of the fire that makes human beings what they are, that makes life as they live it possible. It is equally (according to the legend) the lack of fire, or the lack of ability to make use of fire, that makes the animals what they are, that cuts them off from participation in human life.

This, briefly, is the way I would explain the legend mentioned above, and ample confirmation will be forthcoming when we consider some of the other legends. Attention may be called here to a very significant phrase in a version of the fire legend recorded by Mr Portman[1] to the effect that "it was on account of the fire (i.e. of the possession of fire) that the ancestors became alive."

The three stories considered above contain three motives. (1) They express the social value of fire, by making the foundation of human society (through the differentiation of men and animals) depend on the discovery of fire. (2) They express a peculiar notion as to the relation of the human species to other animals, which is found also in other legends. (3) They give a legendary explanation of some of the characteristics of animals, such as the bright colours of certain birds and fishes.

It would seem that these same motives are present in many of the legends relating to the origin of fire. In the common version of the fire legend the fire is stolen from *Biliku* (*Puluga*) by the kingfisher. This bird has a patch of bright red feathers at the neck and these are explained as being where he was struck by the fire or the pearl-shell (lightning) flung by *Biliku*. In one variant the kingfisher swallowed the fire and had his head cut off by the lightning, whereupon the fire came out of his neck where the red feathers now are. In most of the versions it would seem to be implied that though the kingfisher succeeded in obtaining fire for the use of the ancestors, he was himself unable to profit by his own exertions, for he was turned into a bird condemned to eat his fish raw for ever. In one story, however, from the *Aka-Kede* tribe, it would seem that the kingfisher, by the possession of fire, and through the loss of his wings and tail, became a man. There is a lack of logic here which it is worth while to note. Although the kingfisher became a man,

[1] Page 203.

yet the legend is clearly based on the explanation of the red feathers of the bird's neck as due to the action of the fire. The psychological significance of such inconsistencies as this will have to be discussed later on.

Let us now consider another group of legends. We have seen that one explanation (in the mythological sense) of how the birds arose is that they were ancestors who fled from the fire. There are other stories that give a different account and relate that the animals came into existence through a great flood or storm that overwhelmed the ancestors. Both of these legends are to be found in the same tribes. Their incompatibility does not prevent them from being both equally accepted. If it can be shown that the story of the flood is simply an alternative method of expressing the same set of representations that underlie the story of the origin of the animals through the discovery of fire, the interpretation of the latter will be in some degree confirmed.

One account of the flood or storm, variants of which were obtained from both the north and south of the islands, tells how the ancestors only with great difficulty succeeded in saving the fire. Although it is not explicitly stated, we may conclude, I think, that it was because some of the ancestors kept their fire alight that they remained human, while those who lost their fire were turned into animals. If my personal impressions are of any value, this is really the idea that does underlie the legend in the native mind. Thus it would appear that this version of the flood myth is simply a reversal of the fire legend previously considered. They both express the same thing in different ways. They both make the possession of fire the thing on which social (i.e., human) life depends, the fundamental difference between man and animals.

It may be objected to this interpretation that in some of the versions of the flood myth there is no reference to the ancestors being turned into animals, while in others there is no reference to the saving of the fire. The reply to this is that if we are to understand the legends we must not consider each separately, but must seek out the connections between the different stories, connections that are not always obvious. Thus, as there are, in each of the tribes, different versions of a flood myth it might be supposed that the natives believe in several different floods having taken place in the times of the ancestors. Mr Man seems to have come to the conclusion that there were two distinct floods. I am fully satisfied, from personal knowledge, that the natives think of only one flood or catastrophe, and refer to it all the different legends. Sometimes a man will relate how the flood came and the fire was nearly lost, but will make no mention of the origin of animals at this time. At another time the same man will relate how the flood turned the ancestors into animals, but will make no mention of the saving of the fire. To understand the meaning of the legends we must connect these different stories together, for we know that they are connected in the minds of the Andaman Islanders themselves. Every native knows that it was at the time of the flood that the animals came into existence and he may remember this fact when he hears the story of how the fire was nearly lost. Similarly, when he hears the story of how the animals came into existence he remembers the other story of how the fire was nearly lost. Thus one man gave me a legend of the flood which explained the origin of the animals, and at the very end he mentioned as an afterthought "It was at this time that the fire was saved by *Maia Taolu.*"

When we thus connect the different stories relating to the flood we see that they express a definite system of representations or beliefs, which are found in all the tribes, and that this system is sometimes completely and sometimes partially expressed in the different versions. On the interpretation here suggested the major motives of the flood myth are (1) the social value of fire as expressed by making the difference between man and the animals depend on its possession by the former and not by the latter, and (2) the notion of the animals as having once been one with the ancestors. These two motives are both present in the legends of the origin of fire that were previously considered. It can be shown that even the third motive of the fire legend manages to creep into the flood story. In the *Aka-Kede* version[1] the dove is mentioned as having saved the

[1] Page 207.

fire. The connection between the dove and the fire (which appears in other legends)[1] would seem to have its basis in the shining plumage of the bird, just as the kingfisher is connected with the fire through the red feathers of its neck.

The details of the legends may be briefly mentioned. One *Aka-Jeru* version[2] explains how one of the ancestors made a noise by breaking firewood while the cicada was singing and so raised a great storm, in which the fire was nearly lost, and in which many of the ancestors were turned into animals. This version is a fairly complete expression of the fundamental representations on which the whole group of legends is based. There is an elaboration of one point in that an account is given of how the cyclone was brought about. This is a separate motive which will be discussed and explained later in connection with the *Biliku* myth.

Another legend from the same tribe[3] relates to a storm that was caused in the same way, and that resulted in the destruction of the whole world. The fire, which was nearly extinguished, was saved by one of the ancestors. No mention was made of the ancestors being turned into animals. This version, however, as I have recorded it, is incomplete. I was unfortunately unable to understand some of what the narrator told me.

The *Aka-Kede* version[4] similarly does not distinctly state that the ancestors who were destroyed by the flood were turned into animals, but the fact that the three persons mentioned in the legend are all birds suggests that it was at this time that the birds originated. The bird called *čarami-lebek*, having lowered the surviving ancestors to the ground with their fire, remained at the top of the *Dipterocarpus* tree and has been there ever since. The *Aka-Kọl* version of the same story[5] simply states that the ancestors were turned into animals in a cyclone, but contains no mention of the rescue of the fire.

In a number of these legends it is stated that the ancestors saved themselves by climbing up into a tall tree or into the trees. This is to be explained by the fact that the birds all live up in the trees, and a great many of them can never be seen save overhead. The top of the forest is where the birds live, it

---

[1] Page 202.   [2] Page 206.   [3] *Ibid.*   [4] Page 207.   [5] Page 208.

is their world, raised above the world of men and women. The flood drove the inhabitants up to the tops of the trees. The birds remained there and only the human beings came down again. As the original inhabitants were driven up into the trees by water covering the land we may complete the myth by saying that those who failed to reach the upper world were on that account compelled to spend the rest of their existence in the water as fish and turtle. This is, I think, what the legend really means. Thus the story of the flood gives a picture of a three-fold world, the waters below with their inhabitants the fishes and turtle and other marine creatures, the solid earth, and the upper region of the top of the forest where the flowers bloom and the butterflies and other insects and the birds pass their lives. This representation of the top of the forest as a world in itself may seem strange to one who has never seen a tropical forest, but to one who has spent months beneath it the forest-top of the Andamans does seem a world in itself, near yet inaccessible, a world where there is a gay and interesting life in the sunshine above, of which the wanderer in the deep shade beneath can only catch occasional glimpses as he gazes up through the tangle of boughs and leaves. For the natives of the islands therefore the top of the forest is an alien world into which they can only penetrate with extreme difficulty, by climbing, and with the life of which they have little to do. Similarly the waters of the sea are another world into which they can only penetrate for a few moments at a time by diving[1].

It may be said that, on this view, no allowance is made for the existence of terrestrial animals. That is true, but it must be remembered that there are very few such animals in the Andamans. The civet-cat and the monitor lizard and some of the snakes are as much arboreal in their habits as they are terrestrial. There remain only the pig and the rat as true terrestrial animals, and it may be noted that neither of these two animals ever figures in the legends as an ancestor. There are independent legends that relate to the origin of the pig, and the

---

[1] The same threefold division of the world is seen in the beliefs about the three kinds of spirits, those of the forest, those of the sea, and the *Morua* who, while spoken of as spirits of the sky, are often thought of as living in the tops of the tall trees.

rat seems to be of so little importance that no explanation of its origin would seem to be necessary. Moreover the monitor lizard and the civet-cat, which are partly terrestrial, occupy for this reason exceptional positions in the legends. Thus there is a legend recorded from the *Aka-Kede* tribe which accounts for the simultaneous origin of the civet-cat and the pigs through a game of the ancestors[1]. The monitor lizard is in an altogether exceptional position in that it is equally at home in the trees, on the ground and in the water of a creek. It is in a way free of all the three divisions of the world. This helps us to understand why in some of the tribes the monitor lizard is regarded as the original ancestor not only of the Andamanese but also of all the animals, including the birds of the forest and the fishes of the sea. The civet-cat cannot live in the water as the lizard can[2], but can climb trees and run on the ground. In many of the legends the civet-cat is said to be the wife of the monitor lizard. It will be remembered that in the *Akar-Bale* story it is the civet-cat, the wife of the first ancestor (the monitor lizard), who saved the fire from the flood by climbing up to the top of a steep hill with it. Thus it may be seen that the position of the monitor lizard and the civet-cat in the legends of the Andamanese is partly determined by the position that these two animals occupy in relation to the threefold division of the world revealed in the story of the flood.

The repeated mention of the *Dipterocarpus* tree in these legends would seem to indicate that it is a motive of importance. The tree is the tallest tree of the Andaman forests, and is very common, but it is probable that this does not afford an adequate explanation, and that there are other ideas connected with it in the minds of the Andamanese that would justify the place it occupies in the mythology. In one *Aka-Jeru* story the whole forest is said to have sprung from a *Dipterocarpus* seed dropped by *Biliku* after she had destroyed the original forest in her anger. It may be noted in passing that in the languages of the North Andaman the word for this tree is the same as the word for dugong.

[1] Page 218.
[2] It is worth while to recall here the belief that if a man goes into the water after eating civet-cat he will not be able to swim.

VI] CUSTOMS AND BELIEFS: MYTHS AND LEGENDS 349

Let us now briefly examine the story of the origin of animals as recorded from the *Akar-Bale* tribe[1]. There are three variants of this story. The one recorded from an *A-Pučikwar* informant[2] must really be regarded, I believe, as an imperfect reproduction of the *Akar-Bale* version. The version given by Mr Man[3] is also of *Akar-Bale* origin, as is shown by the fact that the phrases in it are in the *Akar-Bale* language. A comparison of these variants shows that the main purpose of the story is to relate how a great storm or cyclone visited the islands in the times of the ancestors and turned many of them into animals. The storm was brought about by the action of one of the ancestors who in anger did some of the things that are known to anger *Puluga* and cause a storm.

In some of the other legends we find the same motive. Thus in an *Aka-Jeru* legend[4] the flood is said to have been caused by one of the ancestors breaking firewood while the cicada was singing. In an *Aka-Kede* version[5] this part of the story is further elaborated, and a reason is given for this action on the part of the ancestor. *Kopo-tera-wat* was angry with the rest of the ancestors because they refused to give him any of the honey they had collected, and he therefore deliberately performed the action that brought the storm. The purpose of these elements of the legend is to explain how the great flood came about, by tracing it to the anti-social action of some one or more of the ancestors, just as the night is supposed to have been produced by an ancestor who performed a forbidden action. In the *Aka-Kede* version and also, as we shall see, in the *Akar-Bale* story, the matter is traced still further back and the anti-social action of the ancestor is explained as being caused by his anger which had been aroused by a disagreement with the ancestors. The origin of the catastrophe that separated the once united ancestors into animals and human beings is thus traced to the fact that they could not live together sociably and in harmony.

In the *Akar-Bale* story the part which explains how one of the ancestors came to give way to anger is highly elaborated. It starts with the quarrel of the tree-lizard with some of the ancestors. (It may be noted in passing that the tree-lizard is quarrelsome in reality.) This leads to the death of the lizard (or

[1] Page 208.   [2] *Ibid.*   [3] Page 209.   [4] Page 206.   [5] Page 207.

his transformation into an animal that still bears the name), and so to the grief of his mother and her anger against the ancestors who have killed her son. This elaboration of one part of the story tends to obscure the meaning of the whole. This is particularly the case in the version recorded by myself in which the anger of the tree-lizard is the direct cause of the change of some of the ancestors into animals. The narrator sets out to explain how a flood or cyclone came and turned the ancestors into fishes and birds. He elaborates the details of the first part of the story to such an extent that he loses sight of the conclusion. The purpose of the story as explaining the origin of animals remains in his mind, however, and gives rise to the description of how some of the animals had their origin as animals (i.e., were cut off from the human society) by being thrown by the lizard into the forest or into the sea. The legend in this form may therefore be regarded as giving an alternative explanation of the separation of the animals from the human society, the cause of the separation being a great quarrel in which they were all involved. In other words, human society is only possible if personal anger be subordinated to the need of good order; the animals are cut off from human society because they could not live peaceably together without quarrelling.

The examination of the variants of the flood-myth has taken us away from the main argument. In the various stories there are two separable elements. There is first the explanation of how a disastrous flood or storm was caused by the non-observance of ritual prohibitions connected with *Biliku* (*Puluga*). This element will have to be considered in relation to the *Biliku* myth. There is secondly the account of how through the flood or storm the birds and fishes became separated from the human race, and the three regions of the world, as the Andaman Islander knows it, became established. It is this second element that I have sought to explain. To repeat the argument, I would hold that it is really through the loss of the fire that the birds and fishes became cut off from mankind, and that therefore this element of the legends of the flood expresses exactly the same notion as the legend of the catastrophe that followed the discovery of fire. The two groups of legends result from the way the

VI]   CUSTOMS AND BELIEFS: MYTHS AND LEGENDS   351

Andaman Islander feels about the fire as being the one thing on which the society most completely depends for its welfare.

The preceding analysis has shown that the legends relating to the origin of animals, whether through the action of fire, or by the flood, serve to express the social value of fire. If this interpretation be correct we have a close parallel to the explanation of the story of the origin of night. In both cases, it has been argued, what the legend really expresses is the way in which a particular phenomenon (fire, in one case, the alternation of day and night in the other) affects the life of the society and the sentiments on which that life depends. The legends of the catastrophe, however, obviously contain another element of importance, revealing as they do a certain way of thinking about the animals. This element has not yet been explained. The representation of the birds, etc., as ancestors is not confined to one particular legend or group of legends, but runs through them all. Its explanation is therefore better postponed until we come to deal with the general features of the mythology, and will then have to be undertaken.

Let us now turn to the legends that concern *Biliku* (*Puluga*) and *Tarai* (*Deria*), which are of capital importance in the Andaman mythology. The clue to the understanding of them lies in the Andamanese notions about the weather and the seasons. In the Andaman Islands the year may be divided into four seasons. There is the cool season lasting from the beginning of December to the middle of February; immediately following this is the hot season from February to the middle of May; then comes the rainy season, from May to the end of September; October and November constitute a short season to themselves. In the cool season the weather is uniformly cool there is very little rain, and storms are almost unknown; the wind blows uniformly from the N.E. In the hot season there is little or no rain; the wind is generally N.E., but may be variable; summer lightning is frequent, but there are no violent storms except at the very end of the season. During the rainy season, after a short period of uncertain stormy weather with which it begins, the wind blows uniformly from the S.W.; it rains heavily, sometimes every day for weeks together, but violent storms (cyclones) are very rare. Between the rainy season proper and the cool season there is a period of six or eight weeks in which the weather is unsettled; the wind is variable; fine weather alternates with storms that are sometimes of terrific violence; waterspouts are frequent; it is at this season that violent cyclonic storms are likely to occur. This season is called by the Andamanese *Kimil* (*Gumul* of *Aka-Bea*). We have seen in the last chapter that the word *kimil* denotes a condition of social danger, or of contact with the power possessed by all things that can affect the life and safety of the society. It is obviously in this sense, and not as meaning "hot," that it is applied to the season in question, for the months of October and November are fairly cool, certainly very much cooler than February and March. We shall find that this is an important point in connection with the *Biliku* myth.

The life of the Andaman Islander is profoundly affected by the alternation of the seasons. There are, first of all, the violent cyclonic storms that occasionally occur. Such a storm may uproot the jungle for miles, making it impassable for years to come, and thus destroying some of the native hunting grounds. The wind is sometimes so violent as to tear every leaf from the trees in its path. While the storm lasts there is danger to the lives of the natives. An old man recounted to me how on the occasion of a violent cyclone he and the others of his village took refuge in the sea and on the open shore from the danger of falling trees, and remained there till the violence of the storm had abated. The usual name for a cyclone in *Aka-Jeru* is *toko-por*, i.e. "falling wood" or "falling trees." Even if all the natives escape the danger of death or injury, there is still the extreme fear and discomfort of the experience. If a storm lasts for any length of time the natives, who are unable or afraid to go out hunting, have to do without food until it is over. Incidentally the storm may destroy their huts, canoes, and other property and thus cause loss that has to be made up by toil.

The second important effect of the seasons on the life of the Andamanese is through the food supply. During the cool season, and the succeeding hot season, a number of vegetable foods, including the very important roots and some of the most prized fruits, are available. On the other hand, during these seasons the land animals are in poor condition. In the hot season, at any rate, lizards, snakes and the civet-cat are not eaten. Pigs are breeding and are in such poor condition that often a pig that has been killed is left in the jungle as being not good enough to eat. The hot season is pre-eminently the season of honey, which is so abundant that the natives are able to obtain much more than they can consume. In the rainy season there are few vegetable foods and very little honey, but on the other hand the jungle animals are in good condition and flesh food is abundant; fish are more plentiful in this season than during the dry weather. In the *Kimil* season (October and November) the natives add to their food supply two varieties of grub (the larvæ of the cicada and of a beetle) which are regarded as great delicacies. Roughly we can say that the rainy season is the season of flesh food, the *Kimil* season is the season of grubs, the cool season is the season of fruits and roots, and the hot season is the season of honey.

By reference to the prevailing wind the year may be divided into two parts, the N.E. monsoon from November to May, and the S.W. monsoon from May to November.

I propose to show that the Andaman Islanders express the social value of the phenomena of the weather and the seasons, i.e., the way these phenomena affect the social life and the social sentiments, by means of legends and beliefs relating to the two mythical beings whom they call *Biliku* and *Tarai*. Using the word personification in a sense to be defined later in the chapter, we may say that the Andamanese personify the weather and the seasons in the persons of *Biliku* and *Tarai*. *Biliku* is associated with the N.E. monsoon; she lives in the N.E.; the wind from that quarter is called "the *Biliku* wind"; to *Biliku*, therefore, belong the cool and the hot seasons, these being the seasons of the N.E. monsoon. *Tarai* is associated with the S.W. monsoon; he lives in the S.W.; the wind from that quarter is called "the *Tarai* wind," or, in *Aka-Bea*, simply *Deria*; to *Tarai* therefore belongs the rainy season. It is possible to show that the Andaman Islanders associate with these two beings all the phenomena of the weather and the seasons, and are able to represent the changes of the latter as though they were the actions of human or anthropomorphic beings.

In the mass of beliefs and stories relating to *Biliku* and *Tarai* there are some elements on which there is absolute agreement in all the tribes of the Great Andaman Division. I propose to treat these as being the most important elements. There is absolute unanimity, for instance, as to the connection of *Biliku* and *Tarai* with the N.E. and the S.W. respectively, and with the winds that blow from these two points of the compass. Further, this belief does not conflict in any way with any other belief of the Andamanese. There is similar unanimity in the beliefs that *Biliku* is angry at the digging up of yams, and at the melting of bees'-wax. There are other matters on which the agreement is fairly general but not absolute. For instance, there is a common belief that it was *Biliku* who first discovered fire, but there are also legends as to the origin of fire in which *Biliku* does not figure. I propose to treat such elements as these as being of secondary importance. Finally there are other elements with regard to which the beliefs of different tribes are not in agreement. For instance, in the South Andaman *Puluga* is regarded as male, while in the North Andaman *Biliku* is female. I propose to regard such elements as being of only minor importance, i.e., as not being closely connected with the central notion or notions expressed in the myth.

Applying the strict method outlined above, we may begin by noting that there is complete unanimity in regard to the connection of *Biliku* and *Tarai* with the N.E. and the S.W. respectively, and therefore with the monsoons. No interpretation of the myth can be adequate unless it sets out from this fact. The connection is so firmly fixed that it appears in the names of the winds themselves[1]. Even in this matter of the winds, however, there is a slight difference in the detail of the beliefs in different tribes. In the North Andaman it would seem that only the two principal winds are recognized; the S.W. wind (more accurately W.S.W.) is called "the *Tarai*

---

[1] It appears also in geographical names. *Puluga-l'ar-mugu*, meaning 'the Puluga front' is the name of a part of the Archipelago facing the N.E. and means 'the side facing Puluga.'

wind" (not, be it noted, "the wind of *Tarai*"); the N.E. (or more accurately N.N.E.) wind is called "the *Biliku* wind." These two winds are by far the most important, as the former blows steadily throughout the rainy season and the latter blows with almost equal steadiness throughout a good part of the cool and hot seasons. In the *Aka-Bea* and *Akar-Bale* tribes the general belief seems to be precisely the same as in the North Andaman. Only the two principal winds are considered to be of importance and one is associated with *Deria* and the other with *Puluga*. In these two tribes, as in the North Andaman, practically no notice is taken of the existence of winds from other quarters. In the *A-Pučikwar* tribe there is a notable difference, of great importance to the true interpretation of the legend. There is a dual division of the winds; the S.W. wind is called *Teria*; the other winds (of which a number are recognized) are all called *Bilik*. Thus *Bilik* is a generic name for a number of winds, namely for all the northerly or easterly winds, including not only the N.E., but also the N.W. and S.E. winds. The S.W. wind is called by a simple name, *Teria*, or as it would be better rendered in English "the *Teria*." The other winds are called by compound names such as *Mẹtepur Bilik*, *Kọičo Bilik*, etc., which we can only translate as "the N.E. *Bilik*," "the East *Bilik*," etc.

Two things of importance are shown by the consideration of these facts. The first is that there is a sense in which it may be said that the Andaman Islanders personify the winds in the persons of *Biliku* and *Tarai*; they apply to the natural phenomenon a name which is also the name of a mythological person, and they apply it directly and not in a possessive form, i.e., they say "the *Bilik*" or "the *Biliku* wind" and not "*Biliku's* wind." The second is that only the S.W. wind is associated with *Tarai* and all the other winds are associated with *Biliku*.

The last point is one of considerable importance in the interpretation of the myth. If we divide the year by reference to the prevailing winds, then the rainy season, with the exception of its beginning and its end, belongs to the S.W. wind; the hot season (save its end) and the cool season may be regarded as belonging to the N.E. wind, though the wind may be variable in the hot season; there remain two portions of the year, at the change of the monsoon, when the wind is variable, which cannot be classified as belonging strictly to the S.W. or to the N.E. wind. The fact that all these variable winds are denoted in the *A-Pučikwar* tribe by the name *Bilik* shows that in this tribe they are all classified with the N.E. wind. In this way the year is divided into two slightly unequal parts, one belonging to *Teria* or *Tarai* including the whole of the rainy season except the end and the very beginning, the other belonging to *Bilik* (*Biliku*) including the *Kimil* season, the cool season, the hot season, and even the first few days of the rainy season. This strict division only appears in the *A-Pučikwar* tribe, but it will be shown that an approximation to the same notion is found in the other tribes.

There is general agreement in all the tribes in the belief that storms are due to *Biliku* or *Tarai*. Both of them send rain and thunder and lightning, but whenever mention is made in the legends of a violent storm it is always *Biliku* who is mentioned as causing it, and never by any chance *Tarai*. Thus, in regard to this matter of storms, it is evident that *Biliku* is more important than *Tarai*, and this is only one example of the preponderance of *Biliku* over her consort. This preponderance will need to be explained as one of the essentials of the myth[1].

We have already seen how the Andaman Islander represents any natural phenomenon having negative social value as though it were the result of the action of a person in anger, this being the one anti-social passion with which he is most familiar in his own life. Thus the withdrawing of the light of the moon after the full is explained as being due to the anger of the moon. The negative social value of a violent storm is obvious. In accordance with the general principles of his mythology the Andaman Islander therefore explains the storm as being due to the anger of a personal mythical being. But storms are intimately connected with the winds, so that it must be *Biliku* and *Tarai* (in whom the winds are personified) who are responsible for the storms. Further, in the Andamans, violent storms are very rare except at two special periods of the year, at the

---

[1] Although it is generally believed that storms (or more exactly, violent storms or cyclones) are the results of the anger of *Biliku*, yet there is a conflicting belief that storms are made by the spirits, particularly the spirits of the sea.

change of the monsoon. This gives a further ground of association with *Biliku* and *Tarai* between whom the seasons are divided. We have seen that in classifying the winds the natives (of one tribe at any rate) associate with *Tarai* only the steady S.W. wind which brings not cyclones and violent storms but steady rain, while all the other winds are associated with *Biliku*. If this be so it is clear that a cyclone, with its wind veering from one quarter to another, must be the work of *Biliku*. Further, if the *Biliku* season be regarded as including all the periods of variable northerly and easterly winds as well as the period of the steady N.E., then we can say that it is only in the *Biliku* period that violent storms are likely to occur. It is evident therefore that an examination of the natural phenomena themselves gives us an adequate reason for the preponderance of *Biliku* over *Tarai* in the legends. This will be made even more evident as we proceed.

Another law of the Andaman mythology is that a person, such as the moon, is never angry without cause. There are a number of actions that are believed by the Andamanese to cause the anger of *Biliku*; of these there are three of extreme importance, all the others being certainly of much less importance. It is necessary, therefore, to examine these three carefully and find their meaning.

There is absolute agreement in all the tribes with regard to the belief that *Biliku* is angry and sends bad weather when bees'-wax is melted or burnt. The season of honey is the hot season from February to May. During the rainy season scarcely any honey is to be found and that only of the inferior (black) variety. It is clear therefore that honey belongs particularly to the *Biliku* portion of the year. During the hot season honey is abundant and large quantities are collected. As the natives make use of the wax, and as this is useless till it has been melted, this is the special season of the melting of bees'-wax. At the beginning of the season the *Biliku* wind blows calmly from the N.N.E. As the season draws to a close the wind becomes variable, uncertain, and in some years violent storms occur ushering in the rains of the S.W. monsoon. Year after year the wax-melting season comes to a close in stormy weather.

Now stormy weather and the anger of *Biliku* are, for the Andaman Islander, one and the same thing, so that to say that the anger of *Biliku* follows the melting of bees'-wax is in one sense simply a statement of actual observable fact.

Another belief about which there is absolute unanimity in all parts of the Islands is that *Biliku* is angry when certain plants are cut down or dug up. These plants include some of the most valuable vegetable foods of the Andamanese, such as the yams and the pith of the *Caryota* palm. Amongst the roots and fruits associated with *Biliku* there are one or two that were not botanically identified. All of them, however, about which I was able to obtain any information whatever, are available as food during the cool and hot seasons, and either not at all or in very small quantities during the rainy season. On the other hand, of the vegetable foods that are available during the rainy season, not one is ever mentioned as being in any way connected with *Biliku*. Further, amongst all the foods of the cool and hot seasons only those are intimately connected with *Biliku* which begin to be available during the *Kimil* season. A few examples may be mentioned. The yams and other edible roots are not found at all in the rainy season, but the tubers begin to form in the *Kimil* season (October and November) and small quantities of these roots are available for food at that time. By the time the cool season has set in the roots become abundant, and they continue to be found until well on into the hot season. All these roots are regarded as being specially connected with *Biliku* and are spoken of as her foods. The same thing applies to the *Caryota sobolifera* of which the pith is eaten either raw or cooked. The pith begins to form in the *Kimil* season, and this highly prized food is available right through the cool season. The fruit of the *Cycas*, which is another of those belonging to *Biliku*, also begins to ripen at the beginning of the cool weather. As regards the *Entada scandens*, Kurz, in his *Burmese Flora*, mentions it as seeding in the "cold season." I neglected to take note of the relation of this plant to the seasons, but the statement of Kurz may be relied on. Thus it is seen that the vegetable foods that are associated with *Biliku* are those that begin to be available for food during the *Kimil* season and are abundant during the cool season. Now the *Kimil* season, which is really the opening of the N.E. or *Biliku* monsoon, is the season at which cyclonic storms are likely to occur. Here again therefore, as in the case of bees'-wax, there is a definite ground of association in familiar natural phenomena. Year after year, as these foods begin to ripen and to be eaten, the islands are visited with stormy weather, sometimes of exceptional violence. When the Andaman Islander says that the stormy weather which is the sign of the anger of *Biliku* follows the digging up of yams and the cutting down of the *Caryota* palm or the gathering of the seeds of the *Cycas* or *Entada*, he is stating what is an actual fact.

The case of these vegetable foods is in one way different from that of bees'-wax. The melting of the wax goes on for some weeks before the anger of *Biliku* is finally aroused, when storms come to punish the offenders, and the change of season cuts short the supply of honey. In the case of the roots, etc., it would seem that it is only the first step that counts. The danger lies in the beginning of the season. Once the anger of *Biliku* has burst forth the bad weather ceases, the danger is past, and weeks of fine weather ensue, during which the natives may eat freely of the foods in question without fear of consequences. In this connection considerable importance may be attached to a statement made to me on more than one occasion, to the effect that the most efficient way of stopping a storm is to go into the forest and destroy the plants that belong to *Biliku*, i.e., do the very things that make her angry. We may apply this to the events of the *Kimil* season. The natives begin to dig up yams and collect other vegetable foods, and thereupon *Biliku* becomes angry and stormy weather follows. All that the natives have to do is to show sufficient persistence in continuing to eat yams, etc., and the anger of *Biliku* is bound to subside and the stormy weather to cease.

There is a third belief that is generally accepted in all parts of the Great Andaman, that *Biliku* is angry if a cicada be killed, or if a noise be made while the cicada is singing in the morning or the evening. The interpretation of this belief is made difficult by the fact that there is also an association between the cicada and the day and night. Thus Mr Man states that the prohibition against making a noise at dawn (while the cicada is singing) is associated not with *Puluga* but with the sun[1].

The grub of the cicada is eaten during the *Kimil* season, and at no other time of the year. Here the association is simple enough. The killing of the cicada (grub) takes place only during a brief season, and this is the season when cyclones occur. However, the grub of a beetle is eaten at the same season and yet I never heard of any connection between *Biliku* and this other grub. Certainly if there is a belief in such a connection it is very much less important than the belief relating to the cicada. Further, there is the belief that if the imago of the cicada be killed or if a noise be made while the cicada is singing, *Biliku* will be angry and will send bad weather, which is obviously not simply the result of the custom of eating the grub of the cicada during the *Kimil* season.

The relation of the cicada to *Biliku* is almost certainly due to the connection of the insect with the seasons. Unfortunately, not then recognizing the importance of the matter, I did not, while in the Andamans, take particular note of the relation of the life-cycle of the cicada to the revolution of the seasons, and I am reluctant to trust to vague memories of matters to which I did not pay special attention. Mr Man states, apparently on the authority of a native, that during the cold and dry seasons the cicada is seldom seen (and is therefore presumably also seldom heard). What I believe to be the life-cycle of the insect is as follows. During the rainy season only the adult insects are to be found. They lay their eggs at some period during the rainy season, possibly towards the end. In October and November the eggs have developed into pupæ, and it is these that the natives eat; but apparently the adult insects, or some of them, still survive at this time and are to be seen and heard. By about December the last of the adult insects die out and the grubs have not yet attained the adult form, so that there is a period during which no adult insects are either seen or heard. It is probable that the new generation makes its first appearance in adult form as soon as the first rains of the rainy season begin.

[1] Page 154.

The essential point, on which we can base an interpretation of the myth, is that the cicada is not seen or heard during the fine weather (December to March). It probably, as stated above, makes its reappearance just at the period of the stormy weather that ushers in the rainy season. Similarly, it does not disappear until after the end of the stormy period of the *Kimil* season. (I have certainly heard and seen the insect in October, and to the best of my recollection in November also.) Thus the cicada is definitely associated with the part of the year including the rainy season and the two stormy periods at its beginning and end. I believe that this is the fundamental fact that explains the Andamanese beliefs about the connection of the insect with the weather.

I was told of a ceremony that was held at the end of the *Kimil* season in the *Akar-Balɛ* tribe (and possibly in other tribes also) the purpose of which was said to be to ensure fine weather for some months and which is called "Killing the cicada." The ceremony consists of doing the very thing that is believed to produce storms, viz., making a noise while the cicada is singing in the evening. As soon as the cicadæ begin to sing all the persons in camp make as much noise as they can by banging bamboos on the ground, striking the sounding-board, or hammering on the sides of canoes, thus making just the kinds of noise that are said to be most disliked by the cicada. According to the statement of my informant this ceremony results in "killing" all the cicadæ so that they are not heard again for many weeks, and while this silence lasts fine weather is assured. The meaning of this little ceremony is plain when we recall the fact that though the digging up of yams and the cutting down of the *Caryota* palm anger *Biliku* and result in storms yet sufficient persistence in these actions, and therefore in any others that are displeasing to *Biliku*, results in dispelling the bad weather. Thus it is seen that although the matter is a little more complicated, yet the belief in the connection of the cicada with *Biliku* and with bad weather can be explained on exactly the same lines as the beliefs about bees'-wax and vegetable foods. The fact that the same explanation can be given of the three most important prohibitions connected with *Biliku* gives a high degree of probability to the interpretation here offered. These three beliefs are the only ones of real importance. I am unable to explain the connection of *Biliku* with the species of fish, the bird and the two kinds of wood mentioned on page 156. In the North Andaman there is a definite association between *Biliku* and spiders, the generic name for "spider" being *biliku*. I believe that this could be explained on the same basis as the connection with the cicada, i.e., through the connection of spiders with the changes of the seasons, but as I unfortunately neglected to take note of the habits of the spiders of the Andamans I cannot speak with any certainty and therefore prefer not to enter into a discussion of the subject[1].

The explanation that I have to offer of these beliefs relating to *Biliku* and to the things that offend her is that they are simply the statement in a special form of observable facts of nature. The rainy season comes to an end, the wind becomes variable, yams and other vegetable products begin to ripen and are used for food, and stormy weather comes, some years bringing cyclones of exceptional violence. Then follows a period of steady N.E. winds with fine weather and abundance of vegetable foods, during which the noise of the cicada is not to be heard. Then comes the honey season, when everyone is busy collecting honey and melting bees'-wax. The wind becomes very variable, storms come, the fine weather comes to an end and the rainy season begins again. These facts affect the feelings of the Andaman Islander and he expresses his impressions by regarding all these happenings as if they were the actions of an anthropomorphic being The vegetable products, the cicada, and the honey all belong to *Biliku*. When the yams are dug up she is angry, or in other words, storms occur; a storm

[1] The application of the name *biliku* to the spider is clearly a minor motive, and probably a late accretion. The name of the N.E. monsoon is the same in all the divisions of the Andamans about which we have information, with dialectic differences only. In the Little Andaman the form of the name is *Öluga*, and the same name is given to the monitor lizard. Presumably, therefore, there was originally one name throughout the Andamans for the N.E. monsoon (*Öluga, Puluga, Bilik, Bilika, Biliku*) and later this name was applied to the spider in the North Andaman and to the monitor lizard in the Little Andaman. It may be noted that the name of the monitor lizard varies from one language to another in the Great Andaman

is the anger of *Biliku*. The cessation of the song of the cicada removes one of the possible causes of the anger of *Biliku*, and therefore marks the period of fine weather. That anger appears once more when the natives busy themselves with melting bees'-wax.

It may be noted that these beliefs about *Biliku* give an expression of the social value of honey and bees'-wax and of vegetable foods such as yams. The Andaman Islands provide few fruits containing natural sugar. Yet the natives are inordinately fond of sweet things; they greatly enjoy the sugar that they now obtain from the Settlement of Port Blair. Honey, which was almost their only sweet food in former times, was therefore very greatly valued. Apart from the yams and other foods associated with *Biliku* there are very few productions of the Andamans containing starch in a palatable form. To the native who has been living during the rainy season almost entirely on meat and fish, the starchy foods of the stormy season (yams, *Caryota*, etc.) are of great value, and they are very highly prized. Thus the foods associated with *Biliku* all have a high value.

We all know how the value of an object is increased if, in order to obtain it, we have to make some considerable effort or sacrifice, or put ourselves in danger of some evil. Reversing this mental process, the Andaman Islander expresses his sense of the value of honey and yams by the statement that to obtain them he must be prepared to risk the anger of *Biliku* with its results. It was shown in the last chapter that the value of food in general is expressed in the belief that all food is more or less dangerous to eat, and that ritual precautions must be observed if the danger is to be avoided. Here in the *Biliku* myth, we have a further example of the same sort of mental process, in relation not to all foods in general but to a few foods of special value. Yet another example may be given. Roast pork is highly relished by the natives, and they believe that the roasting of pork offends certain spirits of the sky and is therefore dangerous[1].

---

[1] It is to be noted that these tabus connected with *Biliku* are not absolute prohibitions; they are beliefs that if certain things are done *Biliku* will be angry (i.e., there may be storms); if you do these things you must risk the danger. It is exactly the same with the roasting of pork.

364 THE INTERPRETATION OF ANDAMANESE [CHAP.

Returning now to the subject of *Biliku* as the sender of cyclones, it is necessary for the argument, even at the risk of repetition, to show (1) that this is by far the most important attribute of *Biliku*, and (2) that it follows immediately from her connection with the N.E. monsoon.

Taking the second point first, we may note, in the first place, that while *Tarai* is associated with the steady S.W. wind which blows with very little variation for months at a time, *Biliku* is associated with the variable winds of the hot season. Now a characteristic of a cyclonic storm is the way in which the wind

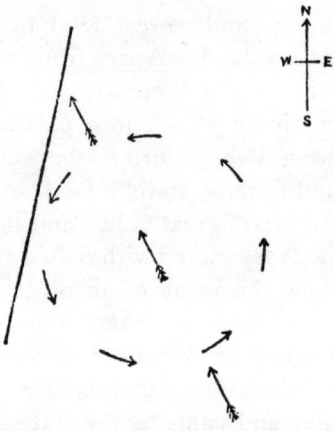

The line represents the position of the Andaman Islands. The larger arrows show the direction in which the cyclonic disturbance is moving. The smaller arrows show the direction of the wind.

veers from one quarter to another. Further, as most of the cyclones that cross the Andamans travel from the south-east in a north-westerly direction, and the movement of the cyclone is in a counter-clockwise direction, the first wind of a cyclonic storm when it strikes the islands comes from the north-east. This may be seen from the accompanying diagram. It is only at the very end of the storm, when the storm centre has passed, that the wind blows from the south-west. Thus it is clear that the association of cyclones with *Biliku* and not with *Tarai* is determined by the nature of the phenomena which the *Biliku-Tarai* myth sets out to explain.

That the most important attribute of *Biliku* is her connection with the cyclones is evident when we consider the legends in which she is mentioned. In most of the legends in which her name occurs[1] she is spoken of as being angry with the ancestors, and we know that a cyclone and the anger of *Biliku* are, for the Andaman Islander, one and the same thing. In some of the stories mention is made of a great storm that *Biliku* sent which nearly destroyed the world. All through the legends we find her pictured as a being whose anger is to be feared, who has the power to destroy human life and human property. *Tarai* is never mentioned in this way, for the rains of the south-west monsoon themselves have no such power.

We are now in a position to compare the characters of *Biliku* and *Tarai* and explain their relative positions in the myth. The reason for the preponderance of *Biliku* lies in the fact that it is she who sends cyclones, while *Tarai* sends nothing more than heavy showers of rain. *Tarai* is never responsible for the destruction of life and property, whereas *Biliku* is. Thus the preponderance of *Biliku* follows from the essentials of the myth. Secondly, *Tarai* is constant, ever the same, whereas *Biliku* is changeable. The rainy season of one year is exactly like that of another, and during the time it lasts the weather is consistent throughout. On the contrary, one year the *Biliku* season brings a terrific storm, and another year it is much less violent, while, from day to day during certain parts of the *Biliku* season the weather is unsettled, so that you cannot tell what the morrow will bring with it. It is obvious that this uncertainty about the actions of *Biliku*, the fact that she cannot altogether be reckoned with, would tend to make her of greater importance in the eyes of the Andamanese than her consort *Tarai*.

Let us now consider the question of the sex of *Biliku*. On this matter there is a lack of agreement. In the North Andaman *Tarai* is declared to be male and *Biliku* female. It can readily be shown that this results from the position of *Biliku* and *Tarai*

---

[1] See, for instance, the Aka-Jeru legend on pages 197—198, the Aka-Kede on page 200 and that from the Akar-Bale tribe on pages 200—201, and also the legends on pages 207, 208.

as regulating the seasons. *Tarai* rules over the rainy season, in which the chief food is the flesh of animals of the land and of the sea; it is the business of men to provide flesh-food. On the contrary *Biliku* rules over the seasons in which the chief foods are vegetable products of different kinds; it is the business of women to provide such foods. It is only men who go out hunting for pigs or turtle or who harpoon or shoot fish, and it is always the men who attend to the first part of the cooking of pig, turtle and dugong; it is the women who dig up the yams and collect the fruits and seeds, and it is the women also who cook them. There is a very real sense, then, in which flesh foods may be called the foods of men, and vegetable foods may be called the foods of women, and, since flesh foods are the foods of *Tarai* and vegetable foods are the foods of *Biliku*, there is a sound reason for calling *Tarai* male and *Biliku* female.

This way of thinking of *Biliku* as female is in harmony with her character as outlined above. Women (in the Andamans) are notoriously uncertain, changeable creatures. You can always reckon fairly well what a man will do, but not so with a woman. Moreover, when the Andaman Islander wishes to picture to himself a pair of closely associated beings, it is natural that he should compare them to the most closely associated couple with which he is familiar,—husband and wife. This tendency leads him to make the sun and moon man and wife in many of his legends, and it may well be expected to have its influence on the *Biliku* myth also.

In the South Andaman however, both *Puluga* and *Daria* are said to be male. It can be shown that this view is also appropriate in its way. The *Akar-Bale* say that *Puluga* and *Daria* were once friends, but have quarrelled and now live at opposite ends of the earth and are perpetually renewing their quarrel. *Daria* has things to himself for a few months (the S.W. monsoon) and sends his wind; then *Puluga* makes an attack on him; some weeks of unsettled weather ensue while they are fighting, until *Daria* is beaten and *Puluga* takes over the control of the weather and sends the N.E. wind. By and by, however, *Daria* shows himself again and there is another quarrel, with its unsettled and stormy weather, which ends in the defeat of *Puluga* and the reinstatement for a period of *Daria*. Even the bald language in which it is stated does not quite hide the poetical grandeur of this conception of the world as the arena of two battling giants in a never-ending quarrel. Those who have lived through a tropical cyclone with its wind changing from one quarter to another, its consummate violence, its sudden onslaught, its pause (that is felt to be merely a pause) as the centre of the disturbance reaches and passes you, and then its sudden renewal of the mad combat with the wind coming now from the opposite quarter, cannot but recognize in the *Akar-Bale* myth a successful attempt to describe such a storm in figurative language.

Such a combat could only be pictured by the Andamanese as taking place between two men, and the myth in this form therefore necessarily involves the belief that both *Puluga* and *Daria* are male. It is evident, therefore, that this view has some justification, that it does enable the Andaman Islander to express the feelings and impressions evoked in him by the phenomena of the weather. I venture to think, however, that the southern myth is not quite so satisfactory as the northern one, does not translate quite so well all the different features of the natural phenomena with which it deals[1].

A most important element of the myth is the connection of *Biliku* (*Puluga*) with fire. In all the tribes there are legends that represent *Biliku* as the first possessor of fire, which was, according to some versions, given by her to the ancestors, and according to others stolen from her by one of them. There can be no doubt that these legends owe their origin to the connection between *Biliku* the storm-sender and lightning.

There are several different beliefs about the lightning. According to one of these the lightning (*Ele*) and the thunder (*Korude*) are persons, who produce the phenomena of the same name. Another belief is that thunder and lightning are produced by *Biliku* and *Tarai*. On the whole, it would seem that

---

[1] In a paper in *Folk-lore*, vol. XX, 1909, I put forward the hypothesis that probably at one time all the tribes of the Andamans regarded *Biliku* (*Puluga*) as female, and *Tarai* (*Daria*) as male. I am still inclined to think that there is some evidence for this, but a discussion of what the Andamanese beliefs may have been in the past is entirely outside the scope of this chapter and is therefore omitted.

the latter belief is the one which is most frequently present to the minds of the natives. A man seeing lightning in the sky will say, according to the season, the prevailing wind, etc., *Biliku čatobom*, or *Tarai čatobom* ; " *Biliku* (or *Tarai*) is at work." There are different accounts, however, of the way in which *Biliku* makes the lightning. One belief is that it is a fire-brand flung by her through the sky; a second is that it is a mother-of-pearl shell (*be*) similarly flung; yet a third statement is that she produces the lightning by striking a pearl shell (*be*) on a red stone.

There is no doubt that the Andamanese regard lightning as fire; the charring of trees struck by it is sufficient to convince them of this. Thus lightning and the sun are the only two natural fires that they know. (With the relation of *Biliku* to the sun I shall deal later.) As the wielder of lightning *Biliku* thus becomes the possessor of fire. The simplest of the different beliefs, the one following immediately from the natural phenomena, would be, therefore, that which makes the lightning a fire-brand. This is, on the whole, the one that is most usually expressed, at any rate in the South Andaman.

The explanation of lightning as a shell depends not only upon the pearly lustre of this kind of shell, but also on other features of it. The shell in question (*be*) is used by women alone, and its use is confined to slicing yams and other vegetables in preparing them for food. Its association with *Biliku* therefore follows from the view of *Biliku* as female and as being especially associated with yams and other vegetable foods. Granting this fundamental connection, then the brightness of the shell, its keen edge and the way in which it can be made to skim through the air, will explain the statement that lightning is just such a shell thrown by *Biliku*. In the South Andaman, where *Puluga* is regarded as male, this belief about the pearl shell would be out of harmony with the rest of the myth, and, as we should expect, it is not found. However, the *Aka-Bea* word for lightning (*be-iŋa*, the *-iŋa* or *-ŋa* being a suffix) suggests that they may have had a similar belief in the past[1].

In the North Andaman the two views of lightning as a firebrand and as a shell are both held, because they both, in

---

[1] The stem *be* seems to be connected with the idea of cutting.

different ways, fit in well with the rest of the myth. There is yet a third view in which these two contradictory beliefs are, as it were, reconciled. This is that *Biliku* produces lightning by striking a pearl shell against a red stone.

In the North Andaman the action of throwing a shell or a fire-brand is regarded as typical of *Biliku*; this is the way in which she is pictured by the native, and in which she would doubtless be portrayed if the Andamanese had a pictorial art. In the dance described in an earlier chapter, in which the dancer gave representations of various mythical beings, *Biliku* was represented by the dancer holding a shell in his hand and dancing round threatening to throw the shell at the spectators.

The representation of *Biliku* or *Puluga* as throwing her lightning in the form of a fire-brand or a shell appears in several of the legends of the origin of fire, and in particular in the legend of which different versions are found in all parts of the islands that tells how the kingfisher stole fire from *Biliku* and how the latter flung a fire-brand or a shell at the thief.

The most usual form of the fire legend, and the only one that I ever heard, is that in which the fire is stolen. Mr Man has recorded a version in which *Puluga* is represented as *giving* the fire to the ancestors. Considerable importance attaches to this motive of the story as it reveals to us the way in which the Andamanese usually think of *Biliku* and of their own relation to her. She is not, so far as these stories go, a benefactress who by the invention of fire has earned the gratitude of men, but rather a person with whom the human society, both in the time of the ancestors and at the present day, is in a condition of opposition. Though *Biliku* had fire, yet she kept it for herself and it was only obtained from her by stealth. She was angry when her fire was stolen and tried to punish the offender.

This opposition between *Biliku* and the ancestors is shown in other legends. In some of the stories she is represented not as living with the ancestors, but as living on one side of a narrow strait while the ancestors lived on the other, as in the *Akar-Bale* and *A-Pučikwar* legends. She is thus separated from the ancestors in the minds of the natives. In the *Aka-Kede* legend the ancestors eat the foods that *Bilika* regards as specially belonging to her, and she kills them. As a result the ancestors join together and kill *Bilika*. In the *Akar-Bale* version something of the same sort appears; *Puluga* is always getting angry with the ancestors because they eat vegetable foods, and in his anger he destroys their huts and other property (as a cyclone does, and as an Andaman Islander is sometimes known to do in a fit of temper); at last the ancestors send him away out of the world. In the *A-Pučikwar* legend *Bilik* goes away from the world in anger because the ancestors steal his fire. In the *Aka-Jeru* version *Biliku* eats up all the food of the ancestors, and so they go away and leave her; she then destroys them with her shells (lightning) and finally perishes in an attempt to cross the sea on a stone. All these legends seem to express much the same thing in different ways, namely the existence of a condition of hostility between *Biliku* and human beings, based on the fact that the latter venture to make use of the things (yams, etc.) that *Biliku* regards as peculiarly her property. There can be no doubt that this is the usual way in which the Andamanese conceive the relation between *Biliku* and the ancestors, and therefore, since the ancestors represent the society in its beginnings, between *Biliku* and themselves. This relation is quite in agreement with what we have seen to be the essential basis of the myth. The natives obtain from the N.E. monsoon things highly valued, such as yams and honey, but they are given as it were grudgingly after a period of storms, and finally taken away in another period of storms.

This view of *Biliku* as hostile to mankind is not, however, absolutely universal if we are to accept Mr Man's account of the myths of the South Andaman. Mr Man describes *Puluga* as the creator of the world and the beneficent ruler of mankind. Although I could not find a native who held exactly the same views about *Puluga* as those that Mr Man represents as being the views commonly held in the tribes he studied (*Aka-Bea* and *A-Pučikwar*), yet there is no doubt that at times, and more particularly in the southern tribes, the natives do regard *Puluga* as the benefactor and even the creator of the human race[1].

[1] In dealing with the account given by Mr Man of the Andaman mythology it is necessary to remember that he was undoubtedly influenced by a very strong desire to

The representation of *Biliku* as hostile to mankind depends upon her position as the angry storm-sender, and this, as the legends show, does seem to be the more usual way of regarding her. But there is another and contrary aspect of *Biliku*. The revolution of the seasons brings to the Andamanese new supplies of relished foods,—the grubs of the *Kimil* season, the yams and honey of the cool and hot seasons. One of the Andamanese names for the season of the N.E. monsoon means "the season of abundance." Therefore *Biliku*, as the personification of this season, is herself the giver of good things. This aspect finds a partial expression in the legends. *Biliku* is regarded as having created or discovered the use of all the natural productions associated with her. (In one legend it is *Perjido*, the son of *Biliku*, who discovers honey with his mother's help.) She thus occupies a position similar to that of the other ancestors, towards whom the men of the present feel grateful for the benefits they have bestowed on mankind. This view of *Biliku* as benefactress is often extended in the North Andaman to the belief that it was she who invented all the arts now practised by women, and there are traces of a belief that it was her son *Perjido* who was similarly responsible for the arts practised by men.

This view of *Biliku* as a benefactress, although it conflicts to some extent with the view of her as on the whole hostile to mankind, yet, since it springs from the essential basis of the myth, cannot be overlooked. During the stormy season the Andaman Islander may well forget every aspect of *Biliku* save that she is responsible for the storms of which he goes in fear, but during the fine weather of the N.E. monsoon, when there is no longer any fear of a violent storm and when he is enjoying an abundance of the good things that he regards as especially belonging to *Biliku*, his feeling towards her must be of a very different nature; she is then the being who gives him the fine weather, the relished foods. Thus, contrary though they be,

show that the beliefs of the Andamanese about *Puluga* were really fundamentally the same as the beliefs of the Christian about his God. It may be taken as certain that he did not consciously allow this wish to affect his record of the Andaman beliefs, but it is very improbable that it did not unconsciously have a great deal of influence both on Mr Man and on his informants.

these two aspects of *Biliku* are both integral parts of the myth.

But *Biliku* is also the first possessor of fire, and we have seen that fire is regarded by the Andamanese as the source of the life of society, and therefore, in a way, of all life. *Biliku* as the source from which comes the fire is also the source of life. This view of *Biliku* is certainly to be found in all parts of the islands, though it has been developed more in the South than in the North. *Biliku* thus becomes responsible for the beginning of the society, and since the whole universe centres in the society, of the whole universe. She becomes the being who created or arranged the order in which men live.

For the honour of this position *Biliku* has, however, a competitor. Besides the lightning there is another natural source of fire, the sun. We find therefore two different (and contrary) developments of the myth of the beginning of the world. In one of these the sun is associated with *Biliku*, is regarded as belonging to her or made by her. For instance, in an *Aka-Kede* legend, she is stated to have made the sun by throwing a flaming brand into the sky. By this means *Biliku* becomes the sole source of fire and therefore of life. This is the position that *Puluga* occupies in the versions of the legends recorded by Mr Man. In those legends *Puluga* gives fire to the first human beings by making the sun come down to earth and ignite a pile of wood. The alternative development makes the sun independent of *Biliku* and it is then the sun, or a mythical person associated directly with the sun, who becomes the maker of the world, the source of life. Unfortunately, I did not obtain much detailed information about this development of the myth. In the North Andaman the being named *Čara* is associated with the sun and with fine weather, and is certainly sometimes regarded as the maker of the world. In the South Andaman it is *Tomo* who is associated with the sun. Men and women, when they die, go to live with *Tomo* in the sky. It is *Tomo* who is responsible for all things being as they are. He was the first being; it was he who arranged the order of nature; and similarly it was he who created the social order, so that a question as to why some custom is observed is often answered by saying that it was

Tomo who made it so. In Mr Man's account *Tomo* is degraded to the position of being merely the first man made by *Puluga*, but in the accounts that were given to me by the natives of the *Akar-Bale* and *A-Pučikwar* tribes *Tomo* was a rival of *Puluga*; sometimes one and sometimes the other was spoken of as being the supreme maker of all things. An *Akar-Bale* man of very high intelligence, who had been educated as a Christian, in trying to explain to me statements about *Tomo* made by another *Akar-Bale* who was regarded as an authority on the legends of his tribe, said that *Tomo* was the same thing to the *Akar-Bale* that God is to the Christian. When I asked him if it was not rather *Puluga* who was the Andaman equivalent of God, he said that some people might think so, but that according to the old man to whom I was talking it was *Tomo* and not *Puluga* who occupied the position[1].

There is only one more point that needs to be discussed, and that is the connection of *Biliku* with the spirits. It is clear that *Biliku* and *Tarai* must be distinguished from the spirits (*Lau*), yet at the same time *Biliku* is brought into relation with the spirits by the existence of two alternative explanations of bad weather. One of the explanations is that storms are due to *Biliku*, while the other is that they are due to the spirits, particularly the spirits of the sea. Both these beliefs, contradictory as they seem, are held by the Andamanese. The connection of the spirits with the weather is due to the fact that

---

[1] To complete the discussion of this part of the subject it would be necessary to deal with many points in the legends of the real meaning of which I do not feel satisfied. I have, for instance, given no explanation of the position of *Perjido* in the *Biliku-Tarai* myth, although this is probably an important matter. Nor have I traced to its source the connection of *Biliku* (with her net, and her hole, or cave, in which she shuts herself up to sleep and from which she comes out to bring rain and storm) with the spider. Besides *Tomo*, *Biliku* has yet another competitor for the position of control over the fine weather of the hot season, namely the snake, *or-čubi* (*wara-jobo*), which is regarded as being in some way the guardian of honey and of fine weather. There are legends that show the connection of this snake with honey (page 227) and the same connection is shown in the honey-eating ceremony (page 105). According to Mr Man, when the natives of the South Andaman see a dark cloud approaching and they do not wish it to rain they threaten *Puluga* that they will call up the *wara-jobo* to bite him. The snake, like other snakes, is only to be seen during the hot weather of the honey season. It may be remembered that it is from this snake that the pattern used in decorating the body with white clay is named.

the weather is a thing that can limit the activity of the society, and we saw in the last chapter that there is a tendency to associate with the spirits of the dead all things that in any way interfere with the smooth progress of social life. When it is said that a storm can be stopped by swishing arrows in the sea, or by placing in the sea a piece of *Anadendron* creeper, it is to the spirits of the sea, who are afraid of arrows and of the *Anadendron*, that the storm is attributed, and not to *Biliku*.

In the *A-Pučikwar* tribe I found an association of *Bilik* with the spirits. One man of this tribe (a medicine-man or dreamer) stated that the *Bilik* are a distinct class of spirits, distinct from the *Lau* and the *Jurua*, yet similar to them. It is the *Bilik* who control the weather. Certain men, when they die, become not *Lau* or *Jurua*, but *Bilik*. Thus in one of his dreams that he related to me he met and conversed with the spirit of a deceased friend whom he spoke of as *Boičo Bilik*, *Boičo* having been his name when he was alive. A medicine-man is able to control the weather through his communication with the *Bilik* in dreams. In this tribe therefore we find a doctrine according to which *Bilik* is not the name of a single being but of a class of beings similar in essentials to the other two classes of spirits. It seemed to me possible that these beliefs are a comparatively late introduction by some of the medicine-men of the tribe. The *Boičo* about whom my informant *Tora* dreamed seemed to have had some part in the development of the doctrine. This does not, however, in the least detract from its value as affording us an insight into the beliefs of the Andamanese.

These beliefs clearly spring from an attempt to distinguish from one another the different northerly and easterly winds, each of the recognizable winds being regarded as a separate person, and from the merging together of the two contrary beliefs in the weather as regulated by spirits and by *Bilik* and *Teria*. The general system of beliefs about spirits as being responsible for all things that may affect human well-being inevitably leads to the notion that the weather is controlled by the spirits, and this is implied also in the belief that a medicine-man (whose power is derived from contact with the spirits) is also able to influence the weather to some extent. This doctrine, however, conflicts with the view of the weather and the seasons as controlled by *Biliku* and *Tarai*, who are not spirits but personifications of natural phenomena. It is perhaps this conflict between doctrines, both of them important and indeed necessary, that has led to the elaboration of the peculiar beliefs met with in the *A-Pučikwar* tribe.

I have dealt with most of the more important details of the *Biliku-Tarai* myth, and have tried to show that the whole myth is an expression of the social value of the phenomena of the weather and the seasons. These phenomena affect the social life in certain definite ways and thereby become the objects of certain sentiments; these sentiments are expressed in the legends. *Biliku* and *Tarai* are personifications of the N.E. and S.W. monsoons; as such they are responsible for the weather; feelings awakened by the weather are therefore referred to *Biliku* and *Tarai*; thus the fear of a cyclone at certain periods of the year is expressed as a fear of the anger of *Biliku*. Since the time when men go in fear of storms is also the time when they are just beginning to dig up yams and eat them, the myth connects the anger of *Biliku* with the digging up of yams, and similarly in the cases of honey and the cicada. As *Biliku* is associated with vegetable foods, and these are things with which women chiefly have to do, *Biliku* (in the North Andaman) is regarded as female; *Tarai*, being associated with flesh foods, is male; the two are therefore conceived as wife and husband. As the maker of storms *Biliku* is responsible for the lightning and is therefore possessed of fire. She thus comes to be regarded as the first possessor of fire. This gives rise to stories of how the ancestors obtained their fire from *Biliku*, and as she is generally regarded as being hostile rather than friendly towards mankind, the stories relate how the fire was stolen from her. But besides being the maker of storms *Biliku* is also the dispenser of the good things of the season of the N.E. monsoon and when this aspect of the procession of the seasons is prominent before their minds the natives think of *Biliku* as a benefactress of mankind. As she is the possessor of fire, and as fire is the source of the life of the society, she comes to be regarded as herself the source of life, though there is an alternative myth that gives this position to a being associated with the sun.

Such is a brief outline of the explanation that I have tried to demonstrate. It may be objected that there are a few important details and several minor details that I have not explained. To that extent my explanation is incomplete, but I hope that I have given sufficient evidence for it to justify us in using it as an integral part of the explanation of the meaning and function of the Andaman mythology in general.

It is not necessary, for the purpose of this chapter, to examine one by one all the legends recorded. Indeed, there are many details of the Andaman mythology that I cannot explain, owing simply, I believe, to my lack of insight into the ways of thought of the natives. The examples already considered are sufficient for the argument. If the interpretations given of these be correct we can base on them certain general conclusions.

I have explained some of the more important of the legends as being expressions or statements of the social value of natural phenomena. The alternation of day and night, for example, affects the life of the society in a certain definite manner and this gives rise to a certain way of thinking and feeling about the phenomenon in question. These thoughts and feelings, however, remain vague and without fixity until they are formulated and expressed either in the form of some definite rule of behaviour, such as the prohibition against noise while the cicada is singing, or in some concrete statement, such as that afforded by the legend of the origin of night. Similarly the legends relating to the origin of fire or the saving of the fire during the flood serve to give definite and permanent form to the vague feelings that result from the way in which the possession of fire affects the social life. Finally, I have tried to show that the myths relating to *Biliku* and *Tarai* are nothing but the expression in concrete form of the ideas and feelings that result from the effects of the weather and the seasons on the life of the Andaman Islanders. From these examples I now propose to draw a general conclusion. All the legends, I wish to maintain, are simply the expression in concrete form of the feelings and ideas aroused by things of all kinds as the result of the way in which these things affect the moral and social life of the Andaman Islanders. In other words the legends have for their function to express the social values of different objects,—to express in general the system of social values that is characteristic of the Andaman social organisation. To justify this general statement it will be necessary to show how it comes about that these representations are expressed in the form of myths and legends dealing with the ancestors and with such anthropomorphic beings as *Biliku* and *Tarai*.

Throughout the myths we meet with examples of what I have called the personification of natural phenomena. It is now necessary to give a more exact definition of this term. By it I mean the association of a natural phenomenon with the idea of a person in such a way that the characteristics of the phenomenon may be regarded as though they were actions or characteristics of the person. The simplest form is that in which the phenomenon itself is spoken of and thought of as if it were an actual person. Thus the sun and the moon are spoken of as Lady Sun and Sir Moon. Similarly, in the North Andaman, the night is personified and is called Lady Night (*Mimi Bat*). In many cases of personification however, while the person may or may not possess the same name as the phenomenon, the latter is said to be produced by the former. Thus, in the North Andaman, *Ele* is the name of the lightning, and *Ele* is spoken of as a person; yet, if we enquire further, we are told that *Ele* (the person) produces the lightning by shaking his leg. A somewhat similar case is that of *Biliku* and *Tarai*. These two beings are said to produce the winds that blow from the different quarters of the compass. But when we enquire as to the names of the winds, we find that in the South Andaman (*A-Pučikwar* tribe) the S.W. wind is called *Teria*, and the other winds are all called *Bilik*. Thus the name of the person is also used as the name of the phenomenon of which he is (in the phraseology here used) the personification. In the North Andaman we find a difference, the winds being called "the *Biliku* wind" and "the *Tarai* wind." It is necessary to insist on this translation of the native *Biliku boto* and *Tarai boto*. We should expect, if *Biliku* were simply a person who produced the winds, that the latter would be called "the wind of *Biliku*," a possessive form (*Biliku ičo bọto*) being used, but this is not so, and the phrase habitually used can only be properly translated "the *Biliku* wind" just as we might say "the north wind." Thus, even in the North Andaman *Biliku* and *Tarai* are used as the names of the two chief winds.

In all these cases, sun and moon, *Biliku* and *Tarai*, etc., I propose to use the term personification, as being the most convenient and not liable to be misunderstood after having been carefully defined. We have now to seek an explanation of this process of personification. A great deal has been written on the subject of personification in mythology, and it is therefore not without diffidence that I venture to put forward an explanation which can only be very briefly stated in this place and would require for its full exhibition a lengthy psychological explanation.

An insight into the process of personification is afforded by considering our own use of figurative language. We talk of the angry storm, the raging sea. In such cases we allow ourselves for a moment to regard the natural phenomenon as if it were a person or the action of a person, and we do not even trouble distinctly to express the "as if." We use such phrases in order to attain a more forcible expression of our thoughts and feelings. How is it that such expressions succeed in the purpose for which they are used?

The reason would seem to be that our knowledge and understanding of persons is much more intimate than our knowledge of things. The fact that we are able, by the action of sympathy, to know what persons with whom we are in contact are feeling, gives us an understanding of them that we can never reach with inanimate objects.

In all human society the most important elements of the experience of the individual are due to his relations with other persons. In the development of the emotional life of the child, persons intervene at every turn, and there is thus built up a system of sentiments and representations which forms the very foundation of the individual's affective life. In other words the first organised experience that the individual attains is all connected with persons and their relations to himself. This early experience provides a basis on which we may and do organise later experiences. The perception of the leaping waves and lashing spray of a sea in tempest arouses in us a vague emotional reaction, but it is an experience that we have not learned to formulate exactly. The feeling awakened in us is, so to speak, unclassified, there is no exact word by which we can express it. We therefore fall back upon that system of affective experiences that have been classified, and for which we do have adequate words, and we apply the word "angry" to the scene before us. At the utterance of the word, with its appeal to infantile memories and to the long series of experiences that have been associated with it, the emotion becomes more definite, if not more intense. We are thus enabled to classify our present experience, to associate it with past experiences that have been arranged in our minds in an organised system, and to find a place for it in that system.

Applying this to the case of the myths we must first of all note that the Andaman Islander has no interest in nature save in so far as it directly affects the social life. Scientific and artistic interest in nature are products of civilisation. The Andaman Islander has no desire to understand the processes of nature as a scientist would wish to do, nor has he any conception of nature as a subject of esthetic contemplation. Natural phenomena affect him immediately by their influence on his own life and on the life of his fellows, and are thereby the source of a number of emotional experiences. In order to express these he has to make use of that part of his own experience that is already thoroughly organised, namely, that relating to the actions of one person as affecting another or as affecting the society. Only in this way is he able to organise his experiences arising from the processes of nature, to classify and render definite the vague impressions that are aroused in him. He interprets nature in terms of the world with which he is most familiar, the world of persons, being enabled to do so by the presence within him of a regulated and definite body of experience which he has derived from his relations with persons from the time of his first awakening to the consciousness of the external world.

There is a parallelism here, as in many other matters, between the psychological development of the individual and that of the race. The fundamental need for the child is to learn to accommodate himself to his environment. In this environment by far the most important objects are persons— parents and other children—and the first business of the growing child is to learn to adapt his actions to the requirements of this intercourse with persons. This is so overwhelmingly important that the other need (of adapting himself to inanimate objects) is quite overshadowed by it. The child has to make experiments and observations upon persons, to learn how they will act. He meets with such a phenomenon as anger, for example, the anger of a parent, or of another child, and by means of a succession of experiences he comes to a satisfactory understanding of this particular thing, and what it means with reference to himself and his actions. This notion of the anger of a parent becomes the nucleus around which is organised the experience of similar phenomena. In play or sometimes in earnest, the child treats all sorts of inanimate objects and events connected with them as if they were persons or the actions of persons. By this means, and by this means alone, he is able to exercise himself in his newly acquired experience and to extend and organise it yet further.

In the history of the race the development of society depends upon the organisation of personal relations. The task of man in primitive society is therefore similar to the task of the child. The needs of his life compel him above everything else to devote himself to organising that part of his experience that relates to the actions of persons upon one another; all else is subordinated to this supreme need; and just as the child organises and develops his experience by treating inanimate objects as if they were persons in such a way that we can hardly tell if he is in play or in earnest, so primitive man, in exactly the same way, organises and develops his social experience by conceiving the whole universe as if it were the interaction of personal forces.

This explanation of the nature of personification helps us to understand some of the Andamanese beliefs. Natural phenomena such as the alternation of day and night, the changes of the moon, the procession of the seasons, and variations of the weather, have important effects on the welfare of the society. The latter, in so far as it is regulated from within, depends on the adaptation of persons to one another. Men must learn to live in harmony, to sacrifice their own desires at times to the needs of others, to avoid occasions of giving offence, and not readily to give way to anger when offence is given. The Andaman Islander represents this fundamental law of the society as though it were the fundamental law of the whole universe. When any evil befalls the society it is as though some personal power were in question, as though some one were angry at some offence. Thus the moon and *Biliku* are represented as persons who can be offended and whose anger has unpleasant results. Conversely when all goes well it is because there is harmony or solidarity between men and the nature beings which affect men's lives. In a word, the forces with which the Andaman Islander is most familiar as affecting his welfare are those of solidarity and opposition; it is solidarity that maintains the harmony of social life, opposition that destroys it. The forces of nature in so far as they affect the society are therefore represented as being of the same nature; there can be either solidarity or opposition between men and nature; the former leads to well-being, the latter to misfortune.

Thus the personification of natural phenomena is one of the methods by which the Andaman Islander projects into the world of nature the moral forces that he experiences in the society. The process is essentially similar to that described in the last chapter in connection with the ceremonial, save that there the forces we were considering were largely impersonal. Perhaps, rather than speaking of it as a projection of moral forces into nature, we should regard it as a process of bringing within the circle of the social life those aspects of nature that are of importance to the well-being of the society, making the moon and the monsoons a part of the social order and therefore subject to the same moral forces that have sway therein.

The personification of natural phenomena is not, however, the only method by which their social value can be expressed.

The *Akar-Bale* legend of the origin of day and night, as we saw at the beginning of the chapter, expresses the social value of the alternation of light and darkness by means of a story of how it originated in the time of the ancestors. If we seek to understand all that this legend means we must ask why the Andaman Islanders believe in the existence of the ancestors, and why they attribute to them the characteristics that are exhibited in the stories they tell about them. The ground of the belief in the ancestors is to be found in the existence of a sentiment fundamental in all human society, which I shall call the feeling of tradition. When an Andaman Islander is asked the question "Why do you do so and so?" he very frequently replies "Because our fathers did so before us." This answer expresses in its simplest form the feeling of tradition. In all his actions, in the way he obtains and cooks his food, in the way in which he makes his various implements and weapons, in the moral and ritual customs that he is required to observe, the native acts in accordance with tradition. If he should ever feel inclined to deviate from it he finds himself in conflict with a powerful compulsive force. In tradition, therefore, the individual is aware of a force stronger than himself, to which he must submit whether he will or not. Further, he is aware that the power which he possesses, as a member of the society, whereby he is able to face the hostile or at best indifferent forces of nature and provide himself with food and maintain himself in security and happiness, is not simply a product of his own personality, but is derived by him from the past. Towards this past, therefore, on which his own life so obviously depends, he feels a grateful dependence. So long as he acts in conformity with tradition he can enjoy safety and happiness, because he is relying on something much greater than his own qualities of mind and body.

To put the matter in a few words, the individual finds himself in relation with an ordered system—the social order—to which he has to adapt himself. The two chief moments in his affective attitude towards that order are his sense of his own dependence upon it and of the need of conforming to its requirements in his actions. It is this,—his sense of his own relation to the social order,—that the Andaman Islander expresses in the legends about the ancestors, which recount how that order came into existence as the result of actions of anthropomorphic beings.

Some of the legends recount the invention of weapons or implements or the discovery of the uses of natural objects. In one of the North Andaman stories it is said that all the weapons and implements now used by men were invented by the first man, whose name, *Jutpu*, probably means "alone," i.e., the man who was at first by himself. This first man made himself a wife from the nest of the white ant. The regulated society of the ants, and the numerous population that a nest contains, give this story its symbolic meaning.

Besides what may be called general culture legends, of which the story of *Jutpu* is an example, there are several special culture legends relating to various discoveries and inventions, such as the tale of how the use of yams for food was first discovered, or that which tells how the monitor lizard discovered quartz and scarified himself with it. By means of these legends the Andaman Islander expresses his sense of his own dependence on the past. He pictures a time when the social order as it now is had not begun, or was just beginning; the knowledge he now possesses was then being acquired, the weapons he uses were being invented, the moral and ritual laws that he obeys were in process of being formulated.

It is obvious that the Andaman Islander cannot regard the ancestors as being persons exactly like himself, for they were responsible for the establishment of the social order to which he merely conforms and of which he has the advantage. He says, therefore, that they were bigger men than himself, meaning by this that they were bigger mentally or spiritually, rather than physically, that they were endowed with powers much greater than those even of the medicine-men of the present time. This explains the magical powers that are attributed to many, or indeed to all, of the ancestors; the belief in the existence in the past of men or beings endowed with what we may almost call supernatural powers is the inevitable result of the way in which the man of to-day feels towards the men of the past on whose inventions and discoveries he is dependent for his daily nourishment[1].

Besides the social order there is another, the order of nature, which is constantly acting upon the social order. To this also the individual has to adapt himself, and his knowledge of how to do so is equally derived from the past. The order of nature only affects him through the social order, and the two therefore necessarily seem to him merely two parts of one whole,—the order of the universe. In the legends he tells how not only the social order but also the order of nature came into existence; an example is the story of the origin of night.

The Andaman Islander finds himself in an ordered world, a world subject to law, controlled by unseen forces. The laws are not to him what natural laws are to the scientist of to-day, they are rather of the nature of moral laws. He recognizes only one meaning of the word right and of the word wrong; right action is that which is in conformity with law, wrong action is that in opposition to the law; it is wrong to give way to anger, it is wrong to kill a cicada, or to have a bright light in camp when the moon is rising in the third quarter, and it is wrong also to try and use unsuitable material for an implement or weapon. Wrong actions always lead to harm; if you use unsuitable wood for your bow it will break and your labour be wasted; if you kill a cicada it will rain heavily; if you give way to anger readily you will earn the dislike of your fellows that may some day lead to your undoing. Right and wrong mean acting in accordance with the laws of the world or in opposition to them, and this means acting in accordance with or in opposition to custom. Custom and law are indeed here two words for the same thing.

The forces of the world, as the Andaman Islander conceives them, are not the blind mechanical forces of modern science: rather are they moral forces. Their action upon human beings is not only to be witnessed in external events, but is to be

---

[1] In the last chapter it was shown that the attribution of magical force to such things as foods and human bones is simply the means by which the social values of these things are represented and recognized. Similarly here the magical powers of the ancestors are simply the representation of their social value, i.e. of the social value of tradition.

experienced in the man's own consciousness or conscience. He feels within himself their compulsion when he would run counter to them, and their support when he leans upon them. The law of the world, then, is a moral law, its forces are moral forces, its values moral values; its order is a moral order.

This view of the world is the immediate and inevitable result of the experience of man in society. It is a philosophy not reached by painful intellectual effort, by the searching out of meanings and reasons and causes; it is impressed upon him in all the happenings of his life, is assumed in all his actions; it needs only to be formulated. And the argument of this chapter has been that it is as the expression or formulation of this view of the world as an order regulated by law that the legends have their meaning, fulfil their function.

The legends of the Andamanese then, as I understand them, set out to give an account of how the order of the world came into existence. But the Andaman Islander has no interest in any part of it except in so far as it affects his own life. He is interested in the procession of the seasons or the alternation of day and night, or the phases of the moon, only in so far as these things have effects upon the community. In other words he is interested in natural phenomena only in so far as such phenomena are really parts of the social order. This I have expressed earlier in the chapter by saying that the legends deal not with all aspects of natural phenomena but only with their social values.

A fundamental character of the natural order (as of the social order) is uniformity; the same processes are for ever repeated. This character of nature the legends take for granted; they assume that if a force is once set into action it will continue to act indefinitely. They assume also a period in which the present order did not exist. Anything that happened in that period has gone on happening ever since. One of the ancestors discovered how to cook yams, and men have been cooking yams in the same way down to the present day. A cicada was crushed and cried out and the night came, and since then the darkness has come every evening as soon as the cicada sings. In one of the legends the tree lizard was quarrelsome, and has remained so. Thus the legends represent the social order, including such natural phenomena as may be said to belong to it, as being due to the interaction of forces of a special character that came into existence in the beginning and have continued to act uniformly ever since. In this way they express two most important conceptions, that of uniformity (or law) and that of the dependence of the present on the past.

It is the need of expressing these two conceptions that gives the legends their function. They are not merely theoretical principles but are both intensely practical. The law of uniformity means that certain actions must be done and others not done if life is to run smoothly; any deviation from uniformity in conduct is dangerous as being contrary to the law that regulates the universe. What actions are to be done and what are to be left undone was determined once for all in the past when the present order came into existence. The knowledge of what to do and what to avoid doing is what constitutes the tradition of the society, to which every individual is required to conform.

The legends, then, set out to express and to justify these two fundamental conceptions. They do so by telling how the social order itself came into existence, and how, also, all those natural phenomena that have any bearing on the social well-being came to be as they are and came to have the relation to the society that they possess.

One group of facts that have an obvious relation to the society consists of the geographical features of the islands. The more notable features of the part of the country in which a man lives, and which he regards as his own, are intimately connected with his moral sentiments. His attachment to his group necessarily involves an attachment to the country of the group. The same sort of thing exists amongst ourselves. This attachment of the members of a group to their own country explains, I think, the part played by what may be called "local motives" in the legends of the Andamanese. Such motives are of considerable importance, of much more importance than would appear from the stories that I have transcribed. The recent

VI] CUSTOMS AND BELIEFS: MYTHS AND LEGENDS 387

changes in their mode of life have had far more influence on the local organisation of the tribes than on any other part of their social organisation, and this has not been without its effect on the legends. We may say, briefly, that the local motives of the legends serve to express the social values of localities. In general each locality has its own versions of the legends, in which the events related are supposed to have taken place at some spot or other in the neighbourhood. Thus all the more prominent features of a locality are associated with the events of the legends. In some cases tales are told that explain these features as having come into existence when the ancestors were alive; a reef of rocks was formerly a canoe, for instance. A few such legends were recorded in an earlier chapter, but it is probable that there were a vast number of similar tales that I did not hear. In some cases a locality has a special social value and therefore a special place in the legends. Thus *Wota-Emi* was the great meeting-place for the natives who lived on Baratang and on parts of the South Andaman and the Middle Andaman, and was also sometimes visited by the natives of the Archipelago. Consequently *Wota-Emi* is represented in the legends of the *A-Pučikwar* tribe as being the great meeting-place or dwelling-place of the ancestors. The effect of these associations between the places with which he is familiar and the events of the legendary epoch in the mind of the Andaman Islander probably is similar to the effect on ourselves of the historical associations of our own country; they serve to make him aware of his attachment to his country or to express his sense of that attachment.

There still remains a most important feature of the legends which has not yet been explained, namely the position of the animals as ancestors. Many of the actors in the legends bear the names of animals but at the same time are spoken of as though they were human beings. Many of the legends explain how some species of animal arose from some one of the ancestors who became an animal and the progenitor of the species. Thus, in the North Andaman, *Kolo* was one of the ancestors; he made wings for himself out of palm-leaves, and so was able to fly; he lived a solitary life in his home at the top of a tree, and was in the habit of stealing men's wives; in the end he became the sea-eagle, and this species still bears the name *kolo*. It is necessary to define as exactly as possible what meaning these stories have to the natives. It is not simply that the legendary person is a man with the name and some of the characteristics of an animal; nor is it simply that the legendary person is the ancestor of the species of which he bears the name. We can only adequately express the thought of the Andamanese by saying that he regards the whole species as if it were a human being. When, in the legends, he speaks of " Sea-eagle " he is thereby personifying the species in the sense in which the word personification has been used throughout this chapter; he is regarding the characteristics of the species as if they were characteristics or actions or results of actions of a person. Admittedly this is a vague description, but the vagueness is in the mental phenomenon described; the Andamanese do not, in this matter, think clearly and analyse their own thoughts. However, we can help ourselves to understand their thoughts by recalling the tales that amused us as children, in which the fox or the rabbit of the tale was an embodiment of the whole species.

The part played in the legends by any particular animal is determined either immediately or indirectly by its observable characteristics. Thus the connection of the kingfisher with fire is due to the fact that he is a fish-eating bird, and that he has a patch of bright red feathers, red being, in the Andamanese mind, always associated with fire. The other birds that are mentioned in the different versions of the fire legend either possess remarkable plumage (as the dove, and the parrot) or are fish-eating birds. The Andamanese regard fish as the fundamental human food, having only one word for "food" and "fish," and they never eat their fish raw as the kingfisher does. In the *Akar-Bale* story of the origin of the animals the tree lizard is characterised by his quarrelsomeness, and by the fact that he is very difficult to catch hold of; these are both actual characteristics of the animal itself. The crab appears in the same legend as a person with a very powerful grip, and with a hard shell to his body. The monitor lizard has his place in the legends determined by the fact that he can climb trees, run on the ground and swim in the water, and is thus equally at home at the top of the trees, on the ground, or in the creek. I have already given this as one of the reasons why he is chosen as the first ancestor of all the animals and of human beings. The lizard also seems to be regarded by the Andamanese as a particularly libidinous animal, and is therefore regarded as the inventor of sexual intercourse and of procreation. Why he should have this sexual reputation I do not know[1]. The tale of how the lizard invented scarification depends on the fact that the marks on the lizard's skin bear a strong resemblance to the marks that the natives make on their own skins with sharp fragments of quartz. The position of the *Paradoxurus* or civet-cat in the stories in which she appears is due to the fact that while she can live in the trees or on the ground she cannot swim; hence, when the flood came, she fled from the water and climbed a steep hill and thus kept the fire alight. In the light of these examples we are justified, I think, in assuming that in all cases, even when the meaning is not clear, the part played by any animal in the legends is due to some actual characteristic of it.

There is thus a parallelism between the personification of natural phenomena and the personification of animal species. I have shown that the characteristics of such beings as *Biliku* and *Tarai* are all to be explained by a consideration of the actual characteristics of the phenomena of which they are the personification (the winds) and of the phenomena immediately connected therewith. The same thing has now been shown to be true with regard to the personified animals. The process of personification is carried out in exactly the same way in the two different classes of cases. I gave as the reason for personifying natural phenomena the fact that in this way, and in this way only, the Andaman Islander is able to express the sentiments that are aroused in him by them. We must see

---

[1] In Central Australia it is believed that if a boy who has not been initiated eats large lizards he will develop an abnormal and diseased craving for sexual intercourse. (Spencer and Gillen, *Native Tribes of Central Australia*, p. 471.) A friend who has observed the monitor lizard in Australia tells me that the animal fully deserves its reputation.

if we can justify the personification of animals by a similar argument.

The habits of observation fostered in the mind of the Andaman Islander by his method of winning his sustenance lead him to take a lively interest in all the creatures of the jungle and the sea, about whose ways he therefore has a great store of knowledge. Every tree and plant of the forest, every bird and insect, every creature that lives in the sea or on the reef has its name. His interest, however, in the case of many of the animals has little or no relation to practical life, for he does not make use of them for food or in any other way. There is here therefore something that contradicts the fundamental assumption of the philosophy that is expressed in the legends, there is a lack of mental unity. These interests in the birds and insects are not correlated with the central mass of interests that control the Andamanese mind and give it its unity. Although his philosophy assumes that everything in which he takes an interest has some meaning in reference to his own life, yet here are things that at first sight have no such meaning. The correlation that is lacking in his experience is brought about by means of the legends; a meaning is provided for the apparently meaningless. The fundamental interest of the Andaman Islander, as of all men in primitive societies, is his interest in persons and personal relations. By regarding the animals as persons and relating stories about them he is able to correlate his interest in them with the fundamental basis of his mental life.

This explanation does not perhaps sound very satisfactory. We do not at present understand the forces that compel the normal mind to strive after unity in its experience. Let us examine the matter a little more closely. All the thoughts and feelings of the Andaman Islander (or at any rate all those that are expressed in the legends) centre in the society; for him the world is merely a stage on which the social drama is perpetually enacted. He coordinates all his thoughts, emotions, and interests around the society, and in the legends he builds up a picture showing the connection between the society and those phenomena of nature that affect it. The majority of the animals (the birds, the insects, and innumerable kinds of fish), not being used for food, or in any other way, bear no apparent relation to the social life. Yet by reason of the woodcraft developed by the necessities of his life he is compelled to take notice of these creatures and to become interested in their ways. Here, therefore, are two conflicting elements in his consciousness, (1) his belief that the whole of nature derives its meaning and interest from its relation to the society, and (2) his consciousness of an alien world (of the birds, etc.) which seems to have no direct relation to the society, and which nevertheless he cannot help being constantly aware of. The Andaman Islander, as I have stated more than once, does not possess any scientific or abstract interest in nature. He never asks himself "What is the meaning of this?" in the same way that a scientist of our own civilisation might do. He asks "What is the meaning of this thing in relation to me and my interests and feelings, and to the social life of which my life is a fragment?" It is because he does feel the need of answers to questions of this kind that the conflict we have noticed arises. This conflict has to be resolved, and there are apparently three alternatives: (1) to admit that there is a meaning in nature apart from its relation to the society, (2) to refuse to take any interest in birds and insects, (3) to explain away the apparent lack of relation. It is this third alternative that is chosen by the Andaman Islander, and there are obvious reasons why it should be so. The explanation is accomplished in a direct and simple manner. In the beginning men and animals were one; then came an event or series of events (the discovery of fire, the great flood, or a great quarrel amongst the ancestors) whereby the men and the animals became cut off from one another, to live henceforward in the same world, but separated by an unseen barrier.

The argument may be put in another way that may perhaps be more convincing. The actual sentiment that is aroused in the mind of the native by the animals is that here is an important and interesting part of the universe that is alien to him, from which he is cut off in some strange way. It is this real sentiment, itself the inevitable result of his life and his surroundings, that is expressed in the belief in the animals as ancestors.

If this explanation be correct we should expect to find that the animals that figure in the legends are those that have no immediate social value either as food or in any other way, while on the other hand the animals that are used for food will not appear in the legends, or will occupy therein a very different place from the others. The only land animal that is regularly used for food is the pig. It is therefore a confirmation of the explanation that we find that the pig is never under any circumstances regarded as one of the ancestors, that is to say, is never personified in the same way that other animals are. One legend about the pig[1] explains, not how the animal came into existence (that seems to be assumed), but how it acquired its senses. Another legend[2] tells how the civet-cat persuaded some of the ancestors to play a game in which they pretended to be pigs, and they were turned into these animals. Here we are clearly dealing with something different from the ordinary process of personification, for we have not one ancestor in whom the species is personified, but a number of persons who were suddenly changed from men and women into pigs by the magical performance of the civet-cat. In the sea there are several animals that are regularly used for food. The dugong is spoken of as an ancestor in an *Akar-Bale* legend, but in the North Andaman there is a story of how the dugong originated from a pig that *Perjido* tried to roast without first disembowelling it and cutting the joints of its legs. There is also in the North Andaman a story of how turtles originated[3]. The existence of these legends shows that the pig, the turtle and the dugong occupy a different position in the minds of the Andamanese from that of the other animals. This serves, in some measure, to confirm the explanation given above.

We may briefly consider what may be regarded as a kind of negative instance by which to test the argument. The world of the stars constitutes a part of the universe just as alien, just as devoid of apparent meaning as that of the birds. We may ask therefore how it is that the Andaman Islanders have no star

[1] Page 217.   [2] Page 218.   [3] Page 218.

myths of the kind that are common in other primitive societies. The answer is, I think, that the Andamanese do not have their attention called to the stars. As their camps are in the dense forest there are very few occasions on which they see the sky at night. When fishing at night on the reefs or in canoes they are too busy to pay much attention to the stars. They have not learnt to relate the procession of the stars and the change of the seasons, nor have they learnt to tell the time at night from their declination. Their navigation is only along the coast and they have therefore no use for the stars as guides of direction. On the contrary, wherever we find a developed star-mythology we find that the stars are studied either as guides to navigation or journeying overland, or as giving indications of the changes of the seasons.

We have considered all the more important aspects of the subject matter of the legends; it remains for us to turn to the form and enquire how it comes about that the representations which analysis reveals are expressed in just the way they are, in a word, why the expression takes the form of a story. It is obvious that in this place no attempt can be made to deal with the general problems of the psychology of story-telling. All that I wish to do is to point out one or two reasons why the legend is an appropriate form (perhaps we might say, the only possible form) for the expression of the view of the world that is revealed in the Andaman mythology.

The Andamanese, like other savages, have not acquired the power of thinking abstractly. All their thought necessarily deals with concrete things. Now the story form provides a means of expressing concretely what could otherwise only be put in an abstract statement. (A large part of the interpretation of the legends, as here undertaken, consists in restating the content of the legends in abstract terms.) Moreover, even if the Andaman Islanders were capable of thinking abstractly, yet, since what they need to express are not thoughts so much as feelings (not intellectual so much as affective processes), they would still need a concrete form of expression. For it is a familiar fact that the concrete has a much greater power of awakening or appealing to our feelings than has the abstract.

In particular the story has ever been a popular medium by which to appeal to sentiments of all kinds.

The chief ground for the interest in stories shown by children and by savages is, I believe, that they afford the means of exercising the imagination in certain specific directions and thereby play an important part in enabling the individual to organise his experience. The course of the development of the human mind (from childhood to adolescence, and from the earliest human ancestor to ourselves) depends upon or involves the existence at certain stages of growth (and to a certain extent throughout the whole process) of a conscious egoistic interest. Mankind, to develop what we call character and conscience, must learn to take a conscious interest in himself, in his own actions, and their motives. The development of this self-consciousness in children is a process of great interest to the psychologist and has already been studied in an imperfect fashion. You have only to watch a child playing a game in which he or she enacts some imaginary part to see how such games afford a means by which the child develops and widens his interest in himself. Children, and many grown-up people (particularly during conditions of lessened mental activity), indulge in what are called daydreams, which take the form of an imaginary succession of adventures of which the dreamer is always the hero. The character of daydreams is that they are always frankly egoistic and boastful. Now this sort of interest in stories is found in the Andamanese, though not in the legends. At the end of a day a group of Andamanese may often be seen seated round a fire listening while one of them recounts adventures. The narration may be merely an exaggerated account of real happenings, but is more often purely fictitious. The narrator will tell, with few words, but with many expressive gestures, how he harpooned a turtle or shot a pig. He may, if his hearers are content to remain and listen, as they sometimes are, go on killing pig after pig for an hour or two together. The point to be noted is that these tales are always frankly egoistic and boastful, and it is for this reason that they may well be compared with the daydreams of the more civilised.

Besides this egoistic interest in stories there is another that is closely connected with it in origin and function. The necessities of social life, particularly in childhood and in primitive societies where a small number of people are constantly reacting upon one another, involve an intense degree of interest in persons and personal qualities. This interest is aroused and fostered by the constant play of personal forces in the social life. Its strength accounts, I believe, for the power of appeal to sentiments that is possessed by stories.

It is a commonplace that in many forms of play the child or the adult (and it is also true of animals) exercises faculties that are important parts of the system of habits or dispositions by which the individual adapts himself to his surroundings. We may regard the interest in stories as similar to play-interests in general. Life in society requires the individual to develop a faculty of what may be called character-estimation, whereby he may judge the motives that are likely to influence the conduct of another person. I have myself noticed that savages such as the Andaman Islanders and the Australian aborigines are as a rule good judges of character. They can quickly estimate how to adapt their conduct and conversation to the character of a person they meet for the first time. They are often excellent mimics, being able to imitate exactly the tone of voice or manner of walking or any other idiosyncrasy of a person whom they have only seen for a short time. I believe, then, that the legends of the Andamanese may be regarded as a means whereby they give exercise to their interest in human character, just as in other kinds of play they exercise other interests and faculties that are integral parts of their adaptation to their environment. By means of the personification of natural phenomena and of species of animals, and through the assumption of the existence of the ancestors and their times, they are able to develop a special kind of unwritten literature, which has for them just the same sort of appeal that much of our own literature has for us. Doubtless it is not a very polished form of art; the characterisation that it exhibits is simple and even crude; the story is not told very skilfully, and indeed the story-teller relies much on his use of expressive gesture to convey his meaning; nevertheless it does fulfil amongst the Andamanese the same sort of function that more developed literary art does in civilised society.

There remains one other matter to be dealt with briefly. I have pointed out on several occasions that the legends contain inconsistencies. Some of these only appear when the real meaning of the legend is discovered, but others are on the surface. It is clear that the Andamanese do not always apply to their legends the laws of logical consistency. It must not, however, be supposed that they are equally illogical in other matters, for this is not so. In matters of everyday practical life the Andamanese show just as much sound commonsense as the inhabitants of a civilised country. They are excellent observers of natural phenomena and are capable of putting their observations to practical use. In any attempt to explain their mythology, therefore, it is necessary to show why in this sphere they do not apply their powers of reasoning. We can understand this when we recall the purpose of the legends as here described, which is, not to give rational explanations, but to express sentiments. When there are two alternative rational explanations of a phenomenon between which we cannot definitely choose we say that either one or other is probably true. In those mental processes in which the purpose is to find a symbolic expression for sentiments or desires, the *either-or* relation is inadmissible owing to the very nature of the thought-process itself. If two expressions of the same sentiment are present, both equally adequate, we must either reject one of them or by making use of both on different occasions admit the possibility of inconsistency. Where the inconsistency becomes more or less obvious we expect the reason to step in and insist that a choice shall be made. But a mind intent on expressing certain feelings, faced with two alternative and equally satisfactory but inconsistent symbols, will hesitate to choose between them even at the command of the desire for logical consistency. It will cling as long as possible to both of them. This is just what the Andaman Islander seems to do in his mythology. The view of lightning as a person who shakes his leg seems to express in some way certain notions of the natives about the lightning. The alternative explanation of lightning as a fire-brand thrown by *Biliku* also satisfies in some way his need of expressing the impressions that the phenomena make upon him. In spite of the inconsistency he clings to both symbols as best he can.

The very existence of inconsistencies of this kind proves without any doubt that the mental processes underlying the legends of the Andamanese are not similar to those that we ourselves follow when we attempt to understand intelligently the facts of nature and of life, but rather are to be compared to those that are to be found in dreams and in art,—processes of what might conveniently be called symbolic thought. It would perhaps hardly be necessary to point this out were it not that many ethnologists still try to interpret the beliefs of savages as being the result of attempts to *understand* natural facts, such as dreams, death, birth, etc. Such writers assume that the savage is impelled by the same motive that so strongly dominates themselves, the desire to understand,—scientific curiosity—and that such beliefs as animism or totemism are of the nature of scientific hypotheses invented to explain the facts of dreaming and of death on the one hand and of conception and birth on the other. If this view of the nature of primitive thought were correct it would be impossible to conceive how such inconsistencies as those that we meet with among the Andamanese could be permitted. On the view that the myths of primitive societies are merely the result of an endeavour to express certain ways of thinking and feeling about the facts of life which are brought into existence by the manner in which life is regulated in society, the presence of such inconsistencies need not in the least surprise us, for the myths satisfactorily fulfil their function not by any appeal to the reasoning powers of the intellect but by appealing, through the imagination, to the mind's affective dispositions.

The thesis of this chapter has been that the legends are the expression of social values of objects of different kinds. By the social value of an object is meant the way in which it affects the life of the society, and therefore, since every one is interested in the welfare of the society to which he belongs, the way in which it affects the social sentiments of the individual. The system of social values of a society obviously depends upon the manner in which the society is constituted, and therefore the legends can only be understood by constant reference to the mode of life of the Andamanese.

The legends give us in the first place a simple and crude valuation of human actions. Anger, quarrelsomeness, carelessness in observing ritual requirements are exhibited as resulting in harm. This is the moral element of the stories strictly so called, and is to be observed in many of them. The young men who failed to observe the rules laid down for those who have recently been through one of the initiation ceremonies were turned to stone. The quarrelsomeness of the lizard led to the ancestors being turned into animals. The bad temper of one of the ancestors resulted in darkness covering the earth, or in a great cyclone in which many were destroyed.

Secondly, the legends as a whole give expression to the social value of the past, of all that is derived from tradition, whether it be the knowledge by which men win their sustenance, or the customs that they observe. In the wonderful times of the ancestors all things were ordered, all necessary knowledge was acquired, and the rules that must guide conduct were discovered. It remains for the individual of the present only to observe the customs with which his elders are familiar.

The legends of a man's own tribe serve also to give a social value to the places with which he is familiar. The creeks and hills that he knows, the camping sites at which he lives, the reefs and rocks that act as landmarks by reason of any striking feature they may present, are all for him possessed of a historic interest that makes them dear to him. The very names, in many cases, recall events of the far-off legendary epoch.

Again, many of the legends express the social value of natural phenomena. By reference to *Biliku* and *Tarai*, for instance, the native can express what he feels with respect to the weather and the seasonal changes that so profoundly affect the common life. Finally, in the legends he is able to express what he feels about the bright plumaged birds and the other creatures with which he is constantly meeting in the jungles, which are a source of perennial interest, and are yet so clearly a part of the world cut off from himself and his life, having no immediately discernible influence upon his welfare.

This system of social values, or rather this system of sentiments, that we find expressed in the legends is an essential part of the life of the Andamanese; without it they could not have organised their social life in the way they have. Moreover the sentiments in question need to be regularly expressed in some way or another if they are to be kept alive and passed on from one generation to another. The legends, which are related by the elders to the young folk, are one of the means (the various ceremonial customs analysed in the last chapter being another) by which they are so expressed, and by which their existence is maintained.

Although the term "social value" has been used as a convenient expression, yet the meaning of the legends might be expressed in other ways. We may say, for instance, that they give a representation of the world as regulated by law. The conception of law which they reveal is not, however, that to which we are accustomed when we think of natural law. We may perhaps adequately state the Andaman notion by saying that moral law and natural law are not distinguished from one another. The welfare of the society depends upon right actions; wrong actions inevitably lead to evil results. Giving way to anger is a wrong action, as being a cause of social disturbance. In the legends the catastrophes that overwhelmed the ancestors are in many instances represented as being caused by some one giving way to anger. There is a right way and a wrong way to set about making such a thing as a bow. We should explain this by saying that the right way will give a good serviceable weapon, whereas the wrong way will give an inferior or useless one. The Andaman Islander tends to look at the matter from a different angle; the right way is right because it is the one that has been followed from time immemorial, and any other way is wrong, is contrary to custom, to law. Law, for the Andaman Islander, means that there is an order of the universe, characterised by absolute uniformity; this order was established once for all in the time of the ancestors, and is not to be interfered with, the results of any such interference being evil, ranging from merely minor ills such as disappointment or discomfort to great calamities. The law of compensation is absolute. Any deviation from law or custom will inevitably bring its results, and inversely any evil that befalls must be the result of some lack of observance. The legends reveal to our analysis a conception of the universe as a moral order.

Here I must conclude my attempt to interpret the customs and beliefs of the Andaman Islanders, but in doing so I wish to point out, though indeed it must already be fairly obvious, that if my interpretation be correct, then the meaning of the customs of other primitive peoples is to be discovered by similar methods and in accordance with the same psychological principles. It is because I have satisfied myself of the soundness of these methods and principles, by applying them to the interpretation of other cultures, that I put forward the hypotheses of these two chapters with an assurance that would not perhaps be justified if I relied solely on a study of the Andamanese. To put the matter in another way, I have assumed a certain working hypothesis, and I have shown that on the basis of this hypothesis there can be built up a satisfactory explanation of the customs and beliefs of the Andamanese. But the hypothesis is of such a nature, stating or involving as it does certain sociological or psychological laws and principles, that if it be true for one primitive people it must be true for others, and indeed, with necessary modifications, must be true of all human society. Such a hypothesis, it is obvious, cannot be adequately tested by reference only to one limited set of facts, and it will therefore be necessary, if it is to become something more than a hypothesis, to test its application over a wider range of ethnological facts.

The matter is so important that it is necessary, even at the risk of wearisome repetition, to give a final statement of the hypothesis that, in this chapter and the last, has been applied to and tested by the facts known to us concerning the Andaman Islanders.

In an enquiry such as this, we are studying, I take it, not isolated facts, but a "culture," understanding by that word the whole mass of institutions, customs and beliefs of a given people.

For a culture to exist at all, and to continue to exist, it must conform to certain conditions. It must provide a mode of subsistence adequate to the environment and the existing density of population; it must provide for the continuance of the society by the proper care of children; it must provide means for maintaining the cohesion of the society. All these things involve the regulation of individual conduct in certain definite ways; they involve, that is, a certain system of moral customs.

Each type of social organisation has its own system of moral customs, and these could be explained by showing how they serve to maintain the society in existence. Such an explanation would be of the psychological, not of the historical type; it would give not the cause of origin of any custom, but its social function. For example it is easy to see the function of the very strong feelings of the Andamanese as to the value of generosity in the distribution of food and of energy in obtaining it, and as to the highly reprehensible nature of laziness and greediness (meaning by the latter word, eating much when others have little). It has only been by the cultivation of these virtues, or by the eradication of the opposite vices, that the Andaman society has maintained itself in existence in an environment where food is only obtainable by individual effort, where it cannot be preserved from day to day, and where there are occasional times of scarcity. It could be shown, to take a further example, how the manner in which the life of the family is organised is closely related to certain fundamental social needs. If we were attempting an explanation of the Andamanese culture as a whole and in all its details it would be necessary to examine all the moral customs of the people and show their relations one to another and to the fundamental basis on which the society is organised.

The necessary regulation of conduct in a given society depends upon the existence in each individual of an organised system of sentiments. That system of sentiments or motives will clearly be different in different cultures, just as the system of moral rules is different in societies of different types. Yet there is, so to speak, a general substratum that is the same in all human societies. No matter how the society may be organised there must be in the individual a strong feeling of attachment to his own group, to the social division (nation, village, clan, tribe, caste, or what not) to which he belongs. The particular way in which that sentiment is revealed in thought and action will depend upon the nature of the group to which it refers. Similarly, no society can exist without the presence in the minds of its members of some form or other of the sentiment of moral obligation—the sentiment that certain things must be done, certain other things must not be done, because those are right, good, virtuous, these are wrong, bad, vicious or sinful. Further, though perhaps less important, yet not less necessary, there is the sentiment of dependence in its various forms—dependence on others, on the society, on tradition or custom.

For a culture to exist, then, these sentiments (and others connected with them, that need not be enumerated) must exist in the minds of individuals in certain definite forms, capable of influencing action in the direction required to maintain the cohesion of the society on its actual basis of organisation. This, we may say, is the social function of these sentiments.

Leaving aside altogether the question of how sentiments of these kinds come into existence, we may note that they involve the existence of an experience of a particular type. The individual experiences the action upon himself of a power or force—constraining him to act in certain ways not always pleasant, supporting him in his weakness, binding him to his fellows, to his group. This force is clearly something not himself—something outside of him therefore, and yet equally clearly it makes itself felt not as mere external compulsion or support, but as something within his own consciousness—within himself, therefore. If we would give a name to this force we can only call it the moral force of society. The very existence of a human society, the argument has run, necessarily involves the existence of this actual experience of a moral force, acting through the society upon the individual, and yet acting within his own consciousness. The experience, then, is there, but it does not follow that the primitive man can analyse his own experience; it is obvious enough that such analysis is beyond him. Still the experience does lead him to form certain notions or representations, and it is possible to show how these notions are psychologically related to the experience of a moral force.

The experience of this moral force comes to the individual in definite concrete experiences only. We first learn to experience our own dependence in our dealings with our parents, and thus we derive the concrete form in which we clothe our later adult feeling of our dependence upon our God. Or, to take an example from the vast number provided by the customs of the Andamanese, the Andaman Islander, like other savages, the main concern of whose lives is the getting and eating of food, inevitably finds his experience of a moral force most intimately associated with the things he uses for food. Inevitably, therefore, he regards food as a substance in which, in some way, the moral force is inherent, since it is often through food that the force actually affects him and his actions. The psychology of the matter can be traced, I hope, in the arguments of the last chapter. From the analysis there given of different customs and beliefs it should be obvious that the way in which the Andaman Islander regards all the things that influence the social life is due to the way in which they are associated with his experience of the moral force of the society.

In this way there arises in the mind of primitive man, as the result of his social life and the play of feeling that it involves, the more or less crude and undefined notion of a power in society and in nature having certain attributes. It is this power that is responsible for all conditions of social euphoria or dysphoria because in all such conditions the power itself is actually experienced. It is the same power that compels the individual to conform to custom in his conduct, acting upon him both within as the force of conscience and without as the force of opinion. It is the same force on which the individual feels himself to be dependent, as a source of inner strength to him in times of need. It is this force also that carries him away during periods of social excitement such as dances, ceremonies or fights, and which gives him the feeling of a sudden great addition to his own personal force.

The Andamanese have not reached the point of recognizing by a special name this power of which they are thus aware. I have shown that in some of its manifestations they regard it, symbolically, as being a sort of heat, or a force similar to that which they know in fire and heat. In more developed societies, however, we find a nearer approach to a definite recognition of this power or force in its different manifestations by means of a single name. The power denoted by the word *mana* in Melanesia, and by the words *orenda, wakan, nauala*, etc., amongst different tribes of North America, is this same power of which I have tried to show that the notion arises from the actual experience of the moral force of the society.

These sentiments and the representations connected with them, upon the existence of which, as we have seen, the very existence of the society depends, need to be kept alive, to be maintained at a given degree of intensity. Apart from the necessity that exists of keeping them alive in the mind of the individual, there is the necessity of impressing them upon each new individual added to the society, upon each child as he or she develops into an adult. Even individual sentiments do not remain in existence in the mind unless they are exercised by being expressed. Much more is this the case with collective sentiments, those shared by a number of persons. The only possible way by which such collective sentiments can be maintained is by giving them regular and adequate expression.

Here then, according to the argument of the last chapter, we find the function of the ceremonial customs of primitive peoples such as the Andamanese. All these customs are simply means by which certain ways of feeling about the different aspects of social life are regularly expressed, and, through expression, kept alive and passed on from one generation to another. Thus the customs connected with foods serve to maintain in existence certain ways of feeling about foods and the moral duties connected with them, and similarly with other customs.

Affective modes of experience (sentiments, feelings or

emotions) can be expressed not only in bodily movements but also by means of language. I have tried to show that the function of the myths and legends of the Andamanese is exactly parallel to that of the ritual and ceremonial. They serve to express certain ways of thinking and feeling about the society and its relation to the world of nature, and thereby to maintain these ways of thought and feeling and pass them on to succeeding generations. In the case of both ritual and myth the sentiments expressed are those that are essential to the existence of the society.

Throughout these two chapters I have avoided the use of the term religion. My reason for this is that I have not been able to find a definition of this term which would render it suitable for use in a scientific discussion of the beliefs of such primitive peoples as the Andamanese.

When we use the term religion we inevitably think first of what we understand by that term in civilised society. It is not possible, I believe, to give an exact definition which shall retain all the connotations of the word as commonly used and which shall at the same time help us in the study of the customs of undeveloped societies. The definition of religion that seems to me on the whole most satisfactory is that it consists of (1) a belief in a great moral force or power (whether personal or not) existing in nature, and (2) an organised relation between man and this Higher Power. If this definition be accepted it is clear that the Andamanese have religious beliefs and customs. They do believe in a moral power regulating the universe, and they have organised their relations to that power by means of some of their simple ceremonies. Yet it does not seem possible to draw a sharp dividing line between those beliefs and customs that properly deserve to be called religious, and others which do not deserve the adjective. It is not possible, in the Andamans, to separate a definite entity which we can call religion from things that may more appropriately be regarded as art, morality, play, or social ceremonial.

Nevertheless the purpose of these two chapters has been to explain the nature and function of the Andamanese religion.

Amongst the fundamental conditions that must be fulfilled if human beings are to live together in society is the existence of this thing that we call religion, the belief in a great Unseen Power, between which and ourselves it must ever be the great concern of life to establish and maintain harmony. The Andaman Islander with his somewhat childish faith, the Australian blackfellow decorated with paint and feathers impersonating his totemic ancestor, the Polynesian sacrificing human victims on the *marae* of his god, the Buddhist following the Holy Eight-Staged Path, are all following in however different ways the same eternal quest.

APPENDIX A

THE TECHNICAL CULTURE OF THE ANDAMAN ISLANDERS

In this appendix I shall give a brief account of the technical culture of the Andaman Islanders, with a few comparative notes on the technology of the Semang of the Malay Peninsula and the Negritos of the Philippine Islands. The Andamanese, the Semang and the Philippine Negritos are so similar in physical characteristics that it is reasonable to suppose that they are descended from a single stock. It is on the basis of this hypothesis that they are all spoken of as belonging to one race, the Negrito race. It is therefore of some interest to compare the culture of these three different peoples to see if we can determine what was the culture of their ancestors.

In such hypothetical reconstructions of the past it is necessary to proceed with extreme caution, as there is no means of controlling results. The method I have adopted is to compare first of all the different types of technological products or activities found in different parts of the Andamans in order to determine as far as possible what was the technical culture of the ancestors of the Andamanese when they first reached the islands, and what changes have taken place since the islands were occupied. It is only this primitive or generalised Andamanese culture that can be compared with that of the Semang or the Philippine Negritos.

From the point of view of technical culture the natives of the Andamans must be separated into two main divisions, which will be spoken of as the Great Andaman Division and the Little Andaman Division respectively[1]. The most plausible explanation of the differences of culture and language between these two divisions has been mentioned already. We must assume that when the islands were first peopled, or at some later time, the inhabitants of the Little Andaman became isolated from those of the Great Andaman. The language and the

[1] See Introduction, p. 12.

technical culture of each of the two groups underwent a number of changes during the many centuries that followed. At a much later date, after the differences between the two divisions had been developed, and probably not many centuries ago, a party or several parties of natives must have made their way from the Little Andaman as far as Rutland Island. Here they came in conflict with the natives of the Great Andaman Division, and in this way arose the antagonism between the Jarawa (the immigrants from the Little Andaman) and the other natives of the South Andaman (who formed in 1858 the Aka-Bea tribe), which has lasted down to the present day. We shall find that the technical culture of the Jarawa has been only very slightly influenced by contact with the natives of the Great Andaman Division, and therefore differs very little from that of the Little Andaman at the present day.

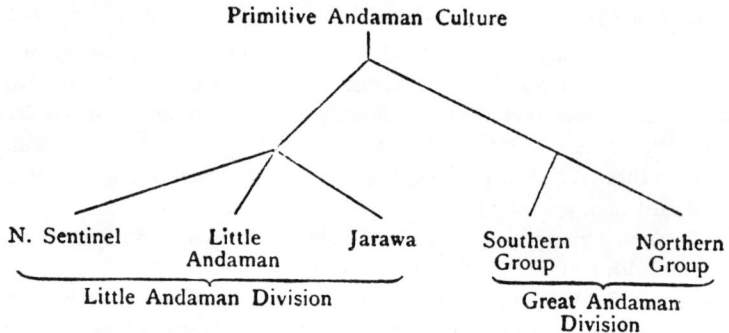

I have provisionally included the natives of the North Sentinel Island in the Little Andaman Division. The ground for so doing is that the form of bow in use in the North Sentinel Island is similar to that of the Little Andaman and unlike that of the Great Andaman. Unfortunately, almost nothing is known about the technology of the North Sentinel, and nothing whatever about the language. It is possible that the natives of this outlying islet have been isolated for many centuries from both the Little Andaman and the Great Andaman, and further information about them might show that their technology is different in important respects from that of the Little Andaman.

Within the Great Andaman Division there are a number of differences in technology between the tribes of the North Andaman and those of the South Andaman and Middle Andaman.

In order to render the exposition and argument that follows more easily understood the supposed relations of the different types of culture are shown in the form of a diagram or tree. The justification for this arrangement will appear as we proceed.

There is only very scanty information available about the technical culture of the Negritos of the Malay Peninsula, whom we may speak of as the Semang. There are differences of technology between the Semang of different parts, and a careful study of these differences would serve to throw much light on changes that have been introduced since the Semang were isolated from the rest of their race. There is no doubt that the Semang have adopted many elements of their present culture from their neighbours the Sakai and others. In some instances it is possible to trace this external influence, but in others it is doubtful whether we are dealing with a primitive Semang form or with a form adopted from their neighbours[1].

The same thing must be said about the Philippine Negritos. Our information is not sufficient to enable us to discuss the local differences, nor to determine what elements of the culture have been introduced by contact with other races[2].

HABITATIONS.

The huts of the Andamanese are best understood by considering first of all the simplest and most temporary structures. A man away from the main camp at night (on a hunting expedition) erects for himself a simple shelter of leaves. Such hunting shelters vary considerably according to circumstances. In the rainy season they are built much more substantially than in the dry season. Sometimes shelter is found between the buttresses of large trees, a few leaves being added. There is, however, one type of hunting shelter that is usual. Two poles are cut and erected perpendicularly in the ground so that they stand about four feet apart and about four feet high. To the top of these is tied, with cane or creeper, a horizontal pole. A few poles or sticks of sufficient length are placed so as to lean against the horizontal pole at an angle of about 45°, the ends resting on the ground. On these are placed any leaves that can be obtained,

---

[1] The information here given as to the Semang is derived from two works, Skeat and Blagden, *Pagan Races of the Malay Peninsula*, vol. I, quoted as *Skeat*, and Rudolf Martin, *Die Inlandstämme der Malayischen Halbinsel*, 1905, quoted as *Martin*.

[2] The information about the Philippine Negritos is derived from Reed, *Negritos of Zambales*, Manila, 1904, quoted as *Reed*, and A. B. Meyer, *Die Philippinen, II, Die Negritos*, Dresden, 1893, quoted as *Meyer*.

preferably the leaves of canes and other palms. The shelter thus consists of a single rectangular roof, one end of which rests on the ground, while the other rests on a horizontal bar attached to the top of two perpendicular supports. The shelter is built facing to leeward.

The usual family hut of the Andamans is built on exactly the same principles as a hunter's shelter, but, being intended for occupation for some weeks or even months, is more carefully built. For a small hut, to be occupied by one family, four posts are erected, two at the back being from two to four feet high above the ground, while two at the front are from five to seven feet high. Two horizontal poles are attached, one to the top of the front posts and the other to the back posts, with strips of cane. If poles of a convenient size and forked at the top are available these may be used for the posts of the hut, the horizontal poles being supported in the forks, but a native would not trouble to search for such timbers, being satisfied with an unforked post. A few slender timbers, preferably of mangrove wood (*Bruguiera*), are placed on the two horizontal poles and bound to them with cane. These rafters, as they may be called, project for a foot or two above or beyond the higher horizontal, and similarly project a foot beyond the lower one so as almost to reach the ground.

In the better kind of hut a mat is made of palm leaves, and this mat is placed on the rafters and tied to them with strips of cane. To make a mat a number of strips of bamboo or cane of sufficient length are taken and placed on the ground parallel to each other. Leaves of a species of cane are collected and each leaf is divided into two parts down the middle. These half-leaves are then attached to the strips of bamboo or cane, by means of strips of the outside of canes, the technique being wrapped-twined work. The half-leaves are attached so that the leaflets, which are attached to the leaf-stem at an angle, incline alternately to one side and the other. The photograph reproduced in Plate VII shows a hut of the kind here described. Mats in course of making are shown lying on the ground in Plates VI and VII.

A quicker, but less efficient way of thatching the hut is to take the half-leaves such as are used for making a mat and fasten them in bundles of five or six directly to the rafters.

Huts of this type, each occupied by a single family, are built by the natives of the Great Andaman Division in the form of villages. The Jarawa and the natives of the Little Andaman build similar huts in their hunting camps, occupied during the fine weather.

Some huts of this type are provided with a floor raised above the ground. Such a floor is erected on short posts, and may be made of bamboos or of planks or pieces of broken-up canoes. A floor of this kind, raised a foot or so above the ground, is shown in Plate VII. Huts are sometimes to be seen with a floor raised as much as three feet above the ground.

The simple Andaman hut as above described is entirely open at the front and on each side. In an exposed situation screens of palm-leaves may be erected at the side. If still more shelter is required, a hut may be built with two roofs. Such a hut requires six posts, two taller ones six or seven feet high, and four shorter ones, two on each side. For such a hut two mats are made, and are so attached that one mat projects above the other. No attempt is made to fasten the two mats together at the top, but on the contrary a space of several inches is left between them to allow the smoke of the fire to escape, rain being excluded by the overhang of one of the mats. Huts of this type may be seen in Plate VI.

Each of the huts hitherto described is occupied by a single family. In order to understand the communal huts it is necessary to consider the arrangement of small huts in a camp or village. In the tribes of the Great Andaman there are two main types of such arrangement. The first type is that of the hunting camp, which is occupied for a few nights only. In this all the huts are placed facing in the same direction (to leeward) and in a line with one another. The second type is that of a village to be occupied for some weeks or months. In this the huts are arranged round an open space, all facing inwards, as described earlier in this book[1]. All encampments in the Great Andaman tend to conform to one or other of these types, but variations are introduced according to the nature of the site occupied. Thus in a hunting camp the site may not permit of the erection of the huts in one line. A village is, as a rule, only put up at a spot that has been used from time immemorial, where there is an open space of sufficient size, but if, for any reason, a site is selected where there is not room to arrange all the huts around the dancing ground, the arrangement of the village may be irregular.

The hunting camps of the Jarawa are sometimes arranged on the same principle as those of the tribes of the Great Andaman Division, i.e., all facing in one direction and as nearly in one line side by side as the site will allow.

The natives of the Little Andaman erect hunting camps in the fine

[1] See p. 34.

weather. In the only one that I have seen the huts were arranged irregularly so as to make the best use of the available space.

A few words must be said on the sites chosen for encampments. It must be remembered that the islands are entirely covered with forest. The natives will not, if they can avoid it, put their camp under high trees, for fear of the danger of falling branches in a storm. At the same time they prefer a situation where there is an open space surrounded with forest so that they are sheltered from the wind. The coast-dwellers always camp immediately within the jungle on the shore of the sea or of a creek. The forest-dwellers usually choose a position on a hill or ridge, and this is particularly the case with the Jarawa. The camp must be close to a supply of fresh water. In the tribes of the Great Andaman Division no precautions are taken against a possible attack by enemies, but the Jarawa do take precautions, clearing the trees around their camps so that they have a good view of the approaches, and even, apparently, placing look-out stations at the tops of the paths[1].

Amongst the coast-dwelling tribes there are sites that have been used for encampments for many centuries. At these spots there are found heaps of refuse that have accumulated year by year. These kitchen-middens, as they are sometimes called, consist of the shells of molluscs, bones of animals, stones that have been used for cooking, fragments of pottery, and loam produced from decayed wood and other refuse.

The two types of camp arrangement which are seen in the village and the hunting camp are exhibited in two different types of communal hut. One of these, corresponding to the hunting camp, may be termed the long shelter. It is apparently only used in the North Sentinel Island. A hut of this type was seen by Mr Gilbert Rogers in 1903. It was rectangular, 40 feet long and 12 feet wide. The roof was supported on three rows of small posts ranging in height from 3 feet at the back to 6 feet at the front of the hut. The roof projected about 2 feet in either direction beyond the posts and was about 2 feet from the ground at the back and 7 feet above the ground at the front. There were twelve places for fires, six in front and six at the back of the hut, and near each, on the right-hand side, was a platform supported on four sticks, of the usual Andamanese type, for keeping food. There were two rows of sleeping places which were separated by small poles, making rectangles on the ground about 5 feet

---

[1] See *Census Report*, 1901.

by 4 feet, each of which was probably occupied by a man and his wife and small children[1].

The relation of this type of communal hut, in which all the members of one local group are brought together under a single roof of one slope, to the ordinary family hut of the Andamans, and the arrangement of the hunting camp in a line, is obvious.

To the arrangement of huts in a village around a central open space corresponds the second type of communal hut, which may be called the round hut. Communal huts of this type were formerly built by the natives of the Great Andaman Division, but have fallen into disuse in recent times, owing to the natives having become much more migratory in their habits. Huts of the same type are built at the present day by the natives of the Little Andaman and by the Jarawa.

In its typical form this kind of hut is built by erecting two circles of posts, a smaller circle of tall posts, and a wider circle of shorter posts. The tops of these posts are connected by horizontal and sloping timbers, which make the framework of the roof. The roof is made of a number of mats of palm-leaves, which are laid on the rafters and tied to them with strips of cane. The mats are made in exactly the same way as the smaller mats used for the small huts and already described. They are sometimes rectangular in shape, though occasionally an attempt is made to make them narrower at the top and broader at the bottom. They are arranged on the roof so as to overlap one another and thus make the hut rain-proof. They are not joined in the centre, but a small space is left for the smoke of the fires to escape, and the rain is prevented from entering by letting one or two of the mats overhang the others at the top.

In the round huts of the Jarawa and the Little Andaman there is no centre-post, and according to the statements made to me by the natives of the Great Andaman they did not use a centre-post for their huts. In the description attached to a photograph in the British Museum Mr Portman speaks of the centre-post of a communal hut, which is shown in the photograph still standing, although the hut had been pulled down. It would therefore seem that in the Great Andaman the natives did sometimes erect a centre-post for their round huts. The typical round hut, however, has no centre-post.

It is clear that the round hut has been developed from the village. If all the small huts of a village be drawn together so as to touch each

---

[1] Supplement to the *Andaman and Nicobar Gazette*, January 2, 1904.

other, and if the mats of thatching be lengthened so as to meet and overlap in the middle, we have a round hut in its typical form. The evidence that this is so is afforded by the thatching, consisting of separate mats, often rectangular in shape (like the mats used for family huts), placed so as to overlap one another. This crude way of thatching could hardly have originated in any other way. Further evidence is afforded, as we shall see, by the internal arrangement of the hut.

Although the hut is here called a round hut, it must not be supposed that the shape is always regularly circular. It may be somewhat oval, and in any case is rarely very regularly constructed. In general, however, the shape approaches more or less nearly to a circle.

Huts of this kind vary in size according to the number of families occupying them. The height in the middle may be as much as 30 feet and the diameter may be 60 feet. The smallest I have seen was a Jarawa hut on Rutland Island, which was only nine feet high and 15 feet maximum diameter. In exposed situations the mats of thatching reach as far as the ground, but huts are sometimes built in sheltered situations with a space of a foot or two left between the ends of the thatch and the ground. A low doorway is provided on one side.

Within the hut there is a central space that is the common part of the hut and corresponds to the dancing ground of the village. In the wet season the communal fire is situated in this open space, and here the communal cooking is performed. In Jarawa huts the roof of the central part of the hut is hung with trophies of the chase consisting of pigs' skulls bound with cane. In former times the natives of the Great Andaman Division hung similar trophies in their round huts. Around the central space are the spaces allotted to the different families, these being marked off by means of short lengths of wood laid on the ground.

It is thus clear that the basis of Andamanese architecture is the use of a single rectangular roof giving a shelter open at the front. This is the usual form of the hunter's shelter and of the family hut in the village. For additional shelter two such roofs may be used, but no attempt is made to join them, one being made to overlap the other. There are two customary modes of arranging huts, either side by side facing in the same direction or round an open space facing inwards. Where, instead of separate roofs for each family, we have a united roof, these two arrangements of the camp give rise to two different types of communal hut, the long hut and the round hut.

In a village each hut is occupied by one family. In the communal hut (of either type) each family has a special portion of the hut marked off for its special use. Whether in a village or in a communal hut each family has its own small fire, at which the family meals are prepared At one side of this fire is erected a small platform about a foot above the ground, supported on either three or four upright sticks. This platform is used for storing food. The natives of the Little Andaman erect low bamboo platforms to serve as beds, arranged round the communal hut, each family having its own. In the Great Andaman the natives, as a rule, make a bed of leaves on the ground and lay a sleeping mat on the top of this. In damp situations, however, they sometimes, as already mentioned, make a floor to the hut, raised a foot or two above the ground, and sleep on that. The Jarawa have a habit of sleeping in the wood-ashes of their fires in their cold weather hunting camps.

Turning now to the Semang, we find some differences in respect to their habitations. Those of the Semang who have not been influenced to a great extent by their neighbours and have not settled down to agricultural pursuits, never camp in the same spot for more than a few days, and have therefore no need to build anything except temporary shelters[1].

The Semang often erect their shelters in trees, well above the surface of the ground. This is a feature which distinguishes them from the Andamanese. It seems probable that these tree-shelters have been adopted by the Semang as a protection against wild beasts[2]. As there are no dangerous beasts in the Andamans, the extra labour involved in building a shelter in the branches of a tree instead of on the ground would serve no useful purpose. The difference in this respect between the Semang and the Andamanese is therefore due to a difference in the circumstances in which they live.

The typical form of Semang shelter, occupied by one family, is erected by planting three or four stout sticks or poles in the ground in a row at an angle of about 60° or 75° and lashing palm-leaves across these. The screen or roof thus formed is further supported, if necessary, with one or two poles used as props in front[3]. These shelters are similar to the Andaman shelters in having a single sloping rectangular roof, but differ from them in being supported, not by upright posts, but in an altogether less adequate manner.

[1] Skeat, p. 172. [2] Skeat, p. 174.
[3] Skeat, p. 176, and plate. See also Annandale, *Fasciculi Malayensis, Anthropology*, Part I, Plate IV.

However, the Semang shelters are apparently very easy to erect, and as they are only occupied for a night or two there is no inducement to the natives to make them more substantial.

The Semang sometimes make a shelter by planting a number of palm-leaves in the ground in a semicircle so that the overhanging ends meet in the centre[1].

As the Semang are constantly moving from place to place, they have little use for a communal hut of substantial build. One communal shelter has been described, which contained eleven sleeping-places arranged in two long rows. The upright timbers of the shelter consisted of young saplings planted in two opposite rows, across them being lashed the leaves of a palm. There were, besides, two central posts or pillars, each about a third of the distance from either end of the shelter, and a dozen poles placed as props or wind-braces in various positions and at various angles, in order to strengthen the structure and keep it from being blown over in a high wind. The two slopes of the roof were not united over a ridge-pole, but a longitudinal aperture was left between them for about two-thirds of the entire length of the roof, and through the gap thus caused the greater part of the smoke from the many fireplaces issued. All round the walls were ranged a number of bamboo sleeping-platforms, five to six feet in length by about three feet in breadth. The owner of each sleeping-platform or family unit possessed a separate fire or hearth[2].

We have only scanty information about the huts of the Philippine Negritos. In Zambales (Luzon) a certain number of the Negritos have adopted a settled mode of life and depend on agriculture for some part of their subsistence. The most advanced of these have adopted the form of hut common amongst their neighbours. The less settled Negritos of Zambales erect huts which are almost exactly the same as the family huts of the Andamanese. Two short upright posts are erected for the back of the hut, and two taller ones for the front, and on these four posts a rectangular roof of one slope is erected. A bamboo floor or platform is erected a foot or so above the ground, just as in some Andaman huts[3]. In the Zambales huts the upright posts are forked and the horizontal poles are supported in the fork.

At Casiguran the Negritos erect palm-leaf shelters similar to those of the Semang. A few poles are thrust into the ground at an angle and in a row and palm-leaves are attached to these, the screen being further supported with props[4].

[1] Skeat, p. 174. [2] Skeat, p. 177. [3] Reed, Plate XXXVIII. [4] Meyer, Plate X.

A comparison of the three branches of the Negrito race in the light of present information shows that the usual form of habitation amongst them is a sloping roof or screen of palm-leaves. One form of this, the simplest to construct, but only suitable as a temporary shelter, is in common use amongst the Semang and is found amongst the Negritos of Casiguran. The other form, more permanent but requiring more labour to erect, is in common use in the Andamans and amongst the Negritos of Zambales. Of communal huts we have no evidence in the Philippines. The communal shelter of the Semang consists of two screens leaning towards one another. The two types of communal hut of the Andamans are both derived from the family hut.

Hunting, Fishing, etc.

The Andaman Islanders depend for their subsistence entirely upon the natural productions of the forest and the sea. They make no attempt whatever to cultivate the soil. Until the introduction of dogs in 1858 they had no domestic animals. Young pigs are occasionally kept in captivity till they are grown, but they are killed for food and are not bred in captivity. Thus the Andamanese provide themselves with food by three different forms of activity: (1) collecting such things as roots and fruits and honey, (2) fishing in the sea and in the creeks, (3) hunting the wild animals of the forest.

For hunting the Andamanese rely entirely on the bow and arrow. Since they have had dogs they occasionally make hunting spears, but they did not do so in former times. They make no use whatever of any method of trapping game or birds. For fishing they also make use of the bow and arrow, wading out on to the reefs and shooting the fish, and in this they are very skilful. Crustaceans, such as crabs and crayfish, are captured in the same way. In the North Andaman a sort of short fish spear was formerly in use as an occasional substitute for the bow and arrow. In all parts of the islands small nets are used by the women for catching small fish and prawns. In the Great Andaman large nets were formerly used for capturing turtle, dugong and large fish near the shore. At the present time the natives of the Great Andaman Division make use of harpoons with which they capture turtle, dugong and large fish from their canoes. Harpoons are not used in the Little Andaman. The Andamanese are also aware of methods of poisoning or stupefying fish in pools by means of certain plants that they crush and place in the water, but I have never seen them use this method of fishing, although they say that they formerly did so. They have no fish hooks and no fish traps. At the present time a few of the natives have learnt to take fish with hook and line, but they are unable to make hooks for themselves, and have to obtain them from the Settlement at Port Blair.

In collecting roots a digging stick is used, and a hooked pole is used for gathering fruit, but they have no other special implements in use in collecting natural productions, and have no need of any. The adze is used for obtaining molluscs and for cutting honey-combs from hollow trees.

It is thus clear that by far the most important utensil of the Andamanese is the bow and arrow. We may say that they are essentially a bow and arrow people. This is even more true of the natives of the Little Andaman Division than of those of the Great Andaman Division.

It may be noted here that the Andamanese have no weapons that are used only for fighting. They fight with their chief hunting weapon, the bow and arrow. Nor have they any special defensive weapons, the shield being unknown.

The Semang in their natural condition depend for their subsistence on collecting roots and fruits from the forest, on catching fish in the streams, and on hunting animals. Their mode of subsistence is thus essentially the same as that of the Andamanese. One difference is that they have not the sea from which to draw supplies, and another is that the forests in which they live afford a much larger variety of game. A number of the Semang now practice a little rude agriculture which they have undoubtedly adopted in imitation of their neighbours of other races[1].

The principal weapon of the Semang, as of the Andamanese, is the bow and arrow. In hunting they also use spears[2], thus showing a difference from the Andamanese. Some of the Semang make use of the blow-pipe with poisoned darts, but it is practically certain that they have adopted the use of this weapon from their neighbours the Sakai[3]. They also make use to some extent of traps with which to capture jungle animals and birds. The wilder Semang living in the mountains have little opportunity of obtaining fish. Those of them that dwell near rivers use fish-spears and harpoons for catching large fish, and a small basket-work scoop for catching small fry[4]. They also fish with

[1] Skeat, p. 341.
[2] Skeat, p. 270.
[3] Skeat, p. 280.
[4] Skeat, p. 205.

rod and line, the hooks being, as a rule, roughly manufactured from bits of brass or other wire[1]. The Semang have no special fighting weapons either offensive or defensive.

In the Philippines some of the Negritos practice a little rude agriculture[2]. It is practically certain that they have only adopted this mode of subsistence through contact with agricultural peoples of other races. They originally depended entirely upon collecting, fishing and hunting, and even those who now grow a few scanty crops devote a large part of their energies to hunting and collecting the natural products of the jungles[3]. The chief weapon of the Negritos of the Philippines, as of the Andamanese and the Semang, is the bow and arrow. They use the bow and arrow for shooting fish, having special fish-arrows[4]. It seems doubtful if they use spears, unless they have adopted them from their neighbours. In hunting deer the Negritos of Zambales use large nets like fish nets. They are acquainted with the use of traps for game but they seem to prefer to depend on the bow and arrow[5]. In the larger streams of Zambales they make fishing weirs of bamboo, after the manner of the Christianised natives of the same part[6].

As the most important weapon of the Andamanese, and indeed of the Negritos in general, is the bow, we may consider this first. Different kinds of bow are in use in different parts of the Andamans, but by a careful comparison of them it is possible to show how they are all derived from one original pattern.

The first kind of bow to be described is that in use in the Little Andaman. These bows are all made of a reddish-brown wood (possibly *Mimusops littoralis*). They are cut with an adze from a straight piece of wood, and are planed but not polished. The length varies within fairly wide limits. Six specimens selected as typical have lengths of 131, 150, 159·5, 163, 168 and 188 centimetres, giving an average of about 160 centimetres (= 63 inches). In section the bow is markedly convex on the one side and slightly convex on the other. The two figures (Fig. 1) show the section at the middle and at a point 7 cm. from the end of a typical specimen. The shape in section varies a little from one example to another, and the dimensions of breadth and thickness also vary. At the broadest point, which is in the middle, the average breadth of six bows is 3·2 cm., the broadest being 3·7 cm., and the narrowest 2·3 cm. The average thickness in the middle is 1·8 cm.,

[1] Skeat, p. 205.   [2] Reed, p. 44.   [3] Reed, p. 44.
[4] Reed, p. 47.   [5] Reed, p. 47.   [6] Reed, p. 48.

the actual figures ranging from 2·1 to 1·3 cm. From the middle the bow tapers slightly towards each end. At a distance of 7 cm. from the end of the bow the average breadth is 1·8 cm., and the average thickness 1·2 cm.

The flatter side is the inside of the bow. Referring to the figures, the side marked A is that which faces a man as he holds the bow ready to shoot (called here the inside). C is thus the right-hand side and D the left-hand. By breadth is meant the distance from C to D, and by thickness the distance from A to B.

At each end of the bow there is a shoulder, as shown in Fig. 2. The length from the shoulder to the end of the bow, i.e. the length of

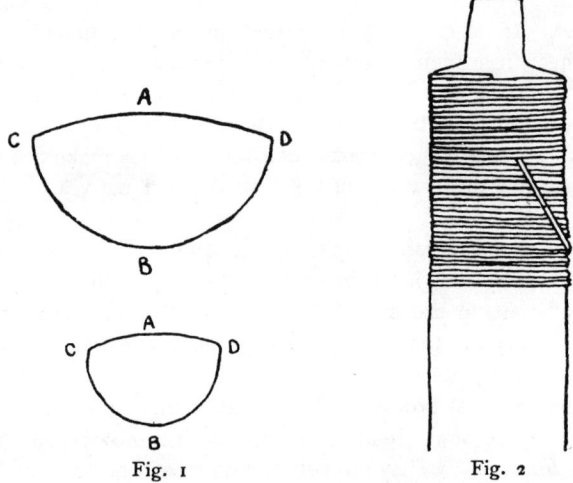

Fig. 1. Section of Little Andaman bow, in the middle and near the end
Fig. 2. Shoulder of Little Andaman bow

the point on which the string is looped, is about 10 to 12 mm. Both ends are the same. For a few centimetres below the shoulder the bow is served over with string or fibre. In a carefully finished bow the serving is usually done with ornamental string, i.e. with string round which is twisted the dried yellow skin of the *Dendrobium*. In other examples plain string is used, or a strip of twisted *Ficus* fibre, or even nowadays a twisted strip of cotton cloth.

Bows are never ornamented in the Little Andaman either with paint or with incised patterns.

The bow-string of the Little Andaman is made of strips of the bark of the *Ficus laccifera*. The number and width of the strips used depend on the size of the bow. In a small bow now in the Cambridge Museum the string is made of a single strip of bark about 1 cm. in width. This strip is simply twisted, the twist being that of a right-hand or male screw. When two strips are used they are not twisted around one another in the way that a two-ply rope is made, but are laid flat together and twisted together, so that when the string is finished only one of the strips is visible, the other being inside. In a stout string for a large bow three or four strips may be twisted together in this way. The bow-string is not a rope, but a twisted strand (Fig. 3.)

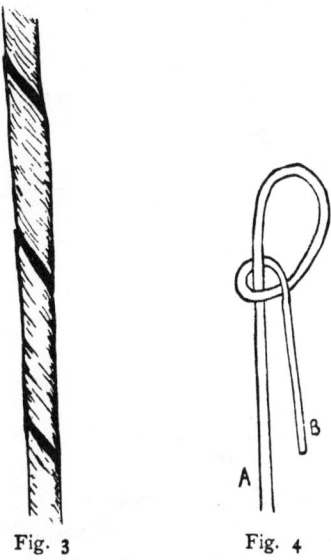

Fig. 3. Fig. 4.

Fig. 3. Bow-string of twisted fibre, Little Andaman
Fig. 4. Diagram showing the method of making the loop in the end of the Little Andaman bow-string

At one end of the string a loop is made, as shown in Fig. 4. The end is doubled over to make a loop of the right size, a round turn is made over the standing part (A) and the end (B) is twisted in with the standing part by untwisting the latter, laying the end in, and twisting up again. If this splicing, as it may perhaps be loosely called, be not sufficiently secure, it is served over or stopped with finer fibre of the same kind. This loop is of sufficient size to slip down over the shoulders. At the other end the string is attached to the peg either with a knot, or else by means of a small loop (just large enough to go over the peg, but not large enough to slip over the shoulder) made in exactly the same way as the loop already described. When the bow is to be strung the larger loop is slipped over the peg at the top end of the bow and is pushed down over the shoulder. The other end (with the smaller loop) is then slipped on the peg at the lower end, resting on the shoulder. The lower end is placed on the ground, while the top end is held in the hand. The man places his foot against the middle of the bow and draws the top towards him until he is able to slip the top loop of the string up over the shoulder so that it catches the peg or tip. The bow is then ready for use.

Toy bows are made for small boys of exactly the same general pattern as the large bows. A toy bow of this kind, now in the Cambridge Museum, is 107 cm. long and 18 mm. broad in the middle.

The next type of bow to be considered is that used by the natives of the North Sentinel Island. I have only been able to see one specimen

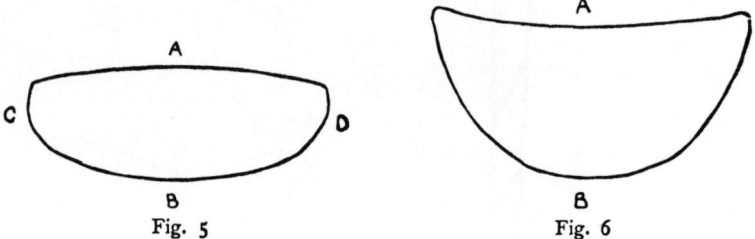

Fig. 5. Section of bow from North Sentinel Island
Fig. 6. Section of Jarawa bow

of this type, which is in the British Museum. It is made of a different kind of wood from that used in the Little Andaman. The length is 155·5 cm., and the breadth at the middle is 4·3 cm. The section in the middle, which is shown in Fig. 5, is slightly different from that of the average Little Andaman bow, but it has the same feature of greater convexity on the outside and less convexity on the inside, and it lies just within the range of variation of the Little Andaman type. The ends of the bow are shaped in the same way as those of the Little Andaman bow. The breadth at the shoulder, however, is 2·5 cm., which is greater than the corresponding measurement of the Little Andaman bow. The bow is not ornamented either with a painted or incised pattern. The string is missing. There is no binding at the ends below the shoulders, but this has possibly been present and come off, as the specimen is one that has been thrown away by its owner owing to the wood having split. So far as we can tell from this single specimen the bow of the North Sentinel differs very little from that of the Little Andaman.

We now come to the bows of the Jarawa of the South Andaman. The Jarawa of Rutland Island, of whom there are now very few, but of whom there were a larger number twenty or thirty years ago, make bows exactly like those of the Little Andaman, and apparently do not make any other kind. The Jarawa to the north of Port Blair, who have been driven northwards by the spread of the Penal Settlement, also make bows of this type, which it is not possible to distinguish from Little Andaman bows. These northern Jarawa, however, also make bows of a different kind. These will be spoken of as belonging to the "modified Jarawa type." They are larger than Little Andaman bows, having an average length of about 185 cm., with a breadth of about 5 cm. The section, throughout the greater part of the length, is either plano-convex, or, more frequently, concavo-convex. The section of a typical example is shown in Fig. 6. At the middle of the bow, where it is held in the

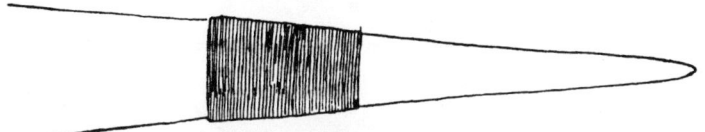

Fig. 7. Upper end of South Andaman bow

hand, there is a slight thickening produced by a protuberance on the inside, i.e. on the flat or concave side. In a certain number of specimens the bow, instead of being straight, is slightly recurved outwards. Finally, the wood from which these bows are cut is not the same as that used in the Little Andaman.

The Little Andaman bow, the North Sentinel bow and the Jarawa bow are all varieties of one type. The Little Andaman form is probably nearest to the original of the type, and I shall show later how the modifications found in the modified Jarawa type came to be adopted.

We now come to bows of a different type, of which there are two varieties, one used in the South and Middle Andaman, and the other used in the North Andaman.

The bow of the South Andaman tribes is not cut from a straight piece of wood, but is cut from a tree that has bent in the course of its growth into a suitable curve. A tree has to be found that will provide a piece of wood of the required shape. From this the bow is shaped with an adze, and is finished by planing with a boar's tusk.

Bows of this kind vary in length between 180 and 210 cm., the most usual length being between 190 and 195 cm. At the upper end the bow is brought to a point approximately circular in section. From this point it broadens out until, at a distance of about 50 or 55 cm., or between one-quarter and one-third of the length of the bow, it reaches its maximum breadth, which is, on the average, about 5·5 cm. The section of the bow at this point is convex on the outer side, while on the inner side it may be flat or slightly concave, or even in rare instances slightly convex. In many specimens there is a very slightly raised keel running down the middle of the inside of the bow. The thickness of the bow at the point mentioned is usually 1·5 to 1·75 cm., and there is little variation in this respect in different specimens. (See Fig. 8.)

At the middle the bow decreases in breadth and increases in thickness to form a handle. At the handle the usual section may be described as pear-shaped, the greatest diameter being the thickness (from inside to outside) and not the breadth.

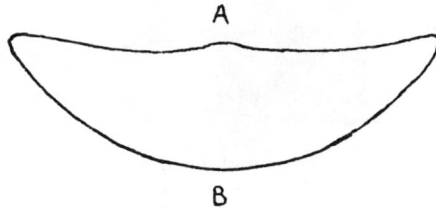

Fig. 8. Section across the blade of a South Andaman bow

From the handle towards the lower end the bow again increases in breadth, so that the lower portion is about the same breadth and thickness as the upper portion. At the lower end it tapers to a point, circular in section, but the point is blunter than at the upper end.

Thus the whole bow consists of a leaf-shaped upper portion or blade which is straight (i.e. neither curved inwards nor outwards), a waist or handle, and a lower blade that is curved backwards or outwards at about its middle, this being the position of the bend in the wood from which it is cut. A bow of this type is shown in Plate v.

Near each end the bow is served over with string for a distance of 3 or 4 cm., leaving a bare point at the upper end of about 7 cm. long, and a point at the lower end of about 1·5 cm. (Fig. 7.)

A bow-string is made from the fibre of the *Anadendron*. A number of strands of the fibre are taken and are waxed with black bees'-wax. Four of these strands are taken, three of them are placed together and the fourth is wound spirally round them. When the end of the active strand (the one being twisted round the others) is neared, a new strand is taken and laid in. The twisting is continued for a few turns and the newly inserted one is then taken, the end of the first active strand being laid in and wound over in its turn. The process continues in this way, new strands being added until a cord of sufficient length has been made. This is again waxed over on the outside.

At one end of the cord a knot is tied. At the other end a loop or eye is formed. To make this eye, when the cord is of sufficient length, the end of it is bent over to form a loop of about 1 cm. or a little more in diameter. This loop is then served over with thread made of *Anadendron* fibre. The serving is continued over the neck of the loop for about 1·5 cm. This gives an eye with the appearance shown in Fig. 9. A loose strand of fibre is left at the neck of the loop. This is wound spirally over the cord, as described before, new strands being added one after another until the cord has been treated in this way for about 35 cm. from the eye. It is then stopped by serving it over for

Fig. 9. Loop of bow-string, South Andaman

about 2 cm. with *Anadendron* thread. It is clear from this description that the cord is somewhat thicker for about 35 cm. from the end with the eye than it is in the rest of its length.

To string the bow the knotted end of the bow-string is fastened round the top end of the bow with a slip knot, so that it rests on the top of the string serving. The bow is then turned upside down and the top end (now temporarily at the bottom) is fixed in the ground or against a stone, so that it will not slip. The other end of the bow is taken by the left hand, while the cord is held in the right, the right foot is placed against the handle or middle of the bow and the bow is bent, the end held by the hand being drawn towards the operator until he is able to slip over it the eye or loop at the end of the string.

After the bow has been strung the upper portion, which before was straight, is now curved inwards, and the bow therefore appears as S-shaped when seen from the side. When a man starts out hunting or fishing he strings his bow and tests it, and it remains strung till he returns, when he unstrings it and places it in his hut.

The advantage of having a knot at one end of the string seems to be that should the string be stretched by use it can be tightened by altering the position of the knot.

At the point where the nock of the arrow is placed when the bow is drawn, it is usual to serve the string over with thread of *Anadendron* fibre.

The peculiar features of the South Andaman bow depend on the fact that the bow takes advantage of the greater toughness and elasticity of wood that has been compressed in the course of its growth. When the bow is drawn the strain does not fall evenly, but, by reason of the shape of the bow, is concentrated on one portion, namely the lower portion of the bow where it is curved outwards. This is easily seen when a bow is strongly drawn, for from the S-shape that it has before, it becomes very nearly true arc-shaped when fully drawn. The lower portion of the bow works as though hinged, and thus the strain is largely borne by the curved portion of the bow. Now this portion is cut from the concave side of a tree that has been bent while growing, and consequently the fibres of the wood are here stronger, tougher and

Fig. 10. Ornament on South Andaman bow

more elastic. The result is that for a given amount of energy spent in drawing the bow a greater force of propulsion is given to the arrow than with a bow of the Little Andaman type.

The breadth of the bow is necessitated by its shape, for if it were narrow the string would slip round on to the outside of the bow. The narrowing at the handle is necessary for holding the bow. The adoption of tapered ends instead of shoulders is a definite improvement as it makes the bow less liable to split at the ends.

The bows of the South Andaman group of tribes are always decorated with incised patterns. The conventional pattern is shown in Fig. 10. One line of such pattern runs down each edge of both the inside and the outside of the bow, and on the inside a similar line of pattern runs down the middle. When bows are newly made they are often also decorated with designs in red paint and white clay, particularly if they are intended as gifts. These painted designs soon wear off and are not renewed.

In these tribes bows are sometimes made of a size so large as to be almost useless for hunting. One such bow, now in the Cambridge

Museum, is 220 cm. long and with a maximum breadth of 10 cm. Such bows are very carefully made and decorated and are intended as gifts. A man generally makes such a bow with the deliberate intention of giving it to some person whom he wishes to please. The bow that I have was specially made to give to me in this way. A man who possessed such a bow would not dream of using it in hunting, but he might use it in a shooting match, in order to show his skill.

In the South Andaman tribes toy bows are made for boys of somewhat the same shape as the ordinary hunting bow. An example of such a bow, now in the Cambridge Museum, is 121 cm. long. It is cut from a bent piece of wood in such a way that the lower portion is curved outwards. The section in the middle is plano-convex, very nearly the half of a circle, the breadth being 26 mm. and the thickness 13 mm. It is broadest in the middle, and tapers towards each end. When strung it assumes the typical S-shape of the South Andaman bow. It is served over with thread at one end and with a strip of

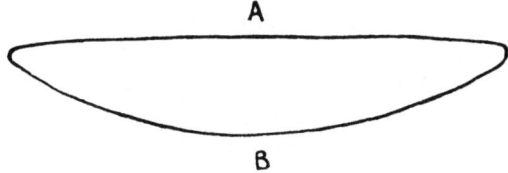

Fig. 11. Section across the blade of a North Andaman bow

cotton cloth at the other, leaving two points for the string. The latter is of the usual South Andaman type, but of smaller dimensions.

We must turn now to the bow used by the four tribes of the North Andaman, which is of a somewhat different pattern from that just described. It is, in the first place, shorter, lighter and more slenderly made. Of ten typical specimens the shortest is 153 cm. long, and the longest is 182 cm. The usual length is about 160 to 165 cm. In its broadest part the North Andaman bow is broader than the South Andaman bow, the breadth varying from 6·5 to 7·5 cm. in different specimens.

Although the North Andaman bow is, as a rule, cut from a curved piece of wood, it may, on occasion, be cut from a piece that is practically straight.

At the upper end of the bow there is a long point. In a specimen that is in every way typical, at about 5 cm. from the point the section is circular and the diameter is about 5 mm.; at about 30 cm.

from the end the section is slightly flattened or oval, and the maximum diameter (the breadth from side to side) is about 1·5 cm. From this the bow broadens fairly rapidly, until at a distance of about 60 cm. from the end it is 7 cm. broad. The section at a point 60 cm. from the end is shown in Fig. 11, where it may be seen to be convex on the outside and only very slightly convex on the inside. At about 75 cm. from the end the bow narrows in breadth to form a handle, at the same time increasing slightly in thickness. The handle is approximately circular in section in the middle, which is about 95 cm. from the upper end, and about 80 cm. from the lower end, the diameter being about 2·2 cm. Below the handle the bow broadens out once more into a lower blade which in shape and section is similar to the upper blade. At a distance of about 30 cm. from the lower end the bow once more narrows off to a point approximately circular in section. The lower point of the bow is not so long or so tapering as the upper point.

The whole bow thus consists of two blade-shaped portions tapering to a point at each end, and with a waist or handle between them. The upper blade is straight, i.e. is not curved either outwards or inwards. The lower blade is curved outwards (like that of the South Andaman bow) in nearly every newly made bow and in every bow that has been in use.

The upper part of the bow is served over with string for about 1·5 cm. (at a distance of 15·5 cm. from the end in the bow that has been described), and the lower end is similarly served (at a distance of 6 cm. from the end). The general shape of the bow as seen from inside is shown in Fig. 12.

The bow-string of the North Andaman is made from *Anadendron* fibre in much the same way as described in connection with the South Andaman bow, but in the North there is a loop or eye at both ends of the string. As soon as the first few centimetres of the cord have been made (by the method previously described) it is bent over into a loop, and this loop is served with *Anadendron* thread, just as in the case of the South Andaman string. The making of the string then proceeds in the usual way until a sufficient length has been made, this depending, of course, on the length of the bow for which it is intended. The end is then bent over into a loop, and this loop is served over with thread. The loose end of fibre is not in this case (as it is in the South Andaman string) twisted round the standing part of the cord, but is laid beside it, and the thread that has been used for serving is wound spirally round them both for a distance of about 10 cm. from the neck of the loop, so that the end is stopped.

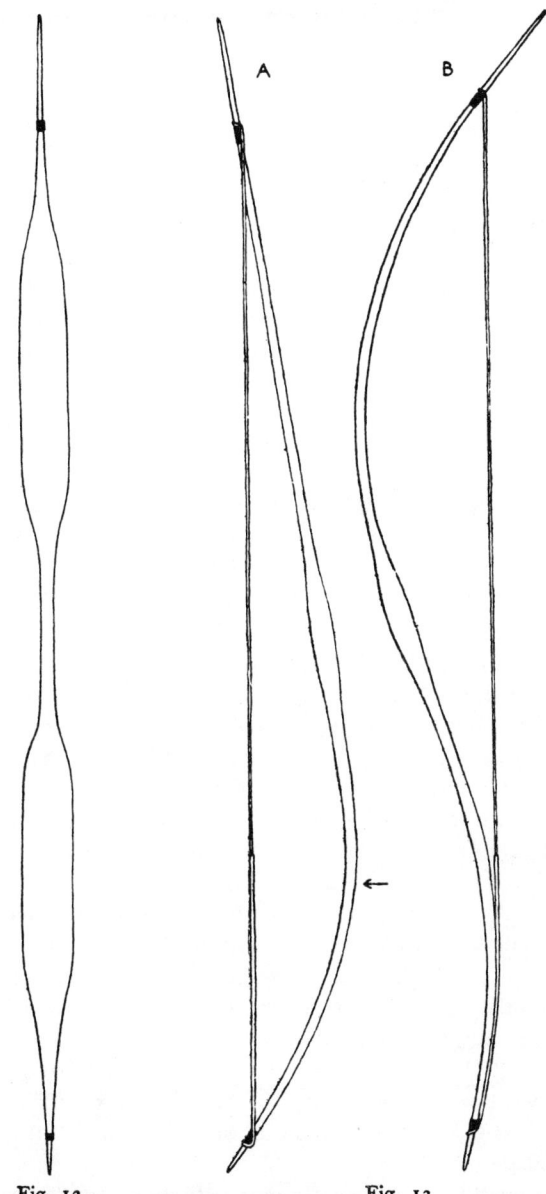

Fig. 12.
Fig. 13.

Fig. 12. North Andaman bow seen from the front
Fig. 13. North Andaman bow; *A*, in the half-strung or reversed position, *B*, in the fully strung position. The arrow shows the point where the bow is seasoned over the fire.

When the bow is to be strung the first made loop is slipped over the top end of the bow so that it rests on the thread serving already mentioned, the neck of the loop being on the inside of the bow. The bow is then laid on the ground, inside downwards, a foot is placed on the middle, and the lower end of the bow is bent upwards (and therefore outwards) far enough to allow the other loop of the cord to be slipped over the end. The bow is now in what may be called the half-strung position, and in order to understand the mechanical principles of this type of bow it is necessary to make quite clear what this position is. It is shown in Fig. 13, *A*. The string passes from the top to the bottom on the outside of the bow, so that the bow is, so to speak, reversed, and is subjected to a strain that causes it to curve outwards. In most bows, when they are first made, there is an outward curve in the lower portion, owing to the bow having been cut from a curved piece of wood. When the bow is half strung this outward curvature is increased. If a bow be made from a straight piece of wood, an outward curve is produced by the operation of stringing it, as described above.

As soon as a bow is completed it is strung in the reversed position described, and is then placed over a fire, in such a position that the lower (curved) blade is immediately above the fire. The smoke and heat of the fire season the wood of this portion of the bow. Any specimen of a bow of this type, unless it has been newly made and not seasoned, is blackened on the inner surface of its lower part. The bow is left to season in this way for some time. A man places his bow over the fire of his own hut, which is kept constantly burning day and night. It must be remembered that all the time it is being seasoned the bow is subjected to a slight strain curving it outwards.

After the bow has been sufficiently seasoned it is brought into use. When a bow that is half strung or strung in a reversed way is to be used, it is taken by the handle in the left hand, with the string away from the body, the bow being upside down. The lower part of the bow (i.e. what is really the top of the bow when it is in its normal position) is rested against the thigh. The string is taken in the right hand and pulled over towards the body, so that the bow reverses itself and appears in the fully strung position shown in Fig. 13, *B*. It is then ready for immediate use.

A bow of this type is hardly ever entirely unstrung. When a man has finished with his bow for the time being, he puts it once more in the half-strung position, by an action the reverse of that described above, and then hangs the bow over the fire. Thus while the bow is in active use it is in the fully strung position, and at all other times it is kept in the half-strung position.

It is clear that the North Andaman bow depends on a principle that is not made use of in the South Andaman bow, which we may state by saying that if a piece of wood be subjected to the influence of heat and smoke while it is bent in one position it will acquire greater strength and elasticity to react against a strain that bends it in the opposite direction. When the bow is fully strung it is S-shaped. When it is drawn the greater part of the strain falls on the lower portion where it is curved outwards. It is this portion of the bow that is strengthened by seasoning.

The North Andaman bow is very much lighter than the South Andaman bow and is much more elastic. I always found it very difficult to shoot with a South Andaman bow, but on the other hand I found the North Andaman bow very easy to use. In drawing it only a slight pull is required in order to send an arrow with considerable velocity. The disadvantage of the northern bow is that, owing to its slighter build, it does not last very long, and is liable to be broken. However, it only takes a man a few days to make a new bow, string included, and the very definite superiority of the North Andaman bow over that of the South Andaman amply compensates for its shorter life.

Bows of exactly the same shape but of smaller dimensions are made in the North Andaman for boys, the length varying from about 90 cm. to about 120 cm. For very small boys toy bows of a different pattern are made. The bow is formed of a piece of wood about 90 cm. long and from 2 to 2·5 cm. broad in the middle. The section in the middle is convexo-convex, with a high degree of convexity on the outside and a much slighter convexity on the inside. The bow tapers to a point at each end, but it tapers more gradually at the top than at the bottom. The bow-string is a simple piece of string (two-ply) made of *Anadendron* fibre. It is tied to the lower end of the bow at a distance of 1·5 to 3 cm. from the end, and at the top it is tied at from 4 to 7 cm. from the end. The shape of a toy bow of this kind as seen from the side is shown in Fig. 14. It is not S-shaped, like the toy bow of the South Andaman previously described, but the curvature is asymmetrical.

I obtained a specimen of a toy bow made of bamboo. Unfortunately there was no string, but it was probably intended to be strung in the fashion of the North Andaman toy bow just described. The outer surface of the bamboo was the outside of the bow, with the result that in section the inner side of the bow was more convex than the outer side. This is the only bow in the whole of the Andamans in which I ever saw this feature. In all other bows of whatever type the outer side is markedly convex and the inner side is either concave, flat or only slightly convex.

It is now possible to compare one with another the different forms of bow in use in the Andamans. It would seem almost certain that the North Andaman bow can only have been derived from the form in use in the South Andaman or from one very similar to it. It is only after they were in the habit of making bows with an outward curve in the lower portion that the natives could have devised the method of seasoning this portion of the bow and keeping it in the reversed or half-strung position. It is unnecessary to argue the matter in detail, and we may conclude that the North Andaman type is derived from the South Andaman type.

It is less certain, but still highly probable, that the South Andaman form was derived from a bow similar to that still in use in the Little Andaman. The South Andaman toy bow shows a stage intermediate between the Little Andaman bow and the usual South Andaman form. The section of this toy bow is very similar to that of the Little Andaman bow. It has no blades, and therefore no waist for the handle. The shape, however, is asymmetrical. Owing to the different method of stringing it, the shoulder at the end of the bow is unnecessary, and the bow is strengthened (prevented from splitting so easily) by tapering the end to a point instead. The difference between the toy bow and the general South Andaman bow is the presence in the latter of the two blades and the waist. The broadening of the bow into the blades is necessary in order to prevent it from accidentally reversing itself.

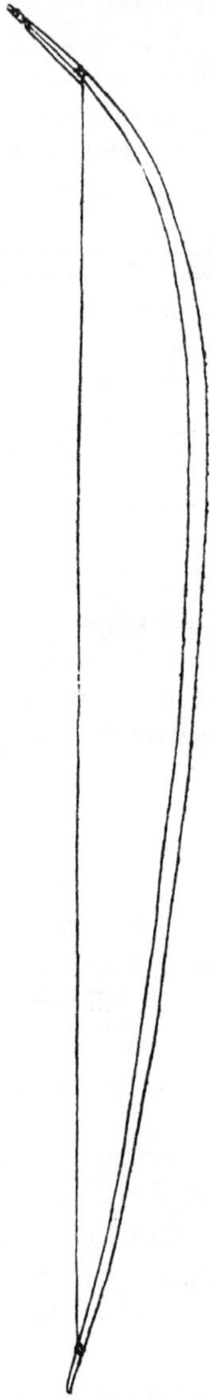

We have still to consider the modified form of the Jarawa bow. The origin of this is easy to discover by the examination of a few typical specimens. Since the Jarawa have been in the South Andaman they have been in hostile contact with the tribes of

Fig. 14. Toy bow of the North Andaman

the South Andaman Division. They have had opportunities of handling bows of the kind made by these tribes, and they have apparently discovered that these bows are more efficient than their own, but they have had no opportunity, such as only friendly intercourse would give, of discovering the principles on which the South Andaman bow is made. They have attempted to imitate it to the best of their ability, and this they have done (1) by making their bows longer and broader, (2) by making them concavo-convex in section instead of convexo-convex, (3) by cutting them occasionally from wood that gives them an outward curve in the

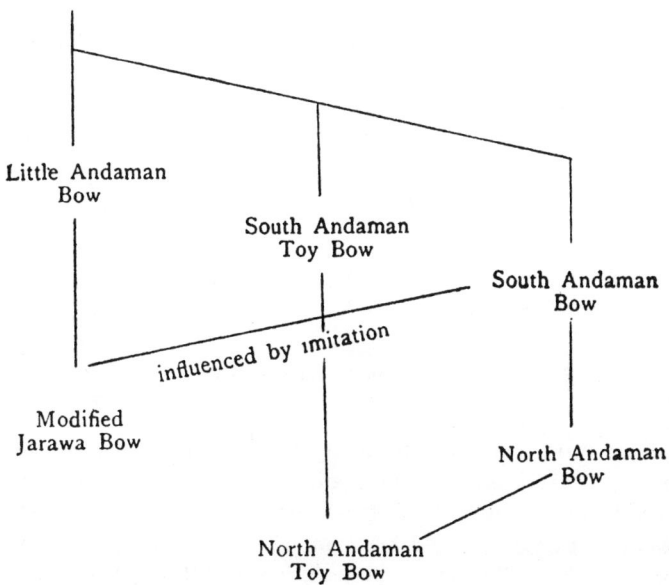

lower portion, (4) by imitating the shape of the handle without, however, giving the bow a waist, (5) by serving over the bow-string with thread at the point where the arrow touches it, (6) by ornamenting their bows with incised and painted patterns. These are the only differences between the modified Jarawa type and the Little Andaman type, and all these may be explained as attempts to imitate the bows of the South Andaman Division. In not a single one of the modified Jarawa bows that I have seen is the fundamental principle of the South Andaman bow successfully applied.

We may conclude that the ancestors of the Andamanese at one time used a bow resembling that in use in the Little Andaman at the present day, and that the S-shaped bow of the Great Andaman has been invented since the separation of the two main divisions of the race.

It is not possible, owing to lack of sufficient information, to determine exactly the types of bow used by the Semang. The following notes are based on only six specimens, two of which are in the Museum of Ethnology at Cambridge[1], while the others are in the British Museum. Four of the specimens are sufficiently similar to one another to be regarded as belonging to one type, which seems to be the usual type of Semang bow. In length they are 165, 174·5, 182 and 197·5 cm., and at the middle they vary in breadth between 2·5 and 3 cm. Three are of palm-wood, and the other is of a light-coloured

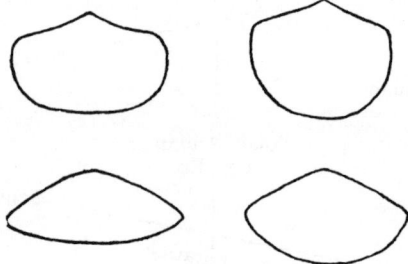

Fig. 15. Section across the middle of four Semang bows

but tough kind of wood. The shape of the section in the middle of the bow varies considerably in the different specimens, as shown in Fig. 15. There is some uncertainty as to which is the inside, and which is the outside of the bow. At each end there is a shoulder, the point or tip at one end being in every instance considerably longer than the other. The string in each case is a three-ply rope, having a spliced eye at one end and being fastened to the bow with a knot at the other end.

The other two specimens do not conform to this type. One is of wood, 134 cm. long, and 3·5 cm. broad in the middle. One end is provided with a notch on each side for the string, while the other end has three pairs of notches. The string is a three-ply cord with a loop or eye at each end. The other specimen is made of bamboo, and is 147 cm. long and 2·25 cm. broad in the middle. One end has one

[1] For information about the two specimens at Cambridge I am indebted to the kindness of Mr J. W. Layard.

pair of notches and the other has two pairs. The string is two-ply with a loop at each end.

What we may perhaps regard as the usual type of Semang bow thus differs from the bow of the Little Andaman in three important respects, (1) in having a longer point at one end than at the other[1], (2) in having a string of three-ply rope instead of a strand of twisted fibre, and (3) in the variations in the section at the middle. From the four specimens available it is not possible to determine around what norm or norms the section of different specimens varies.

Turning to the Negritos of the Philippine Islands, although a number of bows have been described by Meyer[2], the available information is not sufficient to enable us to determine what are the different types, and what is their relation one to another. Amongst the different varieties of bow used by the Negritos there is one which is very similar to the bow of the Little Andaman. It has a rounded or convex outer side, and a flattened inner side. The string loops on to a point at each end, and the string itself is formed of twisted fibre.

From a study of the available material it seems that we are justified in concluding that the primitive Negrito bow was made of wood, with a shoulder at each end, probably with a section rounded on one side and flattened or keeled on the other, and that it had a string of twisted fibre with a loop or eye at one end, the other end being attached with a knot.

The Andaman Islanders use two different kinds of arrows, one for shooting fish and the other for shooting pigs.

The common fish-arrow, as at present used in all parts of the Great Andaman Division, consists of three parts—a shaft, a fore-shaft, and a point. The shaft is a length of bamboo straightened by means of heat, and may vary in length from 70 to 110 cm. At one end the bamboo is cut off about 3 cm. beyond one of the nodes, and a nock is made (Fig. 16). At this end the shaft is roughened with a *Cyrena* shell so as to give a firm grip for the fingers. At the other end the shaft is tapered for about a centimetre. At this end the bamboo is roughened with a shell to give a hold to the thread with which it is bound. The fore-shaft is a length of wood from 15 to 40 cm. long. One end is slightly tapered so that it fits tightly into the end of the bamboo shaft. The other end is tapered to a point, which is flattened on one side. The

---

[1] According to Skeat the end with the longer point is the lower end of the bow (Skeat, p. 273), but Martin (p. 785) describes a bow of this type and states that the longer point is the upper end.
[2] Meyer, pp. 13—17 and Plates VI—VIII.

fore-shaft is inserted into the end of the shaft and the joint is bound over for a distance of about 2·5 cm. with thread. The point consists of a piece of iron wire, sharply pointed at both ends. This is laid against the flattened side of the fore-shaft and is bound to it with thread in such a way that one point projects at the back to form a barb (Fig. 16). When the binding is completed it is covered entirely over with a composition made by melting together bees'-wax, resin and red ochre. The composition is melted over a fire, is applied with a short piece of wood and is then smoothed over with a hot *Cyrena* shell. Only the binding attaching the point to the fore-shaft is covered with composition, and not that at the joining of the fore-shaft and the shaft.

Arrows of this kind are used for shooting fish, but they also serve to shoot snakes or rats and on rare occasions birds.

Similar fish-arrows are made in the Little Andaman, but they are larger (i.e. both longer and thicker) than those of the Great Andaman Division. The two ends of the bamboo shaft are not roughened, and the binding attaching the point to the fore-shaft is not covered with composition (which seems to be unknown in the Little Andaman) but with bees'-wax only.

This seems to be the traditional form of fish-arrow of the Andamans. Before iron was plentiful the point consisted either of the serrated bone from the tail of the sting-ray or of a piece of the tibia of a pig ground down to the requisite dimensions on a piece of stone, and sharpened at each end.

In the Little Andaman fish-arrows are sometimes used with two or four prongs attached to a bamboo shaft. In the British Museum there is an arrow from the North Sentinel Island with four prongs tied on to a wooden shaft, each prong being barbed by a detached piece of wood at the end.

A simple form of arrow is made in both the Great Andaman and the Little Andaman consisting of a bamboo shaft with a pointed wooden head, the point being hardened in the fire. Such arrows are now very rarely used, save for shooting at a mark, but it is probable that before iron was plentiful they were used as a substitute for the fish-arrow described above, being easier to make although less serviceable.

The pig-arrow in use in the Great Andaman consists of a shaft, and a fore-shaft to which is attached a head. The shaft is a piece of the wood of the *Tetranthera lancæfolia*, cut from the tree and straightened by means of heat. At the narrower end a nock about 1 cm. deep is

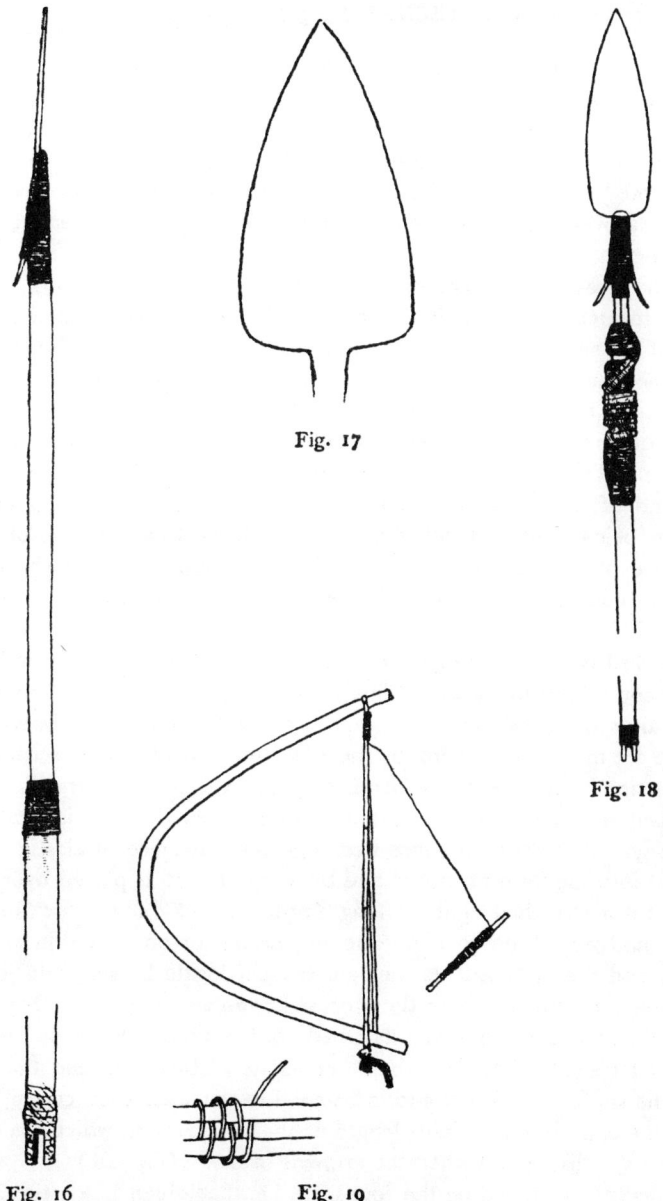

Fig. 16. Fish-arrow of the Great Andaman
Fig. 17. Head of pig-arrow, Great Andaman
Fig. 18. Pig-arrow with detachable head, Great Andaman
Fig. 19. Method of making the cord of the Great Andaman pig-arrow

cut, and the arrow is served with thread of *Anadendron* fibre for about 1·6 cm. above the nock, in order to prevent splitting. At the other end the shaft is hollowed out to a depth of about a centimetre. This hollowing is done with the point of a fish-arrow or other similar piece of pointed iron. For a distance of about 1·5 cm. the end of the shaft is served over with thread of *Anadendron* fibre, so as to prevent it from splitting.

The fore-shaft consists of a piece of tough wood one end of which is cut to such a size that it will fit fairly tightly into the hollow at the end of the shaft. At the other end it is split so as to admit the head.

The head consists of a piece of iron broken into shape with the aid of a stone hammer and then ground down and sharpened on a whetstone or with a file if one be obtainable. The usual shape is shown in Fig. 17. The head is inserted into the split end of the fore-shaft and the end of the latter is then served over with thread. A few centimetres below the head either one or two sharp-pointed pieces of iron wire are placed against the fore-shaft in the same plane as the head and are bound firmly to it with the thread, so as to provide a barb or barbs.

A cord is made and one end of it is attached to the shaft and the other end to the fore-shaft. This cord is made as follows. A number of strands of *Anadendron* fibre are taken and waxed with bees'-wax. These are made into a cord by the same method as that described in connection with the Great Andaman bow-string, one strand being wrapped round the others. About 40 cm. of single cord is made in this way and the two ends are tied together. A piece of elastic wood is bent into the form of an arc and the loop of cord is placed over this so that it is stretched tight. A length of thread (of *Anadendron* fibre) is made and wound on to a fine netting needle or on to a thin slip of wood, and the two cords as they are stretched side by side are bound together with this thread by the process known as "nippering" (Fig. 19). In this way a firm and strong flattened cord is produced. One end of this is fastened to the fore-shaft immediately above the end that fits into the shaft. The other end is fastened to the shaft a few centimetres from the end, leaving a short length of the shaft around which the cord may be spirally wound when the arrow is in use. (Fig. 18.)

Finally, the thread on the fore-shaft, i.e. that which holds the head and barbs in place, and also that which serves to attach the end of the cord, are covered with the composition already described as used on fish-arrows.

Arrows of this kind are used in pig-hunting. The fore-shaft is inserted into the end of the shaft, the cord attaching the two being wound spirally round the end of the shaft. When a pig is struck the barbs prevent the head from coming out of the wound. As the pig attempts to run away the shaft catches against the undergrowth of the jungle and comes loose from the fore-shaft. Sooner or later the shaft becomes entangled in the undergrowth and holds the wounded pig fast till the hunters can come up with it and despatch it. It is obvious that the cord of the arrow needs to be so strong that the pig cannot break it.

The natives of the Great Andaman tribes say that before they had plenty of iron they made similar pig-arrows with heads of shell and barbs of pig's bone.

The natives of the Little Andaman make a pig-arrow very similar to that of the Great Andaman tribes, but on the average somewhat longer. The cord attaching the fore-shaft to the shaft consists of a length of double two-ply rope of *Hibiscus* fibre. The binding of the arrow is done with thread of the *Gnetum* fibre instead of *Anadendron*, and is not coated with composition but is smeared with bees'-wax. The barb (there being usually only one) is not fixed in the same plane as the head, but in the plane at right angles to it. (Fig. 20.)

Amongst the Jarawa the head of the pig-arrow is attached to the fore-shaft by a different method, holes being made in the iron through which the thread that holds it is passed. (Fig. 21.)

Another kind of pig-arrow is sometimes made in the Great Andaman that has not a detachable head. The shaft is a length of bamboo into one end of which is fitted a fore-shaft of wood. The end of this fore-shaft is split and a head of iron is inserted into it and bound there. Such an arrow may be without barbs or may have one or two barbs of iron. It is used only rarely and then chiefly for despatching a pig that has already been struck by an arrow of the usual kind. The natives say that in former times arrows of this kind were used in fighting in preference to ordinary pig-arrows, which, however, were also used.

In former times the natives of the Great Andaman, according to their own statements, made an arrow consisting of a bamboo shaft at the end of which was inserted a head made of *Areca* wood. An arrow of this kind, made for me by a native, is shown in Fig. 22.

None of the arrows made in any part of the Andamans is feathered.

In a comparison of the arrows of the Andamanese with those of the Semang and the Philippine Negritos the most interesting point is that

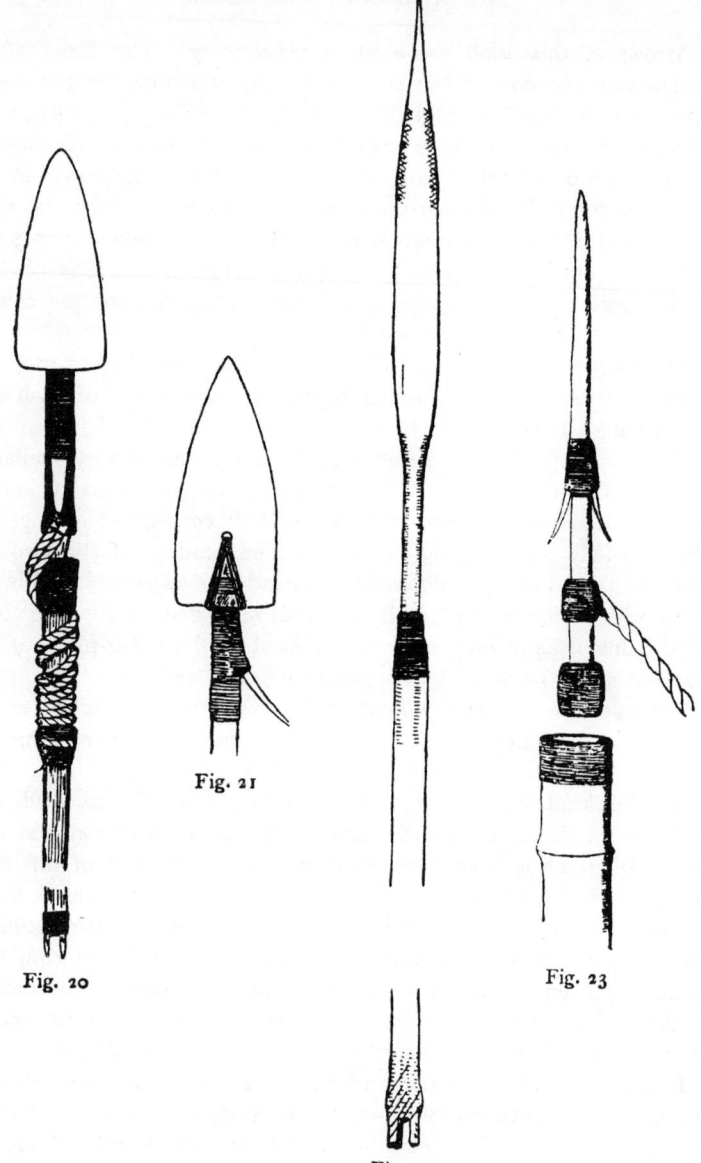

Fig. 20. Pig-arrow, Little Andaman
Fig. 21. Head of Jarawa pig-arrow
Fig. 22. Arrow with head of *Areca* wood, Great Andaman
Fig. 23. Harpoon, Great Andaman

APP. A]   TECHNICAL CULTURE OF ANDAMAN ISLANDERS   441

all three branches of the Negrito race use arrows with detachable heads. Arrows of this kind from the Philippines are described by Meyer[1].

An important point of difference would seem to be that while the Andamanese do not feather their arrows the Semang and the Negritos of the Philippines do so. It would seem, however, from the account of Semang arrows given by Skeat[2] that the feathering is such that it is of no actual service in directing the flight of the weapon, and that it is doubtful whether the Semang really understand the principle of feathering, or whether they do not employ it as the mutilated survival of more intelligent methods or perhaps make use of it for solely magical purposes.

Another important point of difference is that the Semang poison their arrows, while the Andamanese do not. In this connection it must be remembered that the former people have for long been neighbours of people who use blow-pipes with poisoned darts.

After the bow and arrow the most important hunting weapon of the Great Andaman is the harpoon which is used in capturing dugong, turtle, porpoise, and large fish. The harpoon consists of a head, a shaft and a line. The line is a length of rope of *Hibiscus* fibre of as much as twenty fathoms or more in length. The shaft is a bamboo of about 18 feet in length. One end is cut off fairly near a node and is then served over with thread, and slightly hollowed. The head consists of a long piece of iron, such as a stout nail, brought to a sharp point at one end. The other end is served over with thread in such a way as to make it fit fairly tightly into the end of the bamboo shaft. Some distance from the point of the head two barbs of iron are attached by thread, and between this point and the lower end the line is attached. (See Fig. 23.)

A man using the harpoon stands on the forward platform of the canoe, holding the bamboo shaft in his hand. The head is inserted in the upper end of this, and the line passes over his shoulder and is coiled in the bottom of the canoe, the other end being attached to the forward out-rigger boom or to the thwart that takes its place in a large canoe. He poles the canoe along the reef with the harpoon shaft. When about to make a throw he raises the shaft till he can hold the butt end in his right hand, with the point directed towards the fish or turtle, and he then leaps forward so that if he succeeds in his aim the weapon strikes with all the force of his weight behind it. When the turtle or fish is struck the bamboo shaft floats loose and this is secured

[1] Meyer, Plates VI and VIII.   [2] Skeat, p. 274.

by the man in the water, who returns to the canoe. It may be necessary to strike the prey with a second harpoon, but if the first was well thrown the animal is firmly held by the line.

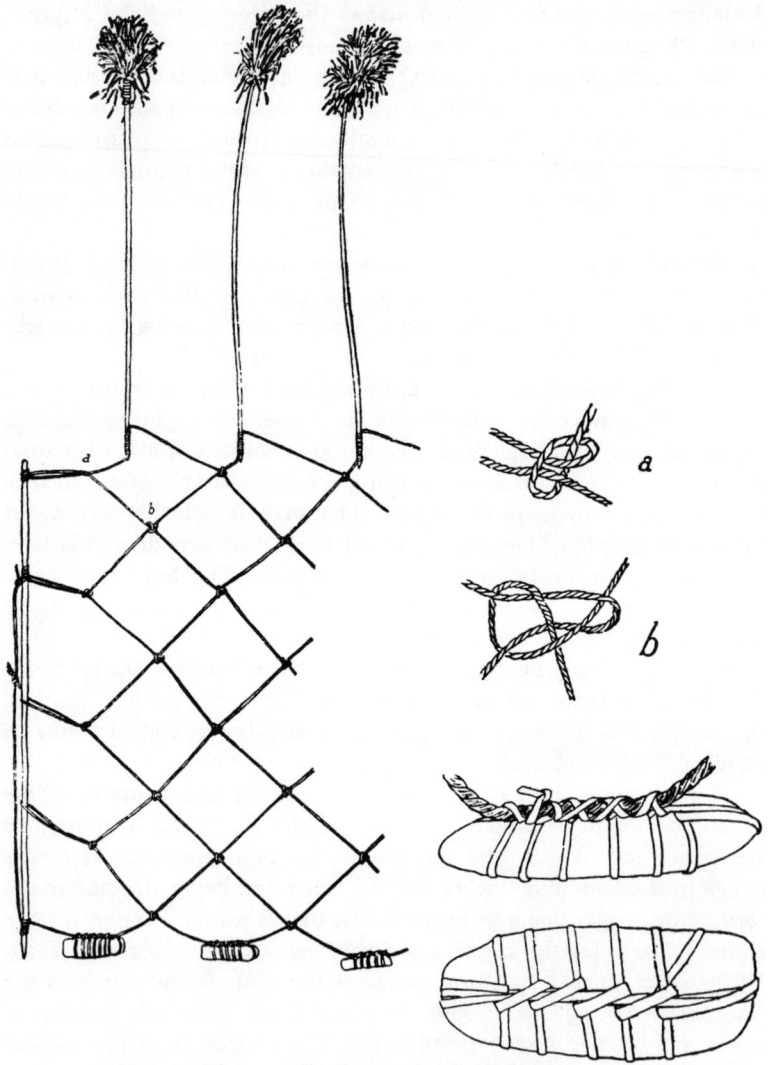

Fig. 24. Turtle net, South Andaman

Harpoons are not used in the Little Andaman. The natives of the Great Andaman say that they themselves have only used them since they were able to obtain iron and that before that time they could only capture turtle and dugong in nets. It would seem therefore that the harpoon has been invented or adopted by the tribes of the Great Andaman Division in comparatively recent times, and was not an element of the primitive Andamanese culture.

The turtle net is no longer used, as the natives prefer the harpoon and have all the iron they need. Such nets were formerly made of rope of *Hibiscus* fibre. A net was about 150 cm. in width and of variable length. One specimen that was made for me had an open mesh of about 25 cm. square, while another had a smaller mesh. The knot used in a net from the South Andaman is the ordinary fisherman's knot shown in Fig. 24 b. In a net from the North Andaman the knot used is a slip-knot, one strand being tied with an overhand knot over another which it crosses at right angles as shown in Fig. 25.

Each end of the turtle net is attached to a stake pointed at the lower end. The lower edge of the net is weighted with stones attached as shown in Fig. 24, while to the upper edge are attached a number of floats, each consisting of a long thin stick of *Hibiscus* wood to the upper end of which is attached a tassel of fibre.

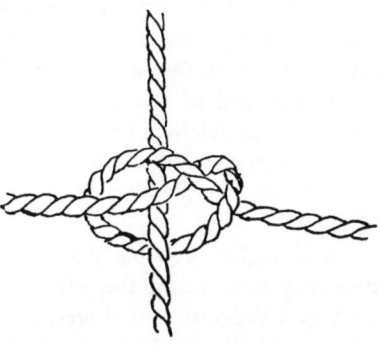

Fig. 25. Knot used in making the North Andaman turtle net

The net was placed in shallow water so that the stones rested on the bottom while the tassels at the upper ends of the floats appeared above the surface. As soon as a turtle was entangled in the net the agitation could be observed by those watching who would proceed to the spot to secure their capture.

So far as is known it would seem that nets of this description are not used in the Little Andaman.

The Andamanese make practically no use of spears. At the present time the natives of the Great Andaman Division sometimes make pig-spears of a length of stout cane or rattan with a head of iron attached. The natives themselves say that such spears have only been made since the occupation of the islands, and it is probable that they were first made in imitation of spears used by Burmese convicts for pig-hunting. They are hardly ever used, the pig-arrow being preferred.

The true fish-spear is unknown in the Andamans though use is sometimes made of a harpoon similar to the turtle harpoon, but of smaller dimensions and with a finer line, for harpooning fish.

In the North Andaman a sort of fish-gig was formerly in use made of about twelve pieces of *Areca* wood of about 105 to 110 cm. long and 1 cm. or less broad and with tapered and sharp-pointed ends. These were fastened side by side by means of a strip of wood near one end, as shown in Fig. 26. This weapon was used for spearing small fish in pools on the reef.

CUTTING IMPLEMENTS.

At the present time the Andamanese make use of iron for their cutting implements. It is uncertain when they first learnt the use of iron, but it was certainly before the end of the eighteenth century. What iron they had was obtained from wrecks, of which there have always been a number on the Andamans. The metal has only become plentiful since the European settlement of 1858.

It is highly probable that the Andamanese, though they may have learnt the use of iron from implements used by visitors to their shores, have not learnt from any other people the method of working the metal. Even at the present day they do not make any use of heat in the manufacture of their iron implements, the metal being worked cold. It seems highly probable that they have simply adopted in connection with iron the methods they formerly used in dealing with other materials, particularly shells.

The materials used by the Andamanese, apart from iron, are wood, bone, shell and stone. We may begin by considering their use of stone.

Fig. 26. North Andaman fish-gig

In former times quartz flakes were used by the Andamanese for the two purposes of shaving and scarifying the skin, and for hardly any other purpose. (Among minor uses of stone flakes may be mentioned those of cutting the finger-nails, and sharpening boars' tusks.) A quartz pebble is held in the left hand and is struck with a hard rounded pebble of any suitable kind. A flake is thus knocked off and falls into the palm of the left hand. The flake is examined, and if it be suitable it is at once used. If it be unsuitable it is thrown away and another made. For shaving, flakes with a sharp blade-like edge are required; for scarifying, flakes with a fine point are preferred. A flake is used till its fine edge is lost and is then thrown away and another made. Thus a woman who is shaving some one's head may use as many as twenty flakes one after another, and to obtain twenty suitable flakes she probably makes as many as forty or even more. The kitchen-middens or heaps of refuse that are found on the sites of old encampments contain thousands of quartz pebbles that have been used as cores, and thousands of flakes.

Besides quartz there is a flinty kind of stone that is used in much the same way for making flakes. Suitable pieces of the stone are obtained and are placed in the fire for a few hours. They are taken out, and when they are cold are used in exactly the same way as a quartz pebble.

At the present time quartz is hardly ever used in this way, for the natives greatly prefer glass, and they obtain sufficient old bottles from Port Blair to satisfy their requirements. The bottom of a bottle is treated in every way as though it was a quartz pebble, a flake being knocked off and used, and then another and so on till the operation in hand (whether shaving or scarifying) is completed. The flake is held between the thumb and first finger when it is being used. In no case is a flake of quartz or glass ever kept. It is only made when required and after having been used is thrown away.

The natives themselves say that they formerly never made any use of stone for cutting purposes save in the case of stone flakes as described above. As against this there are three statements that must be considered. Colebrooke, who visited the islands in 1789, says of the Andamanese that "their canoes are hollowed out of the trunks of trees by means of fire and instruments of stone, having no iron in use amongst them, except such utensils as they have procured from the Europeans and sailors who have lately visited these islands; or from the wrecks of vessels formerly stranded on their coasts." The accuracy of Colebrooke's statement is made doubtful by the fact that at the present time (since 1858) the natives do not use fire in making their canoes, and it seems improbable that if they had this custom in 1789 they should have discontinued it and have entirely forgotten that it ever existed. Further if they used implements of stone in 1789 it is certainly strange that by 1858 they should have entirely forgotten that they ever did so. When Mr Man was making his enquiries the oldest men all agreed in stating that they never used stone for their adzes. We may conclude that Colebrooke's statement is untrustworthy.

Stoliczka records the finding in the South Andaman of a stone celt and a stone arrow-head in the kitchen-middens of the South Andaman. The chief reason for doubting the value of this find is that Stoliczka states that these implements were made of tertiary sandstone, which it is very hard to believe would be of any use whatever. We may therefore adopt the opinion of M. Lapicque[1] that Stoliczka had found fragments of a whet-stone of sandstone and had been mislead into thinking that he had found an axe and an arrow-head.

A third statement that needs to be considered is one by Mr Portman, who presented to the British Museum an arrow with a head of stone made specially for him by a native of the North Andaman who stated that in former times such arrow-heads were used by the Andamanese. At the present time the arrow-head is broken and it would seem to be so fragile as to be entirely worthless for the purpose to which it was supposed to be put. The natives of the North Andaman whom I questioned stated that they did not use stone for their arrow-heads, but shell. We may therefore hold that the evidence given by Mr Portman is not at all satisfactory.

In the Akar-Bale tribe I heard a legend that at a certain spot there is a kind of stone which was used by the ancestors for making adzes. I visited the spot and the stone was pointed out to me. Unfortunately the specimen that I took was lost and I am therefore unable to state what the stone was, but it was such that it would have been utterly impossible to make any sort of adze out of it. It was of a crystalline nature and was easily fractured by a blow against even a soft substance such as wood. It was clear that the native statements about it were merely a legend having no historical value.

We may justifiably conclude that it is probable that the statement of the natives to the effect that before they possessed iron in any quantity they made their adzes and arrow-heads out of shell and not out of stone, is correct. Their use of stone for cutting was therefore confined to the flakes which have been described.

The most important material to the Andamanese seems to have been shell. Mollusc shells were used in the natural form or after having been manufactured. The chief shell used in its natural form is

---

[1] Lapicque, "Ethnographie des Iles Andaman," *Bulletin de la Société d'Anthropologie de Paris*, 1894, p. 370.

the *Cyrena* which serves at the present time as a knife, a scraper and a spoon. Even when they have knives of iron and steel they still use the *Cyrena* shell in preference for some purposes. It is used as a scraper in preparing fibres for rope and thread, in making arrows, as a knife for cutting thatching leaves and cane and even thread and rope, and for making incised patterns on bows and arrows. The shells are always to be found lying about their encampments, and a few are always carried with them when they migrate to a fresh camp. Those living inland obtain their supply of shells from their friends on the coast.

When in use the shell is clasped between the thumb and first finger, the thumb passing over the convex side and the finger round the hinged edge. The remaining fingers are used to clasp the object that is being scraped or cut. In cutting, the motion is away from the body, being produced by a twist of the wrist. In scraping the motion is away from the body, or from left to right. A knife of iron or steel is held in this way by the natives whenever it is used for any purpose for which they formerly would have used a shell. The blade is clasped near the handle between the thumb and first finger, the back of the blade pressing against the root of the thumb, and the handle away from the body.

Another shell that is used in its natural form is a small whelk shell that is used as a scraper for scraping off the outer skin of mangrove seeds in preparing them for food.

A shell that is used in very nearly its natural form is a kind of pearl shell that grows along creeks through the mangrove swamps. The shell is only very slightly curved and it is for this reason that it is selected as suitable. The weak edge or lip of the valve is broken away, and the edge is then slightly ground on a stone. This implement is used by women for slicing yams and certain other vegetables such as some kinds of seeds when they are being prepared for food.

The natives say that before iron was plentiful they used shells for the heads of their pig-arrows. Several different species of shell seem to have been used, the chief concern being to obtain a piece of sufficient size that was as nearly flat as possible. Such shells are those belonging to the larger bivalves. The natives state that their method of working the shell was to break it roughly into shape with stones and then grind it down on a whet-stone until it was given a sufficiently sharp point and edge. Some arrow-heads of shell were made for me by this method at my request by one of the old men of the North Andaman.

The natives state that before they had iron they made their adzes of shell. Two different men of the North Andaman made two shell adzes for me, one of *Pinna* shell, and the other of a shell that I omitted to identify. The *Pinna* shell adze seemed to me only suitable for light work such as finishing off a bow or a canoe, as it seemed likely to break under a strong blow. The other adze was much stronger and therefore capable of heavy work, and although the edge seemed to me to make it a poor implement with which to cut down a tree yet it certainly did not seem less suitable than the stone adzes used by many primitive peoples. If I were given a choice of implements with which to fell a tree, between the shell adze of the Andamanese and a stone axe of South-western Australia I should certainly choose the former.

According to the natives they formerly used bone for the points of their fish-arrows and for the barbs of their pig-arrows. For both of these purposes they now use iron. The bone was broken into a piece of suitable length and then ground down with a whet-stone. Apparently the bone most frequently used was the tibia of the pig. For their fish-arrows they also made use of the bone of the tail of the sting-ray,— its "sting." When the fish was caught the bone was knocked off and reserved for use. It required no treatment whatever, being simply bound on to the point of the fore-shaft in the same way that an iron point is now attached.

Colebrooke, in 1789, described their arrows as "headed with fish-bones or the tusks of wild hogs, sometimes merely with a sharp bit of wood hardened in the fire." By fish-bone he probably means the bone of the sting-ray. Where he writes the tusks of wild hogs we should probably read "the bones." A boar's tusk is curved, and it seems impossible to imagine how it could possibly be used as an arrow-head or arrow-point.

The boar's tusk is used by the Andamanese as an implement, however, making a very efficient sort of spokeshave. The edge which is used is kept sharp by scraping with a quartz or glass flake or with a *Cyrena* shell. The edge is near the point (at *a* in Fig. 27) and the tusk is clasped at the other end between the forefinger and the root of the thumb (at *b* in Fig. 27), the movement being away from the body. It is used for planing bows and paddles, and in the

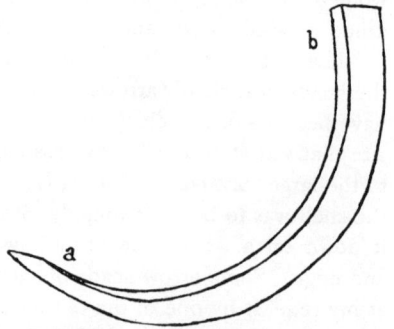

Fig. 27. Boar's tusk, used as a spokeshave

hands of an Andaman Islander is a very efficient implement, producing a beautifully smooth and even surface.

Of wood the Andamanese formerly made knives and arrow-points. The knives were made of a slip of bamboo or cane shaped and sharpened with a *Cyrena* shell. Such knives were used for cutting meat and apparently for no other purpose. A knife was always attached by a short length of cord to a skewer of pointed *Areca* wood. The double implement was used in cooking and eating, the skewer serving to lift pieces of meat in and out of a pot, while the knife served to cut them. At the present time the cane or bamboo knife is replaced by a knife made from hoop-iron, but the shape of the original implement is retained as nearly as possible and a skewer of *Areca* wood is generally attached to it.

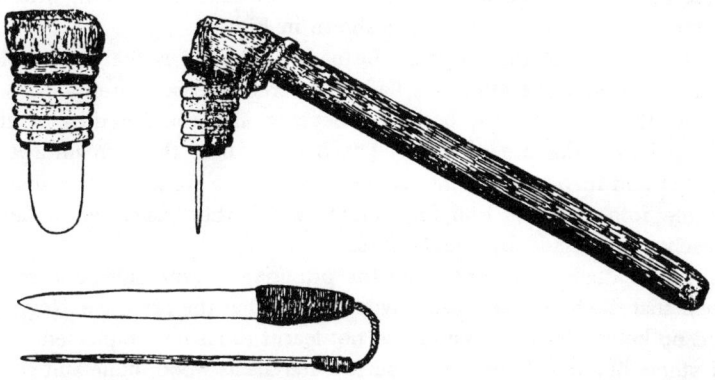

Fig. 28. Adze and knife

As has been already stated the Andamanése formerly used hard wood such as that of the *Areca* palm for the points and heads of their arrows. They do not seem to have made use of bamboo in this way.

At the present time iron is used for the blades of adzes, for the heads and barbs of pig-arrows, the points of fish-arrows, the heads of harpoons, and for knives. The method of working the metal is apparently exactly the same as the method they formerly used for working shell and bone. For the head of a pig-arrow a suitable piece of iron is taken and a fragment of about the right size is broken off by means of a stone hammer. This is then roughly broken into the required shape, no heat being used, and no advantage being taken of the malleability of the metal. The next process is to grind it on a whet-stone. The natives are always eager to obtain files which enable them to do this part of the work much more rapidly. When the arrow-head has been ground into shape the edges are sharpened. Blades for adzes are made in exactly the same way from any suitable piece of iron or steel, such as a cutlass or an old file or a piece of thick hoop-iron. The adze-blade is attached to a handle of mangrove wood by the method shown in Fig. 28.

The barbs of pig-arrows and the points of fish-arrows are made in the same way by breaking the metal into a suitable shape and then grinding it on a whet-stone. It is probable that this was the method that was formerly used for dealing with bone for these purposes.

In the case of the knife, iron or steel is now substituted for cane or bamboo, but the knife has retained its shape in spite of the change of material. The shape of a knife, whether of cane or of iron, with its attached skewer of *Areca* wood is shown in Fig. 28.

In the case of the harpoon the native tradition is that this implement was only made after they had discovered the use of iron.

At the present time both the Semang and the Negritos of the Philippines make use of iron. The Semang heat the iron until it is red-hot and then batter it into shape between two stones[1]. The shapes of the iron weapons and implements which they make follow fairly closely those made by the Malays.

In an attempt to reconstruct the primitive Negrito culture it would seem that the most reasonable hypothesis is that the primitive Negritos had no knowledge of iron and had not learnt to fashion implements out of stone, but relied entirely on such materials as wood, bone and shell. The Andamanese, becoming possessed of iron through wrecks upon their islands, applied to it the technique that they had developed for dealing with shell, and thereby invented their present method of working iron without heating it. The Semang and the Negritos of the Philippines probably first learnt the use of iron from their neighbours of other races. There is not at present any evidence to show that the Negritos ever had any method of working stone except the very simple one at present in use in the Andamans for making flakes.

String, Rope, Mats, Baskets, and Netting.

For string, rope and thread the Andaman Islanders make use of a number of different vegetable substances, but they make no use what-

[1] Skeat, p. 383.

ever of any animal substances. Some of the more important fibres, with their uses and the methods of preparing them, are mentioned below.

The bark of the *Hibiscus tiliaceus*, which occurs in the beach vegetation in all parts of the islands, provides the Andamanese with one of their most important fibres. By the coast-dwellers of the Great and Little Andaman Divisions it is used for making rope. In the Great Andaman Division the rope made from it was formerly used for making turtle nets, and is now used for the lines of turtle harpoons, and for hawsers to attach a canoe either to a stone used as an anchor or to a tree. No other fibre is used for these purposes. The *Hibiscus* rope does not seem to be much affected by salt water. The forest-dwellers of the Great Andaman have less use for rope, and at the same time are not able to obtain so readily the *Hibiscus* fibre. What rope they do have is therefore obtained from the coast-dwellers or is made of some other fibre. In the Little Andaman the *Hibiscus* is regularly used for rope. It is also used for the short cord by which the detachable head of the pig-arrow is attached to the shaft. In the Great Andaman a strip of the bark of the *Hibiscus* is used for the sling in which children are carried. Strips of the bark are worn by the women of the Little Andaman across their shoulders and breasts, as a sort of ornament.

To obtain the fibre young straight shoots of about 120 cm. in length are cut from the tree, those free from gnarls, and having a smooth bark, being chosen. The bark (inner and outer layers) is peeled off in strips of from 1·5 to 3 cm. in width. The inner or liber layer is then separated from the outer layer of the bark, is well scraped with a *Cyrena* shell and dried in the sun or over a fire. When dry it is worked in the hands until the various layers of fibre separate one from another. It is then ready to be made into rope. The fibre is interlacing, and when freshly made is a lustrous greyish brown. After exposure to salt water it turns a dark brown.

Mr E. H. Man, in his work on the Andamans, speaks of the *Melochia velutina* as providing fibre for rope. This is an error. The tree to which Mr Man refers is the *Hibiscus tiliaceus*. It is extremely common on the shores of the islands, as it is in many other parts of the tropics. It is very easily identified, as it bears its characteristic yellow flowers for a long time every year. There is no doubt whatever that this is the tree from which the natives regularly obtain the fibre for the rope they use in turtle-hunting and fishing and in their canoes. Other writers, following Mr Man, have repeated his error in calling it the *Melochia velutina*, for example Sir Richard Temple and Mr Portman. In Mr Portman's collection of photographs in the British Museum there is a good photograph of a *Hibiscus tiliaceus* tree labelled "*Melochia velutina*." I looked carefully in the Andaman jungles for the *Melochia velutina* but was unable to find it, and I am quite certain that in any case, even if it be found there, it is not commonly used by the natives for rope.

The bark of a number of other trees provides fibre of which the natives occasionally make use. Amongst these are one or more species of *Sterculia* (*S. villosa* ?), and a tree that I identified somewhat doubtfully as *Grewia laevigata*. The coarse fibre of the liber layer of these trees may be made into rope by the same method as that employed in dealing with *Hibiscus tiliaceus*. Very little actual use is made of them however. A fibre which looks very like that obtained from one species of *Sterculia* is frequently used by the natives of the Little Andaman (and also by the Jarawa) for their personal ornaments. Mr Portman says that this fibre is obtained from the *Celtis cinnamonea*.

A species of *Hibiscus*, which I believe is *Hibiscus scandens*, growing in the jungles and not along the shore, provides a fibre that is prized by the natives of the Great Andaman tribes for making string or fine rope. The fibre is less easily obtained than that of the *Hibiscus tiliaceus*, but owing to its quality (it is not so interlacing) is capable of being made into finer rope and string. It is often made into string and then used for making netted bags. I did not find this fibre in use in the Little Andaman, but as it is not very often met with even in the Great Andaman, it may possibly be used in the Little Andaman.

There are several species of *Ficus* in the Andaman forests, and the natives know that they can obtain fibre from the bark of these trees. The only one that is regularly made use of is the *Ficus laccifera*. The natives of the Great Andaman Division use the bark of this tree for making their personal ornaments. In the Little Andaman it is used for bow-strings. A fibre called in the Little Andaman *ulu*, and said by Mr Portman to be obtained from the *Ficus hispida*, is used in that island, and by the Jarawa, for making personal ornaments.

The *Gnetum edule*, a climbing plant that is fairly common, is used in all parts of the Andamans for thread and string. The creeper is cut into short lengths at the nodes and is dried for a few days. The outer layer of bark is then scraped off with a *Cyrena* shell, and the liber layer beneath it is peeled off in fine strips and these are made into thread or string. This string is used in the Great Andaman Division for making netted bags and fishing nets. In the Little Andaman it is used for binding their arrows, as well as for netting.

The most valuable fibre of the Great Andaman tribes is that of the *Anadendron paniculatum*, which is used for string and thread and for bow-strings. Until recent times the method of preparing the fibre was not known to the natives of the Little Andaman, but they have now learnt it from the natives of the Great Andaman with whom they have been brought in contact, and the use of the fibre for string and thread is coming in amongst them.

The fibre is not easy to prepare. Long thin branches of the creeper are cut, which must be neither too young nor too old. To obtain these it is often necessary to climb up into high trees, for the *Anadendron* is a climbing plant. The creeper is cut into lengths of from 20 to 40 cm. The bark (inner and outer layers) is peeled off these in strips of from 7 to 10 mm. in width. A strip of the bark is taken and placed on the thigh, inner surface downwards, and is scraped with a *Cyrena* shell until the outer bark is entirely removed and the fibres remain clean and separate. These are dried in the sun or over a fire and, if not needed for immediate use, are stored for future occasion. The fibre is fine and of a light greyish brown colour. In its qualities it somewhat resembles ramie fibre. It is extremely strong.

There are a number of other trees and plants that are known by the natives to afford fibre, but they are not used, or if they are, it is extremely rarely.

The Andaman jungles have a number of different species of *Calamus*, and the canes or rattans of these are put to all sorts of uses, such as the making of baskets, the lashings and furnishings of canoes, and in building huts. In the Little Andaman one species of cane is used to provide the fibre for women's belts. The outer skin is removed and the remainder of the cane is divided into fine strips or threads. A bundle of these tied together constitutes the belt worn by the women of the Little Andaman. The outer sheath of the leaf-stem of the *Calamus tigrinus* is used by the natives of the Great Andaman Division for making mats. Lengths of the leaf-stem are cut and the outer skin is removed in strips of about 3 to 5 mm. in width. The still adhering pith is removed with a *Cyrena* shell, and the strips are dried in the sun and then made into mats.

The leaf-stem of a species of palm is cut while green and is then shredded into long strips. The fibre thus obtained really consists of the leaflets of the young unopened leaves of the palm. It is used in the

Little Andaman to make the tassel that women wear over the pudenda. The women of the North Andaman formerly wore a tassel of this fibre, but have now discontinued the custom, since their contact with the South Andaman. In the Great Andaman tribes this material has important ceremonial uses. It is called *koro* in Aka-Jeru and *ara* in Aka-Bea, and has been frequently mentioned in this volume. A tassel of the fibre is suspended near the grave of a dead person and at the entrance of the village at which the death took place. In the North Andaman a suspended cane hung with a fringe of the fibre is erected for the peace-making ceremony. (See Plate XIX.)

Two plants that were not identified are used in the North Andaman for making baskets. The methods of preparing these will be described later.

The natives of the Great Andaman Division make use of the leaves of the *Pandanus Andamanensium* for making belts for women and ornaments that are worn on ceremonial occasions. These leaves do not seem to be used in the Little Andaman.

The pods of one or more species of *Dendrobium* are collected by the natives of both Great Andaman and Little Andaman. They are roasted in the fire, until the outer skin turns a bright yellow, and this is torn off in strips and used for ornamenting nets, baskets, rope, etc.

The above description includes all the more important vegetable substances used by the Andamanese for their rope, string, netting, and basket-work. There are many other substances that they might use if they wished, of the properties of which they are fully aware. Their knowledge of the trees and plants of the forests and of the peculiar properties of each is very extensive. They themselves say that they use only those that best serve their purposes.

The Andamanese make rope and string or thread, but in all cases it is only two-ply. Rope is made by men only, and is used for the lines of turtle harpoons, and was formerly used for turtle nets. The ropes made from *Hibiscus* fibre are very strong and durable, being quite as good as the best hempen ropes of the same diameter. In rope-making the *Hibiscus* or other fibre (*Sterculia* or *Grewia*) is taken and twisted into a long strand, either with the fingers, or on the thigh by rolling beneath the palm of the hand, short lengths of fibre being added until a single twisted strand of sufficient length and uniform thickness is produced. The middle of this strand is passed over a piece of wood held by the toes, one half of it being wound on to a reel (*kutobi* in Aka-Jeru) made by tying together crossways two pieces of cane or wood each about 20 cm. long and 6 mm. in diameter. The other half of the strand is loose, and is held (near the point where it is tied to the wood held in the toes) between the finger and thumb of the left hand, the rest of it passing across the palm, over the left forearm, under the armpit, across the back and over the right shoulder, hanging down loosely to the worker's right side. This arrangement is in order that the loose strand shall not become entangled or get in the man's way as he works. The reel is held in the right hand and is passed first under the left hand, then back again over it, the two strands being thus twisted into a firm two-ply cord.

The natives of the Little Andaman make rope in much the same way, but they pass the reel from right to left over the other strand and back under it, the twist being thus in the opposite direction from that used in the Great Andaman.

String or thread is made by both men and women. It is put to many uses, the chief being for binding the heads of arrows, harpoons and spears and the ends of bows, and in making nets, baskets, mats and personal ornaments. In making string the man or woman sits down with legs outstretched. Thin strands of fibre, varying in thickness according to the thickness of the string required, are taken and each twisted singly by being rolled between the palm of the right hand and the right thigh, the motion being away from the body. When a sufficient number of short single strands has been thus made, two of them are taken and placed together on the thigh, being held at one end in the left hand. The two strands are rolled together beneath the palm of the right hand, the motion being inwards towards the body. A well twisted thread is thus produced. When some 10 cm. or so have been thus twisted, the thread is rolled once beneath the palm of the hand in the opposite direction, i.e. away from the body, this action rendering it more compact. As soon as the end of the two strands that are being twisted is neared, two more are taken and joined on, first one and then the other, by being rolled in with the first two. Fresh strands are thus continually added as the string grows in length. String of any desired length is made in this way, of considerable strength and of surprisingly uniform thickness.

String is made in this way from the fibre of *Anadendron*, *Gnetum* and *Hibiscus scandens* in the Great Andaman Division, and from *Gnetum* and *ulu* fibre in the Little Andaman. In the Great Andaman string made from *Anadendron* fibre is rendered more durable by being waxed with black bee's-wax, but this treatment is not considered necessary for string made from *Gnetum* fibre or from *Hibiscus scandens*.

Ornamental rope is made for men's belts in the Great Andaman. *Hibiscus* fibre is twisted into a single strand. Around this strand strips of *Dendrobium* skin are wound spirally so that it is entirely covered, and the strand itself is twisted into a two-ply cord.

Two other forms of cord have been already mentioned, namely the bow-string, of twisted fibre of the *Ficus laccifera* in the Little Andaman, and of wrapped fibre of the *Anadendron* in the Great Andaman Division, and the special cord used in the Great Andaman for attaching the head of a pig-arrow to the shaft. The Andamanese make very little use of plaited cord. I have only met with it in personal ornaments made of *Pandanus* leaf in the Great Andaman.

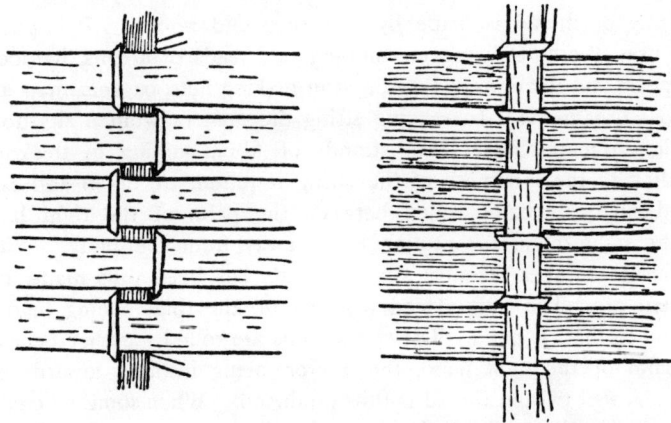

Fig. 29. Method of making bamboo mat, Little Andaman

The mat-work of the Andamanese is very simple. The natives of the Little Andaman make bamboo mats on which they sleep. Strips of bamboo of about 120 cm. in length and ·75 cm. in width are attached by means of thin strips of cane to other strips of bamboo at right angles to the first series. The technique is illustrated in Fig. 29 which shows the back and the front of a portion of such a mat. It is that usually known as wrapped-twined work.

A similar technique is used in both the Little Andaman and the Great Andaman in making thatching of cane-leaves. There is a difference, however, the wrapping used in making thatch being that shown diagrammatically in Fig. 30.

The natives of the Great Andaman make sleeping mats from the outer sheath of the leaf-stem of the *Calamus tigrinus*. Lengths of the material are prepared and cleaned and are cut to a uniform length, generally about 60 to 80 cm., having a breadth of 3 to 5 mm. A length

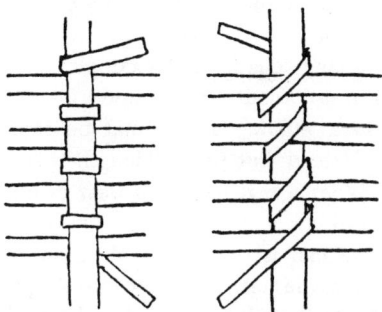

Fig. 30. Diagram showing the technique used in making mats of thatch

of thread, generally of the less valuable *Gnetum* fibre, but occasionally of *Anadendron* fibre, is made and is wound on to two netting needles, one half on each. With this thread the strips of cane-leaf are fastened together. The technique is different in the North Andaman and in the South Andaman.

In the North the technique, which is represented diagrammatically in Fig. 31, *A* is that known as wrapped-twined work. One of the two threads of which the work is composed is held taut, the needle on

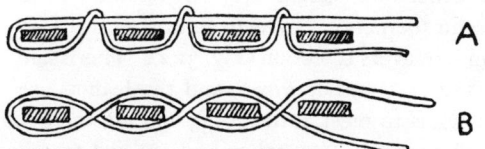

Fig. 31. Diagram showing the technique used in Great Andaman mats
A, North Andaman; *B*, South Andaman

which it is wound being held in the toes, and the other thread is wrapped spirally round it, one of the strips of cane-leaf sheath being enclosed at every turn. Thus the method is exactly the same as that adopted in making mats of thatch.

In the South the technique is that known as twined work or fitching. The two wefts (i.e. the threads) are twisted together in the same direction one under the other, enclosing at each half turn one of the strips of leaf-sheath. This is shown diagrammatically in Fig. 31, *B*.

The mat is made by parallel lines of such twining or wrapped-twining. At each side of the mat the line of threading is quite close to the ends of the strips of which the mat is made. In the South Andaman the work on each side of the mat is different from that in the middle. Each of the two threads is alternately given a complete turn round one of the strips of material.

Mats may be of any length, and examples vary from 1 metre to 10 metres. When in use about a metre and a half is unrolled and the remainder serves as a pillow. If the mat be short a split log does service as a pillow instead, but the full-length mat is certainly a more comfortable bed. When a mat begins to wear or fall to pieces in some part it is not thrown away, but this part is kept rolled up, and an unbroken part of the mat is unrolled to sleep on, the remainder being kept rolled up either at the head, where it forms a pillow, or at the foot. An old mat may be continually increased in length by additions made to it. The work of making these mats is performed by women only.

The Jarawa and the natives of the Little Andaman make mats of a somewhat similar pattern, but I have not been able to secure one so as to see how it is made.

To explain the different forms of the Andamanese baskets, it is most convenient to begin by considering the way in which the natives of the North Andaman tie up their pots. The small cooking-pots of the North Andaman are fragile things and are not easily made, and it is therefore necessary to take care of them. A leaf of the *Licuala* palm is taken. The leaflets are plaited over one another, close to the point of their insertion in the petiole, so as to form a sort of rosette with leaflets radiating from it in every direction (Fig. 32 a). This is laid on the ground, the pot is placed on it upside down, and the leaflets are brought up all round the pot so as to meet at the point, and are there roughly fastened. Three strips of cane are then taken and are tied together crossways in the middle so as to form a sort of six-rayed star with six approximately equal angles. This is laid on the ground with the outer surface of the canes downwards, the pot is placed on it upside down, and the strips of cane are bent upwards over the pot so as to meet at the point. The ends of two opposite strips of cane are left projecting for a few centimetres above the point, and the ends of the other four are fastened firmly down. Another strip of cane is now fastened round the middle of the pot, being applied to the six canes previously mentioned by wrapping, i.e. a turn is taken with it round each of the six strips in turn. The pot is now safely tied up and can be hung in the hut or

carried on a journey without much fear of its coming to grief. To use
the pot it is of course necessary to untie it. A pot wrapped up in this
way is shown in Fig. 32 *a* and *b*.

In the South Andaman the pots have rounded bottoms. They are
not tied up in the same way as in the North Andaman, but for purposes
of safety and carriage each pot is provided with a rude basket. The
basket is made so as to fit the pot. Six strips of cane are taken and
tied together in the middle, as previously described. A stout strip of

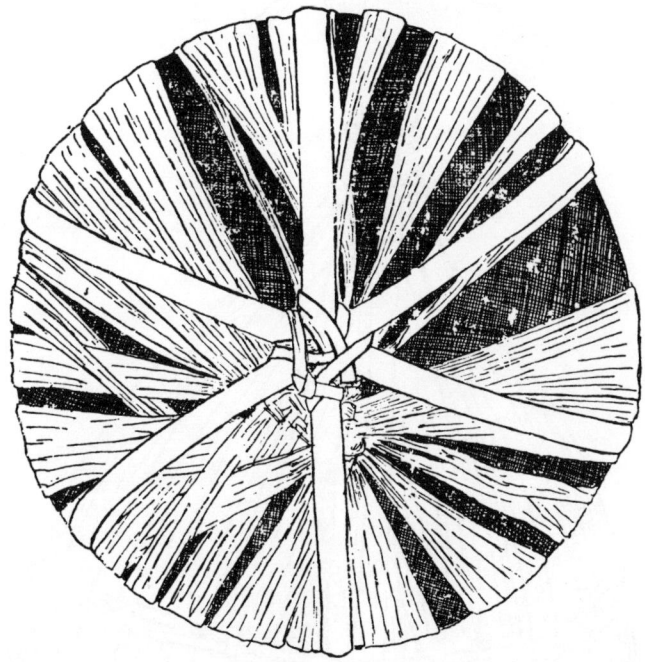

Fig. 32 *a*

cane is then taken and is bent round into a circle so as to be just a little
larger than the outside rim of the pot. This, which is to form the rim
of the basket, is placed in position and the six strips of cane before
mentioned are bent round and attached to it. The manner of attaching
the uprights of the basket to the rim is shown in Fig. 33. The strip of
cane forming the upright is thinned down beyond the point where it
reaches the rim. It is given one turn round the rim, ascending on the
outside and descending inside, then a half turn round the standing part
of itself, immediately below the rim from left to right, then another

complete turn round the rim ascending inside and descending outside, a half turn behind its own standing part below the rim, a third complete turn round the rim, and the end is fastened with an overhand knot.

A thinner strip of cane is now taken and wound round the six uprights (the warp of the basket) being given a turn round one after

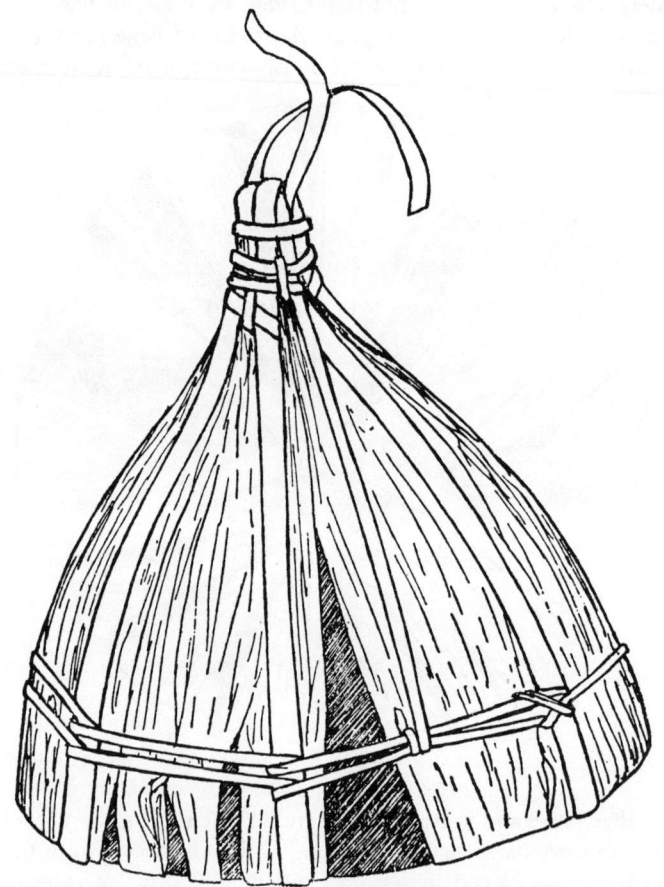

Fig. 32 *b*. Pot, tied up for carrying, North Andaman

another. The technique is that known as wrapped work. If the strip be not long enough another is joined to it with a reef or sailor's knot. The weft (as this thinner strip may be called) is given five or six spiral turns, and thus leaves a very open and rather weak basket. The basket is then further strengthened by other strips of cane attached by one end to the rim and carried downwards, with one turn round each of the horizontal canes (weft) and the other end attached to the centre of the bottom of the basket. A strip of cane or bark is attached to the rim by its two ends to provide a strap by which the basket with its pot may be carried on the back. Before the pot is placed in it the basket is lined with the leaflets of the *Licuala* palm.

We may now turn to the baskets of the Little Andaman, of which there are two varieties, one made with more care than the other. As regards shape both varieties are the same, and the shape is exactly that of the Little Andaman pots.

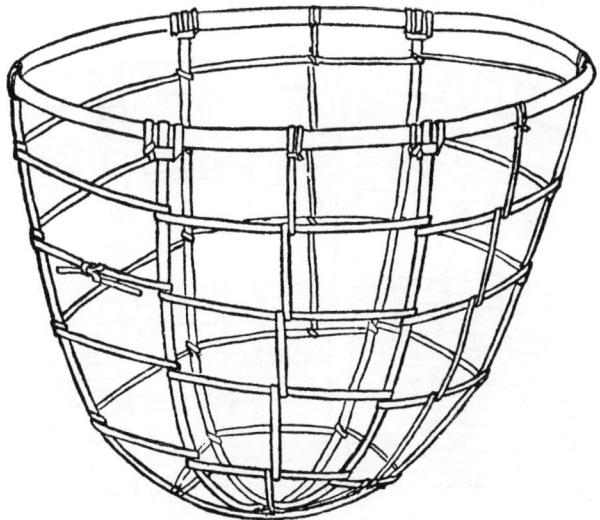

Fig. 33. Basket for carrying pot, South Andaman

The following is a description of a small but typical specimen of the better variety of Little Andaman basket. The foundation consists of twelve whole canes. A little under 80 cm. of the cane is left whole, and at each end it is thinned down to a strip. The twelve canes are taken in four bundles of three each and placed so as to cross each other in the middle. They are bent into a somewhat conical shape, and the ends (where the cane is thinned) are attached to a rim composed of a whole cane bent into a circle and tied. The method by which each of the uprights or stakes is attached to the rim is shown in Fig. 34. It is almost identical with that used in the South Andaman pot basket. The weaving is then begun near the bottom of the basket. A thin strip of the outside of a cane is taken, and is applied to the uprights (warp or stakes) by wrapped work, i.e. it is given a complete turn round each of them in turn. This wrapped weaving is continued spirally from near the bottom of the basket to near the rim. Near the top of the basket, between 4 and 5 cm. from the rim, the weaving is so arranged that for about three-quarters of the way round the basket there is a gap of about 1·5 cm. between two rows of weft (see Fig. 34). The purpose of this will be mentioned later. The basket now consists of a rim to which are attached twelve uprights forming the warp of the basket, around which a fine strip of cane has been spirally wrapped from the bottom to the top. Twelve fine strips of the outside of a

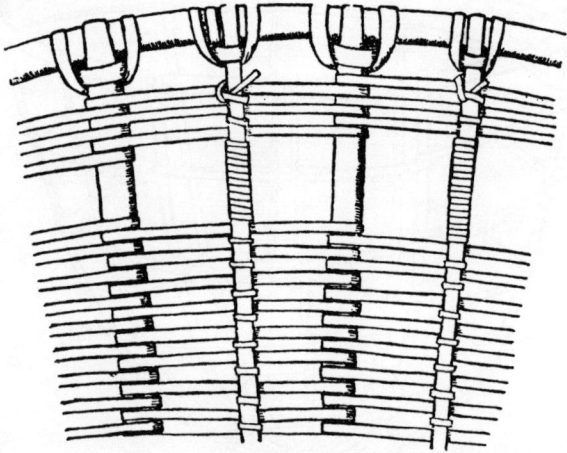

Fig. 34. Portion of basket of Little Andaman

cane are now taken. One end of each is fastened to the rim in between two of the stakes, the mode of fastening being shown in Fig. 34. The strip is then carried down the basket, on the outside, as far as the bottom row of weaving, round which it is doubled, and is then wound spirally, from the bottom to the top of the basket, around its own standing part, including at each spiral turn one of the wefts. Thus each of these twelve strips of cane is attached to the outside of the basket by the process known as wrapped-twined work. The basket is furnished with a handle of bark fibre which is attached by its two ends to the rim on that side where there is no gap between the rows of weft near the top.

In the less carefully made baskets of the Little Andaman there are a few important differences. The stakes of the basket are not thin whole canes, but are strips of larger canes. The weft is applied in wrapped work, as in the basket already described, but the rows of weft are not so close together and are therefore not so numerous. After the first process, when the basket consists of stakes and horizontal (spiral) weft only, vertical strengthening strips are added, but these are applied, not in wrapped-twined work as in the basket described, but in wrapped work, in exactly the same way as in the South Andaman pot-basket. Thus, apart from its shape, which is that of the Little Andaman pot, the Little Andaman basket of this kind is very similar to the South Andaman pot-basket.

The natives of the Little Andaman make pots that are much larger and deeper than those of the South Andaman, and have a more rounded bottom than those of the North Andaman. For every pot a basket is made that exactly fits it, and in this basket it is stored and carried. Every basket that is made in the Little Andaman, whether it be used for carrying a pot or for any other purpose, is made of exactly the same shape.

The purpose of the gap that is left near the top of the basket as described above is in order that strips of string or fibre may be tied across the mouth of the basket, from side to side, in order to keep its contents safe.

We may now return to the Great Andaman and consider the baskets of the South Andaman Group of tribes. These are made from the best canes. From 80 to 120 fine strips of cane are taken which are to form the stakes or uprights. A slight hollow is made in the ground, and the strips of cane are placed crossways across one another in this hollow, the inner surfaces of the canes being downwards. As the strips are being arranged, and when the weaving is begun, the centre, i.e., the point where the strips cross one another in the middle of the hollow, is pressed firmly beneath the heel so as to maintain them in position. The first few strips are sometimes tied together in the middle, but this is not always done. When all the strips are arranged evenly the weaving of the basket is begun with a length of thread, which is slewed in and out between the strips of cane, beginning as near the centre as possible, the stroke being that of ordinary wicker-work. After four or five spiral turns have been taken with the thread it is fastened. The bottom of the basket is then reversed, the stakes being bent over, and the weaving proper is begun with a fine strip of cane.

This is applied by wicker-work nearly as far as the top of the basket. At the top, the weaving is finished off with three or four spiral turns of wrapped-twined work in cane (see Fig. 35). The rim of the basket is formed of a thin piece of wood (circular in section) bent round into a circle of the right size and the two ends tied together. The stakes or uprights are attached to this rim (after the weaving is finished) but a space of about 5 cm. is left between the top of the weaving and

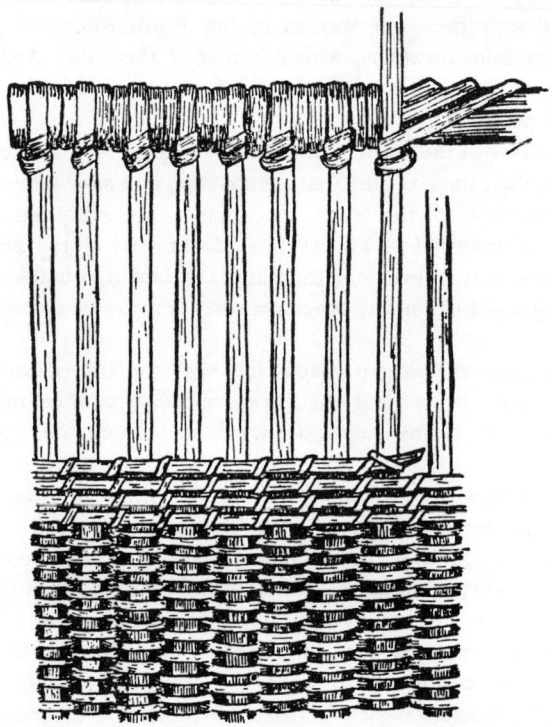

Fig. 35. Portion of basket of South Andaman

the rim. The mode of attaching the uprights to the rim is shown in Fig. 35.

The South Andaman basket is really a conical basket with the bottom reversed or dented inwards to form a "kick" like the kick of a bottle. If it were not for the kick it would be the same shape as the Little Andaman basket. The kick enables it to stand upright, although it is inclined to be top-heavy, but renders it unfit for carrying pots.

The space between the top of the weaving and the rim is to admit of strings being tied across the mouth of the basket to keep its contents safe.

A handle of *Hibiscus* fibre is attached to the rim and rests across the front of the chest when the basket is carried on the back.

South Andaman baskets are sometimes ornamented, in the process of making, with strips of *Dendrobium* skin, applied horizontally by overlaid interlacing. The strip of *Dendrobium* skin is laid over the weft and woven in with it for one turn round the basket. I have never seen ornamentation with *Dendrobium* skin applied to the South Andaman baskets by any method save this one.

Patterns of red paint and white clay are occasionally painted on baskets when they are newly made. Shells are sometimes attached to different parts of the basket by thread, for the purpose of ornament.

In the North Andaman, baskets are made that differ in several important features from those of the South Andaman. They are not made of cane but of two different materials. One of these is the stem of a creeper called *čup-tọi*. Lengths of the creeper are cut and dried and then split lengthways into two or three pieces according to their size. The outer bark or skin is then scraped off with a *Cyrena* shell. These strips are to form the stakes or warp of the basket. The other material is another creeper called *bobi*. The long tough tendrils of this plant are taken and the soft outer sheath removed by drawing the tendril through a piece of split cane or bamboo bent double so that the tendril is scraped between the two inner surfaces. The fibre that remains is split longitudinally into two pieces and dried.

A bundle of strips of the *čup-tọi* is taken, sufficient in length and number for the required size of basket. The bundle is divided into two equal bundles and these are tied together in the middle crossways with thread. This cross forms the beginning of the basket. The weaving is begun with thread, which is slewed in and out between the warp, from 4 to 7 spiral turns being made. During this process the centre of the basket, i.e., the cross, is pressed beneath the heel into a slight hollow made in the ground, to give it a curve which, in the finished basket, will form the "kick." The thread is tied, the bottom is turned upside down, the stakes are bent back and the weaving is continued, not with thread but with strips of *bobi*, till a short distance from the top of the basket, and then three or four rows of wrapped-twined work are made, the strip of *bobi* being coiled round the basket and attached to the uprights with thread. A rim is made of a strip of cane bent into a circle. This is placed inside the uprights and tied to them in two or three places. The remaining portion of each of the uprights, projecting above the rim, is bent down outside and slightly obliquely, and tied down by a thread passing over each in turn and round the rim. A very rough and untidy rim is thus produced, and this is again served or bound over with thread. A handle of *Hibiscus* fibre is added.

In the North Andaman baskets, as in those of the South Andaman, a space of a few centimetres is left between the top of the weaving and the rim, there being for that space only warp or uprights and no weft. This allows string to be tied in any direction across the mouth of the basket, so as to keep its contents safe.

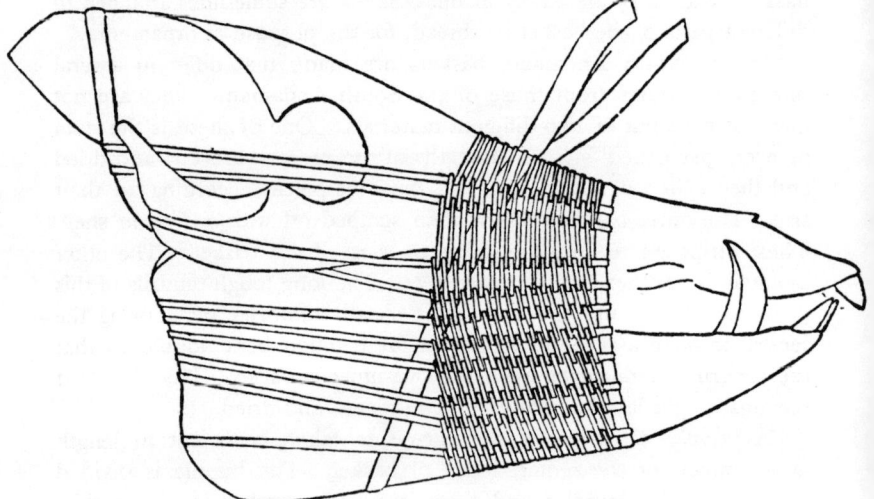

Fig. 36. Pig's skull with basket-work, Jarawa

The shape of the North Andaman baskets is different from that of the southern baskets, the former having a sort of belly at the bottom and narrowing somewhat above. The result is that the northern baskets will stand more firmly, being less top-heavy when either full or empty than those of the south.

In the North Andaman baskets are ornamented as they are made with worked-in strips of *Dendrobium* fibre. There are several different methods of working this ornamentation, resulting in different patterns. Baskets are also ornamented, when new, with painted patterns in white and red, though this is not general, and occasionally shells are attached to them by thread.

One more form of basket-work remains to be briefly mentioned. The natives of all parts of the islands were formerly in the habit of preserving as trophies the skulls of pigs and turtle that were killed in the chase. The natives of the Great Andaman Division do not now trouble to preserve all the skulls of the pigs they kill, and they give as their reason for this that now that they have dogs the hunting of pigs is not a sport that requires any great skill. The Jarawa however still keep up the old custom, and they go so far as carefully to encase every skull in basket-work. As may be seen from Fig. 36 the basket-work in question is of simple wrapped work, the material being strips of cane.

It is of some interest to consider the different forms of technique used by the Andamanese in dealing with flexible materials. Rope and string are only made two-ply. It would seem that the Andamanese have not discovered that three-ply cord is stronger for a given diameter than two-ply. They have, in the bow-string of the Great Andaman, an interesting form of cord that may perhaps best be described as wrapped cord. The making of a rope involves the twisting of two strands of material around one another. The making of a wrapped cord involves the spiral wrapping of one strand of material round another. This is exactly the same process as "serving," and it is one that is used by the Andamanese in all sorts of ways. In serving their arrows with thread and in serving the ends of bows and the heads of harpoons the Andamanese have several different methods of making fast the ends, and I regret that I did not take more detailed notes on this subject. Their skill in handling this technique is shown in the strength of the binding on their arrows.

This spiral wrapping of one strand round a flexible or rigid object lies at the base of much else in their technique. We have seen that they make considerable use of wrapped-twined work. In this work a strip of material crosses at right angles a number of strips of the same or other material, and a weft is wound round the former, taking in one of the latter at each turn. There are two methods of doing this, either by simple spiral wrapping, as in the mats of thatch, or by what may be called "right and left" or "zig-zag" wrapping, as in the bamboo mat of the Little Andaman. A difference is also made according as the strip of material around which the weft is wrapped is rigid, as in the Little Andaman bamboo mat or in thatching, or flexible, as in the North Andaman mat, where it is one thread while the weft is another thread.

Wrapped work, in which a strip of weft is wound successively round one after another of a number of rigid stakes, is another very simple process that is employed in a number of different ways by the Andamanese. The most important development of wrapped work amongst them is seen in the pot-basket of the South Andaman, in the baskets of the Jarawa and Little Andaman and in the pig's-skull basket-work of the Jarawa.

Simple twined work is rare in the Andamans. There is hardly any example of it except in the mats of the South Andaman. It would seem probable that the North Andaman mat technique of wrapped-twined work is the earlier, being more in agreement with what we may call the technical habits of the Andamanese, and that the South Andaman mat technique is a later elaboration. In this connection it may be remembered that plaiting, in which also several wefts are twisted one over another, is rarely used in the Andamans.

The process of nippering, by which the natives of the Great Andaman make the cord of their pig-arrows, and the somewhat similar process used in the Little Andaman in making personal ornaments, are quite in accordance with the general trend of the technique, but when such a process is applied to a number of parallel strips of material instead of to two only it constitutes a step towards wicker-work. It is notable, however, that it is only in the Great Andaman that wicker-work is used, and this suggests that it has only been invented or adopted since the separation of the two divisions of the Andamanese.

It is very tempting to regard the different forms of basket, in the order in which they are described above, as so many stages of a process of evolution. It is, at any rate, worth while to state the argument, and to show what the differences between them exactly are. In the North Andaman pot-covering we have (1) the technique simple wrapped work, and (2) the basis six strips of cane tied together in the middle. In the South Andaman pot-basket we have both these features, but the difference in the shape of the pots allows them to be carried in a true basket and we have therefore (3) a rim, with (4) a peculiar method of attaching the uprights to the rim, (5) a number of horizontal (wrapped) wefts instead of one or two, and (6) strengthening strips applied to the horizontal wefts in wrapped work. In the rougher kind of basket made in the Little Andaman we have nearly all the features of the South Andaman pot-basket. The only differences, apart from the shape of the basket, which in each case follows the shape of the pot, are (2) more than six uprights may be used, and (5) the number of horizontal wefts, i.e. the number of spiral turns taken round the basket, is as a rule greater. In the more carefully made Little Andaman basket there are several differences. The uprights are fine whole canes instead of strips of split cane. It is undoubtedly more difficult to procure whole canes of the proper size than simply to split up larger canes, but where the technique is wrapped work the circular section of the uprights improves the quality of the resulting basket, as a strip of cane is more easily wound round a whole cane than round a split cane, and there is less chance of it breaking when a strain is put upon it. Another difference is that in the better Little Andaman baskets the rows of weft are as close together as the peculiar technique will allow. This makes a finer and stronger basket, and is an obvious improvement. The third difference is that in these baskets the strengthening strips are applied not in wrapped work, but in wrapped-twined work, which, however, we have seen is a common technique in the Andamans. In the better baskets of the Little Andaman we find a special feature of some interest in the gap that is left in the weaving near the rim, to allow of strings being tied across the mouth.

When we look at the South Andaman basket the first thing that strikes us is that it is really a conical basket of much the same shape as the Little Andaman basket, but with the bottom dented in to make a kick, so allowing the basket to stand on its bottom. This denting is only rendered possible, however, by the fact that the uprights of the South Andaman basket are thin strips of cane that can be easily bent, and this again depends on the use of wicker-work in the basket instead of wrapped work. It must be remembered that the top of the weaving is finished off with three rows of wrapped-twined work, and this suggests that there may possibly have been a stage of development between the Little Andaman basket and the South Andaman form, in which the uprights were thin strips of cane, and the weft was applied in wrapped-twined work from top to bottom. This, however, is only a surmise. It does certainly seem probable that the South Andaman basket is derived immediately from a form of basket similar to that of the Little Andaman, the great difference being the change to wicker-work technique. The method of attaching the uprights to the rim was doubtless introduced owing to the fact that the original method is unsatisfactory when the uprights are thin and easily broken strips, instead of stout ones.

The North Andaman basket seems to have been derived from one similar to that of the South Andaman by the introduction of two changes, (1) the use of different materials, and (2) the change of shape. The materials used in the north are such as to give a basket on the whole stronger and more durable than that of the south. If a heavy weight be carried in a southern basket the pressure of the basket on the back tends to crack the canes of which it is composed. In the case of a northern basket it may lose its shape, but the materials of which it is composed will give or bend without cracking so readily. The shape of the northern basket is certainly an improvement, as it avoids the top-heaviness of the southern shape. Both the northern and the southern baskets have a gap between the top of the weaving and the rim, like the basket of the Little Andaman.

Thus every step, or nearly every step, in a hypothetical process of evolution is exhibited in the different forms of basket-work. First we have the pot-covering of the North Andaman, then the pot-basket of the South Andaman, then the rougher kind of Little Andaman basket, of the same shape as the pot, then the South Andaman basket of cane with a kick and finally the basket of the North Andaman. The better kind of Little Andaman basket is simply an independent improvement of the other, involving no new technique.

However much or little probability we may attach to this hypothetical reconstruction of the history of basket-work in the Andamans, one thing does seem fairly certain, and that is that the original ancestors of the Andamanese were not acquainted with wicker-work, or had no use for it. In the Little Andaman Division only wrapped work and wrapped-twined work are used, and the wicker-work of the Great Andaman Division has almost certainly been adopted since the two divisions were separated. The consideration of the general technical bias of the Andamanese in their dealings with flexible materials supports the view that in their case wicker-work is later than wrapped work and wrapped-twined work. It seems more than likely that the Andamanese of the larger island have invented wicker-work in its simplest form on the basis of a previous technique of wrapped and wrapped-twined work. To us wicker-work seems such a simple process as almost to need no inventing. It must be recognized however that the general bias of the Andamanese is against using materials in this way. The Andaman Islander shows a decided preference for those processes in which he uses a single flexible material which he winds or wraps round other rigid or flexible material, as in nippering, or wrapped work or wrapped-twined work.

It is impossible to obtain confirmation of this view, however, from a comparison of the Andamanese with the Semang and the Philippine Negritos. The Semang make mat-work bags and wallets of check, and they make (or use) baskets of hexagonal work. Both check and hexagonal work are used by other races in the Malay Peninsula and in Malaysia generally. The present mats and baskets of the Semang cannot therefore be regarded as original Negrito productions. They have almost certainly been adopted through contact with other cultures.

The same thing would seem to apply to the present basket-work of the Philippine Negritos, of which however we know very little.

Netted bags of string are made by the women of both the Great Andaman and the Little Andaman Divisions, and are used for carrying or storing small objects such as shells, fruit, roots, etc. The string used for these is made from the fibre of the *Gnetum edule* in the Little

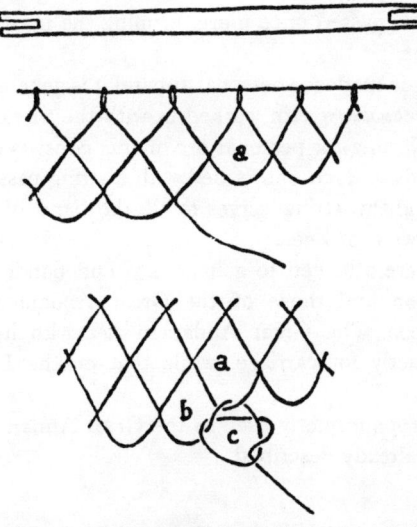

Fig. 37. Diagram showing netting needle, and method of netting

Andaman, and is generally made from the same fibre in the Great Andaman, but in the latter division the fibre of *Hibiscus scandens* is prized for this purpose and is used instead of that of the *Gnetum* when it is available. Small hand fishing nets are made by the women in both divisions from thread of *Gnetum* fibre. In the Great Andaman Division netting is also used for personal ornaments, the thread used for this purpose being generally made from *Anadendron* fibre.

The mode of netting is always the same. Netting needles are used, made from slips of bamboo or cane, and varying in size according to the work for which they are intended. The netting string or thread is wound on to this needle. For the foundation of the net a short length of string is taken and the two ends tied together, the loop thus formed being placed over the big toe as the woman sits on the ground.

The knot used in netting is that known as the fisherman's knot, in use all over the world. The needle is held in the right hand, is passed from above downwards through the loop marked a in the figure, and is drawn through far enough to leave a new loop b of the required size. This loop is held between the thumb and forefinger of the left hand, the uniformity in mesh being apparently obtained largely by the sense of touch. The needle is then passed through the new loop b again from above and is drawn out leaving a loop c, through which the needle is passed once more, forming the finished knot, which is then drawn taut.

When netting is made for personal apparel it is generally ornamented with strips of *Dendrobium* skin worked in with the thread in the course of the netting. Netting for personal ornaments consists of a sort of bag open at both ends. Each end is tied with a string passed through the ultimate loops, and this string serves to tie the band of net round the waist or neck or wrist or knee.

Fishing nets are attached to a handle. The handles of the Little Andaman Division and those of the Great Andaman Division are different in shape. The Great Andaman net with its hoop can be folded up compactly for carriage, while that of the Little Andaman cannot.

The nets of rope formerly used in the Great Andaman for catching turtle have been already described.

Domestic Implements and Utensils.

The Andamanese are perhaps the only people in the world who have no method of their own of making fire. At the present time they obtain matches from the Settlement of Port Blair, and a few of them have learnt, either from Burmese or from Nicobarese, a method of making fire by the friction of pieces of split bamboo. Formerly, however, they had no knowledge of any method by which fire could be produced. Fires were and still are carefully kept alive in the village, and are carefully carried when travelling. Every hunting party carries its fire with it. The natives are very skilful in selecting wood that will smoulder for a long time without going out and without breaking into flame.

The most interesting of the Andamanese domestic utensils is undoubtedly the cooking-pot. Pots are made in all parts of the Andamans where suitable clay is to be found. The clay is obtained and is freed as far as possible from stones and gritty matter with the hands. It is then moistened with water and kneaded on a board consisting of a portion of a broken canoe. It is worked very stiff and after kneading is rolled beneath the palm of the hand into long thin rolls. These are built up into a pot by coiling, the requisite degree of thickness being obtained by pressure of the thumb and first finger. When the pot has been built up to the required size and shape, the surface, inside and out, is moistened and is scraped over in all directions with an *Arca* shell. The pot is dried in the sun for a few hours and is then baked by placing inside and around it pieces of burning wood. The pot often cracks in the baking, and another has to be made.

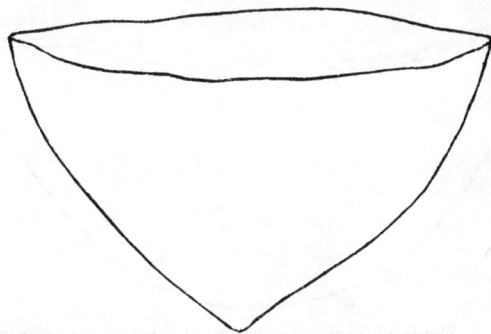

Fig. 38. Shape of North Andaman pot; actual diameter 17 cm.

In the North Andaman the pots are made with pointed bottoms, and are generally small, the largest having a capacity of only six or seven pints. They are made by women only. In the South Andaman the pots have rounded bottoms and, on the average, are larger and thicker than those of the North Andaman. They are made by both men and women, the best being made by men. In the Little Andaman the pots are larger, and, particularly, deeper than those of the South Andaman, and have somewhat pointed bottoms. The pots of the Jarawa are similar to those of the Little Andaman.

In the North Andaman pots are not ornamented, but in the South Andaman they are decorated with usually simple patterns of dots and lines made with a small pointed stick. The Little Andaman pots that I have seen were not decorated.

The pots are used for cooking, i.e. for boiling meat and vegetables. In the North Andaman small pots are specially made for melting the composition used for covering the binding on the heads of arrows.

Neither the Semang nor the Philippine Negritos make any kind of pottery. The origin of Andamanese pottery therefore is a problem of some interest. It is almost certain that the early Andamanese were acquainted with pottery before they were divided into the Great Andaman and Little Andaman Divisions. One of the very few words which is the same in all Andamanese languages is the word for pot, *buču* in the Little Andaman, *buj* in Aka-Bea and *peč* in Aka-Jeru The most reasonable hypothesis would therefore seem to be that the Andamanese learnt the method of making pottery by coiling before they reached the Andaman Islands but after they had become separated

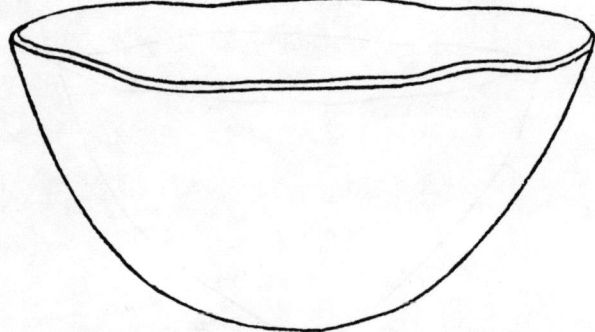

Fig. 39. Shape of South Andaman pot; actual diameter 24 cm.

from that part of the Negrito race from which the Semang and the Philippine Negritos are descended. Of course it is possible that the art of pottery may have been an original possession of the Negritos and that the Semang and Philippine Negritos may have lost it. A people could easily lose the art if they were compelled in the course of their migrations to spend three or four generations in a region that lacked clay suitable for the purpose.

The Andamanese make buckets of wood, which they use for carrying and holding a supply of water. A solid piece is cut from the trunk of a soft-wooded tree and is hollowed out with a chisel made by attaching the blade of an adze to a stick. The natural form of the wood is retained, only the bark being removed from the outside while the inside is chiselled out to leave sides of about a centimetre thick and a bottom of somewhat greater thickness. In order to render the bottom of the bucket water-tight the natives of the Little Andaman pour over it on the inside melted bees'-wax. The natives of the Great Andaman use for this purpose the same composition with which they cover the bindings of their arrows, which certainly is superior to bees'-wax.

A bucket of the shape used in the Great Andaman is shown in Plate VII, on the left. A strip of cane is attached round the middle of the bucket, and to this in turn is attached another strip of cane which, being passed across the front of the chest, enables the bucket to be carried on the back.

The buckets of the Little Andaman are cut with thinner sides than those of the Great Andaman. A strip of cane is fastened round the bucket near the top. From this two other strips of cane are attached by both ends, passing under the bottom, and a third strip is attached which passes over the head and supports the bucket when it is carried on the back. In the Little Andaman the outside of the bucket is charred with fire.

Occasionally pieces of the giant bamboo, which does not grow in the Andamans, are found on the shore, having drifted from the Burma coast. When a sound piece is found it is made into buckets each formed of a single joint.

Water vessels are made from bamboos that do grow in the islands. A length of bamboo of good diameter is cut, containing three joints. The partition of the lowest node is preserved to serve as a bottom, and the other partitions are broken through with an arrow. This is the usual vessel used for carrying water on a journey by land or in a canoe, and for keeping a supply of drinking water in the hut.

A single joint of the same kind of bamboo is used as a cooking vessel. It is cleaned, washed, and dried, and is then filled with meat tightly packed. The top is closed with leaves and the bamboo is placed on the fire until the meat is cooked. Meat is not cooked in this way for immediate consumption. It will keep for twenty-four hours or even longer if not opened. To obtain the contents the bamboo is split open with an adze.

Trays used for food are cut from soft wood of a species of *Sterculia* with an adze. They are shallow and somewhat long and narrow, with pointed ends.

A large *Pinna* shell is occasionally used as a tray or dish for holding food, or for mixing clay with water for painting. A *Nautilus* shell forms a fairly convenient cup or drinking vessel and is frequently used for that purpose, as well as for baling out water from a canoe.

Bamboo tongs are made by bending double a piece split from a bamboo, and cutting the ends to the required shape. They are used for lifting from the fire anything too hot to be taken in the hand and are chiefly of service in cooking.

Digging sticks are made from various kinds of wood, being simply pointed at one or both ends. These sticks are not as a rule preserved, but made as required with an adze and thrown away after use. They are used for digging up edible roots.

Hooks for picking fruit, such as the *Artocarpus*, are made by attaching a small piece of wood to the end of a bamboo. Hooks for catching crabs are made from the wood of the *Rhizophora* by taking advantage of the natural form where a small branch joins a larger one.

The fan-shaped leaf of a *Licuala* palm is made use of in many ways. The edges of the leaflets are sewn together with fine strips of cane, and the sewn leaf is then used either as a sunshade or umbrella for protection from sunshine or rain, as a sleeping mat if the proper article be lacking, as a screen to make the roof or sides of a hut more wind or rain proof, as a wrapper for making objects of all sorts into bundles, and as a winding sheet for a corpse.

Torches are made from resin, which is broken into small pieces and wrapped up in leaves of a species of *Crinum* (? *lorifolium*), a few pieces of smouldering charcoal being added before it is tied up. The torch is then parcelled by marling with a strip of cane or a length of some tough creeper. These resin torches are used in turtle-hunting and fishing expeditions on dark nights.

Other torches are made of fragments of rotten *Dipterocarpus* wood. They are used only in the village.

PERSONAL ORNAMENT; GREAT ANDAMAN.

At the present time the natives of the Great Andaman Division obtain from the Settlement of Port Blair cloth which both men and women wear round the loins. They also obtain beads from which they make necklaces.

The following is a list of the various personal ornaments made by the natives of the Great Andaman Division, and worn by them.

Rope girdle. Every man wears some sort of girdle round his waist, and this was formerly the only object that was constantly worn by men. The girdle may consist of a length of rope of *Hibiscus* fibre or a length of ornamental cord made by wrapping the yellow skin of the *Dendrobium* over two strands of *Hibiscus* fibre and then twisting these into a two-ply cord.

Necklaces and garters of string. Both men and women are often to be seen with a simple piece of string, usually of *Anadendron* fibre, tied round the neck or around the leg just below the knee.

Ornaments of *Pandanus* leaf. Every married woman always wears a belt of *Pandanus* leaf which she is never without for even a moment. When the belt she is wearing needs renewing she puts the new one on before taking the other off. To make such a belt two leaves of the *Pandanus Andamanensium* are taken and cut to a sufficient length (about 20 cm.). The thorns at the edge of the leaf are removed by cutting off a strip of about 3 mm. wide from the edge, leaving a strip of leaf about 4 cm. broad. The two leaves are placed one on the other and are wound spirally round in three turns so as to give a belt of six thicknesses of leaf, the upper surface of the leaf being on the outside of the belt. The leaves are secured together by tying with thread at the back where the two ends just overlap. At the point where the leaves are tied one or two bundles of strips of *Pandanus* leaf are attached with thread. The bundle is made of a number of strips of leaf about 90 cm. long and 2·5 cm. broad which are chewed in the mouth to make them soft and then placed together and served over with thread for about 12 cm. in the middle. Belts of this kind are generally worn by married women, but precisely similar belts are worn by men on certain ceremonial occasions. They are called *toto t'er-bua* in Aka-Jeru.

A very similar belt is made in exactly the same way save that the tassel of leaves at the back consists of narrow strips of *Pandanus* leaf instead of broad strips. This kind of belt is worn by women only. Examples may be seen in Plate IV (the lower belt of the two) and in Plate XVIII. It is called *toto t'er-nyarab* in Aka-Jeru.

A belt is made in much the same way out of *Pandanus* leaves split in half down the midrib, giving strips of about 2·5 cm. broad. Such belts have only a scanty tassel of thin strips of leaf at the back. They are worn by girls and women only. They are called *kudu* in Aka-Jeru.

Yet another variety of belt is made of whole leaves in exactly the same way as the *toto t'er-bua* but has no tassel at the back. An example may be seen in Plate IV (the upper belt). It is worn by women.

Girdles are made of strips of *Pandanus* leaf of about 1·25 cm. broad without any tassel, but with strings of *Dentalium* shell attached at various points. A girdle of this kind is shown in Plate XV.

Girdles are also made by cutting a number of strips of leaf and softening them by chewing them in the mouth. These strips are laid together and either served over or marled with thread so as to make a girdle of round section. A tassel of leaves similar to that of the *toto t'er-bua* is attached to the back, and very frequently strings of *Dentalium* shell are attached at various points. Such a girdle may be worn by either men or women. It is called *toto t'er-ŋau* in Aka-Jeru.

Yet another kind of girdle is made by splitting *Pandanus* leaves into thin strips and making them into a kind of wrapped cord, one strip being wrapped spirally round one or more others by the same technique as that used in making bow-strings. A number of coils of strands made in this way are tied together with thread at various points and a tassel similar to that of the *toto t'er-bua* is added at the back. Such girdles are usually improved by the addition of a few pendent strings of *Dentalium* shell. They may be worn by either men or women. Their name in Aka-Jeru is *toto t'er-moi*.

Ornaments of *Pandanus* leaf to be worn either round the leg just below the knee or round the wrist are made in exactly the same way as the belt called *toto t'er-bua*, each having a tassel of *Pandanus* leaf strips attached. Such garters and bracelets are worn at a dance by men.

Other ornaments for wearing round the wrist or knee when dancing are made by the same method as the girdle called *toto t'er-ŋau*, each having a tassel of strips of leaf.

Similar dancing ornaments are made by plaiting strips of leaf into a three-plait cord of the right length, a tassel of loose leaf strips being left at each end. These are tied round the wrist or knee.

Ornaments for the knee or wrist, such as those shown on the legs of the man in Plate XII, are made by winding spirally a narrow strip of leaf and sewing it. A number of pendent strings of *Dentalium* shell are attached round it, and often strings are attached at the end of which small shells hang suspended which rattle against one another as the wearer walks or dances.

Chaplets or headdresses worn by men when dancing, and occasionally by women, are made of fairly broad strips of leaf in the same way as the *toto t'er-bua*. Such a chaplet may have a tassel of narrow strips of *Pandanus* leaf at the back to which are attached shells that rattle as the wearer moves, or it may have pendent strings of *Dentalium* shells round the hinder half of its circumference.

In making ornaments of *Pandanus* leaf such as the *toto t'er-bua* the upper surface of the strip of leaf is usually ornamented with a design scratched on it with a pointed piece of wood. The design usually covers not only the portion of leaf that is visible when the belt or other object is finished, but also that portion which is not visible, being underneath. Many ornaments of this kind are further decorated when finished with the composition used for covering the bindings of arrows, which is applied with a pointed stick in simple geometrical patterns. The woman shown in Plate x is wearing two belts that have been ornamented with composition in this way.

Woman's leaf apron. In the South Andaman the women wear a sort of small apron consisting of a number of leaves of the *Mimusops littoralis* laid one over the other, the stalk ends of the leaves being tucked in between the layers of a belt of *Pandanus* leaf. The leaves thus hang suspended so as to cover, somewhat inadequately, the pudenda. The natives say that the leaves of the *Mimusops* are chosen because they remain green longer than those of any other species. As soon as the leaves fade and turn yellow they are renewed. The appearance of the leaf apron may be seen in Plates iv and xv.

The women of the North Andaman have within recent years adopted the fashion of those of the South Andaman in this matter, but formerly they made a similar use of a different kind of leaf from a plant called *čainyo* in Aka-Jeru, and over the top of the leaves they wore a tassel of the fibre called *ḳoro*.

Ornaments of netting and *Dentalium* shells. Bands of netting (in shape of a cylinder or bag open at both ends) are made of suitable size to tie round the waist, the neck, the leg below the knee or the wrist. Such netting is generally ornamented as it is being made with strips of *Dendrobium* skin worked in the net. Along the lower edge of the band of netting are attached a number of threads each having *Dentalium* shells strung on to it like beads. Ornaments of this kind are shown in Plates v and ix. They are worn by both men and women, but usually only on the occasion of a dance or some other ceremony.

Ornaments of bone, etc. These are made with human bones, with the bones of such animals as pig, turtle, dugong, *Paradoxurus*, monitor lizard, or with pieces of wood or cane, or of coral, of suitable shape. A length of cord, of the fibre of the *Hibiscus tiliaceus* or of the *Ficus laccifera*, is taken, and the bones are attached to it by thread. As a rule, strips of *Dendrobium* skin are worked in, being laid on the bone and bound over with the thread.

Ornaments of shell. Various kinds of shells are perforated and attached to string and are worn round the neck, the head, the knee, or the wrist. A necklace of fresh-water shells (*ino kolo toi* in Aka-Jeru) is shown in Plate IX. A necklace of small sea-shells is shown in Plate XIII. The favourite shell of the Great Andaman tribes is the *Dentalium octogonum*. The shells are collected from the shore by the women. The closed end of each is bitten off with the teeth and the shells, which thus form cylindrical beads, are strung on to a piece of thread. These strings of shell are worn as necklaces, as shown in Plates IV and XII, and are tied round the wrist and knee and ankle as shown in Plate IV.

Ornaments of seed. The seed-tops of two or three species of mangrove are collected and strung on to thread and worn round the neck. Fig. 40 shows the two kinds of mangrove seed commonly used in this way.

Bamboo necklaces. A necklace is sometimes made of a number of short pieces of bamboo arrow-shaft threaded on to a string. The pieces of bamboo are ornamented with simple designs scratched or cut on them with a shell.

Sling of bark. Another object that may perhaps be mentioned amongst objects of personal ornament is the sling used in carrying children. It is made of a broad strip of the bark of the *Hibiscus tiliaceus*. Some slings are covered entirely with netting, while others are ornamented with shells in various ways. Plate XIV shows one with strings of *Dentalium* shell sewn on to it.

Dancing ornaments of *Tetranthera* wood. A piece of *Tetranthera* wood, usually part of the shaft of an old pig-arrow, about 30 to 35 cm. long, is taken and made into shavings with a *Cyrena* shell. The wood is shaved carefully round and round, so as to make a continuous sheet of fibre, as though unwinding a roll of material. A bundle of these shavings is tied at one end and covered with red paint, and forms an object that is carried in the hand or worn in the belt at dances.

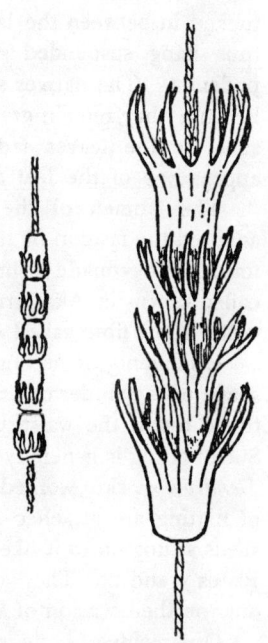

Fig. 40. Necklaces of mangrove seed-tops, Great Andaman

PERSONAL ORNAMENT; LITTLE ANDAMAN.

The personal ornaments of the Little Andaman and of the Jarawa are different from those of the Great Andaman Division, and therefore need to be described separately.

Ornaments of bark. Strips of bark (? *Celtis cinnamonea*) are worn by the men round the waist and round the arm.

Ornamental cord. These are the ornaments most frequently met with both in the Little Andaman and amongst the Jarawa. The basis is a strip of cane, varying in breadth in different examples. On one side of this are laid strips of the yellow skin of the *Dendrobium*, varying in number according to the breadth of the cane, and the whole is served over or bound with thread. The technique in shown in Fig. 41, which represents diagrammatically the method adopted when there are two strips of *Dendrobium* skin. . Such ornamental cord is made in pieces of considerable length. Often tassels of thread (of *Ficus hispida* fibre) are attached to it at intervals. The cord is worn wound round the waist, the neck, or the arm. Both men and women wear it.

Woman's girdle. In the Little Andaman this is made of a number of fine strips of cane tied together with thread. At the front is attached

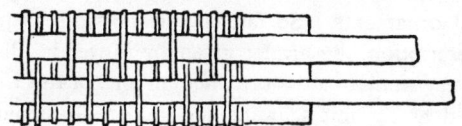

Fig. 41. Diagram showing method of making ornamental cord, Little Andaman

a tassel of fibre made from young unopened palm-leaves (the fibre called *kọro* in Aka-Jeru).

Woman's shoulder strap. The women of the Little Andaman wear a strip of bark over the shoulders, crossing over the chest and passing beneath the breasts.

The above brief description of the ornaments of the Andamanese is perhaps sufficient for the purpose of this appendix, which is to determine as far as possible the elements of a primitive Negrito culture. Any complete account of the subject would need a large number of figures and a discussion of many comparatively unimportant details. The first point of importance to be noted is that the personal ornaments of the Little Andaman Division differ markedly from those of the Great Andaman Division. One difference is that the *Pandanus* leaf, which is used so much and in so many ways in the Great Andaman, seems not to be used at all in the Little Andaman. Another is that shells, which are much used in the Great Andaman, are used to a far less extent in the Little Andaman. The natives of the Little Andaman told me that they sometimes make ornaments of *Dentalium* shell, but I did not see any such ornament, nor any other ornament of shell, in use. The ornaments of netting worn in the Great Andaman, and forming the usual dancing costume, seem not to be used in the Little Andaman. Finally, perhaps most important of all, there is at present no evidence that the natives of the Little Andaman make ornaments of either human or animal bones. In the Little Andaman the lower jaw of a child is preserved by the parents and is worn by them, but I never saw a human skull (whether of child or adult) so worn, and I was not able to obtain any evidence of the use of strings of human bones such as are constantly seen in a camp of the Great Andaman.

The points of similarity between the ornaments of the Little Andaman and those of the Great Andaman are very few. One of the most striking is the great use that is made in both divisions of the yellow skin of the *Dendrobium*. It seems probable that here we have evidence of one element of a primitive Negrito culture, for the Negritos of the Philippines also are fond of using a yellow vegetable fibre for their personal ornaments. So far as it is possible to judge from the figure and description, the armlet given by Meyer in Plate III, No. 11, seems to be very similar to the ornamental cord of the Little Andaman. It is described as a "mit schwarz und gelben Grasstreifchen umflocktener Bambus-reif."

Another point of resemblance between the Great Andaman and the Little Andaman is that in both very little use is made of feathers or flowers. The natives of the Great Andaman never make use of the feathers of birds. The Jarawa occasionally wear in a chaplet a feather of the king-crow (*Dicrurus macrocercus*) if we may judge from a specimen in the British Museum. The natives of the Little Andaman certainly do not as a rule make any use of feathers. It would seem, from all accounts, that the Semang and the Philippine Negritos do not make any considerable use of feathers for personal ornament. We may perhaps hazard the conclusion that this is a mark of the Negrito culture distinguishing them from such people as the Papuans or Australians in whose personal ornaments the feathers of birds occupy an important place.

In the Great Andaman flowers are not used as personal ornaments. In the British Museum there is an ornament from the Little Andaman consisting of a strip of bark-fibre with a few flowers attached.

As regards personal ornament, therefore, the only elements of a primitive Negrito culture that we seem to be able to trace in the Andamans at the present day are (1) the use of yellow vegetable fibre, and (2) the absence of any considerable use of feathers.

One element of a primitive Andamanese culture, though not necessarily of a primitive Negrito culture, would seem to be the use of a tassel of the fibre obtained from an unopened palm-leaf which is used by women to cover their genitals in the Little Andaman, and was similarly used until recently in the North Andaman.

HAIR-DRESSING, SCARIFICATION, AND BODY-PAINTING.

At the present time the usual method of hair-dressing in the Great Andaman is to shave a portion of the scalp all round so as to leave a sort of skull-cap of hair, as may be seen in many of the plates of this volume. In some cases a "parting" is made by shaving a narrow strip over the crown. (See Plate xv, for example.) When the hair grows so long as to be uncomfortable the whole head is shaved, and it is then permitted to grow again. In these days the natives cut their hair whenever they have an opportunity of obtaining a pair of scissors. In the Little Andaman women and old men are frequently to be seen with the head entirely shaved. The younger men shave away the lower edge of the hair all round in the same way as the natives of the Great Andaman, but this may be a recent practice.

The fashion of hair-dressing, at any rate for women, has changed within recent times, for Mr Man wrote in 1882 that "the majority of the women every week or ten days shave their heads almost entirely, leaving only two narrow parallel lines of hair, termed *gor*, from the crown to the nape of the neck[1]." At the present time this style of hair-dressing has fallen entirely into disuse, and the women do their hair in the same way as the men.

The operation of shaving, which is done with a flake of glass or quartz, is performed by women, and never, or very rarely, by men.

Mention has been made in an earlier part of the work of the way in which the natives of the Great Andaman scarify the skin of the body and limbs with a flake of glass or quartz. The Semang do not scarify themselves in this way, but some, at any rate, of the Negritos of the Philippines do.

The natives of the Great Andaman, as described earlier in this work, paint their bodies with a grey clay called *odu* or *og*, with a fine

---

[1] Man, *op. cit.* p. 77.

white clay, and with red paint made by mixing burnt oxide of iron with fat or oil. The natives of the Little Andaman use the same kind of clay as that called *odu* or *og* in the Great Andaman, but instead of applying it in patterns they smear it roughly on the back and front of the trunk. They also use red paint, with which they smear their hair, a practice never met with in the Great Andaman.

ORNAMENTATION.

The Andamanese have simple designs which they paint or incise

Fig. 42. Designs incised or painted on belts of *Pandanus* leaf, Great Andaman

on their bodies and on a great number of the objects that they make and use. A few typical designs such as are incised or painted on belts of *Pandanus* leaf are shown in Fig. 42. A very large number of designs are based on the zig-zag line. Examples are shown in Fig. 42 *c*, *e*, and *g*. In all parts of the Great Andaman and also in the Little Andaman the zig-zag line is associated with snakes. Thus in the Little Andaman the simple zig-zag line is called *dobo kwolage* (*dobo* = snake). In the North Andaman the design of zig-zag lines painted on the body with white clay is called *or-čubi t'era-bat*, *or-čubi* being the name of a species of large snake.

A number of other common designs consist of parallel lines of dots or of short strokes, an example of which is shown in Fig. 42 *f.*

By far the greater number of the Andamanese designs are based on the following elements, (1) parallel lines crossing a surface from side to side at right angles to the edge or else in a sloping direction (about 45°), (2) parallel lines of dots or of short lines, i.e. parallel broken lines, as in Fig. 42 *f,* (3) zig-zag lines, which may be single, or parallel or opposed so as to make lines of lozenges. As an example of the way in which these elements may be combined two designs copied from bamboo necklaces are shown in Fig. 43.

It would perhaps be possible to show that there is a real connection between the ornamentation of the Andamanese and that of the Semang, as there is certainly a considerable degree of superficial resemblance, but at present we understand so little the psychological processes underlying the use of ornament amongst primitive peoples that the subject is one of considerable difficulty.

Fig. 43. Designs on bamboo necklace from the North Andaman

CANOES.

Canoes are in regular use on the coast in all parts of the islands. There are three types of canoe. (1) The Little Andaman canoe, with one outrigger, propelled with paddles or with a pole. (2) The Great Andaman small canoe, with one outrigger, propelled with paddles or with a pole. (3) The Great Andaman large canoe, without outrigger, propelled with oars.

The third kind of canoe mentioned above is a recent innovation. The natives themselves say that such canoes have only been made in recent times, since they have been able to obtain a plentiful supply of iron tools, and so have been able to cut down and hollow out large trunks[1]. They seem to have been invented by the natives of the South Andaman, and copied by those of the Middle and North Andaman.

[1] Man, *Journ. Anthr. Inst.* XII, p. 367, note 4.

Canoes of this type are propelled by rowing with short oars, except in shallow water where they are poled. This method of propulsion (rowing as opposed to paddling) was adopted in imitation of the boats with which they have become familiar since the European occupation.

For the small canoe of the Great Andaman five or six species of soft-wooded trees are used, of which three are species of *Sterculia*. A suitable tree is selected near the shore or a creek, and is felled. Care is taken to make it fall in a particular direction. Thus, if the trunk is curved, the convex side of the curve will have to be the bottom of the canoe, and the tree should fall so that this side lies on the ground. Trees are very rarely regular and before beginning the work of cutting the natives have to decide how it should be cut so as to give the best result, i.e., the greatest stability.

After the tree is felled the trunk is cut to the requisite length. The inside of the canoe is first roughly hollowed out with the adze, no use being made of fire. The bark is then removed from the outside of the trunk and the two ends are shaped. Finally, the inside is carefully finished with the adze so as to reduce the sides and bottom to the requisite thickness.

Except at the stem and stern, the canoe retains the shape of the tree, only the bark being removed, and the sides and bottom being formed of the alburnum or sap-wood. At the stern a small platform is cut projecting over the water, which serves as a seat for the steersman. At the prow a larger platform is cut, on which the harpooner stands when he is harpooning turtle or fish. Below these two platforms the ends are not cut away squarely but are rounded from side to side. The prow of the canoe is in every case the lower and therefore broader end of the trunk. It is only in this way that a sufficiently large platform can be provided for the harpooner.

The trees used for canoes have a pithy core and there is therefore a small patch in both the prow and the stern which would admit the water. In former times these two places were caulked with bees'-wax. At the present time the natives often nail a piece of tin (part of an old kerosene tin, for example), with some rags beneath it, on the outside of the canoe at these two places.

When the hull of the canoe is finished it is moved to the shore or to the bank of a creek and the outrigger is attached. The float is a straight spar of light wood. In the North Andaman the wood of the *Hibiscus tiliaceus* is often used, but Mr Man says that in the South Andaman the float is always made from a species of *Sterculia* (*mai* in

Aka-Bea)[1]. The ends of the float are only roughly shaped. The broader end of the float is forward.

The float is attached to a number of booms, of which there are never less than three in the smallest canoes, while there may be as many as eight or nine in a large canoe. A medium-sized canoe has five or six booms. The boom is a thin straight piece of tough wood, of which one end is sharpened and thrust right through two holes cut in the gunwales of the canoe opposite to one another, the sharpened end projecting for a few inches on the port side of the canoe. The boom thus projects about three feet on the starboard side on the level of the gunwale.

Where the boom passes through the gunwales of the canoe it is bound with cane, and the cane is bound round the whole of that part of the boom that is within the canoe between the two gunwales. (See

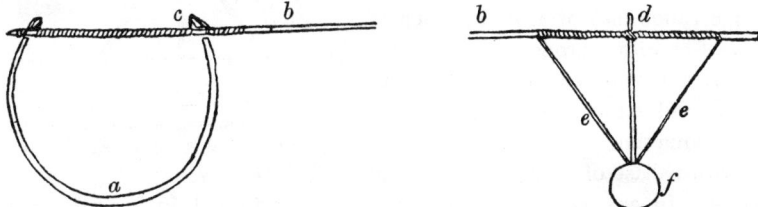

Fig. 44. Transverse section of canoe and outrigger. *a*, hull; *b*, boom; *c*, cane binding over boom; *d*, stick attaching boom to float; *e*, stays of cane; *f*, float

Fig. 44.) This portion of the boom forms a seat for the man paddling the canoe, so that he sits on a level with the gunwale with his feet on the floor of the canoe.

The boom is attached to the float by means of sticks of tough wood. These sticks, having pointed ends, are driven into the float, one perpendicular, and the other two at an angle on each side. The tops of the three sticks are fastened to the boom a few inches from its end by means of a strip of cane. The arrangement of the three sticks is shown in Fig. 45.

The strip of cane with which the sticks are bound to the boom is wound spirally round the boom itself for a few inches and is then carried down round the float and back to the boom again on the other side. The three sticks provide an efficient resistance against a longitudinal thrust (i.e., a thrust in the same direction as the line of the

[1] Man, *op. cit.* p. 397.

canoe). The strip of cane passing from the boom round the float and back to the boom again provides a resistance against any lateral thrust on the float. The three sticks, being driven in when the wood of the float is dry, do not readily work loose, as the water in which it is constantly immersed keeps the wood swollen. The cane binding, including the stays on each side, may work loose, but can readily be tightened or renewed. Each of the booms is attached to the float in exactly the same way, and the whole arrangement is very efficient in keeping the float rigidly attached to the hull in such a position that it rests on the surface of the water when the hull itself rides freely balanced.

Canoes of this type vary in dimensions within wide limits. A small canoe with only three booms, which would carry three persons, measured 4·85 metres in length over all with a beam of about 35 centimetres. A large canoe may measure as much as 9 metres with a proportionate beam.

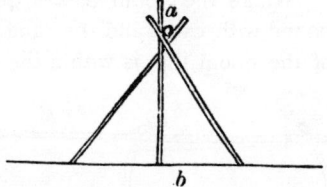

Fig. 45. Showing manner in which the boom (*a*) is connected with the float (*b*).

A well-made canoe will often balance well enough as it stands, but it is sometimes necessary to balance it with ballast of stones or pieces of coral. In any case the canoe is easily overturned in a rough sea unless the occupants can maintain the balance with their bodies. As the canoe is made of light wood it cannot sink even when full of water, and the natives easily right an overturned canoe, bale it out, and get in again, even in a rough sea.

The furniture of a canoe consists of the ballast (of stone), a piece of stone (or sometimes a piece of tin) on which to keep a small fire smouldering, an anchor consisting of a lump of coral or stone attached to a length of rope, a *Nautilus* shell or two for baling out the canoe, a bamboo pole of about 18 feet in length for poling the canoe in shallow water, and paddles.

In the platform overhanging the prow a few holes are cut. These holes are sometimes used to attach the rope by which the canoe is fastened to an anchor. One or more turtle skulls are often attached so as to hang down beneath the platform. In turtle-hunting expeditions on dark nights a torch is slung beneath the forward platform so as to shed its light on the water while the harpooner remains in shadow.

When a canoe is finished it is decorated with designs painted on it with red paint and white clay, particularly on the forward platform and along the gunwale. These designs soon wear off when the canoe is in use and are not renewed.

The paddles used by the Andamanese vary considerably in size and to some extent in shape, but the following description with its accompanying figure gives a fair idea of a typical specimen. The whole paddle has a length of 123·5 centimetres, the shaft being 85 centimetres and the blade 38·5 centimetres. The diameter of the shaft from the blade to the middle is 2·6 centimetres, and from the middle towards the handle end it tapers to a point. The shaft is circular in section throughout its length. The blade is leaf-shaped, pointed bluntly at the apex. In section it is plano-convex, with a maximum thickness of 1·3 centimetres and a width of 8·7 centimetres. Paddles are cut with an adze from the wood of the *Myristica longifolia* and planed with a boar's tusk. They are often ornamented, when new, with painted designs in red and white.

In deep water the canoe is paddled. Each of the occupants sits facing forward. The steersman sits on the stern platform. The others sit on the seats provided by the outrigger booms. Each man paddles on which side he chooses. It rests with the steersman to maintain the canoe in its proper course. In shallow water the canoe is propelled with a pole. A man stands on the forward platform and poles the canoe, steering as he does so. In a fairly large canoe a man at the stern may also take a pole and, standing up, help to propel the canoe.

All the work connected with the making of canoes and paddles is done by men alone, except the painting, which is usually done by women. It is the men also who make most use of canoes.

Fig. 46. Paddle

The large canoe, that is now made by all the tribes of the Great Andaman Division, is simply a canoe of the same general shape as the Great Andaman outrigger canoe, cut from a larger tree and without the outrigger. The shape of the hull, with its platforms fore and aft, is exactly the same. It seems that when the natives obtained a plentiful supply of iron tools (after 1858) they began to cut down and hollow out larger trees than formerly. Having made these larger canoes they found that they would, when well cut and ballasted with stone, float quite well without an outrigger. (It may be mentioned that the hull of a small canoe is always tested on the water before the outrigger is attached.) Indeed a well cut canoe of large size floats and balances better in a rough sea than a smaller one with an outrigger. It is possible that at first these large canoes were propelled with paddles just as the outrigger canoes are, the paddlers facing forward. Having learnt to understand the principle of the oar, through their contact with the Penal Settlement, the natives applied this principle to their own canoes. It could not, of course, be applied to the small canoes, as the shape of the canoe and the position of the paddler make the use of an oar impossible. It could be applied very easily, however, to the new large canoes. In these the oarsman does not sit on a level with the gunwale, but sits down in the hull itself on a piece of wood resting on the two sides of the hull a few inches above the floor. The gunwale of the canoe is thus about on a level with the bottom of his sternum. A number of holes are made in the gunwale on each side, and by means of these, loops of cane are attached to the gunwale. The oar, which is shaped in imitation of European oars, but with a short shaft, is thrust through the loop of cane, which serves as a fulcrum or rowlock. The rowers face aft. A man at the stern steers with a paddle. In shallow water the large canoes are propelled with poles in exactly the same way as the smaller canoes.

In the bow, at about the position that would be occupied by the foremost boom in an outrigger canoe, holes are made in the gunwale on each side and a piece of wood is thrust through them as a sort of thwart. This is to provide a means of making fast the end of the harpoon line or the anchor line, and thus serves a purpose that is served by the foremost boom in the outrigger canoe.

The large canoes are not quite so useful in turtle-hunting as the smaller outrigger variety, as they cannot be so quickly turned when the pursued turtle doubles. Very often a large canoe and a small canoe are taken together on an expedition, the harpooning being mostly done from the smaller one while the captured turtles are placed in the larger one. A small canoe with three or four men cannot hold more than one or at most two big turtles, whereas as many as ten or a dozen can be stowed in one of the large canoes.

The chief use of the large canoes is to make journeys from place to place. One of the largest will hold as many as thirty men and women with their baggage, whereas an outrigger canoe would never carry more than nine or ten. Further, there is less chance of an even heavily laden big canoe capsizing in a rough sea than of an outrigger canoe doing so. One result of the introduction of the large canoe has therefore been to enable the natives to move much more freely about the islands than formerly. The passage from the South Andaman to Ritchie's Archipelago, for instance, would only be attempted in an outrigger canoe on a very calm day, whereas in a large canoe it can be successfully accomplished even when there is something of a sea running.

The small canoe of the Little Andaman is fairly similar to that of the Great Andaman. There are three differences. (1) The stem and stern are squarely cut in the Little Andaman, instead of being rounded off. (2) The outrigger booms are attached to the top of the gunwale by cane binding which passes through holes made in the gunwales, instead of being themselves passed through holes in the gunwale. (3) The float is attached to the booms in a different and less efficient manner. Three pointed hard-wood sticks are driven into the float, but they are all three approximately perpendicular. They are bound at the top to the boom, but there are no stays of cane to maintain the float rigid against a lateral thrust. In other respects the Little Andaman canoe is the same as the Great Andaman canoe.

The Jarawa of the South Andaman do not at the present time make use of canoes. This is apparently because, through their hostility with the Aka-Bea, they have been confined to the interior of the island. They make rafts of bamboos lashed together for crossing creeks and inlets. The forest-dwellers of the Great Andaman Division seem also to have made occasional use of similar rafts for the same purpose.

A canoe of the North Sentinel was seen by Mr Gilbert Rogers during a visit to that island in 1903[1]. It had been hollowed out of a tree and was about 15 feet long. The ends of the canoe were cut off perpendicularly to its length leaving a piece of the tree about one inch thick projecting for about three inches beyond either end to form a small but rickety seat. The log from which the canoe was cut was curved so that the ends were slightly higher than the middle. It had a float supported by six booms passing through holes cut in the sides of the canoe. These booms were fastened to smaller pieces of stick fixed into the sides of the canoe beneath them. The outrigger was attached to each boom by two small pointed sticks driven into the float and tied to the boom above with cane. There was one small paddle, a *Nautilus* shell for a baler, and five poles resting on the outrigger booms. These point to the canoe being poled along in the lagoon, which is quite shallow, rather than to its being used for long journeys or outside the reefs which surround the island. The

[1] Supplement to the *Andaman and Nicobar Gazette*, January 2, 1904.

canoe was 18 inches in diameter at the smaller end and perhaps 30 inches wide at the larger end.

This description shows that the canoe of the North Sentinel is on the whole more like that of the Little Andaman than like that of the Great Andaman.

It seems probable that the Andaman Islands were peopled by sea from the coast of Burma. If this were so, then the original ancestors of the Andamanese must have been in possession of canoes. A consideration of the present Andaman canoes suggests that their ancestors had canoes with a single outrigger on the starboard side, with a number of booms. Of the different methods of attaching the booms to the float, it is possible that the method now in use in the Little Andaman (and apparently also in the North Sentinel) is primitive, and that the Great Andaman attachment is an improvement that has been invented since the separation of the two divisions. On the other hand it is not impossible that the Great Andaman attachment is primitive, and that in the Little Andaman we have a degeneration that might be due to the fact that the Little Andaman (and equally the North Sentinel) provides much less scope for maritime pursuits than the Great Andaman.

The recent invention of the large canoe in the Great Andaman and the adoption of the principle of the oar shows that the Andamanese readily adopt new inventions when these are clearly of service to them.

Turning now to the Semang, as these people live inland they have no use for canoes. They make rafts of bamboos lashed together with which they float down the rivers, returning overland.

Some of the Philippine Negritos seem to live on the coast and possibly have canoes, but nothing is known about these.

Conclusion.

The examination of the technical culture of the Andamanese given above has been sufficient to enable us to make a few statements as to what was probably the culture of the Negritos before they were split up into isolated groups. It is highly probable that they obtained their subsistence solely by hunting and collecting vegetable products. They had bows and arrows, the form of bow being probably fairly similar to that used at the present day in the Little Andaman, while for hunting the larger animals they had arrows with detachable heads. They possibly had no knowledge of any way of making implements of stone, but made use only of such materials as wood, bone, and shell. It is not probable that they possessed the art of making pottery, and their basketry and mat-work were probably confined to very simple forms. In their personal ornaments there is reason to think that they showed a fondness for bright yellow vegetable fibre, and made little or no use of the feathers of birds. The ornamentation of their utensils was probably confined to the use of the simplest forms of geometric design with a preponderance of the zig-zag and the lozenge. Finally their huts consisted of a single sloping roof sufficient to afford shelter for a single family or larger huts consisting of such small huts joined together.

We have seen that since the Andamanese have occupied their present home, or at any rate since the Great Andaman Division and the Little Andaman Division have been separated from one another, many changes, some of considerable importance, have taken place in the Andaman technology. In general it would seem that the technical culture of the Great Andaman has changed more than that of the Little Andaman. Putting aside the effect on the technology of the introduction of iron, there is no evidence that any of the changes that have taken place in the Great Andaman have been due to outside influence. Important modifications have taken place in the form of the bow, in the forms and technique of baskets, and in personal ornaments, and in all these instances there is no reason to think that these changes have not been brought about by the natives themselves without the influence of contact with other people. Their method of working iron, based as it is, to all appearance, on their former method of working shell, shows that even here, though the iron itself came to them from outside, and even though they may have learnt its use from seeing it used by aliens, still they have not learnt from others how to fashion the metal into shape by heating it. Thus, so far as their technical culture is concerned, there is no evidence whatever that the Andamanese have ever been influenced by contact with any other race since the time, now many centuries ago, when they first reached the islands.

On the other hand there is some probability that the ancestors of the Andamanese, before they first reached the islands, or at any rate before the isolation of the Little Andaman from the Great Andaman, had learnt from some other race how to make pottery, and it is possible that at the same time they may have acquired other elements of their culture, such as the outrigger canoe. We may even give a guess as to the particular culture from which the ancestors of the

Andamanese may have adopted these elements, which may well have been that of a branch of that people of whom an offshoot peopled the Nicobars.

Confirmation of these hypotheses, if confirmation be ever forthcoming, can only be obtained in the study of the history of races and of culture in south-eastern Asia. Until we have much fuller knowledge of the culture of the Semang and the Negritos of the Philippines, any conclusions that may be drawn from the study of the Andamanese alone must be regarded as provisional working hypotheses only, and it is as such that they are here put forward.

APPENDIX B

THE ANDAMAN LANGUAGES

The languages of the Andamans have been studied by Man, Temple and Portman. Man's study of the Bea language of the South Andaman was begun in 1877 but was only published, in the form of a *Dictionary of the South Andaman Language*, in the *Indian Antiquary* for the years 1919, 1920, 1921. Sir Richard Temple has on various occasions published accounts of the grammar based on the materials provided by Man and Portman. The fullest of these is contained in the *Report of the Census of India*, 1901, Vol. III, *The Andaman and Nicobar Islands*. Portman published in 1887 a *Manual of the Andamanese Languages* which is full of errors and of no use for scientific purposes. In 1898 he published *Notes on the Languages of the South Andaman Group of Tribes*. Man's *Dictionary* and Portman's *Notes*, if used in conjunction, and critically, give fairly adequate material for the languages of the South Andaman. My own linguistic investigations were chiefly concerned with the four languages of the North Andaman, which are closely related, and the northern dialect of the language of the Little Andaman.

The Andaman languages constitute a separate family having no apparent affinity with any other family of languages. Disregarding the North Sentinel Island, about the language of whose inhabitants nothing is known, the family includes twelve languages which fall into two main divisions. One of the divisions includes the Little Andaman language (hereafter denoted by the abbreviation L.A.) and the language of the Jarawa. The other division includes the ten languages of the Great Andaman tribes. Within most of the languages, in spite of the small size of the linguistic community, there are variations of dialect from one part of the tribe to another.

The following signs are used in this book for consonantal sounds:

$$
\begin{array}{cccccc}
k & g & & y & \eta & \\
 & & \check{c} & \check{\jmath} & & \\
 & & & & \acute{n} & \\
t & d & & & n & l & r \\
p & b & & & w & m &
\end{array}
$$

The sign *ŋ* is used for the nasalised guttural or velar stop and *ñ* for palatalised *n*; the sounds denoted by *č* and *ǰ*, while varying somewhat in different dialects, frequently approximate more nearly to palatalised *t* and *d* than to the affricates *tʃ* and *dʒ*; there are variations in the pronunciation of the dental stops *t* and *d*, predental, dental or alveolar, and cerebral enunciation being heard, but it is not evident that these variations constitute distinct phonemes in any of the languages; in L.A. there is a sound intermediate between *l* and *r* but I could not decide if this is a phoneme distinct from *l* or a special local or individual variant of the *l* phoneme; the *r* in L.A. tends to approximate to *d* (in trying to speak Hindustani a L.A. boy to whom I was teaching that language pronounced every initial *r* as *d*); I did not find *p* in L.A. but cannot be sure that it is really absent; the *b* of L.A. is often pronounced as a voiced bilabial fricative; in some of the Great Andaman languages *p* is similarly sometimes pronounced as a bilabial fricative.

The vowels are denoted as follows:

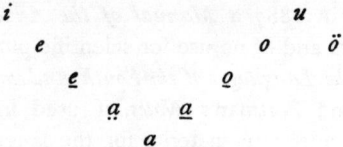

There is some variation in the pronunciation of vowels in different languages and dialects. The sign *ę* is used for the open *e* (ɛ) and *ǫ* for the open *o* (ɔ); *ạ* is the front *a* as in English "man"; *a̱* is the back *a* as in Southern English "father"; *a* is the neutral *a* approximating to the sound in French "pas" though sometimes varying towards the vowel of English "but"; *ö* is not properly identical with German *ö* but approximates somewhat towards the vowel heard in English "fur."

In transcribing the languages of the five tribes of the South Andaman Portman distinguishes fourteen vowels, while Man, in writing Bea, distinguishes sixteen. Both seem to have treated as different phonemes what are only divergent pronunciations of the same phoneme. In Bea the transcriptions of the two writers are frequently different. Thus for such a common word as *jabag*, bad, Portman gives the first vowel the value of *a* in "father." Man gives it the value of the vowel in "cur" and Temple gives it the value of the vowel in "cut." Actually the two vowels are both the neutral middle *a*, the second unstressed and open, the first stressed and slightly less open. Both Man and Portman use diacritics to indicate variations of vowels but their two systems are quite different, in neither are the diacritical marks used with any logical reference to the phonetic relationships of the vowels so differentiated, and neither system conforms to any of the various recognised phonetic alphabets which have been used in writing native languages[1]..

A comparison of the languages on the basis of vocabulary shows that the ten languages of the Great Andaman Division have many words in common, with certain phonetic changes. If there are any regular laws of phonetic shift they are not simple and it has not been found possible to formulate them. Common pairs of phonemes between which shifts do occur are *p-b*, *t-d*, *č-ǰ*, and more rarely *k-g*, i.e. where a word occurs in one language with an unvoiced consonant it may appear in another with the corresponding voiced consonant. It is impossible to say in which direction the shift has occurred. Thus Bea *barata*, Caryota palm, is *poroto* in Jeru, and Bea *parepa*, mat, is *baraba* in Jeru; *buf*, pot, in Bea and Bale is *peč* in all the other Great Andaman languages; snake is *jobo* in Bea, *čubi* in Jeru. Initial *k* in one language is sometimes omitted in another, as Jeru *koroin*, Dipterocarpus, Bea *arain*. Medial *k*, *g* and *ŋ* in some languages are occasionally omitted in others, as Jeru *reŋo*, Ficus, Bea *rao*, Bea *dakar*, bucket, Jeru *tar*. There is occasional equivalence between *č* or *ǰ* and *t* or *d*, as Bea *dogota*, Mimusops, Jeru *čugoto*. These few examples also illustrate sufficiently the variations in vowels.

While there are thus a considerable number of words which are common to all the Great Andaman languages, there are innumerable instances in which the same object or concept is denoted in different languages by entirely different words. Thus "good" is *beriŋa* in Bea, *dem* in Pučikwar and *e-nol* in Jeru.

When the vocabulary of L.A. is compared with the ten Great Andaman languages there is little evidence of relation, not enough, without reference to morphology, to prove that it belongs to the same family. In a fairly extensive vocabulary of L.A. there are less than a dozen words that are clearly related to corresponding Great Andaman words.

In the Andaman languages connected speech is made up by the combination of stems and affixes (prefixes and suffixes). Stems may consist of one, two or three syllables. There are a number of stem-words, each consisting of a single stem; such are most personal names and most names of animal and vegetable species (the exceptions being compound

---

[1] In reviews by Sir Richard Temple of the first edition of this book I have been severely criticised for not using Man's alphabet. I do not think it would be possible for any one except Man himself to apply his system of spelling to the languages of the North Andaman.

words), most names of natural phenomena and of articles in common use; for example, pig, L.A. *kui*, Bea *reg*, Jeru *ra*; sun, L.A. *eke*, Bea *bodo*, Jeru *diu*; bucket, L.A. *uku*, Bea *dakar*, Jeru *ta̱r*; mat, L.A. *emai*, Bea *parepa*, Jeru *baraba*; Cyrena shell used as knife, L.A. *uage*, Bea *uta*, Jeru *bun*. Such stems cannot normally have prefixes attached to them. On the other hand there are a number of stems which cannot be used without a prefix. We come here on one of the fundamental categories of Andamanese thought and speech, a distinction between objects thought of as independent, as "things" and objects thought of as dependent, as being parts, qualities, states or actions of "things." Thus a pig is thought of as a "thing" in this sense, a separate independent entity, and is denoted by a stem-word. But the head of a pig is a dependent object or concept and is therefore denoted by a word formed of a stem and a formation prefix, L.A. *o-tabe*, Jeru *ot-čo*. These stems -*tabe* and -*čo* cannot be used as words without a prefix. Properly the word *ot-čo* is not to be translated "head" but "its head" or "the head of something," the reference to something of which it is the head being expressed by the prefix. It should be noted that there are also some stems which can be used alone or combined with a prefix. Stems of this kind are more numerous in Bea than in N.A. or L.A. Thus "bad" in Bea is *jabag* which can be used as a stem-word in certain contexts or with a prefix, as *ab-jabag*, in others, while in Jeru it is *e-čai*, the stem of which is never used by itself as a word.

The formation of compound words by uniting two or occasionally three stems, with the necessary prefixes, is a common procedure in all the languages; examples, Jeru, *čokbi-tei*, turtle-blood, *e-tomo-t-ot-lam*, muscularly powerful, from *e-tomo*, muscle, and *ot-lam*, strong.

One of the most distinctive features of the Andaman languages is the system of formative prefixes already referred to. The system varies from one language to another, but in this brief sketch all that can be attempted is to indicate the most important features of the system in general. L.A. seems to have five formative prefixes, *i-*, *o-*, *a-*, *e-* and *u-*; *wo-* seems to be a variant of *o-*; *oi-* may be a separate prefix or a form of *i-*. In N.A. the most important prefixes are *e-*, *e̱r-*, *ot-*, *i-*, *aka-*, *oŋ-* and *u-*. Some of these have variant forms; *e-* before a labial may be *em-*; *e̱r-*, *e̱ra-*, *ara-*, *arai-* seem to be all variants of a single prefix.

The first function of these prefixes is to show that the word in which they are used denotes a dependent object, a part, quality, state or action of some person or thing. In L.A. *i-* and in N.A. *e-* can be used as a neutral prefix having no other function except to convey this reference.

Bea has no such neutral prefix, since *ab-*, the nearest equivalent to N.A. *e-*, conveys a specific reference to the human body. A result of this is that certain words indicating qualities, states, and actions which in L.A. have the prefix *i-* and in N.A. *e-* take the form in Bea of a stem which can be used without a prefix if no specific reference is required, or with one when such a reference is made. Thus "small" is *i-tai* in L.A., *e-leo* in N.A., but in Bea is *ketia* which takes the prefix *ab-* when it refers to human beings.

A further function of the formative prefixes is to convey specific references to certain concepts or categories. The system of references is very far from simple and no complete discussion but only a brief series of examples can be given here. One set of special references is to parts of the human or animal body. Thus in L.A. words which refer to states or qualities of a thing as a whole normally take the prefix *i-* as *i-kutu*, big, *i-kulu*, hot, *i-baro*, good. This prefix can therefore refer to the body as a whole. The prefix *o-* can convey a special reference to the head, *e-* to the face, and *u-* to the foot. Thus *i-daŋe* means "bone" of any part of the body, but *o-daŋe* means head-bone, i.e. skull. In N.A. *e-* refers to the body as a whole as *e-taru*, male, *e-buku*, female, *e-leo*, small, *em-pilo*, dead, *ot-* conveys a reference to the head, *aka-* to the mouth and therefore to food and speech, *oŋ-* to the hand or foot. Thus *tei* is the word for blood, *e-tei* means "fever" and *ot-tei* means headache (which is treated by blood-letting by scarification of the forehead).

The relation of the head to the body is generalised so that it becomes a principle of classification. (Compare the English use of "chief," "capital" and "head" itself.) Thus the prow of a canoe is called its head, *roa-t-ot-čo* in Jeru (*roa*, canoe). The fruit of a tree or plant is its *ot-čo*. In L.A. the hand is regarded as standing to the arm in the same relation as a head to a body, so that *i-bi-le* being arm *o-bi* can be used for hand. L.A. carries the analogy of head-body even further, for the thumb is called the head of the hand *o-b-o-tabe* and the big toe the head of the foot *u-kw-o-tabe* (*u-ge*, foot). Apparently connected with the use of *ot-* in the Great Andaman languages to refer to the head and to fruits is its occasional use to refer to things spherical or approximately spherical in shape. There are other special references that can be expressed by *ot-* which are not immediately or very obviously connected with its reference to the head. Thus in N.A. *ot-* may be used to indicate kinship relations; *arai-čulu* means after, following, later in order; *ot-arai-čulu-te* means younger brother; *e-tire* means young offspring of an animal or human being and therefore "a child"; *ot-tire* conveys a special reference to the child of a particular person—"his child"; so also from *e-bui*, marry, is formed the word *ot-e-bui*, consort, the husband or wife of somebody. In Bea the reference to kinship is conveyed by the prefix *ab-* (referring to the human body as a whole). The Bea equivalent of *-tire* is *-dereka*; *ab-dereka* is therefore baby, while *ot-dereka* is used of a fruit in the early stages of its growth. This example illustrates the way in which the idiomatic use of the prefixes varies in different languages.

In the Great Andaman languages the prefixes *er-, era-, ar-, ara-, arai-* seem to be variant forms of a single prefix, the primary reference of which is to place, position, order. (It may be noted that Bea has a stem *er* meaning place.) Any word which refers to position in time or space therefore normally takes this prefix, as Jeru *arai-čulu*, after, *ara-miku*, under, *t-erai-čiro*, yesterday, Bea *ar-tam*, ancient. In Jeru the word for long or tall when referring to an object such as a canoe or a tree is *e-lobuŋ*; when referring to distance between two points it is *era-lobuŋ*, as in *ti-t-era-lobuŋ*, a long way. In some instances the implication of the prefix is not very obvious at first sight. Thus in Jeru *era-meo* is an anchor, i.e. a heavy stone attached by rope to a canoe, *meo* being "stone"; the anchor is what keeps the canoe fixed in one place, therefore the "place-stone." A further, apparently secondary, use of this prefix is in reference to trees, trees being things fixed in one place and frequently serving to identify the place, as when many place names are formed from names of trees (Bale *Moi-lepto*, the place of *moi* trees). An example in Jeru is *era-tire*, the young shoots of a tree or plant, from *e-tire*, offspring. In relation to the human body *era-* refers to the region of the loins, perhaps because when a man is "placed" he is seated. In Jeru *e-tomo* is flesh or muscle of a human or animal body generally; *era-tomo* is the buttocks. This reference to the region of the loins permits the use of this prefix to refer to the genitals as in Jeru *era-tei*, menstruation, from *tei*, blood. In Bea the prefix *ar-* refers to the loins but is extended also to the legs, *ar-čag*.

Although the idiomatic uses of the various prefixes vary considerably from one language to another, yet there are certain features of the system as a whole which are common to all the languages and thus characterise the Andaman family. I have called the prefixes formative because they provide for the expression of derivational concepts by permitting several words of different meaning to be formed from one stem, as illustrated in the examples above. In doing this they give expression to a number of rather indefinite categories. Further, the prefixes have a syntactical function in that the presence of one in a word indicates a reference to some thing of which a part, quality, state or action is being spoken of.

In connection with the formative prefixes we must note the existence of a prefix which may be called integrative. It has two forms *t-* and *l-*. In L.A. *t-* is commonly used and *l-* more rarely; in Bea *l-* is more frequent and *t-* used only occasionally; in N.A. *t-* is used, apparently exclusively. The prefix has two uses. In compound words in which the second stem is preceded by a formative prefix this in turn is preceded by the integrative prefix, as Jeru *e-tomo-t-ot-lam*, muscle strong, Bea *kuk-l-ar-beriŋa*, happy (heart-place-good); L.A. *e-bo-t-a-ti*, eyelid, from *e-bọi*, eye, *a-ti*, skin. It is also used at the beginning of a word before a formative prefix. In Bea *ar-olo* and in Jeru *arai-čulu* mean "after"; *t-ar-olo* and *t-arai-čulu* have to be translated as "the afterwards," "the after time" and *t-ar-olo-lik* or *t-ar-olo-len* and *t-arai-čul-ik*, which are used where we should use the adverb "afterwards," must be literally translated "in the afterwards" or "at a later time," *ik* or *en* having the force of "in" or "at." In Bea the integrative prefix is also used before certain particles of relation when these are not preceded by a pronominal prefix.

Personal pronouns may be either words or prefixes. In N.A. the prefixes are *t-*, I, *ŋ-*, thou, *m-*, we, *ŋil-*, you, *n-*, they. They are used preceding the formative prefixes, as *t-ot-čo*, my head, *n-u-ben-om*, they sleeping. They are also used with certain particles of relation to be referred to later. It will be noted that there is no prefix for the third person singular. This is because in any given context the reference to a person or thing is felt to be sufficiently indicated by the formative prefix itself. Thus *ot-čo* means the head of something, or, in a specific context, his, her or its head; similarly *u-ben-om* means someone sleeping or he sleeping. When personal pronouns occur as words in Jeru they have the form *tio*, *ŋio*, *io* (he, she, it), *mio*, *ŋilio*, *nio*. Examples of use are *kule-l io*, there he (is), *tio ŋ-arai-čulutu-bom*, I follow thee, *ŋilio t-ače-bom*, you (pl.) come with (accompany) me.

While in the Great Andaman languages the third person singular is not indicated before a formative prefix, L.A. on the contrary has two forms of the third person, *gi* (*g-* before a prefix) and *öni* (*ön-* before a prefix). These may be distinguished as definite and indefinite forms respectively of the pronoun. Thus *ön-o-tabe* means "the head of somebody or something" while *g-o-tabe* means "his head" or "its head" with reference to some definite person or thing indicated by the context.

In Bea and Bale there is no pronominal prefix for the third person plural. (All the other Great Andaman languages and L.A. have *n-*.) There is also no distinction between the singular and the plural of the second person. (N.A. has singular *ŋ-*, plural *ŋil-*.) A distinction between singular and plural is therefore made in these two languages by adding *t-* for the plural *after* the formative prefix. Thus with the prefix *ar-* we get *d-ar-*, my, *ŋ-ar-*, thy, *ar-*, his, *m-ara-t-*, our, *ŋ-ara-t-*, your, *ara-t-*, their, and similarly with most of the other prefixes. A somewhat similar construction occurs in Pučikwar which has *ŋe* for thou and *ŋel* for your, but with a prefix such as *ar- ŋ-ar* is thy and *ŋ-ar-el* is your, the *-l* which is distinctive of the plural being placed after the formative prefix.

All the Andaman languages have certain suffixes which may be spoken of as verbal. In Bea those in constant and regular use are *-ke, -ka, -ŋa, -re, -yate* (*-ate, -iate*) and *-ba*. The addition of *-ke* or *-ka* to a stem produces the Andaman equivalent of a finite verb, in the present tense with *-ke* and the past or imperfect with *-ka*, as *mami-ke*, is sleeping, *mami-ka*, was sleeping. The suffix *-ŋa* produces a word which in different contexts may be translated by a noun, an adjective or a present participle, thus *mami-ŋa* may be "sleeping," "asleep" or "the sleeping person." In general *-ŋa* indicates a condition, state or quality rather than an action or happening. The suffixes *-re* and *-yate* are similar to *-ŋa* except that they refer to past time, either to a condition existing in the past or to one resulting from the completion of some action or event. Thus the word *ab-ik-yate* means a recently married wife, *ab-* prefix referring to human beings, *ik* stem meaning "take," *-yate* suffix indicating a completed action, therefore the person who has been "taken" (as a wife). (Man regularly translates *-yate* by the relative "who" or "which" but this is a failure to understand the native idiom.) The suffix *-re* is used in the same way. Thus an older brother is *en-toba-re* or *en-toba-ŋa*, *en-toba* meaning before in time, so that the first form means he who preceded and the second he who precedes. Portman gives *l-at-re* which he translates "has come"; *-at* means "to (a place)" and *l-* is the integrative prefix, so that *l-at-re* refers to the completed action of going to a place and so "arrived." But though the words formed by *-ŋa*, *-re* and *-yate* are not finite verbs (as those formed with *-ke* and *-ka* are) yet they can be used, as can many words that we should call nouns and adjectives, to form a nexus[1]. With *-ke* and *-ka* the nexus is specifically expressed by the suffix, otherwise it is merely understood. The prefix *-ba* or *-bo* expresses negation. When "not" has to stand by itself it takes the form *ya-ba*.

The N.A. verbal system differs from Bea by reason of the existence of a verbal particle *bi* which may be placed either before or after the nexus word to give predicative force, as *kidi koroin bi*, this is a dugong,

[1] For the terms junction and nexus as here used see Jespersen, *The Philosophy of Grammar*, 1924.

kidi t-ičo bi, this is mine, *tio bi tuŋ-om*, I want (I am wanting), *Buio ĵo bi ewur-om*, Buio is singing a song. The *bi* may be contracted to *b'* as in *deko b' era-lio*, well! it is finished. There is also in N.A. an occasional use of *j'* as a substitute for *b'* so that instead of *b' era-lio* one may hear *j era-lio* in some dialects. The equivalent of Bea *-ŋa* is *-om*, sometimes contracted to *-m*, thus *u-ben-om*, sleeping, is exactly equivalent to Bea *mami-ŋa*. The N.A. equivalent of *mami-ke*, is sleeping, is *u-beno-bom*; *-bom* is a true suffix forming a finite verb in the present term, although it may be derived from a synthesis of *bi* and *-om*; *-nom* or *-kom* may be substituted for it. The past or imperfect tense is formed by the suffix *-ba*, *u-beno-ba*, he slept or was sleeping, *t-u-boto-ba*, I fell. The negative suffix in N.A. is *-pu*.

Bea has two substantival suffixes, *-la* (*-ola*) used for persons and *-da* for things. Similar suffixes are found in the other South Andaman languages. The first is added to personal names and personal pronouns, as *Buluba-la, dol-la* (I). The latter is added to words other than those denoting persons, as *karama-da*, bow, *ot-četa-da*, head, *beriŋa-da*, good, *yaba-da*, not, *mami-ŋa-da*, sleeping.

Certain elements in the Andaman languages are best described as particles of relation. The particle meaning "belonging to" is *ijai* in L.A., *ia* (*iya*) in Bea, *ičo* in N.A. It is used with the pronominal prefixes, thus "mine" is L.A. *m-ijai*, Bea *d-ia*, N.A. *t-ičo* and so for other persons. When *ia* is used as a word in Bea the integrative prefix *l-* is added, *l-ia*, belonging to him or it, but in N.A. *ičo* can stand by itself, as *Bora ičo roa*, Bora's canoe.

Bea has three forms of reflexive particles which are chiefly used as prefixes, *ekan, oyun* and *iji*, as *eb-jabag-ike*, hurt (in the sense of damage), *eb-ekan-jabag-ike*, hurt oneself.

In Bea five of the most important particles of relation are *l-en*, in or at, *t-ek*, from, *l-at*, to, towards, *l-ik*, after, on account of, *l-eb*, for. The forms given all contain the integrative particle *l-* or *t-* and are words which fulfil the function of post positions, as *bud l-en*, in the hut, *t-ar-olo l-en*, afterwards. The particles themselves, without the *l-* or *t-* prefix, are used with the pronominal prefixes of the first and second persons, as *ŋ-ik*, with thee. In N.A. the equivalent particles are words which do not need and do not take the integrative prefix *t-*, as *il*, in, *ko*, in or at a place, *kak*, to (motion towards); examples, *čup il*, in the basket, *ŋ-oŋ-koro ko*, in thy hand, *Lau-tiče kak*, to Port Blair. These N.A. particles of relation might perhaps be regarded as suffixes as they seem never to be used except following the word to which the relation is indicated. The particle *il* very frequently does become a suffix *-l*. By the very nature of the Andaman language a distinction between affix and particle is difficult to draw.

In speech the Andamanese express themselves in short disconnected sentences or phrases. Though the languages provide specific mechanisms for indicating nexus these are frequently not used and the nexus is left to be understood. Thus, while nexus is definitely expressed in such N.A. sentences as *t-ot-tau-bom*, I am cold, *ŋio t-ače-bom*, you are coming with me, *u-boto-ba*, he or it fell, *kidi t-ičo bi*, this is mine, *io biwu bi moič-om*, he is making a torch (*biwu*, resin, *biwu-moič*, torch of resin), the nexus is left to be understood in *kule-l io*, there it (is), *kidi e-nol*, this (is) good, *n-u-ben-om*, they (are) sleeping, *t-ičo roa t-er-kuro*, my canoe (is) big.

In nexus the primary precedes the adnex, or in other words the nominative precedes the verb. With transitive verbs the order is subject, object, verb (nominative, accusative, verb). In junctions of the form adjective + noun the primary precedes the adjunct as *koroin t-er-kuro*, a big dugong. There is a marked tendency to unite the two words into a single compound word as *ra-taru*, boar (i.e. male pig), the prefix of *e-taru*, male, being omitted. On the other hand, in junction when the adjunct is a personal pronoun or the equivalent of a genitive the adjunct precedes the primary, as *ŋ-ot-čo*, thy head, *t-ičo roa*, my canoe, *Buio ičo roa*, Buio's canoe.

With reference to Sapir's classification of languages into morphological types[1] we may note that the Andaman languages express concrete concepts by means of stems; they use many derivational concepts, the mechanism for forming these being provided by the formative prefixes and by the facility with which compound words are formed; pure relational concepts are expressed by the juxtaposition of words in the proper order, by particles (*bi* and *ičo* of N.A.), by the verbal and substantival suffixes and by the prefixes; concrete relational concepts are expressed in only a very limited degree by grammatical mechanisms (e.g. present and past time in the verbal suffixes).

[1] Sapir, *Language*.

INDEX

Address, terms of, 44, 53; used in legends, 191
Adoption of children, 77; effects of, on regulation of marriage, 72
Adultery, 50
Adze, 450
Age, distinctions of, 80
Aka-, prefix referring to mouth and speech, 23
Aka-op, term applied to boy or girl during adolescence, 94; foods avoided by, 95; interpretation of avoidances imposed on, 279
Aka-yat relationship, 81
Alebe, name given to girl at first stage of initiation, 93
Alpinia, leaves used in honey-eating ceremony, 105; used as remedy for sickness, 183
Anadendron, magical properties of, 157; 180; protective value of, 261; dangerous to use, 273; uses of fibre, 453; preparation of fibre, 453
Ancestors, legends of the, 190; names applied to the, 137, 190; with animal names, 191; legends of the dispersion of the, 212
Andaman Islands, description of, 1; fauna, 3; climate, 4; early accounts of, 7; area of, 15
Andamanese home, 19
Animal bones, protective power of, 184, 273
Animals, legendary, 225; in the legends, 191; personification of, 388; legends of the origin of, 206 sqq., 341 sqq.
Ant's nest (*Kọt*), human race descended from, 192
Arabian travellers, description of Andamans by, 7
Areca wood, skewer of, 449; arrows of, 439
Arrows, 435 sqq.; protective power attributed to, 259; used to stop a storm, 157
Artocarpus fruit, 40
Ar-yoto, coast-dwellers, 26
Authority of chiefs, 47

Bachelors' hut, 34
Bain (civet-cat), as the first woman, 196
Bamboo, necklaces of, 259, 480; vessels of, 475; used for fish arrows, 435

Bark sling for carrying children, 480; worn by man who desires children, 90
Basket-work, 458 sqq.; Little Andaman, 461; South Andaman, 463; North Andaman, 465; Semang, 470; Philippine Negritos, 471
Be, pearl shell, associated with *Biliku*, 152
Bees'-wax, burning of, angers *Biliku*, 152, 357; magical properties of, 183; protective power of, 263
Belt, men's, 125, 476; women's, 477
Beyan (civet-cat), as the first woman, 193
Bido Těč Lau, 136, 165
Bilik, generic name for winds, 149; name of a class of spirits, 169
Bilika, *Aka-Kede* form of *Biliku*, 199
Biliku, associated with the N.E. wind, 147, 353; associated with the season of the N.E. monsoon, 149; statements concerning her husband and children, 150; meaning of the name, 151; actions that anger, 152; punishes offences with storms, 156; legends about, 197; represented in pantomimic dance, 165
Biliku and *Tarai*, beliefs concerning, 147 sqq.; legends of, 197 sqq.; interpretation of beliefs about, 351 sqq.
Birth of children, customs relating to, 89
Birth-rate, decrease of, 18
Boar's tusk, used as a spokeshave, 448
Bone arrow points, 448
Bones, animal, magical properties of, 184
Bones of the dead, recovered from the grave, 112; worn to prevent sickness, 126, 184; interpretation of customs relating to, 292
Bow, 419 sqq.; Little Andaman, 419; North Sentinel Island, 422; Jarawa, 423; South Andaman, 423; North Andaman, 427; comparison of different forms, 432; Semang, 434; Philippine Negritos, 435; an element of primitive Negrito culture, 492
Buckets, 474
Burial customs, 196 sqq.; weeping over corpse, 106; preparation of corpse, 106; interment, 107; tree-burial, 108; use of *kọro* fibre, 108; burial of children, 109; of strangers, 109; recovery of bones, 112; interpretation of, 285 sqq.

INDEX

Čainyo leaf, used in girl's initiation ceremony, 93; formerly worn by women of North Andaman, 93 note
Čaitan, the abode of spirits of the dead, 171
Calamus, uses of, 453; associated with spirits, 136, 165, 292
Camping sites, 29
Camps, kinds of, 31; hunting, 33, 409
Canoes, 485 sqq.; Little Andaman, 491; North Sentinel Island, 492; ownership of, 42
Čara, equivalent of Tomo, 144; legends of, 193
Caryota, associated with spirits of the dead, 147, 171, 290; belongs to Biliku, 152, 358
Čatlo, stars, children of sun and moon, 141
Čatlo, beetle, associated with Biliku, 156
Čauga, spirits of the dead, 136, 170
Čauga ta, bones of the dead, 137
Čauga tabaŋa, the ancestors, 190, 137
Caves, use of, 33
Celtis cinnamonea, use of fibre of, 452
Ceremonial customs, definition of, 89; nature of, 233, 325
Chiefs, 47
Child, sex of unborn, 90; reincarnation of dead, 90
Childbirth, 89
Children, treatment of, 51; and parents, 76; naming of, 89
Chinese records of Andamans, 7
Cicada, associated with Biliku, 150, 152, 154, 198, 206, 208, 359; associated with day and night, 155, 214, 330; may not be killed, 155; may not be disturbed by noise at dawn or sunset, 154; ceremony of killing the, 155
Čirikli, the moon, 141
Civet-cat, beliefs concerning, 184; as wife of first ancestor, 193, 196; position in legends explained, 348
Clan organisation, absence of, in Andamans, 23
Classificatory system of relationship, 53
Clay, used for making pots, 473; men and women made of, by Jutpu, 192
Clay (odu), newly born child painted with, 90; used in initiation ceremonies, 99, 102; used in mourning, 106, 111; summary of uses of, 122; used after eating food, 122, 265; interpretation of uses of, 275, 289, 312
Clay, white (tọl-odu), use of, after initiation ceremonies, 99, 102; used for decorating corpse, 102; may not be used by mourners, 111, 112; used for ornamenting bones of the dead, 113; summary of uses of, 124; use of, in purification of homicide, 133; interpretation of uses of, 254, 256, 315 sqq.
Climate of Andamans, 4
Coast-dwellers and forest-dwellers, 26
Čoinyop, legend of, 142
Čol, 161; legend of origin of, 224
Colebrooke, 445, 448
Communal huts, 31, 35, 413
Convict Settlement, see Penal Settlement
Cramp, caused by civet-cat, 184
Creeks and islands, legends of origin of, 217
Crime, punishment of, 48
Cyclones, 5, 344, 364
Cyrena shell, uses of, 447

Da, term of address, 44
Dance, 128 sqq.; rhythm of, 130; of women, 131; before a fight, 132, 252; at turtle-eating ceremony, 100, 282; at end of mourning, 114; pantomimic, representing supernatural beings, 164; legend of origin of, 215, 334; social function of, 246 sqq.
Dance meetings, 40, 253
Day, personified, 144; made by Tautǫbitatmǫ, 144; made by Čara, 144
Day and night, legend of origin of, 214; interpreted, 330
Death, legend of origin of, 236, 299
Dendrobium, use of skin of, for ornament, 454
Dentalium shell, ornaments of, 126, 479
Deria, see Tarai
Diu, the sun, 141
Division of labour, 43
Dogs, 36, 417
Domestic implements and utensils, 472 sqq.
Dove, as first woman, 195
Dreams, beliefs concerning, 167, 304; communication with spirits in, 177; power of medicine-man exercised in, 178; provide means of representing the spirit world, 303
Dugong, legend of origin of, 218
Duku (monitor lizard), as first ancestor, 196
Dula, the moon, 141

Eagle (Kǫlo), legend of, 227
Earthquakes, made by the spirits, 146
Education, 276
Elders, respect for, 44; influence of, 50
Ele, personification of lightning, 145; represented in pantomimic dance, 166
Entada scandens, belongs to Biliku, 152

INDEX 507

Era-puli, patterns painted on body, 122; explanation of, 265, 312
Erem-ċauga, spirits of the jungle, 136; Mr Man's account of, 140
Erem-taga, forest-dwellers, 26

Family, 23
Fibres used for making rope and string, 450 sqq.; protective powers attributed to, 259
Ficus laccifera, home of souls of unborn children, 91; storm will come if tree is damaged, 157; leaves used for stopping storm, 157; abode of spirits of dead infants, 174; magical properties of, 181; protective value of, 262; use of fibre of, 452
Fighting, 85
Fire, absence of method of producing, 472; magical properties of, 184; legends of origin of, 201; protective value of, 258; used in initiation ceremonies, 95, 98, 280; interpretation of legends of origin of, 341; social value of, expressed in legends of flood, 345; relation to *Biliku*, 367
Fishing, 417
Flood, legends of, 206; Mr Man's version of, 209; interpretation of legends of, 344
Flower-names of girls, 119; interpretation of, 311
Flying-fox, remedy for rheumatism, 184
Food, distribution of, 43; avoidance of certain, during pregnancy, 89; avoidance of certain, at menstrual periods, 94; avoidance of certain, during adolescence, 95; avoidance of certain, during mourning, 111; customs connected with, 114 sqq., 272; patterns painted on body after eating, 122, 265, 312; belief in dangers of, 270; social value of, 270; used in treatment of sickness, 273
Frederike, Master Caesar, description of Andamans, 8
Frog, legends of, 221; eaten by woman who desires children, 90
Funeral customs, 106 sqq.; interpretation of, 285 sqq.

Gnetum edule, use of fibre of, 452; magical properties of, 181; protective power of, 261
Government, absence of, 44
Grewia laevigata, use of fibre of, 452
Gumul, see *Kimil*

Habitations, 31 sqq., 409 sqq.
Hair-dressing, 483

Harpoon, 441
Hibiscus tiliaceus, use of fibre for rope, 451; method of preparation of fibre, 451; leaves used in turtle-eating ceremony, 98, 99, 100; wood used for cooking turtle, 116; protective power of, explained, 259
Hiccough, said to be caused by lizard, 184
Homicide, customs relating to, 133
Honey, 39; legend of discovery of, 221; associated with the snake *or-ċubi*, 227
Honey-eating ceremony, 105
Hunting, 36, 417
Huts, 32 sqq., 409 sqq.

In, term of address, 44
India, natives of, called *Lau*, 137
Initiation ceremonies, 91 sqq.; interpretation of, 276 sqq.
Initiation into the world of the dead, 146, 290
Interpretation of customs, methods of, 329
Iron, use of, 9, 444, 449

Jarawa, 10, 11, 12, 86; their relation to the *Önge*, 13
Jereg, the abode of the dead, 171, 173
Jereg-l'ar-mugu, the abode of the dead, 170, 171, 173, 174
Jirmu, a legendary animal, 226
Jurua, spirits of the sea, 136
Juruwin, Mr Man's account of, 140
Jutpu, the first being, legend of, 192

Kara-duku, said to be the crocodile, 194
Kimil, term applied to initiation ceremonies, 101; meaning of the word, 266, 307
Kimil season, 39, 153; association with *Biliku*, 359
Knives, 449
Kolo, sea-eagle, legend of, 227
Kolotat (ebony), as the first woman, 194
Koro, fibre, 453; used in burial ceremonies, 108; used in peace-making ceremony, 134; formerly worn by women, 479; explanation of uses of, 290
Korude, thunder, personified, 145
Kot (ant's nest), as the first woman, 192

Land, ownership of, 29
Languages of the Andaman Islands, 11
Lapicque, M. L., 31, 446
Lau, the spirits, 136; term applied to natives of India, 137
Lau toi, bones of the dead, 137
Laziness, condemned, 50

Legends, 186 sqq.; interpretation of, 330 sqq.
Lightning, personified, 145; made by *Ele*, 145; made by *Tarai* and *Biliku*, 145; connection with *Biliku* discussed, 367
Little Andaman, 12; former connection with Great Andaman, 14; huts, 413; bow, 419; arrows, 439; basket-work, 461; personal ornament, 483
Local groups, 23, 26; size of, 27; names of, 28; membership of, 28; meetings of, 40; relations between, 82
Loito, edible root associated with *Biliku*, 199

Maia, term of address, 44; used in legends, 191
Man, E. H., 20
Marco Polo, description of Andamans, 7
Marriage, 70 sqq.; regulation of, 71; of cousins, 71; ceremony of, 73; ceremony, interpretation of, 255
Mats, 456
Medicine-men, 48, 51, 175 sqq.; powers of, how acquired, 176; cure sickness, 178; control the weather, 178; skilled in legendary lore, 186; beliefs concerning, discussed, 301
Melochia velutina, 451
Menstruation, ideas about, 94; avoidances during, 94; ceremony at first occurrence of, 92
Mimi, term of address, 44; used in legends, 191
Mimusops leaves, worn by women, 127; used to frighten *Biliku*, 157
Mincopie, as name of Andaman Islanders, 12
Mode of life, changes in, 19
Monitor lizard, as the first ancestor, 193, 196, 211, 213, 225; identified with *Biliku* (*Öluga*) in Little Andaman, 151; inventor of scarification, 219; position in the legends explained, 388
Moon, personified, 141; beliefs relating to, 142; can turn into a pig, 141; anger of, how caused, 142; waxing and waning of, 143; eclipse of, 143; as wife of *Tomo*, 195; interpretation of beliefs concerning, 340
Morgan, Lewis, 53
Morua, spirits of the sky, 136, 160; angry if pork is roasted, 160
Mourners, names avoided, 111; terms of address used for, 112; cut off from normal social life, 288
Mourning, customs of, 166 sqq.; duration of, 110; ceremony at end of, 114; interpretation of customs of, 285 sqq.
Murder, 48
Myristica, leaves used in initiation ceremonies, 92, 98; explanation of protective power of, 260

Names, 89, 117 sqq.; flower names of girls, 93, 119, 312; avoidance of, 121; of parents avoided after birth of child, 89; of initiates avoided during ceremonies, 93, 95, 101; of deceased avoided during mourning, 111; of mourners avoided during mourning, 111; new, given at turtle-eating ceremony, 101; interpretation of customs relating to, 294 sqq.
Negrito race, 2, 6
Netting, 471 sq.
Nicobar Islands, 2
Night, personified, 144; made by spirits, 145; legend of origin of, 213; legend of origin of, interpreted, 330 sqq.
Nila, beliefs concerning, 163
Nomadism, 30
North Sentinel Island, 15; huts, 412; bow, 422; canoe, 492

Odour, symbolism of, 311
Odu, clay, used in turtle-eating ceremony, 98; used by mourners, 106, 111; uses of, in general, 122; interpretation of use of, after eating food, 265; interpretation of use of, in initiation ceremonies, 281; interpretation of use of, in mourning, 289; interpretation of uses of, in general, 312
Ogar, the moon, 142
Oko-jumu, see Medicine-men
Oko-paiad, see Medicine-men
Önge, 12; see also Little Andaman
Qr-čubi, 124, 162, 227; see also *Wara-Jobo*
Qr-čubi t'era-bat, name of pattern of white clay, 124
Origin of mankind, legends of, 191 sqq.
Ornament, personal, 121 sqq., 476 sqq., 483; interpretation of customs relating to, 254 sqq., 315 sqq.
Ornamentation, character of, 484
Ornamentation of utensils, 323
Ot-kimil, see *Kimil*
Ot-jumulo, double or soul, 166, 304

Painting the body, 121 sqq., 315 sqq.; see also *Odu*, Clay, white (*tol-odu*)
Pandanus leaf, belts, and ornaments of, 477; belts of, worn by women, 127; used in girl's initiation ceremony, 92
Paradoxurus, see Civet-cat
Parents and children, 76

INDEX

Peace-making ceremony, 134; interpretation of, 238
Pearl shell (*be*), used as a knife, 447; associated with *Biliku*, 198, 201, 202, 206, 367, 368
Penal settlement, first, 9; present, 10
Perjido (*Pijĉor*), son of *Biliku*, 150, 160, 198, 199, 217, 371, 373 footnote; and origin of dugong, 218; first discoverer of honey, 221
Personal ornament, see Ornament
Personal qualities, respect for, 45
Personification of natural phenomena, 141 sqq., 377 sqq.; of animals, 388
Petie, monitor lizard, as first ancestor, 193
Philippine Islands Negritos, 6; huts, 416; bows, 435; basket-work, 471
Phonetics, 495
Pig, method of hunting, 36; method of cooking, 37; method of cutting up prescribed by custom, 116, 161, 272; belief in danger of roasting, 160, 363 footnote; skulls preserved, 274; skulls encased in basket-work by Jarawa, 467; the moon can take the form of, 141; legend of how the pig got its senses, 217; legend of the origin of, 218; position of, in legends, 347
Pigeon, connection with conception of children, 91
Pijĉor, see *Perjido*
Poiĉo-tobut, the first ancestor, 192
Population of the Andaman Islands, 15, 16; estimate of former, 18; decrease of, 17; density of, 19, 25
Pork, dangerous to roast, 160
Porokul, husband of *Biliku* in *Aka-Kede* legend, 199
Port Blair, 2, 9, 10
Portman, M. V., 21
Pottery, 473
Prefixes in Andamanese languages, 23, 498
Pregnancy, avoidances during, 89
Presents, as expression of good will, 237
Property, 41; in land, 29
Protective power of amulets explained, 257
Pterocarpus, peculiar beliefs concerning, 182
Pteropus, see Flying-fox
Puki, the moon, 142
Puluga, Mr Man's account of, 157 sqq.; see also *Biliku*
Punishment of crime, 48
Purchas: his Pilgrimes, quoted, 8
Puto, the sun, 142

Quarrels, 48

Rainbow, beliefs concerning, 145
Red paint, used in initiation ceremonies, 99, 102; used on corpse, 106; use prohibited to mourners, 111, 112; used for decorating the bones of the dead, 112; uses of, in general, 125; use of, by homicide, 133; used in treatment of illness, 179; uses of, explained, 318; used for ornamenting utensils, 323
Reflection (*ot-jumulo*) and the notion of soul, 166, 304
Reincarnation of dead infant, 90, 109
Relationship, system of, 52 sqq.; terms of, North Andaman, 54; terms of, *Akar-Bale*, 57
Resin, used for torches, 476; legendary origin of use of, 214, 335
Rheumatism, caused by *Anadendron*, 180
Ritchie, John, 9
Rope, 450, 452, 454; ornamental, 456

Scarification, 92, 483; as remedy for illness, 184; of boy's back at initiation, 94; legend of origin of, 219; interpretation of customs of, 315
Sea-eagle (*Kolo*), legend of, 227
Seasons, 4, connected with *Biliku* and *Tarai*, 149, 351 sqq.
Semang, 6; huts, 415; bow, 434; basket-work, 470
Septs, 28
Shadow, and notion of soul, 166, 304
Shell, implements of, 446
Skewer, 449
Sleep, as condition of danger, 302; prohibited to initiate during ceremonies, 99, 102
Social Organisation, 22 sqq.
Social personality, definition of, 284, 285; not annihilated by death, 285; connection between name and, 294
Social value, definition, 264; expressed in beliefs in protective power of common objects, 264; of food, 270; of night and day expressed in legend, 331; of moonlight, 341; of fire, 342; of weather and seasons expressed in myth of *Biliku* and *Tarai*, 353; explanation of legends as expressing, 397
Songs, 131, 247
Soul, notion of, 106, 304
Sounding-board used in dances, 128
Spelling of Andamanese words, 495
Spirits, 136 sqq., 168 sqq., 297 sqq.; of the jungle, 136; of the sea, 136; of the sky, 136; invisible, 137; appearance of, 138; live in villages, 138; contact with, dangerous, 139; cause illness, 139; more dangerous at night, 139; attracted by whistling, 139; feed on flesh of the dead, 140; Mr Man's account of, 140; night made by, 145;

rainbow belongs to, 145: dead men initiated by, 146
Spirits of the dead, 168 sqq.; remain in the jungle and the sea, 168; go to *Maramiku*, 168; go to the east, 169; live with *Tomo* in the sky, 169; medicine-men become *Bilik*, 169; go to *Jereg-l'ar-mugu*, 170; Mr Man's account of, 171
Stars, beliefs concerning, 141; children of sun and moon, 141; constellations not recognized, 141
Sterculia, use of fibre of, 453
Stoliczka, 446
Stone implements, 444, 450
Storms, 5; made by *Biliku*, 156; caused by spirits of the sea, 157; methods of stopping, 157
String, 455
String figures, 182
Subsistence, 36, 417
Sun, personified, 141, 142; eclipse of, 144; made by *Bilika*, 203

Tarai, husband or child of *Biliku*, 150, 198; statements about, 199; identified with the S.W. wind, 353; see also *Biliku* and *Tarai*
Tautọbitatmọ, makes the daylight, 144
Temple, Sir Richard, 21
Tetranthera, leaves used in girl's puberty ceremony, 92; leaves used in pig-eating ceremony, 102; skewer of wood used in pig-eating ceremony, 102; plumes of shredded wood used in war-dance, 133; plumes of, worn by homicide, 133; plumes of, used in eclipse of the moon, 144; magical properties of, 182; explanation of beliefs concerning, 260
Thunder and Lightning, personified, 145; made by *Biliku* and *Tarai*, 145, 152
Tides, beliefs concerning, 146: soul of dying man goes out with the tide, 175
Ti-miku Lau, spirits of the jungle, 136
Tọlitọn, makes the rainbow, 146
Tomo, connected with sun and fine weather, 142, 195; moon made by, 142, 195; spirits of dead live with, 142, 169; moon as wife of, 195; as first man, 195
Tomo-la, name for the ancestors, 191
Toto (*Pandanus*), name given to girl at first initiation ceremony, 93
Trees, ownership of, 41
Tribal names, 12, 24
Tribes, 12, 23 sqq.; boundaries of, 15; extent of territory of, 25
Trigonostemon, leaves used in sickness, 182
Turtle, legend of origin of, 218, 392; method of killing, prescribed by custom, 116; must only be cooked with *Hibiscus* wood, 116
Turtle-eating ceremony, 98 sqq.; interpretation of, 279
Turtle net, 443

Uču, legend of, 225

Vegetable foods, 38; associated with *Biliku*, 152, 198, 199, 200
Villages, 32; arrangement of, 34
Vital principle, 166

War, 85
Wara-Jobo, *Puluga* threatened with, 162; mentioned in honey-eating ceremony, 105; legend concerning, 227
Weather, 4; connection with *Biliku* and *Tarai*, 147 sqq., 351 sqq.; controlled by medicine-men, 178; fine, associated with *Tomo*, 142, 195
Weeping, ceremony of, 116; interpretation of, 239 sqq., 281
Whistling, attracts spirits, 139
Widows, 75; marriage of, with deceased husband's brother, 75
Winds, names of, 147, 148
Women, position of, 47; costume of, 127; dance of, 131

Yams, associated with *Biliku*, 152, 198; legend of first discovery of, 220

MAP I

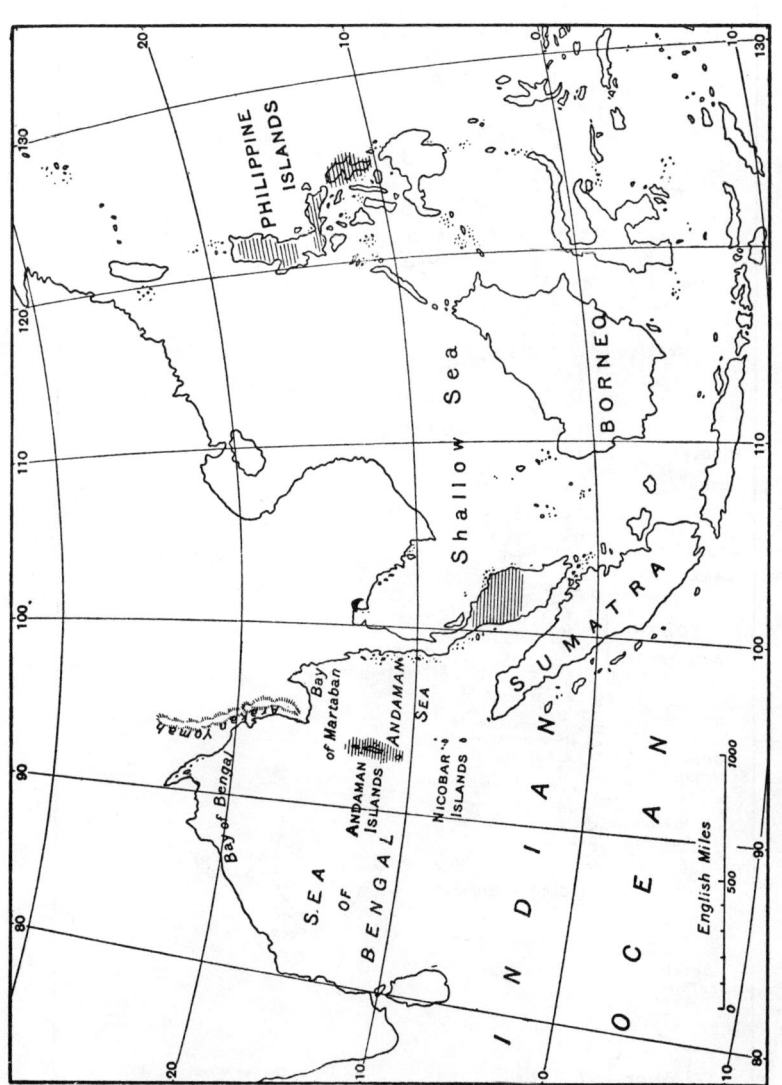

South-eastern Asia, showing the present distribution of the Negrito Race

Map II

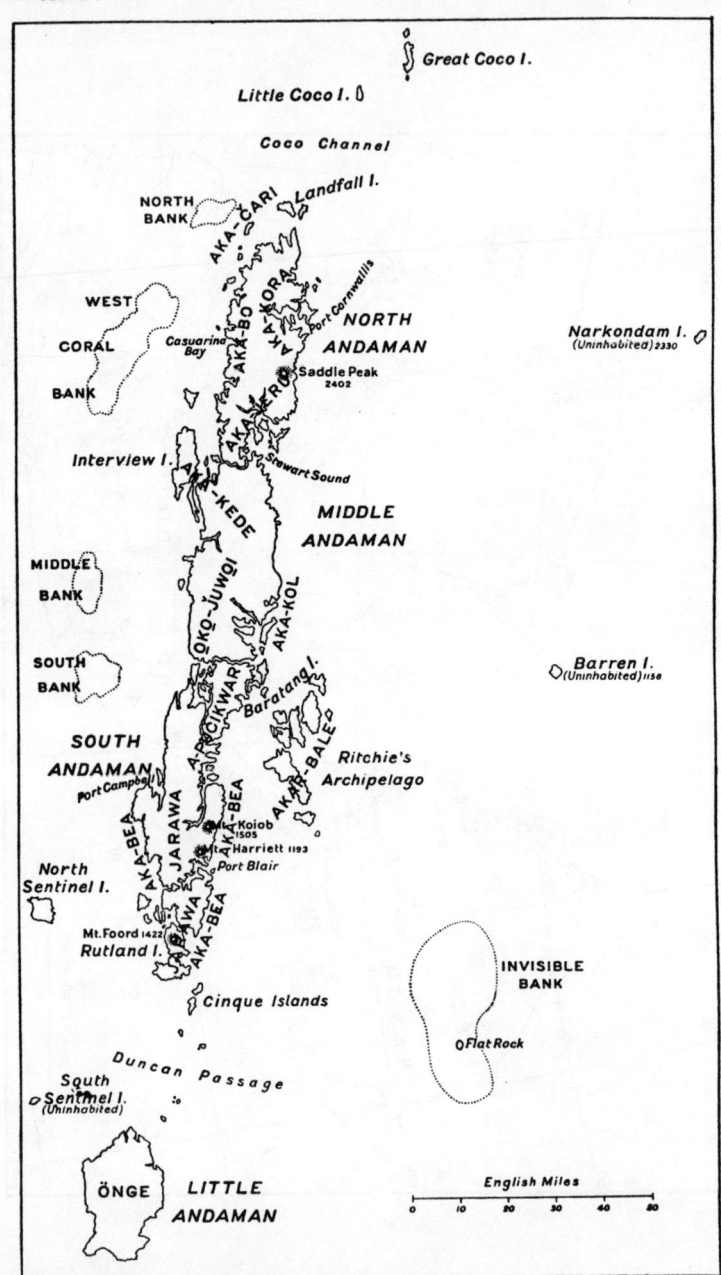

The Andaman Islands, showing the distribution of tribes